LIST OF APPLICATIONS

Application 9.4: The Endless Saga of Steel Protectionism

Application 9A.1: Gains from Free Trade and the NAFTA Debate

Chapter 10

Application 10.1: Should You Need a License to Shampoo a Dog?

Application 10.2: Who Makes Money at Casinos?

Application 10.3: Pricing Problems in Dallas

Application 10.4: Financial Aid at Private Colleges

Application 10.5: Pricing at the Magic Kingdom

Application 10.6: Bundling of Cable and Satellite Television Offerings

Application 10.7: Can Anyone Understand Telephone Pricing?

Chapter 11

Application 11.1: The De Beers Cartel

Application 11.2: Cournot in California

Application 11.3: Price Leadership in Financial Markets

Application 11.4: Competition in Breakfast Space

Application 11.5: Airline Deregulation Revisited

Chapter 12

Application 12.1: Nash Equilibrium on the Beach

Application 12.2: How Is the Price Game Played?

Application 12.3: The Great Electrical Equipment Conspiracy

Application 12.4: First-Mover Advantages for Alcoa, DuPont, Procter & Gamble, and Wal-Mart

Application 12.5: The Standard Oil Legend

Chapter 13

Application 13.1: Hiring by Nonprofit Firms

Application 13.2: Controversy over the Minimum Wage

Application 13.3: Why Is Wage Inequality Increasing?

Application 13.4: Monopsony in the Market for Sports Stars

Application 13A.1: The Opportunity Cost of Time

Application 13A.2: Changing Labor Force Participation for Younger Women and Older Men

Chapter 14

Application 14.1: Do We Need Tax Breaks for Savers?

Application 14.2: Do Taxes Affect Investment?

Application 14.3: Inflation-Indexed Bonds

Application 14.4: Discounting Cash Flows and Derivative Securities

Application 14.5: Are Any Resources Scarce?

Application 14A.1: Compound Interest Gone Berserk

Application 14A.2: Zero-Coupon Bonds

Application 14A.3: Continuous Compounding

Chapter 15

Application 15.1: Blackjack Systems

Application 15.2: Do HMO Patients Need a Bill of Rights?

Application 15.3: Mutual Funds

Application 15.4: The Equity Premium Puzzle

Application 15.5: Safe Driver Insurance Policies

Application 15.6: Looking for Lemons

Chapter 16

Application 16.1: Secondhand Smoke

Application 16.2: Property Rights in Nature

Application 16.3: Regulating Power Plant Emissions

Application 16.4: Why Is There So Much Fundraising on Public Broadcasting?

Application 16.5: Referenda on Public Spending

9e

Intermediate Microeconomics
And Its Application

Walter Nicholson
Amherst College

THOMSON
™
SOUTH-WESTERN

Australia · Canada · Mexico · Singapore · Spain · United Kingdom · United States

THOMSON

SOUTH-WESTERN

Intermediate Microeconomics and Its Application, 9e
Walter Nicholson

VP/Editorial Director:
Jack W. Calhoun

VP/Editor-in-Chief:
Michael P. Roche

Senior Acquisitions Editor:
Peter Adams

Senior Developmental Editors:
Jeff Gilbreath
Susanna C. Smart

Marketing Manager:
Janet Hennies

Production Editor:
Chris Hudson

Media Development Editor:
Peggy Buskey

Media Production Editor:
Pam Wallace

Manufacturing Coordinator:
Sandee Milewski

Compositor:
Shepherd, Inc.

Printer:
Phoenix Color Corp.
Hagerstown, Maryland

Design Project Manager:
Stacy Jenkins Shirley

Cover and Internal Designer:
Craig Ramsdell

Cover Image:
© The Image Bank

Library of Congress Control
Number: 2002116499

ISBN: 0-324-17163-3 (InfoTrac
package)

0-324-27379-7 (package)

0-324-27419-X (text only)

To Beth, Sarah, and David—glad you're here.

About the Author

Walter Nicholson is the Ward H. Patton Professor of Economics at Amherst College. He received a B.A. in mathematics from Williams College and a Ph.D. in economics from MIT. Professor Nicholson's primary research interests are in the econometric analyses of labor market policies including job training, unemployment insurance, welfare, and the impact of trade-adjustment assistance. He is also the author of *Microeconomic Theory: Basic Principles and Extensions, 8th Edition* (South-Western/Thomson Learning, 2002). He and his wife Susan live in Amherst, Massachusetts.

Brief Contents

Preface   xx

Part 1: Introduction   1
1   Economic Models   3
   Appendix to Chapter 1: Mathematics Used in Microeconomics   29

Part 2: Demand   53
2   Utility and Choice   55
3   Individual Demand Curves   89
4   Market Demand and Elasticity   126

Part 3: Production, Costs, and Supply   155
5   Production   157
6   Costs   187
7   Profit Maximization and Supply   221

Part 4: Models of Market Equilibrium   251
8   Perfect Competition   253
9   Applying the Competitive Model   284
   Appendix to Chapter 9: General Equilibrium   312
10   Monopoly   329
11   Imperfect Competition   362
12   Strategy and Game Theory   387

Part 5: Further Topics   417
13   Labor Markets   419
   Appendix to Chapter 13: Labor Supply   448
14   Capital Markets   458
   Appendix to Chapter 14: Compound Interest   482
15   Uncertainty and Information   500
16   Externalities and Public Goods   530

Solutions to Odd-Numbered Problems   565
Brief Answers to MicroQuizzes   587
Glossary   596
Index   603

Contents

Preface   xx

PART 1: INTRODUCTION   1

Chapter 1: Economic Models   3

What Is Microeconomics?   4

A Few Basic Principles   4

Application 1.1: Do Animals Understand Economics?   7

Uses of Microeconomics   8

Application 1.2: Is It Worth Your Time to Be Here?   9

Application 1.3 Saving Blockbuster   11

Application 1.4: Microsoft and Antitrust   12

The Basic Supply-Demand Model   14

Adam Smith and the Invisible Hand   14 • David Ricardo and Diminishing Returns   15 • Marginalism and Marshall's Model of Supply and Demand   16 • Market Equilibrium   17 • Nonequilibrium Outcomes   18 • Change in Market Equilibrium   18

How Economists Verify Theoretical Models   19

Application 1.5: Economics According to Bono   20

Testing Assumptions   21 • Testing Predictions   21 • The Positive-Normative Distinction   22

Application 1.6: Do Economists Ever Agree?   23

Summary   24 • Review Questions   25 • Problems   26 • Internet Exercises   28

Appendix to Chapter 1: Mathematics Used in Microeconomics   29

Functions of One Variable   29

Graphing Functions of One Variable   31

*Linear Functions: Intercepts and Slopes   31   •   Slope and Units of
Measurement   33   •   Changes in Slope   33   •   Changes in Intercept   34
Nonlinear Functions   36   •   The Slope of a Nonlinear Function   36   •   Marginal
and Average Effects   36*

Application 1A.1: Property Tax Assessment   37

Calculus and Marginalism   39

Application 1A.2: Can a "Flat" Tax Be Progressive?   40

Functions of Two or More Variables   41

A Simple Example   42

Graphing Functions of Two Variables   42

Simultaneous Equations   44

*Changing Solutions for Simultaneous Equations   45   •   Graphing Simultaneous
Equations   45*

Empirical Microeconomics and Econometrics   46

Application 1A.3: Can Iraq Affect Oil Prices?   47

Random Influences   49   •   The Ceteris Paribus *Assumption   50*

Summary   51

PART 2: DEMAND   53

Chapter 2: Utility and Choice   55

Utility   55

Ceteris Paribus *Assumption   55   •   Utility from Consuming Two Goods   56
Measuring Utility   57*

Assumptions about Utility   57

Basic Properties of Preferences   57

Application 2.1: Can Money Buy Health and Happiness?   58

More Is Better: Defining an Economic "Good"   59

Voluntary Trades and Indifference Curves   60

*Indifference Curves   61   •   Indifference Curves and the Marginal Rate of
Substitution   62   •   Diminishing Marginal Rate of Substitution   62   •   Balance
in Consumption   63*

Indifference Curve Maps   64

Illustrating Particular Preferences   65

Application 2.2: Product Positioning in Marketing   66

Utility Maximization: An Initial Survey   68

Choices Are Constrained   69   •   A Simple Case   69

Graphic Analysis of Utility Maximization   70

The Budget Constraint   70 • *Budget Constraint Algebra*   71 • *Utility Maximization*   72

Using the Model of Choice   74

Application 2.3: Ticket Scalping   75

Generalizations   78

Many Goods   78

Application 2.4: The Sad Tale of Willie and His Uncle   79

Complicated Budget Constraints   81 • *Composite Goods*   81

Application 2.5: Quantity Discounts and Frequent-Flier Programs   82

Summary   83 • Review Questions   84 • Problems   85 • Internet Exercises   87

Chapter 3: Individual Demand Curves   89

Demand Functions   89

Homogeneity   90

Changes in Income   90

Normal Goods   91

Application 3.1: Engel's Law   92

Inferior Goods   93

Changes in a Good's Price   94

Substitution and Income Effects from a Fall in Price   94 • *Substitution and Income Effects from an Increase in Price*   97 • *Substitution and Income Effects for a Normal Good: Summary*   98 • *Substitution and Income Effects for Inferior Goods*   98 • *Giffen's Paradox*   99

Application 3.2: The Consumer Price Index and Its Biases   100

The Lump-Sum Principle   103

A Graphical Approach   103 • *Generalizations*   104

Application 3.3: Wouldn't Cash Be a Better Way to Help Poor People?   105

Changes in the Price of Another Good   106

Substitutes and Complements   107

Construction of Individual Demand Curves   108

Application 3.4: Why Are So Many "Trucks" on the Road?   109

Shape of the Demand Curve   112

Shifts in an Individual's Demand Curve   112

Be Careful in Using Terminology   114

Consumer Surplus   114

Application 3.5: Fads, Seasons, and Health Scares   115

Demand Curves and Consumer Surplus   116 • *Consumer Surplus and Utility*   117

Application 3.6: Valuing Clean Air   118

Summary   121 • Review Questions   121 • Problems   122 • Internet
Exercises   124

Chapter 4: Market Demand and Elasticity   126

Market Demand Curves   126

*Construction of the Market Demand Curve   126 • Shifts in the Market
Demand Curve   127 • A Simplified Notation   128*

Application 4.1: Why the 2001 Tax Cut Was a Dud   129

Elasticity   130

Price Elasticity of Demand   131

*Values of the Price Elasticity of Demand   132 • Price Elasticity and the Shape
of the Demand Curve   132 • Price Elasticity and the Substitution
Effect   132 • Price Elasticity and Time   133 • Price Elasticity and Total
Expenditures   133*

Application 4.2: Brand Loyalty   134

Application 4.3: Volatile Farm Prices   136

Demand Curves and Price Elasticity   137

*Linear Demand Curves and Price Elasticity   137 • A Unitary Elastic
Curve   140*

Income Elasticity of Demand   141

Application 4.4: An Experiment in Health Insurance   142

Cross-Price Elasticity of Demand   144

Empirical Studies of Demand   144

*Estimating Demand Curves   145 • Some Elasticity Estimates   145 • Some
Cross-Price Elasticity Estimates   147*

Application 4.5: Alcohol Taxes as Drunk Driving Policy   148

Summary   149 • Review Questions   150 • Problems   151 • Internet
Exercises   154

PART 3: PRODUCTION, COSTS, AND SUPPLY   155

Chapter 5: Production   157

Production Functions   157

Two-Input Production Function   158

Marginal Product   158

Application 5.1: Everyone Is a Firm   159

*Diminishing Marginal Product   160 • Marginal Product Curve   161
Average Product   162 • Appraising the Marginal Product Concept   162*

Isoquant Maps   163

Application 5.2: Why Do the Japanese Have a Cost Advantage in Making Cars? 164

*Rate of Technical Substitution 165 • The RTS and Marginal Products 166
Diminishing RTS 166*

Returns to Scale 167

Adam Smith on Returns to Scale 167

Application 5.3: Engineering and Economics 168

A Precise Definition 169 • Graphic Illustrations 169

Input Substitution 171

Application 5.4: Returns to Scale in Beer Brewing 172

*Fixed-Proportions Production Function 173 • The Relevance of Input
Substitutability 174*

Changes in Technology 174

Technical Progress versus Input Substitution 175

A Numerical Example 176

The Production Function 176

Application 5.5: Multifactor Productivity 177

*Average and Marginal Productivities 178 • The Isoquant Map 179
Technical Progress 180*

Summary 181 • Review Questions 182 • Problems 183 • Internet
Exercises 185

Chapter 6: Costs 187

Basic Concepts of Costs 187

*Labor Costs 188 • Capital Costs 188 • Entrepreneurial Costs 189 • The
Two-Input Case 189*

Application 6.1: Stranded Costs and Electricity Deregulation 190

Economic Profits and Cost Minimization 191

Cost-Minimizing Input Choice 192

*Graphic Presentation 192 • An Alternative Interpretation 193 • The Firm's
Expansion Path 194*

Cost Curves 195

*Average and Marginal Costs 197 • Marginal Cost Curves 198 • Average
Cost Curves 199*

Application 6.2: Findings on Firms' Costs 201

Distinction between the Short Run and the Long Run 202

Application 6.3: Airlines' Costs 203

Holding Capital Input Constant 204 • *Types of Short-Run Costs* 205 • *Input Inflexibility and Cost Minimization* 205

Per-Unit Short-Run Cost Curves 206

Application 6.4: Can We Do Anything about Traffic Snarls? 208

Shifts in Cost Curves 209

Changes in Input Prices 209 • *Technological Innovation* 210 • *Economies of Scope* 210

Application 6.5: Economies of Scope in Banks and Hospitals 211

A Numerical Example 212

Long-Run Cost Curves 214 • *Short-Run Costs* 214

Summary 216 • Review Questions 216 • Problems 218 • Internet Exercises 220

Chapter 7: Profit Maximization and Supply 221

The Nature of Firms 221

Firms' Goals 222

Profit Maximization 222

Marginalism 222 • *The Output Decision* 222

Application 7.1: Corporate Profits Taxes and the Leveraged Buyout Craze 223

The Marginal Revenue/Marginal Cost Rule 224 • *Marginalism in Input Choices* 226

Marginal Revenue 226

Marginal Revenue for a Downward-Sloping Demand Curve 226 • *A Numerical Example* 227 • *Marginal Revenue and Price Elasticity* 228

Marginal Revenue Curve 231

Shifts in Demand and Marginal Revenue Curves 231

Supply Decision of a Price-Taking Firm 232

Application 7.2: How Did Airlines Respond to Deregulation? 233

Short-Run Profit Maximization 234 • *Showing Profits* 235 • *The Firm's Short-Run Supply Curve* 236 • *The Shutdown Decision* 236

Profit Maximization and Managers' Incentives 237

Application 7.3: Why Is Drilling for Crude Oil Such a Boom or Bust Business? 238

Nature of the Principal-Agent Relationship 239 • *Conflicts in the Agent Relationship* 240 • *Incentive Contracts* 241

Application 7.4: Principals and Agents in Franchising and Medicine 242

Application 7.5: The Good and Bad Effects of Stock Options 244

Summary 245 • Review Questions 245 • Problems 247 • Internet Exercises 249

PART 4: MODELS OF MARKET EQUILIBRIUM   251

Chapter 8: Perfect Competition   253

Timing of a Supply Response   253

Pricing in the Very Short Run   254

Shifts in Demand: Price as a Rationing Device   254 • Applicability of the Very-Short-Run Model   254

Short-Run Supply   255

Application 8.1: Internet Auctions   256

Construction of a Short-Run Supply Curve   257

Short-Run Price Determination   258

Functions of the Equilibrium Price   258 • Effect of an Increase in Market Demand   260

Shifts in Supply and Demand Curves   260

Short-Run Supply Elasticity   260 • Shifts in Supply Curves and the Importance of the Shape of the Demand Curve   261 • Shifts in Demand Curves and the Importance of the Shape of the Supply Curve   263 • A Numerical Illustration   264

Application 8.2: Ethanol Subsidies in the United States and Brazil   265

The Long Run   267

Equilibrium Conditions   267 • Profit Maximization   268 • Entry and Exit   268 • Long-Run Equilibrium   268

Long-Run Supply: The Constant Cost Case   269

Market Equilibrium   269 • A Shift in Demand   269 • Long-Run Supply Curve   270

Application 8.3: Movie Rentals   271

Shape of the Long-Run Supply Curve   272

The Increasing Cost Case   272 • Long-Run Supply Elasticity   274 Estimating Long-Run Elasticities of Supply   274 • The Decreasing Cost Case   275 • Infant Industries   276

Application 8.4: How Do Network Externalities Affect Supply Curves?   277

Summary   279 • Review Questions   279 • Problems   280 • Internet Exercises   283

Chapter 9: Applying the Competitive Model   284

Consumer and Producer Surplus   284

Short-Run Producer Surplus   285 • Long-Run Producer Surplus   286 Ricardian Rent   286 • Economic Efficiency   288 • A Numerical Illustration   288

Application 9.1: Does Buying Things on the Internet Improve Welfare?   289

Price Controls and Shortages   291

Tax Incidence   293

Application 9.2: Rent Control: Why This Bad Idea Never Dies   294

Long-Run Shifting of the Tax   296 • Long-Run Incidence with Increasing Costs   296 • Incidence and Elasticity   296

Application 9.3: The Tobacco Settlement Is Just a Tax   298

Taxation and Efficiency   299 • A Numerical Illustration   300 • Transactions Costs   300

Trade Restrictions   301

Gains from International Trade   301 • Tariff Protection   303 • Other Types of Trade Protection   304

Application 9.4: The Endless Saga of Steel Protectionism   305

Summary   306 • Review Questions   307 • Problems   308 • Internet Exercises   310

Appendix to Chapter 9: General Equilibrium   312

A Perfectly Competitive Price System   312

Why Is General Equilibrium Necessary?   313

Disturbing the Equilibrium   313 • Reestablishing Equilibrium   314

A Simple General Equilibrium Model   315

The Efficiency of Perfect Competition   316

Prices, Efficiency, and Laissez-Faire Economics   318

Why Markets Fail to Achieve Economic Efficiency   319

Imperfect Competition   319 • Externalities   319

Application 9A.1: Gains from Free Trade and the NAFTA Debate   320

Public Goods   322 • Imperfect Information   322

Efficiency and Equity   323

Defining and Achieving Equity   323 • Equity and Competitive Markets   324

The Edgeworth Box Diagram for Exchange   324

Mutually Beneficial Trades   325 • Efficiency in Exchange   326 • Contract Curve   326 • Efficiency and Equity   327

Summary   328

Chapter 10: Monopoly   329

Causes of Monopoly   329

Technical Barriers to Entry   329 • Legal Barriers to Entry   330

Application 10.1: Should You Need a License to Shampoo a Dog?   331

Profit Maximization   332

A Graphic Treatment 332 • Monopoly Supply Curve 333 • Monopoly Profits 334

What's Wrong with Monopoly? 334

Profitability 334

Application 10.2: Who Makes Money at Casinos? 336

Distortion of Resource Allocation 337

Monopolistic Distortions and Transfers of Welfare 339

Allocational Effects 339 • Distributional Effects 339 • Monopolists' Costs 340

Application 10.3: Pricing Problems in Dallas 341

A Numerical Illustration of Deadweight Loss 342

Price Discrimination 343

Perfect Price Discrimination 344 • Quantity Discounts 345

Application 10.4: Financial Aid at Private Colleges 346

Two-Part Tariffs 347 • Market Separation 348

Application 10.5: Pricing at the Magic Kingdom 349

Pricing for Multiproduct Monopolies 351

Application 10.6: Bundling of Cable and Satellite Television Offerings 352

Regulation of Natural Monopolies 353

Marginal Cost Pricing and the Natural Monopoly Dilemma 353 • Two-Tier Pricing Systems 355 • Rate of Return Regulation 355

Application 10.7: Can Anyone Understand Telephone Pricing? 356

Summary 357 • Review Questions 357 • Problems 358 • Internet Exercises 361

Chapter 11: Imperfect Competition 362

Pricing of Homogeneous Goods 362

Quasi-Competitive Model 362 • Cartel Model 363 • Other Pricing Possibilities 364

Application 11.1: The De Beers Cartel 365

The Cournot Model 366

Market Conditions 366 • Duopoly Model 367 • Cournot Equilibrium 369 • Generalizations 370

Price Leadership Model 370

Application 11.2: Cournot in California 371

Product Differentiation 373

Application 11.3: Price Leadership in Financial Markets 374

Market Definition 375 • Firms' Choices 376 • Market Equilibrium 376

Entry by New Firms   376

Monopolistic Competition   376

Application 11.4: Competition in Breakfast Space   377

Sustainability of Monopolistic Competition   378 • Determination of Industry Structure   379 • Barriers to Entry   380

Application 11.5: Airline Deregulation Revisited   381

Summary   382 • Review Questions   382 • Problems   383 • Internet Exercises   385

Chapter 12: Strategy and Game Theory   387

Basic Concepts   387

Players   388 • Strategies   388 • Payoffs   388

Equilibrium Concepts   389

An Illustrative Advertising Game   389

The Game in Extensive Form   389 • The Game in Normal Form   390 Dominant Strategies and Nash Equilibria   391 • Nature of Nash Equilibria   391

The Prisoner's Dilemma   392

Application 12.1: Nash Equilibrium on the Beach   393

Applications   395 • Cooperation and Repetition   395

Many-Period Games   396

Credible Threats   397

Models of Pricing Behavior   398

The Bertrand Equilibrium   398 • Two-Stage Price Games and Cournot Equilibrium   398 • Comparing the Bertrand and Cournot Results   399 Tacit Collusion   400

Application 12.2: How Is the Price Game Played?   401

Generalizations and Limitations   403

Entry, Exit, and Strategy   403

Sunk Costs and Commitment   403

Application 12.3: The Great Electrical Equipment Conspiracy   404

First-Mover Advantages   405 • Entry Deterrence   406 • A Numerical Example   407 • Limit Pricing   407

Application 12.4: First-Mover Advantages for Alcoa, DuPont, Procter & Gamble, and Wal-Mart   408

Incomplete Information   409 • Predatory Pricing   410

Application 12.5: The Standard Oil Legend   411

N-Player Game Theory   412

Summary   413 • Review Questions   413 • Problems   414 • Internet Exercises   416

PART 5: FURTHER TOPICS   417

Chapter 13: Labor Markets   419

Marginal Productivity Theory of Input Demand   419

Profit-Maximizing Behavior and the Hiring of Inputs   419 • Price-Taking Behavior   420 • Marginal Revenue Product   420 • A Special Case—Marginal Value Product   421

Responses to Changes in Input Prices   422

Single-Variable Input Case   422

Application 13.1: Hiring by Nonprofit Firms   423

A Numerical Example   425 • Two-Variable Input Case   425 • Substitution Effect   426 • Output Effect   426 • Summary of Firm's Demand for Labor   427

Responsiveness of Input Demand to Price Changes   428

Ease of Substitution   428 • Costs and the Output Effect   428

Input Supply   429

Application 13.2: Controversy over the Minimum Wage   430

Labor Supply and Wages   431

Equilibrium Input Price Determination   432

Shifts in Demand and Supply   432

Application 13.3: Why Is Wage Inequality Increasing?   434

Monopsony   435

Marginal Expense   435 • A Numerical Illustration   436 • Monopsonist's Input Choice   437 • A Graphical Demonstration   437 • Monopsonists and Resource Allocation   438 • Causes of Monopsony   439

Application 13.4: Monopsony in the Market for Sports Stars   440

Bilateral Monopoly   441

Summary   442 • Review Questions   443 • Problems   444 • Internet Exercises   446

Appendix to Chapter 13: Labor Supply   448

Allocation of Time   448

A Simple Model of Time Use   448 • The Opportunity Cost of Leisure   449 Utility Maximization   450

Application 13A.1: The Opportunity Cost of Time   451

Income and Substitution Effects of a Change in the Real Wage Rate   452

A Graphical Analysis   453

Market Supply Curve for Labor   455

Application 13A.2: Changing Labor Force Participation for Younger Women and Older Men   456

Summary   457

Chapter 14: Capital Markets   458

Time Periods and the Flow of Economic Transactions   458

Individual Savings—The Supply of Loans   459

   Two-Period Model of Saving   459 • *A Graphical Analysis*   460 • *Substitution and Income Effects of a Change in r*   461

Firms' Demand for Capital and Loans   462

   Rental Rates and Interest Rates   462

Application 14.1: Do We Need Tax Breaks for Savers?   463

   Ownership of Capital Equipment   465

Determination of the Real Interest Rate   465

Application 14.2: Do Taxes Affect Investment?   466

   Changes in the Real Interest Rate   467

Present Discounted Value   468

   Single-Period Discounting   468

Application 14.3: Inflation-Indexed Bonds   469

   Multiperiod Discounting   470 • *Present Value and Economic Decisions*   471

Pricing of Exhaustible Resources   472

   Scarcity Costs   472 • *The Size of Scarcity Costs*   473

Application 14.4: Discounting Cash Flows and Derivative Securities   474

   Time Pattern of Resource Prices   475

Application 14.5: Are Any Resources Scarce?   476

Summary   477 • Review Questions   478 • Problems   479 • Internet Exercises   481

Appendix to Chapter 14: Compound Interest   482

Interest   482

Compound Interest   483

   Interest for 1 Year   483 • *Interest for 2 Years*   483 • *Interest for 3 Years*   484 • *A General Formula*   484 • *Compounding with Any Dollar Amount*   485

Application 14A.1: Compound Interest Gone Berserk   486

Present Discounted Value   487

   An Algebraic Definition   487 • *General PDV Formulas*   488

Application 14A.2: Zero-Coupon Bonds   489

Discounting Payment Streams   490

   An Algebraic Presentation   490 • *Perpetual Payments*   491 • *Varying Payment Streams*   493 • *Calculating Yields*   493 • *Reading Bond Tables*   494

Frequency of Compounding   494

Semiannual Compounding   494 • *A General Treatment   495*

The Present Discounted Value Approach to Investment Decisions   496

Application 14A.3: Continuous Compounding   497

Present Discounted Value and the Rental Rate   498

Summary   499

Chapter 15: Uncertainty and Information   500

Probability and Expected Value   500

Application 15.1: Blackjack Systems   502

Risk Aversion   503

Diminishing Marginal Utility   503 • *A Graphical Analysis of Risk Aversion   504* • *Willingness to Pay to Avoid Risk   505*

Methods for Reducing Risk   505

Insurance   505

Application 15.2: Do HMO Patients Need a Bill of Rights?   508

Diversification   509

Pricing of Risk in Financial Assets   511

Application 15.3: Mutual Funds   512

Investors' Market Options   513 • *Choices by Individual Investors   514*

Application 15.4: The Equity Premium Puzzle   515

The Economics of Information   517

A Utility-Maximizing Model   518 • *Balancing the Gains and Costs of Information   519* • *Information Differences among Economic Actors   520*

Information and Economic Efficiency   520

Application 15.5: Safe Driver Insurance Policies   521

Asymmetric Information and the "Lemons" Problem   522 • *Adverse Selection   523* • *Acquisition and Provision of Information   523*

Application 15.6: Looking for Lemons   524

Summary   525 • Review Questions   525 • Problems   526 • Internet Exercises   529

Chapter 16: Externalities and Public Goods   530

Defining Externalities   530

Externalities between Firms   531 • *Externalities between Firms and People   531* • *Externalities between People   532* • *Reciprocal Nature of Externalities   532*

Externalities and Allocational Efficiency   532

Application 16.1: Secondhand Smoke   533

A Graphical Demonstration   534

Property Rights, Bargaining, and the Coase Theorem   536

*Costless Bargaining and Competitive Markets   536 • Ownership by the
Polluting Firm   536 • Ownership by the Injured Firm   537 • The Coase
Theorem   537 • Distributional Effects   537 • The Role of Transactions
Costs   538*

Externalities with High Transactions Costs   538

Application 16.2: Property Rights in Nature   539

*Legal Redress   540 • Taxation   541 • Regulation of Externalities   542
Optimal Regulation   543 • Fees, Permits, and Direct Controls   543*

Public Goods   544

Attributes of Public Goods   544

Application 16.3: Regulating Power Plant Emissions   545

Nonexclusivity   546 • Nonrivalry   547 • Categories of Public Goods   547

Public Goods and Market Failure   548

A Graphical Demonstration   548

Solutions to the Public Goods Problem   550

*Nash Equilibrium and Underproduction   550 • Compulsory Taxation   551
The Lindahl Equilibrium   551*

Revealing the Demand for Public Goods   552

Application 16.4: Why Is There So Much Fundraising on Public Broadcasting?   553

Local Public Goods   554

Direct Voting and Resource Allocation   554

*Majority Rule   555 • The Paradox of Voting   555 • Single-Peaked
Preferences and the Median Voter Theorem   556 • Voting and Resource
Allocation   557*

Application 16.5: Referenda on Public Spending   558

Representative Government and Bureaucracies   559

Summary   560 • Review Questions   561 • Problems   561 • Internet
Exercises   564

Solutions to Odd-Numbered Problems   565

Brief Answers to MicroQuizzes   587

Glossary   596

Index   603

Preface

In some respects, this new edition is the same tried and true book. It has always been my hope that *Intermediate Microeconomics and Its Application* will provide for students a clear and concise introduction to the ways in which economists explain the operations of markets. I hope that each successive edition of this book continues to approach this goal ever more closely.

In many other respects, however, this is a new book. I have tried to simplify some of the more opaque sections of prior editions and have worked hard to make certain that the analysis in the book is phrased in ways that make more intuitive sense to students. In addition, this is my first edition with South-Western/Thomson Learning and they have managed to give the book a fresh new look and a clearer presentation. All in all, I think both students and faculty will be happy with this latest incarnation.

NEW TO THE NINTH EDITION

Some of the specific changes and additions I have made to the theoretical material in the ninth edition include:

- A simplified presentation of both demand (consumer surplus) and cost concepts so that much extraneous material can now be avoided
- Some reorientation of the material on the competitive model that especially focuses on providing a more compact coverage of general equilibrium ideas
- Major revisions to the factor market material in the text
- Some extensions of the theory of externalities and public goods to illustrate to students further uses of these important concepts

APPLICATIONS AND INTERNET EXERCISES

This edition again features many new applications on such topics as:

- The California Electricity Crisis
- Internet Auctions
- Casino Gambling
- New Protectionism in Steel
- Derivative Securities and Fannie Mae
- Regulation of HMOs

In addition, I have tried to provide updates to all of the applications that I have retained from the eighth edition, with a special emphasis on such current issues as accounting fraud, stock options, and changes in airlines' operational strategies.

This edition also features a series of Internet Exercises that have been designed by my colleague Lisa Takeyama. The exercises are intended to show students how they can make use of Web resources to study important and timely economic questions.

TEXT FEATURES

I am very proud of the features in this text that are designed to facilitate learning. These include:

- Review Questions in each chapter that are intended to build intuition for students
- InfoTrac margin notes that highlight key words throughout the text for further study of chapter topics through the InfoTrac database of articles on the Internet
- Extensive problems in each chapter that are intended to drive home important analytical points (Solutions to many of these problems are also provided as an aid to independent learning.)
- About five short-answer MicroQuizzes in each chapter that provide a check for students as they read
- Questions associated with each Application that motivate students to put the material presented into a broader perspective
- A detailed Glossary that is available both in the margins of the text and gathered together at the end

All of these aids have been revised and updated for this edition when appropriate.

SUPPLEMENTS TO THE TEXT

A helpful array of supplements are available with this edition to both students and instructors.

- An *Instructor's Manual with Test Bank,* by Walter Nicholson, Amherst College, contains summaries, lecture and discussion suggestions, list of glossary terms, solutions to problems, multiple-choice test bank, and suggested test problems. The *Instructor's Manual with Test Bank* is available on the text Web site to instructors only.
- A *Study Guide and Workbook,* by Brett Katzman, Kennesaw College, includes learning objectives, fill-in summaries, multiple-choice questions, glossary questions, exercises involving quantitative problems, graphs, and answers to all questions and problems.
- *Microsoft PowerPoint Slides,* revised by Mark Karscig, Central Missouri State University, are available on the text Web site for use by students as an aid to note taking and by instructors for enhancing their lectures.
- A *text Web site* at *http://nicholson.swcollege.com* contains links to the end-of-chapter Internet Exercises, on-line quizzes, InfoTrac, instructor and student resources, economic applications, and more.
- *Economic Applications (e-con @pps)* at *http://econapps.swcollege.com* is the site for South-Western's dynamic Web features: EconNews On-Line, EconDebate On-Line, and EconData On-Line. Organized by pertinent economic topics and searchable by topic or feature, these features are easy to integrate into the classroom. EconNews, EconDebate, and EconData all deepen your understanding of theoretical concepts through hands-on exploration and analysis for the latest economic news stories, policy debates, and data. These features are updated on a regular basis. The Economic Applications Web site is complementary to every new book buyer via an access card that's packaged with the books. Used book buyers can purchase access to the site at *http://econapps.swcollege.com.*
- *InfoTrac College Edition* has passwords packaged with every new copy of the textbook. InfoTrac is a fully searchable on-line university library containing complete articles and their images. Its database allows access to hundreds of scholarly and popular publications—all reliable sources, including magazines, journals, encyclopedias, and newsletters—with the key words provided in the text.

TO THE INSTRUCTOR

Using this new edition should prove easy both for new adopters and for users of the previous edition. New adopters will find that the book proceeds in a very standard way through demand, supply, and market structure. It is possible to adopt a "bare bones" approach to the subject by covering only this material, or one may add extra topics from the final section of the book that covers factor markets, uncertainty, and externalities.

For previous users of the text, there are virtually no changes here that should affect class scheduling. The most important change is my deletion of the chapter on general equilibrium and inclusion of some of its material in an appendix to the perfect competition chapter. This change was made on the advice of many reviewers who pointed out that the general equilibrium material was somewhat out of keeping with the applied nature of the remainder of the text. I have bowed to their collective judgment.

As always, any comments on the text and its accompanying ancillaries would be most appreciated. Ever since the advent of the Internet, I have accumulated a vast collection of e-mail correspondence. I especially encourage users of the book to contact me in this way (the address is *wenicholson@amherst.edu*).

TO THE STUDENT

This book really is intended to make it easier for you to learn microeconomics. Although the book pulls no punches in terms of insisting you learn "the real thing," it has been extensively reworked over the years to make that process as clear and streamlined as possible. Of course, there may still be places in the text that you don't like or find confusing. I would very much like to hear from you about these. I would also be interested in knowing whether you find the applications useful and enjoyable or, if not, how they might be improved. Prior editions of the book owe a great debt to the perceptive comments of students, and I expect that will be the case for this new version as well. If you feel so inclined, drop me an e-mail (*wenicholson@amherst.edu*).

ACKNOWLEDGMENTS

The first debt of gratitude I must acknowledge for this edition is to Jeff Gilbreath of South-Western/Thomson Learning. He introduced me to the company and helped me in planning this edition. His death in the summer of 2002 cut short what I had hoped would turn into a highly productive, long-term working relationship. I am very grateful to Peter Adams who gave me good advice in Jeff's absence and especially to Susan Smart who, despite being overworked in the extreme, helped to pick up where Jeff had left off and got the text done pretty much on schedule. I hope this book justifies Jeff's faith in it.

As to the specifics of this new edition, I drew especially on a series of very useful reviews of the eighth edition that were kindly provided by Hassan Y. Aly, Ohio State University; Laurie J. Bates, Bryant College; Tibor Besedes, Rutgers University; Donald R. Booth, Chapman University; Barry Haworth, University of

Louisville; Gerrit Knaap, University of Illinois at Urbana-Champaign; Tim Sass, Florida State University; and Mark Walker, University of Arizona.

The suggestions of these reviewers about what should be covered in the book (and what should be omitted) proved to be good advice that I hope I have followed as faithfully as possible. These reviewers' thoughts on the suitability of various applications in the text were also most helpful.

Amherst students who assisted me with this and previous editions include: Mark Bruni, Stephanie Cogen, Morgan Delano, Adrian Dillon, David Macoy, Katie Merrell, Jeff Rodman, and Sujith Vijayan. To them and to all of their colleagues who used the text, I owe a debt of appreciation for keeping me "on message." I also appreciate all of the useful comments I have received from my Amherst colleagues who use this text, Lisa Takeyama and Frank Westhoff. I am thankful that they appear to use it voluntarily and actually seem none the worse for it.

I have been very impressed by the professional staff at South-Western/Thomson Learning who made this edition happen. In addition to Peter Adams and Susan Smart, I owe special gratitude to Chris Hudson who guided the production of the book. On more than one occasion, he caught my errors and made sure everything was here. C. Jeanne Patterson did an exceptional job in copyediting the text; I believe that the writing style here is much improved and hopefully devoid of the professor-speak that inevitably sneaks into my prose if I am not careful. The attractive and innovative design for this edition is the work of Stacy Shirley. I believe users will appreciate the fine job she did in making the appearance of the book more lively and interesting.

Because all of my children (Kate, David, Tory, and Paul) have now become adults, it is only my wife Susan and our sedate dog Tobler who have to put up with my "new edition" moods. This year was a very difficult one for Susan; we are all grateful that it is ending better than it began. I hope that working on this edition did not take too much of my time away from what is really important.

It is hard to pretend to be young when you have three grandchildren (Beth, Sarah, and David). My dedication of this edition to them is not only a feeble attempt to lure them into reading it someday but also a statement about how happy I am that they are here.

Walter Nicholson
Amherst, Massachusetts
April 2003

Part 1

Introduction

"Economics is the study of mankind in the ordinary business of life."

Alfred Marshall, *Principles of Economics*, 1890

Part 1 consists of only a single background chapter. In it we review some basic principles of supply and demand, which should look familiar from your introductory economics course. This review is especially important because supply and demand models serve as a starting point for most of the material covered later in this book.

Mathematical tools are now widely used in practically all areas of economics. Although the math used in this book is not especially difficult, the appendix to Chapter 1 provides a brief summary of what you will need to know. These basic principles are usually covered in an elementary algebra course. Most important for our purposes are the relationships between algebraic functions and the representation of these functions in graphs. Because we will be using graphs heavily throughout the book, it is important to be sure you understand this basic material before proceeding.

1

Economic Models

Why are the prices of airline tickets so crazy? I have made the same trip four times in the past year. I have paid as little as $203 for the trip and as much as $865. I am sure my fellow passengers have paid an even more bewildering variety of prices; in fact, I always worry that the person next to me has gotten a much better deal. Surely, the cost of carrying me on a plane has not changed all that much in the past year; so how can you explain the fares?

Or, consider gas prices. During the past year, I have paid as little as $0.89 per gallon for unleaded regular and as much as $1.59. Although I have been warned by environmentalists about how our "wasteful" use of fossil fuels must be cut back before it is too late, I very much doubt that such price trends have anything to do with geology. The amount of available crude oil just has not changed that much over the past year. So what explains the price movements?

Last night I saw Bono of U2 fame on the television talking about how U.S. farm subsidies will hurt farmers in Ghana, West Africa. Should I be worried about that? And why do we have farm subsidies in the first place, for that matter? Am I paying them?

If these are the kinds of questions that interest you, this is the right place to be. As the quotation in the introduction to this part states, economics (especially microeconomics) is the study of "the ordinary business of life." That is, economists take such things as airfares, gas prices, and farm subsidies as interesting topics, worthy of detailed study. Why? Because understanding these everyday features of our world goes a long way toward understanding the welfare of the actual people who live here. Our intention is to cut through the garble of television sound bites and the hot air of politicians that often obscure rather than enlighten these issues. By developing a thorough analysis of market forces, the goal here is to help you to understand better the many economic trends that affect all of our lives.

WHAT IS MICROECONOMICS?

Economics
The study of the allocation of scarce resources among alternative uses.

As you probably learned in your introductory course, **economics** can be formally defined as the "study of the allocation of scarce resources among alternative uses." This definition stresses that there simply are not enough basic resources (such as land, labor, and capital equipment) in the world to produce everything that people want. Hence, every society must choose, either explicitly or implicitly, how its resources will be used. Of course, such "choices" are not made by an all-powerful dictator who specifies every citizen's life in minute detail. Instead, the way resources get allocated is determined by the actions of many people who engage in a bewildering variety of economic activities. Many of these activities involve participation in some sort of market transaction. Flying in airplanes, buying gasoline, or purchasing food are just three of the practically infinite number of things that people do that have market consequences for them and for society as a whole. **Microeconomics** is the study of all of these choices and of how well the resulting market outcomes meet basic human needs.

Microeconomics
The study of the economic choices individuals and firms make and of how these choices create markets.

Of course, any real-world economic system is far too complicated to be described in detail. Just think about how many items are available in the typical hardware store (not to mention in the typical Home Depot megastore). Surely it would be impossible to study in detail how each hammer or screwdriver was produced and how many were bought in each store. Not only would such a description take a very long time, but also no one would care to know such trivia, especially if the information gathered could not be used elsewhere. For this reason, all economists build simple **models** of various activities that they wish to study. These models may not be especially realistic, at least in terms of their ability to capture the details of how a hammer is sold; but, just as scientists use models of the atom or architects use models of what they want to build, so too economists use simplified models to describe the basic features of markets. Of course, these models are "unrealistic." But maps are unrealistic too—they do not show every house or parking lot. Despite this lack of "realism," maps help you see the overall picture and get you where you want to go. That is precisely what a good economic model should do. The economic models that you will encounter in this book have a wide variety of uses, even though, at first, you may think that they are unrealistic. The applications scattered throughout the book are intended to stress that point. But they only hint at the ways in which the study of microeconomics can help you understand the vast number of economic events that impact your life.

Models
Simple theoretical descriptions that capture the essentials of how the economy works.

A FEW BASIC PRINCIPLES

Production possibility frontier
A graph showing all possible combinations of goods that can be produced with a fixed amount of resources.

Much of microeconomics consists of simply applying a few basic principles to new situations. We can illustrate some of these by examining an economic model with which you already should be familiar—the **production possibility frontier.** This graph shows the various amounts of two goods that an economy can produce during some period (say, one year). Figure 1.1, for example, shows all the

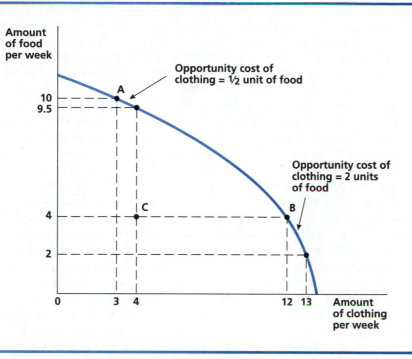

FIGURE 1.1 Production Possibility Frontier The production possibility frontier shows the different combinations of two goods that can be produced from a certain amount of scarce resources. It also shows the opportunity cost of producing more of one good as the quality of the other good that cannot then be produced. The opportunity cost at two different levels of production of a good can be seen by comparing points A and B. Inefficiency is shown by comparing points B and C.

combinations of two goods (say, food and clothing) that can be produced with this economy's resources. For example, 10 units of food and 3 units of clothing can be made, or 4 units of food and 12 units of clothing. Many other combinations of food and clothing can also be produced, and Figure 1.1 shows all of them. Any combination on or inside the frontier can be produced, but combinations of food and clothing outside the frontier cannot be made because not enough resources are available.

This simple model of production illustrates five principles that are common to practically every situation studied in microeconomics:

- *Resources are scarce.* Some combinations of food and clothing (such as 10 units of food together with 12 units of clothing) are unattainable given the resources available. We simply cannot have all of everything we might want.
- *Scarcity involves opportunity costs.* That is, producing more of one good necessarily involves producing less of something else. For example, if this economy produces 10 units of food and 3 units of clothing per year at

Opportunity cost
The cost of a good as measured by the alternative uses that are forgone by producing it.

point A, producing 1 more unit of clothing would "cost" ½ unit of food. In other words, to increase the output of clothing by 1 unit means the production of food would have to decrease by ½ unit.

- *Opportunity costs are usually increasing.* Expanding the output of one particular good will usually involve increasing opportunity costs as diminishing returns set in. Although the precise reasons for this will be explained later, Figure 1.1 shows this principle clearly. If clothing output were expanded to 12 units per year (point B), the opportunity cost of clothing would rise from ½ a unit of food to 2 units of food. Hence, the opportunity cost of an economic action is not constant but varies with the circumstances.

- *Opportunity costs should be measured in real terms.* The opportunity costs involved in producing more of something involve sacrificing some amount of another actual good. Although it is often convenient to talk of opportunity costs in terms of money (dollars, yen, pesos, and so forth), this can sometimes be misleading. Suppose, for example, that an economy operating at point A in Figure 1.1 had a price of clothing of $10 and of food of $20. The opportunity cost of clothing would be ½ unit of food (as the production possibility frontier shows). If prices doubled, the price of clothing would rise to $20 and the price of food would rise to $40. But the opportunity cost of 1 unit of clothing would remain ½ unit of food. Focusing on the change in dollar costs would be misleading since, in real terms, prices have not changed. Practically all of microeconomics deals only in such real terms. Issues involving the price level are usually studied in macroeconomics.

- *Inefficiency involves real opportunity costs.* An economy operating inside its production possibility frontier is said to be performing "inefficiently"—a term we will be making far more precise later. Producing, say, 4 units of clothing and 4 units of food (at point C in Figure 1.1) would involve such an inefficient use of this economy's resources. Such a production would involve the loss of, say, 8 units of clothing that could have been produced along with the 4 units of food. When we study why markets might produce such inefficiencies, it will be important to keep in mind that such losses are not purely conceptual, being of interest only to economic researchers. These are real losses. They involve real opportunity costs. Seeking to avoid such costs should make people in society better off.

In the next section, we show how applying these basic concepts helps in understanding a number of important economic topics. In Application 1.1: Do Animals Understand Economics?, we show how the problem of scarcity and the opportunity costs it entails are universal. It appears that these basic principles can even help us to understand the choices made by wolves, hawks, or finches.

MicroQuiz 1.1

Consider the production possibility frontier shown in Figure 1.1:

1. Why is this curve called a "frontier"?

2. This curve has a "concave" shape. Would the opportunity cost of clothing production increase if the shape of the curve were convex instead?

Scarcity is a dominant feature in nature. Indeed, the effect of scarcity is easier to study in biological societies because they are less complex than modern human societies. In trying to understand the pressures that scarcity imposes on actions, economists and biologists have used models with many similarities. Charles Darwin, the founder of modern evolutionary biology, was well acquainted with the writings of the major eighteenth- and nineteenth-century economists. Their thinking helped to sharpen his insights in *The Origin of Species*. Here we look at the ways in which economic principles are illustrated in the behavior of individual animals and in the evolution of species.

Foraging for Food

All animals must use time and energy in their daily search for food. In many ways, this poses an "economic" problem for them in deciding how to use these resources most effectively. Biologists have developed general theories of animal foraging behavior that draw largely on economic notions of weighing the benefits and costs associated with various ways of finding food.[1]

Two examples help to illustrate this "economic" approach to foraging. First, in the study of birds of prey (eagles, hawks, and so forth), biologists have found that the length of time a bird will hunt in a particular area is determined both by the prevalence of food in that area and by the flight time to another location. These hunters recognize a clear trade-off between spending time and energy looking in one area and using those same resources to go somewhere else. Factors such as the types of food available and the mechanics of the bird's flight can explain observed hunting behavior.

A second, related observation about foraging behavior is the fact that no animal will stay in a given area until all of the food there is exhausted. For example, once a relatively large portion of the prey in a particular area has been consumed, a hawk will go elsewhere. Similarly, studies of honeybees have found that they generally do not gather all of the nectar in a particular flower before moving on. To collect the last drop of nectar is not worth the time and energy the bee must expend to get it. Such weighing of benefits and costs is precisely what an economist would predict.

Scarcity and Evolution

Charles Darwin's greatest discovery was the theory of evolution. Later research has tended to confirm his views that species evolve biologically over long periods of time in ways that adapt to their changing natural environments. In that process, scarcity plays a major role. Adaptations that meet the challenges of a changing environment will allow species to thrive. The failure to adapt rapidly enough can, in extreme cases, cause extinction (as was the case for the dinosaurs).

Many of Darwin's original insights were drawn from his visits to the Galapagos Islands, off the coast of Ecuador. Recent research on the many types of finches Darwin discovered on

[1] See, for example, David W. Stephens and John R. Krebs, *Foraging Theory* (Princeton, NJ: Princeton University Press, 1986).

(continued)

these islands has provided data with which to test his theories.[2] The environmental event that most affected the finches was a severe drought in the early 1980s. Only those finches with extra strong beaks were able to survive, because of their ability to break open what few seeds remained. Succeeding generations of finches have tended to have larger beaks than previous generations. The finches evolved in ways that met the shortage of seeds.

The reactions of economic markets to changing scarcities and to costs, benefits, and trade-offs tend to resemble these evolutionary trends. Rising prices signal the need to economize, and market participants respond by altering their behavior.

To Think About

1. Does it make sense to argue that animals consciously *choose* an optimal strategy for dealing with the scarcity of resources?
2. Evolution selects those genetic traits that favor long-term survival. How does this explain the fact that most animals care for their young even when that takes time and energy?

---

[2] This discussion is based on the summaries contained in J. Weiner, *The Beak of the Finch* (New York: Knopf, 1995).

USES OF MICROECONOMICS

Microeconomics has been applied to study practically every aspect of human behavior. The insights gained by applying a few basic principles to new problems can be far reaching. For example, in Chapter 10, we see how one economist's initial fascination with the way prices were set for the rides at Disneyland opened the way for understanding pricing in such complex areas as air travel or the bundling and pricing of cable television and Internet connections; or, in Chapter 15, we look at another economist's attempt to understand the pricing of used cars. The resulting model of the pricing of "lemons" offers surprising insights about the markets for such important products as health care and legal services. Hence, one must be careful in trying to list the ways in which microeconomics is used because new uses are being discovered every day. Today's seemingly trivial discovery may aid in understanding complex transactions that may not occur until some distant future date.

One way to categorize the uses of microeconomics might be to look at the types of users. At the most basic level, microeconomics has a variety of uses for people in their own lives. An understanding of how markets work can help you make decisions about future jobs, about the wisdom of major purchases (such as houses), or about important financial decisions (such as retirement). Of course, economists are not much better than anyone else in predicting the future. There are legendary examples of economists who in fact made disastrous decisions—most recently illustrated by the financial collapse of a "hedge fund" run by two Nobel Prize–winning economists. But the study of microeconomics can help you to conceptualize the important economic decisions you must make in your life and that can often lead to better decision making. For example, Application 1.2: Is It Worth Your Time to Be Here? illustrates

Those of you who are studying microeconomics as part of your college education are probably paying quite a bit to be in college. It is reasonable to ask
whether this spending is somehow worth it. Of course, many of the benefits
of college (such as the better appreciation of culture, friendship, etc.) do not
have monetary value. In this application, we ask whether the cost is worth it
purely in dollar terms.

Measuring Costs Correctly

The typical U.S. college student pays about $18,000 per year in tuition, fees, and room and
board charges. So one might conclude that the "cost" of 4 years of college is about
$72,000. But this would be incorrect for at least three reasons—all of which derive from a
simple application of the opportunity cost idea:

- Inclusion of room and board fees overstates the true cost of college because these costs
  would likely be incurred whether you were in college or not;
- Including only out-of-pocket costs omits the most important opportunity cost of college attendance—foregone earnings one might make on a job; and
- College costs are paid over time so one cannot simply add 4 years of costs together to
  get the total.

The costs of college can be adjusted for these factors as follows. First, room and board
costs amount to about $6,000 annually, so tuition and fees alone come to $12,000. To
determine the opportunity cost of lost wages, we must make several assumptions, one of
which is that you could earn about $20,000 per year if you were not in school and can only
make back about $2,000 in odd jobs. Hence, the opportunity cost associated with lost
wages is about $18,000 per year, raising the total annual cost to $30,000. For reasons to be
discussed in Chapter 15, we cannot simply multiply $4 \times \$30,000$ but must allow for the fact
that these dollar payments are made at different times. In all, this adjustment would result
in a total cost figure of about $110,000.

The Earnings Gains to College

A number of recent studies have suggested that college graduates earn much more than
those without such an education. A typical finding is that annual earnings for otherwise
identical people are about 50 percent higher if one has attended college. Again, using our
assumption of $20,000 in annual earnings for someone without a college education, this
would imply that earnings gains from graduation might amount to $10,000 per year.
Looked at as an investment, going to college yields about 9 percent per year (that is, 10/110
= .09). This is a relatively attractive real return, exceeding that on long-term bonds (about
2 percent) and on stocks (about 7 percent). Hence, being here does seem worth your time.

Will the Good Times Last?

These calculations are not especially surprising—most people know that college pays
off. Indeed, college attendance in the United States has been expanding rapidly, presumably in response to such rosy statistics. What is surprising is that this large increase

(continued)

in college-educated people does not seem to have reduced the attractiveness of the invest-ment. It must be the case that for some reason the demand for college-educated workers has managed to keep up with the supply. Possible reasons for this have been the subject of much investigation.[1]

To Think About

1. When making the opportunity cost calculations associated with college attendance, how should you take into account the possibility that you might not be able to find a job if you were not in school?
2. The estimated earnings gains from college attendance are based on averages. How might individual peculiarities affect the size of such gains?

[1] For a discussion, see D. Acemoglu, "Technical Change, Inequality, and the Labor Market," *Journal of Economic Literature* (March 2002): 7–72.

how notions of opportunity cost can clarify whether college attendance is really a good investment. Similarly, our discussion of home ownership in Chapter 6 should be of some help in deciding whether owning or renting is the better option.

Businesses also use the tools of microeconomics. Any firm must try to under-stand the nature of the demand for its product. A firm that stubbornly continues to produce a good or service that no one wants will soon find itself in bankruptcy. Application 1.3: Saving Blockbuster illustrates how one firm had to reorganize its entire method of doing business in order to meet customers' expectations. As the example shows, some of the most elementary concepts from microeconomics can aid in understanding why the changes undertaken worked.

Firms must also be concerned with their costs; for this topic, too, microeco-nomics has found many applications. For example, in Chapter 6 we look at some of the research on airline company costs, focusing especially on why Southwest Airlines has been able to make such extensive inroads into U.S. markets. As any-one who has ever flown on this airline knows, the company's attention to keeping costs low verges on the pathological; though passengers may feel a bit like bag-gage, they certainly get to their destinations on time and at very attractive prices. Microeconomic tools can help to understand such efficiencies. They can also help to explore the possible implications of introducing these efficiencies into such notoriously high-cost markets as that for air travel within Europe.

Microeconomics is also often used to evaluate broad questions of government policy. At the deepest level, these investigations focus on whether certain laws and regulations contribute to or detract from overall welfare. As we see in later chap-ters, economists have devised a number of imaginative ways of measuring how various government actions affect consumers, workers, and firms. These measures often play crucial roles in the political debate surrounding the adoption or repeal of such policies. Of course, as Application 1.4: Microsoft and Antitrust illustrates,

Blockbuster is the largest video rental company in the world. The company's rapid growth during the 1980s and 1990s can be attributed both to the increased ownership of VCRs and DVD players in the home and to the related changing patterns of how people view movies. By 1997, however, Blockbuster had encountered significant problems in its core rental business, taking a huge financial loss in that year. The company at first tried to stem its losses by adding new products such as games, music, and candy to its offerings, but that solution proved inadequate to the task. The company was forced to pay closer attention to the nature of the demand for its basic product—the rental of first-run movies.

Blockbuster faced a major problem in renting popular first-run movies. It had to pay very high prices for each tape or DVD—about $65 per copy for most major movies, a very high cost when each outlet may have to stock 30 to 50 copies of each new film. Given such high pricing for this basic input, Blockbuster had to make sure that few, if any, copies sat on its shelves even on low-demand nights (Tuesdays, say). Consequently, it pursued a policy of failing to meet the demand on its busiest nights (Fridays and Saturdays). Customers quickly came to realize that they could not get what they wanted when they wanted it. Movie rentals plummeted.

Nature of the Demand for Rentals

A bit of simple economic analysis can shed some light on the nature of Blockbuster's problem. The company is selling a product that is nonessential. Hence one might expect that people respond significantly to changes in the price of this product (in the terms of Chapter 4, demand is probably quite elastic). But the rental fee is only part of the "price" of renting a movie. Probably equally important in people's decisions are the costs associated with getting to the store and spending time selecting the actual movie to rent. If Blockbuster's shelves are bare, these other components of price rise dramatically. When a customer discovers that the movie he or she wishes to rent isn't there, the customer must either come back later (and face the prospect of being disappointed again) or select a second-best choice. In either case, the consumer is likely to act as if the price has risen, ultimately choosing to rent fewer movies.

Blockbuster's Solution

The only way for Blockbuster to restore demand for its rentals was to find some way to reduce the empty-shelf problem. So a solution rested directly on getting copies of films from the major studios at much lower prices. In a turnabout in policy, Blockbuster agreed to give the studios a substantial share (as much as 40 percent) of the revenues from their movie rentals in exchange for price reductions of up to 90 percent. They then adopted a huge advertising blitz that "guaranteed" the availability of first-run films.

The revenue-sharing solution solved two of the major problems Blockbuster faces in the nature of the demand for its product. First, it allows the firm to add many more copies of popular films to its shelves at very low cost. That in turn reduced the effective price to consumers, who no longer had to cope with the frustrations of empty shelves. Because demand responds significantly to such price changes, the company could easily make up for

(continued)

whatever revenue had to be paid to the studios. The revenue-sharing plan also helped the company address difficulties in predicting the rentals of specific films, making the studios effective partners in sharing this risk.

Evolution of the Movie Rental Business

The immediate effect of revenue sharing was remarkable. Blockbuster's financial statistics improved substantially, and its national share of movie rentals grew rapidly. Clearly, people responded to the end of empty shelves. But the long-run success of the company's business is not assured. Costs associated with obtaining and returning movie rentals still bulk large in the "full price" of the product. New technologies such as DVD rental by mail, pay-per-view options over cable networks, and, perhaps, movie delivery over the Internet all threaten to provide films at much lower full prices than can Blockbuster. Clearly the firm will have to continue to pay very close attention to the demand for its product.

To Think About

1. Which types of consumers would you expect to respond most significantly to Blockbuster's empty shelves?
2. Why did the movie studios agree to the revenue-sharing option?

APPLICATION 1.4

Microsoft and Antitrust

In May 1998 a trial began in federal district court in Washington, D.C., that pitted the U.S. Department of Justice and 20 states against the Microsoft Corporation—the largest computer software firm in the world. At issue was whether Microsoft had illegally "monopolized" various segments of the software industry and thereby violated the Sherman Antitrust Act.

Economic Issues

The central issue in the Microsoft case was whether the firm's dominance of its industry allowed it to follow practices that were ultimately harmful to consumers. In particular, there was the concern that the firm would be able to use its dominance in operating systems for personal computers (Windows 2000 and its predecessors) to harm competitors in other areas. For example, the Netscape Corporation claimed that Microsoft made it intentionally difficult for users to install Netscape's Navigator Web browser in place of Microsoft's own Internet Explorer. Similarly, there were fears that the firm would gain unfair advantages in various types of word processing or spreadsheet software.

(continued)

The Consent Decree

This was not the first time that the Microsoft Corporation had been in the legal spotlight. In 1994 it had signed a consent decree with the U.S. Department of Justice in which the company agreed to end such practices as tying the sale of Microsoft Word or Excel to the licensing of Windows. It also agreed to change the ways in which it charged computer makers such as Compaq and Dell for the basic Windows operating system. But the decree said little about Internet issues—thereby leaving cause for concern that intensified with the rapid increase in Internet usage in the late 1990s.

Dueling Economists

Some of the most important testimony on both sides of the Microsoft case came from economists.[1] The government's primary economic witness, MIT professor Franklin Fisher, argued that control of the Windows operating system gave Microsoft significant power over most PC applications and that the firm had used that power specifically to make it difficult for users to install other firms' software—notably Netscape Navigator. Fisher expressed some caution in evaluating the harm that such actions caused to current consumers. After all, Microsoft was giving away its browser free of charge. Instead, he argued, the real danger was that permitting Microsoft to gain domination of the browser market would allow the firm to eliminate any potential competition in operating systems.

Microsoft countered with an expert witness of its own, Richard Schmalensee (also a professor at MIT and once a student of Fisher's). He argued that fears of Microsoft's ability to deter the development of new operating systems in the future were purely hypothetical and that the company did not in fact currently operate as a monopoly. He cited estimates that Microsoft, if it had true monopoly power, could probably have charged more than $1,000 for its Windows operating system though in fact the system routinely sold for much less than $100.

The Law Works Slowly

As in most large antitrust cases, legal proceedings in the Microsoft case have moved slowly. Initially, Microsoft was found guilty of violating Section II of the Sherman Act, but a major portion of that finding was sent back for further review by an appeals court. In an attempt to hasten matters, the U.S. Department of Justice reached a proposed settlement with Microsoft that, it was claimed, would encourage competition in "middleware" (such as Internet browsers). But several states (who had also sued Microsoft) declined to go along with this settlement on the basis that it was not tough enough. Whether the legal system can ever fashion a remedy for Microsoft's allegedly monopolistic conduct in the rapidly changing computer industry remains an open question.

To Think About

1. How can two economists come to such different opinions on this case? Are they using different methods of analysis? Or are they focusing on different issues?
2. If you had to craft a plan for limiting the possible monopoly power of Microsoft, how would you do it?

---

[1] All of the documents in the Microsoft case are available from the U.S. Justice Department Web site: *http://www.usdoj.gov/atr/cases/ms_index.htm*. The Spring 2001 issue of *The Journal of Economic Perspectives* features a symposium on the Microsoft case.

there are often two sides to such policy questions; and economists are no more immune than anyone else from the temptation to bend their arguments to fit a particular political point of view. Knowledge of microeconomics does provide a basic framework—that is, a common language—in which many such discussions are conducted.

THE BASIC SUPPLY-DEMAND MODEL

As the saying goes, "Even your pet parrot can learn economics—just teach it to say 'supply and demand' in answer to every question." Of course, there is often more to the story. But economists tend to insist that market behavior can usually be explained by the relationship between preferences for a good (demand) and the costs involved in producing that good (supply). The basic **supply-demand model** of price determination is a staple of all courses in introductory economics— in fact, this model may be the first thing you studied in your introductory course. Here we provide a quick review of the model, adding a bit of historical perspective.

Supply-demand model
A model describing how a good's price is determined by the behavior of the individuals who buy the good and of the firms that sell it.

Adam Smith and the Invisible Hand

The Scottish philosopher Adam Smith (1723–1790) is generally credited with being the first true economist. In *The Wealth of Nations* (published in 1776), Smith examined a large number of the pressing economic issues of his day and tried to develop economic tools for understanding them. Smith's most important insight was his recognition that the system of market-determined prices that he observed was not as chaotic and undisciplined as most other writers had assumed. Rather, Smith saw prices as providing a powerful "invisible hand" that directed resources into activities where they would be most valuable. Prices play the crucial role of telling both consumers and firms what resources are "worth" and thereby prompt these economic actors to make efficient choices about how to use them. To Smith, it was this ability to use resources efficiently that provided the ultimate explanation for a nation's "wealth."

Because Adam Smith placed great importance on the role of prices in directing how a nation's resources are used, he needed to develop some theories about how those prices are determined. He offered a very simple and only partly correct explanation. Since, in Smith's day (and, to some extent, even today), the primary costs of producing goods were costs associated with the labor that went into a good, it was only a short step for him to embrace a labor-based theory of prices. For example, to paraphrase an illustration from *The Wealth of Nations,* if it takes twice as long for a hunter to catch a deer as to catch a beaver, one deer should trade for two beavers. The relative price of a deer is high because of the extra labor costs involved in catching one.

Smith's explanation for the price of a good is illustrated in Figure 1.2(a). The horizontal line at P* shows that any number of deer can be produced without affecting the relative cost of doing so. That relative cost sets the price of deer (P*),

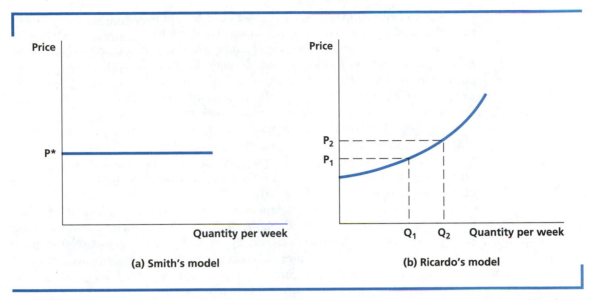

FIGURE 1.2 Early Views of Price Determination To Adam Smith, the relative price of a good was determined by relative labor costs. As shown in the left-hand panel, relative price would be P* unless something altered such costs. Ricardo added the concept of diminishing returns to this explanation. In the right-hand panel, relative price rises as quantity produced rises from Q_1 to Q_2.

which might be measured in beavers (a deer costs two beavers), in dollars (a deer costs $200, whereas a beaver costs $100), or in any other units that this society uses to indicate exchange value. This value will change only when the technology for producing deer changes. If, for example, this society developed better running shoes (which would aid in catching deer but be of little use in capturing beavers), the relative labor costs associated with hunting deer would fall. Now a deer would trade for, say, 1.5 beavers, and the supply curve illustrated in the figure would shift downward. In the absence of such technical changes, however, the relative price of deer would remain constant, reflecting relative costs of production.

David Ricardo and Diminishing Returns

The early nineteenth century was a period of considerable controversy in economics, especially in England. The two most pressing issues of the day were whether international trade was having a negative effect on the economy and whether industrial growth was harming farmland and other natural resources. It is testimony to the timelessness of economic questions that these are some of the same issues that dominate political discussions in the United States (and elsewhere) today. One of the most influential contributors to the earlier debates was the British financier and pamphleteer David Ricardo (1772–1823).

Ricardo believed that labor and other costs would tend to rise as the level of production of a particular good expanded. He drew this insight primarily from his consideration of the way in which farmland was expanding in England at the time. As new and less-fertile land was brought into use, it would naturally take more labor (say, to pick out the rocks in addition to planting crops) to produce an extra bushel of grain. Hence, the relative price of grain would rise. Similarly, as deer hunters exhaust the stock of deer in a given area, they must spend more time locating their prey, so the relative price of deer would also rise. Ricardo believed that the phenomenon of increasing costs was quite general, and today we refer to his discovery as the law of **diminishing returns**. This generalization of Smith's notion of supply is reflected in Figure 1.2(b), in which the supply curve slopes upward as quantity produced expands.

Diminishing returns
Hypothesis that the cost associated with producing one more unit of a good rises as more of that good is produced.

I N F O T R A C©
COLLEGE EDITION
Exclusively from Gale Group and Thomson Learning
www.infotrac-college.com
Keywords: Microeconomics, Dismal science, Alfred Marshall

The problem with Ricardo's explanation was that it really did not explain how prices are determined. Although the notion of diminishing returns undoubtedly made Smith's model more realistic, it did so by showing that relative price was not determined by production technology alone. Instead, according to Ricardo, the relative price of a good can be practically at any level depending on how much of it is produced.

To complete his explanation, Ricardo relied on a subsistence argument. If, for example, the current population of a country needs Q_1 units of output to survive, Figure 1.2(b) shows that the relative price would be P_1. With a growing population, these subsistence needs might expand to Q_2, and the relative price of this necessity would rise to P_2. Ricardo's suggestion that the relative prices of goods necessary for survival would rise in response to diminishing returns provided the basis for much of the concern about population growth in England during the 1830s and 1840s. It was largely responsible for the application of the term *dismal science* to the study of economics.

Marginalism and Marshall's Model of Supply and Demand

Contrary to the fears of many worriers, relative prices of food and other necessities did not rise significantly during the nineteenth century. Instead, as methods of production improved, prices tended to fall and levels of material well-being improved rather dramatically. As a result, subsistence became a less plausible explanation of the amounts of particular goods consumed and economists found it necessary to develop a more general theory of demand. In the latter half of the nineteenth century, they adapted Ricardo's law of diminishing returns to this task. Just as diminishing returns mean that the cost of producing one more unit of a good rises as more is produced, so too, these economists argued, the willingness of people to pay for that last unit declines. Only if individuals are offered a lower price for a good will they be willing to consume more of it. By focusing on the value to buyers of the last, or *marginal,* unit purchased, these economists had at last developed a comprehensive theory of price determination.

The clearest statement of these ideas was presented by the English economist Alfred Marshall (1842–1924) in his *Principles of Economics,* published in 1890. Marshall showed how the forces of demand and supply *simultaneously* determine price. Marshall's analysis is illustrated by the familiar cross diagram shown in Figure 1.3.

As before, the amount of a good purchased per period (say, each week) is shown on the horizontal axis and the price of the good appears on the vertical axis. The curve labeled "Demand" shows the amount of the good people want to buy at each price. The negative slope of this curve reflects the marginalist principle: Because people are willing to pay less and less for the last unit purchased, they will buy more only at a lower price. The curve labeled "Supply" shows the increasing cost of making one more unit of the good as the total amount produced increases. In other words, the upward slope of the supply curve reflects *increasing* marginal costs, just as the downward slope of the demand curve reflects *decreasing* marginal usefulness.

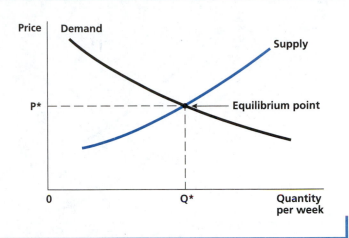

FIGURE 1.3 **The Marshall Supply-Demand Cross** Marshall believed that demand and supply together determine the equilibrium price (P*) and quantity (Q*) of a good. The positive slope of the supply curve reflects diminishing returns (increasing marginal cost), whereas the negative slope of the demand curve reflects diminishing marginal usefulness. P* is an equilibrium price. Any other price results in either a surplus or a shortage.

Market Equilibrium

In Figure 1.3, the demand and supply curves intersect at the point P*, Q*. At that point, P* is the **equilibrium price.** That is, at this price, the quantity that people want to purchase (Q*) is precisely equal to the quantity that suppliers are willing to produce. Because both demanders and suppliers are content with this outcome, no one has an incentive to alter his or her behavior. The equilibrium P*, Q* will tend to persist unless something happens to change things. This illustration is the first of many we encounter in this book about the way in which a balancing of forces results in a sustainable equilibrium outcome. To conceptualize

MicroQuiz 1.2

Another way to describe the equilibrium in Figure 1.3 is to say that at P*, Q* neither the supplier nor the demander has any incentive to change behavior. Use this notion of equilibrium to explain:

1. Why the fact that P*, Q* occurs where the supply and demand curves intersect implies that both parties to the transaction are content with this result; and

2. Why no other P, Q point on the graph meets this definition of equilibrium.

Equilibrium price
The price at which the quantity demanded by buyers of a good is equal to the quantity supplied by sellers of the good.

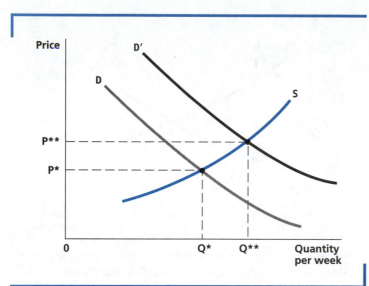

FIGURE 1.4 An Increase in Demand Alters Equilibrium Price and Quality If the demand curve shifts outward to D′ because there is more desire for the product, P*, Q* will no longer be an equilibrium. Instead, equilibrium occurs at P**, Q**, where D′ and S intersect.

the nature of this balancing of forces, Marshall used the analogy of a pair of scissors: Just as both blades of the scissors work together to do the cutting, so too the forces of demand and supply work together to establish equilibrium prices.

Nonequilibrium Outcomes

The smooth functioning of market forces envisioned by Marshall can, however, be thwarted in many ways. For example, a government decree that requires a price to be set in excess of P* (perhaps because P* was regarded as being the result of "unfair, ruinous competition") would prevent the establishment of equilibrium. With a price set above P*, demanders would wish to buy less than Q*, whereas suppliers would produce more than Q*. This would lead to a surplus of production in the market—a situation that characterizes many agricultural markets. Similarly, a regulation that holds a price below P* would result in a shortage. With such a price, demanders would want to buy more than Q*, whereas supplies would produce less than Q*. In Chapter 9, we look at several situations where this occurs.

Change in Market Equilibrium

The equilibrium pictured in Figure 1.3 can persist as long as nothing happens to alter demand or supply relationships. If one of the curves were to shift, however, the equilibrium would change. In Figure 1.4, people's demand for the good increases. In this case, the demand curve moves outward (from curve D to curve D′). At each price, people now want to buy more of the good. The equilibrium price increases (from P* to P**). This higher price both tells firms to supply more goods and restrains individuals' demand for the good. At the new equilibrium price of P**, supply and demand again balance—at this higher price, the amount of goods demanded is exactly equal to the amount supplied.

A shift in the supply curve also affects market equilibrium. In Figure 1.5, the effects of an increase in supplier costs (for example, an increase in wages paid to workers) are illustrated. For any level of output, marginal costs associated with the supply curve S′ exceed those associated with S. This shift in supply causes the price of this product to rise (from P* to P**), and consumers respond to this price rise by reducing quantity demanded (from Q* to Q**) along the demand curve, D. As for the case of a shift in demand, the ultimate result of the shift in supply depicted in Figure 1.5 depends on the shape of both the demand curve and the supply curve.

Marshall's model of supply and demand should be quite familiar to you since it provides the principal focus of most courses in introductory economics. Indeed, the concepts of marginal cost, marginal value, and market equilibrium encountered in this model provide the starting place for most of the economic models you will learn about in this book. Application 1.5: Economics According to Bono shows that even rock stars can sometimes get these concepts right.

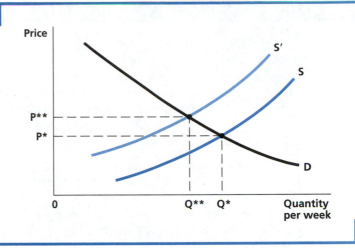

FIGURE 1.5 A Shift in Supply Alters Equilibrium Price and Quality
A rise in costs would shift the supply curve upward to S′. This would cause an increase in equilibrium price from P* to P** and a decline in quantity from Q* to Q**.

MicroQuiz 1.3

Supply and demand curves show the relationship between the price of a good and the quantity supplied or demanded when other factors are held constant. Explain:

1. What factors might shift the demand or supply curve for, say, personal computers.

2. Why a change in the price of PCs would shift neither curve. Indeed, would this price ever change if all of the factors identified previously did not change?

HOW ECONOMISTS VERIFY THEORETICAL MODELS

Not all models are as useful as Marshall's model of supply and demand. An important purpose of studying economics is to sort out bad models from good ones. Two methods are used to provide such a test of economic models. **Testing assumptions** looks at the assumptions upon which a model is based;

Testing assumptions
Verifying economic models by examining validity of the assumptions on which they are based.

Economics According to Bono

The Spring 2002 trip to Africa by the Irish rock star Bono and the U.S. Treasury Secretary Paul O'Neill sparked much interesting dialogue about economics.[1] Especially intriguing was Bono's claim that recently enacted agricultural subsidies in the United States were harming struggling farmers in Africa—a charge that O'Neill was forced to attempt to refute. A simple supply-demand analysis shows that, overall, Bono did indeed have the better of the arguments, though he neglected to mention a few fine points.

Graphing African Exports

Figure 1 shows the supply and demand curves for a typical crop that is being produced by an African country. If the world price of this crop (P^*) exceeds the price that would prevail in the absence of trade (P_D), this country will be an exporter of this crop. The total quantity of exports is given by the distance $Q_S - Q_D$. That is, exports are given by the difference in the quantity of this crop produced and the quantity that is demanded domestically. Such exporting is quite common for many African countries because they have large agrarian populations and generally favorable climates for many types of food production.

In May 2002, the United States adopted a program of vastly increased agricultural subsidies to U.S. farmers. From the point of view of world markets, the main effect of such a program is to reduce world crop prices. This would be shown in Figure 1 as a drop in the world price to P^{**}. This fall in price would be met by a reduction in quantity produced of the crop to Q'_S and an increase in the quantity demanded to Q'_D. Crop exports would decline significantly.

So, Bono's point is essentially correct—U.S. farm subsidies do harm African farmers, especially those in the export business. But he might also have pointed out that African consumers of food do benefit from the price reduction. They are able to buy more food at lower prices. Effectively, some of the subsidy to U.S. farmers has been transferred to African consumers.

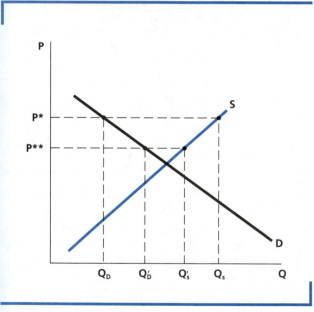

FIGURE 1 **U.S. Subsidies Reduce African Exports** U.S. farm subsidies reduce the world price of this crop from P^* to P^{**}. Exports from this African country fall from $Q_S - Q_D$ to $Q'_S - Q'_D$.

[1] This odd sojourn is well covered in various issues of *The Economist* during May 2002.

Hence, even disregarding whether farm subsidies make any sense for Americans, their effects on the welfare of Africans is somewhat ambiguous.

Other Barriers to African Agricultural Trade

Agricultural subsidies by the United States and the European Union amount to nearly $400 billion per year. Undoubtedly they have a major effect in thwarting African exports. Perhaps even more devastating are the large number of special measures adopted in various developed countries to protect favored domestic industries such as peanuts in the United States, rice in Japan, and livestock in the European Union. Because expanded trade is one of the major avenues through which poor African economies might grow, these restrictions have become very controversial.

To Think About

1. Why do agricultural subsidies in the United States or the European Union reduce world crop prices?
2. How would you diagram the effects of trade restrictions in Figure 1?

---

testing predictions, on the other hand, uses the model to see if it can correctly predict real-world events. This book uses both approaches to try to illustrate the validity of the models that are presented. We now look briefly at the differences between them.

Testing predictions
Verifying economic models by asking if they can accurately predict real-world events.

Testing Assumptions

One approach to testing the assumptions of an economic model might begin with intuition. Do the model's assumptions seem reasonable? Unfortunately, this question is fraught with problems, since what appears reasonable to one person may seem preposterous to someone else (try arguing with a noneconomics student about whether people usually behave rationally, for example).

Assumptions can also be tested with empirical evidence. For example, economists usually assume that firms are in business to maximize profits—in fact, much of our discussion in this book is based on that assumption. Using the direct approach to test this assumption with real-world data, you might send questionnaires to managers asking them how they make decisions and whether they really do try to maximize profits. This approach has been used many times, but the results, like those from many opinion polls, are often difficult to interpret.

Testing Predictions

Some economists, such as Milton Friedman, do not believe that a theory can be tested by looking only at its assumptions. They argue that all theories are based on unrealistic assumptions; the very nature of theorizing demands that we make what may appear to be unrealistic assumptions.[1] Such economists believe that, in order to decide if a theory is valid, we must see if it is capable of explaining and predicting real-world events. The real test of any economic model is whether it is consistent with events from the economy itself.

Friedman gives a good example of this idea by asking what theory explains the shots an expert pool player will make. He argues that the laws of velocity, momentum, and angles from physics make a suitable theoretical model, because the pool player certainly shoots *as if* he or she followed these laws. If we asked the players whether they could state these physical principles, they would undoubtedly answer that they could not. That does not matter, Friedman argues, because the physical laws give very accurate predictions of the shots made and are therefore useful as theoretical models.

Going back to the question of whether firms try to maximize profits, the indirect approach would try to predict the firms' behavior by assuming that they do act *as if* they were maximizing profits. If we find that we can predict firms' behavior, then we can believe the profit-maximization hypothesis. Even if these firms said on questionnaires that they don't really try to maximize profits, the theory will still be valid, much as the pool players' disclaiming knowledge of the laws of physics does not make these laws untrue. The ultimate test in both cases is the theory's ability to predict real-world events.

The Positive-Normative Distinction

Positive-normative distinction

Distinction between theories that seek to explain the world as it is and theories that postulate the way the world should be.

Related to the question of how the validity of economic models should be tested is the issue of how such models should be used. To some economists, the only proper analysis is "positive" in nature. As in the physical sciences, they argue, the correct role for theory is to explain the real world as it is. In this view, developing "normative" theories about how the world *should be* is an exercise for which economists have no more special skills than anyone else. For other economists, this **positive-normative distinction** is not so clear-cut. They argue that economic models invariably have normative consequences that should be recognized. Application 1.6: Do Economists Ever Agree? shows that, contrary to common perceptions, there is considerable agreement among economists about issues that are suitable for positive scientific analysis. There is far less agreement about normative questions related to what should be done. In this book, we take primarily a positive approach by using economic models to explain real-world events. The book's applications pursue these explanations in greater detail. You should feel free to adapt these models to whatever normative goals you believe are worth pursuing.

---

[1] Milton Friedman, *Essays in Positive Economics* (Chicago: University of Chicago Press, 1953), Chapter 1. Another view stressing the importance of realistic assumptions can be found in H. A. Simon, "Rational Decision Making in Business Organizations," *American Economic Review* (September 1979): 493—513.

To the general public, economists are confusing. In many conversations, economists bear the brunt of pointed jokes. Some of my favorites are the following:

If all economists in the world were laid end-to-end, they would never reach a decision.

How many economists does it take to change a light bulb? Two—one to turn the bulb and one to say, "Turn it the other way."

Positive versus Normative Economics

These jokes convey the perception that economists never agree on anything. But that perception arises primarily from an inability to differentiate between the positive and normative arguments that economists make. Economists (like everyone else) often disagree over political questions. They may, therefore, find themselves on opposite sides of controversial policy questions. Economists may also differ on empirical matters. For instance, they may disagree about whether a particular effect is large or small. But on basic theoretical questions there is far less disagreement. Because most economists use the same tools, they tend to "speak the same language" and disagreements on positive questions are far less frequent.

Survey Results

This conclusion is supported by surveys of economists, a sample of which is described in Table 1. The table shows a high degree of agreement among U.S., Swiss, and German economists about relatively positive questions such as the effects of tariffs or of rent controls.[1]

TABLE 1 Percentage of Economists Agreeing with Various Propositions in Three Nations

Proposition	United States	Switzerland	Germany
Tariffs reduce economic welfare	95	87	94
Flexible exchange rates are effective for international transactions	94	91	92
Rent controls reduce the quality of housing	96	79	94
Government should redistribute income	68	51	55
Government should hire the jobless	51	52	35

Source: B. S. Frey, W. W. Pommerehue, F. Schnieder, and G. Gilbert, Consensus and Dissension among Economists: An Empirical Inquiry," *American Economic Review* (December 1984): 986–994. Percentages represent fraction that "Generally Agree" or "Agree with Provisions."

[1]Surveys also tend to show considerable agreement over the likely size of many economic effects. For a summary, see Victor R. Fuchs, Alan B. Krueger, and James M. Poterba, "Economists' Views about Parameters, Values, and Policy," *Journal of Economic Literature* (September 1998): 1387–1425.

(continued)

There is considerably less agreement about broad normative questions, such as whether the government should redistribute income or act as the employer of last resort. For these types of questions, economists' opinions are as varied as those of any other group of citizens.

To Think About

1. Economists from the United States, Switzerland, and Germany may not reflect the views of economists from lower-income countries. Do you think such economists might answer the questions in Table 1 differently?
2. What is the difference between a _____ and an economist? Answer: _____. (An annual prize is being offered by the author for the best completion of this joke.)

SUMMARY

This chapter provides you with some background to begin your study of microeconomics. Much of this material should be familiar to you from your introductory economics course, but that should come as no surprise. In many respects, the study of economics repeatedly investigates the same questions with an increasingly sophisticated set of tools. This course gives you some more of these tools. In establishing the basis for that investigation, this chapter reminds you of several important ideas:

- Economics is the study of allocating scarce resources among possible uses. Because resources are scarce, choices have to be made on how they will be used. Economists develop theoretical models to explain these choices.
- The production possibility frontier provides a simple illustration of the supply conditions in two markets. The curve clearly shows the limits imposed on any economy because resources are scarce. Producing more of one good means that less of something else must be produced. This reduction in output elsewhere measures the opportunity cost involved in such additional production.
- The most commonly used model of the allocation of resources is the model of supply and demand developed by Alfred Marshall in the latter part of the nineteenth century. The model shows how prices are determined by creating an equilibrium between the amount people want to buy and the amount firms are willing to produce. If supply and demand curves shift, new prices are established to restore equilibrium to the market.
- Proving the validity of economic models is difficult and sometimes controversial. Occasionally the validity of a model can be determined by whether it is based on reasonable assumptions. More often, however, models are judged by how well they explain actual economic events.

REVIEW QUESTIONS

1. "To an economist, a resource is 'scarce' only if it has a positive price. Resources with zero prices are, by definition, not scarce." Do you agree? Or does the term *scarce* convey some other meaning?

2. In many economic problems, time is treated as a scarce resource. Describe how problems in using time meet our definition of "economics." Can you think of something that is different about using time than about using physical resources?

3. Provide a formal economic analysis of why honeybees find it in their interest to leave some nectar in each flower they visit. Can you think of any human activities that produce a similar outcome?

4. Classical economists struggled with the "Water-Diamond Paradox," which seeks an explanation for why water (which is very useful) has a low price, whereas diamonds (which are not particularly important to life) have a high price. How would Smith explain the relative prices of water and diamonds? Would Ricardo's concept of diminishing returns pose some problem for this explanation? Can you resolve matters by using Marshall's model of supply and demand? Is water "very useful" to the demanders in Marshall's model?

5. Marshall's model pictures price *and* quantity as being determined simultaneously by the interaction of supply and demand. Using this insight, explain the fallacies in the following paragraph:

   A rise in the price of oranges reduces the number people who want to buy. This reduction by itself reduces growers' costs by allowing them to use only their best trees. Price, therefore, declines along with costs, and the initial price rise cannot be sustained.

6. "Gasoline sells for $1.40 per gallon this year, and it sold for $1.10 per gallon last year. But consumers bought more gasoline this year than they did last year. This is clear proof that the economic theory that people buy less when the price rises is incorrect." Do you agree? Explain.

7. "A shift outward in the demand curve always results in an increase in total spending (prices times quantity) on a good. On the other hand, a shift outward in the supply curve may increase or decrease total spending." Explain.

8. A recent news report suggested that the current supply of personal computers exceeds the demand for those computers. Use a supply and demand graph to see whether you can make any sense out of this assertion.

9. A key concept in the development of positive economic theories is the notion of "refutability"—a "theory" is not a "theory" unless there is some evidence that, if true, could prove it wrong. Use this notion to discuss whether one can conceive of evidence with which the following theories might be refuted:

   - Friedman's claim that pool players play as if they were using the rules of physics
   - The theory that firms operate so as to maximize profits
   - The theory that demand curves slope downward
   - The theory that adoption of capitalism makes people who are poor more miserable

10. The following conversation was heard among four economists discussing whether the minimum wage should be increased:

    Economist A. "Increasing the minimum wage would reduce employment of minority teenagers."

    Economist B. "Increasing the minimum wage would represent an unwarranted interference with private relations between workers and their employers."

    Economist C. "Increasing the minimum wage would raise the incomes of some unskilled workers."

    Economist D. "Increasing the minimum wage would benefit higher-wage workers and would probably be supported by organized labor."

    Which of these economists are using positive analysis and which are using normative analysis in arriving at their conclusions? Which of these predictions might be tested with empirical data? How might such tests be conducted?

PROBLEMS

Note: These problems involve mainly the mathematical material from the Appendix to Chapter 1.

1.1 The following data represent 5 points on the supply curve for orange juice:

Price ($ per gallon)	Quantity (millions of gallons)
1	100
2	300
3	500
4	700
5	900

a. Graph these points with price on the vertical (Y) axis and quantity on the horizontal (X) axis.
b. Do these points seem to lie along a straight line? If so, what is that line?
c. Use the equation calculated in part b to state how much will be supplied when $P = 0$ or when $P = 6$.

1.2 The following data represent 5 points on the demand curve for orange juice:

Price ($ per gallon)	Quantity (millions of gallons)
1	700
2	600
3	500
4	400
5	300

a. Graph these points with price on the vertical (Y) axis and quantity on the horizontal (X) axis.
b. Do these points seem to lie along a straight line? If so, which line?
c. Use the equation calculated in part b to state how much orange juice will be demanded when $P = 0$ or when $P = 6$.

1.3 Marshall defined an equilibrium price as one at which the quantity demanded equals the quantity supplied.

a. Using the data provided in problems 1.1 and 1.2, show that $P = 3$ is the equilibrium price in the orange juice market.
b. Using these data, explain why $P = 2$ and $P = 4$ are not equilibrium prices.
c. Graph your results and show that the supply-demand equilibrium resembles that shown in Figure 1.3.
d. Suppose the demand for orange juice were to increase so that people want to buy 300 million more gallons at every price. How would that change the data in problem 1.2? How would it shift the demand curve you drew in part c?
e. What is the new equilibrium price in the orange juice market given this increase in demand? Show this new equilibrium in your supply-demand graph.

1.4 Suppose that a freeze in Florida reduces orange juice supply by 300 million gallons at every price listed in problem 1.1.

a. How would this shift in supply affect the data in problem 1.1? How would it affect the algebraic supply curve calculated in that problem?
b. Given this new supply relationship together with the demand relationship shown in problem 1.2, what is the equilibrium price in this market?
c. Explain why $P = 3$ is no longer an equilibrium in the orange juice market. How would the participants in this market know $P = 3$ is no longer an equilibrium?
d. Graph your results for this supply shift.

1.5 This problem involves solving demand and supply equations together to determine price and quantity.

a. Consider a demand curve of the form

$$Q_D = -2P + 20$$

where Q_D is the quantity demanded of a good and P is the price of the good. Graph this demand curve. Also draw a graph of the supply curve

$$Q_S = 2P - 4$$

where Q_S is the quantity supplied. Be sure to put P on the vertical axis and Q on the horizontal axis. Assume that all the Qs and Ps are nonnegative for parts a, b, and c. At what values of P and Q do these curves intersect—that is, where does $Q_D = Q_S$?

b. Now suppose at each price that individuals demand four more units of output—that the demand curve shifts to

$$Q_{D'} = -2P + 24$$

Graph this new demand curve. At what values of P and Q does the new demand curve intersect the old supply curve—that is, where does $Q_{D'} = Q_S$?

c. Now, finally, suppose the supply curve shifts to

$$Q_{S'} = 2P - 8$$

Graph this new supply curve. At what values of P and Q does $Q_{D'} = Q_{S'}$? You may wish to refer to this simple problem when we discuss shifting supply and demand curves in later sections of this book.

1.6 Taxes in Oz are calculated according to the formula

$$T = .01I^2$$

where T represents thousand of dollars of tax liability and I represents income measured in thousands of dollars. Using this formula, answer the following questions:

a. How much in taxes is paid by individuals with incomes of $10,000, $30,000, and $50,000? What are the average tax rates for these income levels? At what income level does tax liability equal total income?

b. Graph the tax schedule for Oz. Use your graph to estimate marginal tax rates for the income levels specified in part a. Also show the average tax rates for these income levels on your graph.

c. Marginal tax rates in Oz can be estimated more precisely by calculating tax owed if persons with the incomes in part a get one more dollar. Make this computation for these three income levels. Compare your results to those obtained from the calculus-based result that, for the Oz tax function, its slope = .02I.

1.7 The following data show the production possibilities for a hypothetical economy during one year:

Output of X	Output of Y
1000	0
800	100
600	200
400	300
200	400
0	500

a. Plot these points on a graph. Do they appear to lie along a straight line? What is that straight line production possibility frontier?

b. Explain why output levels of X = 400, Y = 200 or X = 300, Y = 300 are inefficient. Show these output levels on your graph.

c. Explain why output levels of X = 500, Y = 350 are unattainable in this economy.

d. What is the opportunity cost of an additional unit of X output in terms of Y output in this economy? Does this opportunity cost depend on the amounts being produced?

1.8 Suppose an economy has a production possibility frontier characterized by the equation

$$X^2 + 4Y^2 = 100$$

a. In order to sketch this equation, first compute its intercept. What is the value of X if Y = 0? What is the value of Y if X = 0?

b. Calculate three additional points along this production possibility frontier. Graph the frontier and show that it has a general elliptical shape.

c. Is the opportunity cost of X in terms of Y constant in this economy or does it depend on the levels of output being produced? Explain.

d. How would you calculate the opportunity cost of X in terms of Y in this economy? Give an example of this computation.

1.9 Suppose consumers in the economy described in problem 1.8 wished to consume X and Y in equal amounts.

a. How much of each good should be produced to meet this goal? Show this production point on a graph of the production possibility frontier.

b. Assume that this country enters into international trading relationships and decides to produce only good X. If it can trade one unit of X for one unit of Y in world markets, what possible combinations of X and Y might it consume?

c. Given the consumption possibilities outlined in part b, what final choice will the consumers of this country make?

d. How would you measure the costs imposed on this country by international economic sanctions that prevented all trade and required the country to return to the position described in part a?

1.10 Consider the function

$$Y = \sqrt{X \cdot Z}$$

where $X > 0$, $Z > 0$. Draw the contour lines (in the positive quadrant) for this function for $Y = 4$, $Y = 5$, and $Y = 10$. What do we call the shape of these contour lines? Where does the line $20X + 10Z = 200$ intersect the contour line $Y = 50$? (Hint: It may be easier to graph the contour lines for Y^2 here.)

INTERNET EXERCISES

1. *Opportunity costs.* Imagine that you have just received your bachelor's degree. You are wondering whether or not to spend an additional 2 years in college and earn a master's degree. What is the estimated return on this additional investment? Let's find out (you probably wish to review Application 1.2 first, however). Go to the Statistical Abstract of the United States at *http://www.census.gov/statab/www* and click on the most recent edition. Click on Section 4. Education. First, find the table for "Educational Attainment by Selected Characteristics." What percentage of the population holds a bachelor's degree as their highest level of educational attainment? A master's? Now find the table for "Earnings by Highest Degree Earned," and restrict your attention to the row showing average data for all persons. Use the data to estimate the opportunity cost of obtaining a master's degree. Explain your reasoning. Add to this the explicit cost of tuition and fees (use the same annual tuition/fees cost as in Application 1.2) to obtain an estimate of your overall 2-year economic cost of obtaining a master's degree (don't worry about discounting here). Next, use the table to estimate the gain from attaining a master's degree. Finally, compute the annual return on your investment. Why might your estimated return tend to overstate the actual return? (Hint: consider whether the differences in salaries in the table reflect primarily benefits from the various degrees or, rather, the personal characteristics of individuals who pursue those degrees.)

2. *Economic jokes.* Have you heard any good jokes lately? How about this one? Q: How many economists does it take to screw in a lightbulb? A: None—if it really needed changing, market forces would have caused it to happen. . . . Believe it or not, these and other jokes about economics and economists can be found at *http://netec.wustl. edu/JokEc.html*. In fact, many, if not most, of the jokes posted at this Web site were contributed by economists themselves. Now who said economists had no sense of humor?

Mathematics Used in Microeconomics

Mathematics began to be widely used in economics near the end of the nineteenth century. For example, Marshall's *Principles of Economics,* published in 1890, included a lengthy mathematical appendix that developed his arguments more systematically than the book itself. Today, mathematics is indispensable for economists. They use it not to hide behind symbols or to make their arguments hard to understand but to move logically from the basic assumptions of a model to deriving the results of those assumptions. Without mathematics, this process would be both more cumbersome and less accurate.

This appendix reviews some of the basic concepts of algebra. We also discuss a few issues that arise in applying those concepts to the study of economics. We use the tools introduced here throughout the rest of the book.

FUNCTIONS OF ONE VARIABLE

The basic elements of algebra are called **variables.** These can be labeled X and Y and may be given any numerical value. Sometimes the values of one variable (Y) may be related to those of another variable (X) according to a specific functional relationship. This relationship is denoted by the **functional notation**

$$Y = f(X) \tag{1A.1}$$

This is read, "Y is a function of X," meaning that the value of Y depends on the value given to X. For example, if we make X calories eaten per day and Y body weight, then Equation 1A.1 shows the relationship between the amount of food intake and an individual's weight. The form of Equation 1A.1 also shows causality. X is an **independent variable** and may be given any value. On the other hand, the value of Y is completely determined by X; Y is a **dependent variable.** This functional notation shows that "X causes Y."

Variables
The basic elements of algebra, usually called X, Y, and so on, that may be given any numerical value in an equation.

Functional notation
A way of denoting the fact that the value taken on by one variable (Y) depends on the value taken on by some other variable (X) or set of variables.

Independent variable
In an algebraic equation, a variable that is unaffected by the action of another variable and may be assigned any value.

Dependent variable
In algebra, a variable whose value is determined by another variable or set of variables.

TABLE 1A.1 **Values of X and Y for Linear and Quadratic Functions**

Linear Function		Quadratic Function	
X	$Y = f(X)$ $= 3 + 2X$	X	$Y = f(X)$ $= -X^2 + 15X$
−3	−3	−3	−54
−2	−1	−2	−34
−1	1	−1	−16
0	3	0	0
1	5	1	14
2	7	2	26
3	9	3	36
4	11	4	44
5	13	5	50
6	15	6	54

The exact functional relationship between X and Y may take on a wide variety of forms. Two possibilities are:

1. Y is a *linear function* of X. In this case

$$Y = a + bX \qquad \text{(1A.2)}$$

where a and b are constants that may be given any numerical value. For example, if a = 3 and b = 2, this equation would be written as

$$Y = 3 + 2X \qquad \text{(1A.3)}$$

We could give Equation 1A.3 an economic interpretation. For example, if we make Y the labor costs of a firm and X the number of labor hours hired, then the equation could record the relationship between costs and workers hired. In this case there is a fixed cost of $3 (when X = 0, Y = $3), and the wage rate is $2 per hour. A firm that hired 6 labor hours, for example, would incur total labor costs of $15 [= 3 + 2(6) = 3 + 12]. Table 1A.1 illustrates some other values for this function for various values of X.

2. Y is a *nonlinear function* of X. This case covers a wide variety of possibilities including quadratic functions (containing X^2), higher-order polynomials (containing X^3, X^4, and so forth), and those based on special functions such as logarithms. All of these have the property that a given change in X can have different effects on Y depending on the value of X. This contrasts with linear functions for which a given change in X always changes Y by the same amount.

To see this, consider the quadratic equation

$$Y = -X^2 + 15X \tag{1A.4}$$

Y values for this equation for values of X between −3 and + 6 are shown in Table 1A.1. Notice that as X increases by one unit, the values of Y go up rapidly at first but then slow down. When X increases from 0 to 1, for example, Y increases from 0 to 14. But when X increases from 5 to 6, Y increases only from 50 to 54. This looks like Ricardo's notion of diminishing returns—as X increases, its ability to increase Y diminishes.[1]

GRAPHING FUNCTIONS OF ONE VARIABLE

When we write down the functional relationship between X and Y, we are summarizing all there is to know about that relationship. In principle, this book, or any book that uses mathematics, could be written using only these equations. Graphs of some of these functions, however, are very helpful. Graphs not only make it easier for us to understand certain arguments; they also can take the place of a lot of the mathematical notation that must be developed. For these reasons, this book relies heavily on graphs to develop its basic economic models. Here we look at a few simple graphic techniques.

A graph is simply one way to show the relationship between two variables. Usually, the values of the dependent variable (Y) are shown on the vertical axis and the values of the independent variable (X) are shown on the horizontal axis.[2] Figure 1A.1 uses this form to graph Equation 1A.3. Although we use heavy dots to show only the points of this function that are listed in Table 1A.1, the graph represents the function for every possible value of X. The graph of Equation 1A.3 is a straight line, which is why this is called a **linear function**. In Figure 1A.1, X and Y can take on both positive and negative values. The variables used in economics generally take on only positive values, and therefore we only have to use the upper right-hand (positive) quadrant of the axes.

Linear function
An equation that is represented by a straight-line graph.

Linear Functions: Intercepts and Slopes

Two important features of the graph in Figure 1A.1 are its slope and its **intercept** on the Y-axis. The Y-intercept is the value of Y when X is equal to 0. For

Intercept
The value of Y when X equals zero.

---

[1] Of course, for other nonlinear functions, increases in X may result in increasing amounts of Y (consider, for example, $X^2 + 15X$).

[2] In economics, this convention is not always followed. Sometimes a dependent variable is shown on the horizontal axis as, for example, in the case of demand and supply curves. In that case, the independent variable (price) is shown on the vertical axis and the dependent variable (quantity) on the horizontal axis.

example, as we can see in Figure 1A.1, when X = 0, Y = 3; this means that 3 is the Y-intercept.[3] In the general linear form of Equation 1A.2,

$$Y = a + bX$$

the Y-intercept will be Y = a, since this is the value of Y when X = 0.

We define the **slope** of any straight line to be the ratio of the change in Y to the change in X for a movement along the line. The slope can be defined mathematically as

Slope
The direction of a line on a graph; shows the change in Y that results from a unit change in X.

$$Slope = \frac{Change\ in\ Y}{Change\ in\ X} = \frac{\Delta Y}{\Delta X} \qquad (1A.5)$$

where the Δ ("delta") notation simply means "change in." For the particular function shown in Figure 1A.1, the slope is equal to 2. We can clearly see from the dashed lines, representing changes in X and Y, that a given change in X is met by a change of twice that amount in Y. Table 1A.1 shows the same result—as X increases from 0 to 1, Y increases from 3 to 5. Consequently

$$Slope = \frac{\Delta Y}{\Delta X} = \frac{5-3}{1-0} = 2 \qquad (1A.6)$$

It should be obvious that this is true for all the other points in Table 1A.1. Everywhere along the straight line, the slope is the same. Generally, for any linear function, the slope is given by b in Equation 1A.2. The slope of a straight line may be positive (as it is in Figure 1A.1), or it may be negative in which case the line would run from upper left to lower right.

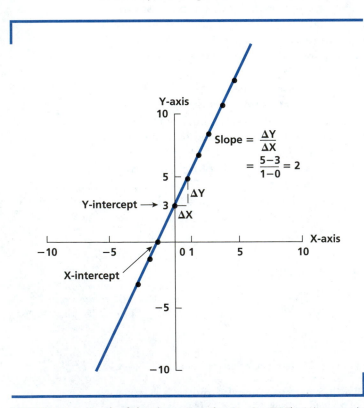

FIGURE 1A.1 Graph of the Linear Function Y = 3 + 2X The Y-intercept is 3; when X = 0, Y = 3. The slope of the line is 2; an increase in X by 1 will increase Y by 2.

[3] One can also speak of the X-intercept of a function, which is defined as that value of X for which Y = 0. For Equation 1A.3 it is easy to see that Y = 0 when X = –3/2, which is then the X-intercept. The X-intercept for the general linear function in Equation 1A.2 is given by X = –a/b, as may be seen by substituting that value into the equation.

A straight line may also have a slope of 0, which is a horizontal line. In this case the value of Y is constant; changes in X will not affect Y. The function would be $Y = a + 0X$, or $Y = a$. This equation is represented by a horizontal line (parallel to the X-axis) through point a on the Y-axis.

Slope and Units of Measurement

The slope of a function depends on the units in which X and Y are measured. For example, a study of a family's consumption of oranges might reveal that the number of oranges (Y) purchased in a week is equal to $3 + 2X$, where X is the family's income measured in hundreds of dollars per week. Consequently, $\Delta Y / \Delta X = 2$; that is, a $100 increase in income one week causes 2 more oranges to be purchased. If income (X) is measured in single dollars, the relationship is $Y = 3 + .02X$ and $\Delta Y / \Delta X = .02$. In this case, although the interpretation of this slope is the same (a $100 increase in income still increases orange purchases by 2 per week), the numerical value of the slope is very different. Similarly, if Y were measured in dozens of oranges per week and X in hundreds of dollars, the relationship would be $Y = \frac{1}{4} + \frac{1}{6} X$. An increase in family income of $100 still increases orange purchases by 2 ($\frac{1}{6}$ of a dozen), but now the slope is different again. Clearly, one must be very careful when discussing *the* slope of a function to know how the variables are measured.

> ### MicroQuiz 1A.1
>
> Suppose that the quantity of flounder caught each week off New Jersey is given by $Q = 100 + 5P$ (where Q is the quantity of flounder measured in thousands of pounds and P is the price per pound in dollars). Explain:
>
> **1.** What are the units of the intercept and the slope in this equation?
>
> **2.** How would this equation change if flounder catch were measured in pounds and price measured in cents per pound?

Changes in Slope

Quite often in this text we are interested in changing the parameters (that is, a and b) of a linear function. We can do this in two ways: We can change the Y-intercept, or we can change the slope. Figure 1A.2 shows the graph of the function

$$Y = -X + 10 \qquad\qquad (1A.7)$$

This linear function has a slope of −1 and a Y-intercept of $Y = 10$. Figure 1A.2 also shows the function

$$Y = -2X + 10 \qquad\qquad (1A.8)$$

We have doubled the slope of Equation 1A.7 from −1 to −2 and kept the Y-intercept at $Y = 10$. This causes the graph of the function to become steeper

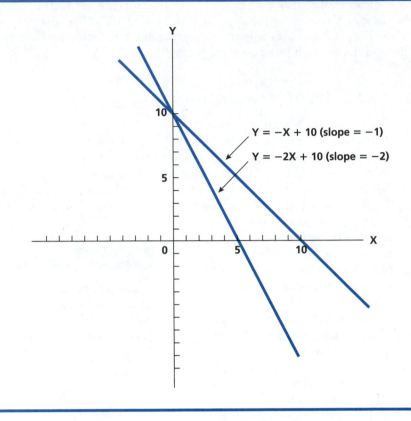

FIGURE 1A.2 Changes in the Slope of a Linear Function When the slope of a linear function is changed but the Y-intercept remains fixed, the graph of the function rotates about the Y-intercept.

and to rotate about the Y-intercept. In general, a change in the slope of a function will cause this kind of rotation without changing the value of its Y-intercept. Since a linear function takes on the value of its Y-intercept when X = 0, changing the slope will not change the value of the function at this point.

Changes in Intercept

Figure 1A.3 also shows a graph of the function Y = –X + 10. It shows the effect of changes in the constant term, that is, the Y-intercept only, while the slope stays at –1. Figure 1A.3 shows the graphs of

$$Y = -X + 12 \qquad (1A.9)$$

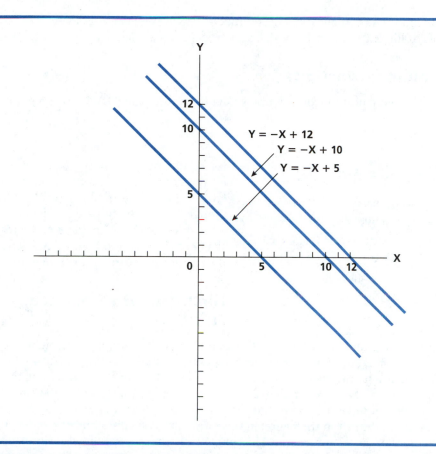

FIGURE 1A.3 Changes in the Y-Intercept of a Linear Function When the Y-intercept of a function is changed, the graph of the function shifts up or down and is parallel to the other graphs.

and

$$Y = -X + 5 \qquad\qquad (1A.10)$$

All three lines are parallel; they have the same slope. Changing the Y-intercept only makes the line shift up and down. Its slope does not change. Of course, changes in the Y-intercepts also cause the X-intercepts to change, and you can see these new intercepts.

In many places in this book we show how economic changes can be represented by changes in slopes or in intercepts. Although the economic context varies, the mathematical form of these changes is of the general type shown in Figure 1A.2

and Figure 1A.3. Application 1A.1: Property Tax Assessment uses these linear concepts to illustrate one such use that may be depressingly familiar to home owners.

Nonlinear Functions

Graphing nonlinear functions is also straightforward. Figure 1A.4 shows a graph of

$$Y = -X^2 + 15X \qquad\qquad (1A.11)$$

MicroQuiz 1A.2

In Figure 1A.2, the X-intercept changes from 10 to 5 as the slope of the graph changes from −1 to −2. Explain:

1. What would happen to the X-intercept in Figure 1A.2 if the slope changed to −⅚?

2. What do you learn by comparing the graphs in Figure 1A.2 to those in Figure 1A.3?

for relatively small, positive values of X. Heavy dots are used to indicate the specific values identified in Table 1A.1, though, again, the function is defined for all values of X. The general concave shape of the graph in Figure 1A.4 reflects the nonlinear nature of this function.

The Slope of a Nonlinear Function

Because the graph of a nonlinear function is, by definition, not a straight line, it does not have the same slope at every point. Instead, the slope of a nonlinear function *at a particular point* is defined to be the slope of the straight line that is tangent to the function at that point. For example, the slope of the function shown in Figure 1A.4 at point B is the slope of the tangent line illustrated at that point. As is clear from the figure, in this particular case, the slope of this function gets smaller as X increases. This graphical interpretation of "diminishing returns" to increasing X is simply a visual illustration of fact already pointed out in the discussion of Table 1A.1.

Marginal and Average Effects

Marginal effect
The change in Y brought about by a one unit change in X at a particular value of X. (Also the slope of the function.)

Average effect
The ratio of Y to X at a particular value of X. (Also the slope of the ray from the origin to the function.)

Economists are often interested in the size of the effect that X has on Y. There are two different ways of making this concept precise. The most usual is to look at the **marginal effect**—that is, how does a small change in X change Y? For this type of effect, the focus is on $\Delta Y/\Delta X$, the slope of the function. For the linear equations illustrated in Figure 1A.1 to Figure 1A.3, this effect is constant—in economic terms, the marginal effect of X on Y is constant for all values of X. For the nonlinear equation graphed in Figure 1A.4, this marginal effect diminishes as X gets larger. Diminishing returns and diminishing marginal effects amount to the same thing.

Sometimes economists speak of the **average effect** of X on Y. By this, they simply mean the ratio Y/X. For example, as shown in Chapter 5, the average productivity of labor in, say, automobile production is measured as the ratio of total

Property Tax Assessment

In most U.S. communities, property taxes pay for schools, the local police force, the fire department, and so forth. Conceptually, figuring what a property owner owes in taxes is a simple matter—the town assessors multiply the tax rate by the market value of the property. A major problem with this procedure, however, is that current market values for most properties are not known because properties only rarely change hands. To come up with accurate market values, localities increasingly turn to sophisticated computer methods to assess properties.

A Simple Linear Method

Local property assessors begin by collecting information on all houses that were recently sold in the area. With these data, they can estimate a relationship between sale price (Y) and a relevant characteristic of the house, say, its square footage (X). Such a relationship might be stated as

$$Y = \$10{,}000 + \$50X \qquad (1)$$

This equation means that a house with zero square footage (X = 0) should sell for $10,000 (because of the value of its land) and each square foot of living space adds $50 to the value of the house. Using the square footage of a house, the assessor can predict its current value by using Equation 1. This procedure is shown in Figure 1. According to the figure, a house with 2,000 square feet would have a market value of $110,000 and one with 3,000 square feet would be worth $160,000.

Valuing Other Features of Homes

Of course, assessors must take into account more features of a house than just square footage. Suppose current sales suggest that a nice view is worth $30,000 in the current housing market. Assuming Equation 1

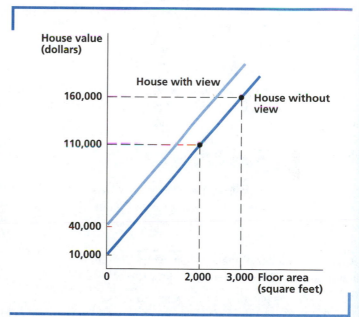

FIGURE 1 Relationship between the Floor Area of a House and Its Market Value Using data on recent house sales, real estate appraisers can calculate a relationship between floor area (X, measured in square feet) and market value (Y). The entire relationship shifts upward by 30,000 if a house has a nice view.

(continued)

reflects the values of houses without views, the values of houses with views can be computed by:

$$Y = \$30,000 + \$10,000 + \$50X =$$
$$\$40,000 + \$50X \qquad (2)$$

Equation 2 shows that the entire relationship between square footage and house value shifts upward by $30,000 if a house has a nice view. This relationship is also shown in Figure 1.

Hedonic Prices

Use of this procedure is not limited only to appraisers. Any analyst who wishes to examine how the features of a property affect its value can apply such "hedonic" procedures using information from sales prices. This approach has been used to study the effects of air or noise pollution on house values and to examine the effects of safety features on the values of used cars.

To Think About

1. Suppose spectacular views are more valuable in large houses than in small ones. How would this effect be represented with algebra?
2. How would you measure the effect of aircraft noise on housing values?

---

auto production (say, 10 million cars per year) to total labor employed (say, 250,000 workers). Hence, average productivity is 40 (= 10,000,000 ÷ 250,000) cars per year per worker.

MicroQuiz 1A.3

Suppose that the relationship between grapes harvested per hour (G, measured in pounds) and the number of workers hired (L, measured in worker- hours) is given by $G = 100 + 20L$.

1. How many additional grapes are harvested by the 10th worker? The 20th worker? The 50th worker?

2. What is the average productivity when 10 workers are hired? When 20 workers are hired? When 50 workers are hired?

Showing average values on a graph is a bit more complex than showing marginal values (slopes). To do so, we take the point on the graph that is of interest (say, point A in Figure 1A.4 whose coordinates are $X = 4$, $Y = 44$) and draw the chord OA. The slope of OA is then $Y/X = 44/4 = 11$—the average effect we seek to measure. By comparing the slope of OA to that of OB (= 54/6 = 9), it is easy to see that the average effect of X on Y also declines as X increases in Figure 1A.4. This is another reflection of the diminishing returns in this function. In later chapters, we show the relationship between marginal and average effects in many different contexts. Application 1A.2: Can a "Flat" Tax Be Progressive? shows how the concepts arise in disputes about revising the U.S. personal income tax.

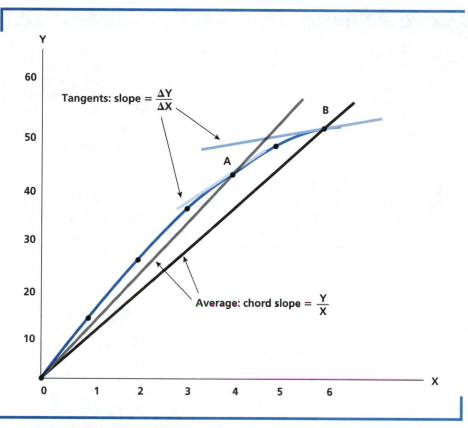

FIGURE 1A.4 Graph of the Quadratic Function Y = –X² + 15X The quadratic equation $Y = -X^2 + 15X$ has a concave graph—the slopes of the tangents to the curve diminish as X increases. This shape reflects the economic principle of diminishing marginal returns. The slope of a chord from the function to the origin shows the ratio $\frac{y}{x}$.

Calculus and Marginalism

Although this course in microeconomics does not require that you know calculus, it should be clear that many of the concepts that we cover were originally discovered using that branch of mathematics. Specifically, many economic concepts are based on looking at the effect of a small (marginal) change in a variable X on some other variable Y. You should be familiar with some of these concepts (such as marginal cost, marginal revenue, or marginal productivity) from your introductory economics course. Calculus provides a way of making the definitions for these ideas more precise. For example, in calculus, mathematicians develop the idea of the *derivative* of a function, which is simply defined as the

Can a "Flat" Tax Be Progressive?

Ever since the U.S. federal income tax (FIT) was first enacted in 1913, there has been a running debate about its fairness, particularly about whether the rates of taxation fairly reflect a person's ability to pay. Historically, the FIT had steeply rising tax rates, though these were moderated during the 1970s and 1980s.

Recently, a "flat tax" with a single tax rate has been proposed as a solution to some of the complexities and adverse economic incentives that arise with multiple rates. These ideas have been attacked as unfair in that they would eliminate the prevailing increasing rate structure.

Progressive Income Taxation

Advocates of tax fairness usually argue that income taxes should be "progressive"—that is, they argue that richer people should pay a *higher fraction* of their incomes in taxes because they are "more able to do so." Notice that the claim is that the rich should pay *proportionally* more, not just *more,* taxes. To achieve this goal, lawmakers have tended to specify tax schedules with increasing marginal rates. That is, an extra dollar of income is taxed at a higher rate the higher a person's income is. Figure 1 illustrates these increasing rates by the line OT.[1] The increasing slope of the various segments of OT reflects the increasing marginal tax rate structure.

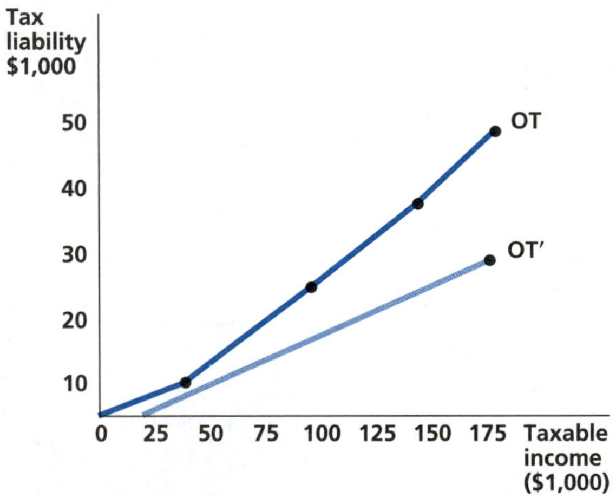

Flat Tax Proposals

Unfortunately, this progressive rate structure poses a variety of difficulties. It complicates the income tax withholding system (because it is unclear what rate should apply to, say, dividends and interest), and the system requires some type of multiyear averaging to prevent unfairness to people whose income fluctuates. For these and other reasons, some tax reformers have proposed a flat tax—one characterized by only a single marginal rate. Under one such proposal by former House Majority Leader Richard Armey, the first $26,000 of

FIGURE 1 Progressive Rates Compared to a Flat Tax Schedule
The line OT shows tax liabilities under the current rate schedule. OT' shows tax liabilities under one flat tax proposal.

[1] The tax does permit various deductions in calculating "taxable income." Hence, Figure 1 does not reflect the relationship between total income and taxes paid.

taxable income for a couple would not be taxed. All income above this level would be taxed at a flat rate of 17 percent. Tax collections under this schedule are shown by the line OT' in Figure 1.

Progressivity of the Flat Tax

The flat tax proposal illustrated in Figure 1 is also "progressive" in that individuals with higher incomes pay a higher fraction of their income in taxes. For example, a couple with $50,000 in taxable income would pay 8.2 percent of income in taxes (taxes would be 0.17[50,000 − 26,000] = 4,080), whereas a couple with $200,000 in taxable income would pay 14.8 percent. Hence, a flat tax can be "progressive." It would be very difficult to approximate the degree of progressivity in the current income tax structure with a flat tax, however.[2]

To Think About

1. Is the flat tax (OT' revenue) neutral? Are as many dollars in taxes collected as under the current tax?
2. How could a flat tax be made more progressive than the current tax represented by OT?

[2] A broadening of the definition of income used would help to achieve this purpose under a flat tax. For an updated version of Armey's proposal see his Web site at *http://www.flattax.gov*

---

limit of the ratio $\frac{\Delta Y}{\Delta X}$ as ΔX gets very small. In graphical terms, the derivative of a function and its slope are the same concept. Both provide a measure of the marginal impact of X on Y. Derivatives provide a convenient shorthand way of studying marginal effects. All of the major results in this book were discovered by making use of this connection between mathematics and economics. For example, the French economist A. Cournot (about whom we learn more later in the text) discovered the concept of marginal revenue in the early nineteenth century when he was given the very practical problem of setting prices for water in Paris. His application of calculus to this problem today provides the basic approach to all studies of monopoly pricing.

FUNCTIONS OF TWO OR MORE VARIABLES

Economists are usually concerned with functions of more than just one variable, since there is almost always more than a single cause of an economic outcome. To see the effects of many causes, economists must work with functions of several variables. A two-variable function might be written in functional notation as

$$Y = f(X, Z) \tag{1A.12}$$

TABLE 1A.2 Values of X, Z, and Y That Satisfy the Relationship Y = X · Z		
X	**Z**	**Y**
1	1	1
1	2	2
1	3	3
1	4	4
2	1	2
2	2	4
2	3	6
2	4	8
3	1	3
3	2	6
3	3	9
3	4	12
4	1	4
4	2	8
4	3	12
4	4	16

This equation shows that Y's values depend on the values of two independent variables, X and Z. For example, an individual's weight (Y) depends not only on calories eaten (X) but also on how much the individual exercises (Z). Increases in X increase Y, but increases in Z decrease Y. The functional notation in Equation 1A.12 hints at the possibility that there might be trade-offs between eating and exercise. In Chapter 2, we start to explore such trade-offs because they are central to the choices that both individuals and firms make.

A Simple Example

In general, we could have Y depend on the values of more than two variables, but a simple two-variable function can be used to explain most of the relevant facts about how multiple variable functions work. Suppose the relationship between Y, X, and Z is given by

$$Y = X \cdot Z \qquad \text{(1A.13)}$$

The form of this particular function is widely used in economics. Later chapters use a closely related form to show the utility (Y) that an individual receives from using two goods (X and Z) and also to show the production relationship between an output (Y) and two inputs (say, labor X and capital Z). Here, however, we are interested mainly in this function's mathematical properties.

Some values for the function in Equation 1A.13 are recorded in Table 1A.2. Two important facts are shown by this table. First, even if one of the variables is held constant (say, at X = 2), changes in the other independent variable (Z) will cause the value of the dependent variable (Y) to change. The value of Y increases from 4 to 6 as Z rises from 2 to 3, even though X is held constant. In economic terms, this illustrates the "marginal" influence of variable Z. Second, several different combinations of X and Z will result in the same value of Y. For example, Y = 4 if X = 2, Z = 2 or if X = 1, Z = 4 (or, indeed, for an infinite number of other X, Z combinations if fractions are used). Using this equality of values of Y for a number of X, Z combinations, functions of two variables can be graphed rather simply.

GRAPHING FUNCTIONS OF TWO VARIABLES

We would need to use three-dimensions to graph a function of two variables completely: one axis for X, one for Z, and one for Y. Drawing three-dimensional graphs in a two- dimensional book is very difficult. Not only must an artist be good enough to be able to show depth in only two dimensions, but the reader

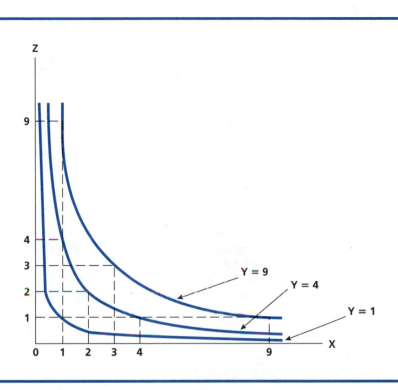

FIGURE 1A.5 Contour Lines for Y = X · Z Contour lines for the function Y = X · Z are rectangular hyperbolas. They can be represented by making Y equal to various supplied values (here Y = 1, Y = 4, Y = 9) and then graphing the relationship between the independent variables X and Z.

must have enough imagination to read the graph as a three-dimensional model. Since economists are not necessarily good artists (and some would argue because economists lack imagination), they graph these functions another way that is much like the techniques mapmakers use.

Mapmakers are also confined to working with two-dimensional drawings. They use **contour lines** to show the third dimension. These are lines of equal altitude that outline the physical features of the territory being mapped. For example, a contour line labeled "1,000 feet" on a map shows all those points of land that are 1,000 feet above sea level. By using a number of contour lines, mapmakers can show the heights and steepness of mountains and the depths of valleys and ocean trenches. In this way, they add the third dimension to a two-dimensional map.

Economists also use contour lines—that is, lines of equal "altitude." Equation 1A.13 can be graphed in two dimensions (one dimension for the values of X and another dimension for values of Z), with contour lines to show the values of Y, the third dimension. This equation is graphed in Figure 1A.5, with three contour lines: one each for Y = 1, Y = 4, and Y = 9.

Contour lines
Lines in two dimensions that show the sets of values of the independent variables that yield the same value for the dependent variable.

Each of the contour lines in Figure 1A.5 is a rectangular hyperbola. The contour line labeled "Y = 1" is a graph of

$$Y = 1 = X \cdot Z \tag{1A.14}$$

"Y = 4" is a graph of

$$Y = 4 = X \cdot Z \tag{1A.15}$$

and the line labeled "Y = 9" is a graph of

$$Y = 9 = X \cdot Z \tag{1A.16}$$

Some of the values along these contour lines are shown in Table 1A.2. It would be easy to compute other points on the curves. Other contour lines for the function could also be drawn by making Y equal to the desired level and graphing the resulting relationship between X and Z. Since we can give Y any value we want, an infinite number of contour lines can be drawn. In this way, we can show the original function in Equation 1A.13 as accurately as we want without resorting to three dimensions.

SIMULTANEOUS EQUATIONS

MicroQuiz 1A.4

Figure 1A.5 shows three contour lines for the function Y = X · Z. How do these lines compare to the following contour lines?

1. Contour lines for Y = 3, 2, and 1 for the function $Y = \sqrt{X \cdot Z}$

2. Contour lines for Y = 81, 16, and 1 for the function $Y = X^2 \cdot Z^2$.

Another mathematical concept that is often used in economics is **simultaneous equations.** When two variables (say, X and Y) are related by two different equations, it is sometimes, though not always, possible to solve these equations together for a single set of values of X and Y that satisfies both of the equations. For example, it is easy to see that the two equations

$$\begin{aligned} X + Y &= 3 \\ X - Y &= 1 \end{aligned} \tag{1A.17}$$

Simultaneous equations
A set of equations with more than one variable that must be solved together for a particular solution.

have a unique solution of

$$\begin{aligned} X &= 2 \\ Y &= 1 \end{aligned} \tag{1A.18}$$

These equations operate "simultaneously" to determine the solutions for X and Y. One of the equations alone cannot determine a specific value for either variable—the solution depends on both of the equations.

Changing Solutions for Simultaneous Equations

It makes no sense in these equations to ask how a change in, say, X would affect the solution for Y. There is only one solution for X and Y from these two equations. As long as both equations must hold, the values of neither X nor Y can change. Of course, if the equations themselves are changed, then their solution will also change. For example, the equation system

$$X + Y = 5$$
$$X - Y = 1 \qquad \text{(1A.19)}$$

is solved as

$$X = 3$$
$$Y = 2 \qquad \text{(1A.20)}$$

Changing just one of the parameters in Equation Set 1A.17 gives us an entirely different solution set.

Graphing Simultaneous Equations

These results are illustrated in Figure 1A.6. The two equations in Equation Set 1A.17 are straight lines that intersect at the point (2,1). This point is the solution to the two equations since it is the only one that lies on both lines. Changing the constant in the first equation of this system gives us a different intersection for Equation Set 1A.19. In that case, the lines intersect at point (3,2), and that is the new solution. Even though only one of the lines shifted, both X and Y take on new solutions.

The similarity between the algebraic graph in Figure 1A.6 and the supply and demand graphs in Figure 1.3 and Figure 1.4 is striking. The point of intersection of two curves is called a "solution" in algebra and an "equilibrium" in economics, but in both cases we are finding the point that satisfies both relationships. The shift of the demand curve in Figure 1.4 clearly resembles the change in the simultaneous equation set in Figure 1A.6. In both cases, the shift in one of the curves results in new solutions for both of the variables. Marshall's analogy of the blades of the supply and demand "scissors" determining market price and quantity can be seen in the algebraic notion of simultaneous systems and their

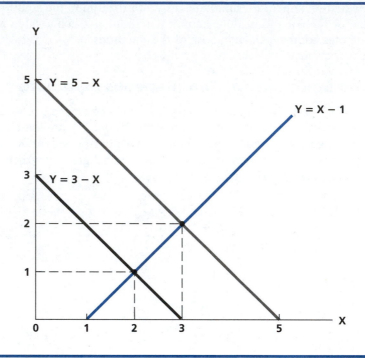

FIGURE 1A.6 Solving Simultaneous Equations The linear equations X + Y = 3 (Y = 3 − X) and (X − Y = 1) can be solved simultaneously to find X = 2, Y = 1. This solution is shown by the point of intersection of the graphs of the two equations. If the first equation is changed (to Y = 5 − X), the solution will also change (to X = 3, Y = 2).

MicroQuiz 1A.5

Economists use the *ceteris paribus* assumption to hold "everything else" constant when looking at a particular effect. How is this assumption reflected in simultaneous equations? Specifically:

1. Explain how the changes illustrated in Figure 1A.6 represent a change in "something else"; and

2. Explain how the changes illustrated in Figure 1A.6 might occur in a supply-demand context in the real world.

solutions. Throughout this book, we use such graphs to show how markets arrive at equilibrium outcomes that satisfy both supply and demand relationships simultaneously. Application 1A.3: Can Iraq Affect Oil Prices? provides a first glimpse of this sort of analysis.

EMPIRICAL MICROECONOMICS AND ECONOMETRICS

As we discussed in Chapter 1, economists are not only concerned with devising models of how the economy works. They must also be concerned with establishing the validity of those models, usually by

Ongoing disputes between the United States and Iraq have caused much concern about how these might affect world oil prices. Specifically, can Iraq, by withholding some of its oil production, affect world oil prices and potentially cause harm to the U.S. economy? A simple supply-demand model can be used to suggest the potential size of such a problem.

A Short-Run Model

Crude oil is traded in a world market, so a starting place is to model that market. A simple demand curve for the market might be[1]

$$Q_D = 80 - 0.4\ P \tag{1}$$

where Q_D is the quantity of crude oil demanded in millions of barrels per day and P is the price in dollars per barrel. Supply might be represented by

$$Q_S = 55 + 0.6\ P \tag{2}$$

Market Equilibrium

Market equilibrium in this market can be found by equating Q_D and Q_S:

$$80 - 0.4\ P = 55 + 0.6\ P \text{ or } P = 25,\ Q = 70 \tag{3}$$

These equilibrium values are shown by the intersection D and S in Figure 1. The price of $25 per barrel and an output of 70 million barrels per day are approximately the values for the world oil market prevailing in mid-2002.

The Effectiveness of Threats by Iraq

Iraq produces about 2.5 million barrels of oil per day. The impact of a decision to sell no oil can be evaluated by assuming that the supply curve in Figure 1 shifts to S' whose equation is given by:

$$Q_S = (55 - 2.5) + 0.6\ P = 52.5 + 0.6\ P \tag{4}$$

Repeating the algebra yields a price of $27.50 and a quantity produced of 69 million barrels per day. Hence, such a decision by Iraq would have some impact, but it would certainly not be catastrophic.[2] Notice that the impact of an Iraqi boycott would be significantly cushioned by the willingness of other producers to increase output when price rises. Although Iraqi production is cut by 2.5 million barrels under our scenario, world output falls by only 1 million barrels because other producers increase output by 1.5 million barrels in response to the $2.50 price increase.

---

[1] This equation and the supply equation are chosen to be roughly consistent with empirical evidence that shows that the short-run price of elasticity of demand for crude oil is about –.15 and the short-run supply elasticity is about 0.25.
[2] Of course, the decision would definitely harm Iraq, who would see its daily oil revenues reduced from $62.5 million to zero.

(continued)

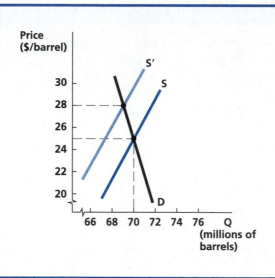

FIGURE 1 Effect of Iraqi Oil Embargo on World Market
A decision by Iraq to eliminate oil exports would shift the world supply curve to S¹, raising the price to $27.50 from $25.00.

To Think About

1. Would the impact of a decision by Iraq to produce no oil have a larger or smaller impact on prices if it were continued for several years?
2. How would a decision by Iraq to refuse to sell oil only to the United States (but to sell its oil to everyone else) affect world oil prices?

looking at data from the real world. The tools used for this purpose are studied in the field of *econometrics* (literally, "economic measuring"). Because many of the applications that appear in this book are taken from econometric studies, and because econometrics has come to play an increasingly important role in all of economics, here we briefly discuss a few aspects of this subject. Any extended treatment is, of course, better handled in a full course on econometrics; but discussion of a few key issues may be helpful in understanding how economists draw conclusions about their models. Specifically, we look at two topics that are relevant to all of econometrics: (1) random influences; and (2) the *ceteris paribus* assumption.

Random Influences

If real-world data fit economic models perfectly, econometrics would be a very simple subject. For example, suppose an economist hypothesized that the demand for pizza (Q) was a linear function of the price of pizza (P) of the form

$$Q = a - bP \qquad (1A.21)$$

where the values for a and b were to be determined by the data. Because any straight line can be established by knowing only two points on it, all the researcher would have to do is: (1) find two places or time periods where "everything else" was the same (a topic we take up next); (2) record the values of Q and P for these observations; and (3) calculate the line passing through

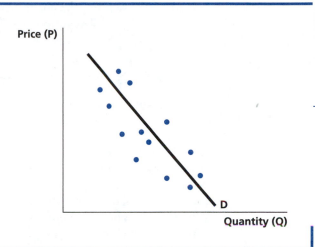

FIGURE 1A.7 Inferring the Demand Curve from Real-World Data Even when the *ceteris paribus* assumption is in force, actual data (shown by the points) will not fit the demand curve (D) perfectly because of random influences. Statistical procedures must be used to infer the location of D.

the two points. Assuming that the demand equation 1A.21 holds in other times or places, all other points on this curve could be determined with perfect accuracy.

Unfortunately, no economic model exhibits such perfect accuracy. Instead, the actual data on Q and P will be scattered around the "true" demand curve because of the huge variety of random influences (such as whether people get a yearning for pizza on a given day) that affect demand. This situation is illustrated in Figure 1A.7. The true demand curve for pizza is shown by the black line, D. Unfortunately, researchers do not know this line. They can "see" only the actual points shown in color. The problem the researcher faces then is how to infer what the true demand curve is from these scattered points.

Technically, this is a problem in **statistical inference.** The researcher uses various statistical techniques in an attempt to abstract from all of the random things that affect the demand for pizza and to *infer* what the relationship between Q and P actually is. A discussion of the techniques actually used for this purpose is beyond the scope of this book, but a glance at Figure 1A.7 makes clear that no technique will find a simple line that fits the points perfectly. Instead, some compromises will have to be made in order to find a demand curve that is "close" to most of the data points. Careful consideration of the nature of the random

Statistical inference
Use of actual data and statistical techniques to determine quantitative economic relationships.

influences present in a problem can help in devising which technique to use.[4] A few of the applications in this text describe how researchers have adapted techniques to their purposes.

The *Ceteris Paribus* Assumption

All economic theories employ the assumption that "other things are held constant." In the real world, of course, many things do change. If the data points in Figure 1A.7 come from different weeks, for example, it is unlikely that conditions such as the weather or the prices of pizza substitutes (hamburgers?) have remained unchanged over these periods. Similarly, if the data points in the figure come from, say, different towns, it is unlikely that all factors that may affect pizza demand are exactly the same in every town. Hence, a researcher might reasonably be concerned that the data in Figure 1A.7 do not reflect a single demand curve. Rather, the points may lie on several different demand curves, and attempting to force them into a single curve would be a mistake.

To address this problem, two things must be done: (1) Data should be collected on all of the other factors that affect demand, and (2) appropriate procedures must be used to control for these measurable factors in analysis. Although the conceptual framework for doing this is fairly straightforward,[5] many practical problems arise. Most important, it may not in fact be possible to measure all of the other factors that affect demand. Consider, for example, the problem of deciding how to measure the precise influence of a pizza advertising campaign on pizza demand. Would you measure the number of ads placed, the number of ad readers, or the "quality" of the ads? Ideally, one might like to measure people's perceptions of the ads—but how would you do that without an elaborate

---

MicroQuiz 1A.6

An economic consulting firm is hired to estimate the demand for DVD movies among several cities. Explain using a graph why each of the following "solutions" to the *ceteris paribus* problem is in fact no solution at all—why would the demand curves developed by applying each assumption probably be wrong?

Approach 1: Use statistical procedures to control for what is easily measured (i.e., average income) and forget about what cannot be easily measured (i.e., the number of homes with DVD players).

Approach 2: Control for "everything" that affects demand; don't worry about the possibility that the supply of DVDs may differ from city to city.

---

[4] In many problems the statistical technique of "ordinary least squares" is the best available. This technique proceeds by choosing the line for which the sum of the squared deviations from the line for all of the data points is as small as possible. For a discussion, see R. Ramanathan, *Introductory Econometrics with Applications,* 5th ed. (Mason, OH: South-Western College Publishing, 2001).

[5] To control for the older measurable factors (X) that affect demand, the demand curve given in Equation 1A.21 must be modified to include these other factors as $Q = a - bP + cX$. Once the parameters a, b, and c have been determined, this allows the researcher to hold X constant (as is required by the *ceteris paribus* assumption) while looking at the relationship between Q and P. Changes in X shift the entire Q-P relationship.

and costly survey? Ultimately, then, the researcher will often have to make some compromises in the kinds of data that can be collected, and some uncertainty will remain about whether the *ceteris paribus* assumption has been imposed faithfully. Many controversies over testing the reliability of economic models arise for precisely this reason.

SUMMARY

This chapter reviews material that should be familiar to you from prior math and economics classes. The following results will be used throughout the rest of this book:

- Linear equations have graphs that are straight lines. These lines are described by their slopes and by their intercepts with the Y-axis.
- Changes in the slope cause the graph of a linear equation to rotate about its Y-intercept. Changes in the Y-intercept cause the graph to shift in a parallel way.
- Nonlinear equations have graphs that have curved shapes. Their slopes change as X changes.
- Economists often use functions of two or more variables because economic outcomes have many

causes. These functions can sometimes be graphed in two dimensions by using contour lines.

- Simultaneous equations determine solutions for two (or more) variables that satisfy all of the equations. An important use of such equations is to show how supply and demand curves determine equilibrium prices. For that reason, such equations are widely encountered in economics.
- Testing economic models usually requires the use of real-world data together with appropriate econometric techniques. An important problem in all such applications is to ensure that the *ceteris paribus* assumption has been imposed correctly.

Part 2

Demand

"Utility is that principle which approves or disapproves every action whatsoever according to the tendency it . . . (has) to augment or diminish . . . happiness. . . ."

Jeremy Bentham, *Introduction to the Principles of Morals and Legislation,* 1789

Part 2 examines how economists model people's economic decisions. Our main goal is to develop Marshall's demand curve for a product and to show why this demand curve is likely to be downward sloping.

Chapter 2 describes how economists treat the consumer's decision problem. We first define the concept of utility, which represents a consumer's preferences. The second half of the chapter discusses how people decide to spend their incomes on different goods to get the greatest satisfaction possible—that is, to "maximize" their utility.

Chapter 3 investigates how people change their choices when their income changes or as prices change. This allows us to develop an individual's demand curve for a product. Chapter 3 also illustrates a few additional applications of the economic model of individual's choices.

Chapter 4, the final one in this part, shows how individual demand curves can be "added up" to make market demand curves. These curves provide a basic building block for our study of the price determination process.

2

Utility and Choice

Every day you must make many choices: when to wake up; what to eat; how much time to spend working, studying, or relaxing; and whether to buy something or save your money. Economists investigate all these decisions because they all affect the way any economy operates. In this chapter we look at the general model used for this purpose.

The economic **theory of choice** begins by describing people's preferences. This simply amounts to a complete cataloging of how a person feels about all the things he or she might do. But people are not free to do anything they want—they are constrained by time, income, and many other factors in the choices open to them. Our model of choice must also describe how these constraints affect the ways in which individuals actually are able to make choices based on their preferences.

Theory of choice
The interaction of preferences and constraints that causes people to make the choices they do.

UTILITY

Economists model people's preferences using the concept of **utility,** which we define as the satisfaction that a person receives from his or her activities. This concept is very broad, and in the next few sections we define it more precisely. We use the simple case of a single consumer who receives utility from just two commodities. We will eventually analyze how that person chooses to allocate income between these two goods, but first we need to develop a better understanding of utility itself.

Utility
The pleasure or satisfaction that people get from their economic activity.

Ceteris Paribus Assumption

To identify all the factors affecting a person's feelings of satisfaction would be a lifelong task for an imaginative psychologist. To simplify matters, economists focus on basic, quantifiable economic factors and look at how people choose among them. Economists clearly recognize that all sorts of factors (aesthetics, love, security, envy, and so forth) affect behavior, but they develop models in which these kinds of factors are held constant and are not specifically analyzed.

Much economic analysis is based on this *ceteris paribus* (other things being equal) **assumption.** We can simplify the analysis of a person's consumption decisions by assuming that satisfaction is affected only by choices made among the options being considered. All other effects on satisfaction are assumed to remain constant. In this way we can isolate the economic factors that affect consumption behavior. This narrow focus is not intended to imply that other things that affect utility are unimportant; we are conceptually holding these other factors constant so that we may study choices in a simplified setting.

Ceteris paribus assumption
In economic analysis, holding all other factors constant so that only the factor being studied is allowed to change.

Utility from Consuming Two Goods

This chapter concentrates on an individual's problem of choosing the quantities of two goods (which for most purposes we will call simply "X" and "Y") to consume. We assume that the person receives utility from these goods and that we can show this utility in functional notation by

$$\text{Utility} = U(X, Y; \text{other things}) \tag{2.1}$$

This notation indicates that the utility an individual receives from consuming X and Y over some period of time depends on the quantities of X and Y consumed and on "other things." These other things might include easily quantifiable items such as the amounts of other kinds of goods consumed, the number of hours worked, or the amount of time spent sleeping. They might also include such unquantifiable items as love, security, and feeling of self-worth. These other things appear after the semicolon in Equation 2.1 because we assume that they are held constant while we examine the individual's choice between X and Y. If one of the other things should change, the utility from some particular amounts of X and Y might be very different than it was before.

For example, several times in this chapter we consider the case of a person choosing how many hamburgers (Y) and soft drinks (X) to consume during one week. Although our example uses trivial commodities, the analysis is quite general and will apply to any two goods. In analyzing the hamburger–soft drink choices, we assume that all other factors affecting utility are held constant. The weather, the person's basic preferences for hamburgers and soft drinks, the person's exercise pattern, and everything else are assumed not to change during the analysis. If the weather, for instance, were to become warmer, we might expect soft drinks to become relatively more desirable, and we wish to eliminate such effects from our analysis, at least for the moment. We usually write the utility function in Equation 2.1 as

$$\text{Utility} = U(X, Y) \tag{2.2}$$

with the understanding that many other things are being held constant. All economic analyses impose some form of this *ceteris paribus* assumption so that the relationship between a selected few variables can be studied.

Measuring Utility

You might think that economists would try to measure utility directly, but that goal has proven to be very elusive. The problems are of two general types. First, economists have found it very difficult to impose the *ceteris paribus* assumption. In the real world, things are constantly changing in people's lives so it is hard to measure the utility of a few specific economic goods. Some progress has been made in this regard by using controlled experiments in laboratories (usually with students as subjects), but experimental economics remains in its infancy.

A second pervasive problem with measuring utility is in defining a unit of measurement. Economists have been rather unsuccessful in developing some sort of scale that might measure utility in, say, "happiness units" and allow comparisons of one person's units to those of someone else. One natural way for economists to think about this issue might be to treat income and utility synonymously. This would provide a direct measure of "happiness" and permit such statements as "a person with $50,000 per year is twice as happy as someone with $25,000." As Application 2.1: Can Money Buy Health and Happiness? shows, however, this approach, though widely used, poses pitfalls of its own.

Fortunately, we do a fairly complete job of studying economic choices without actually measuring utility on any sort of a numerical scale. To do so, we only have to be willing to assume that people have well-defined preferences so that they can clearly state whether they prefer situation A to situation B or *vice versa*. That is, people can order the options available from most to least favorable, though they may not be able to give numerical values to the options. Together with a few more seemingly reasonable assumptions, this is all we need to get started.

ASSUMPTIONS ABOUT UTILITY

What do we mean by saying that people's preferences are "consistent"? How can we describe the voluntary deals that people are willing to make? Can these preferences (utility) be shown graphically? We explore these questions as we begin our study of economists' model of choice.

Basic Properties of Preferences

Although we cannot measure utility, we might expect people to express their preferences in a reasonably consistent manner. Between two consumption bundles, A and B, we might expect a person to be able to state clearly either "I prefer A to B," or "I prefer B to A," or "A and B are equally attractive to me." We do not expect

Can Money Buy Health and Happiness?

Although measuring utility directly may be impossible, economists have been quite willing to explore various approximations. Perhaps the most widely used measure is annual income. As the old joke goes, even if money can't buy happiness, it can buy you any kind of sadness you want. Here we focus specifically on the connections between income, health and happiness.

Income and Health

An individual's health is certainly one aspect of his or her utility, and the relationship between income and health has been intensively studied. Virtually all of these studies conclude that people who have higher incomes enjoy better health. For example, comparing men of equal ages, life expectancy is about 7 years shorter for those with incomes in the bottom quarter of the population than for those in the top quarter. Similar differences show up in the prevalence of various diseases—rates of heart disease and cancer are much lower for those in the upper-income group. Clearly it appears that money can "buy" good health.

There is less agreement among economists about *why* more income "buys" good health.[1] The standard explanation is that higher incomes allow people greater access to health care. Higher incomes may also be associated with taking fewer health-related risks (e.g., smoking or excessive alcohol consumption). In fact, these factors play relatively little role in determining an individual's health. For example, the connection between income and health persists in countries with extensive national health insurance systems and after controlling for the risky things people do. These findings have led some economists to question the precise causality in the income-health linkage. Is it possible that the health is affecting income rather than vice versa? Workers' earnings are clearly affected by their health, and large, health-related expenses may make it difficult for some people to accumulate much wealth. Sorting out these various possibilities is important to understanding precisely how the distribution of income is related to the distribution of health.

Income and Happiness

A more general approach to the relationship between income and utility asks people to rank how happy they are on a numerical scale. Although people's answers show considerable variability, the data do show certain regularities. People with higher incomes report that they are happier than are those with lower incomes in virtually every survey. For example, the economic historian Richard Easterlin reports on measured happiness in the United States on a 4-point scale.[2] He finds that people with incomes above $75,000 per year have an average happiness ranking of 2.8 whereas those with incomes below $20,000 per year have a ranking below 2. Surveys from other countries show much the same result.

One puzzle in the association between income and happiness is that a person's happiness does not seem to rise as he or she becomes more affluent during his or her lifetime. But people always seem to think they are better off than they were in the past and will be

---

[1] For a more complete discussion of the issues raised in this section, see James P. Smith, "Healthy Bodies and Thick Wallets: The Dual Relationship between Health and Economic Status," *Journal of Economic Perspectives* (Spring 1999): 145–166.

[2] Richard A. Easterlin, "Income and Happiness: Toward a Unified Theory," *Economic Journal* (July 2001): 465–484.

even better off in the future. Easterlin argues that such findings can be explained by the fact that people's aspirations rise with their incomes—getting richer as one gets older is offset by rising expectations in its total effect on happiness. Clearly the relationship is a complex one and measuring happiness has become a major area of inquiry for economists.

To Think About

1. Because a higher income makes it possible for a person to consume bundles of goods that were previously unaffordable, isn't he or she necessarily better off? Isn't that all we need to know?
2. Sometimes people are said to be poor if they have to spend more than, say, 25 percent of their income on food, Why would spending a large fraction of one's income on food tend to indicate some degree of economic deprivation?

the individual to be paralyzed by indecision but, rather, to be able to say precisely how he or she feels about any potential consumption possibilities. This rules out such situations as the mythical jackass, who, finding himself midway between a pile of hay and a bag of oats, starved to death because he was unable to decide which way to go. Formally, we are assuming preferences are **complete**—that people can always make a choice between any two options presented to them.

In addition to expecting people to be able to state preferences clearly and completely, we might also expect people's preferences not to be self-contradictory. We do not expect a person to make statements about his or her preferences that conflict with each other. In other words, we assume that preferences are **transitive**. If a person says, "I prefer A to B," and "I prefer B to C," then he or she can be expected to say, "I prefer A to C." A person who instead states the contrary (that is, "I prefer C to A") would appear to be hopelessly inconsistent. We wish to rule out such inconsistency.

Complete preferences
The assumption that an individual is able to state which of any two options is preferred.

Transitivity of preferences
The property that if A is preferred to B, and B is preferred to C, then A must be preferred to C.

More Is Better: Defining an Economic "Good"

A third assumption we make about preferences is that a person prefers more of a good to less. In Figure 2.1, all points in the darkly shaded area are preferred to the amounts of X* of good X and Y* of good Y. Movement from point X*, Y* to any point in the shaded area is an unambiguous improvement, since in this area this person gets more of one good without taking less of another. This idea of preferences is implicit in our definition of an "economic good" as an item that yields positive benefits to people.[1] That is, more of a good is, by definition, better. Combinations of goods in the lightly shaded area of Figure 2.1 are definitely inferior to X*, Y* since they offer less of *both* goods.

---

[1] Later in this chapter, we briefly describe a theory of "bads"—items for which less is preferred to more. Such items might include toxic wastes, mosquitoes, or, for this author, lima beans.

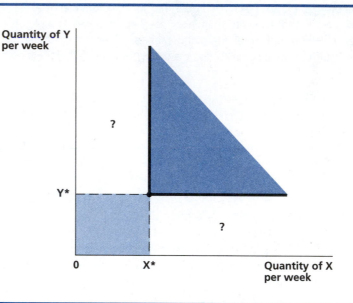

FIGURE 2.1 More of a Good Is Preferred to Less The darkly shaded area represents those combinations of X and Y that are unambiguously preferred to the combination X*, Y*. This is why goods are called "goods"; individuals prefer having more of any good rather than less. Combinations of X and Y in the lightly shaded area are inferior to the combination X*, Y*, whereas those in the questionable areas may or may not be superior to X*, Y*.

VOLUNTARY TRADES AND INDIFFERENCE CURVES

How people feel about getting more of some good when they must give up an amount of some other good is probably the most important reason for studying preferences. The areas identified with question marks in Figure 2.1 are difficult to compare to X*, Y* since they involve more of one good and less of the other. Whether a move from X*, Y* into these areas would increase utility is not clear. To be able to look into this situation, we need some additional tools. Because giving up units of one commodity (for example, money) to get back additional units of some other commodity (say, candy bars) is what gives rise to trade and organized markets, these new tools provide the foundation for the economic analysis of demand.

MicroQuiz 2.1

How should the assumption of completeness and transitivity be reflected in Figure 2.1? Specifically:

1. What does the assumption of completeness imply about all of the points in the figure?

2. If it were known that a particular point in the "?" area in Figure 2.1 was preferred to point X*, Y*, how could transitivity be used to rank some other points in that area?

Indifference Curves

To study voluntary trades, we use the concept of an **indifference curve.** Such a curve shows all those combinations of two goods that provide the same utility to an individual; that is, a person is *indifferent* about which particular combination on the curve he or she actually has. For example, Figure 2.2 records the quantity of soft drinks consumed by a person in one week on the horizontal axis and the quantity of hamburgers consumed in the same week on the vertical axis. The curve U_1 in Figure 2.2 includes all those combinations of hamburgers and soft drinks with which this person is equally happy. For example, the curve shows that he or she would be just as happy with six hamburgers and two soft drinks per week (point A) as with four hamburgers and three soft drinks (point B) or with

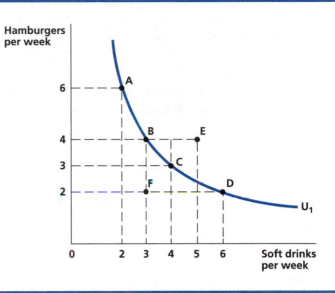

FIGURE 2.2 Indifference Curve The curve U_1 shows the combinations of hamburgers and soft drinks that provide the same level of utility to an individual. The slope of the curve shows the trades an individual will freely make. For example, in moving from point A to point B, the individual will give up two hamburgers to get one additional soft drink. In other words, the marginal rate of substitution is approximately 2 in this range. Points below U_1 (such as F) provide less utility than points on U_1. Points above U_1 (such as E) provide more utility than U_1.

three hamburgers and four soft drinks (point C). The points on U_1 all provide the same level of utility, therefore, he or she does not have any particular reason for preferring any point on U_1 to any other point.

    The indifference curve U_1 is similar to a contour line on a map (as discussed in Appendix to Chapter 1) in that it shows those combinations of hamburgers and soft drinks that provide an identical "altitude" (that is, amount) of utility. Points to the northeast of U_1 promise a higher level of satisfaction and are preferred to points on U_1. Point E (five soft drinks and four hamburgers) is preferred to point C because it provides more of both goods. As in Figure 2.1, our definition of goods assures that combination E is preferred to combination C. Similarly, our assumption of transitivity assures that combination E is also preferred to combinations A, B, and D and to all other combinations on U_1.

    Combinations of hamburgers and soft drinks that lie below U_1, on the other hand, are less desirable since they offer less satisfaction. Point F offers less of both goods than does point C. The fact that the indifference curve U_1 has a negative slope (that is, the curve runs from the upper left portion of the figure to the lower right portion) indicates that if a person is forced to give up some hamburgers, he

Indifference curve
A curve that shows all the combinations of goods or services that provide the same level of utility.

or she must receive additional soft drinks to remain equally well-off. This type of movement along U_1 represents those trades that a person might freely make. Knowledge of U_1 therefore eliminates the ambiguity associated with the questionable areas we showed in Figure 2.1.

Indifference Curves and the Marginal Rate of Substitution

What happens when an individual moves from point A (six hamburgers and two soft drinks) to point B (four hamburgers and three soft drinks)? This person remains equally well-off because the two commodity bundles lie on the same indifference curve. This person will voluntarily give up two of the hamburgers that were being consumed at point A in exchange for one additional soft drink. The slope of the curve U_1 between A and B is therefore approximately $-\frac{2}{1} = -2$. That is, Y (hamburgers) declines two units in response to a one-unit increase in X (soft drinks). We call the absolute value of this slope the **marginal rate of substitution (MRS).** Hence, we would say that the MRS (of soft drinks for hamburgers) between points A and B is 2: Given his or her current circumstances, this person is willing to give up two hamburgers in order to get one more soft drink.

Marginal rate of substitution (MRS)

The rate at which an individual is willing to reduce consumption of one good when he or she gets one more unit of another good. The negative of the slope of an indifference curve.

Diminishing Marginal Rate of Substitution

The MRS varies along the curve U_1. For points such as A, this person has quite a few hamburgers and is relatively willing to trade them away for soft drinks. On the other hand, for combinations such as those represented by point D, the individual has an abundance of soft drinks and is reluctant to give up any more hamburgers to get more soft drinks. The increasing reluctance to trade away hamburgers reflects the notion that the consumption of any one good (here, soft drinks) can be pushed too far. This characteristic can be seen by considering the trades that take place in moving from point A to B, from point B to C, and from point C to D. In the first trade, two hamburgers are given up to get one more soft drink—the MRS is 2 (as we have already shown). The second trade involves giving up one hamburger to get one additional soft drink. In this trade, the MRS has declined to 1, reflecting an increased reluctance to give up hamburgers to get more soft drinks. Finally, for the third trade, from point C to D, the individual is willing to give up a hamburger only if two soft drinks are received in return. In this final trade, the MRS is ½ (the individual is willing to give up one-half of a hamburger to get one more soft drink), which is a further decline from the MRS of the previous trades. Hence, the MRS steadily declines as soft drinks (shown on the X-axis) increase.

Balance in Consumption

Our conclusion of a diminishing MRS is based on the idea that people prefer balanced consumption bundles to unbalanced ones.[2] This assumption is illustrated precisely in Figure 2.3, where the indifference curve U_1 from Figure 2.2 is redrawn. Our discussion here concerns the two extreme consumption options A and D. In consuming A, this person gets six hamburgers and two soft drinks; the same satisfaction could be received by consuming D (two hamburgers and six soft drinks). Now consider a bundle of commodities (say, G) "between" these extremes. With G (four hamburgers and four soft drinks), this person obtains a higher level of satisfaction (point G is northeast of the indifference curve U_1) than with either of the extreme bundles A or D.

The reason for this increased satisfaction should be geometrically obvious. All of the points on the straight line joining A and D lie above U_1. Point G is one of these points (as the figure shows, there are many others). As long as the indifference curve obeys the assumption of a diminishing MRS, it will be convex; any bundle that represents an "average" between two equally attractive extremes

> **MicroQuiz 2.2**
>
> The slope of an indifference curve is negative.
>
> **1.** Explain why the slope of an indifference curve would not be expected to be positive for economic "goods."
>
> **2.** Explain why the MRS (which is the negative of the slope of an indifference curve) cannot be calculated for points E and F in Figure 2.2 without additional information.

---

[2] If we assume utility is measurable, we can provide an alternative analysis of a diminishing MRS. To do so we introduce the concept of the marginal utility of a good X (denoted by MU_X). Marginal utility is defined as the extra utility obtained by consuming one more unit of good X. The concept is meaningful only if utility can be measured and so is not as useful as the MRS. If the individual is asked to give up some Y (ΔY) to get some additional X ($X\Delta$), the change in utility is given by

$$\text{Change in utility} = MU_Y \cdot \Delta Y + MU_X \cdot \Delta X \qquad \text{(i)}$$

It is equal to the utility gained from the additional X less the utility lost from the reduction in Y. Since utility does not change along an indifference curve, we can use Equation i to derive

$$\frac{-\Delta Y}{\Delta X} = \frac{MU_X}{MU_Y} \qquad \text{(ii)}$$

Along an indifference curve, the negative of its slope is given by MU_X/MU_Y. That is, by definition, the MRS. Hence we have

$$MRS = MU_X/MU_Y \qquad \text{(iii)}$$

For example, if an extra hamburger yields two utils (units of utility; $MU_Y = 2$) and an extra soft drink yields four utils ($MU_X = 4$), MRS = 2 since the individual will be willing to trade away two hamburgers to get an additional soft drink. If it is assumed that MU_X falls and MU_Y increases as X is substituted for Y, Equation iii shows that MRS will fall as we move counterclockwise along U_1.

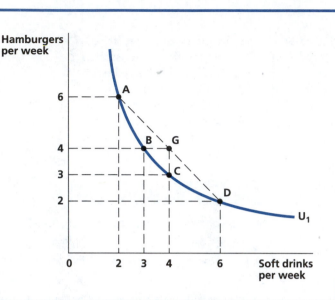

FIGURE 2.3 **Balance in Consumption Is Desirable** The consumption bundle G (four hamburgers, four soft drinks) is preferred to either of the extreme bundles A and D. This is a result of the assumption of a diminishing MRS. Because individuals become progressively less willing to give up hamburgers as they move in a southeasterly direction along U_1, the curve U_1 will have a convex shape. Consequently, all points on a straight line joining two points such as A and D will lie above U_1. Points such as G will be preferred to any of those on U_1.

will be preferred to those extremes. The assumption of a diminishing MRS reflects the notion that people prefer variety in their consumption choices.

INDIFFERENCE CURVE MAPS

Although Figure 2.2 and Figure 2.3 each show only one indifference curve, the positive quadrant contains many such curves, each one corresponding to a different level of utility. Since every combination of hamburgers and soft drinks must yield some level of utility, every point must have one (and only one[3]) indifference curve passing through it. These curves are, as we said earlier, similar to the contour lines that appear on topographical maps in that they each represent a different "altitude" of utility. In Figure 2.4,

three of these curves have been drawn and are labeled U_1, U_2, and U_3. These are only three of the infinite number of curves that characterize an individual's entire **indifference curve map.** Just as a map may have many contour lines (say, one for each inch of altitude), so too the gradations in utility may be very fine, as would be shown by very closely spaced indifference curves. For graphic convenience, our analysis generally deals with only a few indifference curves that are relatively widely spaced.

The labeling of the indifference curves in Figure 2.4 has no special meaning except to indicate that utility increases as we move from combinations of good on U_1 to those on U_2 and then to those on U_3. As we have pointed out, there is no precise way to measure the level of utility associated with, say, U_2. Similarly, we have no way of measuring the amount of extra utility an individual receives from

Indifference curve map

A contour map that shows the utility an individual obtains from all possible consumption options.

---

[3] One point cannot appear on two separate indifference curves because it cannot yield two different levels of utility. Each point in a map can have only a single altitude.

consuming bundles on U_3 instead of U_2. All we can say is that utility increases as this person moves to higher indifference curves. That is, he or she would prefer to be on a higher curve rather than on a lower one. This map tells us all there is to know about this person's preferences. Both economists and marketing experts have made use of these ideas, as Application 2.2: Product Positioning in Marketing illustrates.

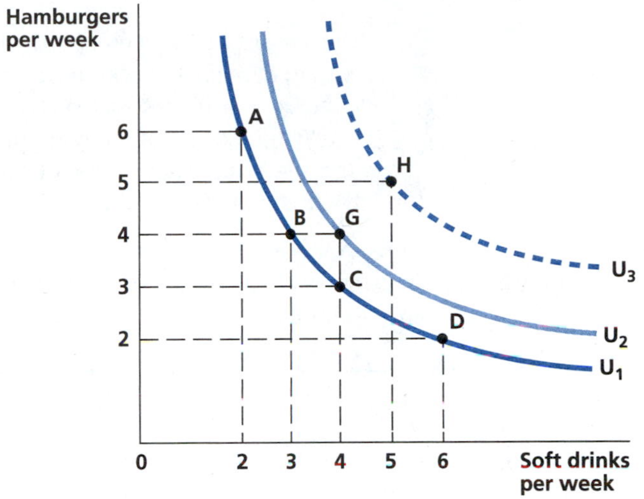

Illustrating Particular Preferences

To illustrate some of the ways in which indifference curve maps might be used to reflect particular kinds of preferences, Figure 2.5 shows four special cases.

FIGURE 2.4 Indifference Curve Map for Hamburgers and Soft Drinks
The positive quandrant is full of indifference curves, each of which reflects a different level of ultility. Three such curves are illustrated. Combinations of goods on U_3 are preferred to those on U_2, which in turn are preferred to those on U_1. This is simply a reflection of the assumption that more of a good is preferred to less, as may be seen by comparing points C, G, and H.

A Useless Good

Figure 2.5(a) shows an individual's indifference curve map for food (on the horizontal axis) and smoke grinders (on the vertical axis). Since smoke grinders are totally useless, increasing purchases of them does not increase utility. Only by getting additional food does this person enjoy a higher level of utility. The vertical indifference curve U_2, for example, shows that utility will be U_2 as long as this person has 10 units of food no matter how many smoke grinders he or she has.

An Economic Bad

The situation illustrated in Figure 2.5(a) implicitly assumes that useless goods cause no harm—having more useless smoke grinders causes no problem since one can always throw them away. In some cases, however, such free disposal is not possible, and additional units of a good can cause actual harm. For example, Figure 2.5(b) shows an indifference curve map for food and houseflies. Holding food consumption constant at 10, utility declines as the number of houseflies increases. Because additional houseflies reduce utility, an individual might even be willing to give up some food (and buy flypaper instead, for example) in exchange for fewer houseflies.

One practical application of utility theory is in the field of marketing. Firms that wish to develop a new product that will appeal to consumers must provide the good with attributes that successfully differentiate it from its competitors. A careful positioning of the good that takes account of both consumers' desires and the costs associated with product attributes can make the difference between a profitable and an unprofitable product introduction.

A Graphic Analysis

Consider, for example, the case of breakfast cereals. Suppose only two attributes matter to consumers—taste and crunchiness (shown on the axes of Figure 1). Utility increases for movements in the northeast direction on this graph. Suppose that a new breakfast cereal has two competitors—Brand X and Brand Y. The marketing expert's problem is to position the new brand in such a way that it provides more utility to the consumer than does Brand X or Brand Y, while keeping the new cereal's production costs competitive. If marketing surveys suggest that the typical consumer's indifference curve resembles U_1, this can be accomplished by positioning the new brand at, say, point Z.

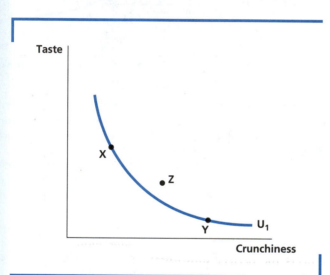

FIGURE 1 **Product Positioning** Market research indicates consumers are indifferent between the characteristics of cereals X and Y. Positioning a new brand at Z offers good market prospects.

Hotels

Hotel chains use essentially the same procedure in competing for business. For example, the Marriott Corporation gathers small focus groups of consumers.[1] It then asks them to rank various sets of hotel attributes such as check-in convenience, pools, and room service. Such information allows Marriott to construct (multidimensional) indifference curves for these various attributes. It then places its major competitors on these graphs and explores various ways of positioning its own product.

Options Packages

Similar positioning strategies are followed by makers of complex products, such as automobiles or personal computers, supplied with various factory-installed options. These makers not only must position their basic product among many competitors but also they must decide when to incorporate options into their designs and how to price them. For example,

[1] This example is taken from Alex Hiam, *The Vest Pocket CEO* (Englewood Cliffs, NJ: Prentice Hall, 1990): 270–272.

throughout the 1980s, Japanese automakers tended to incorporate such options as air conditioning, power windows, and sun roofs into their mid-range models, thereby giving them a "luxury" feel relative to their American competitors. The approach was so successful that most makers of such autos have adopted it. Similarly, in the personal computer market, producers such as Dell or Compaq found they could gain market share by including carefully tailored packages of peripherals (larger hard drives, extra memory, powerful modems) in their packages.

To Think About

1. How is the MRS concept relevant to the positioning analysis illustrated in Figure 1? How could firms take advantage of information about such a trade-off rate?
2. Doesn't the idea of an automobile "options package" seem inferior to a situation where each consumer chooses exactly what he or she wants? How do you explain the prevalence of such packages?

Perfect Substitutes

The illustrations of convex indifference curves in Figure 2.2 through Figure 2.4 reflected the assumption that diversity in consumption is desirable. If, however, the two goods we were examining were essentially the same (or at least served identical functions), we could not make this argument. In Figure 2.5(c), for example, we show an individual's indifference curve map for Exxon and Mobil gasoline. Because this buyer is unconvinced by television advertisements, he or she has adopted the sensible proposition that all gallons of gasoline are pretty much the same. Hence, he or she is always willing to trade one gallon of Exxon for a gallon of Mobil—the MRS along any indifference curve is 1.0. The straight-line indifference curve map in Figure 2.5(c) reflects the perfect substitutability between these two goods.

Perfect Complements

In Figure 2.5(d), on the other hand, we illustrate a situation in which two goods go together. This person (quite naturally) prefers to consume left shoes (on the horizontal axis) and right shoes (on the vertical axis) in pairs. If, for example, he or she currently has three pairs of shoes, additional right shoes provide no more utility (compare this to the situation in panel a). Similarly, additional left shoes alone provide no additional utility. An extra pair of shoes, on the other hand, does increase utility (from U_3 to U_4) since this individual likes to consume these two goods together. Any situation in which two goods have such a strong complementary relationship to one another would be described by a similar map of L-shaped indifference curves.

Of course, these simple examples only hint at the variety in types of preferences that can be illustrated by indifference curve maps. Later in this chapter, we encounter other examples that help to explain observed economic behavior.

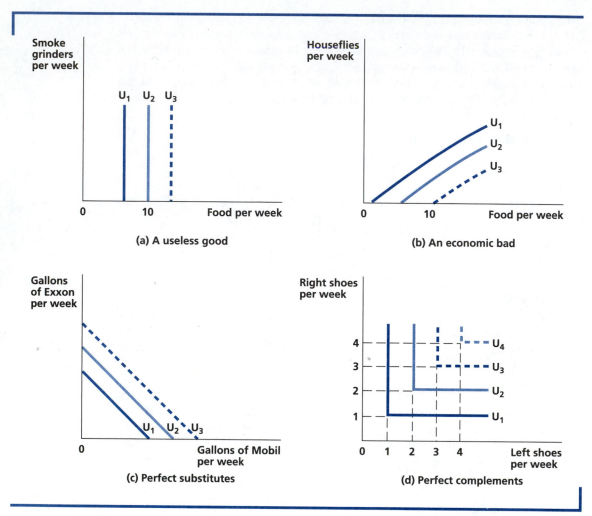

FIGURE 2.5 Illustrations of Specific Preferences The four indifference curve maps in this figure geographically analyze different relationships between two goods.

Because indifference curve maps reflect people's basic preferences about the goods they might select, such maps provide an important first building block for studying demand.

UTILITY MAXIMIZATION: AN INITIAL SURVEY

Economists assume that when a person is faced with a choice from among a number of possible options, he or she will choose the one that yields the highest utility—utility maximization. As Adam Smith remarked more than two centuries ago, "We are not ready to suspect any person of being defective in selfishness."[4] In other words, economists assume that people know their own minds and make choices consistent with their preferences. This section surveys in general terms how such choices might be made.

INFOTRAC©
COLLEGE EDITION
Exclusively from Gale Group and Thomson Learning

www.infotrac-college.com
Keywords: Theory of utility, Theory of choice, Indifference curves, Utility maximization

Choices Are Constrained

The most interesting feature of the utility-maximization problem is that people are constrained in what they can buy by the size of their incomes. Of those combinations of goods that a person can afford, he or she will choose the one that is most preferred. This most preferred bundle of goods may not provide complete bliss; it may even leave this person in misery. It will, however, reflect the best use of limited income. All other combinations of goods that can be bought with that limited income would leave him or her even worse off. It is the limitation of income that makes this an economic problem of allocating a scarce resource (the limited income) among alternative end uses.

A Simple Case

Consider the following trivial problem: How should a person choose to allocate income among two goods (hamburgers and soft drinks) if he or she is to obtain the highest level of utility possible? Answering this question provides fundamental insights into all of microeconomics. The basic result can easily be stated at the outset. In order to maximize utility given a fixed amount of income to spend on two goods, this person should spend the entire amount and choose a combination of goods for which the marginal rate of substitution between the two goods is equal to the ratio of those goods' market prices.

The reasoning behind the first part of this proposition is straightforward. Because we assume that more is better, a person should obviously spend the entire amount budgeted for the two items. The alternative here is throwing the money away, which is obviously less desirable than buying something.

The reasoning behind the second part of the proposition is more complicated. Suppose that a person is currently consuming some combination of hamburgers and soft drinks for which the MRS is equal to 1; he or she is willing to do without one hamburger in order to get an additional soft drink. Assume, on the other hand, that the price of hamburgers is $2.00 and that of soft drinks is $1.00. The ratio of their prices is $1.00/$2.00 = ½. This person is able to afford an extra soft drink by doing without only one-half of a hamburger. In this situation the

[4] Adam Smith, *The Theory of Moral Sentiments* (1759; reprint. New Rochelle, NY: Arlington House, 1969), 446.

individual's MRS is not equal to the ratio of the goods' market prices, and we can show that some other combination of goods provides more utility.

Suppose this person consumes one less hamburger. This frees $2.00 in purchasing power. He or she can now buy one more soft drink (at a price of $1.00) and is now as well-off as before, since the MRS was assumed to be 1. However, another dollar remains unspent that can now be spent on either soft drinks or hamburgers (or some combination of the two). This additional consumption clearly makes the individual better off than in the initial situation.

Our numbers here were purely arbitrary. Whenever a person selects a combination of goods for which the MRS differs from the price ratio, a similar utility-improving change in spending patterns can be made. This reallocation will continue until the MRS is brought into line with the price ratio, at which time maximum utility is attained. We now present a more formal proof of this.

GRAPHIC ANALYSIS OF UTILITY MAXIMIZATION

Budget constraint
The limit that income places on the combinations of goods that an individual can buy.

To develop a graphic demonstration of the process of utility maximization, we will begin by showing how to illustrate an individual's **budget constraint**. This constraint shows which combinations of goods are affordable. It is from among these that the individual can choose the bundle that provides the most utility.

The Budget Constraint

Figure 2.6 shows the combinations of two goods (which we will call simply X and Y) that a person with a fixed amount of money to spend can afford. If all available income is spent on good X, the number of units that can be purchased is recorded as X_{max} in the figure. If all available income is spent on Y, Y_{max} is the amount that can be bought. The line joining X_{max} to Y_{max} represents the various mixed bundles of goods X and Y that can be purchased using all the available funds. Points in the shaded area below the budget line are also affordable, but these leave some portion of funds unspent, so these points would usually not be chosen.

The downward slope of the budget line shows that the individual can afford more X only if Y purchases are cut back. The precise slope of this relationship depends on the prices of the two goods. If Y is expensive and X is cheap, the line will be relatively flat since choosing to consume one less Y will permit the purchasing of many units of X (an individual who decides not to purchase a new designer suit can instead choose to purchase many pairs of socks). Alternately, if Y is relatively cheap per unit and X is expensive, the budget line will be steep.

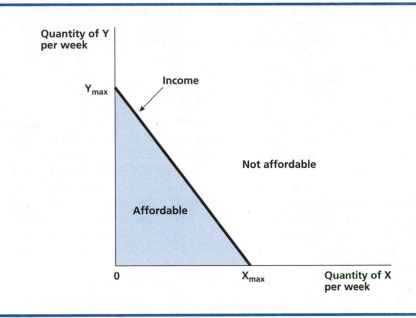

FIGURE 2.6 Individual's Budget Constraint for Two Goods Those combinations of X and Y that the individual can afford are shown in the shaded triangle. If, as we usually assume, the individual prefers more than less of every good, the outer boundary of this triangle is the relevant constraint where all of the available funds are spent on either X or Y. The slope of this straight boundary is given by $-P_x/P_y$.

Reducing Y consumption does not permit very much more of good X to be bought. All of these relationships can be made clearer by using a bit of algebra.

Budget Constraint Algebra

Suppose that the individual has I dollars to spend on either good X or good Y. Suppose also that P_X represents the price of good X and P_Y the price of good Y. The total amount spent on X is given by the price of X times the amount purchased ($P_X \cdot X$). Similarly, $P_Y \cdot Y$ represents total spending on good Y. Since the available income must be spent on either X or Y we have

Amount spent on X + Amount spent on Y = I

or

$$P_X \cdot X + P_Y \cdot Y = I \tag{2.3}$$

Equation 2.3 is an algebraic statement of the budget line shown in Figure 2.6. To study this constraint, we can solve this equation for Y so that the budget line has the standard form for a linear equation (Y = a + bX). This solution gives

$$Y = -\left(\frac{P_X}{P_Y}\right)X + \frac{I}{P_Y} \qquad (2.4)$$

Although the two representations of the budget constraint say exactly the same thing, the relationship between Equation 2.4 and Figure 2.6 is easier to see. It is obvious from that equation that if the individual chooses to spend all available funds on Y (that is, if X = 0), he or she can buy I/P_Y units. If hamburgers cost $2.00 each and this person has decided to spend his or her $20 income only on hamburgers, it is clear that 10 can be bought. That point in the figure is the Y-intercept, which we previously called Y_{max}. Similarly, a slight manipulation of the budget equation shows that if Y = 0, all income will be devoted to X purchases, and the X-intercept will be I/P_X. If $20 is spent only on soft drinks, 20 (= $20 ÷ $1) can be bought. Again, this point is labeled X_{max} in the figure. Finally, the slope of the budget constraint is given by the ratio of the goods' prices, $-P_X/P_Y$. This shows the ratio at which Y can be given up to get more X in the market. In the hamburger–soft drink case, the slope would be –½ (= –$1/$2) showing that the opportunity cost of one soft drink is half a burger. More generally, as we noted before, if P_X is low and P_Y is high, the slope will be small and the budget line will be flat. On the other hand, a high P_X and a low P_Y will make the budget line steep. As for any linear relationship, the budget constraint can be shifted to a new position by changes in its Y-intercept or by changes in its slope. In Chapter 3, we use this fact to study how changes in income or in the prices of goods affect an individual's choices.

MicroQuiz 2.3

Suppose a person has $100 to spend on Frisbees and beach balls.

1. Graph this person's budget constraint if Frisbees cost $20 and beach balls cost $10.

2. How would your graph change if this person decided to spend $200 (rather than $100) on these two items?

3. How would your graph change if Frisbee prices rose to $25 but total spending returned to $100?

Utility Maximization

A person can afford all bundles of X and Y that fall within the shaded triangle in Figure 2.6. From among these, he or she will choose the one that offers the greatest utility. The budget constraint can be used together with the individual's indifference curve map to show this utility-maximization process. Figure 2.7 illustrates the procedure. This person would be irrational to choose a point such as A; he or she can get to a higher utility level (that is, higher than U_1) just by spending some of the unspent portion of his or her income. Similarly, by reallocating expenditures the individual

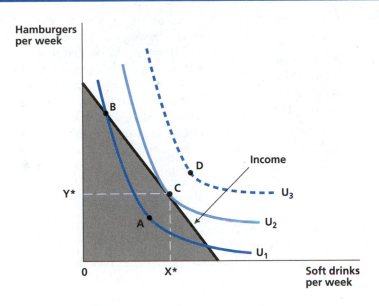

FIGURE 2.7 Graphic Demonstration of Utility Maximization Point C represents the highest utility that can be reached by this individual, given the budget constraint. The combination X*, Y* is therefore the rational way for this person to use the available purchasing power. Only for this combination of goods will two conditions hold: All available funds will be spent; and the individual's psychic rate of trade-off (marginal rate of substitution) will be equal to the rate at which the goods can be traded in the market (P_X/P_Y).

can do better than point B. This is the case in which the MRS and the price ratio differ, and the individual can move to a higher indifference curve (say, U_2) by choosing to consume less Y and more X. Point D is out of the question because income is not large enough to permit the purchase of that combination of goods. It is clear that the position of maximum utility will be at point C where the combination X*, Y* is chosen. This is the only point on indifference curve U_2 that can be bought with I dollars, and no higher utility level can be bought. C is the single point of tangency between the budget constraint and the indifference curve. Therefore all funds are spent and

Slope of budget constraint = Slope of indifference curve   (2.5)

or (neglecting the fact that both slopes are negative)

$$P_X/P_Y = MRS \qquad (2.6)$$

$$\frac{MU_x}{MU_y} = \frac{P_x}{P_y} = MRS$$

The result we started with is proved. For a utility maximum, the MRS should equal the ratio of the prices of the goods. The diagram shows that if this condition is not fulfilled, this person could be made better off by reallocating expenditures.[5] You may wish to try several other combinations of X and Y that this person can afford to show that all of them provide a lower utility level than does combination C. That is why C is a point of tangency—it is the only affordable combination that allows this person to reach U_2. For a point of nontangency (say B), a person can always get more utility because the budget constraint passes through the indifference curve (see U_1 in the figure). In Application 2.3: Ticket Scalping, we examine a case in which people do not have such complete freedom in how they spend their incomes.

USING THE MODEL OF CHOICE

This model of utility maximization can be used to explain a number of common observations. Figure 2.8, for example, provides an illustration of why people with the same income choose to spend this in different ways. In all three panels of Figure 2.8, the budget constraints facing each individual are the same. However, Hungry Joe in panel a of the figure has a clear preference for hamburgers. He chooses to spend his $20 almost exclusively on burgers. Thirsty Teresa, on the other hand, chooses to spend most of her $20 on soft drinks. She does buy two

---

[5] If we use the results of note 2 on the assumption that utility is measurable, Equation 2.6 can be given an alternative interpretation. Because

$$P_X/P_Y = MRS = MU_X/MU_Y \qquad \textbf{(i)}$$

for a utility maximum, we have

$$\frac{MU_X}{P_X} = \frac{MU_Y}{P_Y} \qquad \textbf{(ii)}$$

The ratio of the extra utility from consuming one more unit of a good to its price should be the same for each good. Each good should provide the same extra utility per dollar spent. If that were not true, total utility could be raised by reallocating funds from a good that provided a relatively low level of marginal utility per dollar to one that provided a high level. For example, suppose that consuming an extra hamburger would yield 5 utils (units of utility) whereas an extra soft drink would yield 2 utils. Then each util costs $.40 (=$2.00 ÷ 5) if hamburgers are bought and $.50 (=$1.00 ÷ 2) if soft drinks are bought. Clearly hamburgers are a cheaper way to buy utility. So this person should buy more hamburgers and fewer soft drinks until each becomes an equally costly way to get utility.

Tickets to major concerts or sporting events are not usually auctioned off to the highest bidder. Instead, promoters tend to sell most tickets at "reasonable" prices and then ration the resulting excess demand either on a first-come-first-served basis or by limiting the number of tickets each buyer can purchase. Such rationing mechanisms create the possibility for further selling of tickets at much higher prices in the secondary market—that is, ticket "scalping."

A Graphical Illustration

Figure 1 shows the motivation for ticket scalping for, say, Super Bowl tickets. With this consumer's income and the quoted price of tickets, he or she would prefer to purchase four tickets (point A). But the National Football League has decided to limit tickets to only one per customer. This limitation reduces the consumer's utility from U_2 (the utility he or she would enjoy with tickets freely available) to U_1. Notice that this choice of one ticket (point B) does not obey the tangency rule for a utility maximum—given the price of tickets, this person would prefer to buy more.

In fact, this frustrated consumer would be willing to pay more than the prevailing price for additional Super Bowl tickets. He or she would not only be more than willing to buy a second ticket at the official price (since point C is above U_1) but also would be willing to give up an additional amount of other goods (given by distance CD) to get this ticket. It appears that this person would be more than willing to pay quite a bit to a "scalper" for the second ticket. For example, tickets for major events at the 1996 Atlanta Olympics often sold for five times their face prices, and resold tickets for the 1999 Super Bowl went for upwards of $2000.

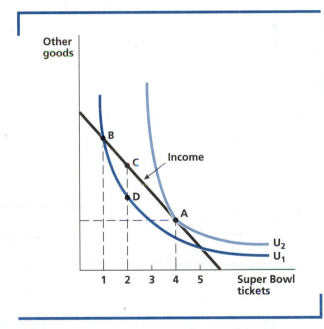

FIGURE 1 Rationing of Tickets Leads to Scalping Given this consumer's income and the price of tickets, he or she would prefer to buy four. With only one available, utility falls to U_1. This person would pay up to CD in other goods for a second ticket at the original price.

Antiscalping Laws

Most economists hold a relatively benign view of ticket scalping. They view the activity as being voluntary between a willing buyer and a willing seller. State and local governments often see things differently, however. Many have passed laws that seek either to regulate

(continued)

the prices of resold tickets or to outlaw ticket selling in locations near the events.[1] The generally cited reason for such laws is that scalping is "unfair"—perhaps because the "scalper" makes profits that are "not deserved." The main effect of such laws, however, appears to ensure profits for licensed ticket brokers at the expense of individuals who might wish to enter into this business on their own.

To Think About

1. Some promoters of sporting events favor antiscalping laws because they believe that such activity cuts into their profits. What do you make of this argument?
2. Scalping is just one example of the "black markets" that arise when goods are rationed by means other than price. What are a few other examples? Are these black markets undesirable?

[1] For a summary of such laws, see "The Folly of Anti-Scalping Laws," *The Cato Journal* (Spring/Summer 1995): 65–80.

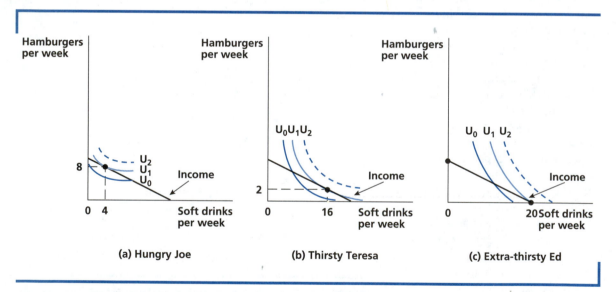

FIGURE 2.8 Differences in Preferences Result in Differing Choices The three individuals illustrated here all have the same budget constraint. They have $20 to spend, hamburgers cost $2, and soft drinks cost $1. These people choose very different consumption bundles because they have differing preferences for the two goods.

hamburgers, however, because she feels some need for solid food: Extra-Thirsty Ed, whose situation is shown in panel c, wants a totally liquid diet. He gets the most utility from spending his entire $20 on soft drinks. Even though he would, with more to spend, probably, buy hamburgers, in the current case he is so thirsty that the opportunity cost of giving up a soft drink to do so is just too high.

Figure 2.9 presents again the four specific indifference curve maps that were introduced earlier in this chapter. Now we have superimposed a budget constraint on each one and indicated the utility-maximizing choice by E. Some obvious implications can be drawn from these illustrations. Panel a makes clear that a utility-maximizing individual will never buy a useless good. Utility is as large as possible by consuming only food. There is no reason for this person to incur the opportunity cost involved in consuming any smoke grinders. A similar result holds for panel b—there is no reason for this person to spend anything on houseflies (assuming there is a store that sells them).

In panel c, the individual buys only Exxon even though Exxon and Mobil are perfect substitutes. The relatively steep budget constraint in the figure indicates that Mobil is the more expensive of the two brands, so this person opts to buy only Exxon. Since the goods are all but identical, the utility-maximizing decision is to buy only the less-expensive brand. People who buy only generic versions of prescription drugs or who buy all their brand-name household staples at a discount supermarket are exhibiting a similar type of behavior.

Finally, the utility-maximizing situation illustrated in Figure 2.9(d) shows that this person will buy shoes only in pairs. Any departure from this pattern would result in buying extra left or right shoes, which alone provide no utility. In similar circumstances involving complementary goods, people also tend to purchase those goods together. Other items of apparel (gloves, earrings, socks, and so forth) are also bought mainly in pairs. Most people have preferred ways of concocting the beverages they drink (coffee and cream, gin and vermouth) or of making sandwiches (peanut butter and jelly, ham and cheese); and people seldom buy automobiles, stereos, or washing machines by the part. Rather, they consume these complex goods as fixed packages made up of their various components.

Overall then, this model of choice provides a very flexible way of explaining why people make the choices that they do. Because people are faced with budget constraints, they must be careful to allocate their incomes so that they provide as much satisfaction as possible. Of course, they will not explicitly engage in the kinds of graphic analyses shown in the figures for this chapter. But this model seems to be a good way of making precise the notion that people "do the best with what they've got." We look at how this model can be used to illustrate a famous court case in Application 2.4: The Sad Tale of Willie and His Uncle.

MicroQuiz 2.5

Figure 2.8 and Figure 2.9 show that the condition for utility maximization must be amended sometimes to deal with special situations.

1. Explain how the condition should be changed for "boundary" issues such as those shown in Figure 2.8(c) and 2.9(c) where people buy zero amounts of some goods. Use this to explain why your author never buys any lima beans.

2. How do you interpret the condition in which goods are perfect complements such as those shown in Figure 2.9(d)? If shoes were sold separately, could any price ratio make you depart from buying pairs?

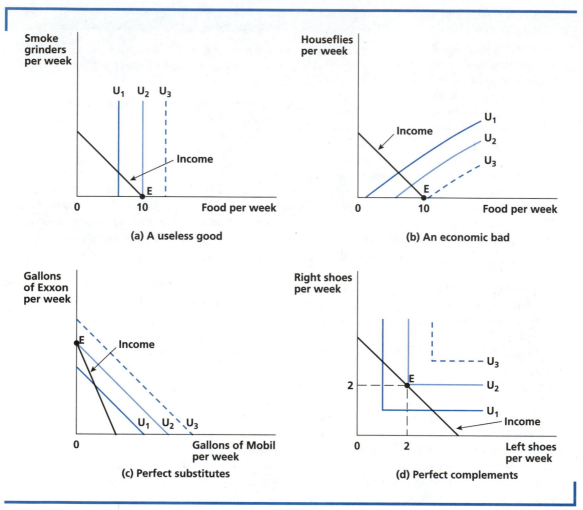

FIGURE 2.9 Utility-Maximizing Choices for Special Types of Goods The four panels in this figure repeat the special indifference curve maps from Figure 2.5. The resulting utility-maximizing positions (denoted by E in each panel) reflect the specific relationships among the goods pictured.

GENERALIZATIONS

The basic model of choice that we have been examining can be generalized in several ways. Here we look briefly at three of these.

Many Goods

Of course people buy more than two goods. Even if we were to focus on very large categories such as "food," "clothing," "housing," or "transportation," it is

One of the strangest legal cases of the nineteenth century was the New York case of *Hamer v. Sidway* in which nephew Willie sued his uncle for failing to carry through on the promise to pay him $5,000 if he did not smoke, drink, or gamble until he reached the age of 21. No one in the case disagreed that the uncle had made this deal with Willie when he was about 15 years old. The legal issue was whether the uncle's promise was a clear "contract," enforceable in court. An examination of this peculiar case provides an instructive illustration of how economic principles can help to clarify legal issues.

Graphing the Uncle's Offer

Figure 1 shows Willie's choice between "sin" (that is, smoking, drinking, and gambling) on the X-axis and his spending on everything else on the Y-axis. Left to his own devices, Willie would prefer to consume point A—which involves some sin along with other things. This would provide him with utility of U_2. Willie's uncle is offering him point B—an extra $5,000 on the condition that sin = 0. In this graph, it is clear that the offer provides more utility (U_3) than does point A, so Willie should take the offer and spend his teenage years sin-free.

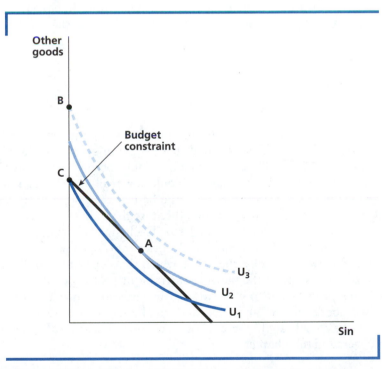

FIGURE 1 Willie's Utility and His Uncle's Promises Left to his own devices, Willie consumes point A and gets utility U_2. His uncle's offer would increase utility to U_3. But, when his uncle reneges, Willie gets U_1 (point C).

(continued)

When the Uncle Reneges

When Willie came to collect the $5,000 for his abstinence, his uncle assured him that he would place the funds in a bank account that Willie would get once he was "capable of using it wisely." But the uncle died and left no provision for payment in his will. So Willie ended up with no money. The consequences of being stiffed for the $5,000 can be shown in Figure 1 by point C—this is the utility Willie would get by spending all his income on non-sin items.

Willie Goes to Court

Not willing to take his misfortune lying down, Willie took his uncle's estate to court, claiming, in effect, that he had made a contract with his uncle and deserved to be paid. The uncle's heirs argued that there was no such contract because the uncle had never received anything in return for his $5,000. But the court eventually ruled that Willie's abstinence was sufficient "consideration" to ensure that a contract existed. Willie finally got paid.

To Think About

1. Suppose that the uncle's heirs had offered to settle by making Willie as well-off as he would have been by acting sinfully in his teenage years. How could you show the amount they would have to pay in Figure 1?
2. Would the requirement that the uncle make Willie "whole" by paying the amount suggested in question 1 provide the right incentives for the uncle not to renege on this contract?

clear that we would need a theory that includes more than two items. Once we looked deeper into the types of food that people might buy or how they might spend their housing dollars, the situation would become very complex indeed. But the basic findings of this chapter would not really be changed in any major way. People who are seeking to make the best of their situations would still be expected to spend all of their incomes (because the only alternative is to throw it away—saving is addressed in Chapter 15). The logic of choosing combinations of goods for which the MRS is equal to the price ratio remains true, too. Our intuitive proof showed that any choice for which the slope of the indifference curve differs from the slope of the budget constraint offers the possibility for improvement. This proof would not be affected by situations in which there are more than two goods. Hence, although the formal analysis of the many-good case is indeed more complicated,[6] there is not much more to learn from what has already been covered in this chapter.

---

[6] For a mathematical treatment, see W. Nicholson, *Microeconomic Theory: Basic Principles and Extensions,* 8th ed. (Mason, OH: South-Western/Thomson Learning, 2002), Chapter 4.

Complicated Budget Constraints

The budget constraints discussed in this chapter all had a very simple form—they could all be represented by straight lines. The reason for this is that the price a person was assumed to pay for a good was not affected by how much of that good he or she bought. There were assumed to be no special deals for someone who purchased many hamburgers or who opted for "super" sizes of soft drinks. In many cases, people do not face such simple budget constraints. Instead, they face a variety of inducements to buy larger quantities or complex bundling arrangements that give special deals only if other items are also bought. For example, the pricing of telephone service has become extremely complex involving cut rates for more extensive long-distance usage, special deals for services such as voice mail or caller ID, and tie-in sales that offer favorable rates to customers who also buy Internet or cable television service from the same vendor. Describing precisely the budget constraint faced by a consumer in such situations can be quite difficult. But a careful analysis of the properties of such complicated budget constraints and how they relate to the utility-maximizing model can be quite revealing in showing why people behave in the ways they do. Application 2.5: Quantity Discounts and Frequent-Flier Programs provides one such illustration.

Composite Goods

Another important way in which the simple two-good model in this chapter can be generalized is through the use of a **composite good.** Such a good is constructed by combining spending on many individual items into one aggregated whole. One way such a good is used is to study the way people allocate their spending among such major items as "food" and "housing." For example, in the next chapter, we show that spending on food tends to fall as people get richer, whereas spending on housing is, more or less, a constant fraction of income. Of course, these spending patterns are in reality made up of individual decisions about what kind of breakfast cereal to buy or whether to paint your house; but adding many things together can often help to illuminate important questions.

Composite good
Combining expenditures on several different goods whose relative prices do not change into a single good for convenience in analysis.

Probably the most common use of the composite good idea is in situations where we wish to study decisions to buy one specific item such as airline tickets or gasoline. In this case, a common procedure is to show the specific item of interest on the horizontal (X) axis and spending on "everything else" on the vertical (Y) axis. This is the procedure we used in Application 2.3 and Application 2.4, and we use it many other times later in this book. Taking advantage of the composite good idea can greatly simplify many problems. Some technical issues arise in using composite goods, though those do not detain us very long in this book. A first problem is how we are to measure a composite good. In our endless hamburger–soft drink example, the units of measurement were obvious. But the only way to add up all of the individual items that constitute "everything else" is to do so in dollars (or some other currency). Looking at dollars of spending on everything else will indeed prove to be a very useful graphical device. But one might have some lingering concerns that, because such

Quantity Discounts and Frequent-Flier Programs

The budget constraints we have studied in this chapter are graphed using straight lines because the prices of goods are unaffected by how much the consumer buys. In cases where consumers receive quantity discounts or may have to pay "excessive use" fees, this assumption is no longer valid and the budget constraint may not have such a simple shape.

Quantity Discounts and the Budget Constraint

The case of a quantity discount is illustrated in Figure 1. Here consumers who buy less than X_D pay full price and face the usual budget constraint. Purchases in excess of X_D entitle the buyer to a lower price (on the extra units), and this results in a flatter budget constraint beyond X_D. The constraint, therefore, has a "kink" at X_D. Effects of this kink on consumer choices are suggested by the indifference curve U_1, which is tangent to the budget constraint at both point A and point B. This person is indifferent between consuming relatively little of X or a lot of X. A slightly larger quantity discount could tempt this consumer definitely to choose the larger amount of X. Notice that such a choice entails not only consuming low-price units of X but also buying more X at full price (up to X_D) in order to get the discount.[1]

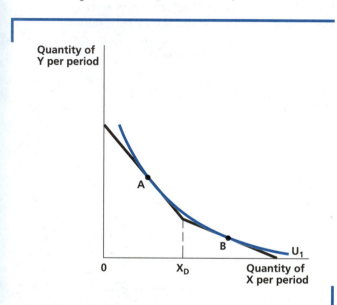

FIGURE 1 Kinked Budget Constraint Resulting from a Quantity Discount A quantity discount for purchases greater than X_D results in a kinked budget constraint. This consumer is indifferent between consuming relatively little X (point A) or a lot of X (point B).

Frequent-Flier Programs

All major airlines sponsor frequent-flier programs. These entitle customers to accumulate mileage with the airline at reduced fares. Because unused-seat revenues are lost forever, the airlines utilize such programs to tempt consumers to travel more. Any additional full-fare travel that the programs may generate provides extra profits for the airline.

Some economists argue that frequent-flier plans reduce competition among airlines by tying a particular consumer to the airline on which he or she maintains such a plan. Of

---

[1] Many other pricing schemes can be shown on a simple utility-maximizing graph. See J. DeSalvo and M. Hug, "Introducing Nonlinear Pricing into Consumer Theory," *Journal of Economic Education* (Spring 2002): 166–179.

course, consumers are free to join a number of plans and some airlines give credit for travel on other airlines. Hence, the overall effect of the plans may simply be to fill seats that would have gone empty, with no anticompetitive effect on full-fare prices.

To Think About

1. Some medical insurance plans cover drug costs only to the extent that they exceed, say, $10 per month. How would such a plan affect an individual's budget constraint and his or her drug purchase decisions?
2. Suppose frequent-flier coupons were transferable among people. How would this affect Figure 1 and, more generally, the overall viability of the program?

---

adding up requires us to use the prices of individual items, we might get into some trouble when prices change. This then leads to a second problem with composite goods—what is the "price" of such a good. In most cases, there is no need to answer this question because we assume that the price of the composite good (good Y) does not change during our analysis. But, if we did wish to study changes in the price of a composite good we would obviously have to define that price first.

In our treatment, therefore, we will not be much concerned with these technical problems associated with composite goods. If you are interested in the ways that some of the problems are solved in practice, you may wish to do some reading on your own.[7]

SUMMARY

This chapter covers a lot of ground. In it we have seen how economists explain the kinds of choices people make and the ways in which those choices are constrained by economic circumstances. The chapter has been rather tough going in places. The theory of choice is one of the most difficult parts of any study of microeconomics, and it is unfortunate that it usually comes at the very start of the course. But that placement clearly shows why the topic is so important. Practically every model of economic behavior starts with the building blocks introduced in this chapter.

The principal conclusions in this chapter are:

*   Economists use the term *utility* to refer to the satisfaction that people derive from their economic activities. Usually only a few of the things that affect utility are examined in any particular analysis. All other factors are assumed to be held constant so that a person's choices can be studied in a simplified setting.
*   Utility can be shown by an indifference curve map. Each indifference curve identifies those bundles of goods that a person considers to be equally attractive. Higher levels of utility are represented by higher indifference curve "contour" lines.

---

[7] For an introduction, see W. Nicholson, *Microeconomic Theory: Basic Principles and Extensions*, 8th ed. (Mason, OH: South-Western/Thomson Learning, 2002), 158–161.

- The slope of indifference curves shows how a person is willing to trade one good for another while remaining equally well-off. The negative of this slope is called the "marginal rate of substitution" (MRS), because it shows the degree to which an individual is willing to substitute one good for another in his or her consumption choices.

- People are limited in what they can buy by their "budget constraints." When a person is choosing between two goods, his or her budget constraint is usually a straight line because prices do not depend on how much is bought. The negative of the slope of this line represents the price ratio of the two goods—it shows what one of the goods is worth in terms of the other in the marketplace.

- If people are to obtain the maximum possible utility from their limited incomes, they should spend all the available funds and should choose a bundle of goods for which the MRS is equal to the price ratio of the two goods. Such a utility maximum is shown graphically by a tangency between the budget constraint and the highest indifference curve that this person's income can buy.

REVIEW QUESTIONS

1. The notion of utility is an "ordinal" one for which it is assumed that people can rank combinations of goods as to their desirability, but that they cannot assign a unique numerical (cardinal) scale for the goods that quantifies "how much" one combination is preferred to another. For each of the following ranking systems, describe whether an ordinal or cardinal ranking is being used: (a) military or academic ranks; (b) prices of vintage wines; (c) rankings of vintage wines by the French Wine Society; (d) press rankings of the "Top Ten" football teams; (e) results of the current U.S. Open Golf Championships (in which players are ranked by stroke play); (f) results of early U.S. Open Golf Championships (which were conducted using match play).

2. How might you draw an indifference curve map that illustrates the following ideas?
   a. Margarine is just as good as the high-priced spread.
   b. Things go better with Coke.
   c. A day without wine is like a day without sunshine.
   d. Popcorn is addictive—the more you eat, the more you want.
   e. If he doesn't wear English Leather, he wears nothing at all.
   f. It takes two to tango.

3. Inez reports that an extra banana would increase her utility by two units and an extra pear would increase her utility by six units. What is her MRS of bananas for pears—that is, how many bananas would she voluntarily give up to get an extra pear? Would Philip (who reports that an extra banana yields 100 units of utility whereas an extra pear yields 400 units of utility) be willing to trade a pear to Inez at her voluntary MRS?

4. Oscar consumes two goods, wine and cheese. His weekly income is $500.
   a. Describe Oscar's budget constraints under the following conditions:
      - Wine costs $10/bottle, cheese costs $5/pound;
      - Wine costs $10/bottle, cheese costs $10/pound;
      - Wine costs $20/bottle, cheese costs $10/pound
      - Wine costs $20/bottle, cheese costs $10/pound, but Oscar's income increases to $1,000/week.
   b. What can you conclude by comparing the first and the last of these budget constraints?

5. While standing in line to buy popcorn at your favorite theater, you hear someone behind you

say, "This popcorn isn't worth its price—I'm not buying any." How would you graph this person's situation?

6. A careful reader of this book will have read footnote 2 and footnote 5 in this chapter. Explain why these can be summarized by the commonsense idea that a person is maximizing his or her utility only if getting an extra dollar to spend would provide the same amount of extra utility no matter which good he or she chooses to spend it on. (Hint: Suppose this condition were not true—is utility as large as possible?)

7. Most states require that you purchase modest automobile insurance when you buy a car. Use an indifference curve diagram to show that this reduces utility for some people. What kinds of people are most likely to have their utility reduced by such a law? Why do you think that the government requires such insurance?

8. Two students are studying microeconomics trying to understand why the tangent condition studied in this chapter means utility is at a maximum. Let's listen:

Student A. If a person chooses a point on his or her budget constraint that is not tangent, it is clear that he or she can manage to get a higher utility by spending differently.

Student B. I don't get it—how do you know he or she can do better instead of worse?

How can you help Student B out with a graph?

9. Suppose that an electric company charges consumers $.10 per kilowatt hour for electricity for the first 1,000 used in a month but $.15 for each extra kilowatt hour after that. Draw the budget constraint for a consumer facing this price schedule and discuss why many individuals may choose to consume exactly 1,000 kilowatt hours.

10. Suppose an individual consumes three items: steak, lettuce, and tomatoes. If we were interested only in examining this person's steak purchases, we might group lettuce and tomatoes into a single composite good called "salad." How would you define this good? What would this person's budget constraint for steak and salad be? What would it mean to say that "the relative price of salad has risen"?

PROBLEMS

2.1 Suppose a person has $8.00 to spend only on apples and oranges. Apples cost $.40 each, and oranges cost $.10 each.

a. If this person buys *only* apples, how many can be bought?
b. If this person buys *only* oranges, how many can be bought?
c. If the person were to buy 10 apples, how many oranges could be bought with the funds left over?
d. If the person consumes one less apple (that is, nine), how many more oranges could be bought? Is this rate of trade-off the same no matter how many apples are relinquished?
e. Write down the algebraic equation for this person's budget constraint, and graph it showing the points mentioned in parts a through d (using graph paper would improve the accuracy of your work).

2.2 Suppose the person faced with the budget constraint described in problem 2.1 has preferences for apples (A) and oranges (O) given by

$$\text{Utility} = \sqrt{A \cdot O}$$

a. If A = 5 and O = 80, what will utility be?
b. If A = 10, what value for O will provide the same utility as in part a?
c. If A = 20, what value for O will provide the same utility as in parts a and b?
d. Graph the indifference curve implied by parts a through c.

e. Given the budget constraint from problem 2.1, which of the points identified in parts a through c can be bought by this person?

f. Show through some examples that every other way of allocating income provides less utility than does the point identified in part b. Graph this utility-maximizing situation.

2.3 Paul Video derives utility only from CDs and DVDs. His utility function is

$$U = \sqrt{C \cdot D}$$

a. Sketch Paul's indifference curves for $U = 5$, $U = 10$, and $U = 20$.

b. Suppose Paul has $200 to spend and that CDs cost $5 and DVDs cost $20. Draw Paul's budget constraint on the same graph as his indifference curves.

c. Suppose Paul spends all of his income on DVDs. How many can he buy and what is his utility?

d. Show that Paul's income will not permit him to reach the $U = 20$ indifference curve.

e. If Paul buys 5 DVDs, how many CDs can he buy? What is his utility?

f. Show that the utility calculated in part e is the highest Paul can achieve with his $200.

2.4 Returning to problem 2.3, suppose Paul's roommates object to his music choices and require him only to buy equal numbers of CDs and DVDs.

a. Given Paul's $200 income, how much of each will he buy? What is his utility?

b. Suppose Paul's roommates wish Paul to accept their restrictions voluntarily. How much extra income would they have to give him to do so?

2.5 Ms. Caffeine enjoys coffee (C) and tea (T) according to the function $U(C,T) = 3C + 4T$. What does her utility function say about her MRS of coffee for tea? What do her indifference curves look like? If coffee and tea cost $3 each and Ms. Caffeine has $12 to spend on these products, how much coffee and tea should she buy to maximize her utility? Draw the graph of her indifference curve map and her budget constraint, and show that the utility-maximizing point occurs only on the T-axis where no coffee is bought. Would she buy any coffee if she had more

money to spend? How would her consumption change if the price of coffee fell to $2?

2.6 Vera is an impoverished graduate student who has only $100 a month to spend on food. She has read in a government publication that she can assure an adequate diet by eating only peanut butter and carrots in the fixed ratio of 2 pounds of peanut butter to 1 pound of carrots, so she decides to limit her diet to that regime.

a. If peanut butter costs $4 per pound and carrots cost $2 per pound, how much can she eat during the month?

b. Suppose peanut butter costs rise to $5 because of peanut subsidies introduced by a politically sensitive government. By how much will Vera have to reduce her food purchases?

c. How much in food stamp aid would the government have to give Vera to compensate for the effects of the peanut subsidy?

d. Explain why Vera's preferences are of a very special type here. How would you graph them?

2.7 Assume consumers are choosing between housing services (H) measured in square feet and consumption of all other goods (C) measured in dollars.

a. Show the equilibrium position in a diagram.

b. Now suppose the government agrees to subsidize consumers by paying 50 percent of their housing cost. How will their budget line change? Show the new equilibrium.

c. Show in a diagram the minimum amount of income supplement the government would have to give individuals instead of a housing subsidy to make them as well-off as they were in part b.

2.8 Suppose low-income people have preferences for nonfood consumption (NF) and for food consumption (F). In the absence of any income transfer programs, a person's budget constraint is given by

$$NF + P_F F = I$$

where P_F is the price of food relative to nonfood items and NF and I are measured in terms of nonfood prices (that is, dollars).

a. Graph the initial utility-maximizing situation for this low-income person.

b. Suppose now that a food stamp program is introduced that requires low-income people to pay C (measured in terms of nonfood prices) in order to receive food stamps sufficient to buy F* units of food (presumably $P_F F^* > C$). Show this person's budget constraint if he or she participates in the food stamp program.

c. Show graphically the factors that will determine whether the person chooses to participate in the program.

d. Show graphically what it will cost the government to finance benefits for the typical food stamp recipient. Show also that some people might reach a higher utility level if this amount were simply given with no strings attached.

2.9 Suppose that people derive utility from two goods—housing (H) and all other consumption goods (C).

a. Show a typical consumer's allocation of his or her income between H and C.

b. Suppose that the government decides that the level of housing shown in part a (say, H^*) is "substandard" and requires that all people buy $H^{**} > H^*$ instead. Show that this law would reduce this person's utility.

c. One way to return this person to the initial level of utility would be to give him or her extra income. On your graph, show how much extra income this would require.

d. Another way to return this person to his or her initial level of utility would be to provide a housing subsidy that reduces the price of housing. On your graph, show this solution as well.

2.10 A common utility function used to illustrate economic examples is the Cobb-Douglas function where $U(X,Y) = X^\alpha Y^\beta$ where α and β are fractional exponents that sum to 1.0 (that is, for example, 0.3 and 0.7).

a. Explain why the utility function used in problem 2.2 and problem 2.3 is a special case of this function.

b. It can be shown that a person with this utility function will spend a fraction α of his or her income on good X and a fraction β on good Y. Use this result to solve part e and part f of problem 2.3.

c. Show that with this utility function, a person's total spending on good X will not change if the price of X changes so long as his or her income stays constant.

d. Show that with this utility function a change in the price of Y will not affect the amount of X purchased.

e. Show that with this utility function, a 50 percent increase in income accompanied by no changes in the price of X or Y will cause purchases of both X and Y to rise by 50 percent.

INTERNET EXERCISES

1. *Budget constraints and income taxes.* As someone once said, "Only two things in life are certain: death and taxes." Suppose you have an income of $52,000 per year (or $1,000 per week). Suppose further you only consume goods X and Y, where the price of X is $10 per unit and the price of Y is $20 per unit. Neatly draw a graph of your weekly budget constraint. Be sure to label your axes and compute the intercepts of your budget constraint. What is the value of its slope? Now consider how the income tax will affect your budget constraint. For simplicity, suppose your entire $52,000 income were taxable. Go to *http://taxes.yahoo.com* and click on Tax Rates. Calculate the amount of your federal tax liability, assuming you are single (note that the tax rates listed are *marginal* tax rates; that is, dollars of income 0 to $A are taxed at one rate, while the next dollars of income $B to $C are taxed at a higher rate, and so on). On the same graph as your original budget constraint, draw your new weekly after-tax budget constraint. Has the slope changed? Why or why not?

2. *Rationing.* In 1942, mandatory rationing of gasoline was implemented across the United States on account of the war. In fact, gasoline was but one of hundreds of goods rationed during this time. An interesting and brief account of the rationing that took place during World War II can be found at *http://www.ibiscom.com/vogas.htm.* Be sure to also listen to the 1942 sound clip, if possible, of Jack Benny, Gracie Allen, and Eddie Cantor giving a humorous account of the gasoline rationing at the time—you should get a chuckle out of it.

For what main purpose was gasoline rationed? How much gasoline was allocated to motorists using their cars for nonessential purposes? Use an analysis similar to that in Application 2.3 to show and explain how the rationing of gasoline may have altered the welfare of motorists. Would *all* motorists be made worse off with rationing? If so, explain. If not, explain, and show using an appropriate graph.

3

Individual Demand Curves

This chapter studies how people change their choices when conditions change. In particular, we study how changes in income or changes in the price of a good affect the amount that people choose to consume. We compare the new choices with those that were made before conditions changed. The main result of this approach is to construct an individual's demand curve for a good. This curve shows the amounts of a good that a person chooses to buy at different prices.

DEMAND FUNCTIONS

Chapter 2 concluded that the quantities of X and Y that a person chooses depend on that person's preferences and on the shape of his or her budget constraint. If we knew a person's preferences and all the economic forces that affect his or her choices, we could predict how much of each good would be chosen. We can summarize this conclusion using the **demand function** for some particular good, say, X:

$$\text{Quantity of X demanded} = d_X(P_X, P_Y, I; \text{preferences}) \qquad (3.1)$$

Demand function
A representation of how quantity demanded depends on prices, income, and preferences.

This function contains the three elements that determine what the person can buy—the prices of X and Y and the person's income (I)—as well as a reminder that choices are also affected by preferences for the goods. These preferences appear to the right of the semicolon in Equation 3.1 because for most of our analysis we assume that preferences do not change. People's basic likes and dislikes are assumed to be developed through a lifetime of experience. They are unlikely to change as we examine their reactions to relatively short-term changes in their economic circumstances caused by changes in commodity prices or incomes.

The quantity demanded of good Y depends on these same general influences and can be summarized by

$$\text{Quantity of Y demanded} = d_Y(P_X, P_Y, I; \text{preferences}) \qquad (3.2)$$

Preferences again appear to the right of the semicolon in Equation 3.2 because we assume that the person's taste for good Y will not change during our analysis.

Homogeneity

One important result that follows directly from Chapter 2 is that if the prices of X and Y and income (I) were all to double (or to change by any identical percentage), the amounts of X and Y demanded would not change. The budget constraint

$$P_X X + P_Y Y = 1 \qquad (3.3)$$

is the same as the budget constraint

$$2P_X X + 2P_Y Y = 2I \qquad (3.4)$$

Graphically, these are exactly the same lines. Consequently, both budget constraints are tangent to a person's indifference curve map at precisely the same point. The quantities of X and Y the individual chooses when faced by the constraint in Equation 3.3 are exactly the same as when the individual is faced by the constraint in Equation 3.4.

This is an important result: The amounts a person demands depend only on the relative prices of goods X and Y and on the "real" value of income. Proportional changes in both the prices of X and Y and in income change only the units we count in (such as dollars instead of cents). They do not affect the quantities demanded. Individual demand is said to be **homogeneous** for proportional changes in all prices and income. People are not hurt by general inflation of prices if their incomes increase in the same proportion. They will be on exactly the same indifference curve both before and after the inflation. Only if inflation increases some incomes faster or slower than prices change does it then have an effect on budget constraints, on the quantities of goods demanded, and on people's well-being.

Homogeneous demand function Quantity demanded does not change when prices and income increase in the same proportion.

CHANGES IN INCOME

As a person's total income rises, assuming prices do not change, we might expect the quantity purchased of each good also to increase. This situation is illustrated in Figure 3.1. As income increases from I_1 to I_2 to I_3, the quantity of X demanded increases from X_1 to X_2 to X_3 and the quantity of Y demanded increases from Y_1

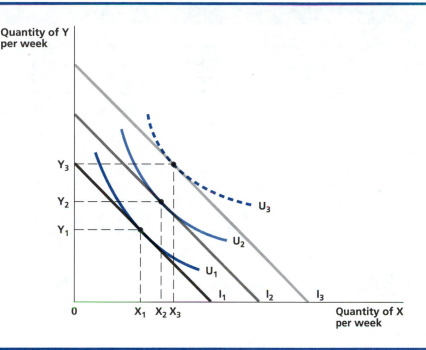

FIGURE 3.1 Effect of Increasing Income on Quantities of X and Y Chosen As income increases from I_1 to I_2 to I_3, the optimal (utility-maximizing) choices of X and Y are shown by the successively higher points of tangency. The budget constraint shifts in a parallel way because its slope (given by the ratio of the goods' prices) does not change.

to Y_2 to Y_3. Budget lines I_1, I_2, and I_3 are all parallel because we are changing only income, not the relative prices of X and Y. Remember, the slope of the budget constraint is given by the ratio of the two goods' prices, and these prices are not changing in this figure. Increases in income do, however, make it possible for this person to consume more; this increased purchasing power is reflected by the outward shift in the budget constraint and an increase in overall utility.

Normal Goods

In Figure 3.1, both good X and good Y increase as income increases. Goods that follow this tendency are called **normal goods.** Most goods seem to be normal goods—as their incomes increase, people tend to buy more of practically everything. Of course, as Figure 3.1 shows, the demand for some "luxury" goods (such as Y) may increase rapidly when income rises, but the demand for "necessities" (such as X) may grow less rapidly. The relationship between income and the amounts of various goods purchased has been extensively examined by economists, as Application 3.1: Engel's Law shows.

Normal good
A good that is bought in greater quantities as income increases.

Engel's Law

One of the most important generalizations about consumer behavior is that the fraction of income spent on food tends to decline as income increases. This finding was first discovered by the Prussian economist, Ernst Engel (1821–1896) in the nineteenth century and has come to be known as Engel's Law. Table 1 illustrates the data that Engel used. They clearly show that richer families spent a smaller fraction of their income on food.

Recent Data

Recent data for U.S. consumers (see Table 2) tend to confirm Engel's observations. Affluent families devote a smaller proportion of their purchasing power to food than do poor families. Comparisons of the data from Table 1 and Table 2 also confirm Engel's Law—even current low-income U.S. consumers are much more affluent than nineteenth-century Belgians and, as might be expected, spend a much smaller fraction of their income on food.

TABLE 1 Percentage of Total Expenditures on Various Items in Belgian Families in 1853

Expenditure Item	Annual Income		
	$225–$300	$450–$600	$750–$1,000
Food	62.0%	55.0%	50.0%
Clothing	16.0	18.0	18.0
Lodging, light, and fuel	17.0	17.0	17.0
Services (education, legal, health)	4.0	7.5	11.5
Comfort and recreation	1.0	2.5	3.5
Total	100.0	100.0	100.0

Source: Based on A. Marshall, *Principles of Economics,* 8th ed. (London: Macmillan, 1920): 97. Some items have been aggregated.

TABLE 2 Percentage of Total Expenditures by U.S. Consumers on Various Items, 2000

Item	Annual Income (000)		
	$15–20	$40–50	$70+
Food	15.4%	14.7%	11.4%
Clothing	4.8	4.7	5.3
Housing	32.9	30.4	30.2
Other items	46.9	50.2	53.1
Total	100.0	100.0	100.0

Source: U.S. Bureau of Labor Statistics Web site: *http://stats.bls.gov/cex/2000/share/income.pdf*

Other Laws?

Whether other Engel-like laws apply to the relationship between income and consumption is open to question. For example, Table 2 shows a weak tendency for the fraction of spending on housing to decline with income, but the pattern is not overwhelming.

To Think About

1. The data in Table 2 includes food both eaten at home and in restaurants. Do you think eating at restaurants follows Engel's law?
2. Property taxes are based on housing values. Are these taxes regressive?

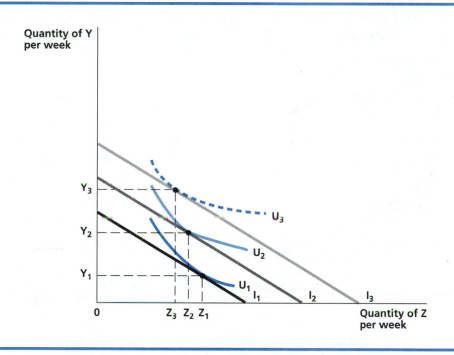

FIGURE 3.2 Indifference Curve Map Showing Inferiority Good Z is inferior because the quantity purchased declines as income increases. Y is a normal good (as it must be if only two goods are available), and purchases of it increase as total expenditures increase.

Inferior Goods

The demand for a few unusual goods may decrease as a person's income increases. Some proposed examples of such goods are "rotgut" whiskey, potatoes, and secondhand clothing. This kind of good is called an **inferior good.** How the demand for an inferior good responds to rising income is shown in Figure 3.2.

Inferior good
A good that is bought in smaller quantities as income increases.

The theory of utility maximization implies that the relationship between a person's income and the amounts of goods he or she buys will be determined solely by his or her preferences. How would the relationship between income and house purchases look in the following circumstances?

1. The person's MRS of housing for other goods is the same along any ray through the origin of the indifference curve map.

2. The person's MRS of housing for other goods follows the pattern in question 1 until housing reaches a certain "adequate" level and then the MRS becomes zero.

The good Z is inferior because the individual chooses less of it as his or her income increases. Although the curves in Figure 3.2 continue to obey the assumption of a diminishing MRS, they exhibit inferiority. Good Z is inferior only because of the way it relates to the other goods available (good Y here), not because of its own qualities. Purchases of rotgut whiskey decline as income increases, for example, because an individual is able to afford more expensive beverages (such as French champagne). Although, as our examples suggest, inferior goods are relatively rare, the study of them does help to illustrate a few important aspects of demand theory.

CHANGES IN A GOOD'S PRICE

Examining how a price change affects the quantity demanded of a good is more complex than looking at the effect of a change in income. Changing the price geometrically involves not only changing the intercept of the budget constraint but also changing its slope. Moving to the new utility-maximizing choice means moving to another indifference curve and to a point on that curve with a different MRS.

When a price changes, it has two different effects on people's choices. There is a **substitution effect** that occurs even if the individual stays on the same indifference curve because consumption has to be changed to equate MRS to the new price ratio of the two goods. There is also an **income effect** because the price change also changes "real" purchasing power. People will have to move to a new indifference curve that is consistent with their new purchasing power. We now look at these two effects in several different situations.

Substitution effect
The part of the change in quantity demanded that is caused by substitution of one good for another. A movement along an indifference curve.

Income effect
The part of the change in quantity demanded that is caused by a change in real income.

Substitution and Income Effects from a Fall in Price

Let's look first at how the quantity consumed of good X changes in response to a fall in its price. This situation is illustrated in Figure 3.3. Initially, the person maximizes utility by choosing the combination X*, Y at point A. When the price of X falls, the budget line shifts outward to the new budget constraint as shown in the figure. Remember that the budget constraint meets the Y-axis at the point where all available income is spent on good Y. Because neither the person's income nor the price of good Y has changed here, this Y-intercept is the same for both constraints. The new X-intercept is to the right of the old one because the lower price of X means that, with the lower price, this person could buy more X if he or she

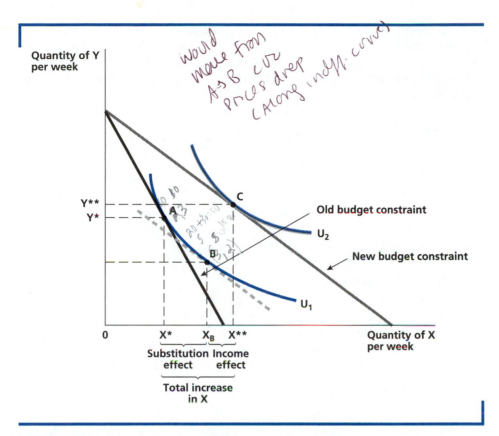

FIGURE 3.3 Income and Substitution Effects of a Fall in Price When the price of X falls, the utility-maximizing choice shifts from A to C. This movement can be broken down into two effects: first, a movement along the initial indifference curve to point B where the MRS is equal to the new price ratio (the substitution effect); second, a movement to a higher level of utility, since real income has increased (the income effect). Both the substitution and income effects cause more X to be bought when its price declines.

devoted all income to that purpose. The flatter slope of the budget constraint shows us that the relative price of X to Y (that is, P_X/P_Y) has fallen.

Substitution Effect

With this change in the budget constraint, the new position of maximum utility is at X**, Y** (point C). There, the new budget line is tangent to the indifference curve U_2. The movement to this new set of choices is the result of two different effects. First, the change in the slope of the budget constraint would have motivated this person to move to point B even if the person had stayed on the original indifference curve U_1. The dashed line in Figure 3.3 has the same slope as the new budget constraint, but it is tangent to U_1 because we are holding "real" income (that is, utility) constant. A relatively lower price for X causes a move from A to B if this person does not become better off as a result of the lower price. This movement is a graphic demonstration of the substitution effect. Even though the individual is no better off, the change in price still causes a change in consumption choices.

Income Effect

The further move from B to the final consumption choice, C, is identical to the kind of movement we described in Figure 3.1 for changes in income. Because the price of X has fallen but nominal income (I) has stayed the same, this person has a greater "real" income and can afford a higher utility level (U_2). If X is a normal good, he or she will now demand more of it. This is the income effect. As is clear from the figure, both the substitution effect and the income effect cause this person to choose more X when the price of X declines.

The Effects Combined

People do not actually move from A to B to C when the price of good X falls. We never observe the point B; only the two actual choices of A and C are reflected in this person's behavior. But the analysis of income and substitution effects is still valuable because it shows that a price change affects the quantity demanded of a good in two conceptually different ways.

We can use the hamburger–soft drink example from Chapter 2 to show these effects at work. Suppose that the price of soft drinks falls to $.50 from the earlier price of $1.00. This price change will increase this person's purchasing power. Whereas earlier 20 soft drinks could be bought with an income of $20.00, now 40 of them can be bought. The price decrease shifts the budget constraint outward and increases utility. This person now will choose some different combination of hamburgers and soft drinks than before, if only because the previous choice of five hamburgers and ten soft drinks (under the old budget constraint) now costs only $15—there is $5 left unspent, and this person will choose to do something with it.

In making the new choices, the individual is influenced by two different effects. First, even if we hold utility constant by somehow compensating for the beneficial effect that the fall in price has, this person will still act so that the MRS is brought into line with the new price ratio (now one hamburger to four soft drinks). This compensated response is the substitution effect. Even with a constant real income, this person will still choose more soft drinks and fewer hamburgers because the opportunity cost of eating a burger in terms of soft drinks forgone is now higher than before.

In actuality, real income has also increased; in order to assess the total effect of the price change on the demand for soft drinks, we must also investigate the effect of the change in purchasing power. The increase in real income would (assuming soft drinks are normal goods) be another reason to expect soft drink purchases to increase.

Substitution and Income Effects from an Increase in Price

We can use a similar analysis to see what happens if the price of good X increases. The budget line in Figure 3.4 shifts inward because of an increase in the price of X. The Y-intercept for the budget constraint again does not change since neither income nor P_Y has changed. The slope of the budget constraint is now steeper, however, because X costs more than it did before.

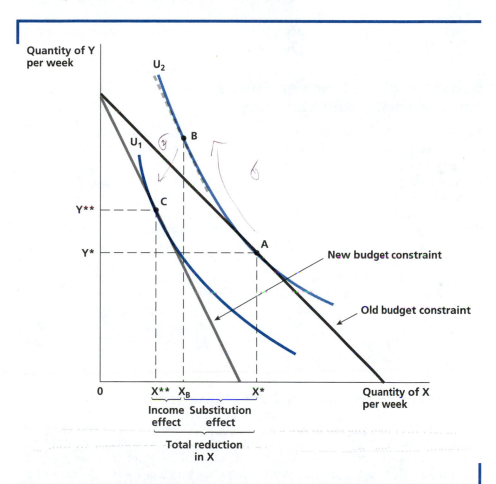

FIGURE 3.4 Income and Substitution Effects of an Increase in Price When the price of good X increases, the budget constraint shifts inward. The movement from the initial utility-maximizing point (A) to the new point (C) can again be analyzed as two separate effects. The substitution effect causes a movement to point B on the initial indifference curve (U_2). The price increase also creates a loss of purchasing power. This income effect causes a consequent movement to a lower indifference curve. The income and substitution effects together cause the quantity demanded of X to fall as a result of the increase in its price.

The movement from the initial point of utility maximization (A) to the new point C is again caused by two forces. First, even if this person stayed on the initial indifference curve (U_2), he or she would substitute Y for X and move along U_2 to point B. At this point, the dashed line (with the same slope as the new budget constraint) is just tangent to the indifference curve U_2. The movement from A to B along U_2 is the substitution effect. However, because purchasing power is reduced by the increase in the price of X (the amount of income remains constant, but now X costs more), the person must move to a lower level of utility, which is the income effect of the higher price. In Figure 3.4, both the income and substitution effects work in the same direction and cause the quantity demanded of X to fall in response to an increase in its price.

Substitution and Income Effects for a Normal Good: Summary

Figure 3.3 and Figure 3.4 show that, for a normal good, substitution and income effects work in the same direction to yield the expected result: People choose to consume more of a good whose price has fallen and less of a good whose price has risen. As we illustrate later, this provides the rationale for drawing downward-sloping demand curves. If other things do not change, price and quantity move in opposite directions along such a curve. Recognizing that price changes lead to both substitution and income effects also helps to analyze whether such moves will be large or small. In general, price changes that induce big substitution effects or that have big effects on purchasing power (because the good is an important component of people's budgets) will have large effects on quantity demanded. Price changes that cause only modest substitutions among goods or that have trivial effects on purchasing power will have correspondingly small effects on quantity demanded. This kind of analysis also offers a number of insights about some commonly used economic statistics, as Application 3.2: The Consumer Price Index and Its Biases illustrates.

Substitution and Income Effects for Inferior Goods

For the rare case of inferior goods, we cannot make such blanket statements about the effects of price changes. In this case, substitution and income effects work in opposite directions. The net effect of a price change on quantity demanded will be ambiguous. Here we show that ambiguity for the case of an increase in price, leaving it to you to explain the case of a fall in price.

Figure 3.5 shows the income and substitution effects from an increase in price when X is an inferior good. As the price of X rises, the substitution effect causes this person to choose less X. This substitution effect is represented by a movement from A to B in the initial indifference curve, U_2. This movement is exactly the same as in Figure 3.4 for a normal good. Because price has increased, however, this person now has a lower real income and must move to a lower indifference curve, U_1. The individual will choose combination C. At C, more X is chosen than at point B.

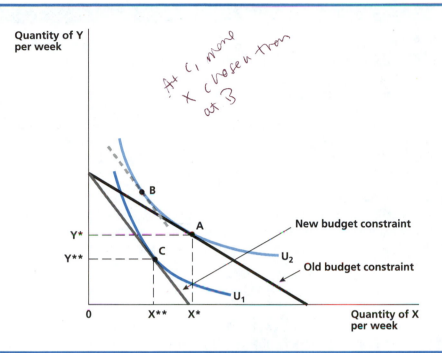

FIGURE 3.5 Income and Substitution Effects for an Inferior Good When the price of X increases, the substitution effect causes less X to be demanded (as shown by a movement to point B on the indifference curve U_2). However, because good X is inferior, the lower real income brought about by its price increase causes the quantity demanded of X to increase (compare point B and point C). In this particular example, the substitution effect outweighs the income effect and X consumption still falls (from X* to X**).

This happens because good X is an inferior good: As real income falls, the quantity demanded of X increases rather than declines as it would for a normal good. In Figure 3.5, however, X** is less than X*; less X is ultimately demanded in response to the rise in its price. In our example here, the substitution effect is strong enough to outweigh the "perverse" income effect from the price change.

Giffen's Paradox

If the income effect of a price change for an inferior good and is strong enough, the change in price and the resulting change in the quantity demanded could move in the same direction. Legend has it that the English economist Robert Giffen observed this paradox in nineteenth-century Ireland—when the price of potatoes rose, people consumed more of them. This peculiar result can be explained by looking at the size of the income effect of a change in the price of potatoes. Potatoes were not only inferior goods but also used up a large portion of the Irish

INFOTRAC©
COLLEGE EDITION
Exclusively from Gale Group and Thomson Learning

www.infotrac-college.com
Keywords: Substitution effect, Giffen goods

The Consumer Price Index and Its Biases

One of the principal measures of inflation in the United States is provided by the Consumer Price Index (CPI), which is published monthly by the U.S. Department of Labor. To construct the CPI, the Bureau of Labor Statistics first defines a typical market basket of commodities purchased by consumers in a base year (1982 is the year currently used). Then data are collected every month about how much this market basket of commodities currently costs the consumer. The ratio of the current cost to the bundle's original cost (in 1982) is then published as the current value of the CPI. The rate of change in this index between two periods is reported to be the rate of inflation.

An Algebraic Example

This construction can be clarified with a simple two-good example. Suppose that in 1982 the typical market basket contained X^{82} of good X and Y^{82} of good Y. The prices of these goods are given by P_X^{82} and P_Y^{82}. The cost of this bundle in the 1982 base year would be written as

$$\text{Cost of bundle in 1982} =$$
$$B^{82} = P_X^{82} \cdot X^{82} + P_Y^{82} \cdot Y^{82} \tag{1}$$

To compute the cost of the same bundle of goods in, say, 2002, we must first collect information on the goods' prices in that year (P_X^{02}, P_Y^{02}) and then compute

$$\text{Cost of bundle in 2002} =$$
$$B^{02} = P_X^{02} \cdot X^{82} + P_Y^{02} \cdot Y^{82} \tag{2}$$

Notice that the quantities purchased in 1982 are being valued at 2002 prices. The CPI is defined as the ratio of the costs of these two market baskets:

$$\text{CPI (for 2002)} = \frac{B^{02}}{B^{82}} \tag{3}$$

The rate of inflation can be computed from this index. For example, if a market basket of items that cost \$100 in 1982 costs \$180 in 2002, the value of the CPI would be 1.80 and we would say there had been an 80 percent increase in prices over this 20-year period.[1] It might (possibly incorrectly) be said that people would need an 80 percent increase in nominal 1982 income to enjoy the same standard of living in 2002 that they had in 1982. Cost-of-living adjustments (COLAs) in Social Security benefits and in many job agreements are calculated in precisely this way. Unfortunately, this approach poses a number of problems.

Substitution Bias in the CPI

One problem with the preceding calculation is that it assumes that people who are faced with year 2002 prices will continue to demand the same basket of commodities that they consumed in 1982. This treatment makes no allowance for substitutions among

---

[1] Frequently, index numbers are multiplied by 100 to avoid computation to several decimal places. Hence, a *value* of 180 would be reported. Each figure shows an 80 percent gain in the index over the base period.

commodities in response to changing prices. The calculation may overstate the decline in purchasing power that inflation has caused because it takes no account of how people will seek to get the most utility for their dollars when prices change.

In Figure 1, for example, a typical individual initially is consuming X^{82}, Y^{82}. Presumably this choice provides maximum utility (U_1), given his or her budget constraint in 1982 (which we call I). Suppose that by 2002 relative prices have changed in such a way that P_X/P_Y falls—that is, assume that good Y becomes relatively more expensive. Using these new prices, the CPI calculates what X^{82}, Y^{82} would cost. This cost would be reflected by the budget constraint I', which is flatter than I (to reflect the changed prices) and passes through the 1982 consumption point. As the figure makes clear, the erosion in purchasing power

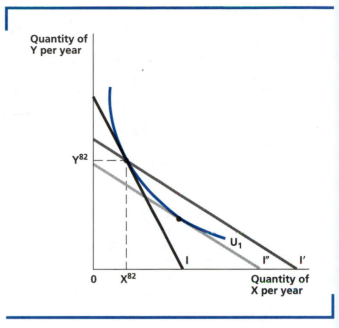

FIGURE 1 **Substitution Bias of the Consumer Price Index** In 1982 with income I the typical consumer chose X^{82}, Y^{82}. If this market basket is with different relative prices, the basket's cost will be given by I'. This cost exceeds what is actually required to permit the consumer to reach the original level of utility, I".

that has occurred is overstated. With I', our typical individual could now reach a higher utility level than could have been attained in 1982. The CPI overstates the decline in purchasing power that has occurred.

A true measure of inflation would be provided by evaluating an income level, say, I", which reflects the new prices but just permits the individual to remain on U_1. This would take account of the substitutions in consumption that people might make in response to changing relative prices (they consume more X and less Y in moving along U_1). Unfortunately, adjusting the CPI to take such substitutions into account is a difficult task— primarily because the typical consumer's utility function cannot be measured perfectly.

New Product Bias

The introduction of new or improved products produces a similar bias in the CPI. New products usually experience sharp declines in prices and rapidly growing rates of acceptance by consumers (consider notebook computers or DVDs, for example). If these goods are not included in the CPI market basket, a major source of welfare gain for consumers will have been omitted. Of course, the CPI market basket is updated every few years to permit new goods to be included. But that rate of revision is often insufficient for rapidly changing consumer markets.

(continued)

Outlet Bias

Finally, the fact that the Bureau of Labor Statistics sends buyers to the same retail outlets each month may overstate inflation. Actual consumers tend to seek out temporary sales or other bargains. They shop where they can make their money go the farthest. In recent years this has meant shopping at giant discount stores such as Wal-Mart or Costco rather than at traditional outlets. The CPI as currently constructed does not take such price-reducing strategies into account.

Consequences of the Biases

Measuring all these biases and devising a better CPI to take them into account is no easy task. Indeed, because the CPI is so widely used as "the" measure of inflation, any change can become a very hot political controversy. Still, there is general agreement that the current CPI may overstate actual increases in the cost of living by as much as 0.75 percent to 1.0 percent per year.[2] By some estimates, correction of the index could reduce projected federal spending by as much as a half trillion dollars over a 10-year period. Hence, some politicians have proposed caps on COLAs in government programs. Such suggestions have been very controversial, and none has so far been enacted. In private contracts, however, the upward biases in the CPI are frequently recognized. Few private COLAs provide full offsets to inflation as measured by the CPI.

To Think About

1. Would more frequent revisions of the market basket used for the CPI ameliorate the various biases outlined here? What problems would arise from using a frequently changing market basket?
2. How should quality improvements be reflected in the CPI? Is a 2003 television the same good as a 1976 television? If not, how will inclusion of "one television" in the CPI market basket affect whether it measures true inflation?

[2] For a detailed discussion, see the compendium of articles in the Winter 1998 issue of *The Journal of Economic Perspectives*.

Giffen's paradox
A situation in which an increase in a good's price leads people to consume more of the good.

people's income. An increase in the price of potatoes therefore reduced real income substantially. The Irish were forced to cut back on other food consumption in order to buy more potatoes. Even though this rendering of events is economically implausible, the possibility of an increase in the quantity demanded in response to the price increase of a good has come to be known as **Giffen's paradox.**[1]

[1] A major problem with this explanation is that it disregards Marshall's observations that both supply and demand factors must be taken into account when analyzing price changes. If potato prices increased because of a decline in supply due to the potato blight, how could *more* potatoes possibly have been consumed? Also, since many Irish people were potato farmers, the potato price increase should have increased real income for them. For a detailed discussion of these and other fascinating bits of potato lore, see G. P. Dwyer and C. M. Lindsey, "Robert Giffen and the Irish Potato," *American Economic Review* (March 1984): 188–192.

THE LUMP-SUM PRINCIPLE

Economists have had a long-standing interest in studying taxes. We look at such analyses at many places in this book. Here we use our model of individual choice to show how taxes affect utility. Of course, it seems obvious (if we don't consider the government services that taxes provide) that paying taxes must reduce a person's utility because purchasing power is reduced. But, through the use of income and substitution effects, we can show that the size of his or her welfare loss will depend on how a tax is structured. Specifically, taxes that are imposed on general purchasing power will have smaller welfare costs than will taxes imposed on a narrow selection of commodities. This "lump-sum principle" lies at the heart of the study of the economics of taxation.

MicroQuiz 3.2

Substitution effects take particularly simple forms in some cases. Describe these effects for:

1. Left shoes and right shoes (as shown in Figure 2.5d).

2. Exxon and Mobil gasoline (as shown in Figure 2.5c).

A Graphical Approach

A graphical proof of the lump-sum principle is presented in Figure 3.6. Initially, this person has I dollars to spend and chooses to consume X^* and Y^*. This combination yields utility level U_3. A tax on good X alone would raise its price, and the budget constraint would become steeper. With that budget constraint (shown as line I' in the figure), a person would be forced to accept a lower utility level (U_1) and would choose to consume the combination X_1, Y_1.

Suppose now that the government decided to institute a general income tax that raised the same revenue as this single-good excise tax. This would shift the individual's budget constraint to I''. The fact that I'' passes through X_1, Y_1 shows that both taxes raise the same amount of revenue.[2] However, with the income tax budget constraint I'', this person will choose to consume X_2, Y_2 (rather than X_1, Y_1). Even though the individual pays the same tax bill in both instances, the combination chosen under the income tax yields a higher utility (U_2) than does the tax on a single commodity.

---

[2] Algebra shows why this is true. With the sales tax (where the tax rate is given by t) the individual's budget constraint is

$$I = I' = (P_X + t) X_1 + P_Y Y_1$$

Total tax revenues are given by

$$T = tX_1$$

With an income tax that collected the same revenue, after-tax income is

$$I'' = I - T = P_X X_1 + P_Y Y_1$$

which shows that I'' passes through the point X_1, Y_1 also.

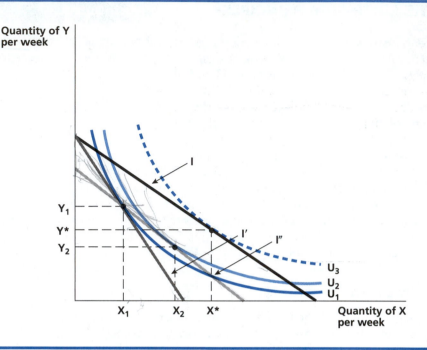

FIGURE 3.6 The Lump-Sum Principle An excise tax on good X shifts the budget constraints to I'. The individual chooses X_1, Y_1 and receives utility of U_1. A lump-sum tax that collects the same amount shifts the budget constraint to I''. The individual chooses X_2, Y_2 and receives more utility (U_2).

An intuitive explanation of this result is that a single-commodity tax affects people's well-being in two ways: It reduces general purchasing power (an income effect), and it directs consumption away from the taxed commodity (a substitution effect). An income tax incorporates only the first effect, and, with equal tax revenues raised, individuals are better off under it than under a tax that also distorts consumption choices.

Generalizations

More generally, the demonstration of the lump-sum principle in Figure 3.6 suggests that the utility loss associated with the need to collect a certain amount of tax revenue can be kept to a minimum by taxing goods for which substitution effects are small. By doing so, taxes will have relatively little welfare effect beyond their direct effect on purchasing power. On the other hand, taxes on goods for which there are many substitutes will cause individuals to alter their consumption plans in major ways. This additional distortionary effect raises the overall utility cost of such taxes to consumers. In Application 3.3: Wouldn't Cash Be a Better Way to Help Poor People, we look at a few implications of these observations for welfare policy.

Most countries provide a wide variety of programs to help poor people. In the United States, there is a general program for cash assistance to low-income families, but most anti-poverty spending is done through a variety of "in-kind" programs such as Food Stamps, Medicaid, and low-income housing assistance. Such programs have expanded very rapidly during the past 30 years, whereas the cash program has tended to shrink (especially following the 1996 welfare reform initiative).

Inefficiency of In-Kind Programs

The lump-sum principle suggests that these trends may be unfortunate because the in-kind programs do not generate as much welfare for poor people as would the spending of the same funds in a cash program. The argument is illustrated in Figure 1. The typical low-income person's budget constraint is given by I prior to any assistance. This yields a utility of U_1. An anti-poverty program that provided, say, good X at a highly subsidized price would shift this budget constraint to I′ and raise this person's utility to U_2. If the government were instead to spend the same funds[1] on a pure income grant to this person, his or her budget constraint would be I″ and this would permit a higher utility to be reached (U_3). Hence, the in-kind program is inefficient in terms of raising the utility of this low-income person.

There is empirical evidence supporting this conclusion. Careful studies of spending patterns of poor people suggest that a dollar spent on food subsidy programs is "worth" only about $.90 to the recipients. A dollar in medical care subsidies may be worth only about $.70, and housing assistance may be worth less than $.60. Spending on these kinds of in-kind programs therefore may not be an especially effective way of raising the utility of poor people.

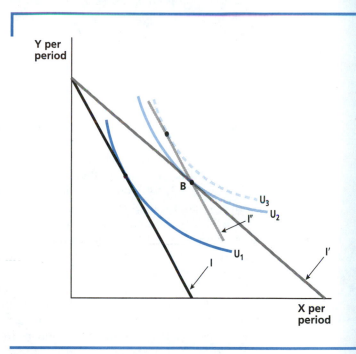

FIGURE 1 Superiority of an Income Grant A subsidy on good X (constraint I′) raises utility to U_2. For the same funds, a pure income grant (I″) raises utility to U_3.

---

[1] Budget constraints I′ and I″ represent the same government spending because both permit this person to consume point B.

(continued)

Paternalism and Donor Preferences

Why have most countries favored in-kind programs over cash assistance? Undoubtedly, some of this focus stems from paternalism—policymakers in the government may feel that they have a better idea of how poor people should spend their incomes than do poor people themselves. In Figure 1, for example, X purchases are indeed greater under the in-kind program than under the cash grant though utility is lower. A related possibility is that "donors" (usually taxpayers) have strong preferences for how aid to poor people should be provided. Donors may care more about providing food or medical care to poor people than about increasing their overall welfare. Political support for (seemingly more efficient) cash grants is simply nonexistent.

To Think About

1. How should the welfare of children be factored into Figure 1 (which may only reflect the decision making of the head-of-household)?
2. Some people fear that cash grants may affect the work incentives of poor people. Would similar concerns apply to in-kind programs?

CHANGES IN THE PRICE OF ANOTHER GOOD

A careful examination of our analysis so far would reveal that a change in the price of X will also have an effect on the quantity demanded of the other good (Y). In Figure 3.3, for example, a decrease in the price of X causes not only the quantity demanded of X to increase but the quantity demanded of Y to increase as well. We can explain this result by looking at the substitution and income effects on the demand for Y associated with the decrease in the price of X.

First, as we see in Figure 3.3, the substitution effect caused less Y to be demanded. In moving along the indifference curve U_1 from A to B, X is substituted for Y because the lower ratio of P_X/P_Y required an adjustment in the MRS. In this figure, the income effect of the decline in the price of good X is strong enough to reverse this result. Because Y is a normal good and real income has increased, more Y is demanded: The individual moves from B to C. Here Y^{**} exceeds Y^*, and the total effect of the price change is to increase the demand for Y.

A slightly different set of indifference curves (that is, different preferences) could have shown different results. Figure 3.7 shows a relatively flat set of indifference curves where the substitution effect from a decline in the price of X is very large. In moving from A to B, a large amount of X is substituted for Y. The income effect on Y is not strong enough to reverse this large substitution effect. In this case, the quantity of Y finally chosen (Y^{**}) is smaller than the original amount. The effect of a decline in the price of one good on the quantity demanded of some other good is ambiguous; it all depends on what the person's preferences, as reflected by his or her indifference curve map, look like. We have

[handwritten margin note: Sub effect of X less Y demanded at B than Sub effect less Y demanded at B from A]

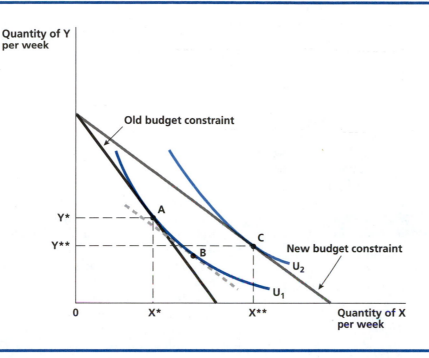

FIGURE 3.7 Effect on the Demand for Good Y of a Decrease in the Price of Good X In contrast to Figure 3.3, the quantity demanded of Y now declines (from Y* to Y**) in response to a decrease in the price of X. The relatively flat indifference curves cause the substitution effect to be very large. Moving from A to B means giving up a substantial quantity of Y for additional X. This effect more than outweighs the positive income effect (from B to C), and the quantity demanded of Y declines. So, purchases of Y may either rise or fall when the price of X falls.

to examine carefully income and substitution effects that (at least in the case of only two goods) work in opposite directions.

Substitutes and Complements

Economists use the terms *substitutes* and *complements* to describe the way people look at the relationships between goods. Complements are goods that go together in the sense that people will increase their use of both goods simultaneously. Examples of complements might be coffee and cream, fish and chips, peanut butter and jelly, or gasoline and automobiles. Substitutes, on the other hand, are goods that can replace one another. Tea and coffee, Hondas and Pontiacs, or owned versus rented housing are some goods that are substitutes for each other.

Whether two goods are substitutes or complements of each other is primarily a question of the shape of people's indifference curves. The market behavior of

Complements

Two goods such that when the price of one increases, the quantity demanded of the other falls.

Substitutes

Two goods such that if the price of one increases, the quantity demanded of the other rises.

individuals in their purchases of goods can help economists to discover these relationships. Two goods are **complements** if an increase in the price of one causes a decrease in the quantity consumed of the other. For example, an increase in the price of coffee might cause not only the quantity demanded of coffee to decline but also the demand for cream to decrease because of the complementary relationship between cream and coffee. Similarly, coffee and tea are **substitutes** because an increase in the price of coffee might cause the quantity demanded of tea to increase as tea replaces coffee in use.

How the demand for one good relates to the price increase of another good is determined by both income and substitution effects. It is only the combined gross result of these two effects that we can observe. Including both income and substitution effects of price changes in our definitions of substitutes and complements can sometimes lead to problems. For example, it is theoretically possible for X to be a complement for Y and at the same time for Y to be a substitute for X. This perplexing state of affairs has led some economists to favor a definition of substitutes and complements that looks only at the direction of substitution effects.[3] We do not make that distinction in this book. In Application 3.4: Why Are So Many "Trucks" on the Road?, we take a brief look at some of the complex relationships between gas prices and what people drive.

MicroQuiz 3.3

Changes in the price of another good create both income and substitution effects in a person's demand for, say, coffee. Describe those effects in the following cases and state whether they work in the same direction or in opposite directions in their total impact on coffee purchases.

1. A decrease in the price of tea

2. A decrease in the price of cream

CONSTRUCTION OF INDIVIDUAL DEMAND CURVES

We have now completed our discussion of how the individual's demand for good X is affected by various changes in economic circumstances. We started by writing the demand function for good X as

$$\text{Quantity of X demanded} = d_X(P_X, P_Y, I; \text{preferences})$$

Then we examined how changes in each of the economic factors P_X, P_Y, and I might affect an individual's decision to purchase good X. The principle purpose

---

[3] For a slightly more extended treatment for this subject, see Walter Nicholson, *Microeconomic Theory: Basic Principles and Extensions*, 8th ed. (Mason, OH: South-Western/Thomson Learning), 154–158. For a complete treatment, see J. R. Hicks, *Value and Capital* (London: Cambridge University Press, 1939), Chapter 3 and the mathematical appendix.

Motor vehicle registrations in the United States have shown a remarkable change over the past 10 years. In 1990, fewer than 30 percent of the vehicles on U.S. roads were "trucks" whereas by 2000 that figure had increased to over 40 percent. Virtually all of the new vehicle registrations during the 1990s were trucks. How is it that people in the United States have such a great need to transport things?

What Is a "Truck"?

Of course, the huge gain in truck registrations does not mean that most people in the United States are driving 18-wheelers. Rather, the issue is one of definition. The U.S. Department of Transportation regards a wide variety of automobile-like vehicles as "trucks" for purposes of data collection. These include vans, minivans, mobile homes, and (most important) sport-utility vehicles (SUVs). The data reflect a huge increase in the popularity of these autolike vehicles during the 1990s. People in the United States have proven more than willing to make substitutions in the types of vehicles they buy.

Relative Price Effects

One of the most important reasons for the trend toward SUVs and their ilk has been a sharp decline in real gasoline prices. In the late 1980s, gasoline sold for about $1.50 per gallon with that price falling to about $1.10 by 1999. In inflation-adjusted terms, the real price of gasoline declined by over 40 percent. This had the effect of significantly reducing the relative costs of operating trucklike vehicles. Suppose that the typical SUV averages about 15 miles per gallon of gasoline and is driven 15,000 miles per year. The savings from lower fuel prices on the 1,000 gallons of gasoline used during the year would amount to perhaps $800. This might be as much as 15 to 20 percent of the overall operating cost of an SUV during the year. For a similarly priced but higher-mileage automobile, the percent reduction might only be in the 5 to 10 percent range. Hence, the relative price (remember, *relative prices* are what matter in consumers' choices) of SUVs fell rather significantly. Clearly, the decline in relative operating costs had a major impact in causing people to substitute away from more traditional automobiles.

The Unintended Effects of Regulations

Part of the increased buying of trucklike vehicles can also be explained as unintended side effects of various governmental regulations that were (perhaps paradoxically) intended to reduce gasoline usage. One set of regulations was the Corporate Average Fuel Economy (CAFE) standards that required automakers to achieve certain average miles-per-gallon goals on their annual car sales. "Trucks" were generally exempt from the CAFE standards, so firms could freely market all types of SUVs but had to be more careful about the numbers of large cars they sold. A 1991 tax on "gas guzzlers" put large automobiles at a further disadvantage relative to trucks by imposing taxes of as much as $5,000 on cars with especially low mileage ratings.

(continued)

The End of the Large SUV Era?

Several factors suggest that U.S. consumers' infatuation with "trucks" may be coming to an end. After 2000, gas prices have tended to move upward, reaching perhaps $1.45 by mid-2002 (still well below the real prices of the 1980s). Congress, perhaps embarrassed by the emergence of super-large SUVs such as the Ford Excursion, the GMC Yukon, or the Toyota Sequoia, has belatedly moved to start the inclusion of SUVs under the CAFE standards. Perhaps most important, several automakers have introduced smaller, more fuel-efficient SUVs that are built on automobile bodies (the Honda CRV, for example, is built on the Civic frame). For many buyers, these may provide a better match to the characteristics they are seeking than do the large SUVs.

To Think About

1. Why does the government have fuel economy standards? Doesn't the attempt to regulate how much gasoline people buy conflict with our more general presumptions that consumers should, within the limits of the law, be able to make up their own minds about what they wish to consume?

2. Passengers in large SUVs are much less likely to suffer injuries in crashes—especially when an SUV collides with a small car. Is this an additional area where the government should seek to limit consumer choices by prescribing size limits for cars? Or should people be able to buy as much "safety" as they would like?

Individual demand curve

A graphic representation of the relationship between the price of a good and the quantity of it demanded by a person, holding all other factors constant.

of this examination has been to permit us to derive individual demand curves and to analyze those factors that might cause a demand curve to change its position. This section shows how a demand curve can be constructed. The next section analyzes why this curve might shift.

An **individual demand curve** shows the *ceteris paribus* relationship between the quantity demanded of a good (say, X) and its price (P_X). Not only are preferences held constant under the *ceteris paribus* assumption (as they have been throughout our discussion in this chapter), but the other factors in the demand function (that is, the price of good Y and income) are also held constant. In demand curves, we are limiting our study to only the relationship between the quantity of a good chosen and changes in its price.

Figure 3.8 shows how to construct a person's demand curve for good X. In panel a, a person's indifference curve map is drawn using three different budget constraints in which the price of X decreases. These decreasing prices are P'_X, P''_X, and P'''_X. The other economic factors that affect the position of the budget constraint (the price of good Y and income) do not change. In graphic terms, all three constraints have the same Y-intercept. The successively lower prices of X rotate this constraint outward. Given the three separate budget constraints, the individual's utility-maximizing choices of X are given by X', X", and X'". These three choices show that the quantity demanded of X increases as the price of X falls.

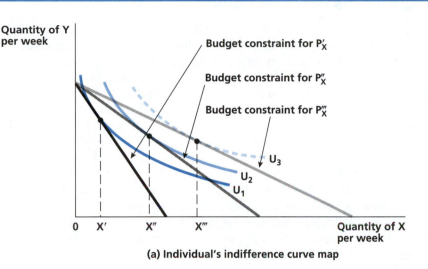

(a) Individual's indifference curve map

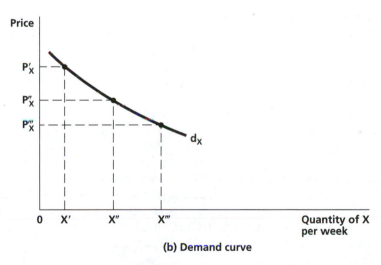

(b) Demand curve

FIGURE 3.8 Construction of an Individual's Demand Curve In panel a, the individual's utility-maximizing choices of X and Y are shown for three successively lower prices of X. In panel b, this relationship between P_x and X is used to construct the demand curve for X. The demand curve is drawn on the assumption that the price of Y and money income remain constant as the price of X varies.

The information in panel a in Figure 3.8 can be used to construct the demand curve shown in panel b. The price of X is shown on the vertical axis, and the quantity chosen continues to be shown on the horizontal axis. The demand curve (d_x) is downward sloping, showing that when the price of X falls, the quantity demanded of X increases. As we have shown, this increase represents both the substitution and income effects of the price decline.

Shape of the Demand Curve

The precise shape of the demand curve is determined by the income and substitution effects that occur when the price of X changes. A person's demand curve may be either rather flat or quite steeply sloped, depending on the nature of his or her indifference curve map. If X has many close substitutes, the indifference curves will be nearly straight lines (such as those shown in Figure 3.7), and the substitution effect from a price change will be very large. The quantity of X chosen may fall substantially in response to a rise in its price; consequently, the demand curve will be relatively flat. For example, consider a person's demand for one particular brand of cereal (say, the famous Brand X). Because any one brand has many close substitutes, the demand curve for Brand X will be relatively flat. A rise in the price of Brand X will cause people to shift easily to other kinds of cereal, and the quantity demanded of Brand X will be reduced significantly.

On the other hand, a person's demand curve for some goods may be steeply sloped. That is, price changes will not affect consumption very much. This might be the case if the good has no close substitutes. For example, consider a person's demand for water. Because water satisfies many unique needs, it is unlikely that it would have any substitutes when the price of water rose, and the substitution effect would be very small. However, since water does not use up a large portion of a person's total income, the income effect of the increase in the price of water would also not be large. The quantity demanded of water probably would not respond greatly to changes in its price; that is, the demand curve would be nearly vertical.

As a third possibility, consider the case of food. Because food as a whole has no substitutes (although individual food items obviously do), an increase in the price of food will not induce important substitution effects. In this sense, food is similar to our water example. However, food is a major item in a person's total expenditures, and an increase in its price will have a significant effect on purchasing power. It is possible, therefore, that the quantity demanded of food may be reduced substantially in response to a rise in food prices because of this income effect. The demand curve for food might be flatter (that is, demand reacts more to price) than we might expect if we thought of food only as a "necessity" with few, if any, substitutes.[4]

SHIFTS IN AN INDIVIDUAL'S DEMAND CURVE

An individual's demand curve summarizes the relationship between the price of X and the quantity demanded of X when all the other things that might affect demand are held constant. The income and substitution effects of changes in that

[4] For this reason, sometimes it is convenient to talk about demand curves that reflect only substitution effects. We do not study such "compensated" demand curves in this book, however.

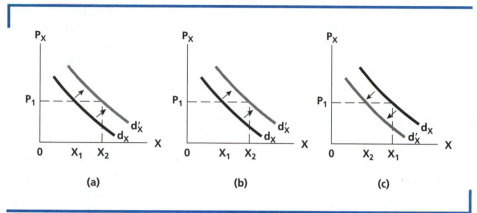

FIGURE 3.9 Shifts in an Individual's Demand Curve In panel a, the demand curve shifts outward because the individual's income has increased. More X is now demanded at each price. In panel b, the demand curve shifts outward because the price of Y has increased, and X and Y are substitutes for the individual. In panel c, the demand curve shifts inward because of the increase in the price Y; that is, X and Y are complements.

price cause the person to move along his or her demand curve. If one of the factors (the price of Y, income, or preferences) that we have so far been holding constant were to change, the entire curve would shift. The demand curve remains fixed only while the *ceteris paribus* assumption is in effect. Figure 3.9 shows the kinds of shifts that might take place. In panel a, the effect on good X of an increase in income is shown. Assuming that good X is a normal good, an increase in income causes more X to be demanded at each price. At P_1, for example, the quantity of X demanded rises from X_1 to X_2. This is the kind of effect we described early in this chapter (Figure 3.1). When income increases, people buy more X even if its price has not changed, and the demand curve shifts outward. Panels b and c in Figure 3.9 record two possible effects that an increase in the price of Y might have on the demand curve for good X. In panel b, X and Y are assumed to be substitutes—for example, coffee (X) and tea (Y). An increase in the price of tea causes the individual to substitute coffee for tea. More coffee (that is, good X) is demanded at each price than was previously the case. At P_1, for example, coffee demand increases from X_1 to X_2.

On the other hand, suppose X and Y are complements—for example, coffee (X) and cream (Y). An increase in the price of cream causes the demand curve for coffee to shift inward. Because coffee and cream go together, less coffee (that is, good X) will now be demanded at each price. This shift in the demand curve is shown in panel c—at P_1, coffee demand falls from X_1 to X_2.

Changes in preferences might also cause the demand curve to shift. For example, a sudden warm spell would undoubtedly shift the entire demand curve for cold drinks outward. More drinks would be demanded at each price because now each person's desire for them has increased. Similarly, increased environmental consciousness during the 1980s and 1990s vastly increased the demand for such items as recycling containers and organically grown food. Application 3.5: Fads, Seasons, and Health Scares explores a few other reasons why demand curves might shift.

MicroQuiz 3.4

The following statements were made by two reporters describing the same event. Which reporter (if either) gets the distinction between shifting a demand curve and moving along it correct?

Reporter 1. The freezing weather in Florida will raise the price of oranges and people will reduce their demand for oranges. Because of this reduced demand, producers will get lower prices for their oranges than they might have and these lower prices will help restore orange purchases to their original level.

Reporter 2. The freezing weather in Florida raises orange prices and reduces the demand for oranges. Orange growers should therefore accustom themselves to lower sales even when the weather returns to normal.

Be Careful in Using Terminology

It is important to be careful in making the distinction between the shift in a demand curve and movement along a stationary demand curve. Changes in the price of X lead to movements along the demand curve for good X. Changes in other economic factors (such as a change in income, a change in another good's price, or a change in preferences) cause the entire demand curve for X to shift. If we wished to see how a change in the price of steak would affect a person's steak purchases, we would use a single demand curve and study movements along it. On the other hand, if we wanted to know how a change in income would affect the quantity of steak purchased, we would have to study the shift in the position of the entire demand curve.

To keep these matters straight, economists must speak carefully. The movement downward along a stationary demand curve in response to a fall in price is called an **increase in quantity demanded.** A shift outward in the entire curve is an **increase in demand.** A rise in the price of a good causes a **decrease in quantity demanded** (a move along the demand curve), whereas a change in some other factor may cause a **decrease in demand** (a shift of the entire curve to the left). It is important to be precise in using those terms; they are not interchangeable.

Increase or decrease in quantity demanded

The increase or decrease in quantity demanded caused by a change in the good's price. Graphically represented by the movement along a demand curve.

Increase or decrease in demand

The change in demand for a good caused by changes in the price of another good, in income, or in preferences. Graphically represented by a shift of the entire demand curve.

CONSUMER SURPLUS

Demand curves provide a considerable amount of information about the willingness of people to make voluntary transactions. Because demand curves are in principle measurable, they are much more useful for studying economic behavior in the real world than are utility functions. One important application uses demand curves to study the consequences of price changes for people's overall welfare. This technique relies on the concept of *consumer surplus*—a concept we

The notion that changes in preferences can influence the demand for products incorporates a wide variety of possible cultural and psychological influences. Let's look at a few.

Fads

Products such as Holiday Barbies, Beanie Babies, and Super Nintendo systems all experienced extremely rapid growth in demand when they were initially introduced, followed by an equally rapid loss of consumer interest. The widespread use of a product among consumers actually generates additional demand until a saturation point is reached. Then, demand falls precipitously. Such temporary bursts of demand (sometimes termed *bandwagon effects*) arise because of the interdependence among people's preferences—everyone wants to be part of the latest craze. This recurring pattern in the product fad's purchasing indicates a rather predictable demand for such products. Predicting exactly which products will catch on, however, is a mystery.

Seasonality

Season-sensitive goods are the polar opposites of fad products when it comes to predictability. Everyone knows that the demand for wedding cakes increases in June, that turkeys are mostly consumed at Thanksgiving, and that Christmas trees are bought in December. Seasonality also affects the demand for less-familiar items. A famous early study of New England fishing, for example, found that the demand for scrod (New Englandese for small cod) regularly increased by about 13 percent during Lent because of the dietary restrictions imposed during this period by the Catholic Church upon its members.[1] All these seasonal patterns show that preferences are formed through a variety of long-term historical and cultural influences. This is one reason why economists tend to treat them as being stable over short periods.

Health Scares

Some of the more rapid shifts in demand in recent years have been associated with changing perceptions by consumers about the health risks associated with various products. Concern about the risks of smoking, for example, has resulted in a long-term reduction in the number of smokers in the United States since the Surgeon General's report of 1964. Concern about cholesterol has led to similar long-term declines in individuals' demands for beef and dairy products.

Health concerns have also had dramatic short-term effects on demand. A 1982 incident in Chicago in which cyanide tablets were inserted into a few Tylenol bottles reduced the demand for that product by more than 50 percent. Finding two cyanide-injected grapes in 1988 caused the demand for Chilean fruits to drop dramatically. A 1993 study of the fat content of Chinese food caused a large decline in sales at Chinese restaurants.

Many times the demand for food items may react strongly to recent "scientific" studies. European demand for American beef dropped sharply in 1997 following some suggestions

[1] F. W. Bell, "The Pope and the Price of Fish," *American Economic Review* (December 1968): 346–350.

(continued)

(subsequently disproved) that growth hormones fed to cattle are unsafe. Studies purporting to show health benefits from eating tomatoes had an important effect on demand in 1998, though many were skeptical of the study's methods.

To Think About
1. Does the unpredictability of demand affect the profits firms might earn on a product? Why might turkeys or Christmas trees yield relatively small profits, whereas fad products often are quite profitable? (See Part 4 for further analysis.)
2. Do you think people often overreact to "scientific" studies of the health effects of consuming certain foods? How should a consumer choose among food items when the science is unclear?

examine in this section. The tools developed here are widely used by economists to study the effects of public policies on the welfare of citizens.

Demand Curves and Consumer Surplus

In order to understand the consumer surplus idea, we begin by thinking about an individual's demand curve for a good in a slightly different way. Specifically, each point on such a demand curve can be regarded as showing what a person would be willing to pay for *one more unit* of the good. Demand curves slope downward because this "marginal willingness to pay" declines as a person consumes more of a given good. On the demand curve for T-shirts in Figure 3.10, for example, this person chooses to consume ten T-shirts when the price is $11. In other words, this person is willing to pay $11 for the tenth T-shirt he or she buys. With a price of $9, on the other hand, this person chooses fifteen T-shirts, so, implicitly, he or she values the fifteenth shirt at only $9. Viewed from this perspective then, a person's demand curve tells us quite a bit about his or her willingness to pay for different quantities of a good.

Because a good is usually sold at a single market price, people choose to buy additional units of the good up to the point at which their marginal valuation is equal to that price. In Figure 3.10, for example, if T-shirts sell for $7, this person will buy twenty T-shirts because the twentieth T-shirt is worth precisely $7. He or she will not buy the twenty-first T-shirt because it is worth less than $7 (once this person already has twenty T-shirts). Because this person would be willing to pay more than $7 for the tenth or the fifteenth T-shirt, it is clear that this person gets a "surplus" on those shirts because he or she is actually paying less than the maximal amount that would willingly be paid. Hence, we have a formal definition of **consumer surplus** as the difference between the maximal amounts a person would pay for a good and what he or she actually pays. In graphical terms, consumer surplus is given by the area below the demand curve and above the market price. The concept is measured in dollars.

Consumer surplus
The extra value individuals receive from consuming a good over what they pay for it. What people would be willing to pay for the right to consume a good at its current price.

Because the demand curve in Figure 3.10 is a straight line, the computation of consumer surplus is especially simple. It is just the area of triangle AEB. When the price of T-shirts is $7, the size of this area is $0.5 \cdot 20 \cdot (\$15 - \$7) = \$80$. When this person buys twenty T-shirts at $7, he or she actually spends $140 but also receives a consumer surplus of $80. If we were to value each T-shirt at the maximal amount this person would pay for that shirt, we would conclude that the total value of the twenty T-shirts he or she consumes is $220, but they are bought for only $140.

A rise in price would reduce this person's consumer surplus from T-shirt

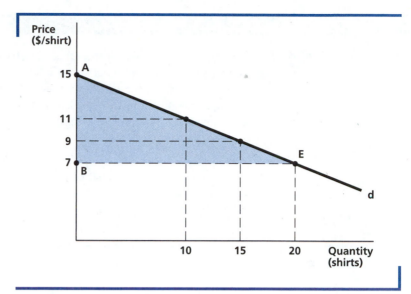

FIGURE 3.10 **Consumer Surplus from T-Shirt Demand Price ($/shirt)** The curve d shows a person's demand for T-shirts. He or she would be willing to pay $11 for the tenth shirt and $9 for the fifteenth shirt. At a price of $7, he or she receives a surplus of $4 for the tenth shirt and $2 for the fifteenth shirt. Total consumer surplus is given by area AEB ($80).

purchases. At a price of $11, for example, he or she buys ten T-shirts and consumer surplus would be computed as $0.5 \cdot 10 \cdot (\$15 - \$11) = \$20$. Hence, $60 of consumer surplus has been lost because of the rise in the price of T-shirts from $7 to $11. Some of this loss in consumer surplus went to shirt-makers because this person must pay $40 more for the ten T-shirts he or she does buy than was the case when the price was $7. The other $20 in consumer surplus just disappears. In later chapters, we see how computations of this type can be used to judge the consequences of a wide variety of economic situations in which prices change. Application 3.6: Valuing Clean Air shows an application of the concept to environmental policy.

Consumer Surplus and Utility

The concept of consumer surplus can be tied directly to the theory of utility maximization we have been studying. Specifically, consumer surplus provides a way of putting a monetary value on the effects that changes in the marketplace have on people's utility. Consumer surplus is not really a new concept but just an alternative way of getting at the utility concepts with which we started the study of demand.

Valuing Clean Air

In recent years, a variety of environmental laws have been passed to clean up the nation's air, water, and land. Many of these actions are quite expensive with costs running into the billions of dollars. In order to determine whether such costs are warranted, economists have devised some ingenious procedures for evaluating the benefits that environmental regulations provide.

Estimating a Demand Curve

One method economists use to evaluate improvements is to look at how environmental factors affect measurable values in related markets. For example, by looking at the *ceteris paribus* relationship between air pollution levels in various locations and the prices of houses in these locations, it is possible to infer the amount that people will pay to avoid dirty air. One study of six metropolitan areas found that home owners were willing to pay between $20 and $80 more for a house in order to avoid one extra microgram of suspended particulates per cubic meter of air.[1] Using this information, it is possible to compute a demand curve for clean air as shown in Figure 1. The vertical axis shows the price home buyers seem willing to pay to avoid air pollution, and the horizontal axis shows the quantity of clear air purchased. Here, clean air is measured by the number of suspended particles and ranges from very dirty (100 micrograms per cubic meter) to very clean (0 micrograms per cubic meter). National average figures are reflected by point E on the demand curve: Home buyers pay about $50 to avoid one extra microgram of particulates and *consume* air containing an average of about 55 micrograms of suspended particulates per cubic meter.

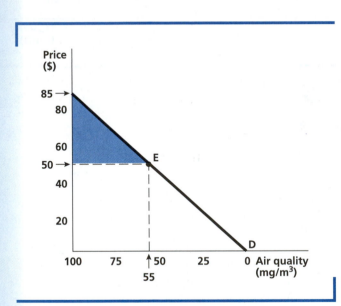

FIGURE 1 Demand Curve for Clean Air In their housing decisions, individuals pay $50 in extra housing costs to avoid 1 mg/m[1] of suspended particles. This improves air quality from 100 to 55 mg/m[1] and costs consumers $2,250. They receive consumer surplus of $788.

Consumer Surplus and the Value of Clean Air

Figure 1 shows that on average people are spending $2,250 (= $50 times a reduction of 45 micrograms of particulates) extra in housing costs to avoid dirty air. But this reflects only

[1] R. B. Palmquist, "Estimating the Demand for Characteristics of Housing," *Review of Economics and Statistics* (August 1989): 394–404. Prices have been updated to 2002 levels.

part of the value of cleaner air to consumers. At point E, individuals also receive a consumer surplus represented by the shaded triangle in the figure. This represents the additional amount that consumers would be willing to pay rather than being forced to live with dirty air. The value represented by this triangle is $788 (= [85 – 50] · [45] ÷ 2). This value can be multiplied by the total number of households to estimate the total consumer surplus from clean air.

To Think About

1. What is the total value of completely clean air for the typical person illustrated in Figure 1? How might this figure be used to evaluate environmental clean-up activities?
2. Does the use of a linear demand curve in Figure 1 seem reasonable? What does the curve imply about individuals' willingness to tolerate extra dirty air (more than 100 mg/m³)?

Figure 3.11 illustrates the connection between consumer surplus and utility. The figure shows a person's choices between a particular good (here again we use the T-shirt example) and "all other" goods he or she might buy. The budget constraint shows that with a $7 price and a budget constraint given by line I, this person would choose to consume twenty T-shirts along with $500 worth of other items. Including the $140 spent on T-shirts, total spending on all items would be $640. This consumption plan yields a utility level of U_1 to this person.

Now consider a situation in which T-shirts were not available—perhaps they are banned by a paternalistic government that objects to slogans written on the shirts. In this situation, this person requires some compensation if he or she is to continue to remain on the U_1 indifference curve. Specifically, an extra income given by distance AB would just permit this person to reach U_1 when there are no T-shirts available. It is possible to show that this dollar value is approximately equal to the consumer surplus figure computed in the previous section—that is, distance AB is approximately $80. Hence, consumer surplus can also be interpreted as measuring the amount one would have to compensate a person for withdrawing a product from the marketplace.

A somewhat different way to measure consumer surplus would be to ask how much income this person would be willing to pay for the right to consume T-shirts at $7 each. This amount would be given by distance BC in Figure 3.11. With a budget constraint given by I', this person can achieve that same utility level (U_0) that he or she could obtain with budget constraint I

MicroQuiz 3.5

Throughout this book, we see that consumer surplus areas are often triangular.

1. Explain why this area is measured in dollars. (Hint: What are the units of the height and width of the consumer surplus triangle?)

2. Suppose that the price of a product rose by 10 percent. Would you expect the size of the consumer surplus triangle to fall by more or less than 10 percent?

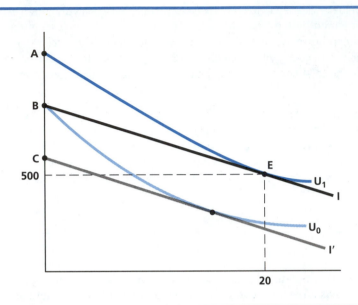

FIGURE 3.11 Consumer Surplus and Utility Initially, this person is at E with utility U_1. He or she would need to be compensated by amount AB in other goods to get U_1 if T-shirts were not available. He or she would also be willing to pay BC for the right to consume T-shirts rather than spending I only on other goods. Both distance AB and distance BC approximate the consumer surplus area in Figure 3.10.

if no T-shirts were available. Again, it is possible to show[5] that this amount also is approximately equal to the consumer surplus figure calculated in the previous section ($80). In this case, the figure represents the amount that a person would voluntarily give up in exchange for dropping a no-T-shirt law. Hence, both approaches reach the same conclusion—that consumer surplus provides a way of putting a dollar value on the utility people gain from being able to make market transactions.

Increases in the market price of T-shirts would again reduce these consumer surplus/utility measures. The correspondence between Fig-ure 3.10 and Fig-ure 3.11 would permit us to continue to study the welfare consequences of price changes using either graph. Because it is usually much easier to study these matters using a demand curve, however, that is the approach we take in later chapters.

[5] For a theoretical treatment of these issues, see R. D. Willig, "Consumer's Surplus without Apology," *American Economic Review* (September 1976): 589–597. Willig shows that distance AB in Figure 3.11 (which is termed the "compensating income variation") exceeds total consumer surplus whereas distance BC (termed the "equivalent income variation") is smaller than consumer surplus. All three measures approach the same value if income effects in the demand for the good in question are small.

SUMMARY

This chapter uses the model of individual choice to examine how people react to changes in income or prices. We have come to several important conclusions about the demand for a good:

- Proportionate changes in all prices and income will not affect choices because such changes do not shift the budget constraint.
- When income alone increases, the demand for a good will increase unless that good is inferior.
- A change in the price of a good has substitution and income effects that together cause changes in consumption choices. Except in the unlikely case of Giffen's paradox, a reduction in a good's price will cause more of it to be demanded. An increase in price will cause less of the good to be demanded.
- A change in the price of one good will usually affect the demand for other goods. If two goods are complements, an increase in the price of one will reduce the demand for the other. If the goods are substitutes, an increase in the price of one will increase the demand for the other.
- The demand for a good is also affected by preferences. Preferences are usually held constant under the *ceteris paribus* assumption in theoretical analysis, but changes in preferences can cause important shifts in real-world demand functions.
- Consumer surplus is the area below the demand curve and above the market price for a good. The area measures what people would pay for the right to consume the good at its current market price. Increases in the market price reduce the amount of consumer surplus that a person gets.

REVIEW QUESTIONS

1. Monica always buys one unit of food together with three units of housing, no matter what the prices of these two goods. Use this information to decide whether the following events would make her better off or worse off or leave her welfare unchanged.

   a. The prices of food and housing increase by 50 percent with Monica's income unchanged.
   b. The prices of food and clothing increase by 50 percent, and Monica's income increases by 50 percent.
   c. The price of food increases by 50 percent, the price of housing remains unchanged, and Monica's income increases by 25 percent.
   d. The price of food remains unchanged, the price of housing increases by 50 percent, and Monica's income increases by 25 percent.
   e. How might your answers to part c and part d change if Monica were willing to alter her mix of food and housing in response to price changes?

2. Suppose a person consumes only two goods, X and Y, and that the prices of these goods are fixed. How would the set of utility-maximizing points traced out by successively higher incomes look if

   a. this person always split his or her income equally between X and Y?
   b. X were a luxury, Y a necessity?
   c. Y were a luxury, X a necessity?
   d. an unchanging amount of X were bought as income expanded above some minimal amount?
   e. X were an inferior good? (Can Y be inferior here too?)

3. Suppose Jennifer always spends half her income on food. How will changes in the price of food affect the quantity of food consumed? How will changes in the price of food affect total spending on food? How large an increase in income would be needed to offset the effect of a 10 percent increase in the price of food?

4. Ivan always buys left and right shoes in pairs. Explain why a sale on right shoes will have an income effect but no substitution effect on his left and right shoe purchases.

5. Suppose George doesn't care what brand of toothpaste he buys. Show graphically why he will always buy the cheapest brand.

6. Is the following statement true or false? Explain. "Every Giffen good must be inferior, but not every inferior good exhibits the Giffen paradox."

7. Suppose that Eve never changes the quantity of water she consumes when the price of water changes. How do income and substitution effects work in this case?

8. When coffee prices rise, John buys more tea but fewer coffee mugs. Explain the substitution and income effects of the price change on these two goods.

9. Does the theory of consumer choice require that an individual's demand curve for a good be downward sloping? In what case would a demand curve be vertical? When might it be positively sloped?

10. Explain whether the following events would result in a move along an individual's demand curve for popcorn or in a shift of the curve. If the curve would shift, in what direction?

   a. An increase in the individual's income
   b. A decline in popcorn prices
   c. An increase in prices for pretzels
   d. A reduction in the amount of butter included in a box of popcorn
   e. The presence of long waiting lines to buy popcorn
   f. A sales tax on all popcorn purchases

PROBLEMS

3.1 Elizabeth M. Suburbs makes $200 a week at her summer job and spends her entire weekly income on new running shoes and designer jeans, since these are the only two items that provide utility to her. Furthermore, Elizabeth insists that for every pair of jeans she buys, she must also buy a pair of shoes (without the shoes, the new jeans are worthless). Therefore, she buys the same number of pairs of shoes and jeans in any given week.

a. If jeans cost $20 and shoes cost $20, how many will Elizabeth buy of each?

b. Suppose that the price of jeans rises to $30 a pair. How many shoes and jeans will she buy?

c. Show your results by graphing the budget constraints from part a and part b. Also draw Elizabeth's indifference curves.

d. To what effect (income or substitution) do you attribute the change in utility levels between part a and part b?

3.2 Consider again the clothing choices of Ms. Suburbs from problem 3.1. Assume again that she always buys running shoes and jeans in combination

and that initially the price of shoes is $20 and that her income is $200.

a. How many pairs of jeans will this person choose to buy if jeans prices are $30, $20, $10, or $5?

b. Use the information from part a to graph Ms. Suburbs's demand curve for jeans.

c. Suppose that her income rises to $300. Graph her demand curve for jeans in this new situation.

d. Suppose that the price of running shoes rises to $30 per pair. How will this affect the demand curves drawn in part b and part c?

3.3 The Jones family spends all its income on food and shelter. It derives maximum utility when it spends two-thirds of its income on shelter and one-third on food.

a. Use this information to calculate the demand functions for shelter and food. Show that demand is homogeneous with respect to changes in all prices and income.

b. Graph the demand curves for shelter and food for the Jones family if family income is $20,000.

c. Show how the demand curves for shelter and food would shift if income rose to $50,000.

d. Explain why a change in food prices does not affect shelter purchases in this problem.

3.4 Mr. Wright, a clothing salesman, is forced by his employer to spend at least $100 of his weekly income of $500 on clothing. Show that his utility level is lower than if he could freely allocate his income between clothing and other goods.

3.5 Pete Moss buys 100 units of fertilizer and 80 units of grass seed along with quantities of other goods. The price of fertilizer rises by $.40 per unit, and the price of grass seed drops by $.50 per unit; other prices and Pete's income remain unchanged. Will Pete buy more, less, or the same amount of fertilizer? Explain. (Hint: How do the price changes affect Pete's budget constraint?)

3.6 David gets $3 per month as an allowance to spend any way he pleases. Since he likes only peanut butter and jelly sandwiches, he spends the entire amount on peanut butter (at $.05 per ounce) and jelly (at $.10 per ounce). Bread is provided free of charge by a concerned neighbor. David is a picky eater and makes his sandwiches with exactly 1 ounce of jelly and 2 ounces of peanut butter. He is set in his ways and will never change these proportions.

a. How much peanut butter and jelly will David buy with his $3 allowance in a week?

b. Suppose the price of jelly were to rise to $.15 per ounce. How much of each commodity would be bought?

c. By how much should David's allowance be increased to compensate for the rise in the price of jelly in part b?

d. Graph your results of part a through part c.

e. In what sense does this problem involve only a single commodity—peanut butter and jelly sandwiches? Graph the demand curve for this single commodity.

f. Discuss the results of this problem in terms of the income and substitution effects involved in the demand for jelly.

3.7 Each year Sam Mellow grows 200 units of wheat and 100 units of sunflower seeds for his own consumption and for sale to the outside world. Wheat and sunflower seeds are the only two items that provide utility to Sam. They are also his only source of income. Sam cannot save his proceeds from year to year.

a. If the price of wheat is $2 per unit and sunflower seeds sell for $10 per unit, Sam chooses to sell 20 units of the sunflower seeds he produces while retaining 80 units for his own use. Show Sam's utility-maximizing situation and indicate both his initial production levels and the amount of additional wheat he will buy with the proceeds from his sunflower seed sales.

b. Suppose sunflower seed prices fall to $6 per unit while wheat prices remain unchanged. Will Sam be made better or worse off by this price decline? Or is the situation ambiguous? Explain carefully using a graphic analysis. Show that if Sam is to be made better off by the price decline he must become a seller of wheat and a buyer of sunflower seeds.

c. Explain using the terms *income effect* and *substitution effect* why the analysis in part b differs from the usual case in which a price decline always increases an individual's utility level.

   (Hint: To begin this problem, show that Sam's budget constraint always passes through the point Wheat = 200, Sunflower seeds = 100.)

3.8 Irene's demand for pizza is given by:

$$Q = \frac{0.3I}{P}$$

where Q is the weekly quantity of pizza bought (in slices), I is weekly income, and P is the price of pizza. Using this demand function, answer the following:

a. Is this function homogeneous in I and P?

b. Graph this function for the case I = 200.

c. One problem in using this function to study consumer surplus is that Q never reaches zero no matter how high P is. Hence, suppose that the function holds only for P ≤ 10 and that Q = 0 for

P > 10. How should your graph in part b be adjusted to fit this assumption?

d. With this demand function (and I = 200), it can be shown that the area of consumer surplus is approximately CS = 198 − 6P − 60 ln(P) where "ln(P)" refers to the natural logarithm of P. Show that if P = 10, CS = 0.

e. Suppose P = 3. How much pizza is demanded and how much consumer surplus does Irene receive? Give an economic interpretation to this magnitude.

f. If P were to increase to 4, how much would Irene demand and what would her consumer surplus be? Give an economic interpretation to why the value of CS has fallen.

3.9 The demand curves we studied in this chapter were constructed holding a person's nominal income constant—hence, changes in prices introduced changes in real income (that is, utility). Another way to draw a demand curve is to hold utility constant as prices change. That is, the person is "compensated" for any effects that the prices have on his or her utility. Such *compensated demand curves* illustrate only substitution effects, not income effects. Using this idea, show that:

a. For any initial utility-maximizing position, the regular demand curve and the compensated demand curve pass through the same price/quantity point.

b. The compensated demand curve is generally steeper than the regular demand curve.

c. Any regular demand curve intersects many different compensated demand curves.

d. If Irving consumes only pizza and chianti in fixed proportions of one slice of pizza to one glass of chianti, his regular demand curve for pizza will be downward-sloping but his compensated demand curve(s) will be vertical.

3.10 The residents of Uurp consume only pork chops (X) and Coca-Cola (Y). The utility function for the typical resident of Uurp is given by

$$\text{Utility} = U(X, Y) = \sqrt{X \cdot Y}$$

In 2002, the price of pork chops in Uurp was $1 each; Cokes were also $1 each. The typical resident consumed 40 pork chops and 40 Cokes (saving is impossible in Uurp). In 2003, swine fever hit Uurp and pork chop prices rose to $4; the Coke price remained unchanged. At these new prices, the typical Uurp resident consumed 20 pork chops and 80 Cokes.

a. Show that utility for the typical Uurp resident was unchanged between the 2 years.

b. Show that using 2002 prices would show an increase in real income between the 2 years.

c. Show that using 2003 prices would show a decrease in real income between the years.

d. What do you conclude about the ability of these indexes to measure changes in real income?

INTERNET EXERCISES

1. *The Food Stamp Program.* If you were offered the choice between $100 in movie tickets and $100 in cash, which would you take? If you are like most people, you would take the cash. As Application 3.3 illustrates, individuals are generally better off with an outright cash grant than they would be under an equivalent in-kind transfer. The Food Stamp Program is one example in which individuals are subsidized with in-kind benefits. Under this program, low-income individuals are given a fixed dollar amount in food coupons that may only be applied toward the purchase of food. Information about the Food Stamp Program can be found at the USDA Food Stamp Program Web site at *http://www.fns.usda.gov/fsp*. Go to Program Data and then click on National Level Annual Summary. For the most recent year listed, on average, how many program recipients were there? What was the dollar value of total benefits distributed? What was the average monthly benefit per person? Go back to the Web site's main page and click on Search to per-

form a search for "participation rate trend." For the most recent year given, what percentage of eligible individuals actually received food stamps? Why do you think this percentage is not closer to 100 percent?

2. *Price indexes and cost of living.* At some point in your career, you may be faced with a tempting job offer that requires you to relocate to another state. Let's assume that you currently live in Hartford, Connecticut, and earn $40,000 per year. Suppose you are offered the opportunity to relocate to San Francisco, California, where your salary would be $55,000 per year. Should you make the move? After all, you would be earning more money, right? Well, you would probably also want to know something about the relative cost of living between the two places. Application 3.2 demonstrates how the consumer price index can be used to compare average price levels over time. Similar price indexes can also be used to compare average price levels across geographic regions. One handy cost of living calculator can be found at *http://www.chelafinancial.com/studentcenter/ studentcenter.cfm?referurl=overture_studctr.* In the drop-down menu, select the cost of living calculator. Use the calculator to estimate what salary you would have to earn in San Francisco to maintain the same standard of living as you presently enjoy in Hartford. *Ceteris paribus,* based on this answer, should you make the move? In light of the discussion of substitution bias in Application 3.2, however, is it possible that you could actually be better off in San Francisco with a salary of $55,000 than in Hartford with a salary of $40,000? Explain.

Market Demand and Elasticity

In this chapter, we show how individual demand curves are "added up" to create the market demand curve for a good. Market demand curves reflect the actions of many people and show how these actions are affected by market prices.

This chapter also describes a few ways of measuring market demand. We introduce the concept of elasticity and show how we can use it to summarize how the quantity demanded of a good changes in response to changes in income and prices.

MARKET DEMAND CURVES

Market demand
The total quantity of a good or service demanded by all potential buyers.

Market demand curve
The relationship between the total quantity demanded of a good or service and its price, holding all other factors constant.

The **market demand** for a good is the total quantity of the good demanded by all potential buyers. The **market demand curve** shows the relationship between this total quantity demanded and the market price of the good, when all other things that affect demand are held constant. The market demand curve's shape and position are determined by the shape of individuals' demand curves for the product in question. Market demand is nothing more than the combined effect of many economic choices by consumers.

Construction of the Market Demand Curve

Figure 4.1 shows the construction of the market demand curve for good X when there are only two buyers. For each price, the point on the market demand curve is found by summing the quantities demanded by each person. For example, at a price of P_X^*, individual 1 demands X_1^*, and individual 2 demands X_2^*. The total quantity demanded at the market at P_X^* is therefore the sum of these two amounts: $X^* = X_1^* + X_2^*$. Consequently the point X^*, P_X^* is one point on the market

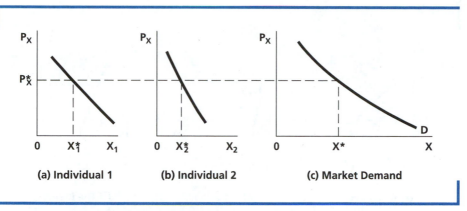

FIGURE 4.1 Constructing a Market Demand Curve from Individual Demand Curves A market demand curve is the horizontal sum of individual demand curves. At each price, the quantity in the market is the sum of the amounts each person demands. For example, at P_X^* the demand in the market is $X_1^* + X_2^* = X^*$.

demand curve D. The other points on the curve are plotted in the same way. The market curve is simply the horizontal sum of each person's demand curve. At every possible price, we ask how much is demanded by each person, and then we add up these amounts to arrive at the quantity demanded by the whole market. The demand curve summarizes the *ceteris paribus* relationship between the quantity demanded of X and its price. If other things that influence demand do not change, the position of the curve will remain fixed and will reflect how people as a group respond to price changes.

Shifts in the Market Demand Curve

Why would a market demand curve shift? We already know why individual demand curves shift. To discover how some event might shift a market demand curve, we must first find out how this event causes individual demand curves to shift and then compare the horizontal sum of these new demand curves with the old market demand. In some cases, the direction of a shift in the market demand curve is reasonably predictable. For example, using our two-buyer case, if both of their incomes increase and both regard X as a normal good, then each person's demand curve would shift outward. Hence, the market demand curve would also shift outward. At each price, more would be demanded in the market because each person could afford to buy more. This situation in which a general rise in income increases market demand is illustrated in Figure 4.2. Application 4.1: Why the 2001 Tax Cut Was a Dud shows how this notion can be used to study the effects of tax cuts, although, as is often the case in economics, the story is not quite as simple as it appears to be.

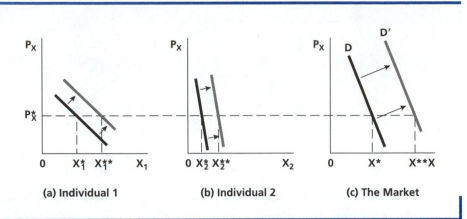

(a) Individual 1   **(b) Individual 2**   **(c) The Market**

FIGURE 4.2 Increases in Each Individual's Income Cause the Market Demand Curve to Shift Outward An increase in income for each individual causes the individual demand curve for X to shift out (assuming X is a normal good). For example, at P_X^*, individual 1 now demands X_1^{**} instead of X_1^*. The market demand curve shifts out to D'. X* was demanded at P_X^* before the income increase. Now X^{**} ($= X_1^{**} + X_2^{**}$) is demanded.

In some cases, the direction that a market demand curve shifts may be ambiguous. For example, suppose that one person's income increases but a second person's income decreases. The location of the new market demand curve now depends on the relative shifts in the individual demand curves that these income changes cause. The curve could either shift inward or shift outward.

What holds true for our simple two-person example also applies to much larger groups of demanders—perhaps even to the entire economy. In this case, the market demand summarizes the behavior of all possible consumers. If personal income in the United States as a whole were to rise, the effect on the market demand curve for pizza would depend on whether the income gains went to people who love pizza or to people who never touch it. If the gains went to pizza lovers, the U.S. market demand for pizza would shift outward significantly. It would not shift at all if the income gains went only to pizza haters.

A change in the price of some other good (Y) will also affect the market demand for X. If the price of Y rises, for example, the market demand curve for X will shift outward if most buyers regard X and Y as substitutes. On the other hand, an increase in the price of Y will cause the market demand curve for X to shift inward if most people regard the two goods as complements.

A Simplified Notation

Often in this book we look at only one market. In order to simplify the notation, we use the letter Q for the quantity of a good demanded (per week) in this market, and we use P for its price. When we draw a demand curve in the Q, P plane,

In May 2001, the U.S. Congress passed one of the largest cuts in personal income taxes in history. The cuts are to be implemented over a 10-year period and will (over that period) amount to more than $1.6 trillion. As a "down payment" on this sum, the law provided that most U.S. taxpayers receive an immediate check for $300 (or $600 for a married couple), and these checks rolled out of the Treasury at the rate of 9 million per week during the summer of 2001. Many politicians argued that such a large tax reduction would have an important effect on fighting the recession that was then beginning by boosting the demand for virtually every good. But such a prediction ignored both economic theory and the realities of the bizarre U.S. tax system. Ultimately, the tax cut seems to have had virtually no impact on consumer spending.

The Permanent Income Hypothesis

Our discussion of demand theory showed that changes in people's incomes do indeed shift demand curves outward. But we were a bit careless in defining exactly what income is. Milton Friedman made one of the most important discoveries that clarify this question in the 1950s. He argued that spending decisions are based on a person's long-term view of his or her economic circumstances.[1] Short-term increases or decreases in income have little effect on spending patterns. Friedman's view that spending decisions are based on a person's "permanent" income is now widely accepted by economists. Virtually all studies of actual spending behavior rely on this insight.

Tax Cuts and Permanent Income

According to Friedman's theory, a tax reduction will affect a person's spending only to the extent that it affects his or her permanent income. This insight suggests that the 2001 tax act had little impact for two reasons. First, consider the $300 checks. These came to people "out of the blue," and everyone knew that such largess would not continue. The checks were too small to stimulate spending on any major goods, so they were largely saved. People made no changes in what they were already intending to buy. In this, they were exhibiting exactly the same sort of nonresponse that they had shown in many previous episodes including temporary tax increases in the late 1960s and temporary reductions in the 1970s.

Now consider the effect of the overall tax act, a plan that was intended to be implemented over a 10-year period. Because of wrangling in Congress, the actual schedule of tax cuts is "back-loaded." That is, most of the cuts do not begin until 2006, and the largest cuts are reserved until 2009–10. Such distant tax cuts probably have little impact on people's perceptions of their economic situations. In purely dollar terms, the present value[2] of such distant tax savings is much smaller than their actual stated amounts. Perhaps more

---

[1] Milton Friedman, *A Theory of the Consumption Function* (Princeton, NJ: Princeton University Press, 1957). Recent amendments to Friedman's theory stress the "life-cycle" nature of income and spending decisions—that is, people are assumed to plan their spending over their entire life.

[2] The present value of a sum payable in the future is less than the actual amount because of forgone interest. For a discussion of this concept, see Chapter 14 and its Appendix.

important, taxpayers have become very familiar with constantly changing tax laws and probably have little faith that tax cuts projected for many years in the future will actually occur. That is, many of the tax reductions promised under the 2001 act were simply not "credible."

Complexities in the Income Tax

Another set of reasons that led to the ineffectiveness of the 2001 tax cuts relate to the complexities in the U.S. income tax itself. First, all of the rate changes in the bill were subject to "sunset" provisions—in 2011, tax rates are supposed to return to 2001 levels. In effect, the entire tax bill is a temporary one. What happens after 2011 is anyone's guess. Second, the bill did not deal with the *alternative minimum tax* (AMT)—a provision of the U.S. income tax originally intended to catch fat cats who pay little taxes, but one that has increasingly affected middle-income taxpayers. Under this arcane provision, much of the effect of the tax reductions promised under the 2001 act will be neutralized by increased taxes collected under the AMT. Finally, many of the tax reductions in the 2001 bill came about through special credits for all sorts of items such as college tuitions and energy conservation. How these actually affect the purchasing power of the average citizen obviously depends on whether they wish to spend their incomes on the especially favored items. Certainly the effect is not just a simple shift outward in people's budget constraints.

To Think About

1. If a person makes economic decisions based on his or her permanent income, how much might be spent currently out of an unexpected $300 check from the government?
2. How might people differ in the ways in which they respond to getting a tax rebate check from the government?

we assume that all other factors affecting demand are held constant. That is, income, the price of other goods, and preferences are assumed not to change. If one of these factors should change, the demand curve would probably shift. As was the case for individual demand curves, the term "change in quantity demanded" is used for a movement along a given market demand curve, and the term "change in demand" is used for a shift in the entire curve.

ELASTICITY

Economists frequently need to show how changes in one variable affect some other variable. They ask, for example, how much does a change in the price of electricity affect the quantity of it demanded, or how does a change in income affect total expenditures on automobiles? One problem in summarizing these kinds of effects is that goods are measured in different ways. For example, steak is typically sold per pound, whereas oranges are generally sold per dozen. A $.10 per pound rise in the price of steak might cause consumption of it to fall by

2 pounds per week, and a \$.10 per dozen rise in the price of oranges might cause orange purchases to fall by one-half dozen per week. But there is no way to compare the change in steak sales to the change in orange sales. When two goods are measured in different units, we cannot make a simple comparison between them to determine which item is more responsive to changes in its price.

In order to make these comparisons, economists use the concept of **elasticity**. In general, the elasticity of variable B with respect to changes in variable A is defined as the percentage change in B brought about by a 1 percent change in A. Elasticity is unit-free—it compares one percentage to another, and the units disappear. In our oranges and steak example, a 1 percent rise in the price of steak might lead to a 2 percent decline in the quantity bought, whereas a 1 percent rise in the price of oranges might lead to only a 1 percent decline in the quantity bought. Steak purchases in this example are more responsive to price than orange purchases are. The fact that steak and oranges are measured in different ways is no longer a problem.

> **MicroQuiz 4.1**
>
> A shift outward in a demand curve can be described either by the extent of its shift in the horizontal direction or by its shift in the vertical direction. How would the following shifts be shown graphically?
>
> **1.** News that nutmeg cures the common cold causes people to demand 2 million pounds more nutmeg *at each price.*
>
> **2.** News that nutmeg cures the common cold causes people to be willing to pay \$1 more per pound of nutmeg *for each possible quantity.*

Elasticity
The measure of the percentage change in one variable brought about by a 1 percent change in some other variable.

PRICE ELASTICITY OF DEMAND

Although there are many different applications of elasticity in this book, probably the most important is the **price elasticity of demand**. Changes in P (the price of a good) will lead to changes in Q (the quantity of it purchased), and the price elasticity of demand measures this relationship. Specifically, the price elasticity of demand ($e_{Q,P}$) is defined as the percentage change in quantity in response to a 1 percent change in price. In mathematical terms,

Price elasticity of demand
The percentage change in the quantity demanded of a good in response to a 1 percent change in its price.

$$\text{Price elasticity of demand} = e_{Q,P} = \frac{\text{Percentage change in Q}}{\text{Percentage change in P}} \quad (4.1)$$

This elasticity records how Q changes in percentage terms in response to a percentage change in P. Because P and Q move in opposite directions (except in the rare case of Giffen's paradox), $e_{Q,P}$ will be negative.[1] For example, a value of $e_{Q,P}$ of –1 means that a 1 percent rise in price leads to a 1 percent decline in quantity,

---

[1] Sometimes the price elasticity of demand is defined as the absolute value of the definition in Equation 4.1. Using this definition, elasticity is never negative; curves are classified as elastic, unit elastic, or inelastic depending on whether $e_{Q,P}$ is greater than, equal to, or less than 1. You need to recognize this distinction as there is no consistent use in economic literature.

TABLE 4.1 Terminology for the Ranges of $e_{Q,P}$	
Value of $e_{Q,P}$ at a Point on Demand Curve	Terminology for Curve at This Point
$e_{Q,P} < -1$	Elastic
$e_{Q,P} = -1$	Unit elastic
$e_{Q,P} > -1$	Inelastic

whereas a value of $e_{Q,P}$ of -2 means that a 1 percent rise in price causes quantity to decline by 2 percent.

Values of the Price Elasticity of Demand

A distinction is often made among values of $e_{Q,P}$ that are less than, equal to, or greater than -1. Table 4.1 lists the terms used for each value. For an elastic curve ($e_{Q,P}$ is less[2] than -1), a price increase causes a more than proportional quantity decrease. If $e_{Q,P} = -3$, for example, each 1 percent rise in price causes quantity to fall by 3 percent. For a unit elastic curve ($e_{Q,P}$ is equal to -1), a price increase causes a decrease in quantity of the same proportion. For an inelastic curve ($e_{Q,P}$ is greater than -1), price increases proportionally more than quantity decreases. If $e_{Q,P} = -\frac{1}{2}$, a 1 percent rise in price causes quantity to fall by only $\frac{1}{2}$ of 1 percent. In general then, if a demand curve is elastic, changes in price along the curve affect quantity significantly; if the curve is inelastic, price has little effect on quantity demanded.

Price Elasticity and the Shape of the Demand Curve

We often classify the market demand for goods by their price elasticities of demand. For example, the demand for most medical services is very inelastic. The market demand curve here may be almost vertical, showing that the quantity demanded is not responsive to price changes. On the other hand, price changes will have a major effect on the quantity demanded of a particular kind of candy bar (the demand is elastic). Here the market demand curve would be relatively flat. If market price were to change even slightly, the quantity demanded would change significantly because people would buy other kinds of candy bars.

Price Elasticity and the Substitution Effect

The discussion of income and substitution effects in Chapter 3 provides a theoretical basis for judging what the size of the price elasticity for particular goods might be. Goods with many close substitutes (brands of breakfast cereal, small cars, brands of electronic calculators, and so on) are subject to large substitution effects from a price change. For these kinds of goods, we can presume that demand will be elastic ($e_{Q,P} < -1$). On the other hand, goods with few close substitutes (water, insulin, and salt, for example) have small substitution effects

---

[2] Remember, numbers like -3 are *less than* -1 whereas $-\frac{1}{2}$ is *greater than* -1. Because we are accustomed to thinking only of positive numbers, comparisons among price elasticities can sometimes be confusing.

when their prices change. Demand for such goods will probably be inelastic with respect to price changes ($e_{Q,P} > -1$; that is, $e_{Q,P}$ is between 0 and −1). Of course, as we mentioned previously, price changes also create income effects on the quantity demanded of a good, which we must consider to completely assess the likely size of overall price elasticities. Still, because the price changes for most goods have only a small effect on people's real incomes, the existence (or nonexistence) of substitutes is probably the principal determinant of price elasticity.

Price Elasticity and Time

Making substitutions in consumption choices may take time. To change from one brand of cereal to another may only take a week (to finish eating the first box), but to change from heating your house with oil to heating it with electricity may take years because a new heating system must be installed. We already have seen in Application 3.4: Why Are So Many "Trucks" on the Road? that trends in gasoline prices may have little short-term impact because people already own their cars and have relatively fixed travel needs. Over a longer term, however, there is clear evidence that people will change the kinds of cars they drive in response to falling real gasoline prices. In general then, it might be expected that substitution effects and the related price elasticities would be larger the longer the time period that people have to change their behavior. In some situations it is important to make a distinction between short-term and long-term price elasticities of demand, since the long-term concept may show much greater responses to price change. In Application 4.2: Brand Loyalty, we look at a few cases where this distinction can be quite important.

Price Elasticity and Total Expenditures

The price elasticity of demand is useful for studying how total expenditures on a good change in response to a price change. Total expenditures on a good are found by multiplying the good's price (P) times the quantity purchased (Q). If demand is elastic, a price increase will cause total expenditures to fall. When demand is elastic, a given percentage increase in price is more than counterbalanced in its effect on total spending by the resulting large decrease in quantity demanded. For example, suppose people are currently buying 1 million automobiles at $10,000 each. Total expenditures on automobiles amount to $10 billion. Suppose also that the price elasticity of demand for automobiles is −2. Now, if the price increases to $11,000 (a 10 percent increase), the quantity purchased would fall to 800,000 cars (a 20 percent fall). Total expenditures are now $8.8 billion. Because demand is elastic, the price increase causes total expenditures to fall. This example can be easily reversed to show that, if demand is elastic, a fall in price will cause total expenditures to increase. The extra sales generated by a fall in price more than compensate for the reduced price in this case. For example, a number of computer software producers have discovered that they can increase

Brand Loyalty

One reason that substitution effects are larger over longer periods than over shorter ones is that people develop spending habits that do not change easily.

For example, when faced with a variety of brands consisting of the same basic product, they may develop loyalty to a particular brand, purchasing it on a regular basis. This behavior makes sense because a person does not need to reevaluate products continually. Thus, decision-making costs are reduced. Brand loyalty also reduces the likelihood of brand substitutions even when there are short-term price differentials. Over the long term, however, price differences can tempt buyers into trying other brands and thereby switch their loyalties.

Automobiles

The competition between American and Japanese automakers provides a good example of changing loyalties. Prior to the 1980s, Americans exhibited considerable loyalty to U.S. automobiles. Repeat purchases of the same brand were a common pattern. In the early 1970s, Japanese automobiles began making inroads into the American market on a price basis. The lower prices of Japanese cars eventually convinced Americans to buy them. Satisfied with their experiences, by the 1980s many Americans developed loyalty to Japanese brands. This loyalty was encouraged, in part, by large differences in quality between Japanese and U.S. cars that became especially wide in the mid-1980s. Although U.S. automakers seem to have closed some of the quality gap in the 1990s, lingering loyalty to Japanese autos has made it difficult to regain market share. By one estimate, U.S. cars would have to sell for approximately $1,600 less than their Japanese counterparts in order to encourage buyers of Japanese cars to switch.[1]

Licensing of Brand Names

The advantages of brand loyalty have not been lost on innovative marketers. Famous trademarks such as Coca-Cola, Harley-Davidson, or even Disney's Mickey Mouse have been applied to products rather different from the originals. For example, Coca-Cola for a period licensed its famous name and symbol to makers of sweatshirts and blue jeans in the hope that this would differentiate the products from their generic competitors. Similarly, Mickey Mouse is one of the most popular trademarks in Japan, appearing on products both conventional (watches and lunchboxes) and unconventional (fashionable handbags and neckties).

The economics behind these moves are straightforward. Prior to licensing, products are virtually perfect substitutes and consumers shift readily among various makers. Licensing creates somewhat lower price responsiveness for the branded product, so producers can charge more for it without losing all their sales. The large fees paid to Coca-Cola, Disney, Michael Jordan, or major league baseball provide strong evidence of the strategy's profitability.

[1] F. Mannering and C. Winston, "Brand Loyalty and the Decline of American Automobile Firms," *Brookings Papers on Economic Activity, Microeconomics* (1991): 67–113.

To Think About

1.   Does the speed with which price differences erode brand loyalties depend on the frequency with which products are bought? Why might differences between short-term and long-term price elasticities be much greater for brands of automobiles than for brands of toothpaste?
2.   Why do people buy licensed products when they could probably buy generic brands at much lower prices? Does the observation that people pay 50 percent more for Nike shoes endorsed by basketball star Michael Jordan than for identical no-name competitors violate the assumptions of utility maximization?

their total revenues by selling at low, cut-rate prices. The extra users attracted by low prices more than compensates for those low prices.[3]

If demand is unit elastic ($e_{Q,P} = -1$), total expenditures stay the same when prices change. A movement of P in one direction causes an exactly opposite proportional movement in Q, and the total price-times-quantity stays fixed. Even if prices fluctuate substantially, total spending on a good with unit elastic demand never changes.

Finally, when demand is inelastic, a price rise will cause total expenditures to rise. A price rise in an inelastic situation does not cause a very large reduction in quantity demanded, and total expenditures will increase. For example, suppose people buy 100 million bushels of wheat per year at a price of $3 per bushel. Total expenditures on wheat are $300 million. Suppose also that the price elasticity of demand for wheat is −0.5 (demand is inelastic). If the price of wheat rises to $3.60 per bushel (a 20 percent increase), quantity demanded will fall by 10 percent (to 90 million bushels). The net result of these actions is to increase total expenditures on wheat to $324 million. Because the quantity of wheat demanded is not very responsive to changes in price, total revenues are increased by a price rise. This same example could also be reversed to show that, in the inelastic case, total revenues are reduced by a fall in price. Application 4.3: Volatile Farm Prices illustrates how inelastic demand can result in highly unstable prices when supply conditions change.

The relationship between price elasticity and total expenditures is summarized in Table 4.2. You should think through the logic of each entry in the table to obtain a working knowledge of the elasticity concept. These relationships are used many times in later chapters.

---

[3] Of course, costs are also important to software producers; but the extra cost of producing more copies of a software program is very low.

Volatile Farm Prices

The demand for agricultural products is relatively inelastic. That is especially true for such basic crops as wheat, corn, or soybeans. An important implication of this inelasticity is that even modest changes in supply, often brought about by weather patterns, can have large effects on the prices of these crops. This volatility in crop prices has been a feature of farming throughout all of history.

The Paradox of Agriculture

Recognition of the fundamental economics of farm crops yields paradoxical insights about the influence of the weather on farmers' well-being. "Good" weather can produce bountiful crops and abysmally low prices, whereas "bad" weather (in moderation) can result in attractively high prices. For example, relatively modest supply disruptions in the U.S. grain belt during the early 1970s caused an explosion in farm prices. Farmers' incomes increased more than 40 percent over a short, 2-year period. These incomes quickly fell back again when more normal weather patterns returned.

This paradoxical situation also results in somewhat misleading news coverage of localized droughts. Television news reporters will usually cover such droughts by showing the viewer a shriveled ear of corn, leaving the impression that all farmers are being devastated. That is undoubtedly true for the farmer whose parched field is being shown (though he or she may also have irrigated fields next door). But the larger story of local droughts is that the price increases they bring benefit most farmers outside the immediate area—a story that is seldom told.

Volatile Prices and Government Programs

Ever since the New Deal of the 1930s, the volatility of U.S. crop prices was moderated through a variety of federal price-support schemes. These schemes operated in two ways. First, through various acreage restrictions, the laws constrained the extent to which farmers could increase their plantings. In many cases, farmers were paid to keep their land fallow. A second way in which prices were supported was through direct purchases of crops by the government. By manipulating purchases and sales from grain reserves, the government was able to moderate any severe swings in price that may have otherwise occurred. All of that seemed to have ended in 1996 with the passage of the Federal Agricultural Improvement and Reform (FAIR) Act. That act sharply reduced government intervention in farm markets.

Initially, farm prices held up quite well following the passage of the FAIR Act. Throughout 1996 and 1997, they remained significantly above their levels of the early 1990s. But the increased plantings encouraged by the act in combination with downturns in some Asian economies caused a decline in crop prices of nearly 20 percent between 1998 and 2000. Though prices staged a bit of a rebound in early 2001, by the end of the year they had again fallen back. Faced with elections in November 2002, this created considerable pressure on politicians to do something. Such pressures culminated in the passage of a 10-year, $83 billion farm subsidy bill in May of 2002. That bill largely reversed many of the provisions of the FAIR Act. It increased assistance to wheat and corn farmers and expanded subsidies to such essential farm products as peanuts, honey, and mohair. The bill also brought threats of retaliation from many U.S. trading partners as its subsidies were perceived to give unfair advantages to American farmers in international markets. Clearly, the volatility of farm prices will continue to exert political influences so long as farmers vote in close elections.

To Think About
1. The volatility of farm prices is both good and bad news for farmers. Since periods of low prices are often followed by periods of high prices, the long-term welfare of farmers is hard to determine. Would farmers be better off if their prices had smaller fluctuations around the same trend levels?
2. How should fluctuations in foreign demand for U.S. crops be included in a supply-demand model? Do such fluctuations make crop prices even more volatile?

TABLE 4.2 Relationship between Price Changes and Changes in Total Expenditure

If demand is	In response to an increase in price, expenditures will	In response to a decrease in price, expenditures will
Elastic	Fall	Rise
Unit elastic	Not change	Not change
Inelastic	Rise	Fall

DEMAND CURVES AND PRICE ELASTICITY

The relationship between a particular demand curve and the price elasticity it exhibits is relatively complicated. Although it is common to talk about *the* price elasticity of demand for a good, this usage conveys the false impression that price elasticity necessarily has the same value at every point on a market demand curve. A more accurate way of speaking is to say that "at current prices, the price elasticity of demand is . . ." and, thereby, leave open the possibility that the elasticity may take on some other value at a different point on the demand curve. In some cases, this distinction may be unimportant because the price elasticity of demand has the same value over the range of demand being examined. In other cases, the distinction may be important, especially when large movements along a demand curve are being considered.

Linear Demand Curves and Price Elasticity

Probably the most important illustration of this warning about elasticities occurs in the case of a linear (straight-line) demand curve. As one moves along such a curve, the price elasticity of demand is always changing value. At high price

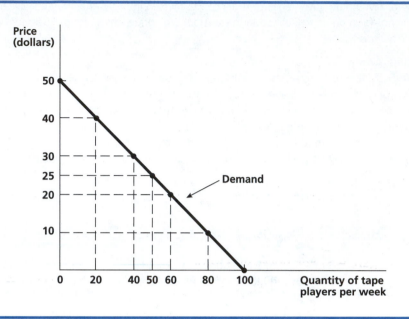

FIGURE 4.3 Elasticity Varies along a Linear Demand Curve A straight-line demand curve is elastic in its upper portion, inelastic in its lower portion. This relationship is illustrated by considering how total expenditures change for different points on the demand curve.

levels, demand is elastic; that is, a fall in price increases quantity purchased more than proportionally. At low prices, on the other hand, demand is inelastic; a further decline in price has relatively little proportional effect on quantity.

This result can be most easily shown with a numerical example. Figure 4.3 illustrates a straight-line (linear) demand curve for, say, portable cassette tape players. In looking at the changing elasticity of demand along this curve, we will assume it has the specific algebraic form

$$Q = 100 - 2P \tag{4.2}$$

where Q is the quantity of players demanded per week and P is their price. The demonstration would be the same for any other linear equation we might choose. Table 4.3 shows a few price-quantity combinations that lie on the demand curve, and these points are also reflected in Figure 4.3. Notice, in particular, that the quantity demanded is zero for prices of $50 or greater.

Table 4.3 also records total expenditures on tape players (P · Q) represented by each of the points on the demand curve. These expenditures are also repre-

TABLE 4.3 Price, Quantity, and Total Expenditures of Tape Players for the Demand Function

Price (P)	Quantity (Q)	Total expenditures (P × Q)
$50	0	$0
40	20	800
30	40	1,200
25	50	1,250
20	60	1,200
10	80	800
0	100	0

sented by the areas of the various rectangles in Figure 4.3. For prices of $50 or above, total expenditures are $0. No matter how high the price, if nothing is bought, expenditures are $0. As price falls below $50, total expenditures increase. At P = $40, total expenditures are $800 ($40 · 20), and for P = $30, the figure rises to $1,200 ($30 · 40).

For high prices, the demand curve in Figure 4.3 is elastic; a fall in price causes enough additional sales to increase total expenditures. This increase in total expenditures begins to slow as price drops still further. In fact, total spending reaches a maximum at a price of $25. When P = $25, Q = 50 and total expenditures on tape players are $1,250. For prices below $25, reductions in price cause total expenditures to fall. At P = $20, expenditures are $1,200 ($20 · 60), whereas at P = $10, they are only $800 ($10 · 80). At these lower prices, the increase in quantity demanded brought about by a further fall in price is simply not large enough to compensate for the price decline itself, and total expenditures fall.

This relationship is quite general. At high prices on a linear demand curve, demand is elastic ($e_{Q,P} < -1$). Demand is unit elastic ($e_{Q,P} = -1$) at a price halfway between $0 and the price at which demand drops to nothing (given by P = $50 in the prior example). Hence, demand is unit elastic at a price of P = $25. Below that price, demand is inelastic. Further reductions in price actually reduce total revenues.

Because of this property of linear demand curves, it is particularly important when using them to note clearly the point at which price elasticity is to be

> **MicroQuiz 4.2**
>
> How would knowledge of the price elasticity of demand for its product help to guide these producers?
>
> *Producer 1 (movie theater owner).* My seats are mainly empty—would a lower price for tickets help my profits?
>
> *Producer 2 (gas station owner).* The state just raised gasoline taxes by $.10—how should I adjust my pump prices?

measured.[4] When looking at economic data from such a demand curve, if the price being examined has not changed very much over the period being analyzed, the distinction may be relatively unimportant. But, if the analysis is being conducted over a period of substantial price change, the possibility that elasticity may have changed should be considered.

A Unitary Elastic Curve

Suppose that instead of being characterized by Equation 4.2, the demand for tape players took the form

$$Q = \frac{1,200}{P}$$

(4.3)

As shown in Figure 4.4, the graph of this equation is a hyperbola—it is not a straight line. In this case, $P \cdot Q = 1,200$ regardless of the price. This can be verified by examining any of the points identified in Figure 4.4. Because total expenditures are constant everywhere along this hyperbolic demand curve, the price elasticity of demand is always −1. Therefore, this is one simple example of a demand curve that has the same price elasticity along its entire length.[5] Unlike the

---

[4] The changing price elasticity along a linear demand curve can be shown algebraically as follows: Assume a demand curve of the form

$$Q = a - bP$$

(i)

Because

$$e_{Q,P} = \frac{\frac{\Delta Q}{Q}}{\frac{\Delta P}{P}} = \frac{\Delta Q}{\Delta P} \times \frac{P}{Q}$$

for the case of the demand curve in equation i,

$$e_{Q,P} = -b \cdot \frac{P}{Q}$$

(ii)

For large P, P/Q is large and $e_{Q,P}$ is a large negative number. For small P, P/Q is small and $e_{Q,P}$ is a small negative number. Equation ii provides a convenient way to compute $e_{Q,P}$: use two points on the demand curve to derive the curve's slope, b, then multiply by P/Q for the point being examined. Alternatively, equation ii can be used to derive −b (the slope of the demand curve) if $e_{Q,P}$, P, and Q are known.

[5] More generally, if demand takes the form

$$Q = aP^b \ (b < 0)$$

(i)

the price elasticity of demand is given by b. This elasticity is the same everywhere along such a demand curve. Equation 4.3 is a special case of equation i for which

$$e_{Q,P} = b = -1$$

(ii)

Taking logarithms of equations i yields

$$\ln Q = \ln a + b \ln P$$

(iii)

which shows that the price elasticity of demand can be found by studying the relationship between $\ln Q$ and $\ln P$.

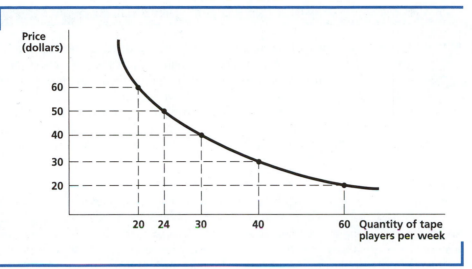

FIGURE 4.4 A Unitary Elastic Demand Curve This hyperbolic demand curve has a price elasticity of demand of −1 along its entire length. This is shown by the fact that total spending on tape players is the same ($1,200) everywhere on the curve.

linear case, for this curve, there is no need to worry about being specific about the point at which elasticity is to be measured. Application 4.4: An Experiment in Health Insurance illustrates how this approach can yield very useful results.

INCOME ELASTICITY OF DEMAND

Another type of elasticity is the **income elasticity of demand** ($e_{Q,I}$). This concept records the relationship between income changes and change in quantity demanded:

$$\text{Income elasticity of demand} = e_{Q,I} = \frac{\text{Percentage change in Q}}{\text{Percentage change in I}} \quad (4.4)$$

Income elasticity of demand
The percentage change in the quantity demanded of a good in response to a 1 percent change in income.

For a normal good, $e_{Q,I}$ is positive because increases in income lead to increases in purchases of the good. For the unlikely case of an inferior good, on the other hand, $e_{Q,I}$ would be negative, implying that increases in income lead to decreases in quantity purchased.

Among normal goods, whether $e_{Q,I}$ is greater than or less than 1 is a matter of considerable interest. Goods for which $e_{Q,I} > 1$ might be called luxury goods, in that purchases of these goods increase more rapidly than income. For example, if the income elasticity of demand for automobiles is 2, then a 10 percent increase in income will lead to a 20 percent increase in automobile purchases. On the

An Experiment in Health Insurance

The provision of health insurance is one of the most universal and controversial social policies throughout the world. Although many nations have comprehensive insurance schemes that cover most of their populations, policymakers in the United States have resisted such an all-inclusive approach. Instead, U.S. policies have evolved as a patchwork, stressing employer-provided insurance for workers together with special programs for the aged (Medicare) and the poor (Medicaid). Regardless of how health insurance policies are designed, however, all face a similar set of problems.

Moral Hazard

One of the most important such problems is that insurance coverage of health care needs tends to increase the demand for services. Because insured patients pay only a small fraction of the costs of the services they receive, they will demand more than they would have if they had to pay market prices. This tendency of insurance coverage to increase demand is (perhaps unfortunately) called "moral hazard," though there is nothing especially immoral about such behavior. Taking the effect into account in planning for the potential costs of health insurance schemes is crucial to getting a realistic picture.

The Rand Experiment

The Medicare program was introduced in the United States in 1965, and the increase in demand for medical services by the elderly was immediately apparent. In order to understand better the factors that were leading to this increase in demand, the government funded a large-scale experiment in four cities. In that experiment, which was conducted by the Rand Corporation, people were assigned to different insurance plans that varied in the generosity of coverage they offered. Specifically, the plans varied the fraction of medical costs that people would have to pay out of their own pockets for medical care.[1] In insurance terms, the experiment varied the "coinsurance" rate from zero (free care) to nearly 100 percent (patients pay everything). By studying the reactions to these variations in price, the researchers were able to estimate the price elasticity of demand for medical services.

Results of the Experiment

Table 1 shows the results from the experiment. People who faced lower out-of-pocket costs for medical care tended to demand more of it. A rough estimate of the elasticity of demand can be obtained by averaging the percentage changes across the various plans in the table. That is,

$$e = \frac{\% \text{ change in Q}}{\% \text{ change in P}} = \frac{+12}{-66} = -0.18$$

So, as might have been expected, the demand for medical care is inelastic, but it clearly is not zero. In fact, the Rand study found much larger price effects for some specific

[1] Details of the experiment are reported in W. G. Manning, J. P. Newhouse, E. B. Keeler, A. Liebowitz, and M. S. Marquis, "Health Insurance and the Demand for Medical Care: Evidence from a Randomized Experiment," *American Economic Review* (June 1987): 251–277.

TABLE 1 Results of the Rand Health Insurance Experiment

Coinsurance rate	Percent change in price	Average total spending	Percent change in quantity
0.95		$540	
0.50	−47%	573	+6.1%
0.25	−50	617	+7.7
0.00	−100	750	+21.6
Average	−66		+12.0

Source: Manning et al. Table 2.

medical services such as mental health care and dental care. It is these kinds of services for which new insurance coverage would be expected to have the greatest impact on market demand. This fact is recognized in the design of medical plans throughout the world that often have stricter limits on the coverage of mental and dental care than on services with smaller price elasticities (such as surgery).

To Think About

1. The data in Table 1 show average spending for families who faced differing out-of-pocket prices for medical care. Why do these data accurately reflect the changes in quantity that are required in the elasticity formula?
2. In recent years, prepaid health plans (i.e., HMOs) have come to be the dominant form of employer-provided health plans. How do prepaid plans seek to control the moral hazard problem? Why are they so controversial? (See also Application 15.2)

other hand, as Engel's Law suggests, food has an income elasticity of much less than 1. If the income elasticity of demand for food were 0.5, for example, then a 10 percent rise in income would result in only a 5 percent increase in food purchases. Considerable research has been done to determine the actual values of income elasticities for various items, and we discuss the results of some of these studies in the final section of this chapter.

MicroQuiz 4.3

Values for the income elasticity of demand are restricted by the fact that consumers are bound by budget constraints. Use this fact to explain:

1. Why is it that not every good can have an income elasticity of demand greater than one? Can every good have an income elasticity of demand less than 1?

2. If a set of consumers spend 95 percent of their incomes on housing, why can't the income elasticity of demand for housing be much greater than 1?

CROSS-PRICE ELASTICITY OF DEMAND

Cross-price elasticity of demand
The percentage change in the quantity demanded of a good in response to a 1 percent change in the price of another good.

In Chapter 3 we showed that a change in the price of one good will affect the quantity demanded of most other goods. To measure such effects, economists use the **cross-price elasticity of demand.** This concept records the percentage change in quantity demanded (Q) that results from a 1 percentage point change in the price of some other good (call this other price P′). That is,

$$\text{Cross-price elasticity of demand} = e_{Q,P} = \frac{\text{Percentage change in Q}}{\text{Percentage change in P}'} \quad (4.5)$$

If these goods are substitutes, the cross-price elasticity of demand will be positive because the price of one good and the quantity demanded of the other good will move in the same direction. For example, the cross-price elasticity for changes in the price of tea on coffee demand might be 0.2. Each 1 percentage point increase in the price of tea results in a 0.2 percentage point increase in the demand for coffee because coffee and tea are substitutes in people's consumption choices. A fall in the price of tea would cause the demand for coffee to fall also, since people would choose to drink tea rather than coffee.

If two goods are complements, the cross-price elasticity will be negative showing that the price of one good and the quantity of the other good move in opposite directions. The cross-price elasticity of doughnut prices on coffee demand might be, say, –1.5. This would imply that a 1 percent increase in the price of doughnuts would cause the demand for coffee to fall by 1.5 percent. When doughnuts are more expensive, it becomes less attractive to drink coffee because many people like to have a doughnut with their morning coffee. A fall in the price of doughnuts would increase coffee demand because, in that case, people will choose to consume more of both complementary products. As for the other elasticities we have examined, considerable empirical research has been conducted to try to measure actual cross-price elasticities of demand.

MicroQuiz 4.4

Suppose that a set of consumers spend their incomes only on beer and pizza.

1. Explain why a fall in the price of beer will have an ambiguous effect on pizza purchases.

2. What does the fact that the demand for pizza must be homogeneous imply about the relationship between the price elasticity of demand for pizza, the income elasticity of demand for pizza, and the cross-price elasticity of the demand for pizza with respect to beer prices?

EMPIRICAL STUDIES OF DEMAND

Economists have for many years studied the demand for all sorts of goods. Some of the earliest studies generalized from the expenditure patterns of a small sample of families. More recent studies have examined a wide variety of goods to estimate both income and price elasticities.

Although it is not possible for us to discuss in detail here the statistical techniques used in these studies, we can show in a general way how these economists proceeded.

INFOTRAC°
COLLEGE EDITION
Exclusively from Gale Group and Thomson Learning

www.infotrac-college.com
Keywords: Price elasticity, Farm prices, Rand health insurance experiment, Moral hazard

Estimating Demand Curves

Estimating the demand curve for a product is one of the more difficult and important problems in econometrics. The importance of the question is obvious. Without some idea of what the demand curve for a product looks like, economists could not describe with any precision how the market for a good might be affected by various events. Usually the notion that a rise in price will cause quantity demanded to fall will not be precise enough—we want some way to estimate the size of the effect.

Problems in deriving such an estimate are of two general types. First are those related to the need to implement the *ceteris paribus* assumption. One must find some way to hold constant all of the other factors that affect quantity demanded so that the direct relationship between price and quantity can be observed. Otherwise, we will be looking at points on several demand curves rather than on only one. We have already discussed this problem in Appendix to Chapter 1, which shows how it can often be solved through the use of relatively simple statistical procedures.[6]

A second problem in estimating a demand curve goes to the heart of microeconomic theory. From the early days in your introductory economics course, you have (hopefully) learned that quantity and price are determined by the simultaneous operation of demand and supply. A simple plot of quantity versus price will be neither a demand curve nor a supply curve, but only points at which the two curves intersect. The econometric problem then is to penetrate behind this confusion and "identify" the true demand curve. There are indeed methods for doing this, though we will not pursue them here.[7] All studies of demand, including those we look at in the next section, must address this issue, however.

Some Elasticity Estimates

Table 4.4 gathers a number of estimated income and price elasticities of demand. As we shall see, these estimates often provide the starting place for analyzing how activities such as changes in taxes or import policy might affect various markets. In several later chapters, we use these numbers to illustrate such applications.

---

[6] The most common technique, multiple regression analysis, estimates a relationship between quantity demanded (Q), price (P), and other factors that affect quantity demanded (X) of the form $Q = a + bP + cX$. Given this relationship, X can be held constant while looking at the relationship between Q and P. Following footnote 5, it is common practice to use logarithms to provide estimates of elasticities.

[7] For a good discussion, see R. Ramanathan, *Introductory Econometrics with Applications*, 5th ed. (Mason, OH: South-Western, 2002), Chapter 13.

TABLE 4.4 Representative Price and Income Elasticities of Demand

	Price elasticity	Income elasticity
Food	−0.21	+0.28
Medical services	−0.18	+0.22
Housing		
Rental	−0.18	+1.00
Owner-occupied	−1.20	+1.20
Electricity	−1.14	+0.61
Automobiles	−1.20	+3.00
Beer	−0.26	+0.38
Wine	−0.88	+0.97
Marijuana	−1.50	0.00
Cigarettes	−0.35	+0.50
Abortions	−0.81	+0.79
Transatlantic air travel	−1.30	+1.40
Imports	−0.58	+2.73
Money	−0.40	+1.00

Sources: Food: H. Wold and L. Jureen, *Demand Analysis* (New York: John Wiley & Sons, Inc., 1953): 203. Medical Services: income elasticity from R. Andersen and L. Benham, "Factors Affecting the Relationship between Family Income and Medical Care Consumption" in *Empirical Studies in Health Economics,* Herbert Klarman, ed. (Baltimore: Johns Hopkins Press, 1970). Price elasticity from Manning et al. "Health Insurance and the Demand for Medical Care: Evidence from a Randomized Experiment, *American Economic Review* (June 1987) 251–277. Housing: income elasticities from F. de Leeuw, "The Demand for Housing," *Review of Economics and Statistics* (February 1971); price elasticities from H. S. Houthakker and L. D. Taylor, *Consumer Demand in the United States* (Cambridge, Mass.: Harvard University Press, 1970): 166–167. Electricity: R. F. Halvorsen, "Residential Demand for Electricity," unpublished Ph.D. dissertation, Harvard University, December 1972. Automobiles: Gregory C. Chow, *Demand for Automobiles in the United States* (Amsterdam: North Holland Publishing Company, 1957). Beer and Wine: J. A. Johnson, E. H. Oksanen, M. R. Veall, and D. Fritz, "Short-Run and Long-Run Elasticities for Canadian Consumption of Alcoholic Beverages," *Review of Economics and Statistics* (February 1992): 64–74. Marijuana: T. C. Misket and F. Vakil, "Some Estimates of Price and Expenditure Elasticities among UCLA Students," *Review of Economics and Statistics* (November 1972): 474–475. Cigarettes: F. Chalemaker, "Rational Addictive Behavior and Cigarette Smoking," *Journal of Political Economy* (August 1991): 722–742. Abortions: M. J. Medoff, "An Economic Analysis of the Demand for Abortions," *Economic Inquiry* (April 1988): 253–259. Transatlantic air travel: J. M. Cigliano, "Price and Income Elasticities for Airline Travel," *Business Economics* (September 1980): 17–21. Imports: M. D. Chinn, "Beware of Econometricians Bearing Estimates," *Journal of Policy Analysis and Management* (Fall 1991): 546–567. Money: "Long-Run Income and Interest Elasticities of Money Demand in the United States," *Review of Economics and Statistics* (November 1991): 665–674. Price elasticity refers to interest rate elasticity.

Although interested readers are urged to explore the original sources of these estimates to understand more details about them, in our discussion we just take note of a few regularities they exhibit. With regard to the price elasticity figures, most are relatively inelastic (between 0 and −1). For the groupings of commodities listed, substitution effects are not especially large, although they may be large within these categories. For example, substitutions between beer and other commodities may be relatively small, though substitutions among

TABLE 4.5 Representative Cross-Price Elasticities of Demand

Demand for	Effect of price of	Elasticity estimate
Butter	Margarine	1.53
Electricity	Natural gas	.50
Coffee	Tea	.15

Sources: Butter: Dale M. Heien, "The Structure of Food Demand: Interrelatedness and Duality," *American Journal of Agricultural Economics* (May 1982): 213–221. Electricity: G. R. Lakshmanan and W. Anderson, "Residential Energy Demand in the United States," *Regional Science and Urban Economics* (August 1980): 371–386. Coffee: J. Huang, J. J. Siegfried, and F. Zardoshty, "The Demand for Coffee in the United States, 1963–77," *Quarterly Journal of Business and Economics* (Summer 1980): 36–50.

brands of beer may be substantial in response to price differences. Still, all the estimates are less than zero, so there is clear evidence that people do respond to price changes for most goods.[8] Application 4.5: Alcohol Taxes as Drunk Driving Policy shows how price elasticity estimates can inform an important policy debate

As expected, the income elasticities in Table 4.4 are positive and are roughly centered about 1.0. Luxury goods, such as automobiles or transatlantic travel ($e_{Q,I} > 1$), tend to be balanced by necessities, such as food or medical care ($e_{Q,I} < 1$). Because none of the income elasticities is negative, it is clear that Giffen's paradox is very rare.

Some Cross-Price Elasticity Estimates

Table 4.5 shows a few cross-price elasticity estimates that economists have derived. All of the pairs of goods illustrated are probably substitutes, and the positive estimated values for the elasticities confirm that view. The figure for the relationship between butter and margarine is the largest in Table 4.5. Even in the absence of health issues, the competition between these two spreads on the basis of price is clearly very intense. Similarly, natural gas prices have an important effect on electricity sales because they help determine how people will heat their homes.

---

[8] Although the estimated price elasticities in Table 4.4 incorporate both substitution and income effects, they predominantly represent substitution effects. To see this, note that the price elasticity of demand ($e_{Q,P}$) can be disaggregated into substitution and income effects by

$$e_{Q,P} = e_S - s_i e_i$$

where e_S is the "substitution" price elasticity of demand representing the effect of a price change holding utility constant, s_i is the share of income spent on the good in question, and e_i is the good's income elasticity of demand. Because s_i is small for most of the goods in Table 4.4, $e_{Q,P}$ and e_S have values that are reasonably close.

Alcohol Taxes as Drunk Driving Policy

Each year more than 40,000 Americans die in automobile accidents. Such accidents are the leading cause of death for teenagers. It is generally believed that alcohol consumption is a major contributing factor in at least half of those accidents. In recent years the government has tried to combat drunk driving by teenagers in two primary ways: by increasing legal minimum ages for drinking and by adopting stricter drunk driving laws. These efforts appear to have had significant effects in reducing teen fatalities. At the same time that these laws were coming into effect, however, real taxes on alcohol declined. Because teens may be especially sensitive to alcohol prices, these reductions may have eroded some of the impact of the more stringent laws. But the connection between teen alcohol consumption and alcohol taxes is actually more complex than it first appears.

Price Elasticity Estimates—The Importance of Beer

Most empirical studies of alcohol consumption show that it is sensitive to price. The figures in Table 4.4 suggest that these elasticities in the United States range from approximately –0.3 for beer to perhaps as large as –0.9 for wine. Studies of alcohol consumption in other countries reach essentially the same conclusion: while all alcohol consumption appears to be relatively price sensitive, price elasticities for beer are usually found to be less than half those for wine (and other spirits). Unfortunately, most teenage alcohol consumption is beer. The lower price elasticity of demand for this product therefore poses a problem for those who would use alcohol taxes as a deterrent to drunk driving.

Why beer should have a lower price elasticity of demand than other alcoholic beverages is somewhat of a puzzle. Two factors may provide a partial explanation. First, a significant portion of beer consumption is done in a group setting (tapping a keg, for example). In this case, the direct impact of higher prices may be less than when goods are purchased individually because, at the margin, drinking more costs the consumer no more in out-of-pocket costs. A second possible reason for the lower price elasticity of beer consumption relates to differences among beer consumers. Most beer is consumed by those who drink quite a lot (say, more than a six-pack at a session). This is a group of consumers for whom demand has been found to be less responsive to price than is the case for most other consumers.

Beer Consumption and Habit Formation

Another possibility, however, is that past studies of alcohol consumption have not modeled this activity correctly and thus consumption may be more price responsive than the elasticity estimates imply. Specifically, some authors have argued that "binge" drinking of beer is primarily a habit, created over several years of increasingly serious drinking. Hence, as for many products, the price elasticity of demand for beer may be much larger over the long run than the short-run estimates imply. One important econometric study[1] that supports this conclusion finds that restoring the real rate of taxation on beer to that prevailing in the

---

[1] C. J. Ruhm, "Alcohol Policies and Highway Vehicle Fatalities," *Journal of Health Economics* (August 1996): 435–454.

1970s would reduce highway fatalities by 7 to 8 percent—a figure about in line with the declines brought on by the stricter laws. Overall, such a price increase might save about 3,500 lives.

To Think About

1. Reducing alcohol consumption through taxation would have a number of effects in addition to those related to drunk driving. What are some of these effects? Do these also provide a rationale for higher alcohol taxes?
2. One principle of efficient taxation is that taxes should be imposed directly on the "problem." Alcohol taxes do not do that because they tax alcohol consumers who do not drive and they do not tax nondrinkers who cause accidents. Still, why might this policy be preferred to a more direct tax on drunk drivers?

SUMMARY

In this chapter, we constructed a market demand curve by adding up the demands of many consumers. This curve shows the relationship between the market price of a good and the amount that people choose to purchase of that good, assuming all the other factors that affect demand do not change. The market demand curve is a basic building block for the theory of price determination. We use the concept frequently throughout the remainder of this book. You should therefore keep in mind the following points about this concept:

- The market demand curve represents the summation of the demands of a given number of potential consumers of a particular good. The curve shows the *ceteris paribus* relationship between the market price of the good and the amount demanded by all consumers.
- Factors that shift individual demand curves also shift the market demand curve to a new position. Such factors include changes in incomes, changes in the prices of other goods, and changes in people's preferences.
- The price elasticity of demand provides a convenient way of measuring the extent to which market demand responds to price changes. Specifically, the price elasticity of demand shows the percentage change in quantity demanded in response to a 1 percent change in market price. Demand is said to be elastic if a 1 percent change in price leads to a greater than 1 percent change in quantity demanded. Demand is inelastic if a 1 percent change in price leads to a smaller than 1 percent change in quantity.

- There is a close relationship between the price elasticity of demand and total expenditures on a good. If demand is elastic, a rise in price will reduce total expenditures. If demand is inelastic, a rise in price will increase total expenditures.
- Other elasticities of demand are defined in a way similar to that used for the price elasticity. For example, the income elasticity of demand measures the percentage change in quantity demanded in response to a 1 percent change in income.
- The price elasticity of demand is not necessarily the same at every point on a demand curve. For a linear demand curve, demand is elastic for high prices and inelastic for low prices.
- Economists have estimated elasticities of demand for many different goods using real-world data. A major problem in making such estimates is to devise ways of holding constant all other factors that affect demand so that the price–quantity points being used lie on a single demand curve.

REVIEW QUESTIONS

1. In the construction of the market demand curve shown in Figure 4.1, why is a horizontal line drawn at the prevailing price, P_X^*? What does this assume about the price facing each person? How are people assumed to react to this price?

2. Explain how the following events might affect the market demand curve for prime filet mignon:

   a. A fall in the price of filet mignon because of a decline in cattle prices
   b. A general rise in consumers' incomes
   c. A rise in the price of lobster
   d. Increased health concerns about cholesterol
   e. An income tax increase for high-income people used to increase welfare benefits
   f. A cut in income taxes and welfare benefits

3. Why is the price elasticity of demand usually negative? If the price elasticity of demand for automobiles is less than the price elasticity of demand for medical care, which demand is more elastic? Give a numerical example.

4. "Gaining extra revenue is easy for any producer—all it has to do is raise the price of its product." Do you agree? Explain when this would be true, and when it would not be true.

5. Suppose that the market demand curve for pasta is a straight line of the form $Q = 300 - 50P$ where Q is the quantity of pasta bought in thousands of boxes per week and P is the price per box (in dollars).

   a. At what price does the demand for pasta go to zero? Develop a numerical example to show that the demand for pasta is elastic at this point.
   b. How much pasta is demanded at a price of zero? Develop a numerical example to show that demand is inelastic at this point.

   c. How much pasta is demanded at a price of $3? Develop a numerical example that suggests that total spending on pasta is as large as possible at this price.

6. Marvin currently spends 35 percent of his $100,000 income on renting his apartment. If his income elasticity of demand for housing is 0.8, will this fraction rise or fall when he gets a raise to $120,000? Would you give a different answer to this question if Marvin's income elasticity of demand for housing were 1.3?

7. J. Trueblue always spends one-third of his income on American flags. What is the income elasticity of his demand for such flags? What is the price elasticity of his demand for flags?

8. Table 4.4 reports an estimated price elasticity of demand for electricity of –1.14. Explain what this means with a numerical example. Does this number seem large? Do you think this is a short- or long-term elasticity estimate? How might this estimate be important for owners of electric utilities or for bodies that regulate them?

9. Table 4.5 reports that the cross-price elasticity of demand for electricity with respect to the price of natural gas is 0.50. Explain what this means with a numerical example. What does the fact that the number is positive imply about the relationship between electricity and natural gas use?

10. An economist hired by a home building firm has been asked to estimate a demand curve for homes. He gathers data on the price of new houses and on the number sold from the top 100 metropolitan areas in the United States. He plots these data, draws a line that seems to pass near the points, and labels that line "demand." How many problems can you identify in this approach to estimating the demand for houses?

PROBLEMS

4.1 Suppose the demand curve for flyswatters is given by

$$Q = 500 - 50P$$

where Q is the number of flyswatters demanded per week and P is the price in dollars.

a. How many flyswatters are demanded at a price of $2? How about a price of $3? $4? Suppose flyswatters were free; how many would be bought?
b. Graph the flyswatter demand curve. Remember to put P on the vertical axis and Q on the horizontal axis. To do so, you may wish to solve for P as a function of Q.
c. Suppose during July the flyswatter demand curve shifts to

$$Q = 1,000 - 50P$$

Answer part a and part b for this new demand curve.

4.2 Suppose that the demand curve for garbanzo beans is given by

$$Q = 20 - P$$

where Q is thousands of pounds of beans bought per week and P is the price in dollars per pound.

a. How many beans will be bought at P = 0?
b. At what price does the quantity demanded of beans become zero?
c. Calculate total expenditures (P · Q) for beans for each whole dollar price between the prices identified in part a and part b.
d. What price for beans yields the highest total expenditures?
e. Suppose the demand for beans shifted to $Q = 40 - 2P$. How would your answers to part a through part d change? Explain the differences intuitively and with a graph.

4.3 Consider the three demand curves

$$Q = \frac{100}{P} \qquad \text{(i)}$$

$$Q = \frac{100}{\sqrt{P}} \qquad \text{(ii)}$$

$$Q = \frac{100}{P^{3/2}} \qquad \text{(iii)}$$

a. Use a calculator to compute the value of Q for each demand curve for P = 1 and for P = 1.1.
b. What do your calculations show about the price elasticity of demand at P = 1 for each of the three demand curves?
c. Now perform a similar set of calculations for the three demand curves at P = 4 and P = 4.4. How do the elasticities computed here compare to those from part b? Explain your results using footnote 5 of this chapter.

4.4 The market demand for potatoes is given by

$$Q = 1,000 + 0.3I - 300P + 299P'$$

where
Q = Annual demand in pounds
I = Average income in dollars per year
P = Price of potatoes in cents per pound
P' = Price of rice in cents per pound.

a. Suppose I = $10,000 and P' = $.25; what would be the market demand for potatoes? At what price would Q = 0? Graph this demand curve.
b. Suppose I rose to $20,000 with P' staying at $.25. Now what would the demand for potatoes be? At what price would Q = 0? Graph this demand curve. Explain why more potatoes are demanded at every price in this case than in part a.
c. If I returns to $10,000 but P' falls to $.10, what would the demand for potatoes be? At what price

would Q = 0? Graph this demand curve. Explain why fewer potatoes are demanded at every price in this case than in part a.

4.5 Tom, Dick, and Harry constitute the entire market for scrod. Tom's demand curve is given by

$$Q_1 = 100 - 2P$$

for $P \leq 50$. For $P > 50$, $Q_1 = 0$. Dick's demand curve is given by

$$Q_2 = 160 - 4P$$

for $P \leq 40$. For $P > 40$, $Q_2 = 0$. Harry's demand curve is given by

$$Q_3 = 150 - 5P$$

for $P \leq 30$. For $P > 30$, $Q_3 = 0$. Using this information, answer the following:

a. How much scrod is demanded by each person at P = 50? At P = 35? At P = 25? At P = 10? And at P = 0?
b. What is the total market demand for scrod at each of the prices specified in part a?
c. Graph each individual's demand curve.
d. Use the individual demand curves and the results of part b to construct the total market demand for scrod.

4.6 Suppose the quantity of good X demanded by individual 1 is given by

$$X_1 = 10 - 2P_X + 0.01I_1 + 0.4P_Y$$

and the quantity of X demanded by individual 2 is

$$X_2 = 5 - P_X + 0.02I_2 + 0.2P_Y$$

a. What is the market demand function for total X (= $X_1 + X_2$) as a function of P_X, I_1, I_2, and P_Y?
b. Graph the two individual demand curves (with X on the horizontal axis, P_X on the vertical axis) for the case $I_1 = 1,000$, $I_2 = 1,000$, and $P_Y = 10$.
c. Using these individual demand curves, construct the market demand curve for total X. What is the algebraic equation for this curve?
d. Now suppose I_1 increases to 1,100 and I_2 decreases to 900. How would the market demand curve shift? How would the individual demand curves shift? Graph these new curves.

e. Finally, suppose P_Y rises to 15. Graph the new individual and market demand curves that would result.

4.7 Suppose that the current market price of VCRs is $300, that average consumer disposable income is $30,000, and that the price of DVD players (a substitute for VCRs) is $500. Under these conditions, the annual U.S. demand for VCRs is 5 million per year. Statistical studies have shown that for this product $e_{Q,P} = -1.3$, $e_{Q,I} = 1.7$, and $e_{Q,P'} = 0.8$ where P' is the price of DVD players.
Use this information to predict the annual number of VCRs sold under the following conditions:

a. Increasing competition from Korea causes VCR prices to fall to $270 with I and P' unchanged.
b. Income tax reductions raise average disposable income to $31,500 with P and P' unchanged.
c. Technical improvements in DVD players cause their price to fall to $400 with P and I unchanged.
d. All of the events described in part a through part c occur simultaneously.

4.8 The market demand for cashmere socks is given by

$$Q = 1,000 + .5I - 400P + 200P'$$

where
Q = Annual demand in number of pairs
I = Average income in dollars per year
P = Price of one pair of cashmere socks
P' = Price of one pair of wool socks
Given that I = $20,000, P = $10, and P' = $5, determine $e_{Q,P}$, $e_{Q,I}$, and $e_{Q,P'}$ at this point. (Hint: Use footnote 4 of this chapter.)

4.9 In Problem 3.9, we introduced compensated demand curves along which utility is held constant and only the substitution effect of price changes is considered. This problem shows how the price elasticity of demand along such a curve is related to the customary measure of price elasticity.

a. Suppose consumers buy only two goods, food and shelter, and that they buy these in fixed proportions—one unit of food for each unit of shelter. In this case, what does the compensated demand curve for food look like? What is the price elasticity of demand along this curve (call this elasticity e_s—the substitution elasticity). Are there any substitution effects in this demand?

b. Under the conditions of part a, what is the income elasticity of demand for food ($e_{F,I}$)?

c. Continuing as in part a, suppose one unit of food costs half what one unit of housing costs. What fraction of income will be spent on food (call this s_F)?

d. Using the information in part c, what is the overall price elasticity of demand (including both substitution and income effects) for food ($e_{F,P}$)? (Hint: A numerical example may help here.)

e. Use your answers to part a through part d to show that the numbers calculated in this problem obey the formula in footnote 8 of this chapter:

$$e_{F,P} = e_s - s_F e_{F,I}$$

This formula is quite general. It is sometimes called the "Slutsky Equation" after its discoverer.

f. Let us change this problem a bit now to assume that people *always* spend ⅓ of their income on food no matter what their income or what the price of food is. What is the demand function for food in this case?

g. Under the conditions of part f, what are the values of $e_{F,P}$, s_F, $e_{F,I}$, and (using the formula in part e) e_s for this case? Explain why the value for e_s differs between this case and the value of calculated in part a.

h. How would your answers to part a through part g change if we focused on shelter instead of food?

4.10 For the linear demand curve shown in the following figure, show that the price elasticity of demand at any given point (say, point E) is given by minus the ratio of distance X to distance Y in the figure. (Hint: Use footnote 4 of this chapter.) Explain how this result provides an alternative way of showing how elasticity varies along a linear demand curve.

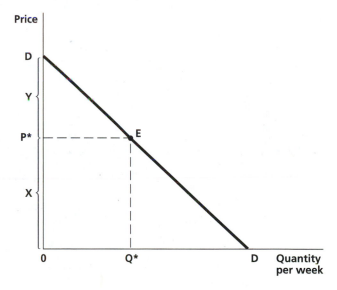

INTERNET EXERCISES

1. *Elasticity and Bus Fares.* Suppose you are the manager of a major city transit system. You are considering increasing bus fares from $0.75 to $0.81, but you need to know the impact of such an increase on transit ridership and revenues before doing so. Consult the analysis of bus fare elasticity at *http://www.apta.com/info/online/elastic.htm,* which is abstracted from an article entitled "Fare Elasticity and Its Application to Forecasting Transit Demand," published by the American Public Transportation Association. Complete the following statement: Using the Simpson-Curtin elasticity, the fare increase from $0.75 to $0.81 will reduce ridership by _____ percent while the newer overall average elasticity estimate suggests the same fare increase will reduce ridership by _____ percent. What do you predict will happen to your total revenue as a result of the fare increase, regardless of which estimate you use? Explain. On average, is the overall peak hour demand for ridership more or less elastic than the overall off-peak demand for ridership? Explain. Is this what you would expect? Why or why not?

2. *Elasticity and Alcohol Duties.* Application 4.5 discusses how elasticities can be used to determine the effectiveness of increasing taxes on alcohol to discourage drunk driving. In a very readable study, Zoë Smith also considers alcohol taxes and elasticities, but as applied to a very different question: Will lowering the tax on alcohol increase government revenue in the United Kingdom by reducing the amount of cross-border shopping, or will the lower tax rate lead to a loss in revenue? Read her briefing note at *http://www.ifs.org.uk/consume/alcohol.pdf.* Explain why, in order to determine whether, for example, lowering the tax on beer will raise or lower total revenue to the government, the following elasticities are important: the price elasticity of demand for beer and the cross-price elasticity of demand for wine with respect to the price of beer. From the information in Table 3 on the Web site, for which good (beer, spirits, or wine) is demand most price responsive? Least price responsive? For each good (the most and least price responsive), predict the resulting percentage change in quantity demanded in response to a 5 percent *decrease* in price. According to the information in Table 4 on the Web site, a reduction in the wine tax will lead to an increase in total wine sales. Refer to the appropriate elasticity from Table 3 to explain why. Use the information in Table 3 to determine whether beer and wine are substitutes or complements. Explain your answer. What does this imply about how tax revenue from beer sales will change if there is a decrease in the wine tax? Explain.

Part 3

Production, Costs, and Supply

"The laws and conditions of production partake of the character of physical truths. There is nothing arbitrary about them."

J. S. Mill, *Principles of Political Economy*, 1848

Part 3 considers the production and supply of economic goods. The organizations that supply goods are called *firms.* They may be large, complex organizations, such as Microsoft or the U.S. Defense Department, or they may be quite small, such as mom-and-pop stores or self-employed farmers. All firms must make choices about what inputs they will use and the level of output they will supply. Part 3 looks at these choices.

To be able to produce any output, firms must hire many inputs (labor, capital, natural resources, and so forth). Because these inputs are scarce, they have costs associated with their use. Our goal in Chapter 5 and Chapter 6 is to show clearly the relationship between input costs and the level of the firm's output. In Chapter 5, we introduce the firm's production function, which shows the relationship between inputs used and the level of output that results. Once this physical relationship between inputs and outputs is known, the costs of needed inputs can be determined for various levels of output. This we show in Chapter 6.

Chapter 7 uses the cost curves developed in Chapter 6 to discuss firms' supply decisions. It provides a detailed analysis of the supply decisions of profit-maximizing firms. The chapter also looks briefly at problems in structuring managers' incentives so that they will seek maximum profits.

5

Production

In this chapter, we show how economists illustrate the relationship between inputs and outputs using production functions. This is the first step in showing how input costs affect firms' supply decisions.

PRODUCTION FUNCTIONS

The purpose of any **firm** is to turn inputs into outputs: General Motors combines steel, glass, workers' time, and hours of assembly line operation to produce automobiles; farmers combine their labor with seed, soil, rain, fertilizer, and machinery to produce crops; and colleges combine professors' time with books and (hopefully) hours of student study to produce educated students. Because economists are interested in the choices that firms make to accomplish their goals, they have developed a rather abstract model of production. In this model, the relationship between inputs and outputs is formalized by a **production function** of the form

$$q = f(K, L, M \ldots) \tag{5.1}$$

where q represents the output of a particular good[1] during a period, K represents the machine (that is, capital) use during the period, L represents hours of labor input, and M represents raw materials used. The form of the notation indicates

Firm
Any organization that turns inputs into outputs.

Production function
The mathematical relationship between inputs and outputs.

---

[1] Sometimes the output for a firm is defined to include only its "value added"; that is, the value of raw materials used by the firm is subtracted to arrive at a net value of output for the firm. This procedure is also used in adding up gross domestic product to avoid double-counting of inputs. Throughout our discussion, a single firm's output is denoted by q.

the possibility of other variables affecting the production process. The production function summarizes what the firm knows about mixing various inputs to yield output.

For example, this production function might represent a farmer's output of wheat during one year as being dependent on the quantity of machinery employed, the amount of labor used on the farm, the amount of land under cultivation, the amount of fertilizer and seeds used, and so forth. The function shows that, say, 100 bushels of wheat can be produced in many different ways. The farmer could use a very labor-intensive technique that would require only a small amount of mechanical equipment (as tends to be the case in China). The 100 bushels could also be produced using large amounts of equipment and fertilizer with very little labor (as in the United States). A great deal of land might be used to produce the 100 bushels of wheat with less of the other inputs (as in Brazil or Australia); or relatively little land could be used with great amounts of labor, equipment, and fertilizer (as in British or Japanese agriculture). All of these combinations are represented by the general production function in Equation 5.1. The important question about this production function from an economic point of view is how the firm chooses its levels of q, K, L, and M. We take this question up in detail in the next three chapters.

Two-Input Production Function

We simplify the production function here by assuming that the firm's production depends on only two inputs: capital (K) and labor (L). Hence, our simplified production function is now

$$q = f(K, L) \tag{5.2}$$

The decision to focus on capital and labor is arbitrary. Most of our analysis here holds true for any two inputs that might be investigated. For example, if we wish to examine the effects of rainfall and fertilizer on crop production, we can use those two inputs in the production function while holding other inputs (quantity of land, hours of labor input, and so on) constant. In the production function that characterizes a school system, we can examine the relationship between the "output" of the system (say, academic achievement) and the inputs used to produce this output (such as teachers, buildings, and learning aids). The two general inputs of capital and labor are used here for convenience, and we frequently show these inputs on a two-dimensional graph. Application 5.1: Everyone Is a Firm shows how the production function idea can yield quite surprising insights.

MARGINAL PRODUCT

The first question we might ask about the relationship between inputs and outputs is how much extra output can be produced by adding one more unit of an

Turning inputs into outputs is something we all do every day without thinking about it. When you drive somewhere, you are combining labor (your time) with capital (the car) to produce economic output (a trip). Of course, the output from this activity is not traded in organized markets; but there is not very much difference between providing "taxi services" to yourself or selling them to someone else. In both cases, you are performing the economic role that economists assign to firms. In fact, "home production" constitutes a surprisingly large segment of the overall economy. Looking at people as "firms" can yield some interesting insights.

The Amount of Home Production

Economists have tried to estimate the amount of production that people do for themselves. By including such items as child care, home maintenance, commuting, physical maintenance (for example, exercise), and cooking, they arrive at quite substantial magnitudes— perhaps more than half of traditionally measured GDP. To produce this large amount of output, people employ significant amounts of inputs. Time-use studies suggest that the time people spend in home production is only slightly less than time spent working (about 30 percent of total time in both cases). Also, people's investment in home-related capital (such as houses, cars, and appliances) is probably larger than business firms' investment in buildings and equipment. Because most of the output produced with these inputs is not sold, it does not enter into common measures of overall economic activity. But our imperfect measures of economic activity should not obscure the importance of what people do at home.

Production of Housing Services

Some of the more straightforward things produced at home are what might be called "housing services." People combine the capital invested in their homes with some purchased inputs (electricity, natural gas) and with their own time (cleaning the gutters) to produce living accommodations. In this respect, people are both producers of housing services and consumers of those same services; and this is precisely how housing is treated in GDP accounts. In 2001, for example, people spent more than $850 billion in (implicitly) renting houses from themselves. They also spent nearly $400 billion on household operations, even if we do not assign any value to the time they spent in household chores. How people change their production of housing services over the business cycle (do they fix the roof when they are laid off, for example) is an important question in macroeconomics.

Production of Health

The production function concept is widely used in thinking about health issues. People are assumed to combine inputs of purchased medical care (such as medicines or physicians' services) together with their own time in order to "produce" health. An important implication of this approach is that people may to some extent find it possible to substitute their own actions for purchased medical care while remaining equally healthy. Whether current medical insurance practices give them adequate incentives to do that is widely debated. The fact that people may know more than their physicians do about their own health and how to produce it also raises a number of complex questions about regulating the medical industry, as we see in Chapter 15.

(continued)

Production of Children

A somewhat more far-fetched application of the home production concept is to view families as producers of children. One of the most important observations about this "output" is that it is not homogeneous—children have both "quantity" and "quality" dimensions, and families will choose which combination of these to produce. Clearly significant amounts of inputs (especially parental time) are devoted to this process—by some estimates the input costs associated with children are second only to housing for typical families. From an economic point of view, one of the more interesting issues involved in producing children concerns the fact that such investments are irreversible (unlike, say, housing where one can always opt for a smaller house). This may cause some people to view this production as quite risky, as any parent of a teen can attest.

To Think About

1. If people produce goods such as housing services and health for their own consumption, how should we define the "prices" of these goods in the model of utility maximization used in prior chapters?
2. How will a family with more than one adult decide how to allocate each person's work time between home production and work in the market?

Marginal product
The additional output that can be produced by adding one more unit of a particular input while holding all other inputs constant.

input to the production process. The marginal physical productivity, or more simply, **marginal product** of an input is defined as the quantity of extra output provided by employing one additional unit of that input while holding all other inputs constant. For our two principal inputs of capital and labor, the marginal product of labor (MP_L) is the extra output obtained by employing one more worker while holding the level of capital equipment constant. Similarly, the marginal product of capital (MP_K) is the extra output obtained by using one more machine while holding the number of workers constant.

As an illustration of these definitions, consider the case of a farmer hiring one more person to harvest a crop while holding all other inputs constant. The extra output produced when this person is added to the production team is the marginal product of labor input. The concept is measured in physical quantities such as bushels of wheat, crates of oranges, or heads of lettuce. We might, for example, observe that 25 workers in an orange grove are able to produce 10,000 crates of oranges per week, whereas 26 workers (with the same trees and equipment) can produce 10,200 crates. The marginal product of the 26th worker is 200 crates per week.

Diminishing Marginal Product

We might expect the marginal product of an input to depend on how much of that input is used. For example, workers cannot be added indefinitely to the harvesting of oranges (while keeping the number of trees, amount of equipment, fertilizer, and so forth fixed) without the marginal product eventually deteriorating. This possibility is illustrated in Figure 5.1. The top panel of the figure shows the relationship between output per week and labor input during the week when the level of capital input is held fixed. At first, adding new workers also increases output significantly; but these gains diminish as even more labor is added and the fixed amount of capital becomes overutilized. The concave shape of the total output curve in panel a therefore reflects the economic principle of diminishing marginal product.

Marginal Product Curve

A geometric interpretation of the marginal product concept is straightforward—it is the slope[2] of the total product curve shown in panel a of Figure 5.1. The decreasing slope of the curve shows diminishing marginal product. For higher values of labor input, the total curve is nearly flat—adding more labor raises output only slightly. The bottom panel of Figure 5.1 illustrates this slope directly by the marginal product of

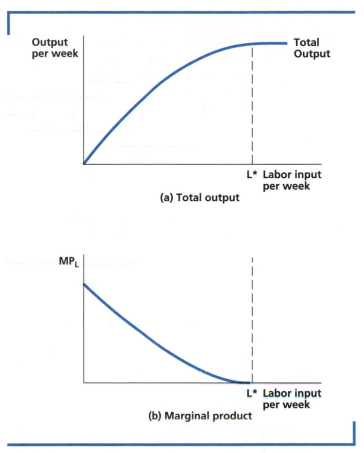

FIGURE 5.1 Relationship between Output and Labor Input Holding Other Inputs Constant Panel a shows the relationship between output and labor input holding other inputs constant. Panel b shows the marginal product of labor input, which is also the slope of the curve in panel a. Here, MP_L diminishes as labor input increases. MP_L reaches zero at L*.

labor curve (MP_L). Initially, MP_L is high because adding extra labor results in a significant increase in output. As labor input expands, however, MP_L falls. Indeed, at L*, additional labor input does not raise total output at all. It might be the case that 50 workers can produce 12,000 crates of oranges per week, but adding a 51st worker (with the same number of trees and equipment) fails to raise this output at all. This may happen because he or she just gets in the way in an already crowded orange grove. The marginal product of this new worker is therefore zero.

---

[2] In mathematical terms, the MP_L is the derivative of the production function with respect to L. Because K is held constant in defining the MP_L, this derivative should be a "partial" derivative.

Average Product

When people talk about the productivity of workers, they usually do not have in mind the economist's notion of marginal product. Rather, they tend to think in terms of "output per worker." In our orange grove example, with 25 workers, output per worker is 400 (= 10,000 ÷ 25) crates of oranges per week. With 50 workers, however, output per worker falls to 240 (= 12,000 ÷ 50) crates per week. Because the marginal productivity of each new worker is falling, output per worker is also falling. Notice, however, that the output-per-worker figures here give a misleading impression of how productive an extra worker really is. With 25 workers, output per worker is 400 crates of oranges per week, but adding a 26th worker only adds 200 crates per week. Indeed, with 50 workers, an extra worker adds no additional output even though output per worker is a respectable 240 crates per week.[3] Because most economic analysis involves questions of adding or subtracting small amounts of an input in a given production situation, the marginal product idea is clearly the more important concept. Figures on output per worker (that is, "average product") can be quite misleading if they do not accurately reflect these marginal ideas.

Appraising the Marginal Product Concept

MicroQuiz 5.1

Average and marginal productivities can be derived directly from the firm's production function. For each of the following cases, discuss how the values of these measures change as labor input expands. Explain why the cases differ.

Case 1. Apples harvested (q) depend on hours of labor employed (L) as: q = 10 + 50L.

Case 2. Books dusted (q) depend on minutes spent dusting (L) as: q = –10 + 5L.

The concept of marginal product itself may sometimes be difficult to apply because of the *ceteris paribus* assumption used in its definition. Both the levels of other inputs and the firm's technical knowledge are assumed to be held constant when we perform the conceptual experiment of, say, adding one more worker to an orange grove. But, in the real world, that is not how such hiring would likely occur. Rather, additional hiring would probably also necessitate adding additional equipment (ladders, crates, tractors, and so forth). From a broader perspective, additional hiring might be accompanied by the opening up of entirely new orange groves and the adoption of improved methods of production. In such cases, the *ceteris paribus* assumptions incorporated in the definition of marginal productivity would be

[3] Output per worker can be shown geometrically in the top panel of Figure 5.1 as the slope of a chord from the origin to the relevant point in the total product curve. Because of the concave shape of the total product curve, this slope too decreases as labor input is increased. Unlike the marginal product of labor, however, average productivity will never reach zero unless extra workers actually reduce output.

violated and the combinations of q and L observed would lie on many different marginal product curves. For this reason, it is more common to study the entire production function for a good, using the marginal product concept to help understand the overall function. Application 5.2: Why Do the Japanese Have a Cost Advantage in Making Cars? provides an illustration of why such an overall view may be desirable.

ISOQUANT MAPS

One way to picture an entire production function in two dimensions is to look at its **isoquant map**. We can again use a production function of the form $q = f(K,L)$, using capital and labor as convenient examples of any two inputs that might happen to be of interest. To show the various combinations of capital and labor that can be employed to produce a particular output level, we use an **isoquant** (from the Greek *iso,* meaning "equal"). For example, all the combinations of K and L that fall on the curve labeled $q = 10$ in Figure 5.2 are capable of producing 10 units of output per period. This single isoquant records the many alternative ways of producing 10 units of output. One combination is represented by point A. A firm could use L_A and K_A to produce 10 units of output. Alternatively, the firm might prefer to use relatively less capital and more labor and would therefore choose a point such as B. The isoquant demonstrates that a firm can produce 10 units of output in many different ways just as the indifference curves in Part 2 showed that many different bundles of goods yield the same utility.

There are infinitely many isoquants in the K–L plane. Each isoquant represents a different level of output. The isoquants record successively higher levels of output as we move in a northeasterly direction since using more of each of the inputs will permit output to increase. Two other isoquants (for $q = 20$ and $q = 30$) are also shown in Figure 5.2. They record those combinations of inputs that can produce the specified level of output. You may notice the similarity between an isoquant map and the individual's indifference curve map

Isoquant map
A contour map of a firm's production function.

Isoquant
A curve that shows the various combinations of inputs that will produce the same amount of output.

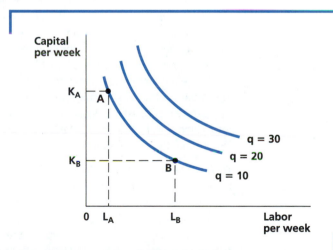

FIGURE 5.2 Isoquant Map Isoquants record the alternative combinations of inputs that can be used to produce a given level of output. The slope of these curves shows the rate at which L can be substituted for K while keeping output constant. The negative of this slope is called the (marginal) rate of technical substitution (RTS). In the figure, the RTS is positive, and it is diminishing for increasing inputs of labor.

In 1979, Japan overtook the United States as the world's largest producer of automobiles. U.S. imports of Japanese cars topped 2 million per year in 1983 and have remained high ever since. The story of the changing auto-buying behavior of Americans provides a major focus for several applications in this book. The following discussion takes a look at production in the two countries.

Labor Productivity

By most estimates, the Japanese enjoy a considerable productivity advantage in making automobiles. In terms of output per worker, for example, it is estimated to take Honda or Toyota about 30 labor hours to produce a car in Japan versus about 45 hours for General Motors or Chrysler in the United States. Similar differences also exist in vehicle production costs.[1]

Despite extensive research, it has not been possible to identify specific differences in the amounts of capital equipment devoted to automobile production that might explain these differences. That is, the differences in output per worker do not seem to be explained by simple substitution of capital for labor along a given isoquant map. Instead, a variety of more complex possibilities have been suggested.

Differences in Production Methods

Some of the productivity differences between U.S. and Japanese producers may be related to production methods. Because most Japanese cars and pickup trucks are about the same size, many types of vehicles can be produced on the same assembly lines. U.S. producers tend to use many more assembly lines to accommodate their greater variability in vehicle size. Automating production (through the use of robots, for example) is, therefore, somewhat easier in Japan.

There are also differences in the way auto production is organized in the United States and Japan. Although firms in both countries tend to buy many components of cars from independent suppliers, in Japan the suppliers are better integrated with the assembly firms. Information and engineering staffs are more widely shared so that redesigning is needed less frequently. This relationship also leads to higher levels of quality control.

Differences in Industrial Relations

In addition to these technical differences, some observers have also suggested that Japanese industrial relations practices may aid productivity. Because many workers effectively cannot be fired, usually belong to a company union, and obtain a large portion of their pay in terms of year-end bonuses, they may feel a greater attachment to their firms than do workers in the United States, where relations between labor and management are more adversarial. Some evidence that Japanese labor-relations practices influence productivity is provided by experiences with Japanese-run automobile plants in the United States (for example, the Honda assembly plant in Marysville, Ohio or Toyota's plant in Kentucky). In

---

[1] Figures reported by J. Ball in "Productivity Improves among U.S. Auto Makers," *The Wall Street Journal* (18 June 1999). Interestingly, the figures reported for Ford are much closer to those for Japanese firms.

these plants, labor productivity appears to be only slightly lower than for the same firms in Japan and higher than productivity in many U.S. auto plants.

To Think About

1. Why would auto producers in Japan and in the United States use different methods to make cars? Given that there are no great secrets surrounding auto production (U.S. and Japanese engineers frequently visit each other's factories), why wouldn't firms everywhere adopt the same production functions?
2. If Japanese industrial relations practices really do make workers more productive, how would you express this in a production function? Is "good labor relations" a separate input? If so, why don't all firms practice better labor relations?

discussed in Part 2. Both are "contour" maps that show the "altitude" (that is, of utility or output) associated with various input combinations. For isoquants, however, the labeling of the curves is measurable (an output of 10 units per week can be measured), and we are more interested in the shape of these curves than we were in the exact shape of indifference curves.

Rate of Technical Substitution

The slope of an isoquant shows how one input can be traded for another while holding output constant. Examining this slope gives some information about the technical possibilities for substituting labor for capital—an issue that can be quite important to firms. The slope of an isoquant (or, more properly, its negative) is called the **marginal rate of technical substitution (RTS)** of labor for capital. Specifically, the RTS is defined as the amount by which capital input can be reduced while holding quantity produced constant when one more unit of labor input is used. Mathematically,

$$
\begin{aligned}
\textit{Rate} \text{ of technical substitution} & \\
\text{(of labor for capital)} \ = RTS \ & \text{(of L for K)} \\
= & -(\text{Slope of isoquant}) \\
= & \ \frac{\text{Change in capital input}}{\text{Change in labor input}} \qquad (5.3)
\end{aligned}
$$

Marginal rate of technical substitution (RTS) The amount by which one input can be reduced when one more unit of another input is added while holding output constant. The negative of the slope of an isoquant.

where all of these changes refer to a situation in which output (q) is held constant. The particular value of this trade-off rate will depend not only on the level of output but also on the quantities of capital and labor being used. Its value depends on the point on the isoquant map at which the slope is to be measured. At a point such as A in Figure 5.2, relatively large amounts of capital can be given up if one more unit of labor is employed—at point A, the RTS is a high positive number. On the other hand, at point B, the availability of an additional unit of labor does not permit a very large reduction in capital input, and the RTS is relatively small.

The RTS and Marginal Products

We can use the RTS concept to discuss the likely shape of a firm's isoquant map. Most obviously, it seems clear that the RTS should be positive; that is, each isoquant should have a negative slope. If the quantity of labor employed by the firm increases, the firm should be able to reduce capital input and still keep output constant. Because labor presumably has a positive marginal product, the firm should be able to get by with less capital input when more labor is used. If increasing labor actually required the firm to use more capital, it would imply that the marginal product of labor is negative, and no firm would be willing to pay for an input that had a negative effect on output.

We can show this result more formally by noting that the RTS is precisely equal to the ratio of the marginal product of labor to the marginal product of capitals. That is,

$$\text{RTS (of L for K)} = \frac{MP_L}{MP_K} \qquad (5.4)$$

Suppose, for example, that $MP_L = 2$ and $MP_K = 1$. Then, if the firm employs one more worker, this will generate two extra units of output if capital input remains constant. Put another way, the firm can reduce capital input by 2 when there is another worker and output will not change. Hence, by definition, the RTS is 2 – the ratio of the marginal products.

Now, applying Equation 5.4, it is clear that if the RTS is negative, one of the marginal products must also be negative. But no firm would pay anything for an input that reduced output. Hence, at least for those portions of isoquants we can observe, the RTS must be positive (and the slope of the isoquant negative).

Diminishing RTS

The isoquants in Figure 5.2 are drawn not only with negative slopes (as they should be) but also as convex curves. Along any one of the curves, the RTS is *diminishing*. For a high ratio of K to L, the RTS is a large positive number indicating that a great deal of capital can be given up if one more unit of labor is employed. On the other hand, when a lot of labor is already being used, the RTS is low, signifying that only a small amount of capital can be traded for an additional unit of labor if output is to be held constant. This shape seems intuitively reasonable: The more labor (relative to capital) that is used, the less able labor is to replace capital in production. A diminishing RTS shows that use of a particular input can be pushed too far. Firms will not want to use "only labor" or "only machines" to produce a given level of output.[4] They will choose a more balanced input mix that uses at least some of each input. In Chapter 6, we see exactly how an optimal (that is, minimum cost) mix of inputs might be chosen. Application 5.3: Engineering and Economics illustrates how isoquant maps can be developed from actual production information.

RETURNS TO SCALE

Because production functions represent actual methods of production, economists pay considerable attention to the form of these functions. The shape and properties of a firm's production function are important for a variety of reasons. Using such information, a firm may decide how its research funds might best be spent on developing technical improvements. Or, public policymakers might study the form of production functions to argue that laws prohibiting very large-scale firms

> **MicroQuiz 5.2**
>
> A hole can be dug in 1 hour with a small shovel and in half an hour with a large shovel.
>
> **1.** What is the RTS of labor time for shovel size?
>
> **2.** What does the "one hole" isoquant look like? How much time would it take a worker to dig a hole if he or she used a small shovel for half the hole, then switched to the large shovel?

would harm economic efficiency. In this section, we develop some terminology to aid in examining such issues.

Adam Smith on Returns to Scale

The first important question we might ask about production functions is, how does the quantity of output respond to increases in all inputs together? For example, suppose all inputs were doubled. Would output also double, or is the relationship not quite so simple? Here we are asking about the **returns to scale** exhibited by a production function, a concept that has been of interest to economists ever since Adam Smith intensively studied (of all things) the production of pins in the eighteenth century. Smith identified two forces that come into play when all inputs are doubled (for a doubling of scale). First, a doubling of scale permits a greater "division of labor." Smith was intrigued by the skill of people who made only pin heads, or who sharpened pin shafts, or who stuck the two together. He

Returns to scale
The rate at which output increases in response to proportional increases in all inputs.

---

[4] An incorrect, but possibly instructive, argument based on Equation 5.4 might proceed as follows. In moving along an isoquant, more labor and less capital are being used. Assuming that each factor exhibits a diminishing marginal product, it might be argued that MP_L would decrease (because the quantity of labor has increased) and that MP_K would increase (because the quantity of capital has decreased). Consequently, the RTS (= MP_L/MP_K) should decrease. The problem with this argument is that *both* inputs are changing together. It is not possible to make such simple determinations about changes in marginal productivities when two inputs are changing, because the marginal product concept requires that all other inputs be held constant.

Engineering and Economics

One way economists manage to derive production functions for a specific good is through the use of information provided by engineers. An illustration of how engineering studies might be used is provided in Figure 1. Suppose engineers have developed three processes (A, B, and C) for producing a given good.

Process A uses a higher ratio of capital to labor than does process B, and process B uses a higher capital-to-labor ratio than does process C. Each process can be increased as much as desired by duplicating the basic machinery involved. The points a, b, and c on each respective ray show a particular output level, say q_0. By joining these points, we obtain the q_0 isoquant, with points between each ray reflecting proportionate use of two techniques.

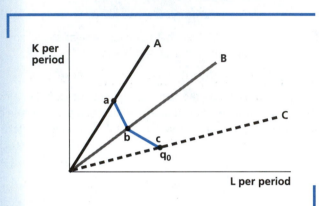

FIGURE 1 Construction of an Isoquant from Engineering Data The rays A, B, and C show three specific industrial processes. Points a, b, and c show the level of operation of each processes necessary to yield q_0. The q_1 isoquant reflects various mixtures of the three processes.

Solar Water Heating

This method was used by G. T. Sav to examine the production of domestic hot water by rooftop solar collectors.[1] Because solar systems require backup hot water generators for use during periods of reduced sunlight, Sav was especially interested in the proper way to integrate the two processes. Sav used engineering data to develop an isoquant map showing the trade-off between fuel use and solar system capital requirements. He showed that isoquant maps differ in various regions of the United States, with the productivity of solar collectors obviously depending upon the amount of sunlight available in the different regions. Solar collectors that work very efficiently in Arizona may be quite useless in often-cloudy New England.

Energy and Capital

More generally, the engineering approach has been used to examine the relationship between energy use and firms' capital input choices. A number of engineering studies suggest that energy and capital substitute for each other in the design of industrial equipment; to economize on energy usage generally requires more sophisticated machinery.

Although the substitutability between energy and capital seems clear to engineers, economists have sometimes found that energy and capital appear to complement each other in production. That is, the two inputs seem to rise and fall together. For example, some economists have claimed that poor productivity performances during the late 1970s

---

[1] G. T. Sav, "The Engineering Approach to Production Functions Revisited: An Application to Solar Processes." *The Journal of Industrial Economics* (September 1984): 21–35.

(see Application 5.5) may have resulted from rising energy prices, which deterred both energy and capital use.

To Think About

1. Governments often offer large tax incentives to people who install solar collectors. Would these incentives affect the technology used to produce domestic hot water? Do the incentives seem to be a good idea?
2. Engineers sometimes talk about the "energy efficiency" of an industrial process. Many systems (such as home heating plants) utilize only about 40 percent of the total energy available in the fuel they use. What does this fact suggest about capital-energy substitutability?

suggested that efficiency might increase—production might more than double—as greater specialization of this type becomes possible.

Smith did not envision that these benefits to large-scale operations would always be available, however. He recognized that large firms may encounter inefficiencies in managerial direction and control if scale is dramatically increased. Coordination of production plans for more inputs may become more difficult when there are many layers of management and many specialized workers involved in the production process.

A Precise Definition

Which of these two effects of scale is more important is an empirical question. To investigate this question, economists need a precise definition of returns to scale. A production function is said to exhibit *constant returns to scale* if a doubling of all inputs results in a precise doubling of output. If a doubling of all inputs yields less than a doubling of output, the production function is said to exhibit *decreasing returns to scale*. If a doubling of all inputs results in more than a doubling of output, the production function exhibits *increasing returns to scale*.

Graphic Illustrations

These possibilities are illustrated in the three graphs of Figure 5.3. In each case, production isoquants for $q = 10, 20, 30,$ and 40 are shown, together with a ray (labeled A) showing a uniform expansion of both capital and labor inputs. Panel a illustrates constant returns to scale. There, as both capital and labor inputs are successively increased from 1 to 2, and 2 to 3, and then 3 to 4, output expands proportionally. That is, output and inputs move in unison. In panel b, by comparison, the isoquants get farther apart as output expands. This is a case of decreasing returns to scale—an expansion in inputs does not result in a proportionate rise in output. For example, the doubling of both capital and labor inputs

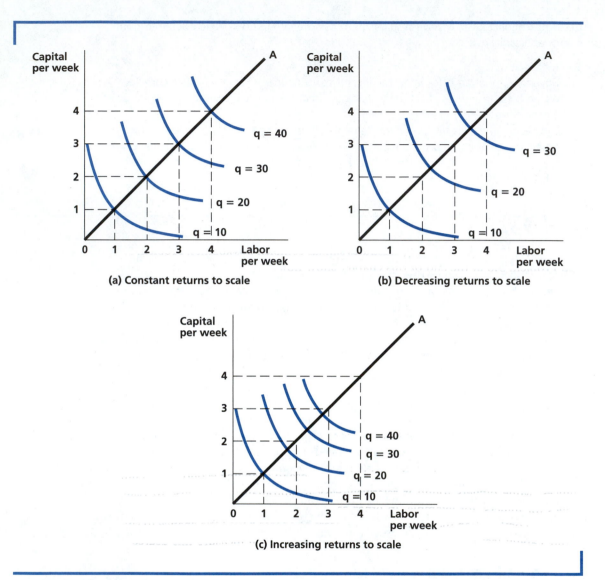

FIGURE 5.3 Isoquant Maps Showing Constant, Decreasing, and Increasing Returns to Scale In panel a, an expansion in both inputs leads to a similar, proportionate expansion in output. This shows constant returns to scale. In panel b, an expansion in inputs yields a less-than-proportionate expansion in output, illustrating decreasing returns to scale. Panel c shows increasing returns to scale—output expands proportionately faster than inputs.

from 1 to 2 units is not sufficient to increase output from 10 to 20. That increase in output would require more than a doubling of inputs. Finally, panel c illustrates increasing returns to scale. In this case, the isoquants get closer together as input expands—a doubling of inputs is more than sufficient to double output. Large-scale operation would in this case appear to be quite efficient.

INFOTRAC©
COLLEGE EDITION
Exclusively from Gale Group and Thomson Learning
www.infotrac-college.com
Keywords: Marginal product, Returns to scale, Input substitution, Multifactor productivity.

The types of scale economies experienced in the real world may, of course, be rather complex combinations of these simple examples. A production function may exhibit increasing returns to scale over some output ranges and decreasing returns to scale over other ranges. Or, some aspects of a good's production may illustrate scale economies, whereas other aspects may not. For example, the production of computer chips can be highly automated; but the assembly of chips into electronic components is more difficult to automate and may exhibit few such scale economies. Application 5.4: Returns to Scale in Beer Brewing illustrates similar complex possibilities. Problem 5.7 and Problem 5.8 at the end of this chapter show how the returns to scale concept can be captured with a simple mathematical function.

INPUT SUBSTITUTION

Another important characteristic of a production function is how "easily" capital can be substituted for labor, or, more generally, how any one input can be substituted for another. This characteristic depends more on the shape of a single isoquant than on the whole isoquant map. So far we have assumed that a given output level can be produced with a variety of different input mixes—that is, we assumed firms could substitute labor for capital while keeping output constant. How easily that substitution can be accomplished may, of course, vary. In some cases, the substitution can be made easily and quickly in response to changing economic circumstances. Mine owners found it relatively easy to automate in response to rising wages for miners, for example. In other cases, firms may have little choice about the input combination they must use. Producers of operas have little chance to substitute capital (scenery) for labor (singers). Economists can measure this degree of substitution very technically, but for us to do so here would take us too far afield.[5] We can look at one special case in which input substitution is impossible, which shows us the kinds of problems in substitution that economists have explored.

---

[5] Formally, the case of input substitution is measured by the *elasticity of substitution*, which is defined as the ratio of the percentage change in K/L to the percentage change in the RTS along an isoquant. For the fixed-proportions case, this elasticity is zero because K/L does not change at the isoquant's vertex.

Returns to Scale in Beer Brewing

The possibility of returns to scale has played a significant role in the evolution of the U.S. beer brewing industry since World War II. For most of that time, the increasing returns available from large-scale operations led to an increasing concentration of the industry's output among fewer firms. More recently, however, this process has been slowed by the rapid growth of local microbreweries.

Sources of Scale Economies

In part, the economies of scale in beer brewing arise from simple geometry. Because beer is produced by volume (usually measured in barrels per year) but the capital involved in brewing equipment (kettles, piping, and so forth) has costs that are proportional to surface area, larger breweries are able to achieve reduced capital costs per barrel. Economies of scale are also associated with container-filling technology—especially for beer cans. Automated control systems have made increasingly high-speed production lines possible. Finally, as for many products sold in a national market, there may also be economies of scale in distribution, advertising, and marketing. Television advertising is an especially important source of such economies.

Increasing Concentration in Beer Production

These factors came to play an increasingly important role in the U.S. beer industry (and in the beer industry in many other countries) in the period following World War II. Prior to the war, beer was produced mainly on a local level. High transportation costs tended to isolate markets. Most large cities had three or more local breweries. But improvements in production techniques (especially those related to producing beer in cans) and in national marketing resulted in a sharp decline in numbers of firms as the market consolidated rapidly. Between 1945 and the mid-1980s, the number of U.S. brewing firms fell by more than 90 percent from 450 to 44. Even more significant was the consolidation of industry output among a few large firms—especially Anheuser-Busch, Miller, and Coors. These firms tended to operate very large breweries (each producing over 4 million barrels per year), usually in multiple locations to reduce shipping costs. Anheuser-Busch alone came to account for more than one-third of industry output, making its Budweiser the largest-selling single brand of beer in the world.

Product Differentiation and the Growth of Microbreweries

The major brewery firms left one significant hole in their market penetration: They neglected premium brands, leaving an opening for local microbreweries to enter this market. Beginning in the mid-1980s, firms such as Anchor (San Francisco), Sierra Nevada (Chico, California), and Redhook (Seattle) began producing significant amounts of premium brew. Because they were able to obtain higher prices for their output than the national brands, they could cover the extra costs that their relatively small scale of operations entailed. The 1990s saw a virtual explosion of new brands, many with odd names (Wicked Pete's, Three Fingered Jake's) or local appeal (Catamount, Telluride). A similar course of events was followed in Great Britain during the 1980s with the "real ale" movement. In that case, many of the most promising microbrews were absorbed into larger national brands. Some movement in that direction has also occurred in the United States. For example, in 1994, Redhook formed a distribution alliance with Anheuser-Busch, hoping to benefit from the larger firm's economies of scale in that stage of the business. Whether the microbrews can retain an identity of their own, therefore, remains an open question.

To Think About

1. How do transport costs affect economies of scale in breweries? Why has Coors, alone among the major producers, chosen to pursue a single-plant strategy? How might a large brewing firm decide on an optimal number of plants?
2. Who buys beer produced by microbreweries? Is this a different market segment from buyers of Budweiser or Miller? How are such differences relevant to beer marketing?

Fixed-Proportions Production Function

Figure 5.4 demonstrates a case where no substitution is possible. This case is rather different from the ones we have looked at so far. Here, the isoquants are L-shaped, indicating that machines and labor must be used in absolutely fixed proportions. Every machine has a fixed complement of workers that cannot be varied. For example, if K_1 machines are in use, L_1 workers are required to produce output level q_1. Employing more workers than L_1 will not increase output with K_1 machines. This is shown by the fact that the q_1 isoquant is horizontal beyond the point K_1, L_1. In other words, the marginal productivity of labor is zero beyond L_1. On the other hand, using fewer workers would result in excess

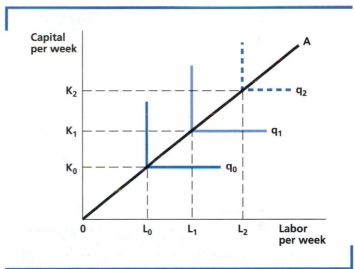

FIGURE 5.4 Isoquant Map with Fixed Proportions The isoquant map shown here has no substitution possibilities. Capital and labor must be used in fixed proportions if neither is to be redundant. For example, if K_1 machines are available, L_1 units of labor should be used. If L_2 units of labor are used, there will be excess labor since no more than q_1 can be produced from the given machines. Alternatively, if L_0 laborers were hired, machines would be in excess to the extent $K_1 - K_0$.

machines. If only L_0 workers were hired, for instance, only q_0 units could be produced, but these units could be produced with only K_0 machines. When L_0 workers are hired, there is an excess of machines of an amount given by $K_1 - K_0$.

The production function whose isoquant map is shown in Figure 5.4 is called a **fixed-proportions production function.** Both inputs are fully employed only if a combination of K and L that lies along the ray A, which passes through the

Fixed-proportions production function
A production function in which the inputs must be used in a fixed ratio to one another.

vertices of the isoquants, is chosen. Otherwise, one input will be excessive in the sense that it could be cut back without reducing output. If a firm with such a production function wishes to expand, it must increase all inputs simultaneously so that none of the inputs is redundant.

The fixed-proportions production function has a wide variety of applications to real-world production techniques. Many machines do require a fixed complement of workers; more than these would be redundant. For example, consider the combination of capital and labor required to mow a lawn. The lawn mower needs one person for its operation, and a worker needs one lawn mower in order to produce any output. Output can be expanded (that is, more grass can be mowed at the same time) only by adding capital and labor to the productive process in fixed-proportions. Many production functions may be of this type, and the fixed-proportions model is in many ways appropriate for production planning.[6]

The Relevance of Input Substitutability

MicroQuiz 5.3

The only inputs required to produce educated students (Q) are teachers' time (T) and textbooks (B).

1. Do you think this production function exhibits increasing, constant, or decreasing returns to scale?

2. What kinds of substitution possibilities do you think are reflected in this production function?

The ease with which one input can be substituted for another is of considerable interest to economists. They can use the shape of an isoquant map to see the relative ease with which different industries can adapt to the changing availability of productive inputs. For example, over the past 100 years, the output of the American economy has shifted markedly away from agricultural production and toward manufacturing and service industries. This shift moved certain factors of production (notably, labor) out of agriculture and into other industries. If production were relatively flexible in terms of input substitutability, the inputs formerly used in agriculture could be easily accommodated in the manufacturing and service industries. On the other hand, if production were closer to fixed proportions, the inputs might not be absorbed in exactly the proportions released by agriculture and unemployment might result.

CHANGES IN TECHNOLOGY

A production function reflects firms' technical knowledge about how to use inputs to produce outputs. When firms improve their production techniques, the produc-

---

[6] The lawn mower example points up another possibility. Presumably there is some leeway in choosing what size and type of lawn mower to buy. Any device, from a pair of clippers to a gang mower, might be chosen. Prior to the actual purchase, the capital-labor ratio in lawn mowing can be considered variable. Once the mower is purchased, however, the capital-labor ratio becomes fixed.

tion function changes. This kind of technical advancement occurs constantly as older, outmoded machines are replaced by more efficient ones that embody state-of-the-art techniques. Workers too are part of this technical progress as they become better educated and learn special skills for doing their jobs. Today, for example, steel is made far more efficiently than in the nineteenth century both because blast furnaces and rolling mills are better and because workers are better trained to use these facilities.

The production function concept and its related isoquant map are important tools for understanding the effect of technical change. Formally, technical progress represents a shift in the production function, such as that illustrated in Figure 5.5. In this figure, the isoquant q_0 summarizes the initial state of technical knowledge. That level of output can be produced using K_0, L_0, or any of a number of input combinations. With the discovery of new production techniques, the q_0 isoquant shifts toward the origin—the same output level can now be produced using smaller quantities of inputs. If, for example, the q_0 isoquant shifts inward to q_0', it is now possible to produce q_0 with the same amount of capital as before (K_0) but with much less labor (L_1). It is even possible to produce q_0 using both less capital and less labor than previously by choosing a point such as A. **Technical progress** represents a real saving on inputs and (as we see in the next chapter) a reduction in the costs of production.

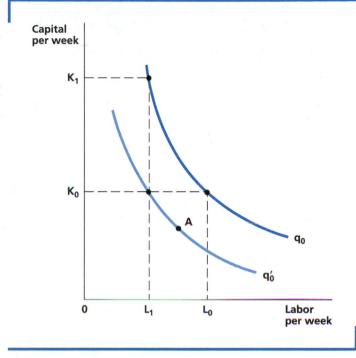

FIGURE 5.5 Technical Change Technical progress shifts the q_0 isoquant to q_0'. Whereas previously it required K_0 L_0 to produce q_0 now, with the same amount of capital, only L_1 units of labor are required. This result can be contrasted to capital-labor substitution, in which the required labor input for q_0 also declines to L_1 more capital (K_1) is used.

Technical progress
A shift in the production function that allows a given output level to be produced using fewer inputs.

Technical Progress versus Input Substitution

We can use Figure 5.5 to show an important distinction between true technical advancement and simple capital-labor substitution. With technical progress, the firm can continue to use K_0, but it produces q_0 with less labor (L_1). The output per unit of labor input rises from q_0/L_0 to q_0/L_1. Even in the absence of technical

TABLE 5.1 Hamburger Production Exhibits Constant Returns to Scale

Grills (K)	Workers (L)	Hamburgers per hour
1	1	10
2	2	20
3	3	30
4	4	40
5	5	50
6	6	60
7	7	70
8	8	80
9	9	90
10	10	100

Source: Equation 5.5.

improvements, the firm could have achieved such an increase by choosing to use K_1 units of capital. This substitution of capital for labor would also have caused the average productivity of labor to rise from q_0/L_0 to q_0/L_1. This rise would not mean any real improvement in the way goods are made, however. In studying productivity data, especially data on output per worker, we must be careful that the changes being observed represent technical improvements rather than capital–labor substitution. Application 5.5: Multifactor Productivity illustrates this distinction.

A NUMERICAL EXAMPLE

Additional insights about the nature of production functions can be obtained by looking at a simple numerical example. Although this example is obviously unrealistic (and, I hope, a bit amusing), it does reflect the way production is studied in the real world.

The Production Function

Suppose we looked in detail at the production process used by the fast-food chain Hamburger Heaven (HH). The production function for each outlet in the chain is

$$\text{Hamburgers per hour} = q = 10\sqrt{KL} \tag{5.5}$$

where K represents the number of grills used and L represents the number of workers employed during an hour of production. One aspect of this function is that it exhibits constant returns to scale.[7] Table 5.1 shows this fact by looking at input levels for K and L ranging from 1 to 10. As both workers and grills are increased together, hourly hamburger output rises proportionally. To increase the number of hamburgers it serves, HH must simply duplicate its kitchen technology over and over again.

---

[7] Since this production function can be written $q = 10K^{1/2}L^{1/2}$, it is a Cobb-Douglas function with constant returns to scale (since the exponents sum to 1.0). See Problem 5.7.

Differences in the way productivity is measured can have an important effect on the economic insights that the data provide. By far the most common way of measuring productivity is in terms of "output per hour." For example, Table 1 shows the rates of change in output per hour in manufacturing during three recent periods in the United States, Germany, and France. Although the data show that the rates of increase were slower in the 1974–91 period than either before or after, gains during that period still averaged more than 2 percent per year, a reasonably respectable showing.

The Multifactor Correction

But these figures can be rather misleading because they may reflect simple capital-labor substitution rather than real technical gains. For that reason, national statistical agencies have begun to compute a "multifactor" productivity measure that attempts to take such substitution into account.[1] Table 2 shows these figures also for the United States, Germany, and France. These adjusted figures bring the abysmal performance of productivity in the 1974–91 period into sharper focus. In all of the countries, rates of productivity gain during this period were less than half of what they were in either earlier or later periods.

TABLE 1 Annual Average Change in Output per Hour in Manufacturing

	1956–73	1974–91	1992–2000
United States	2.84	2.36	4.03
Germany	6.29	2.80	3.08
France	6.22	2.80	4.29

TABLE 2 Annual Average Change in Multifactor Productivity in Manufacturing

	1956–73	1974–91	1992–2000
United States	1.57	0.74	1.96
Germany	3.40	0.94	1.66
France	4.42	1.23	3.05

Source for Tables 1 and 2: Bureau of Labor Statistics web site: http://www.stats.bls.gov/

[1] A simple illustration of how this computation is made is based on the Cobb-Douglas production function $Q = AK^a L^b$ where A is the technical change factor. Taking logs of this expression and differentiating with respect to time yields $G_Q = G_A + aG_K + bG_L$ where G_X means the proportional rate of growth of X ($[dX/dt]/X$). Hence, multifactor productivity (G_A) can be calculated from knowledge of growth rates of output and of the two inputs K and L, and from knowledge about the exponents a and b.

(continued)

Explanations for the Decline

Many explanations have been proposed for the multifactor productivity slowdown after 1973. Some economists blame the rapidly rising energy prices of the period or the accompanying high rates of inflation in all prices, claiming that such forces made production planning especially difficult. Other explanations include such factors as increasing environmental regulations, deteriorating education systems and poorly trained workers, or even a general decline in the work ethic among employees.

Turnaround in the 1990s

Whatever the causes for poor productivity performance in the 1974–91 period, the turnaround in the 1990s has been equally surprising, at least in manufacturing. Table 2 shows that multifactor productivity gains in the 1990s were reasonably close to what they had been in the "good old days" before 1973. Perhaps this turnaround represents a reversal of the earlier trends (maybe workers have rediscovered the work ethic?); or, this may be a reaction to some new factors altogether (such as a response to increasing globalization in all manufacturing industries).

To Think About

1. The figures in Table 1 and Table 2 refer only to manufacturing. Why might it be difficult to measure productivity in such industries as services or the government?
2. The dates used in Table 1 and Table 2 to divide up the entire period are problematic because some of them correspond to major recessions. How does the business cycle affect the measurement of productivity trends?

Average and Marginal Productivities

To show labor productivity for HH, we must hold capital constant and vary only labor. Suppose that HH has four grills (K = 4, a particularly easy number of which to take a square root). In this case

$$q = 10\sqrt{4 \cdot L} = 20\sqrt{L} \qquad (5.6)$$

and this provides a simple relationship between output and labor input. Table 5.2 shows this relationship. Notice two things about the table. First, output per worker declines as more hamburger flippers are employed. Because K is fixed, this occurs because the flippers get in each other's way as they become increasingly crowded around the four grills. Second, notice that the productivity of each additional worker hired also declines. Hiring more workers drags down output per worker because of the diminishing marginal productivity arising from the fixed number of grills. Even though HH's production exhibits constant returns to scale when both K and L can change, holding one input constant yields the expected declining average and marginal productivities.

TABLE 5.2 Total Output, Average Productivity, and Marginal Productivity with Four Grills

Grills (K)	Workers (L)	Hamburgers per hour (q)	q/L	MP$_L$
4	1	20.0	20.0	—
4	2	28.3	14.1	8.3
4	3	34.6	11.5	6.3
4	4	40.0	10.0	5.4
4	5	44.7	8.9	4.7
4	6	49.0	8.2	4.3
4	7	52.9	7.6	3.9
4	8	56.6	7.1	3.7
4	9	60.0	6.7	3.4
4	10	63.2	6.3	3.2

Source: Equation 5.5.

The Isoquant Map

The overall production technology for HH is best illustrated by its isoquant map. Here, we show how to get one isoquant, but any others desired could be computed in exactly the same way. Suppose HH wants to produce 40 hamburgers per hour. Then its production function becomes

$$q = 40 \text{ hamburgers per hour} = 10\sqrt{KL} \qquad (5.7)$$

or

$$4 = \sqrt{KL} \qquad (5.8)$$

or

$$16 = K \cdot L \qquad (5.9)$$

Table 5.3 shows a few of the K, L combinations that satisfy this equation. Clearly, there are many ways to produce 40 hamburgers, ranging from using a lot of grills with workers dashing among them to using many workers gathered around a few grills. All possible combinations are reflected in the "q = 40" isoquant in Figure 5.6. Other isoquants would have exactly the same shape showing that HH has many substitution possibilities in the ways it actually chooses to produce its heavenly burgers.

TABLE 5.3 Construction of the q = 40 Isoquant

Hamburgers per hour (q)	Grills (K)	Workers (L)
40	16.0	1
40	8.0	2
40	5.3	3
40	4.0	4
40	3.2	5
40	2.7	6
40	2.3	7
40	2.0	8
40	1.8	9
40	1.6	10

Source: Equation 5.9.

Technical Progress

The possibility for scientific advancement in the art of hamburger production can also be shown in this simple case. Suppose that genetic engineering leads to the invention of self-flipping burgers so that the production function becomes

$$q = 20\sqrt{K \cdot L} \qquad (5.10)$$

We can compare this new technology to that which prevailed previously by recalculating the q = 40 isoquant:

$$q = 40 = 20\sqrt{KL} \qquad (5.11)$$

or

$$2 = \sqrt{KL} \qquad (5.12)$$

or

$$4 = KL \qquad (5.13)$$

The combinations of K and L that satisfy this equation are shown by the "q = 40 after invention" isoquant in Figure 5.6. One way to see the overall effect of the invention is to calculate output per worker-hour in these two cases. With 4 grills, Figure 5.6 shows that it took 4 workers using the prior technology to produce 40 hamburgers per hour. Average productivity was 10 hamburgers per hour per worker. Now a single worker can produce 40 hamburgers per hour because each burger flips itself. Average productivity is 40 hamburgers per hour per worker. This level of output per worker-hour could have been attained under the old technology, but that would have required using 16 grills and would have been considerably more costly.

MicroQuiz 5.4

Consider the following historical changes in labor productivity. Which of these were "technical progress"? Which were primarily substitution of capital for labor? If the case seems ambiguous, explain why.

1. The increase in coal output per worker when open-pit mining began.

2. The increase in auto output per worker with the introduction of the assembly line.

3. The increase in electricity output per worker with larger power stations.

4. The increase in computer-power output per worker with the availability of better microchips.

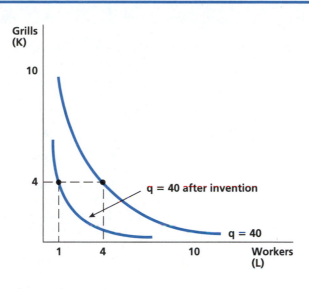

FIGURE 5.6 Technical Progress in Hamburger Production The q = 40 isoquant comes directly from Table 5.3. Technical progress causes this isoquant to shift inward. Previously it took 4 workers with 4 grills to produce 40 hamburgers per hour. With the intervention, it takes only 1 worker working with 4 grills to achieve the same output.

SUMMARY

Chapter 5 shows how economists conceptualize the process of production. We introduce the notion of a production function, which records the relationship between input use and output, and we show how this function can be illustrated with an isoquant map. Several features of the production function are analyzed in the chapter:

- The marginal product of any input is the extra output that can be produced by adding one more unit of that input while holding all other inputs constant. The marginal product of an input declines as more of that input is used.
- The possible input combinations that a firm might use to produce a given level of output are shown on an isoquant. The (negative of the) slope of the isoquant is called the rate of technical substitution (RTS)—it shows how one input can be substituted for another while holding output constant.

- "Returns to scale" refers to the way in which a firm's output responds to proportionate increases in all inputs. If a doubling of all inputs causes output to more than double, there are increasing returns to scale. If such a doubling of inputs causes output to less than double, returns to scale are decreasing. The middle case, when output exactly doubles, reflects constant returns to scale.
- In some cases, it may not be possible for the firm to substitute one input for another. In these cases, the inputs must be used in fixed proportions. Such production functions have L-shaped isoquants.
- Technical progress shifts the firm's entire isoquant map. A given output level can be produced with fewer inputs.

REVIEW QUESTIONS

1. Provide a brief description of the production function for each of the following firms. What is the firm's output? What inputs does it use? Can you think of any special features of the way production takes place in the firm?

   a. An Iowa wheat farm
   b. An Arizona vegetable farm
   c. U.S. Steel Corporation
   d. A local arc welding firm
   e. Sears
   f. Joe's Hot Dog Stand
   g. The Metropolitan Opera
   h. The Metropolitan Museum of Art
   i. The National Institutes of Health
   j. Dr. Smith's private practice
   k. Paul's lemonade stand

2. In what ways are firms' isoquant maps and individuals' indifference curve maps based on the same idea? What are the most important ways in which these concepts differ?

3. Roy Dingbat is the manager of a hot dog stand that uses only labor and capital to produce hot dogs. The firm usually produces 1,000 hot dogs a day with 5 workers and 4 grills. One day a worker is absent but the stand still produces 1,000 hot dogs. What does this imply about the 1,000 hot dog isoquant? Why do Roy's management skills justify his name?

4. A recent news headline read: "Productivity rises by record amount as economy roars out of recession." Assuming that the "productivity" referred to in this headline is the customary "Average Output per Worker Hour" that is usually reported, how would you evaluate whether this increase really is an increase in workers' marginal products?

5. Marjorie Cplus wrote the following answer on her micro examination: "Virtually every production function exhibits diminishing returns to scale because my professor said that all inputs have diminishing marginal productivities. So when all inputs are doubled, output must be less than double." How would you grade Marjorie's answer?

6. Answer question 5 using two specific production functions as examples:

   a. A fixed-proportions production function
   b. A Cobb-Douglas production function of the form

   $$q = \sqrt{K \cdot L}$$

   (See problems 5.4, 5.7, and 5.8 for a discussion of this case.)

7. Universal Gizmo operates a large number of plants that produce gizmos using a special technology. Each plant produces exactly 100 gizmos per day using 5 gizmo presses and 15 workers. Explain why the production function for the entire UG firm exhibits constant returns to scale.

8. Continuing the prior question, suppose that Universal Gizmo devises a new plant design that uses 15 gizmo presses and 5 workers also to produce 100 gizmos per day. How would you construct an isoquant for the firm for 100,000 gizmos per day based on the following assumptions:

   a. The firm uses plants only of the type specified in question 7.
   b. The firm uses plants only of its new type.
   c. The firm uses 500 plants of the type in question 7 and 500 plants of the new type.
   What do you conclude about the ability of UG to substitute workers for gizmo presses in its production?

9. Can a fixed-proportions production function exhibit increasing or decreasing returns to scale? What would its isoquant map look like in each case?

10. Suppose that a firm's production function for each of its many plants exhibits constant returns to scale, but that overall operations must be coordinated by a single boss. With only a few plants to manage the boss rapidly becomes bored—he/she does a better job with more plants to manage—up to a point. But, once there are more than 20 plants to manage, the boss gets very confused and output tumbles. How would the isoquant map for this firm look?

PROBLEMS

5.1 Imagine that the production function for tuna cans is given by

$$q = 6K + 4L$$

where
q = Output of tuna cans per hour
K = Capital input per hour
L = Labor input per hour

a. Assuming capital is fixed at K = 6, how much L is required to produce 60 tuna cans per hour? To produce 100 per hour?
b. Now assume that capital input is fixed at K = 8; what L is required to produce 60 tuna cans per hour? To produce 100 per hour?
c. Graph the q = 60 and q = 100 isoquants. Indicate the points found in part a and part b. What is the RTS along the isoquants?

5.2 Frisbees are produced according to the production function

$$q = 2K + L$$

where
q = Output of Frisbees per hour
K = Capital input per hour
L = Labor input per hour

a. If K = 10, how much L is needed to produce 100 Frisbees per hour?
b. If K = 25, how much L is needed to produce 100 Frisbees per hour?
c. Graph the q = 100 isoquant. Indicate the points on that isoquant defined in part a and part b. What is the RTS along this isoquant? Explain why the RTS is the same at every point on the isoquant.
d. Graph the q = 50 and q = 200 isoquants for this production function also. Describe the shape of the entire isoquant map.
e. Suppose technical progress resulted in the production function for Frisbees becoming

$$q = 3K + 1.5L$$

Answer part a through part d for this new production function and discuss how it compares to the previous case.

5.3 Digging clams by hand in Sunset Bay requires only labor input. The total number of clams obtained per hour (q) is given by

$$q = 100\sqrt{L}$$

where L is labor input per hour.

a. Graph the relationship between q and L.
b. What is the average productivity of labor (output per unit of labor input) in Sunset Bay? Graph this relationship and show that output per unit of labor input diminishes for increases in labor input.
c. It can be shown that the marginal productivity of labor in Sunset Bay is given by

$$MP_L = 50/\sqrt{L}$$

Graph this relationship and show that labor's marginal productivity is less than average productivity for all values of L. Explain why this is so.

5.4 Suppose that the hourly output of chili at a barbecue (q, measured in pounds) is characterized by

$$q = 20\sqrt{KL}$$

where K is the number of large pots used each hour and L is the number of worker hours employed.

a. Graph the q = 2,000 pounds per hour isoquant.
b. The point K = 100, L = 100 is one point on the q = 2,000 isoquant. What value of K corresponds to L = 101 on that isoquant? What is the approximate value for the RTS at K = 100, L = 100?
c. The point K = 25, L = 400 also lies on the q = 2,000 isoquant. If L = 401, what must K be for this input combination to lie on the q = 2,000 isoquant? What is the approximate value of the RTS at K = 25, L = 400?
d. For this production function, it can be shown that a general formula for the RTS is

$$RTS = K/L$$

Compare the results from applying this formula to those you calculated in part b and part c. To convince yourself further, perform a similar calculation for the point K = 200, L = 50.

e. If technical progress shifted the production function to

$$q = 40\sqrt{KL}$$

all of the input combinations identified earlier can now produce q = 4,000 pounds per hour. Would the various values calculated for the RTS be changed as a result of this technical progress, assuming now that the RTS is measured along the q = 4,000 isoquant?

5.5 Grapes must be harvested by hand. This production function is characterized by fixed proportions—each worker must have one pair of stem clippers to produce any output. A skilled worker with clippers can harvest 50 pounds of grapes per hour.

a. Sketch the grape production isoquants for q = 500, q = 1,000, and q = 1,500 and indicate where on these isoquants firms are likely to operate.

b. Suppose a vineyard owner currently has 20 clippers. If the owner wishes to utilize fully these clippers, how many workers should be hired? What should grape output be?

c. Do you think the choices described in part b are necessarily profit-maximizing? Why might the owner hire fewer workers than indicated in this part?

d. Ambidextrous harvesters can use two clippers—one in each hand—to produce 75 pounds of grapes per hour. Draw an isoquant map (for q = 500, 1,000, and 1,500) for ambidextrous harvesters. Describe in general terms the considerations that would enter into an owner's decision to hire such harvesters.

5.6 Power Goat Lawn Company uses two sizes of mowers to cut lawns. The smaller mowers have a 24-inch blade and are used on lawns with many trees and obstacles. The larger mowers are exactly twice as big as the smaller mowers and are used on open lawns

where maneuverability is not so difficult. The two production functions available to Power Goat are:

	Output per hour (square feet)	Capital input (no. of 24″ mowers)	Labor input
Large mowers	8,000	2	1
Small mowers	5,000	1	1

a. Graph the q = 40,000 square feet isoquant for the first production function. How much K and L would be used if these factors were combined without waste?

b. Answer part a for the second function.

c. How much K and L would be used without waste if half of the 40,000-square-foot lawn were cut by the method of the first production function and half by the method of the second? How much K and L would be used if three-fourths of the lawn were cut by the first method and one-fourth by the second? What does it mean to speak of fractions of K and L?

d. On the basis of your observations in part c, draw a q = 40,000 isoquant for the combined production functions.

5.7 The production function

$$q = K^a L^b$$

where $0 \le a, b \le 1$, is called a Cobb-Douglas production function. This function is widely used in economic research. Using the function, show that

a. The chili production function in problem 5.4 is a special case of the Cobb-Douglas.

b. If a + b = 1, a doubling of K and L will double q.

c. If a + b < 1, a doubling of K and L will less than double q.

d. If a + b > 1, a doubling of K and L will more than double q.

e. Using the results from part b through part d, what can you say about the returns to scale exhibited by the Cobb-Douglas function?

5.8 For the Cobb-Douglas production function in problem 5.7, it can be shown (using calculus) that

$$MP_K = aK^{a-1}L^b$$
$$MP_L = bK^aL^{b-1}$$

If the Cobb-Douglas exhibits constant returns to scale (a + b = 1), show that

a. Both marginal productivities are diminishing.
b. The RTS for this function is given by

$$RTS = \frac{bK}{aL}$$

c. The function exhibits a diminishing RTS.

5.9 The production function for puffed rice is given by

$$q = 100\sqrt{KL}$$

where q is the number of boxes produced per hour, K is the number of puffing guns used each hour, and L is the number of workers hired each hour.

a. Calculate the q = 1,000 isoquant for this production function and show it on a graph.
b. If K = 10, how many workers are required to produce q = 1,000? What is the average productivity of puffed-rice workers?

c. Suppose technical progress shifts the production function to

$$q = 200\sqrt{KL}$$

Answer part a and part b for this case.

5.10 Capital and labor are used in fixed proportions to produce airline flights—it takes two operators (pilots) and one plane for each trip made. Technical and safety problems make it impossible for a single pilot to fly a plane.

a. What is the output of this production process and what do the isoquants look like?
b. Suppose an airline hired 30 pilots and 10 planes during a particular period. Explain both graphically and in words why this might be a foolish thing to do.
c. Suppose progress in avionic equipment made it possible for a single pilot to handle each plane. How would that shift the isoquant map described in part a? Would this raise the average productivity of labor in this industry? Would it raise the average productivity of capital (planes)? Explain.

INTERNET EXERCISES

1. *Labor productivity: international comparisons.* How does labor productivity in the United States stack up to that in other countries? The Penn World tables, an exceptionally useful database, particularly for macroeconomic applications, may shed some light on this question. To access the database, go to *http://datacentre2.chass. utoronto.ca/pwt/*. Click on Alphabetical List of Topics. Scroll down and click on Real GDP per Worker (i.e., output per worker). Using 1990 as the selected year, click Submit Query. What country ranks first in output per worker? Last? Where is the United States ranked? By what percentage does the United States' output per worker exceed that of West Germany? Japan? India? Technically, labor productivity is more accurately measured as output per worker *hour*, not output per worker. Consider, for example, that while 1990 output per worker was higher in the United States than in West Germany, 1990 output per worker *hour* was 3 percent higher in West Germany than in the United States. Can you explain what might lead to such a difference?

2. *Household production.* As Application 5.1 suggests, while the amount of household production is substantial, it is not included in standard measures of overall economic activity such as GDP (gross domestic product). Recently, GPI Atlantic has attempted to construct a "Genuine Progress Index" for Canada, which includes the value of such unpaid household economic activity. Some of their findings can be found at *http://www.*

gpiatlantic.org/pr_valhw.shtml. In total, how many hours did Nova Scotians spend on domestic chores and child care? How many total hours did Nova Scotians spend on work for pay? What is the total value of Nova Scotia's household production? If the value of this production were included in Nova Scotia's GDP, by what percent would GDP increase? Including household production, what are the three largest sectors in the entire Nova Scotia economy? The article suggests that increased expenditures on "time-saving" household durable equipment has not really saved labor time in household production at all. What does this imply about the value of the marginal rate of technical substitution of labor for capital in household production? Explain. Does the same implication hold if one also accounts for the fact that household "output" may have increased? Carefully explain and show using an isoquant map.

6

Costs

Production costs are a crucial determinant of firms' supply decisions. In this chapter, we look at such costs. Specifically, we are concerned with defining the costs that are associated with each output level that the firm might consider. To do so, we study how a firm chooses, for each output level, that combination of inputs that makes total costs as small as possible. We also look at why firms might incur relatively higher costs if they have to make short-term changes in their output levels than would be the case if they had more time to adapt to new production levels. When our analysis is finished, you should be in a position to understand the elements that go into determining the cost structure for any firm.

BASIC CONCEPTS OF COSTS

There are at least three different concepts of costs encountered in economics: opportunity cost, accounting cost, and economic cost. For economists, the most general of these is **opportunity cost** (sometimes called *social cost*). Because resources are limited, any decision to produce more of one good means doing without some other good. When an automobile is produced, for example, an implicit decision has been made to do without 15 bicycles, say, that could have been produced using the labor, chrome, and glass that goes into the automobile. The opportunity cost of one automobile is 15 bicycles.

Because it is often inconvenient to express opportunity costs in terms of physical goods, we sometimes choose monetary units instead. The price of a car may often be a good reflection of the costs of the goods that were given up to produce it. We could then say the opportunity cost of an automobile is $20,000 worth of other goods. This may not always be the case, however. If something were produced with resources that could not be usefully employed elsewhere, the true

Opportunity cost
The cost of a good as measured by the alternative uses that are forgone by producing the good.

opportunity cost of this good's production would be close to zero, even though someone may have been paid for the resources.

Although the concept of opportunity cost is fundamental to all economic analysis, it may be too abstract to be of practical use to firms in looking at the costs of their inputs. The two other concepts of cost are directly related to the firm's input choices. **Accounting cost** stresses what was actually paid for inputs, even if those amounts were paid long ago. **Economic cost** (which draws, in obvious ways, on the idea of opportunity cost), on the other hand, is defined as the payment required to keep an input in its present employment, or the remuneration that the resource would receive in its next best alternative use.

To see how the economic definition of cost might be applied in practice and how it differs from accounting ideas, we now consider the economic costs of three general inputs: labor, capital, and the services of entrepreneurs (owners).

Accounting cost
The concept that inputs cost what was paid for them.

Economic cost
The amount required to keep an input in its present use; the amount that it would be worth in its next best alternative use.

Labor Costs

Economists and accountants view labor costs in much the same way. To the accountant, firms' spending on wages and salaries is a current expense and therefore is a cost of production. Economists regard wage payments as an *explicit cost*: labor services (worker-hours) are purchased at some hourly **wage rate** (which we denote by w), and we presume that this rate is the amount that workers would earn in their next best alternative employment. If a firm hires a worker at, say, $10 per hour, we usually assume that this figure represents about what the worker would earn elsewhere. There is no reason for the firm to offer more than this amount, and no worker would willingly accept less. Of course, there are cases in the real world where a worker's wage does not fairly reflect economic cost. The wages of the dunderhead son of the boss exceed his economic cost since no one else would be willing to pay him very much; or, prisoners who are paid $.50/hour to make license plates probably could earn much more were they out of jail. Noticing such differences between wages paid and workers' opportunity costs can provide an interesting start to an economic investigation; but, for now, it seems most useful to start with the presumption that wages paid are about equal to true economic costs.

Wage rate (w)
The cost of hiring one worker for one hour.

Capital Costs

In the case of capital services (machine-hours), accounting and economic definitions of costs differ greatly. Accountants, in calculating capital costs, use the historical price of a particular machine and apply some (more or less) arbitrary depreciation rule to determine how much of that machine's original price to charge to current costs. For example, a machine purchased for $1,000 and expected to last 10 years might be said to "cost" $100 per year, in the accountant's view. Economists, on the other hand, regard the amount paid for a machine as a **sunk cost.** Once such a cost has been incurred, there is no way to get it back.

Sunk cost
Expenditure that once made cannot be recovered.

Because sunk costs do not reflect forgone opportunities, economists instead focus on the *implicit cost* of a machine as being what someone else would be willing to pay to use it. Thus, the cost of one machine-hour is the **rental rate** for that machine in the best alternative use. By continuing to use the machine, the firm is implicitly forgoing the rent someone else would be willing to pay for its use. We use v to denote this rental rate for one machine-hour. This is the rate that the firm must pay for the use of the machine for one hour regardless of whether the firm owns the machine (in which case it is an implicit cost) or rents the machine from someone else such as Hertz Rent-a-Car (in which case it is an explicit cost). In Chapter 15, we examine the determinants of rental rates in more detail. For now Application 6.1: Stranded Costs and Electricity Deregulation looks at a current battle about costs between economists and accountants that has important implications for people's electric bills.

Rental rate (v)
The cost of hiring one machine for one hour.

Entrepreneurial Costs

The owner of a firm is entitled to whatever is left from the firm's revenues after all costs have been paid. To an accountant, all of this excess would be called "profits" (or "losses" if costs exceed revenues). Economists, however, ask whether owners (or entrepreneurs) also encounter opportunity costs by being engaged in a particular business. If so, their entrepreneurial services should be considered an input to the firm, and some cost should be imputed to that input. For example, suppose a highly skilled computer programmer starts a software firm with the idea of keeping any (accounting) profits that might be generated. The programmer's time is clearly an input to the firm, and a cost should be imputed to it. Perhaps the wage that the programmer might command if he or she worked for someone else could be used for that purpose. Hence, some part of the accounting profits generated by the firm would be categorized as entrepreneurial costs by economists. Residual economic profits would be smaller than accounting profits. They might even be negative if the programmer's opportunity costs exceeded the accounting profits being earned by the business.

INFOTRAC©
COLLEGE EDITION
Exclusively from Gale Group and Thomson Learning

www.infotrac-college.com
Keywords: Capital costs, Labor costs, Production costs, Cost minimizing

MicroQuiz 6.1

Young homeowners often get bad advice that confuses accounting and economic costs. What is the fallacy in each of the following pieces of advice? Can you alter the advice so that it makes sense?

1. Owning is always better than renting. Rent payments are just money down a "rat hole"—making house payments as an owner means that you are accumulating a real asset.

2. One should pay off a mortgage as soon as possible. Being able to close out your mortgage and burn the papers is one of the great economic experiences of your life!

The Two-Input Case

We can make two simplifying assumptions about the inputs a firm uses. First, we can assume, as before, that there are only two inputs: labor (L, measured in

Stranded Costs and Electricity Deregulation

For most of its history, the electric power industry in the United States has been a heavily regulated utility. The price of electricity was set by a public regulatory commission in such a way as to allow each firm a "fair" return on its investment in electricity generation and distribution equipment. This regulatory structure began to crumble in the mid-1990s as states began to introduce competition into the pricing of electricity at the wholesale level.[1] The expected decline in wholesale electricity prices raised panic among many tradition-bound electric utilities. The resulting debate over "stranded costs" will continue to plague electricity for many years to come.

The Nature of Stranded Costs

The fundamental problem for the traditional utilities is that some of their generating facilities became "uneconomic" with deregulation because their average costs of producing electricity exceeded the price of electricity on the open market.[2] That was especially true for nuclear power facilities and for generating facilities that use alternative energy sources such as solar or wind power. The historical costs of these facilities have therefore been "stranded" by deregulation, and the utilities believe that fairness dictates that they be able to recover these costs through surcharges on consumers.

From the economist's perspective, of course, this plea rings hollow. The historical costs of electricity-generating facilities are sunk costs. The fact that the facilities are currently uneconomic to operate implies that their market values are zero (no buyer would pay anything for such a facility). Such a decline in the value of productive equipment is common in many industries—machinery for making mechanical calculators, 78 RPM recordings, or high-button shoes is also worthless now (though sometimes collected as an antique), but no one suggests that the owners should be compensated for these losses. Indeed, Joseph Schumpeter coined the term "creative destruction" to refer to this dynamic hallmark of the capitalist system. Why should electricity generation be any different?

Socking It to the Consumer

The utility industry argues that its regulated status does indeed make it different. Because state regulations promised them a "fair" return on their investments, they argue, the firms have the right to some sort of compensation for the impact of deregulation. This argument has had a large effect in some states. In California, for example, utilities were awarded more than $28 billion in compensation for their stranded costs—a figure that will eventually show up on every electricity customer's bill. In one particularly extreme case, the Southern California Edison Company will receive more in stranded-cost compensation than the entire value of the company on the New York Stock Exchange. Most other states will probably enact similar provisions during the next several years.

[1] Prices for the distribution of electricity to local homes and businesses continue to be highly regulated—in part because this segment of the business is regarded as a "natural monopoly" (see Chapter 10).
[2] The debate about stranded costs has been ambiguous about which notion of "unit" cost (marginal or average) is being compared to the price of electricity.

The Future of Deregulation

Allowing electric utilities to charge customers for their stranded costs has reduced the incentives for deregulation in wholesale electric markets because imposing such costs results in reducing sharply the benefits electricity consumers might achieve from using alternative suppliers. Moves toward deregulation have been further stalled by the Enron debacle that broke in late 2001. As one aspect of that case, the firm was accused of conspiring to manipulate wholesale electricity prices, especially in California during the summer of 2000. Although this contention remains unproved (see Application 11.2), the association with Enron has given electricity deregulation an undeserved bad name.

To Think About

1. Many traditional electric utilities believe that they had an "implicit contract" with state regulators to ensure a fair return on their investments. What kind of incentives would such a contract provide to the utilities in their decisions about what types of generating equipment to buy?

2. How would the possibility that equipment may quickly become obsolete be handled in unregulated markets? That is, how could this possibility be reflected in a firm's economic costs?

labor-hours) and capital (K, measured in machine-hours). Entrepreneurial services are assumed to be included in capital input. That is, we assume that the primary opportunity costs faced by a firm's owner are those associated with the capital the owner provides.

A second assumption we make is that inputs are hired in perfectly competitive markets. Firms can buy (or sell) all the labor or capital services they want at the prevailing rental rates (w and v). In graphic terms, the supply curve for these resources that the firm faces is horizontal at the prevailing factor prices.

Economic Profits and Cost Minimization

Given these simplifying assumptions, total costs for the firm during a period are:

$$\text{Total costs} = TC = wL + vK \tag{6.1}$$

where, as before, L and K represent input usage during the period. Assuming the firm produces only one output, its total revenues are given by the price of its product (P) times its total output [q = f(K,L), where f(K,L) is the firm's production function]. **Economic profits** (π) are then the difference between total revenues and total economic costs:

$$\pi = \text{Total revenues} - \text{Total costs} = Pq - wL - vK$$

$$= Pf(K,L) - wL - vK \tag{6.2}$$

Economic profits (π) The difference between a firm's total revenues and its total economic costs.

In general, Equation 6.2 shows that the economic profits obtained by a firm depend only on the amount of capital and labor it hires. If, as we assume in many places in this book, the firm seeks maximum profits, we might study its behavior by examining how it chooses K and L. This would, in turn, lead to a theory of the "derived demand" for capital and labor inputs—a topic we explore in detail in Chapter 13.

Here, however, we wish to develop a theory of costs that is somewhat more general and might apply to firms that pursue goals other than profits. To do that, we begin our study of costs by finessing a discussion of output choice for the moment. That is, we assume that for some reason the firm has decided to produce a particular output level (say, q_1). The firm's revenues are therefore fixed at $P \cdot q_1$. Now we wish to examine how the firm might choose to produce q_1 at minimal costs. Because revenues are fixed, minimizing costs will make profits as large as possible for this particular level of output. The details of how a firm chooses the amount it will produce are taken up in the next chapter.

COST-MINIMIZING INPUT CHOICE

In order to minimize the cost of producing q_1, a firm should choose that point on the q_1 isoquant that has the lowest cost. That is, it should explore all feasible input combinations to find the cheapest one. We now show that this will require the firm to choose that input combination for which the marginal rate of technical substitution (RTS) of L for K is equal to the ratio of the inputs' costs, w/v. To see why this is so intuitively, let's ask what would happen if a firm chose an input combination for which this were not true. Suppose the firm is producing output level q_1 using K = 10, L = 10, and the RTS is 2 at this point. Assume also that w = $1, v = $1, and hence that w/v = 1, which is unequal to the RTS of 2. At this input combination, the cost of producing q_1 is $20, which is not the minimal input cost. Output q_1 can also be produced using K = 8 and L = 11; the firm can give up two units of K and keep output constant at q_1 by adding one unit of L. At this input combination, the cost of producing q_1 is only $19. A proof similar to this one can be made any time the RTS and the ratio of the input costs differ. Therefore, we have shown that to minimize total cost the firm should produce where the RTS is equal to the ratio of the prices of the two inputs. Now let's look at the proof in more detail.

Graphic Presentation

This cost-minimization principle is demonstrated graphically in Figure 6.1. The isoquant q_1 shows all the combinations of K and L that are required to produce q_1. We wish to find the least costly point on this isoquant. Using Equation 6.1, we can see that those combinations of K and L that keep total costs constant lie

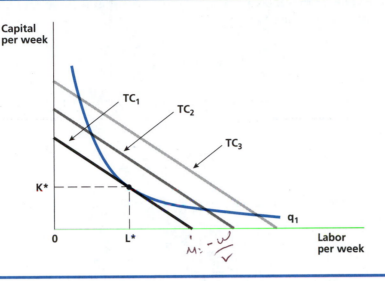

FIGURE 6.1 Minimizing the Costs of Producing q₁ A firm is assumed to choose capital (K) and labor (L) to minimize total costs. The condition for this minimization is that the rate at which L can be substituted for K (while keeping q = q₁) should be equal to the rate at which these inputs can be traded in the market. In other words, the RTS (of L for K) should be set equal to the price ratio w/v. This tangency is shown here in that costs are minimized at TC₁ by choosing inputs K* and L*.

along a straight line with slope −w/v.[1] Consequently, all lines of equal total cost can be shown in Figure 6.1 as a series of parallel straight lines with slopes −w/v. Three lines of equal total cost are shown in Figure 6.1: $TC_1 < TC_2 < TC_3$. It is clear from the figure that the minimum total cost for producing q_1 is given by TC_1 where the total cost curve is just tangent to the isoquant. The cost-minimizing input combination is L*, K*.

We have therefore shown that for a cost minimum the slope of the isoquant should equal −w/v. At that point of tangency, the rate at which the firm is technically able to substitute L for K (the RTS) in production is equal to the rate at which the firm can substitute L for K through market transactions.

An Alternative Interpretation

Another way of looking at the result pictured in Figure 6.1 may provide more intuition about the cost-minimization process. In Chapter 5, we showed that the

---

[1] For example, if TC = $100, Equation 6.1 would read 100 = wL + vK. Solving for K gives K = w/vL + 100/v. Hence, the slope of this total cost line is −w/v, and the intercept is 100/v (which is the amount of capital that can be purchased with $100).

absolute value of the slope of an isoquant (the RTS) is equal to the ratio of the two inputs' marginal productivities:

$$RTS(L \text{ for } K) = \frac{MP_L}{MP_K} \tag{6.3}$$

The cost-minimization procedure shown in Figure 6.1 requires that this ratio also equal the ratio of the inputs' prices:

$$RTS(L \text{ for } K) = \frac{MP_L}{MP_K} = \frac{w}{v} \tag{6.4}$$

Some minor manipulation of this equation yields:

$$\frac{MP_L}{w} = \frac{MP_K}{v} \tag{6.5}$$

This condition for cost minimization essentially says that the firm should employ its inputs so that, at the margin, it gets the same "bang for the buck" from each kind of input hired. For example, consider the owner of an orange grove. If MP_L is 20 crates of oranges per hour and the wage is $10 per hour, the owner is getting two crates of oranges for each dollar he or she spends on labor input. If tree-shaking machinery would provide a better return on dollars spent, the firm would not be minimizing costs. Suppose that MP_K is 300 crates per hour from hiring another tree-shaker and that these wondrous machines rent for $100 per hour. Then each dollar spent on machinery yields three crates of oranges and the firm could make its costs lower by using fewer workers and more machinery. Only if Equation 6.5 holds will each input provide the same marginal output per dollar spent, and only then will costs be truly minimized.

MicroQuiz 6.2

Suppose a firm faces a wage rate of 10 and a capital rental rate of 4. In the following two situations, how much of each input should this firm hire in order to minimize the cost of producing an output of 100 units? How would the firm's input choices change if capital rental rates rose to 10?

1. The firm produces with a fixed-proportions production function that requires 0.1 labor hours and 0.2 machine hours for each unit of output.

2. The firm's production function is given by $Q = 10L + 5K$.

The Firm's Expansion Path

Any firm can perform an analysis such as the one we just performed for every level of output. For each possible output level (q), it would find that input combination that minimizes the cost of producing it. If input costs (w and v) remain constant for all amounts the firm chooses to use, we can easily trace out this set of cost-minimizing choices, as shown in Figure 6.2. This ray records the cost-minimizing tangencies for successively higher levels of output. For example, the minimum cost for pro-

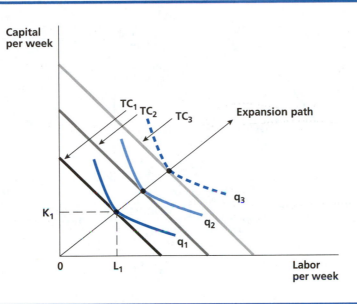

FIGURE 6.2 Firm's Expansion Path The firm's expansion path is the locus of cost-minimizing tangencies. On the assumption of fixed input prices, the curve shows how input use increases as output increases.

ducing output level q_1 is given by TC_1, and inputs K_1 and L_1 are used. Other tangencies in the figure can be interpreted in a similar way. The set of all of these tangencies is called the firm's **expansion path** because it records how input use expands as output expands while holding the prices of the inputs constant. The expansion path need not necessarily be a straight line. The use of some inputs may increase faster than others as output expands. Which inputs expand more rapidly will depend on the precise nature of production.

Expansion path
The set of cost-minimizing input combinations a firm will choose to produce various levels of output (when the prices of inputs are held constant).

COST CURVES

The firm's expansion path shows how minimum-cost input use increases when the level of output expands. The path allows us to develop the relationship between output levels and total input costs. Cost curves that reflect this relationship are fundamental to the theory of supply. Figure 6.3 illustrates four possible shapes for this cost relationship. Panel a reflects a situation of constant returns to scale. In this case, as Figure 5.3 showed, output and required input use are proportional to one another. A doubling of output requires a doubling of inputs. Because input prices do not change, the relationship between output and total

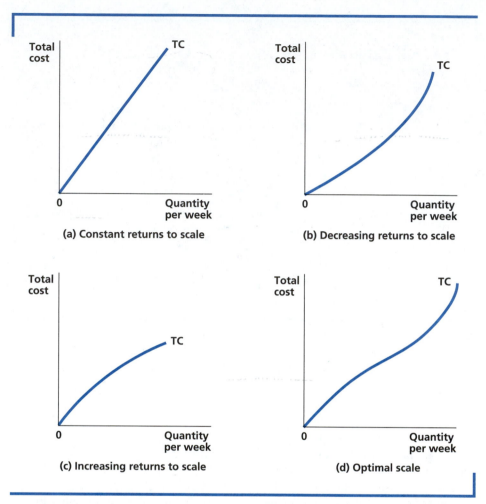

FIGURE 6.3 Possible Shapes of the Total Cost Curve The shape of the total cost curve depends on the nature of the production function. Panel a represents constant returns to scale: As output expands, input costs expand proportionately. Panel b and panel c show decreasing returns to scale and increasing returns to scale, respectively. Panel d represents costs where the firm has an "optimal scale" of operations.

input costs is also directly proportional—the total cost curve is simply a straight line that passes through the origin (since no inputs are required if q = 0).[2]

Panel b and panel c in Figure 6.3 reflect the cases of decreasing returns to scale and increasing returns to scale, respectively. With decreasing returns to

---

[2] A technical property of constant returns to scale production functions is that the RTS depends only on the ratio of K to L, not on the scale of production. For given input prices, the expansion path is a straight line, and cost-minimizing inputs expand proportionately along with output. For an illustration, see the numerical example at the end of this chapter.

scale, successively larger quantities of inputs are required to increase output and input costs rise rapidly as output expands. This possibility is shown by the convex[3] total cost curve in panel b. In this case, costs expand more rapidly than output. With increasing returns to scale, on the other hand, successive input requirements decline as output expands. In that case, the total cost curve is concave, as shown in panel c. In this case, considerable cost advantages result from large-scale operations.

Finally, panel d in Figure 6.3 demonstrates a situation in which the firm experiences ranges of both increasing and decreasing returns to scale. This situation might arise if the firm's production process required a certain "optimal" level of internal coordination and control by its managers. For low levels of output, this control structure is underutilized and expansion in output is easily accomplished. At these levels, the firm would experience increasing returns to scale—the total cost curve is concave in its initial section. As output expands, however, the firm must add additional workers and capital equipment, which perhaps need entirely separate buildings or other production facilities. The coordination and control of this larger-scale organization may be successively more difficult, and diminishing returns to scale may set in. The convex section of the total cost curve in panel d reflects that possibility.

The four possibilities in Figure 6.3 illustrate the most common types of relationships between a firm's output and its input costs. This cost information can also be depicted on a per-unit-of-output basis. Although this depiction adds no new details to the information already in the total cost curves, showing per-unit curves will be quite useful when we analyze the supply decision in the next chapter.

Average and Marginal Costs

Two per-unit-of-output cost concepts are average and marginal costs. **Average cost** (AC) measures total costs per unit. Mathematically,

Average cost
Total cost divided by output; a common measure of cost per unit.

$$\text{Average cost} = AC = \frac{TC}{q} \tag{6.6}$$

This is the per-unit-of-cost concept with which people are most familiar. If, a firm has total costs of $100 in producing 25 units of output, it is natural to consider the cost per unit to be $4. Equation 6.6 reflects this common averaging process.

For economists, however, average cost is not necessarily the most meaningful cost-per-unit figure. In Chapter 1, we introduced Marshall's analysis of demand and supply. In his model of price determination, Marshall focused on the cost of the last unit produced because it is that cost that influences the supply decision.

---

[3] One way to remember how to use the terms "convex" and "concave" is to note that the curve in Figure 6.3(c) resembles (part of) a cave entrance and is therefore "concave."

Marginal cost
The additional cost
of producing one
more unit of output.

To reflect this notion of incremental cost, economists use the concept of **marginal cost** (MC). By definition then,

$$\text{Marginal cost} = MC = \frac{\text{Change in TC}}{\text{Change in q}} \tag{6.7}$$

That is, as output expands, total costs increase, and the marginal cost concept measures this increase only *at the margin*. For example, if producing 24 units costs the firm $98 but producing 25 units costs it $100, the marginal cost of the 25th unit is $2: To produce that unit the firm incurs an increase in cost of only $2. This example shows that the average cost of a good ($4) and its marginal cost ($2) may be quite different. This possibility has a number of important implications for pricing and overall resource allocation.

Marginal Cost Curves

Figure 6.4 compares average and marginal costs for the four total cost relationships shown in Figure 6.3. As our definition makes clear, marginal costs are reflected by the slope[4] of the total cost curve since (as discussed in Appendix to Chapter 1) the slope of any curve shows how the variable on the vertical axis (here, total cost) changes for a unit change in the variable on the horizontal axis (here, quantity). In panel a of Figure 6.3, the total cost curve is linear—it has the same slope throughout. In this case, marginal cost (MC) is constant. No matter how much is produced, it will always cost the same to produce *one more unit*. The horizontal MC curve in panel a of Figure 6.4 reflects this fact.

In the case of decreasing returns to scale (panel b in Figure 6.3), marginal costs are increasing. The total cost curve becomes steeper as output expands, so, at the margin, the cost of one more unit is becoming greater. The MC curve in panel b in Figure 6.4 is positively sloped reflecting these increasing marginal costs.

For the case of increasing returns to scale (panel c in Figure 6.3), this situation is reversed. Because the total cost curve becomes flatter as output expands, marginal costs fall. The marginal cost curve in panel c in Figure 6.4 has a negative slope.

Finally, the case of first concave, then convex total costs (panel d in Figure 6.3) yields a U-shaped marginal cost curve in Figure 6.4. Initially, marginal costs fall because the coordination and control mechanism of the firm is being utilized more efficiently. Diminishing returns eventually appear, however, and the marginal cost curve turns upward. The MC curve in panel d in Figure 6.4 reflects the general idea that there is some optimal level of operation for the firm—if production is pushed too far, very high marginal costs will be the result. We make this idea of optimal scale more precise as we study average costs.

---

[4] If total costs are given by TC(q), then mathematically marginal cost is given by the derivative function $MC = \frac{dTC}{dq}$.

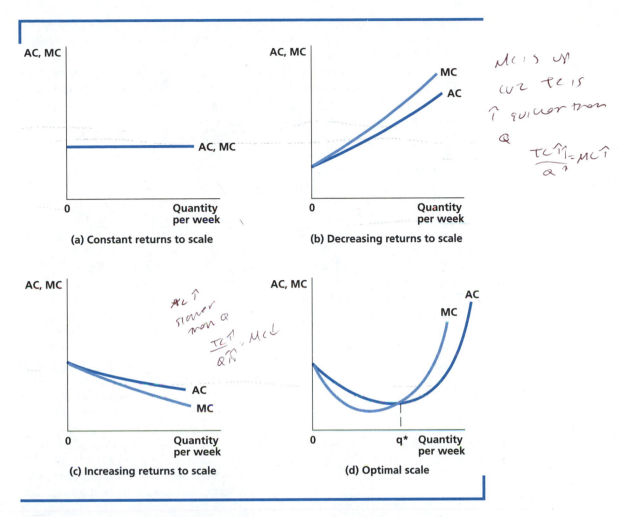

FIGURE 6.4 Average and Marginal Cost Curves The average and marginal cost curves shown here are derived from the total cost curves in Figure 6.3. The shapes of these curves depend on the nature of the production function.

Average Cost Curves

Developing average cost (AC) curves for each of the cases in Figure 6.4 is also relatively simple. The average and marginal cost concepts are identical for the very first unit produced. If the firm produced only one unit, both average and marginal cost would be the cost of that one unit. Graphing the AC relationship begins at the point where the marginal cost curve intersects the vertical axis. For panel a in Figure 6.4, marginal cost never varies from its initial level. It always costs the same amount to produce one more unit, and AC must also reflect this amount. If it always costs a firm $4 to produce one more unit, both average and marginal costs are $4. Both the AC and the MC curves are the same horizontal line in panel a in Figure 6.4.

In the case of decreasing returns to scale, rising marginal costs also result in rising average costs. Because the last unit produced is becoming more and more costly as output expands, the overall average of such costs must be rising. Because the first few units are produced at low marginal costs, however, the overall average will always lag behind the high marginal cost of the last unit produced. In panel b in Figure 6.4, the AC curve is upward sloping, but it is always below the MC curve.

In the case of increasing returns to scale, the opposite situation prevails. Falling marginal costs cause average costs to fall as output expands, but the overall average also reflects the high marginal costs involved in producing the first few units. As a consequence, the AC curve in panel c in Figure 6.4 is negatively sloped and always lies above the MC curve. Falling average cost in this case is, as we shall see in Chapter 10, a principal force leading to relatively large-scale operations for firms with such increasing-returns-to-scale technologies.

The case of a U-shaped marginal cost curve represents a combination of the two preceding situations. Initially, falling marginal costs cause average costs to decline also. For low levels of output, the configuration of average and marginal cost curves in panel d in Figure 6.4 resembles that in panel c. Once the marginal costs turn up, however, the situation begins to change. As long as marginal cost is below average cost, average cost will continue to decline because the last unit produced is still less expensive than the prior average. When MC < AC, producing one more unit pulls AC down. Once the rising segment of the marginal cost curve cuts the average cost curve from below, however, average costs begin to rise. Beyond point q* in panel d in Figure 6.4, MC exceeds AC. The situation now resembles that in panel, b and AC must rise. Average costs are being pulled up by the high cost of producing one more unit. Because AC is falling to the left of q* and rising to the right of q*, average costs of production are lowest at q*. In this sense, q* represents an "optimal scale" for a firm whose costs are represented in panel d in Figure 6.4. Later chapters show that this output level plays an important role in the theory of price determination. Application 6.2: Findings on Firms' Costs looks at how average cost curves can be used to determine which industries might find large-scale firms more appropriate. Application 6.3: Airlines' Costs then looks more closely at cost in one particular industry.

MicroQuiz 6.3

Suppose that there are to be ten quizzes in your economics course. You have scored 80 on every one of the first five quizzes.

1. What will happen to your average for the course if your grade falls to 60 on each of the next two quizzes?

2. What will you have to score on the final three quizzes in the course to get your average back to 80?

3. Explain how this example illustrates the relationship between average and marginal costs studied in this section.

Findings on Firms' Costs

Most studies of long-run cost curves have found that average-cost curves have a modified L-shape, such as the one shown in Figure 1.

Some Evidence

Table 1 reports the results of representative studies of long-run average-cost curves for a variety of industries. Entries in the table represent the long-run average cost for a firm of a particular size (small, medium, or large) as a percentage of the minimal average-cost firm in the industry. For example, the data for hospitals indicate that small hospitals have average costs that are about 29.6 percent greater than average costs for large ones.

The costs of most other industries seem to be similar to those illustrated in Figure 1. Average costs are lower for medium and large firms than for smaller ones; that is, there appears to be a "minimum efficient scale" of operation (termed, appropriately, MES in the field of industrial organization). However, in several cases, the average-cost advantages are not great. For trucking, smaller firms seem to operate with lower average costs.

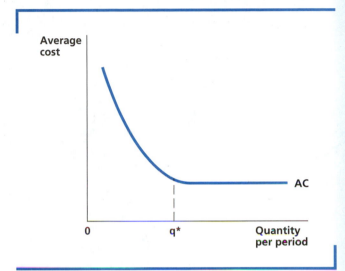

FIGURE 1 Long-Run Average Cost Curve Found in Many Empirical Studies In most empirical studies, the AC curve has been found to have this modified L shape. q* represents the minimum efficient scale for this firm.

To Think About

1. Many of the industries listed in Table 1 seem to exhibit modest cost economies of large-scale operation. Why do you think this does not apply to trucking?
2. The average-cost estimates in Table 1 typically refer to costs for an entire firm. Do you think a study of individual plants would show larger or smaller economies of scale?

(continued)

TABLE 1 Long-Run Average-Cost Estimates

Industry	Firm Size		
	Small	Medium	Large
Aluminum	166.6	131.3	100.0
Automobiles	144.5	122.7	100.0
Electric power	113.2	101.1	101.5
HMOs	118.0	106.3	100.0
Hospitals	129.6	111.1	100.0
Life insurance	113.6	104.5	100.0
Lotteries (state)	175.0	125.0	100.0
Sewage treatment	104.0	101.0	100.0
Trucking	100.0	102.1	105.6

Sources: Aluminum: J. C. Clark and M. C. Fleming, "Advanced Materials and the Economy," *Scientific American* (October 1986): 51–56. Automobiles: M. A. Fuss and L. Waverman, "Costs and Productivity Differences in Automobile Production" (Cambridge, UK: Cambridge University Press, 1992). Electric power: L. H. Christensen and W. H. Greene, "Economics of Scale in U.S. Power Generation," *Journal of Political Economy* (August 1976): 655–676. Hospitals: T. W. Granneman, R. S. Brown, and M. V. Pauly, "Estimating Hospital Costs," *Journal of Health Economics* (March 1986): 107–127; HMOs: D. Wholey, R. Feldman, J. B. Christianson, and J. Engberg, "Scale and Scope Economies among Health Maintenance Organizations," *Journal of Health Economics* 15 (1996): 657–684; Life insurance: R. Geehan, "Returns to Scale in the Life Insurance Industry," *The Bell Journal of Economics* (Autumn 1977): 497–516. Lotteries: C. T. Clotfelter and P. J. Cook, "On the Economics of State Lotteries," *Journal of Economic Perspectives* (Fall 1990): 105–119. Sewage treatment: M. R. J. Knapp, "Economies of Scale in Sewage Purification and Disposal," *Journal of Industrial Economics* (December 1978): 163–183. Trucking: R. Koenka, "Optimal Scale and the Size Distribution of American Trucking Firms," *Journal of Transport Economics and Policy* (January 1977): 54–67.

Short run
The period of time in which a firm must consider some inputs to be fixed in making its decisions.

Long run
The period of time in which a firm may consider all of its inputs to be variable in making its decisions.

DISTINCTION BETWEEN THE SHORT RUN AND THE LONG RUN

Economists sometimes wish to distinguish between the **short run** and the **long run** for firms. These terms denote the length of time over which a firm may make decisions. This distinction is useful for studying market responses to changed conditions. For example, if only the short run is considered, a firm may need to treat some of its inputs as fixed because it may be technically impossible to change those inputs on short notice. If a time interval of only 1 week is involved, the size of a Honda assembly plant would have to be treated as fixed. Similarly, an entrepreneur who is committed to an Internet start-up firm would find it

Costs for airlines have been extensively studied by economists. The interest was sparked by the many changes that have taken place in this industry in recent years, such as deregulation, bankruptcy, and mergers. The analysis of costs provides a first step to understanding the economic forces that have motivated these changes.

Two general findings seem to characterize airlines' costs. First, costs seem to differ substantially among U.S. firms. When average costs are measured on a per-passenger-mile basis, those at high-cost airlines exceed those at low-cost airlines by more than 50 percent. For example, USAirways has costs of nearly 12 cents per passenger mile versus 7 cents for Southwest Airlines. A second generalization is that costs for U.S. airlines appear to be significantly lower than for airlines in other countries. Again, differences on a per-passenger-mile basis of 50 percent or more are common.

Reasons for Differences among U.S. Firms

Economists have explored a wide variety of reasons that might explain the large variation in airlines' costs. Some of the differences may be explained by the nature of airlines' routes. Airlines that fly longer average distances or operate a greater number of flights over a given network tend to have lower costs. In such cases, the firms can spread the fixed costs associated with terminals, maintenance facilities, and reservation systems over a larger output volume. Characteristics of the fleet of planes operated by various airlines can also affect costs. Firms that operate older fleets or that operate fleets with many different types of planes tend to have higher maintenance and fuel costs. One secret of Southwest Airlines' low costs, for example, is that their fleet is composed almost exclusively of relatively fuel-efficient newer Boeing 737s. Wage costs, especially for pilots, also differ significantly among the airlines. Friction over noncompetitive wage contracts has been a repeated cause of labor strife in the airline industry and was one of the primary factors that led to the purchase of United Airlines by its employees in 1991. In exchange for about 55 percent of the company, United employees agreed to wage concessions that may have reduced costs per passenger mile by as much as 25 cents. Similarly, a 1999 strike at American Airlines focused on wages to be paid to pilots of new, smaller jet aircraft.

International Airline Regulation and Costs

The factors leading to differing costs of U.S. airlines also help explain why non-U.S. airline costs are high. Many foreign carriers' route networks are quite inefficient, for example. They have yet to adopt the "hub and spoke" system that has become standard in the United States. An additional source of high costs is the regulatory environment faced by many foreign firms. In the United States such regulation largely ended in 1978 and costs fell significantly thereafter (see Application 7.2 and Application 11.5). Foreign governments have been much slower to deregulate, however. Many countries continue to operate state-owned airlines. Often, labor costs in such airlines are much higher[1] than on private ones and this creates political pressures opposing deregulation.

[1] See C. K. Ng and P. Seabright, "Competition, Privatization, and Productive Efficiency: Evidence from the Airline Industry," *Economic Journal* (July 2001): 591–619.

(continued)

These restrictions are beginning to crack, however. In Europe, low-price airlines have put pressure on such traditionally high-cost firms as Lufthansa and KLM. This, in turn, has led to threatened strikes against these large carriers as their workforces oppose cost-cutting plans. In Australia, the government ended many rigid controls on domestic aviation in the early 1990s, especially those related to entry and importation of aircraft. By some estimates, costs per passenger mile fell by 15 to 20 percent in the three years following these actions. Even airlines serving lucrative Pacific routes have begun to face pressures on their costs. For example, Japan Airlines has abandoned its former high-cost practice of buying all of its in-flight consumables in Japan, instead opting to buy some items in their destination markets.

To Think About

1. How can airlines' costs differ? Don't the firms buy their inputs in the same markets and have similar production functions for producing travel services? Does the theory developed in this chapter permit such differences?
2. The evidence from airline deregulation experiences suggests that competition reduces airline costs. How does this happen? Which kinds of costs seem most likely to be reduced through competition? Which least likely?

impossible (or extremely costly) to change jobs quickly—in the short run, the entrepreneur's input to his or her firm is essentially fixed. Over the long run, however, neither of those inputs needs to be considered fixed, since Honda's factory size can be altered and the entrepreneur can indeed quit the business.

Holding Capital Input Constant

Probably the easiest method to introduce the distinction between the short run and the long run into the analysis of a firm's costs is to assume that one of the inputs is held constant in the short run. Specifically, we assume that capital input is held constant at a level of K_1 and that (in the short run) the firm is free to vary only its labor input. For example, a trucking firm with a fixed number of trucks and loading facilities can still hire and fire workers to change its output. We already studied this possibility in Chapter 5, when we examined the marginal productivity of labor. Here, we are interested in analyzing how changes in a firm's output level in the short run are related to changes in total costs. We can then contrast this relationship to the cost relationships studied earlier, in which both inputs could be changed. We will see that the diminishing marginal productivity that results from the fixed nature of capital input causes costs to rise rapidly as output expands.

Of course, any firm obviously uses far more than two inputs in its production process. The level of some of these inputs may be changed on rather short notice. Firms may ask workers to work overtime, hire part-time replacements from an employment agency, or rent equipment (such as power tools or automobiles) from some other firm. Other types of inputs may take somewhat longer to be adjusted; for example, to hire new, full-time workers is a relatively time-consuming (and costly) process, and ordering new machines designed to unique specifications may involve a considerable time lag. Still, most of the important insights from making the short-run/long-run distinction can be obtained from the simple two-input model by holding capital input constant.

Types of Short-Run Costs

Because capital input is held fixed in the short run, the costs associated with that input are also fixed. That is, the amount of capital costs that the firm incurs is the same no matter how much the firm produces—it must pay the rent on its fixed number of machines even if it chooses to produce nothing. Such **fixed costs** play an important role in determining the firm's profitability in the short run, but (as we shall see) they play no role in determining how firms will react to changing prices because they must pay the same amount in capital costs no matter what they do.

Fixed costs
Costs associated with inputs that are fixed in the short run.

Short-run costs associated with inputs that can be changed (labor in our simple case) are called **variable costs**. The amount of these costs obviously will change as the firm changes its labor input so as to bring about changes in output. For example, although a Honda assembly plant may be of fixed size in the short run (and the rental costs of the plant are the same no matter how many cars are made), the firm can still vary the number of cars produced by varying the number of workers employed. By adding a third shift, for example, the firm may be able to expand output significantly. Costs involved in paying these extra workers would be variable costs.

Variable costs
Costs associated with inputs that can be varied in the short run.

Input Inflexibility and Cost Minimization

The total costs that firms experience in the short run may not be the lowest possible for some output levels. Because we are holding capital fixed short run, the firm does not have the flexibility in input choice that was assumed when we discussed cost minimization and the related (long-run) cost curves earlier in this chapter. Rather, to vary its output level in the short run, the firm will be forced to use "nonoptimal" input combinations.

This is shown in Figure 6.5. In the short run, the firm can use only K_1 units of capital. To produce output level q_0, it must use L_0 units of Labor, L_1 units of labor to produce q_1, and L_2 units to produce q_2. The total costs of these input combinations are given by STC_0, STC_1, and STC_2, respectively. Only for the input combination K_1, L_1 is output being produced at minimal cost. Only at that point is the RTS equal to the ratio of the input prices. From Figure 6.5, it is clear that q_0 is being produced with "too much" capital in this short-run situation. Cost minimization should suggest a southeasterly movement along the q_0 isoquant, indicating a substitution of labor for capital in production. On the other hand, q_2 is being produced with "too little" capital, and costs could be reduced by substituting

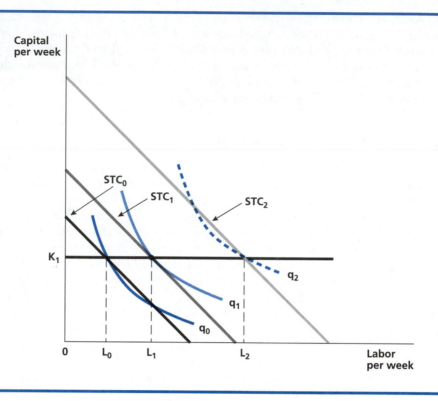

FIGURE 6.5 **"Nonoptimal" Input Choices Must Be Made in the Short Run** Because capital input is fixed at K_1 in the short run, the firm cannot bring its RTS into equality with the ratio of input prices. Given the input prices, q_0 should be produced with more labor and less capital than it will be in the short run, whereas q_2 should be produced with more capital and less labor than it will be.

capital for labor. Neither of these substitutions is possible in the short run. However, over the long run, the firm will be able to change its level of capital input and will adjust its input usage to the cost-minimizing combinations.

PER-UNIT SHORT-RUN COST CURVES

The relationship between output and short-run total costs shown in Figure 6.5 can be used in a way similar to what we did earlier in this chapter to define a number of per-unit notions of short-run costs. Specifically, short-run average cost can be defined as the ratio of short-run total cost to output. Similarly, short-run marginal cost is the change in short-run total cost for a one-unit increase in output. Because we do not use the short-run/long-run distinction extensively in this book, it is unnecessary to pursue the construction of all of these cost curves in detail. Rather, our earlier discussion of the relationship between the shapes of total cost curves and their related per-unit curves will usually suffice.

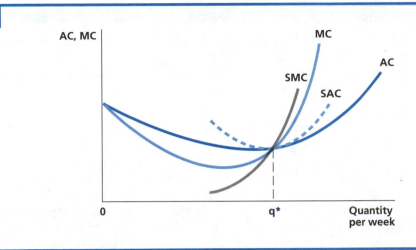

FIGURE 6.6 Short-Run and Long-Run Average and Marginal Cost Curves at Optimal Output Level When long-run average cost is U-shaped and reaches a minimum at q*, SAC and SMC will also pass through this point. For increases in output above q*, short-run costs are higher than long-run costs.

One particular set of short-run cost curves is especially instructive, however. Figure 6.6 shows the case of a firm with a U-shaped (long-run) average cost curve.

For this firm, long-run average costs reach a minimum at output level q*, and, as we have noted in several places, at this output level, MC = AC. Also associated with q* is a certain level of capital usage, K*. What we wish to do now is to examine the short-run average and marginal cost curves (denoted by SAC and SMC, respectively) based on this level of capital input. We now look at the costs of a firm whose level of capital input is fixed at K* to see how costs vary in the short run as output departs from its optimal level of q*.

Our discussion about the total cost curves in Figure 6.5 shows that when the firm's short-run decision causes it to use the cost-minimizing amount of capital input, short-run and long-run total costs are equal. Average costs then are equal also. At q*, AC is equal to SAC. This means that at q*, MC and SMC are also equal, since both of the average cost curves are at their lowest points. At q* in Figure 6.6, the following equality holds:

$$AC = MC = SAC(K^*) = SMC(K^*) \qquad (6.8)$$

For increases in q above q*, short-run costs are greater than long-run costs. These higher per-unit costs reflect the firm's inflexibility in the short run because some inputs are fixed. This inflexibility has important consequences for firms' short-run supply responses and for price changes in the short run. In Application 6.4: Can We Do Anything about Traffic Snarls?, we look at some cases where short-run costs rise rapidly as the traffic (output) increases.

Can We Do Anything about Traffic Snarls?

Automobile traffic congestion is a major problem in most cities. Indeed, transportation economists have estimated that each year traffic delays cost U.S. motorists about $50 billion in lost time.[1] Similar losses are experienced by drivers all over the world.

Nature of Marginal Costs

To understand the origin of traffic congestion, it is important to understand the precise nature of the costs involved. For any traffic facility (road, bridge, tunnel, and so forth), output is measured in number of vehicles per hour. Capital costs associated with this output are largely fixed—depreciation occurs at a more or less uniform rate regardless of the level of traffic. Variable costs associated with traffic facilities consist primarily of motorists' time. Studies of people's willingness to spend time commuting conclude that such time is valued at about one half of the wage people can earn—that is, travel time "costs" about $8 per hour. As traffic congestion increases, travel times lengthen and travel costs rise. The marginal cost of producing "one more trip" is then given by the overall increase in travel time experienced by all motorists when one more vehicle uses a traffic facility. As traffic volume approaches a facility's capacity, such marginal costs increase rapidly.

The high marginal costs associated with adding an extra automobile to an already crowded facility are not, however, directly experienced by the motorist driving that car. His or her decision imposes costs on all other motorists. Hence, there is a divergence between the private costs that enter into a motorist's decision to use a particular traffic facility and the total social costs that this decision entails. It is this divergence that leads motorists to opt for driving patterns that overutilize traffic facilities.

Congestion Tolls

The standard answer given by economists to this problem is the adoption of taxes that bring social and private marginal costs into agreement. In the present context, that would require the adoption of highway, bridge, or tunnel tolls that accurately reflect the social costs that users of such facilities cause. Because these costs vary by time of day (being highest during morning and evening rush hours), tolls should also vary over the day. Indeed, no tolls would be required during off-peak hours when adding one more car to a facility does not result in any time delays.

Toll-Collecting Technology

Although congestion tolls were first suggested in the 1950s, they remained (much like many other economist-inspired remedies) a pie-in-the-sky scheme. Building collection booths for tolls was regarded as very costly and likely to result in more congestion than adoption of a correct pricing mechanism would cure. This changed dramatically in the late 1980s with the development of low-cost, electronic-toll-collection techniques. Toll billing can now be done by mail, charging differing amounts depending on the time of day travel

[1] This figure is taken from R. Arnott and K. Small, "The Economics of Traffic Congestion," *American Scientist* (September–October 1994): 446–455. The author's discussion of three "paradoxes" in traffic economics (in which building additional facilities may increase congestion) is particularly recommended.

occurs (much as is done for long-distance phone calls). Such a system was first installed on an experimental basis in Hong Kong—a city famous for horrendous rush hours. In 1995, Orange County (California) introduced congestion pricing on a short segment of Route 91. As more drivers use toll transponders (such as E-Z Pass in New York and New Jersey), implementing congestion tolls will become easier.

To Think About

1. Some commuter groups argue that congestion tolls are unfair because they hit motorists who have to drive at certain hours rather than those who drive off-peak in their spare time. Wouldn't a system of uniform (by time of day) tolls be fairer? Regardless of toll schedules, how should toll revenues be used?
2. Airports also face congestion since many planes seek to land and take off during morning and evening rush hours. In what ways is this problem similar to the traffic congestion problem? In what ways is it different?

SHIFTS IN COST CURVES

We have shown how any firm's cost curves are derived from its cost-minimizing expansion path. Any change in economic conditions that affects this expansion path will also affect the shape and position of the firm's cost curves. Three kinds of economic changes are likely to have such effects: changes in input prices, technological innovations, and economies of scope.

> ### MicroQuiz 6.4
>
> Give an intuitive explanation for the following questions about Figure 6.6:
>
> **1.** Why does SAC exceed AC for every level of output except $q*$?
>
> **2.** Why does SMC exceed MC for output levels greater than $q*$?
>
> **3.** What would happen to this figure if the firm increased its short-run level of capital beyond $K*$?

Changes in Input Prices

A change in the price of an input tilts the firm's total cost lines and alters its expansion path. A rise in wage rates, for example, causes firms to produce any output level using relatively more capital and relatively less labor. To the extent that a substitution of capital for labor is possible (remember that substitution possibilities depend on the shape of the isoquant map), the entire expansion path of the firm rotates toward the capital axis. This movement in turn implies a new set of cost curves for the firm. A rise in the price of labor input causes the entire relationship between output levels and costs to change. Presumably, all cost curves are shifted upward, and the extent of the shift depends both on how "important" labor is in production and on how successful the firm is in substituting other inputs for labor. If labor is relatively unimportant or if the firm can readily shift to more mechanized methods of production, increases in costs resulting from a rise in wages may be rather small. Wage costs have relatively little impact on the costs of oil refineries because labor constitutes a small fraction of total cost. On the other hand, if labor is a very important part of a firm's costs and input substitution is difficult (remember the case of lawn mowers), production costs may rise significantly. A rise in carpenters' wages raises homebuilding costs significantly.

Technological Innovation

In a dynamic economy, technology is constantly changing. Firms discover better production methods, workers learn how to do their jobs better, and the tools of managerial control may improve. Because such technical advances alter a firm's production function, isoquant maps—as well as the firm's expansion path—shift when technology changes. For example, an advance in knowledge may simply shift all isoquants toward the origin, with the result that any output level can then be produced with a lower level of input use and a lower cost. Alternatively, technical change may be "biased" in that it may save only on the use of one input—if workers become more skilled, for instance, this saves only on labor input. Again, the result would be to alter isoquant maps, shift expansion paths, and finally affect the shape and location of a firm's cost curves. In recent years, some of the most important technical changes have been related to the revolution in microelectronics. Costs of computer processing have been halved every 2 years or so for the past 20 years. Such cost changes have had major impacts on many of the markets we study in this book.

MicroQuiz 6.5

An increase in the wages of fast-food workers will increase McDonald's costs.

1. How will the extent of the increase in McDonald's costs depend on whether labor costs account for a large or a small fraction of the firm's total costs?

2. How will the extent of the increase in McDonald's costs depend on whether the firm is able to substitute capital for labor?

Economies of Scope

A third factor that may cause cost curves to shift arises in the case of firms that produce several different kinds of output. In such multiproduct firms, expansion in the output of one good may improve the ability to produce some other good. For example, the experience of the Sony Corporation in producing videocassette recorders undoubtedly gave it a cost advantage in producing DVD players because many of the underlying electronic circuits were quite similar between the two products. Or, hospitals that do many surgeries of one type may have a cost advantage in doing other types because of the similarities in equipment and operating personnel used. Such cost effects are called **economies of scope** because they arise out of the expanding scope of operations of multiproduct firms. Application 6.5: Economies of Scope in Banks and Hospitals looks at a few of these situations.

Economies of scope

Reductions in the costs of one product of a multiproduct firm when the output of another product is increased.

Banks and hospitals are both complex types of firms that produce many different products. Recently, a large number of mergers has occurred in both of these industries, so economists are naturally interested in whether the resulting larger firms have lower costs. One of the primary reasons for expecting lower costs is that mergers make it possible for firms to offer a broader array of products. If economies of scope are important, this additional production may cause the costs of these firms' traditional business lines to be lower. A comparison of banks and hospitals also provides an interesting contrast between an industry where for-profit firms predominate (banks) and one where nonprofit firms are most common (hospitals).

Banks

All banks are financial intermediaries. They collect deposits from one group of lenders and transfer those funds to another group of borrowers, making gross profits on the spread between borrowing and lending costs. But banks must also incur operating expenses in their deposit and lending activities, so their net profits depend on how efficiently those activities are conducted. Indeed, because the interest rates banks charge and receive are largely determined by external market forces, their actual profit levels are determined primarily by the efficiency of their operations.

Economies of scope can reduce banks' costs if the costs associated with any one particular financial product fall when the bank offers other products. For example, a bank that offers consumer loans may find that the costs of making those loans declines when it also offers loans to retailers because common resources (such as credit checks or loan-payment-collection technology) can be used for both purposes. Similarly, in servicing depositors, banks may find that conducting foreign exchange operations may reduce their costs for international customers.

The possibility for economies of scope has played an important role in the evolution of banking regulations. For example, this was one of the primary arguments in favor of repealing the Glass-Steagall Act in the United States and permitting banks to engage in investment banking activities (such as underwriting). Similarly, the European Community has adopted more flexible merger guidelines for banks—again, with the view of taking advantage of economies of scope. Banking regulators throughout Asia have also taken similar steps.

Hospitals

Examining the costs of hospitals provides an illustration of how the methods introduced in the chapter can be applied to nonprofit firms as well. Although most hospitals are not intended to earn economic profits, they still face revenue constraints that push them toward cost-minimization. Economies of scope arise in a variety of hospital activities. Facilities for surgical operations tend to have lower costs the wider the variety of operations that are done—primarily because similar equipment is required in many surgeries. Hospital staff may also become more efficient in surgeries if a greater diversity of activities helps them to learn to do their jobs better. Other areas where economists have found economies

(continued)

of scope in hospital operations include the provision of outpatient services, running intensive-care units, and establishing hospital-owned pharmacies.

As is the case for banking, the presence of economies of scope in hospitals has been an important force leading to hospital mergers. Smaller institutions (say, fewer than 150 to 200 beds) have found that private and government insurance reimbursement rates do not cover their higher costs of operation, and they have opted to merge with larger institutions. The problem has been especially severe for religion-based hospitals and for hospitals in rural areas in the United States. Indeed, the U.S. government has been forced to adopt a fairly large-scale system of subsidies for rural hospitals in order to ensure that some reasonably nearby service remains available.

To Think About

1. Doesn't the idea of economies of scope in banking conflict with Adam Smith's observations about the benefits of specialization? Why wouldn't a bank have lower costs by specializing in one part of the business and then contracting with similarly specialized banks for other services?
2. Table 1 of Application 6.2 shows that hospitals also exhibit increasing returns to scale in their overall operations. How would you differentiate between increasing returns to scale and economies of scope for such firms?

A NUMERICAL EXAMPLE

If you have the stomach for it, we can continue the numerical example we began in Chapter 5 to derive cost curves for Hamburger Heaven (HH). To do so, let's assume HH can hire workers at $5 per hour and that it rents all of its grills from the Hertz Grill Rental Company for $5 per hour. Hence, total costs for HH during one hour are

$$TC = 5K + 5L \qquad (6.9)$$

where K and L are the number of grills and the number of workers hired during that hour, respectively. To begin our study of HH's cost-minimization process, suppose the firm wishes to produce 40 hamburgers per hour. Table 6.1 repeats the various ways HH can produce 40 hamburgers per hours and uses Equation 6.9 to compute the total cost of each method. It is clear in Table 6.1 that total costs are minimized when K and L are each 4. With this employment of inputs, total cost is $40 with half being spent on grills ($20 = $5 × 4 grills) and the other half being spent on workers. Figure 6.7 shows this cost-minimizing tangency.

TABLE 6.1 Total Costs of Producing 40 Hamburgers per Hour

Output (q)	Workers (L)	Grills (K)	Total cost (TC)
40	1	16.0	$85.00
40	2	8.0	50.00
40	3	5.3	41.50
40	4	4.0	40.00
40	5	3.2	41.00
40	6	2.7	43.50
40	7	2.3	46.50
40	8	2.0	50.00
40	9	1.8	54.00
40	10	1.6	58.00

Source: Table 5.2 and Equation 6.9.

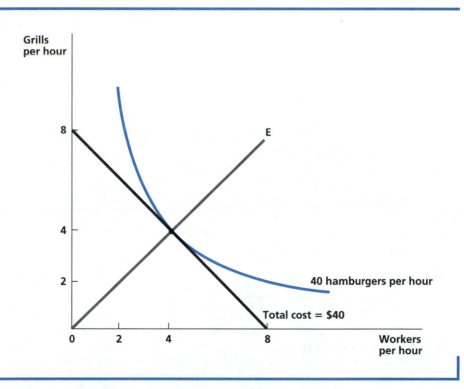

FIGURE 6.7 Cost-Minimizing Input Choice for 40 Hamburgers per Hour Using four grills and four workers is the minimal cost combination of inputs that can be used to produce 40 hamburgers per hour. Total costs are $40.

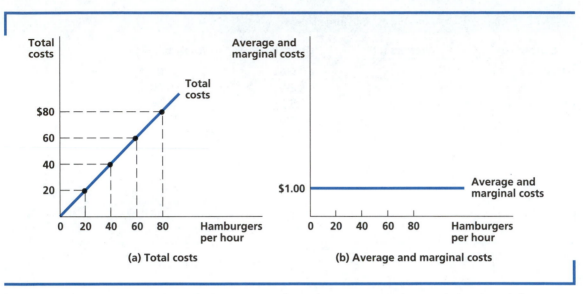

FIGURE 6.8 Total, Average, and Marginal Cost Curves The total cost curve is simply a straight line through the origin reflecting constant returns to scale. Long-run average and marginal costs are constant at $1 per hamburger.

Long-Run Cost Curves

Because HH's production function has constant returns to scale, computing its expansion path is a simple matter; all of the cost-minimizing tangencies will resemble the one shown in Figure 6.7. As long as w = v = $5, long-run cost minimization will require K = L and each hamburger will cost exactly $1. This result is shown graphically in Figure 6.8. HH's long-run total cost curve is a straight line through the origin, and its long-run average and marginal costs are constant at $1 per burger. The very simple shapes shown in Figure 6.8 are a direct result of the constant-returns-to-scale production function HH has.

Short-Run Costs

If we hold one of HH's inputs constant, its cost curves have a more interesting shape. For example, with the number of grills fixed at four, Table 6.2 repeats the labor input required to produce various output levels (see Table 5.3). Total costs of these input combinations are also shown in the table. Notice how the diminishing marginal productivity of labor for HH causes its costs to rise rapidly as output expands. This is shown even more clearly by computing the short-run average and marginal costs implied by those total cost figures. The marginal cost of the 100th hamburger amounts to a whopping $2.50 because of the four-grill limitation in the production process.

TABLE 6.2 Short-Run Costs of Hamburger Production

Output (q)	Workers (L)	Grills (K)	Total cost (STC)	Average cost (SAC)	Marginal cost (SMC)
10	0.25	4	$21.25	$2.125	—
20	1.00	4	25.00	1.250	$0.50
30	2.25	4	31.25	1.040	0.75
40	4.00	4	40.00	1.000	1.00
50	6.25	4	51.25	1.025	1.25
60	9.00	4	65.00	1.085	1.50
70	12.25	4	81.25	1.160	1.75
80	16.00	4	100.00	1.250	2.00
90	20.25	4	121.25	1.345	2.25
100	25.00	4	145.00	1.450	2.50

Source: Table 5.3 and Equation 6.9. Marginal costs have been computed using calculus.

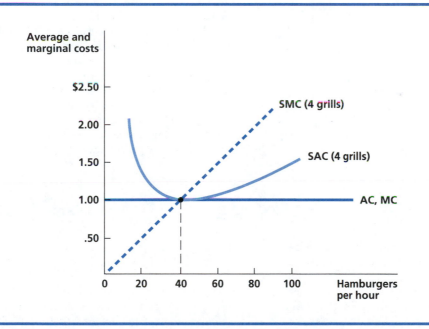

FIGURE 6.9 Short-Run and Long-Run Average and Marginal Cost Curves for Hamburger Heaven For this constant returns-to-scale production function, AC and MC are constant over all ranges of output. This constant average cost is $1 per unit. The short-run average cost curve does, however, have a general U-shape since the number of grills is held constant. The SAC curve is tangent to the AC curve at an output of 40 hamburgers per hour.

Finally, Figure 6.9 shows the short-run average and marginal cost curves for HH. Notice that SAC reaches its minimum value of $1 per hamburger at an output of 40 burgers per hour since that is the optimal output level for four grills. For increases in output above 40 hamburgers per hour, both SAC and SMC increase rapidly.[5]

SUMMARY

This chapter shows how to construct the firm's cost curves. These curves show the relationship between the amount that a firm produces and the costs of the inputs required for that production. In later chapters, we see how these curves are important building blocks for the theory of supply. The primary results of this chapter are:

• To minimize the cost of producing any particular level of output, the firm should choose a point on the isoquant for which the rate of technical substitution (RTS) is equal to the ratio of the inputs' market prices. Alternatively, the firm should choose its inputs so that the ratio of an input's marginal productivity to its price is the same for every input.

• By repeating this cost-minimization process for every possible level of output, the firm's expansion path can be constructed. This shows the minimum-cost way of producing any level of output. The firm's total cost curve can be calculated directly from the expansion path.

• The two most important unit-cost concepts are average cost (that is, cost per unit of output) and marginal cost (that is, the incremental cost of the last unit produced). Average and marginal cost curves can be constructed directly from the total cost curve. The shape of these curves depends on the shape of the total cost curve.

• Short-run cost curves are constructed by holding one (or more) of the firm's inputs constant in the short run. These short-run costs will not generally be the lowest cost the firm could achieve if all inputs could be adjusted. Short-run costs increase rapidly as output expands because the inputs that can be increased experience diminishing marginal productivities.

• Cost curves shift to a new position whenever the prices of inputs change. Improvements in production techniques also shift cost curves because the same level of output can then be produced with fewer inputs. Expanding one output in a multi-product firm may reduce costs of some other output when there are economies of scope.

REVIEW QUESTIONS

1. Trump Airlines is thinking of buying a new plane for its shuttle service. Why does the economist's notion of cost suggest that Trump should consider the plane's price in deciding whether it is a profitable investment but that, once brought, the plane's price is not directly relevant to Trump's profit-maximizing decisions? In such a case of "sunk costs," which cost should be used for the plane?

2. Farmer McDonald was heard to complain, "Although my farm is still profitable, I just can't afford to stay in this business any longer. I'm going to sell out and start a fast-food business." In what sense is McDonald using the word *profitable* here? Explain why his statement might be correct if he means profits in the accountant's sense but would be dubious if he is referring to economic profits.

[5] For some examples of how the cost curves for HH might shift, see problem 6.9 and problem 6.10.

3. Explain why the assumption of cost minimization implies that the total cost curve must have a positive slope: An increase in output must always increase total cost.

4. Suppose a firm had a production function with linear isoquants, implying that its two inputs were perfect substitutes for each other. What would determine the firm's expansion path in this case? For the opposite case of a fixed-proportions production function, what would the firm's expansion path be?

5. Consider two possible definitions of marginal cost:

   a. The extra cost involved in producing one more unit of output.
   b. The cost of the last unit produced.

   Are these definitions identical? If not, which is more correct? Why might the other be misleading?

6. Leonardo is a mechanically minded person who always builds things to help him understand his courses. To help in his understanding of average and marginal cost curves, he draws a TC-q axis pair on a board and attaches a thin wood pointer by a single nail through the origin. He now claims that he can find the level of output for which average cost is a minimum for any cost curve by the following mechanical process: (1) Draw the total cost curve on his graph; (2) Rotate his pointer until it is precisely tangent to the total cost curve he has drawn; and (3) Find the quantity that corresponds to this tangency. Leonardo claims that this is the quantity where average cost is minimized. Is he right? For which of the total cost curves in Figure 6.3 would this procedure work? When would it not work?

7. Late Bloomer is taking a course in microeconomics. Grading in the course is based on 10 weekly quizzes, each with a 100-point maximum. On the first quiz, Late Bloomer receives a 10. In each succeeding week, he raises his score by 10 points, scoring a 100 on the final quiz of the year.

   a. Calculate Late Bloomer's quiz average for each week of the semester. Why, after the first week, is his average always lower than his current week's quiz?
   b. To help Late Bloomer, his kindly professor has decided to add 40 points to the total of his quiz scores before computing the average. Recompute Late Bloomer's weekly averages given this professional gift.
   c. Explain why Late bloomer's weekly quiz averages now have a U shape. What is his lowest average during the term?
   d. Explain the relevance of this problem to the construction of cost curves. Why does the presence of a "fixed cost" of 40 points result in a U-shaped curve? Are Late Bloomer's average and marginal test scores equal at his minimum average?

8. Jana is a mathematical whiz. She has been reading this chapter and remarks, "All this short-run/long-run stuff is a trivial result of the mathematical fact that the minimum value for any function must be as small as or smaller than the minimum value for the same function when some additional constraints are attached." Use Jana's insight to explain the following:

   a. Why short-run total costs must be equal to or greater than long-run total costs for any given output level
   b. Why short-run average cost must be equal to or greater than long-run average cost for any given output level
   c. Whether you can make a definite statement about the relationship between short-run and long-run marginal cost

9. Taxes can obviously affect firms' costs. Explain how each of the following taxes would affect total, average, and marginal cost. Be sure to consider whether the tax would have a different effect depending on whether one discusses short-run or long-run costs:

   a. A franchise tax of $10,000 that the firm must pay in order to operate
   b. An output tax of $2 on each unit of output
   c. An employment tax on each worker's wages
   d. A capital use tax on each machine the firm uses

10. Use Figure 6.1 to explain why a rise in the price of an input must increase the total cost of producing any given output level. What does this result suggest about how such a price increase shifts the AC curve? Do you think it is possible to draw any definite conclusion about how the MC curve would be affected?

PROBLEMS

6.1 A widget manufacturer has an infinitely substitutable production function of the form

$$q = 2K + L$$

a. Graph the isoquant maps for q = 20, q = 40, and q = 60. What is the RTS along these isoquants?
b. If the wage rate (w) is $1 and the rental rate on capital (v) is $1, what cost-minimizing combination of K and L will the manufacturer employ for the three different production levels in part a? What is the manufacturer's expansion path?
c. How would your answer to part b change if v rose to $3 with w remaining at $1?

6.2 A stuffed-wombat manufacturer determined that the lowest average production costs were achieved when eight wombats were produced at an average cost of $1,000 each. If the marginal cost curve is a straight line intersecting the origin, what is the marginal cost of producing the ninth wombat?

6.3 The long-run total cost function for a firm producing skateboards is

$$TC = q^3 - 40q^2 + 430q$$

where q is the number of skateboards per week.

a. What is the general shape of this total cost function?
b. Calculate the average cost function for skateboards. What shape does the graph of this function have? At what level of skateboard output does average cost reach a minimum? What is the average cost at this level of output?
c. The marginal cost function for skateboards is given by

$$MC = 3q^2 - 80q + 430$$

Show that this marginal cost curve intersects average cost at its minimum value.

d. Graph the average and marginal cost curves for skateboard production.

6.4 Trapper Joe, the fur trader, has found that his production function in acquiring pelts is given by

$$q = 2\sqrt{H}$$

where q = the number of pelts acquired in a day, and H = the number of hours Joe's employees spend hunting and trapping in one day. Joe pays his employees $8 an hour.

a. Calculate Joe's total and average cost curves (as a function of q).
b. What is Joe's total cost for the day if he acquires four pelts? Six pelts? Eight pelts? What is Joe's average cost per pelt for the day if he acquires four pelts? Six pelts? Eight pelts?
c. Graph the cost curves from part a and indicate the points from part b.

6.5 A firm producing hockey sticks has a production function given by

$$q = 2\sqrt{K \cdot L}$$

In the short run, the firm's amount of capital equipment is fixed at K = 100. The rental rate for K is v = $1, and the wage rate for L is w = $4.

a. Calculate the firm's short-run total cost function. Calculate the short-run average cost function.
b. The firm's short-run marginal cost function is given by SMC = q/50. What are the STC, SAC, and SMC for the firm if it produces 25 hockey sticks? Fifty hockey sticks? One hundred hockey sticks? Two hundred hockey sticks?
c. Graph the SAC and the SMC curves for the firm. Indicate the points found in part b.
d. Where does the SMC curve intersect the SAC curve? Explain why the SMC curve will always intersect the SAC at its lowest point.

6.6 Professor Smith and Professor Jones are going to produce a new introductory textbook. As true economists, they have laid out the production function for the book as

$$q = \sqrt{SJ}$$

where
q = the number of pages in the finished books
S = the number of working hours spent by Smith
J = the number of working hours spent by Jones
Smith values her labor at $20 per working hour. She has spent 900 hours preparing the first draft. Jones, whose labor is valued at $80 per working hour, will revise Smith's draft to complete the book.

a. How many hours will Jones have to spend to produce a finished book of 150 pages? Of 300 pages? Of 450 pages?
b. What is the marginal cost of the 150th page of the finished book? Of the 300th page? Of the 450th page?

6.7 An enterprising entrepreneur purchases two firms to produce widgets. Each firm produces identical products and each has a production function given by

$$q_i = \sqrt{K_i \cdot L_i}$$

where

$$i = 1, 2$$

The firms differ, however, in the amount of capital equipment each has. In particular, firm 1 has $K_1 = 25$, whereas firm 2 has $K_2 = 100$. The marginal product of labor is $MP_L = 5/(2\sqrt{L})$ for firm 1, and $MP_L = 5/\sqrt{L}$ for firm 2. Rental rates for K and L are given by w = v = $1.

a. If the entrepreneur wishes to minimize short-run total costs of widget production, how would output be allocated between the two firms?
b. Given that output is optimally allocated between the two firms, calculate the short-run total and average cost curves. What is the marginal cost of the 100th widget? The 125th widget? The 200th widget?

c. How should the entrepreneur allocate widget production between the two firms in the long run? Calculate the long-run total and average cost curves for widget production.
d. How would your answer to part c change if both firms exhibited diminishing returns to scale?

6.8 Suppose a firm's constant-returns-to-scale production function requires it to use capital and labor in a fixed ratio of two workers per machine to produce 10 units and that the rental rates for capital and labor are given by v = 1, w = 3.

a. Calculate the firm's long-run total and average cost curves.
b. Suppose K is fixed at 10 in the short run. Calculate the firm's short-run total and average cost cures. What is the marginal cost of the 10th unit? The 25th unit? The 50th unit? The 100th unit?

6.9 In the numerical example of Hamburger Heaven's production function in Chapter 5, we examined the consequences of the invention of a self-flipping burger that changed the production function to

$$q = 20\sqrt{KL}$$

a. Assuming this shift does not change the cost-minimizing expansion path (which requires K = L), how are long-run total, average, and marginal costs affected? (See the numerical example at the end of chapter 6.)
b. More generally, technical progress in hamburger production might be reflected by

$$q = (1 + r)\sqrt{KL}$$

where r is the annual rate of technical progress (that is, a rate of increase of 3 percent would have r = .03). How will the year-to-year change in the average cost of a hamburger be related to the value of r?

6.10 In our numerical example, Hamburger Heaven's expansion path requires K = L because w (the wage) and v (the rental rate of grills) are equal. More generally, for this type of production function, it can be shown that

$$K/L = w/v$$

for cost minimization. Hence, relative input usage is determined by relative input prices.

a. Suppose both wages and grill rents rise to $10 per hour. How would this affect the firm's expansion path? How would long-run average and marginal cost be affected? What can you conclude about the effect of uniform inflation of input costs on the costs of hamburger production?

b. Suppose wages rise to $20 but grill rents stay fixed at $5. How would this affect the firm's expansion path? How would this affect the long-run average and marginal cost of hamburger production? Why does a multiplication of the wage by 4 result in a much smaller increase in average costs?

INTERNET EXERCISES

1. *Costs: employee compensation.* How much do employers pay their employees? Are unionized employees paid more than nonunionized employees? The answer to these and other questions regarding employment compensation can be found at the Bureau of Labor Statistics Web site at *http://stat.bls.gov.* Under Wages, Earnings, and Benefits, click on Employment Costs. Under News Releases, click on Employer Costs for Employee Compensation. What is the most recent estimate of the overall average cost per hour for employee compensation? What percentage of this comes from wages and salaries? Benefits? In private industry, what is the average percentage of total employee compensation made up by health benefits? What is the average total hourly compensation for unionized employees in private industries? Nonunionized employees? Some studies have shown that unionized workers tend to be more productive than their nonunionized counterparts. Keeping in mind both the wage and productivity differentials, can you make any general determination about the impact of unionization on a firm's average total costs? Explain.

2. *Congestion costs on the Internet.* When you download an MP3 (or other large) file from the Internet, do you consider how your download may create costs to others in the form of Internet congestion? Application 6.4 discusses congestion costs on roads and highways, but a similar analysis can be applied to Internet usage. Internet congestion has become increasingly problematic. In fact, there are actually Internet "weather report" sites that detail, in real time, the degree of Internet congestion in various geographic regions. For example, see *http://www.internettrafficreport.com* or *http://www.internetweather.com.* For a good overview of the "economic, institutional, and technological structure" of the Internet, go to Jeffrey Mackie-Mason and Hal Varian's "Economic FAQs about the Internet" at *http://www.sims.berkeley.edu/resources/infoecon/pricing.html.* Link to the Web site and read the sections "How Can the Internet Deal with Increasing Congestion?" and "How Might Prices Be Used to Control Congestion?" Why do the authors suggest that Internet congestion is more serious than say, highway congestion? Discuss how the marginal cost of using the Internet varies with the degree of congestion at the time. What pricing scheme do the authors propose to control congestion? What do you think of such a proposal?

7

Profit Maximization and Supply

In this chapter, we use the cost curves developed in Chapter 6 to study firms' output decisions. This results in a detailed model of supply. First, however, we briefly look at some conceptual issues about firms.

THE NATURE OF FIRMS

As we pointed out earlier, a firm is any institution that turns inputs into outputs. The relationships among providers of inputs to a firm may be quite complicated. Each provider agrees to devote his or her input to production activities under a set of understandings about how the input is to be used and what benefit the provider will receive. In some cases, these relationships are explicitly set down in contracts. Workers often negotiate contracts that specify in considerable detail what hours are to be worked, what rules of work are to be followed, and what rate of pay is to be received. Similarly, capital owners invest in a firm under a set of explicit legal principles about how the capital will be used and the compensation the owners will receive. In addition to these formal arrangements, there are many more implicit relationships among the people in a firm. For example, managers and workers follow certain procedures in making production decisions, and there are many implicit understandings about who has the authority to do what. Capital owners often delegate considerable authority to managers and workers to make decisions on their behalf. General Motors shareholders, for example, are not involved in the decision of how to build cars though, technically, they own the assembly line. All of these explicit and implicit relationships among providers change through time in response to experiences and to events external to the firm. Much as a basketball team tries out new plays and defensive strategies, firms alter the nature of their internal organizations in order to achieve better long-run results.

Firms' Goals

These complicated relationships in a firm pose some problems for economists who wish to develop theoretical generalizations about how firms behave. In our study of demand theory, it made some sense to talk about choices by a rational consumer because we were examining decisions by only a single person. But for firms, many people may be involved in decisions, and any detailed study of such decisions may quickly become deeply mired in questions of psychology, sociology, and group dynamics.

To avoid such complexities, economists treat the firm as a single decision-making unit, an approach that sweeps away all the complicated behavioral issues about relationships among employees and capital owners. This approach assumes that firms' decisions are made by a single dictatorial manager who rationally pursues some goal, usually the maximization of the firm's economic profits. This is the approach we take in this chapter to develop the theory of a firm's supply behavior. A final section of the chapter looks at a few complications raised by the need to provide the right incentives to managers.

PROFIT MAXIMIZATION

If firms pursue the goal of making the most profits possible, by definition, they seek to make the difference between total revenues and total economic costs as big as possible. Here we are using economic concepts of costs and profits. Accounting notions of profits may be relevant to questions about how a firm is taxed (Application 7.1: Corporate Profits Taxes and the Leveraged Buyout Craze looks at this relationship), but maximizing economic profits is the fundamental goal motivating the decisions that firms make.

Marginalism

If firms are profit maximizers, they make decisions in a marginal way. The manager-owner adjusts the things that can be controlled until it is impossible to increase profits further. The manager looks, for example, at the incremental (or marginal) profit from producing one more unit of output or the additional profit from hiring one more employee. As long as this incremental profit is positive, the manager decides to produce the extra output or hire the extra worker. When the incremental profit of an activity becomes zero, the manager has pushed the activity far enough—it would not be profitable to go further.

The Output Decision

We can show this relationship between profit maximization and marginalism most directly by looking at the output level that a firm chooses to produce. A firm sells some level of output, q, and from these sales the firm receives its

Corporate income (or profit) taxes were levied in the United States in 1909, about 4 years before the personal income tax was put into effect. In 2002, corporate income tax revenues amounted to more than $200 billion, more than 10 percent of total federal tax collections. Many people view the tax as a natural complement to the personal income tax. Under U.S. law, corporations share many of the same rights as do people, so it may seem only reasonable that corporations should be taxed in a similar way. Some economists, however, believe that the corporate profits tax seriously distorts the allocation of resources, both because of its failure to use an economic profit concept under the tax law and because a substantial portion of corporate income is taxed twice.

Definition of Profits

A large portion of what is defined as corporate profits under the tax laws is in fact a normal return to shareholders for the equity they have invested in the corporations. Shareholders expect a similar return from other investments they make: If they deposit their money in a bank, for instance, they expect to be paid interest. Hence, some portion of corporate profits should be considered an economic cost of doing business because it reflects what owners have forgone by making an equity investment. If this cost were added to other corporate costs, reported profits would be reduced substantially.

Effects of the Double Tax

The corporate profits tax is not so much a tax on profits as it is a tax on the equity returns of corporate shareholders. Such taxation may have two consequences. First, corporations will find it more attractive to finance new capital investments through loans and bond offerings (whose interest payments are an allowable cost) than through new stock issues (whose implicit costs are not an allowable cost under the tax law). A second effect occurs because a part of corporate income is double taxed—first when it is earned by the corporation and then later when it is paid out to shareholders in the form of dividends. Hence, the total rate of tax applied to corporate equity capital is much higher than that applied to other sources of capital.

The Leveraged Buyout Craze

These peculiarities of the corporate income tax are at least partly responsible for the wave of leveraged buyouts (LBOs) that swept financial markets in the late 1980s. Michael Milken and others made vast fortunes by developing this method of corporate financing. The basic principle of an LBO is to use borrowed funds to acquire most of the outstanding stock of a corporation. Those involved in such a buyout are substituting a less highly taxed source of capital (debt) for a more highly taxed form (equity). Huge deals such as the $25 billion buyout of RJR-Nabisco by the Kohlberg, Kravis, Roberts company were an attempt to maximize the true economic profits that can be extracted from a business (some involved in these deals also used questionable financial practices).

The benefits of leveraged buyouts are larger, of course, when companies can be purchased cheaply. The huge increase in stock prices that started in 1991 made this mechanism

(continued)

much less profitable, despite relatively low interest rates for borrowers. Hence, most buy-outs in the 1990s came about through the use of vastly appreciated share prices. High stock prices made equity finance so cheap that questions of taxation became of secondary concern. With the drop in stock prices after 2000, however, debt-financed buyouts may return to fashion.

To Think About

1. Is it possible to redefine accounting concepts so that only economic profits are taxed?
2. A popular slogan of some tax reformers is: "Corporations don't pay taxes, people do." Do you agree? If so, why do we have a separate tax for corporations? Which "people" pay that tax?

revenues, $R(q)$. The amount of revenues received obviously depends on how much output is sold and on what price it is sold for. Similarly, in producing q, certain economic costs are incurred, $TC(q)$, and these also depend on how much is produced. Economic profits (π) are defined as

$$\pi = R(q) - TC(q) \qquad (7.1)$$

In deciding how much output to produce, the firm chooses the amount for which economic profits are as large as possible. This process is illustrated in Figure 7.1. The top panel of this figure shows rather general revenue and total cost curves. As might be expected, both have positive slopes—producing more causes both the firm's revenues and its costs to increase. For any level of output, the firm's profits are represented by the vertical distance between these two curves. These are shown separately in the lower panel of Figure 7.1. Profits are zero when the revenue and cost curves intersect (q_1 and q_2) and are largest when the vertical distance between revenues and cost are greatest (q^*). Clearly, a firm that is pursuing the goal of profit maximization would opt to produce q^*. Characterizing this output level leads to one of the most useful and familiar results in microeconomics.

The Marginal Revenue/Marginal Cost Rule

In order to examine the conditions that must hold at q^*, consider a firm that produces less than this amount. It would find that, if it were to increase its output by one unit, additional revenues would rise faster than would additional costs—so, profits would grow. In economic jargon, a firm that opted to produce less than q^* would find that its **marginal revenue** would be greater than its marginal production cost—a sure sign that increasing output will raise profits. Increasing output beyond q^* would, however, cause profits to fall. Beyond q^*, the extra revenue from selling one more unit is not as great as the cost of producing that extra unit

Marginal revenue
The extra revenue a firm receives when it sells one more unit of output.

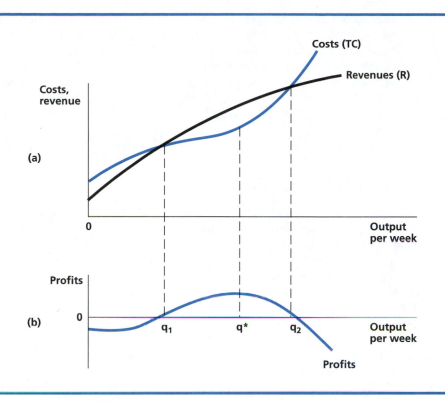

FIGURE 7.1 Marginal Revenue Must Equal Marginal Cost for Profit Maximization Economic profits are defined as total revenues minus total economic costs and can be measured by the vertical distance between the revenue and cost curves. Profits reach a maximum when the slope of the revenue function (marginal revenue) is equal to the slope of the cost function (marginal cost). In the figure, this occurs at q*. Profits are zero at both q_1 and q_2.

so producing it would cause a drop in profits. Hence, the characteristics of output q* are clear—at that output, marginal revenue is precisely equal to marginal cost. More succinctly, at q*

$$\text{Marginal revenue} = \text{Marginal cost} \qquad (7.2)$$

or

$$MR = MC \qquad (7.3)$$

Because both marginal revenue and marginal cost are functions of q, Equation 7.3 can usually be solved for q*. For output levels less than q*, MR > MC, whereas, for output levels greater than q*, MR < MC.

A geometric proof of this key proposition can be developed from Figure 7.1. We are interested in the conditions that must hold if the vertical distance between the revenue and cost curves is to be as large as possible. Clearly this requires that the slopes of the two curves be equal. If the curves had differing slopes, profits could be increased by adjusting output in the direction in which the curves diverged. Only when the two curves are parallel would such a move not raise profits. But the slope of the total cost curve is in fact marginal cost and (as we shall see) the slope of the total revenue curve represents marginal revenue. Hence, the geometric argument also proves the MR = MC output rule for profit maximization.

Marginalism in Input Choices

Similar marginal decision rules apply to firms' input choices as well. Hiring another worker, for example, entails some increase in costs, and a profit-miximizing firm should balance the additional costs against the extra revenue brought in by selling the output produced by this new worker. A similar analysis holds for the firm's decision on the number of machines to rent. Additional machines should be hired only as long as their marginal contributions to profits are positive. As the marginal productivity of machines begins to decline, the ability of machines to yield additional revenue also declines. The firm eventually reaches a point at which the marginal contribution of an additional machine to profits is exactly zero—the extra sales generated precisely match the costs of the extra machines. The firm should not expand the rental of machines beyond this point. In Chapter 13 we look at such hiring decisions in more detail.

MARGINAL REVENUE

Price taker
A firm or individual whose decisions regarding buying or selling have no effect on the prevailing market price of a good.

It is the revenue from selling one more unit of output that is relevant to a profit-maximizing firm. If a firm can sell all it wishes without affecting market price—that is, if the firm is a **price taker**—the market price will indeed be the extra revenue obtained from selling one more unit. In other words, if a firm's output decisions do not affect market price, marginal revenue is equal to price. Suppose a firm was selling 50 widgets at $1 each. Then total revenues would be $50. If selling one more widget does not affect price, that additional widget will also bring in $1 and total revenue will rise to $51. Marginal revenue from the 51st widget will be $1 (= $51 − $50). For a firm whose output decisions do not affect market price, we therefore have

$$MR = P \qquad\qquad (7.4)$$

Marginal Revenue for a Downward-Sloping Demand Curve

A firm may not always be able to see all it wants at the prevailing market price. If it faces a downward-sloping demand curve for its product, it can sell more only by reducing its selling price. In this case, marginal revenue will be less than market price. To see why, assume in our prior example that to sell the 51st widget the firm must reduce the price of all its widgets to $.99. Total revenues are now $50.49 (= $.99 × 51), and the marginal revenue from the 51st widget is only $.49 (= $50.49 − $50.00). Even though the 51st widget sells for $.99, the extra revenue obtained from selling the widget is a net gain of only $.49 (a $.99 gain on the 51st widget less a $.50 reduction in revenue from charging one penny less for each of the first 50). When selling one more unit causes market price to decline, marginal revenue is less than market price:

$$MR < P \tag{7.5}$$

Firms that must reduce their prices to sell more of their products (that is, firms facing a downward-sloping demand curve) must take this fact into account in deciding how to obtain maximum profits.

A Numerical Example

The result that marginal revenue is less than price for a downward-sloping demand curve is illustrated with a numerical example in Table 7.1. There, we have recorded the quantity of, say, tape cassettes demanded from a particular store per week (q), their price (P), total revenues from cassette sales (P · q), and marginal revenue (MR) for a simple linear demand curve of the form

$$q = 10 - P \tag{7.6}$$

Total revenue from tape sales reaches a maximum at q = 5, P = 5. For q > 5, total revenues decline. Increasing cassette sales beyond five per week actually causes marginal revenue to be negative.

In Figure 7.2, we have drawn this hypothetical demand curve and can use the figure to illustrate the marginal revenue concept. Consider, for example, the extra revenue obtained if the firm sells four tapes instead of three. When output is three, the market price per tape is $7 and total revenues (P · q) are $21. These revenues are shown by the area of the rectangle P*Aq*0. If the firm produces four tapes per week instead, price must be reduced to $6 to sell this increased output level. Now total revenue is $24, illustrated by the area of the

---

MicroQuiz 7.1

Use the marginal revenue/marginal cost rule to explain why each of the following purported rules for obtaining maximum profits is *incorrect*.

1. Maximum profits can be found by looking for that output for which profit per unit (that is, price minus average cost) is as large as possible.

2. Because the firm is a price taker, the scheme outlined in point 1 can be made even more precise—maximum profits may be found by choosing that output level for which average cost is as small as possible. That is, the firm should produce at the low point of its average-cost curve.

TABLE 7.1 Total and Marginal Revenue for Cassette Tapes (q = 10 − P)			
Price (P)	Quantity (q)	Total revenue (P · q)	Marginal revenue (MR)
$10	0	$ 0	
9	1	9	$ 9
8	2	16	7
7	3	21	5
6	4	24	3
5	5	25	1
4	6	24	−1
3	7	21	−3
2	8	16	−5
1	9	9	−7
0	10	0	−9

rectangle P**Bq**0. A comparison of the two revenue rectangles shows why the marginal revenue obtained by producing the fourth tape is less than its price. The sale of this tape does indeed increase revenue by the price at which it sells ($6). Revenue increases by the area of the darkly shaded rectangle in Figure 7.2. But, to sell the fourth tape, the firm must reduce its selling price from $7 to $6 on the first three tapes sold per week. That price reduction causes a fall in revenue of $3, shown as the area of the lightly shaded rectangle in Figure 7.2.

The net result is an increase in revenue of only $3 ($6 − $3) rather than the gain of $6 that would be calculated if only the sale of the fourth tape is considered in isolation. The marginal revenue for other points in this hypothetical demand curve could also be illustrated. In particular, if you draw the case of a firm producing six tapes instead of five, you will see that marginal revenue from the sixth tape is negative. Although the sixth tape itself sells for $4, selling it requires the firm to reduce price by $1 on the other five tapes it sells. Hence, marginal revenue is −$1 (= $4 − $5).

Marginal Revenue and Price Elasticity

In Chapter 4, we introduced the concept of the price elasticity of demand ($e_{Q,P}$), which we defined as

$$e_{Q,P} = \frac{\text{Percentage change in Q}}{\text{Percentage change in P}} \tag{7.7}$$

Although we developed this concept as it relates to the entire market demand for a product (Q), the definition can be readily adapted to the case of the demand

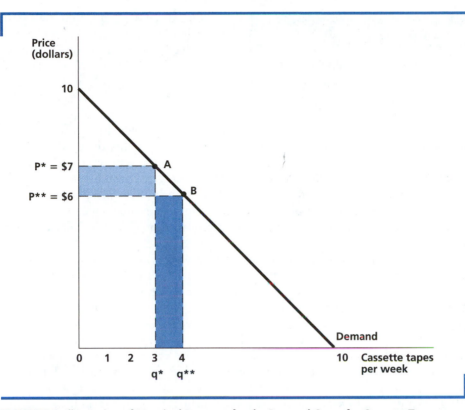

FIGURE 7.2 Illustration of Marginal Revenue for the Demand Curve for Cassette Tapes
(q = 10 − P) For this hypothetical demand curve, marginal revenue can be calculated as the extra revenue from selling one more tape. If the firm sells four tapes instead of three, for example, revenue will be $24 rather than $21. Marginal revenue from the sale of the fourth tape is therefore $3. This represents the gain of $6 from the sale of the fourth tape *less* the decline in revenue of $3 as a result of the fall in price for the first three tapes from $7 to $6.

curve that faces an individual firm. We define the price elasticity of demand for a single firm's output (q) as

$$e_{q,P} = \frac{\text{Percentage change in q}}{\text{Percentage change in P}} \qquad (7.8)$$

where P now refers to the price at which the firm's output sells.[1]

---

[1] This definition assumes that competitors' prices stay the same when the firm varies its own price. Under such a definition, the demand curve facing a single firm may be quite elastic even if the demand curve for the market as a whole is not. Indeed, if other firms are willing to supply all that consumers want to buy at a particular price, the firm cannot raise its price above that level without losing all its sales. Such behavior by rivals would therefore force price-taking behavior on the firm (see the discussion in the next section.) For a more complete discussion of interfirm price competition, see Chapter 9 and Chapter 12.

TABLE 7.2 Relationship between Marginal Revenue and Elasticity	
Demand curve	**Marginal revenue**
Elastic ($e_{q,P} < -1$)	MR > 0
Unit elastic ($e_{q,P} = -1$)	MR = 0
Inelastic ($e_{q,P} > -1$)	MR < 0

Our discussion in Chapter 4 about the relationship between elasticity and total expenditures also carries over to the case of a single firm. Total spending on the good (P · q) is now the same as total revenue for the firm. If demand facing the firm is inelastic ($0 \geq e_{q,P} > -1$), a rise in price will cause total revenues to rise. But, if this demand is elastic ($e_{q,P} < -1$), a rise in price will result in smaller total revenues. Clearly, therefore, there is a connection between the price elasticity and marginal revenue concepts. However, because price elasticity concerns reactions to changing prices whereas marginal revenue concerns the effect of changes in quantity sold, we must be careful to clarify exactly what this connection is.

Table 7.2 summarizes the connection between the price elasticity of the demand curve facing a firm and marginal revenue. Let's work through the entries in the table. When demand is elastic ($e_{q,P} < -1$), a fall in price raises quantity sold to such an extent that total revenues rise. Hence, in this case, an increase in quantity sold lowers price and thereby raises total revenue—marginal revenue is positive (MR > 0). When demand is inelastic ($0 \geq e_{q,P} > -1$), a fall in price, although it allows a greater quantity to be sold, reduces total revenue. Since an increase in output causes price and total revenue to decline, MR is negative. Finally, if demand is unit elastic ($e_{q,P} = -1$), total revenue remains constant for movements along the demand curve so MR is zero. More generally, the precise relation between MR and price elasticity is given by:

$$MR = P\left(1 + \frac{1}{e_{q,P}}\right) \tag{7.9}$$

and all of the relationships in Table 7.2 can be derived from this basic equation.[2] For example, if demand is elastic ($e_{q,P} < -1$), Equation 7.9 shows that MR is positive. Indeed, if demand is infinitely elastic ($e_{q,P} = -\infty$), MR will equal price since, as we showed before, the firm is a price taker and cannot affect the price it receives.

To see how Equation 7.9 might be used in practice, suppose that a firm knows that the elasticity of demand for its product is –2. It may derive this figure from historical data that show that each 10 percent decline in its price has usually led to an increase in sales of about 20 percent. Now assume that the price of the firm's output is $10 per unit and the firm wishes to know how much additional revenue the sale of one more unit of output will yield. The additional unit of out-

[2] The proof requires calculus. See Walter Nicholson, *Microeconomic Theory: Basic Principles and Extensions,* 8th ed. (Cincinnati: South-Western/Thomson Learning, 2002), 339–340.

put will not yield $10 because the firm faces a downward-sloping demand curve: To sell the unit requires a reduction in its overall selling price. The firm can, however, use Equation 7.9 to calculate that the additional revenue yielded by the sale will be $5 [= $10 · (1 + 1/–2) = $10 · 1/2]. The firm will produce this extra unit if marginal costs are less than $5; that is, if MC < $5, profits will be increased by the sale of one more unit of output. Although firms in the real world use more complex means to decide on the profitability of increasing sales (or of lowering prices), our discussion here illustrates the logic these firms must use. They must recognize how changes in quantity sold affect price (or vice versa) and how these price changes affect total revenues.

> **MicroQuiz 7.2**
>
> How does the relationship between marginal revenue and price elasticity explain the following economic observations?
>
> **1.** There are five major toll routes for automobiles from New Jersey into New York City. Raising the toll on one of them will cause total revenue collected on that route to fall. Raising the tolls on all of the routes will cause total revenue collected on any one route to rise.
>
> **2.** A doubling of the restaurant tax from 3 percent to 6 percent only in Amherst, Massachusetts, causes meal tax revenues to fall in that town, but a statewide increase of a similar amount causes tax revenues to rise.

MARGINAL REVENUE CURVE

Any demand curve has a **marginal revenue curve** associated with it. It is sometimes convenient to think of a demand curve as an *average revenue curve* because it shows the revenue per unit (in other words, the price) at various output choices the firm might make. The marginal revenue curve, on the other hand, shows the extra revenue provided by the last unit sold. In the usual case of a downward-sloping curve, the marginal revenue curve will lie below the demand curve because, at any level of output, marginal revenue is less than price.[3] In Figure 7.3, we have drawn a marginal revenue curve together with the demand curve from which it was derived. For output levels greater than q_1, marginal revenue is negative. As q increases from 0 to q_1, total revenues (P · q) increase. However, at q_1, total revenues ($P_1 · q_1$) are as large as possible; beyond this output level, price falls proportionately faster than output rises so total revenues fall.

> **Marginal revenue curve**
> A curve showing the relation between the quantity a firm sells and the revenue yielded by the last unit sold. Derived from the demand curve.

Shifts in Demand and Marginal Revenue Curves

In Chapter 4, we talked in detail about the possibility of a demand curve's shifting because of changes in such factors as income, other prices, or preferences. Whenever a demand curve shifts, its associated marginal revenue curve shifts

---

[3] If demand is infinitely elastic (that is, if the demand curve is a horizontal line at some price), the average and marginal revenue curves coincide. Selling one more unit has no effect on price; therefore, marginal and average revenue are equal.

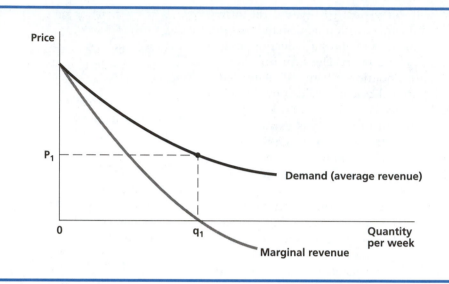

FIGURE 7.3 Marginal Revenue Curve Associated with a Demand Curve Since the demand curve is negatively sloped, the marginal curve will fall below the demand ("average revenue") curve. For output levels beyond q_1, marginal revenue is negative. At q_1, total revenue ($P_1 \cdot q_1$) is a maximum; beyond this point, additional increases in q actually cause total revenues to fall because of the accompanying decline in price.

MicroQuiz 7.3

Use Equation 7.9 and Figure 7.3 to answer the following questions about the relationship between a demand curve and its associated marginal revenue curve.

1. How does the vertical distance between the demand curve and its marginal revenue curve at a given level of output depend on the price elasticity of demand at that output level?

2. Suppose that an increase in demand leads consumers to be willing to pay 10 percent more for a particular level of output. Will the marginal revenue associated with this level of output increase by more or less than 10 percent? Does your answer depend on whether the elasticity of demand changes as a result of the shift?

with it. This should be obvious. The marginal revenue curve is always calculated by referring to a specific demand curve. In later analysis, we will have to keep in mind the kinds of shifts that marginal revenue curves might make when we talk about changes in demand. Application 7.2: How Did Airlines Respond to Deregulation? shows the importance of marginal decisions to the behavior of the airline industry following deregulation.

SUPPLY DECISION OF A PRICE-TAKING FIRM

In this section, we look in detail at the supply decision by a single price-taking firm. This analysis leads directly to the study of market supply curves and price determination—a topic that we take up in the next part. Here, however, we are concerned only with the decisions of a single firm.

Under the Airline Deregulation Act of 1978, a number of laws restricting U.S. airline operations were to be gradually phased out. Regulation of airline fares was reduced or eliminated entirely, and rules governing the assignment of airline routes were relaxed significantly. These dramatic changes in the legal environment in which airlines operated provided economists with an ideal opportunity to observe how firms respond to altered circumstances. In general, the responses were consistent with the profit-maximization hypothesis.

Marginal Revenue

A clear example of airlines' attention to marginal revenue was the development of new fare structures following deregulation. Prices for unrestricted coach fares dropped little because businesspeople, whose demands are relatively inelastic, usually pay these fares. Consequently, little if any extra revenue would have been earned by the airlines' attempting to lure additional full-fare passengers into flying. For special discount fares, however, it was an entirely different story. Discount fares were generally targeted toward people with highly elastic travel demands (tourists, families traveling together, and so forth). In these cases, large price reductions increased passenger demand significantly, thereby improving the passenger levels on many flights. Overall, the increased use of discount fares resulted in a 33 percent decline in the average price per passenger-mile-flown.[1] The structure of the price declines ensured that these discount fares generated far more additional revenue for the airlines than an across-the-board fare cut of a similar magnitude would have. It also resulted in a much wider dispersion among airlines on the same route (averaging 36 percent of average price) than had existed prior to deregulation.[2]

Marginal Cost

Airlines' attention to marginal costs in response to deregulation is also what might have been expected based on the profit-maximization hypothesis. Their fleets of aircraft could not be changed significantly in the short run, so airlines altered their route structures to coincide with those aircraft they already had. As Alfred Kahn has observed, from an economic point of view, their planes represented "marginal costs with wings," which could easily be moved around once deregulation came.

Effects of such reallocations by airlines were readily apparent. Service to many small communities (previously required under Civil Aeronautics Board regulation) was curtailed. Flight lengths were generally brought into greater correspondence with the optimal operating characteristics of the aircraft. Many airlines adopted a hub-and-spoke procedure for connecting flights that also had the effect of allowing them to use different types of aircraft for different routes.

One particularly interesting innovation in airline practices is the creative use of overbooking. Because the marginal cost associated with filling empty seats on a plane is

---

[1] See C. Winston, "U.S. Industry Adjustment to Economic Deregulation," *Journal of Economic Perspectives* (Summer 1998): 89–110.
[2] S. Borenstein and N. L. Rose, "Competition and Price Dispersion in the U.S. Airline Industry," *Journal of Political Economy* (August 1994): 653–682.

(continued)

essentially zero, profits from the last few passengers on a flight are very high. Hence, the airlines have tried very hard to reduce the losses they suffer from "no shows" by selling more space than is available. Waiting for a flight to leave has come to resemble a frantic auction as airline personnel make increasingly attractive offers to get some passengers to give up their seats voluntarily. The value of these giveaways (free fares to anywhere) shows that airlines gain a lot by filling their planes.

To Think About

1. Airline pricing has led to much grousing from passengers that they "paid twice what the guy sitting next to me did." Should the government seek to stamp out such price differences?

2. Some critics of airline deregulation charge that it has caused airlines to skimp on safety. Does this claim make sense?

Short-Run Profit Maximization

The output decision of a price-taking firm has no effect on the price for which it can sell its output. For that reason, the firm treats price as a fact of nature in its decisions—it cannot do anything about the price, so it must adapt to it. For example, farmers can log onto the Internet each morning to check the prevailing prices of the crops they wish to sell. Each farmer feels he or she is "too small" to have any effect on the price. Still, the farmer has considerable flexibility in deciding how much to supply—he or she can choose which crop to harvest, whether to plant something new, or even whether to plow under a healthy crop if harvesting it would not pay. These are the kinds of decisions for which the model in this section is appropriate.

As we saw previously, a firm that acts as a price taker will treat the market price of its output as being synonymous with marginal revenue. Each unit that the firm sells will fetch this price no matter how much is sold. The firm's profit-maximizing decision is then to choose that output level for which price (marginal revenue) is equal to marginal cost. Here, we look only at the short-run aspects of this question. Over the long run, pricing results depend very much on what other firms do, so it is best to leave that discussion until the next chapter.

In Figure 7.4, we show the short-run average and marginal cost curves for this typical firm that we developed in Chapter 6 (see Figure 6.6). We also have drawn a horizontal line at the prevailing price for this firm's product, P*. This line is also labeled MR to show that this is the marginal revenue for this firm—it can sell all it wants and receive this additional revenue from each additional unit sold. Clearly, output level q* provides maximum profits here—at this output level, price (marginal revenue) is indeed equal to marginal cost. You can tell that profits are as large as possible at q* by simply asking what would happen if the firm produced either slightly more or slightly less. For any q less than q*, price (P*) exceeds marginal cost. Hence, an expansion in output would yield more in extra revenues than in extra costs—profits would rise by moving toward q*. Similarly,

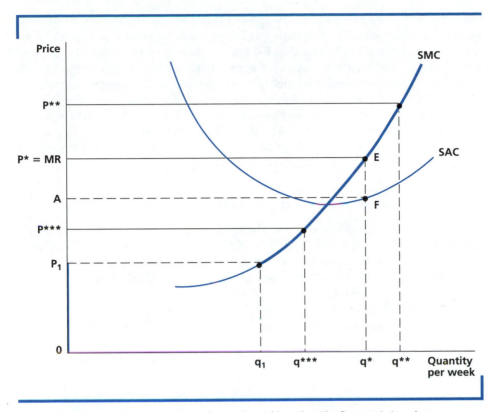

FIGURE 7.4 Short-Run Supply Curve for a Price-Taking Firm The firm maximizes short-run profits by producing that output for which P = SMC. For P < P₁ (P₁ = Minimum short-run average variable cost), the firm chooses to shut down (q = 0). The short-run supply curve is given by the heavy colored lines in the figure.

if the firm opted for q < q*, now marginal cost would exceed P*. Cutting back on output would save more in costs than would be lost in sales revenue. Again, profits would rise by moving toward q*.

Showing Profits

The actual amount of profits being earned by this firm when it decides to produce q* is easiest to show by using the short-run, average-cost curve. Because profits are given by

$$\text{Profits} = \pi = \text{Total revenue} - \text{Total cost} = P^*q^* - \text{STC}(q^*) \qquad (7.10)$$

we can factor q* out of this expression to get

$$\text{Profits} = \pi = q^* \left(P^* - \frac{TC}{q^*} \right) = q^* \left(P^* - \text{SAC}(q^*) \right) \qquad (7.11)$$

So, total profits are given by profits-per-unit (price minus average cost) times the number of units sold. Geometrically, profits per unit are shown in Figure 7.4 by the vertical distance EF. Notice that the average cost used to calculate these per-unit profits is the actual average cost experienced when the firm produces q*. Now, total profits are found by multiplying this vertical distance by the number of units sold, q*. These are therefore given by the area of the rectangle P*EFA. In this case, these profits are positive because P > SAC. These could be zero if P = SAC, or even negative if P < SAC. Regardless of whether profits are positive or negative, we know that they are as large as possible because output level q* obeys the marginal-revenue-equals-marginal-cost rule.[4]

The Firm's Short-Run Supply Curve

Firm's short-run supply curve
The relationship between price and quantity supplied by a firm in the short run.

The positively sloped portion of the short-run marginal cost curve is the **firm's short-run supply curve** for this price-taking firm. That is, the curve shows how much the firm will produce for every possible market price. At a higher price of P**, for example, the firm will produce q** because it will find it in its interest to incur the higher marginal costs q** entails. With a price of P***, on the other hand, the firm opts to produce less (q***) because only a lower output level will result in lower marginal costs to meet this lower price. By considering all possible prices that the firm might face, we can see from the marginal cost curve how much output the firm will supply at each price—if it is to maximize profits.

MicroQuiz 7.4

Use the theory of short-run supply illustrated in Figure 7.4 to answer the following questions:

1. How will an increase in the fixed costs that Burger King must pay to heat its outlets affect the firm's short-run supply curve for Whoppers?

2. How will a $10,000 fine imposed on Burger King for littering by its customers affect the firm's short-run shutdown decision? Would your answer change if the fine were $1,000 per day, to be ended once the littering stopped?

The Shutdown Decision

For very low prices, firms may not follow the P = MC rule. The firm always has another option in the short run—it can choose to produce nothing. We therefore have to compare the profits obtainable if the firm opts to pursue this shutdown strategy to those obtainable if it follows the P = MC rule. To do so, we must return to the distinction introduced in Chapter 6 between fixed and variable costs. In the short run, the firm must pay its fixed costs (for example, rent on its factory)

---

[4] Technically, the P = MC rule is only a necessary condition for a maximum in profits. The value of q found by applying this rule would not yield maximum profits if the marginal cost curve had a negative slope at q*. In that case, either increasing or decreasing q slightly would in fact increase profits. For all of our analysis, therefore, we will assume that the short-run marginal cost curve has a positive slope at the output level for which P = SMC.

whether or not it produces any output. If the firm shuts down, it suffers a loss of these fixed costs because it earns no revenues and incurs no variable costs. Can the firm do better than this dismal outcome? Because fixed costs are incurred in either case, the decision to produce must be based on a comparison between the total revenues a firm can receive for its output and the short-run variable costs (SVC) it incurs in producing this output. In algebraic terms, the firm will opt for $q > 0$ providing

$$P \cdot q \geq SVC$$

or, dividing by q,

$$P \geq SVC/q$$

In words, price must exceed variable cost per unit (that is, average variable cost). In Figure 7.4, the minimum value[5] for average variable cost is assumed to be P_1. This is the **shutdown price** for this firm. For $P \geq P_1$, the firm will follow the $P = MC$ rule for profit maximization (even though profits may still be negative if $P < SAC$) and its supply curve will be its short-run marginal cost curve. For $P < P_1$, price does not cover the minimum average variable costs of production and the firm will opt to produce nothing. This decision is illustrated by the heavy colored segment $0P_1$ in Figure 7.4. The practical importance of shutdown decisions is illustrated in Application 7.3: Why Is Drilling for Crude Oil Such a Boom or Bust Business?

Shutdown price
The price below which the firm will choose to produce no output in the short run. Equal to minimum average variable cost.

PROFIT MAXIMIZATION AND MANAGERS' INCENTIVES

So far in this chapter we have tended to treat the owner of a firm (that is, the owner of a firm's capital) as if he or she were also the manager in charge of making all of the firm's decisions. This approach makes the assumption of profit maximization intuitively reasonable—an owner who maximizes profits will make the income earned on his or her investment as large as possible. Hence, the assumption of profit maximization is in general agreement with the utility-maximization approach to behavior that we studied earlier in this book.

In many cases, however, managers do not own the firms that employ them. Rather, the manager is hired by the owner to act as his or her "agent" in making decisions. That is, the owner turns over decision-making authority to the manager, expecting the manager to maximize profits. In this section, we look briefly at this **principal-agent relationship.**

Principal-agent relationship
An economic actor (the principal) delegating decision-making authority to another party (the agent).

[5] For values of q larger than q_1, following the $P = MC$ rule ensures $P > AVC$ because there $MC > AVC$.

Why Is Drilling for Crude Oil Such a Boom or Bust Business?

The production of crude oil by small operators provides a number of illustrations of the principles of short-run supply behavior by price-taking firms. Because prices for crude oil are set in international markets, these firms clearly are price takers, responding to the price incentives they face. Rising marginal costs for drillers reflect the increased costs that the firms encounter as they drill to greater depths or in less-accessible areas. Hence, we should expect oil well activity to follow our simple model of responding to price changes.

Some Historical Data

Table 1 shows U.S. oil well drilling activity over the past 30 years. The table also shows the average price of crude oil in the various years, adjusted for changing prices or drilling equipment. The tripling of real oil prices between 1970 and 1980 led to a tripling of drilling. In many cases, these additional wells were drilled in high-cost locations (for example, in deep water in the Gulf of Mexico or on the Arctic Slope in Alaska). Clearly, the late 1970s and early 1980s were boom times for oil drillers.

Price Decline and Supply Behavior

Recessions in 1981 and 1990, combined with vast new supplies of crude oil (from the North Sea and Mexico, for example), put considerable pressure on oil prices. By 1990, real crude oil prices had declined by about 40 percent from their levels of the early 1980s. U.S. drillers were quick to respond to these changing circumstances. As Table 1 shows, less than half the number of wells were drilled in 1990 as in 1980. Real prices tended to stabilize during the 1990s, ending the decade much where they started. Drilling activity in the United States fell only modestly during the decade.

The Shutdown Decision

The decline in oil prices during the 1980s also prompted oil well operators to shut down some marginal operations. Especially vulnerable were high-cost wells such as those that used pressurized steam or those that produced fewer than 10 barrels per day. These shutdowns reached nearly 20 percent of all wells before prices stablized.

TABLE 1 World Oil Prices and Oil Well Drilling Activity in the United States

Year	World Price per Barrel	Real Price per Barrel*	Number of Wells Drilled
1970	$3.18	$7.93	21,177
1980	$21.59	$25.16	70,610
1990	$20.03	$16.30	31,555
2000	23.00	$16.40	26,981

*Nominal price divided by producer price index for capital equipment, 1982 = 1, 00.
Source: U.S. Department of Energy, Website: http:/www.eia.doe.gov

Other Margins in Drilling

Of course, the data in Table 1 only hint at the kinds of responses that oil drillers make when prices change. The marginal cost of an oil well depends crucially on such factors as the difficulty of the drilling location, how deep the well is drilled, and whether secondary recovery methods are used to stimulate oil production. A more complete study of the industry would look at how all of these features are affected by changing crude oil prices. In 1980, for example, not only were many wells drilled but also the average depth of these wells was much greater than had previously been the case. As might have been expected, the marginal costs incurred in that year were quite high. Consistent with the lower real oil prices of the 1990s, wells drilled during that decade tended to be lower-cost ventures.

To Think About

1. Are U.S. producers of crude oil accurately described as price takers?
2. How can firms continue to drill many thousands of oil wells in the United States each year? Hasn't all the oil in the United States already been found?

Nature of the Principal-Agent Relationship

Adam Smith understood the basic conflict between owners and managers. In *The Wealth of Nations*, he observed that "the directors of . . . companies, being the managers of other people's money than of their own, it cannot well be expected that they should watch over it with the same anxious vigilance with which [owners] watch over their own."[6] From this observation, Smith went on to look at the behavior of such famous British institutions as the Royal African Company, the Hudson's Bay Company, and the East India Company, which he used to illustrate some of the consequences of management by nonowners. His observations provide an important starting point for the study of modern firms.

www.infotrac-college.com
Keywords: Profit maximization, Marginal revenue, Marginal cost, Shutdown decision, Managers' incentives

The major issue raised by the use of manager-agents is illustrated in Figure 7.5. This figure shows the indifference curve map of a manager's preferences between the firm's profits (which are of primary interest to the owners) and various benefits (such as a fancy office or travel in the corporate jet or helicopter) that accrue mainly to the manager. This indifference curve map has the same shape as those in Part 2, because both profits and benefits provide positive utility to the manager and he or she may be willing to consider trade-offs between the two.

To construct the budget constraint that the manager faces in seeking to maximize his or her utility, assume first that the manager is also the owner of this firm. If the manager chooses to have no special benefits from the job, profits will

---

[6] Adam Smith, *The Wealth of Nations*, 1776 Cannan Edition (New York: Modern Library, 1937), 700.

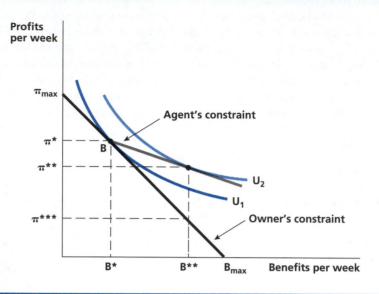

FIGURE 7.5 Incentives for a Manager Acting as an Agent for a Firm's Owners If a manager were the sole owner of a firm, π^*, B* would be chosen since this combination of profits and benefits provides maximum utility. If the manager only owns one-third of the firm, however, the perceived budget constraint will be flatter and B**, π^{**} will be chosen.

be π_{max}. Each dollar of benefits received by the manager reduces these profits by one dollar. The budget constraint will have a slope of –1, and profits will reach zero when benefits total B_{max}.

Given this budget constraint, the owner-manager maximizes utility by opting for profits of π^* and benefits of B*. Profits of π^*, while less than π_{max}, may still represent profit maximization in this situation because any other owner-manager would also wish to receive B* in benefits. That is, B* represents an economic cost of doing business; and, given these costs, the firm's manager really does maximize net profits.

Conflicts in the Agent Relationship

Now suppose that the manager is not the only owner of this firm. Instead, assume that, say, one-third of the capital of the firm is owned by the manager and the other two-thirds is owned by outside investors who play no role in operating the firm. In this case, the manager will act as if he or she no longer faces a budget constraint that requires sacrificing one dollar of the profits for each dollar of benefits. Now, a dollar of benefits costs the manager only $.33 in profits. The other $.67 is effectively paid by the other owners in terms of reduced profits on their investment. Although the new budget constraint continues to include the point B*, π* (the manager could still make the same decision a sole owner could), for benefits greater than B* the slope of the budget constraint to the manager appears to be only –1/3; profits on the manager's portion of the business decline by only $.33 for each dollar in benefits received. Given this apparent budget constraint, the manager would choose point B**, π** to maximize his or her utility. Being only a partial owner of the firm causes the manager to choose a lower level of profits and a higher level of benefits than would be chosen by a sole owner.

Point B**, π** is not really attainable by this firm. Although the cost of one dollar of benefits appears to be only $.33 in profits for the manager, in reality, of course, the benefits cost one dollar to all the owners. When the manager opts for B** in benefits, profits are π***. The firm's owners are harmed by having to rely on an agency relationship with the firm's manager. It appears that the smaller the fraction of the firm that is owned by the manager, the greater the extent of the distortions that will be induced by this relationship.

The situation illustrated in Figure 7.5 is representative of a variety of principal-agent problems that arise in economics. Whenever one actor relies on another actor to make decisions, the motivation of this agent must be taken into account since the agent may make different decisions than the principal would. Examples of this relationship occur not only in the management of firms but also in such diverse applications as hiring investment advisors (do they really put their clients' interests first?); relying on an automobile mechanic's assessment in ordering repairs; and buying a tie for a relative. In Application 7.4: Principals and Agents in Franchising and Medicine, we briefly examine two specific examples of the relationship.

> **MicroQuiz 7.5**
>
> The potential mismatch between the motives of principles and agents should not be overstated. Consider the problem of hiring a mechanic to work on your car. Why would principal-agent problems be less likely if:
>
> **1.** You were quite knowledgeable about car repairs?
>
> **2.** There were many mechanics in town?

Incentive Contracts

The firm's owners would be unlikely to take the kind of behavior illustrated in Figure 7.5 lying down. They are being forced to accept lower profits than might be earned on their investments in exchange of manager-oriented benefits that provide no value to them personally. What can they do? Most obviously, they can refuse to invest in the firm if they know the manager will behave in this manner. In that event, the manager would have two options. First, he or she could go it alone, financing the company completely with his or her own funds. The firm

Principals and Agents in Franchising and Medicine

Problems in principal-agent relationships arise in economic situations as diverse as fast-food operations and the provision of medical care. A closer examination shows that these two situations have much in common.

Franchising

Many large businesses operate their local retail outlets through franchise contracts. The McDonald's Corporation, for example, does not actually own every place that displays the golden arches. Instead, local restaurants are usually owned by small groups of investors who have bought a franchise from the parent company. The problem for the parent company is to ensure that their franchise agents operate in a proper manner.

Various provisions of franchise contracts help to ensure this result. McDonald's franchisees, for example, must meet certain food-quality and service standards and they must purchase their supplies (hamburgers, frozen fries, buns, napkins, and so forth) from firms that also meet standards set by the parent company. In return, the franchisee gets some management assistance and enjoys the reputation of the McDonald's trademark (together with its national advertising). More important, the franchisee gets to keep a large share of the profits generated by the local restaurant, thereby providing significant incentives to operate it efficiently. The existence of these incentives probably explains why McDonald's opted for franchising rather than direct ownership—this form of contract is better suited for controlling the principal-agent problems that arise in fast food.[1]

Doctors and Patients

A similar set of problems occurs between physicians and their patients. When people are sick, they often have very little idea of what is wrong or what the most promising treatment is. They place themselves under a physician's care in the belief that the physician has better information on which to base decisions about the proper course of action. The physician then acts as an agent for the patient. But there are several reasons why a physician might not choose exactly what a fully informed patient would choose. The physician generally pays none of the patient's bills; to the physician, the price of anything prescribed is essentially zero. Indeed, since the physician may in many instances also be the provider of care, he or she may even benefit financially from the services prescribed. A number of studies have gathered evidence on such physician-induced demand, and most have reported relatively small but significant effects.

Physicians as Double Agents

Most medical care consumers have insurance. Because insurance companies must rely on physicians to deliver care, this raises a second principal-agent situation in which the compa-

---

[1] For a summary of empirical evidence, see R. S. Thompson, "Company Ownership vs. Franchising: Issues and Evidence," *Journal of Economic Studies,* 19, no. 4 (1992): 31–42.

nies need some way to ensure that physicians will not overprescribe care. With traditional fee-for-service insurance, providing such incentives to physicians is very difficult because the company cannot monitor every physician decision. This is one reason that many health care plans have adopted "prepaid" features such as those found in health maintenance organizations (HMOs). Under these plans, insured patients pay an annual fee covering all of their medical needs. That annual fee then becomes a budget constraint for physicians who now may more carefully consider the costs of the care they deliver.

To Think About

1. Many states have enacted laws that protect franchisees from their larger parent firms. For example, some states do not allow the establishment of new franchises from the same parent if that would be "unfair" to existing firms. How would such restrictions affect the efficiency of franchise contracts?

2. Why do many medical care consumers hate their HMOs? Do we need an HMO patients' "Bill of Rights" to ensure that such consumers are fairly treated? (See also Application 15.2.)

would then return to the owner-manager situation in which B*, π* is the preferred choice of benefits and profits. Alternatively, the manager may obtain outside financing to operate the firm if the operation is too expensive to finance alone. In this case, the manager has to work out some sort of contractual arrangement with would-be owners to get them to invest.

Writing a contract under which managers pay completely for benefits out of their share of the profits is probably impossible for owners to do. Enforcing the provisions of such a contract would require constant supervision of the manager's activities—something the owners would prefer not to do, since that would force them into a managerial role. Instead, owners may try to develop less-strict contracts that give managers an incentive to economize on benefits and thereby pursue goals closer to pure profit maximization. By offering such contract provisions as profit-sharing bonuses, stock option plans, and company-financed pensions, the owner may be able to give managers an incentive to be careful about the benefits they choose to take. The final agreement will be a compromise between owners' desires to incorporate incentives to encourage profit-maximizing behavior and the costs involved in writing the contract and monitoring that behavior. In Application 7.5: The Good and Bad Effects of Stock Options, we explore how contracts involving stock ownership can help ameliorate the principal-agent conflict, though not without adding some additional concerns.

Stock options grant to the holder the ability to buy shares at a fixed price. If the market price of these shares rises, option holders will benefit because they can buy the stock at less than the market price (and perhaps resell it, making a quick profit). Options are usually granted by firms to their executives as one way of providing incentives to manage the firm in a way that will increase the price of its shares.

The Explosion in Stock Options

Use of stock options as a form of executive compensation has grown rapidly in recent years. In 1980, most firms did not offer options to their executives and, in those that did, the value of options constituted a fairly small percent of total compensation. By 2000, top executives of the largest companies received more than half their total compensation in the form of stock options, sometimes amounting to options worth hundreds of millions of dollars. There are many reasons for the increased popularity of stock options as a form of compensation. Rising stock prices throughout the decade of the 1990s undoubtedly made this form of compensation more attractive to executives. From the perspective of firms, the accounting treatment of options (which are often assigned a zero cost to the firm granting them) made them a low-cost way to pay their executives. A special provision in the tax laws enacted in 1993 specified that firms could not deduct executive pay of more than $1 million per year unless that pay was tied to company performance—a further spur to the use of options.

Incentive Effects of Options

Stock options clearly do succeed in tying an executive's compensation to the performance of a company's stock. By one estimate, stock options provide more than 50 times the pay-to-performance ratio provided by conventional pay packages.[1] Dollar for dollar, options also provide more pay-to-performance incentives than would a simple grant of shares to the executive. But the exact incentive effects of stock options are complex, depending on precisely how the options are granted and the ways in which the stock price for the firm performs. For example, options are less valuable when the firm pays large dividends to its shareholders, so the executive may have an incentive to hold back on dividend increases. On the other hand, options are more valuable when the price of a company's stock is more volatile, so options may induce executives to make more risky investments than they ordinarily would.

Unanticipated Incentive Effects—Accounting Fraud

Executives with significant holdings of stock options can make huge amounts of money if the values of their shares rise. In recent years, it has been common to see executives making hundreds of millions of dollars on such stock price movements. One unintended effect of giving CEOs such a large stake in seeing a higher stock price has been to encourage them to seek to manipulate information that can affect the price of their shares. Executives of the WorldCom Corporation, for example, hid nearly $4 billion in corporate expenses in

[1]B. J. Hall and J. B. Liebman, "Are CEOs Really Paid Like Bureaucrats?" *Quarterly Journal of Economics* (August 1998).

2001 so that their company would look more profitable. The firm's CEO benefited handsomely when he bailed out of the firm's stock. Accounting fiascos such as those at Enron and Tyco also seem to have been motivated in part by the desire to keep stock prices up so options holders could benefit. Whether stock option contracts can be adjusted to reduce the incentives for such actions remains an open question.

To Think About

1. Michael Eisner, CEO of the Walt Disney Corporation, once received over $500 million in stock options. Do you think he managed the company better than if he had been awarded *only* $50 million's worth?
2. If the price of a company's stock declines, stock options may become worthless. What would be the effect of a policy that promised to adjust the purchase price specified in the option contract downward when this happens?

SUMMARY

In this chapter, we examined the assumption that firms seek to maximize profits in making their decisions. A number of conclusions follow from this assumption:

- In making output decisions, a firm should produce the output level for which marginal revenue equals marginal cost. Only at this level of production is the cost of extra output, at the margin, exactly balanced by the revenue it yields.
- Similar marginal rules apply to the hiring of inputs by profit-maximizing firms. These are examined in Chapter 13.
- For a firm facing a downward-sloping demand curve, marginal revenue will be less than price. In

this case, the marginal revenue curve will lie below the market demand curve.

- A price-taking firm maximizes profits by choosing that output level for which price equals marginal cost. The marginal cost curve is the supply curve for such a firm. If price falls below short-run average variable costs, however, the firm will choose to shut down and produce no output.
- Encouraging profit-maximizing behavior raises principal-agent problems in the relationship between a firm's owners and managers. Incentive contracts may ameliorate those problems.

REVIEW QUESTIONS

1. Why do economists assume that firms seek maximum economic profits? Because accounting rules determine what the dollar value of profits actually is, why should firms be concerned with the economists' concept of cost? Which notion of profits do you believe is most important to entrepreneurs who are considering starting a business?
2. For its owners, a firm represents an asset that they own. Why would the pursuit of profit maximization by the firm make this asset as valuable as possible?
3. Explain whether each of the following actions would affect the firm's profit-maximizing decision. (Hint: How would each affect MR and MC?)
   a. An increase in the cost of a variable input such as labor
   b. A decline in the output price for a price-taking firm

c. Institution of a small fixed fee to be paid to the government for the right of doing business

d. Institution of a 50 percent tax on the firm's profits

e. Institution of a per-unit tax on each unit the firm produces

f. Receipt of a no-strings-attached grant from the government

g. Receipt of a subsidy per unit of output from the government

h. Receipt of a subsidy per worker hired from the government

4. Sally Greenhorn has just graduated from a noted business school but does not have the foggiest idea about her new job with a shrink-wrapped dog biscuit firm. She has been given responsibility for a new line of turkey-flavored biscuits and must decide how many to produce. She opts for the following strategy: (1) Begin by hiring one worker and one dog biscuit machine; (2) If the revenues from this pilot project exceed its costs, add a second worker and machine; (3) If the additional revenues generated from the second worker/machine combination exceed what these cost, add a third; (4) Stop this process when adding a worker/machine combination brings less in revenues than it costs. Answer the following questions about SG's approach:

a. Is SG using a marginal approach to her hiring of inputs?

b. Does the approach adopted by SG also imply that she is following a MR = MC rule for finding a profit-maximizing output?

c. SG's distinguished professor of marketing examines her procedures and suggests she is mistaken in her approach. He insists that she should instead measure the profit on each new worker/machine combination employed and stop adding new output as soon as the last one added earns a lower profit than the previous one. How would you evaluate his distinguished advice?

5. What kind of demand curve does a price-taking firm face? For such a curve, what is the relationship between price and marginal revenue?

Explain why an individual firm can be a price taker even though the entire market demand curve for its product may be downward-sloping.

6. Two features of the demand facing a firm will ensure that the firm must act as a price taker:

a. That other firms be willing to provide all that is demanded at the current price, and

b. That consumers of the firm's output regard it as identical to that of its competitors.

Explain why both of these conditions are required if the firm is to treat the price of its output as fixed. Describe what the demand facing the firm would be like if one of the conditions held but not the other.

7. A certain economics professor earns royalties from his textbook that are specified as 12 percent of the book's selling price. Assuming that the demand curve for this text is a downward-sloping straight line, how many copies of this book would the professor wish his or her publisher to sell? Is this the same number that the publisher itself would want to sell?

8. Show graphically the price that would yield exactly zero in economic profits to a firm in the short run. With the price, why are profits maximized even though they are zero? Does this zero-profit solution imply that the firm's owners are starving?

9. Why do economists believe short-run marginal cost curves have positive slopes? Why does this belief lead to the notion that short-run supply curves have positive slopes? What kind of signal does a higher price send to a firm with increasing marginal costs? Would a reduction in output ever be the profit-maximizing response to an increase in price for a price-taking firm?

10. Wildcat John owns a few low-quality oil wells in Hawaii. He was heard complaining recently about the low price of crude oil: "With this $18 per barrel price I can't make any money—it costs me $20 per barrel just to run my oil pumps. Still, I only paid $1 an acre for my land many years ago, so I think I will just stop pumping for a time and wait for prices to get above $20." What do you make of John's production decisions?

PROBLEMS

7.1 John's Lawn Mowing Service is a small business that acts as a price taker (MR = P). The prevailing market price of lawn mowing is $20 per acre. Although John can use the family mower for free (but see problem 7.2), he had other costs given by

$$\text{Total cost} = 0.1q^2 + 10q + 50$$

$$\text{Marginal cost} = 0.2q + 10$$

where q = the number of acres John chooses to mow in a week.

a. How many acres should John choose to mow in order to maximize profit?
b. Calculate John's maximum weekly profit.
c. Graph these results and label John's supply curve.

7.2 Consider again the profit-maximizing decision of John's Lawn Mowing Service from problem 7.1. Suppose John's greedy father decides to charge John for the use of the family lawn mower.

a. If the lawn mower charge is set at $100 per week, how will this affect the acres of lawns John chooses to mow? What will his profits be?
b. Suppose instead that John's father requires John to pay 50 percent of his weekly profits as a mower charge. How will this affect John's profit-maximizing decision?
c. If John's greedy father imposes a charge of $2 per acre for use of the family mower, how will this affect John's marginal cost function? How will it affect his profit-maximizing decision? What will his profits be now? How much will John's greedy father get?
d. Suppose finally that John's father collects his $2 per acre by collecting 10 percent of the revenues from each acre John mows. How will this affect John's profit-maximizing decision? Explain why you get the same result here as for part c.

7.3 Widgets International faces a demand curve given by

$$Q = 10 - P$$

and has a constant marginal and average cost of $3 per widget produced. Complete the following table for the various production levels.

q	P	TR (= P · q)	MR	MC	AC	TC	π
1							
2							
3							
4							
5							
6							
7							
8							
9							
10							

How many widgets will the firm produce in order to maximize profits? Explain briefly why this is so.

7.4 Suppose that a firm faces a demand curve that has a constant elasticity of –2. This demand curve is given by

$$q = 256/P^2$$

Suppose also that the firm has a marginal cost curve of the form

$$MC = 0.001q$$

a. Graph these demand and marginal cost curves.
b. Calculate the marginal revenue curve associated with the demand curve; graph this curve. (Hint: Use Equation 7.9 for this part of the problem.)
c. At what output level does marginal revenue equal marginal cost?

7.5 Suppose a firm faces the following demand curve:

$$q = 60 - 2P$$

a. Calculate the total revenue curve for the firm (that is, TR in terms of q).
b. Using a tabular proof, show that the firm's MR curve is given by MR = 30 – q.
c. Assume also that the firm has an MC curve given by MC = 0.2q. What output level should the firm produce to maximize profits?
d. Graph the demand, MC, and MR curves and the point of profit maximization.

7.6 Universal Widget produces high-quality widgets at its plant in Nevada for sale throughout the world. The cost function for total widget production (q) is given by

$$\text{Total costs} = 10q$$

$$\text{Marginal costs} = 10$$

Widgets are demanded only in Australia (where the demand curve is given by q = 100 − 2P and MR = 50 − q) and Lapland (where the demand curve is given by q = 120 − 4P and MR = 30 − q/2). If Universal Widget can control the quantities supplied to each market, how many should it sell in each location in order to maximize total profits? What are these profits? Graph your results.

7.7 The town where John's Lawn Mowing Service is located (see problem 7.1) is subject to sporadic droughts and monsoons. During periods of drought, the price for mowing lawns drops to $15 per acre, whereas, during monsoons, it rises to $25 per acre.

a. How will John react to these changing prices?
b. Suppose that weeks of drought and weeks of monsoons each occur half the time during a summer. What will John's average weekly profit be?
c. Suppose John's kindly (but still greedy) father offers to eliminate the uncertainty in John's life by agreeing to trade him the weekly profits based on a stable price of $20 in exchange for the profits John actually makes. Should John take the deal?
d. Graph your results and explain them intuitively.

7.8 In order to break the hold of John's greedy father over his struggling son (problems 7.1, 7.2, and 7.7), the government is thinking of instituting an income subsidy plan for the lad. Two plans are under consideration: (1) a flat grant of $200 per week to John; and (2) a grant of $4 per acre mowed.

a. Which of these plans will John prefer?
b. What is the cost of plan (2) to the government?

7.9 Suppose the production function for high-quality brandy is given by

$$q = \sqrt{K \cdot L}$$

where q is the output of brandy per week and L is labor hours per week. In the short run, K is fixed at 100, so the short-run production function is

$$q = 10\sqrt{L}$$

a. If capital rents for $10 and wages are $5 per hour, show that short-run total costs are

$$STC = 1,000 + 0.05q^2$$

b. Given the short-run total cost curve in part a, short-run marginal costs are given by

$$SMC = 0.1q$$

With this short-run marginal cost curve, how much will the firm produce at a price of $20 per bottle of brandy? How many labor hours will be hired per week?
c. Suppose that, during recessions, the price of brandy falls to $15 per bottle. With this price, how much would the firm choose to produce and how many labor hours would be hired?
d. Suppose that the firm believes that the fall in the price of brandy will last for only 1 week, after which it will wish to return to the level of production in part a. Assume also that, for each hour that the firm reduces its workforce below that described in part a, it incurs a cost of $1. If it proceeds as in part c, will it earn a profit or incur a loss? Explain.

7.10 Suppose that candidates for managerial positions at Fly-by-Night Waterbeds, Inc., can command salaries of $10,000 per year in other employment, but on those jobs they are not able to play golf during working hours. Fly-by-Night, however, is located next to a golf course, so it is possible for managers to sneak off to play, though this does harm the company's profits. Suppose that a potential manager's utility functions are given by

$$\text{Utility} = 0.1 \sqrt{s} + 2g$$

where s is the manager's annual salary and g is the number of golf games he or she can play each week during the year, whose value can be only 0, 1, or 2. Annual profits for the firm prior to paying the manager are $19,000 if g = 0, $16,000 if g = 1, and $8,000 if g = 2.

a. Suppose that Fly-by-Night can write a contract that specifies precisely how much golf its manager may play. What will be the profit-maximizing combination of salary and golf that will allow the firm to hire a manager? What will the firm's net profits be in this situation?

b. Suppose that a manager is hired under the contract specified in part a but that the firm's owners cannot monitor how much golf the manager actually plays. What will the manager do? What will the firm's net profits be?

c. Suppose that the firm's owners recognize the principal-agent problem that arises in part b and decides to use a profit-sharing contract to ameliorate the problem. If the manager's salary is to be based only on a share of the firm's profits, what share must be paid? How much golf will the manager choose to play with this contract? Will the firm choose to offer this contract to the manager?

INTERNET EXERCISES

1. *Corporate profits tax.* How much do firms pay in corporate profits taxes? Let's follow up on Application 7.1 and look at some recent data on the corporate profits tax. Go to the Statistical Abstract of the United States at *http://www. census.gov/statab/www.* Click on the tables for Business Enterprise. Scroll down to the tables entitled Corporate Profits, Taxes, and Dividends and Corporate Profits before Taxes by Industry. For the most recent year given, how much did corporations generate in profits before tax and how much tax did they pay? What percentage of after-tax profits were paid out in dividends? Which three industries generated the largest profits? What percentage of overall profits was generated by manufacturing? Retail trade? Now, scroll down to the table entitled Manufacturing, Mining, and Trade Corporations—Profits and Stockholders' Equity Ratios. For the most recent year given, what was the value of profits per dollar of sales for manufacturing? Retail trade? Explain why the profits in these tables are not the same as economic profits. In light of this, does the difference in profits per dollar of sales (and therefore tax liability per dollar of sales) between manufacturing and retail trade suggest that the corporate profits tax is really a tax on equity capital? Explain (it may be helpful here to review the discussion in Application 7.1).

2. *Corporate profits and employee stock options.* As Application 7.5 mentions, firms do not generally treat employee compensation in the form of stock options as an expense. This and other so-called "questionable" accounting practices have recently come under intense scrutiny, as they can all lead to misleadingly inflated statements of net earnings. An interesting and brief account of the problem is given in the CNN/Money article by Justin Lahart entitled "Bracing for an Earnings Hit" at *http://money.cnn.com/2002/07/11/news/ options/index.htm.* According to the study by Merrill Lynch, by how much did the non-expensing of options inflate total earnings of S&P 500 firms in 2001? By what percent would Microsoft's 2002 earnings be reduced? Intel's? For what percentage of the top "Tech Offenders" listed would otherwise positive 2002 earnings per share (EPS) become negative with the expensing of stock options? By what percent would Yahoo!'s 2002 EPS fall with the expensing of stock options? Would you support a requirement that firms expense stock options? Explain.

Part 4

Models of Market Equilibrium

"By directing industry in such a manner as its produce may be of greatest value . . . [the manager] . . . is led by an invisible hand to promote . . . [the interest of] . . . society more effectively than he really intends to promote it."

Adam Smith, *The Wealth of Nations*, 1776

Now that we have studied the behavior of demanders (Part 2) and suppliers (Part 3), we are ready to show how they come together to conduct market transactions. Because the nature of these transactions can be quite different depending on how a market is organized, we have to cover a number of possibilities here. When you finish this part, you should have a good understanding of most of the basic results of microeconomics.

Part 4 begins with a study of perfect competition. This represents an idealized market situation in which there are many demanders and many suppliers. Because each participant constitutes a very small portion of the market, each believes (correctly) that any actions he or she might take will have no effect on market prices. Chapter 8 explores the consequences of this price-taking assumption. Chapter 9 introduces you to a few of the many applications of this model.

Chapter 10 looks at a situation in which there is only a single supplier to a market. A principal conclusion is that markets characterized by monopoly tend to misallocate resources.

Markets that fall between the perfectly competitive and monopoly extremes are examined in Chapter 11 and Chapter 12. The approach taken in Chapter 11 is very similar to that taken in the previous chapters—a few models of equilibrium pricing in imperfectly competitive markets are developed in explicit detail. In Chapter 12, we adopt a rather different approach by utilizing the tools of game theory to study market equilibrium.

8

Perfect Competition

This chapter discusses how prices are determined in perfectly competitive markets. The theory we develop here is an elaboration of Marshall's supply and demand analysis that is at the core of all of economics. We show how equilibrium prices are established and describe some of the factors that cause prices to change. In Chapter 9, we illustrate some of the many applications of this model.

TIMING OF A SUPPLY RESPONSE

In the analysis of pricing, it is important to decide the length of time that is to be allowed for a **supply response** to changing demand conditions. The pattern of equilibrium prices will be different if we are talking about a very short period of time during which supply is essentially fixed and unchanging than if we are envisioning a very long-run process in which it is possible for entirely new firms to enter a market. For this reason, it has been traditional in economics to discuss pricing in three different time periods: (1) the very short run, (2) the short run, and (3) the long run. Although it is not possible to give these terms an exact time length, the essential distinction among them concerns the nature of the supply response that is assumed to be possible. In the *very short run*, there can be no supply response—quantity supplied is absolutely fixed. In the *short run*, existing firms may change the quantity they are supplying but no new firms can enter the market. In the *long run*, firms can further change the quantity supplied and completely new firms may enter a market, this produces a very flexible supply response. This chapter discusses each of these different types of responses.

> **Supply response**
> The change in quantity of output supplied in response to a change in demand conditions.

PRICING IN THE VERY SHORT RUN

Market period
A short period of time during which quantity supplied is fixed.

In the very short run or **market period,** there is no supply response. The goods are already "in" the marketplace and must be sold for whatever the market will bear. In this situation, price acts only to ration demand. The price will adjust to clear the market of the quantity that must be sold. Although the market price may act as a signal to producers in future periods, it does not perform such a function currently since current period output cannot be changed.

Figure 8.1 illustrates this situation.[1] Market demand is represented by the curve D. Supply is fixed at Q^*, and the price that clears the market is P_1. At P_1, people are willing to take all that is offered in the market. Sellers want to dispose of Q^* without regard to price (for example, the good in question may be perishable and will be worthless if not sold immediately). The price P_1 balances the desires of demanders with the desires of suppliers. For this reason, it is called an **equilibrium price.** In Figure 8.1, a price in excess of P_1 would not be an equilibrium price because people would demand less than Q^* (remember that firms are always willing to supply Q^* no matter what the price). Similarly, a price below P_1 would not be an equilibrium price because people would then demand more than Q^*. P_1 is the only equilibrium price possible when demand conditions are those represented by the curve D.

Equilibrium price
The price at which the quantity demanded by buyers of a good is equal to the quantity supplied by sellers of the good.

Shifts in Demand: Price as a Rationing Device

If the demand curve in Figure 8.1 shifted outward to D' (perhaps because incomes increased or because the price of some substitute increased), P_1 would no longer be an equilibrium price. With the demand curve D', far more than Q^* is demanded at the price P_1. Some people who wish to make purchases at a price of P_1 would find that not enough of the good is now available to meet the increase in demand. In order to ration the available quantity among all demanders, the price would have to rise to P_2. At that new price, demand would again be reduced to Q^* (by a movement along D' in a northwesterly direction as the price rises). The price rise would restore equilibrium to the market. The curve labeled S (for "supply") in Figure 8.1 shows all the equilibrium prices for Q^* for any conceivable shift in demand. The price must always adjust to ration demand to exactly whatever supply is available. In Application 8.1: Internet Auctions, we look at how this price-setting mechanism works in practice.

Applicability of the Very-Short-Run Model

The model of the very short run is not particularly useful for most markets. Although the theory may adequately apply to some situations where goods are

---

[1] As in previous chapters, we use Q to represent total quantity bought or sold in a market and q to represent the output of a single firm.

perishable, the far more common situation involves some degree of supply response to changing demand. It is usually presumed that a rise in price prompts producers to bring additional quantity into the market. We have already seen why this is true in Chapter 7 and explore the response in detail in the next section.

Before beginning that analysis, note that increases in quantity supplied need not come only from increased production. In a world in which some goods are durable (that is, last longer than a single market period), current owners of these goods may supply them in increasing amounts to the market as price rises. For example, even though the supply of Rembrandts is absolutely fixed, we would not draw the market supply curve for these paintings as a vertical line, such as that shown in Figure 8.1. As the price of Rembrandts rises, people (and museums) become increasingly willing to part with them. From a market point of view, the supply curve for Rembrandts has an upward slope even though no new production takes place. A similar analysis would follow for many types of durable goods, such as antiques, used cars, 1950s baseball cards, or corporate shares, all of which are not currently being produced. Here, we are more interested in how demand and production are related, however, so we do not look at these other cases in detail.

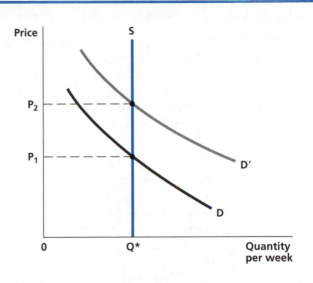

FIGURE 8.1 **Pricing in the Very Short Run** When quantity is absolutely fixed in the very short run, price acts only as a device to ration demand. With quantity fixed at Q*, price P_1 will prevail in the marketplace if D is the market demand curve. At this price, individuals are willing to consume exactly that quantity available. If demand should shift upward to D', the equilibrium price would rise to P_2.

SHORT-RUN SUPPLY

In analysis of the short run, the number of firms in an industry is fixed. There is just not enough time for new firms to enter a market or for existing firms to exit completely. However, the firms currently operating in the market are able to adjust the

---

MicroQuiz 8.1

Suppose that a flower grower brings 100 boxes of roses to auction. There are many buyers at the auction; each may either offer to buy one box at the stated price by raising a bid paddle or decline to buy.

1. If the auctioneer starts at zero and calls off successively higher per-box prices, how will he or she know when an equilibrium is reached?

2. If the auctioneer starts off at an implausibly high price ($1,000/box) and successively lowers that price, how will he or she know when an equilibrium is reached?

Internet Auctions

Auctions on the Internet have rapidly become one of the most popular ways of selling all manner of goods. Web sites offering auctions range from huge, all-inclusive listings such as eBay or Amazon to highbrow specialties (Sothebys). Virtually every type of good can be found on some Web site. There are sites that specialize in collectibles, industrial equipment, office supplies, and even the truly weird (check out Disturbing Auctions). Occasionally, even human organs have appeared in Internet auctions, though, at least in the United States, selling such items is illegal and this may have been a hoax.

Is Supply Fixed in Internet Auctions?

There is a sense in which Internet auctions resemble the theoretical situation illustrated in Figure 8.1—the goods listed are indeed in fixed supply and will be sold for whatever bidders are willing to pay. But this view of things may be too simple because it ignores dynamic elements that may be present in suppliers' decisions. Suppose, for example, that a supplier has ten copies of an out-of-print book to sell. Should he or she list all ten at once? Because buyers may search for what they want only infrequently, such a strategy may not be a good one. Selling all of the books at once may yield rather low prices for the final few sold because, at any one time, there are few demanders who value the books highly. But spreading the sales over several weeks may yield more favorable results. The book supplier will also watch auction prices of other sellers' offerings and will use price patterns in deciding precisely when to list the books to be sold. Hence, although the analysis of Figure 8.1 may be a good starting place for studying Internet auctions, any more complete understanding requires looking at complex sequences of decisions.

Special Features of Internet Auctions

A quick examination of auction sites on the Internet suggests that operators employ a variety of features in their auctions. Amazon, for example, has explicitly stated "reserve" prices that must be met before a bid will be considered. eBay does not explicitly report a reserve price, but many items do have reserve prices that can only be discovered through the bidding process. Some auctions provide you with a bidding history, whereas others only tell you the cumulative number of bids. A few auctions offer you the opportunity of buying a good outright at a relatively high price without going through the bidding process. eBay, for example has a "Buy It Now" price on many items. What purposes do these various features of Internet auctions serve? Presumably, an operator will only adopt a feature that promises to yield it better returns either in terms of attracting more sellers or (what may amount to the same thing) obtaining higher prices for sellers. But why do these features promise such higher returns? And why do auctioneers seem to differ in their opinions about what works? Attempts to answer these questions usually focus on the uncertainties inherent in the auction process and how bidders respond to them.[1]

---

[1] For example, although eBay's Buy It Now prices seem irrational because they impose an upper limit to the bidding, these have been explained as profit maximizing for sellers when some bidders are very risk averse. See E. B. Budish and L. N. Takeyama, "Buy Prices in Online Auctions: Irrationality on the Internet?" *Economic Letters* (September 2001): 325–333.

Internet Auctions and Reputations

Because buyers and sellers are total strangers in Internet auctions, a number of special provisions have been developed to mitigate the risks of fraud that the parties might encounter in such situations. The primary problem facing bidders in the auctions is in knowing that the goods being offered meet expected quality standards. An important way that many of the auctions help to reduce such uncertainty is through a grading process for sellers. Previous bidders provide rankings to the auction sites, and these are summarized for potential buyers. A good reputation probably results in a seller receiving higher bids. For sellers, the primary risk is that they will not be paid (or that a check will bounce). Various intermediaries (such as PayPal) have been developed to address this problem.

To Think About

1. A racetrack recently offered bobble-head dolls of a famous jockey for $3. One patron reportedly bought 100 of these claiming that he could immediately resell them on the Internet for $10 each. What do you think?
2. Why does eBay keep its reserve prices secret? Doesn't this just frustrate bidders who are told that their bids are unacceptable?

---

quantity they are producing in response to changing prices. Because there are a large number of firms each producing the same good, each firm will act as a price taker. The model of short-run supply by a price-taking firm in Chapter 7 is therefore the appropriate one to use here. That is, each firm's short-run supply curve is simply the positively sloped section of its short-run marginal cost curve above the shutdown price. Using this model to record individual firms' supply decisions, we can add up all of these decisions into a single market supply curve.

Construction of a Short-Run Supply Curve

The quantity of a good that is supplied to the market during some period is the sum of the quantities supplied by each firm. Because each firm faces the same market price in deciding how much to produce, the total supplied to the market also depends on this price. This relationship between market price and quantity supplied is called a **short-run market supply curve.**

Figure 8.2 illustrates the construction of the curve. For simplicity, we assume there are only two firms, A and B. The short-run supply (that is, marginal cost) curves for firms A and B are shown in Figure 8.2, (a) and (b). The market supply curve shown in Figure 8.2(c) is the horizontal sum of these two curves. For example, at a price of P_1, firm A is willing to supply q_1^A, and firm B is willing to supply Q_1^B. At this price, the total supply in the market is given by Q_1, which is equal to $q_1^A + q_1^B$. The other points on the curve are constructed in an identical way. Because each firm's supply curve slopes upward, the market supply curve will also slope upward. This upward slope reflects the fact that short-run marginal

Short-run market supply curve
The relationship between market price and quantity supplied of a good in the short run.

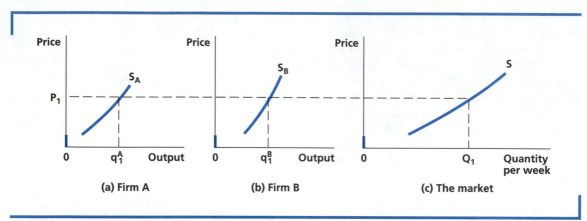

FIGURE 8.2 Short-Run Market Supply Curve The supply (marginal cost) curves of two firms are shown in panel a and panel b. The market supply curve in panel c is the horizontal sum of these curves. For example, at P_1, firm A supplies q_1^A, firm B supplies q_1^B, and total market supply is given by $Q_1 = q_1^A + q_1^B$.

costs increase as firms attempt to increase their outputs. They are willing to incur these higher marginal costs only at higher market prices.

The construction in Figure 8.2 uses only two firms; actual market supply curves represent the summation of many firms' supply curves. Again, the market supply curve has a positive slope because of the positive slope of each firm's underlying short-run marginal cost curve. This market supply curve summarizes the short-run diminishing returns experienced by all firms, the prices of the inputs they use, and the profit-maximizing decisions that each firm makes.

SHORT-RUN PRICE DETERMINATION

We can now combine demand and supply curves to demonstrate how equilibrium prices are established in the short run. Figure 8.3 shows this process. In Figure 8.3 (b), the market demand curve D and the short-run supply curve S intersect at a price of P_1 and a quantity of Q_1. This price-quantity combination represents an equilibrium between the demands of individuals and the supply decisions of firms—the forces of supply and demand are precisely balanced. What firms supply at a price of P_1 is exactly what people want to buy at that price. This equilibrium tends to persist from one period to the next unless one of the factors underlying the supply and demand curves changes.

Functions of the Equilibrium Price

Here, the equilibrium price P_1 serves two important functions. First, this price acts as a signal to producers about how much should be produced. In order to

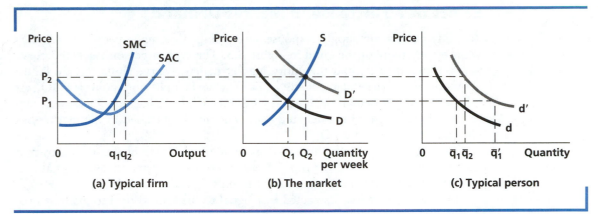

FIGURE 8.3 Interactions of Many Individuals and Firms Determine Market Price in the Short Run Market demand curves and market supply curves are each the horizontal sum of numerous components. These market curves are shown in panel b. Once price is determined in the market, each firm and each individual treat this price as fixed in their decisions. If the typical person's demand curve shifts to d', market demand will shift to D' in the short run, and price will rise to P_2.

maximize profits, firms produce that output level for which marginal costs are equal to P_1. In the aggregate, then, production is Q_1. A second function of the price is to ration demand. Given the market price of P_1, utility-maximizing consumers decide how much of their limited incomes to spend on that particular good. At a price of P_1, total quantity demanded is Q_1, which is precisely the amount that is produced. This is what economists mean by an equilibrium price. No other price brings about such a balancing of supply and demand.

The implications of the equilibrium price (P_1) for a typical firm and for a typical person are shown in Figure 8.3(a) and (c), respectively. For the typical firm, the price P_1 causes an output level of q_1 to be produced. The firm earns a profit at this particular price because price exceeds short-run average total cost. The initial demand curve d for a typical person is shown in Figure 8.3(c). At a price of P_1, this person demands q_1. Adding up the quantities that each person demands at P_1 and the quantities that each firm supplies shows that the market is in equilibrium. The market supply and demand curves are a convenient way of doing that addition.

MicroQuiz 8.2

How does the fact that there are many buyers and sellers in a competitive market enforce price-taking behavior? Specifically suppose that the equilibrium price of corn is $3 per bushel.

1. The owners of Yellow Ear Farm believe they deserve $3.25 per bushel because the farm has to use more irrigation in growing corn. Can this farm hold out for, and get, the price it wants?

2. United Soup Kitchens believes that it should be able to buy corn for $2.75 because it serves the poor. Can this charity find a place to buy at the price it is willing to pay?

Effect of an Increase in Market Demand

To study a short-run supply response, let's assume that many people decide they want to buy more of the good in Figure 8.3. The typical person's demand curve shifts outward to d′, and the entire market demand curve shifts. Figure 8.3(b) shows the new market demand curve, D′. The new equilibrium point is P_2, Q_2: At this point, supply-demand balance is reestablished. Price has now increased from P_1 to P_2 in response to the demand shift. The quantity traded in the market has also increased from Q_1 to Q_2.

The rise in price in the short run has served two functions. First, as shown in our analysis of the very short run, it has acted to ration demand. Whereas at P_1 a typical individual demanded $\bar{q}_1'$, now at P_2 only $\bar{q}_2$ is demanded.

The rise in price has also acted as a signal to the typical firm to increase production. In Figure 8.3(a), the typical firm's profit-maximizing output level has increased from q_1 to q_2 in response to the price rise. That is the firm's short-run supply response: An increase in market price acts as an inducement to increase production. Firms are willing to increase production (and to incur higher marginal costs) because price has risen. If market price had not been permitted to rise (suppose, for example, government price controls were in effect), firms would not have increased their outputs. At P_1, there would have been an excess (unfilled) demand for the good in question. If market price is allowed to rise, a supply-demand equilibrium can be reestablished so that what firms produce is again equal to what people demand at the prevailing market price. At the new price P_2, the typical firm has also increased its profits. This increased profitability in response to rising prices is important for our discussion of long-run pricing later in this chapter.

SHIFTS IN SUPPLY AND DEMAND CURVES

In previous chapters, we analyzed many of the reasons why either demand or supply curves might shift. Some of these reasons are summarized in Table 8.1. You may wish to review the material in Chapter 4, "Market Demand and Elasticity," and Chapter 6, "Costs," to see why these changes shift the various curves. These types of shifts in demand and supply occur frequently in real-world markets. When either a supply curve or a demand curve does shift, equilibrium price and quantity change. This section looks briefly at such change and how the outcome depends on the shapes of the curves.

Short-Run Supply Elasticity

Some terms used by economists to describe the shapes of demand and supply curves need to be understood before we can discuss the effects of these shifts. We already introduced the terminology for demand curves in Chapter 4. There, we developed the concept of the price elasticity of demand, which shows how the

---

TABLE 8.1 Reasons for a Shift in a Demand or Supply Curve

Demand	Supply
Shifts outward (→) because	Shifts outward (→) because
• Income increases	• Input prices fall
• Price of substitute rises	• Technology improves
• Price of complement falls	
• Preferences for good increase	
Shifts inward (←) because	Shifts inward (←) because
• Income falls	• Input prices rise
• Price of substitute falls	
• Price of complement rises	
• Preferences for good diminish	

---

quantity demanded responds to changes in price. When demand is elastic, changes in price have a major impact on quantity demanded. In the case of inelastic demand, however, a price change does not have very much effect on the quantity that people choose to buy. Firms' short-run supply responses can be described along the same lines. If an increase in price causes firms to supply significantly more output, we say that the supply curve is "elastic" (at least in the range currently being observed). Alternatively, if the price increase has only a minor effect on the quantity firms choose to produce, supply is said to be inelastic. More formally:

$$\text{Short-run supply elasticity} = \frac{\text{Percentage change in quantity supplied in short run}}{\text{Percentage change in price}} \qquad (8.1)$$

For example, if the short-run supply elasticity is 2.0, each 1 percent increase in price results in a 2 percent increase in quantity supplied. Over this range, the short-run supply curve is rather elastic. If, on the other hand, a 1 percent increase in price leads only to a 0.5 percent increase in quantity supplied, the **short-run elasticity of supply** is 0.5, and we say that supply is inelastic. As we will see, whether short-run supply is elastic or inelastic can have a significant effect on market performance.

Short-run elasticity of supply
The percentage change in quantity supplied in the short run in response to a 1 percent change in price.

Shifts in Supply Curves and the Importance of the Shape of the Demand Curve

A shift inward in the short-run supply curve for a good might result, for example, from an increase in the prices of the inputs used by firms to produce the good. An increase in carpenters' wages raises homebuilders' costs and clearly affects their

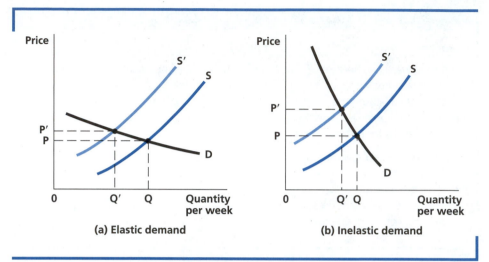

FIGURE 8.4 **Effect of a Shift in the Short-Run Supply Curve Depends on the Shape of the Demand Curve** In panel a, the shift inward in the supply curve causes price to increase only slightly, whereas quantity contracts sharply. This results from the elastic shape of the demand curve. In panel b, the demand curve is inelastic; price increases substantially with only a slight decrease in quantity.

willingness to produce houses. The effect of such a shift on the equilibrium levels of P and Q depends on the shape of the demand curve for the product. Figure 8.4 illustrates two possible situations. The demand curve in Figure 8.4(a) is relatively price elastic; that is, a change in price substantially affects the quantity demanded. For this case, a shift in the supply curve from S to S' causes equilibrium prices to rise only moderately (from P to P'), whereas quantity is reduced sharply (from Q to Q'). Rather than being "passed on" in higher prices, the increase in the firms' input costs is met primarily by a decrease in quantity (a movement down each firm's marginal cost curve) with only a slight increase in price.[2]

This situation is reversed when the market demand curve is inelastic. In Figure 8.4(b), a shift in the supply curve causes equilibrium price to rise substantially but quantity is little changed because people do not reduce their demands very much if prices rise. Consequently, the shift upward in the supply curve is passed on to demanders almost completely in the form of higher prices. The result of this demonstration is almost counterintuitive. The impact, say, of a wage increase on house prices depends not so much on how suppliers react but on the nature of demand for houses. If we asked only how much builders' costs were increased by a wage increase, we might make a very inaccurate prediction of how prices would change. The effect of any given shift upward in a supply curve can only be determined with additional information about demand.

[2] Notice, for example, that on the supply curve S', the marginal cost of producing output level Q is considerably higher than the marginal cost of producing Q'.

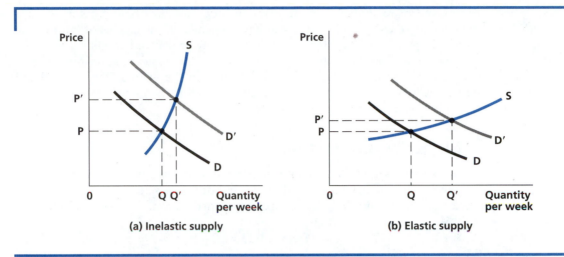

FIGURE 8.5 **Effect of a Shift in the Demand Curve Depends on the Shape of the Short-Run Supply Curve** In panel a, supply is inelastic; a shift in demand causes price to increase greatly with only a small increase in quantity. In panel b, on the other hand, supply is elastic; price rises only slightly in response to a demand shift.

Shifts in Demand Curves and the Importance of the Shape of the Supply Curve

For similar reasons, a given shift in a market demand curve will have different implications for P and Q depending on the shape of the short-run supply curve. Two illustrations are shown in Figure 8.5. In Figure 8.5(a), the supply curve for the good in question is relatively inelastic. As quantity expands, firms' marginal costs rise rapidly, giving the supply curve its steep slope. In this situation, a shift outward in the market demand curve (caused, for example, by an increase in consumer income) causes prices to increase substantially. Yet, the quantity supplied increases only slightly. The increase in demand (and in Q) has caused firms to move up their steeply sloped marginal cost curves. The accompanying large increase in price serves to ration demand. There is little response in terms of quantity supplied.

Figure 8.5(b) shows a relatively elastic short-run supply curve. This kind of curve would occur for an industry in which marginal costs do not rise steeply in response to output increases. For this case, an increase in demand produces a substantial increase in Q. However, because of the nature of the supply curve, this increase is not met by great cost increases. Consequently, price rises only moderately.

These examples again demonstrate Marshall's observation that demand and supply together determine price and quantity. Recall from Chapter 1 Marshall's analogy: Just as it is impossible to say which blade of a scissors does the cutting, so too it is impossible to attribute price solely

INFOTRAC©
COLLEGE EDITION
Exclusively from Gale Group and Thomson Learning

www.infotrac-college.com
Keywords: Perfect competition, Supply response, Internet auctions, Ethanol subsidies

to demand or to supply characteristics. Rather, the effect that shifts in either a demand curve or a supply curve will have depends on the shapes of both of the curves. In predicting the effects of shifting supply or demand conditions on market price and quantity in the real world, this simultaneous relationship must be considered. Application 8.2: Ethanol Subsidies in the United States and Brazil illustrates how this short-run model might be used to examine some of the politics of government price-support schemes.

A Numerical Illustration

Changes in market equilibria can be illustrated with a simple numerical example. Suppose, as we did in Chapter 7, that the quantity of cassette tapes demanded per week (Q) depends on the price of tapes (P) according to the simple relation

$$\text{Demand: } Q = 10 - P \qquad (8.2)$$

Suppose also that the short-run supply curve for tapes is given by

$$\text{Supply: } Q = P - 2 \text{ or } P = Q + 2 \qquad (8.3)$$

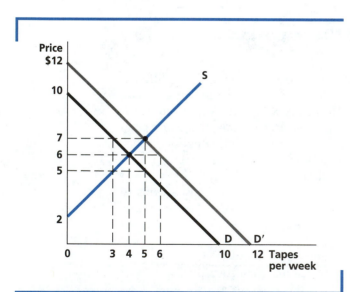

Figure 8.6 graphs these equations. As before, the demand curve (labeled D in the figure) intersects the vertical axis at P = $10. At higher prices, no tapes are demanded. The supply curve (labeled S) intersects the vertical axis at P = 2. This is the shutdown price for firms in the industry—at a price lower than $2, no tapes will be produced. As Figure 8.6 shows, these supply and demand curves intersect at a price of $6 per tape. At that price, people demand four tapes per week and firms are willing to supply four tapes per week. This equilibrium is also illustrated in Table 8.2, which shows the quantity of tapes demanded and supplied at each price. Only when P = $6 do these amounts agree. At a price of $5 per tape, for example, people want to buy five tapes per week but only three will be supplied; there is an excess demand of two tapes

FIGURE 8.6 Demand and Supply Curves for Cassette Tapes With the curves D and S, equilibrium occurs at a price of $6. At this price, people demand four tapes per week and that is what firms supply. When demand shifts to D′, price will rise to $7 to restore equilibrium.

Ethanol is another term for ethyl alcohol. In addition to its role as an intoxicant, the chemical also has potentially desirable properties as a fuel for automobiles because it burns cleanly and can be made from renewable resources such as sugar cane or corn. Ethanol can also be used as an additive to gasoline, and some claim that this oxygenated product reduces air pollution. Indeed, several governments have adopted subsidies to producers of ethanol.

A Diagrammatic Treatment

One way to show the effect of a subsidy in a supply-demand graph is to treat it as a shift in the short-run supply curve.[1] In the United States, for example, producers of ethanol get what amounts to a 54-cents-a-gallon tax credit. As shown in Figure 1, this shifts the supply curve (which is the sum of ethanol producers' marginal cost curves) downward by 54 cents. This leads to an expansion of demand from its pre-subsidy level of Q_1 to Q_2. The total cost of the subsidy then depends not only on its per-gallon amount but also on the extent of this increase in quantity demanded.

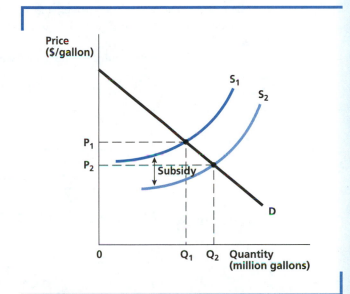

The Ethanol Subsidy and U.S. Politics

Although the scientific basis for using ethanol as a fuel additive to reduce pollution has been challenged, the politics of the subsidy are unassailable. For example, a major beneficiary of the subsidy in the

FIGURE 1 Ethanol Subsidies Shift the Supply Curve Price
Imposition of a subsidy on ethanol production shifts the short-run supply curve from S_1 to S_2. Quantity expands from Q_1 to Q_2, and the subsidy is paid on this larger quantity.

United States is the Archer Daniels Midland Company, a large corn processor. It is also a significant contributor to both major U.S. political parties. The fact that ethanol subsidies are concentrated in Iowa is also politically significant, as that state hosts one of the earliest presidential primary races. The 2002 energy bill proposes that subsidies and other policies be used to triple ethanol use by 2010.

---

[1] A subsidy can also be shown as a "wedge" between the demand and supply curves—a procedure we use in Chapter 9 to study tax incidence.

(continued)

Brazilian Politics

In Brazil, ethanol is made from sugar cane, one of the country's most important agricultural products. For many years, the government subsidized the production of ethanol and required that most cars' engines be adapted to run on it as a fuel. Economic liberalization during the 1990s led to a significant decline in the use of the fuel, however. In June of 1999, thousands of sugar-cane growers rallied in Brasilia, demanding that the government do more to support ethanol. But soaring sugar prices in 2000 made the government worry more about about inflation. The required ethanol content of fuel was reduced by 20 percent.

To Think About

1. Many of the purported benefits of ethanol use are environmental in nature. Assuming that these benefits are real, would an unsubsidized market provide the right level of ethanol use?
2. Who actually benefits from the ethanol subsidy: consumers, farm owners, or farm workers?

TABLE 8.2 Supply and Demand Equilibrium in the Market for Cassette Tapes

	Supply	Demand	
	$Q = P - 2$	Case 1 $Q = 10 - P$	Case 2 $Q = 12 - P$
Price	Quantity supplied (tapes per week)	Quantity demanded (tapes per week)	Quantity demanded (tapes per week)
$10	8	0	2
9	7	1	3
8	6	2	4
7	5	3	5
6	4	4	6
5	3	5	7
4	2	6	8
3	1	7	9
2	0	8	10
1	0	9	11
0	0	10	12

New equilibrium. Initial equilibrium.

per week. Similarly, at a price of $7 per tape, there is an excess supply of two tapes per week.

If the demand curve for tapes were to shift outward, this equilibrium would change. For example, Figure 8.6 also shows the demand curve D′, whose equation is given by

$$Q = 12 - P \qquad (8.4)$$

With this new demand curve, equilibrium price rises to $7 per tape and quantity also rises to five tapes per week. This new equilibrium is confirmed by the entries in Table 8.2, which show that this is the only price that clears the market given the new demand curve. For example, at the old price of $6, there is now an excess demand for tapes because the amount people want (Q = 6) exceeds what firms are willing to supply (Q = 4). The rise in price from $6 to $7 restores equilibrium both by prompting people to buy fewer tapes and by encouraging firms to produce more.

> **MicroQuiz 8.3**
>
> Use the information on Case 1 in Table 8.2 to answer the following questions.
>
> **1.** Suppose that the government confiscated two tapes per week as being "not suitable for young ears." What would be the equilibrium price of the remaining tapes?
>
> **2.** Suppose that the government imposed a $4-per-tape tax resulting in a $4 difference between what consumers pay and what firms receive for each tape. How many tapes would be sold? What price would buyers pay?

THE LONG RUN

In perfectly competitive markets, supply responses are more flexible in the long run than in the short run for two reasons. First, firms' long-run cost curves reflect the greater input flexibility that firms have in the long run. Second, the long run also allows firms to enter and exit a market in response to profit opportunities. These actions have important implications for pricing. We begin our analysis of these various effects with a description of the long-run equilibrium for a competitive industry. Then, as we did for the short run, we show how supply and prices change when conditions change.

Equilibrium Conditions

A perfectly competitive market is in equilibrium when no firm has an incentive to change its behavior. Such an equilibrium has two components: Firms must be content with their output choices (that is, they must be maximizing profits), and they must be content to stay in (or out of) the market. We discuss each of these components separately.

Profit Maximization

As before, we assume that firms seek maximum profits. Because each firm is a price taker, profit maximization requires that the firm produce where price is equal to (long-run) marginal cost. This first equilibrium condition, $P = MC$, determines both the firm's output choice and its choice of a specific input combination that minimizes these costs in the long run.

Entry and Exit

A second feature of long-run equilibrium concerns the possibility of the entry of entirely new firms into a market or the exit of existing firms from that market. The perfectly competitive model assumes that such entry and exit entail no special costs. Consequently, new firms are lured into any market in which (economic) profits are positive because they can earn more there than they can in other markets. Similarly, firms leave a market when profits are negative. In this case, firms can earn more elsewhere than in a market where they are not covering opportunity costs.

If profits are positive, the entry of new firms causes the short-run market supply curve to shift outward because more firms are now producing than were in the market previously. Such a shift causes market price (and market profits) to fall. The process continues until no firm contemplating entering the market would be able to earn an economic profit.[3] At that point, entry by new firms ceases and the number of firms has reached an equilibrium. When the firms in a market suffer short-run losses, some firms choose to leave, causing the supply curve to shift to the left. Market price then rises, eliminating losses for those firms remaining in the marketplace.

Long-Run Equilibrium

In this chapter, we assume that all the firms producing a particular good have the same cost curves; that is, we assume that no single firm controls any special resources or technologies.[4] Because all firms are identical, the equilibrium long-run position requires every firm to earn exactly zero economic profits. In graphic terms, long-run equilibrium price must settle at the low point of each firm's long-run average total cost curve. Only at this point do the two equilibrium conditions hold: $P = MC$ (which is required for profit maximization) and $P = AC$ (which is the required zero-profit condition).

---

[3] Remember, we are using the economic definition of profits here. Profits represent the return to the business owner in excess of that which is strictly necessary to keep him or her in the business. If an owner can just earn what he or she could earn elsewhere, there is no reason to enter a market.

[4] The important case of firms having different costs is discussed in Chapter 9. In that chapter, we see that very low-cost firms can earn positive, long-run profits. These represent a "rent" to whatever input provides the firms' unique low cost (e.g., especially fertile land or a low-cost source of raw materials).

These two equilibrium conditions have rather different origins. Profit maximization is a goal of firms. The $P = MC$ rule reflects our assumptions about firms' behavior and is identical to the output-decision rule used in the short run. The zero-profit condition is not a goal for firms. Firms would obviously prefer to have large profits. The long-run operations of competitive markets, however, force all firms to accept a level of zero economic profits ($P = AC$) because of the willingness of firms to enter and exit. Although the firms in a perfectly competitive industry may earn either positive or negative profits in the short run, in the long run only zero profits prevail. That is, firms' owners earn only normal returns on their investments.

LONG-RUN SUPPLY: THE CONSTANT COST CASE

The study of long-run supply depends crucially on how the entry of new firms affects the costs of inputs. The simplest assumption one might make is that entry has no effect on these prices. Under this assumption, no matter how many firms enter or leave a market, every firm retains exactly the same set of cost curves with which it started. There are many important cases for which this constant input cost assumption may not be made; we analyze these cases later. For the moment, however, we wish to examine the equilibrium conditions for this **constant cost case.**

Constant cost case
A market in which entry or exit has no effect on the cost curves of firms.

Market Equilibrium

Figure 8.7 demonstrates long-run equilibrium for the constant cost case. For the market as a whole, in Figure 8.7(b), the demand curve is labeled D and the short-run supply curve is labeled S. The short-run equilibrium price is therefore P_1. The typical firm in Figure 8.7(a) produces output level q_1, because at this level of output price is equal to short-run marginal cost (SMC). In addition, with a market price of P_1, output level q_1 is also a long-run equilibrium position for the firm. The firm is maximizing profits because price is equal to long-run marginal cost (MC). Figure 8.7(a) also shows a second long-run equilibrium property: Price is equal to long-run average total costs (AC). Consequently, economic profits are zero and there is no incentive for firms either to enter or to leave this market.

A Shift in Demand

Suppose now that the market demand curve shifts outward to D'. If S is the relevant short-run supply curve, then in the short run, price rises to P_2. The typical firm, in the short run, chooses to produce q_2 and (because $P_2 > AC$) earns profits on this level of output. In the long run, these profits attract new firms into the market. Because of the constant cost assumption, this entry of new firms has no effect on input costs. Perhaps this industry hires only a small fraction of the workers in an area and raises its capital in national markets. More inputs can

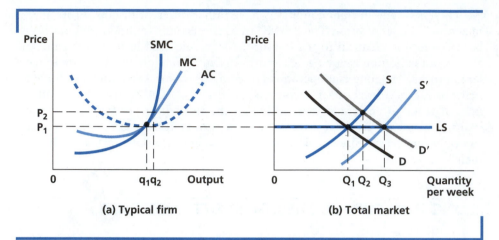

FIGURE 8.7 Long-Run Equilibrium for a Perfectly Competitive Market: Constant Cost Case
An increase in demand from D to D′ causes price to rise from P_1 to P_2 in the short run. This higher price creates profits, and new firms are drawn into the market. If the entry of these new firms has no effect on the cost curves of firms, new firms continue to enter until price is pushed back down to P_1. At this price, economic profits are zero. The long-run supply curve, LS, is therefore a horizontal line at P_1. Along LS, output is increased by increasing the number of firms that each produce q_1.

therefore be employed without affecting firms' cost curves. New firms continue to enter the market until price is forced down to the level at which there are again no pure economic profits. The entry of new firms therefore shifts the short-run supply curve to S′ where the equilibrium price (P_1) is reestablished. At this new long-run equilibrium, the price-quantity combination P_1, Q_3 prevails in the market. The typical firm again produces at output level q_1, although now there are more firms than there were in the initial situation.

Long-Run Supply Curve

By considering many such shifts in demand, we can examine long-run pricing in this industry. Our discussion suggests that no matter how demand shifts, economic forces that cause price always to return to P_1 come into play. All long-run equilibria occur along a horizontal line at P_1. Connecting these equilibrium points shows the long-run supply response of this industry. This long-run supply curve is labeled LS in Figure 8.7. For a constant cost industry of identical firms, the long-run supply curve is a horizontal line at the low point of the firms' long-run average total cost curves. The fact that price cannot depart from P_1 in the long run is a direct consequence of the constancy of input prices as new firms enter. Application 8.3: Movie Rentals looks at some cases where this is approximately true.

Movies have been available for home rental since the 1920s. Although the technology for showing films has changed dramatically over time (making it much cheaper and more widely available), the basic rental business has consistently exhibited the characteristics of a constant cost industry. Here, we look at a few recent implications of this fact.

The VCR Revolution

Once the VHS standard was adopted for videocassette recorders, ownership of the tape players grew phenomenally. By the end of the 1980s, more than 70 percent of U.S. households owned this equipment, thereby creating the demand for movie rentals on videotape. At first the rental industry was quite profitable, but there were no significant barriers to entry. Any would-be entrepreneur could rent space, put up a few shelves, and get in on the action. Because inputs used by the industry (low-wage workers and simple rental space) were readily available at market prices, the industry had a perfectly elastic long-run supply curve—it could easily meet exploding demand with no increase in price. Between 1982 and 1987, the number of tape rental outlets grew fourfold and the standard price for a rental movie fell to about $1.50 per night. Even grocery stores and mini-marts were stocking movies for rental.

New Technology: The DVD

Introduction of digital versatile disk (DVD) technology in the mid-1990s followed a similar path. Once a critical threshold of households owned DVD players, the rental market for movies on DVD emerged quickly. Existing video rental firms found that they could easily add a few DVD racks to their stores, and rental prices for DVDs soon came to approximate those for tapes (as might have been anticipated given the close substitutability between the two products). New outlets for DVD rentals, especially over the Internet, also enhanced the supply response. Again, the absence of barriers to entry together with the ready availability of inputs resulted in a close approximation to the constant cost model.

Sorting Out Future Technologies

This elastic supply response has also dictated a strict market test for innovations in the movie rental business—such innovations must be cost-competitive with existing methods of distribution or they will not be adopted. The fate of "Divx" technology provides an instructive example. This approach (primarily organized by the Circuit City chain of electronic stores) offered movie rentals on nonreturnable DVDs. The rental outlet monitored each showing through computer modems and imposed extra charges for additional viewing. Because consumers had to purchase special equipment, Divx gained few adherents. It was largely abandoned by the start of 1999.

Many other new technologies have been proposed for renting movies. Most of these involve "delivery" over cable television, satellite, or the Internet. Such delivery offers consumers considerable advantages over repeated trips to the rental store. But the technology also poses dangers for consumers, especially if movie studios decide to distribute their products directly. This outcome seems at least possible because such distribution would not require the establishment of a chain of rental outlets. Direct distribution could allow film

(continued)

studios much more monopoly power in renting specific films than they now have with tape and DVD rentals. Still, the studios would have to compete with such existing distribution methods, so the ultimate evolution of the new technologies remains uncertain.

To Think About

1. In Application 1.3, we looked at the Blockbuster chain of movie rental outlets. Why has this large firm been so successful in this highly competitive industry? Can Blockbuster raise its prices for rentals above the competitive level because it is so large?

2. Although the home movie rental industry has been an important source of income to film studios in recent years, they still prefer to open their films in theaters and embargo them for a time until tapes or DVDs are released. Why do the studios follow this practice? Can you think of other cases where products are released for sale in a piecemeal manner?

SHAPE OF THE LONG-RUN SUPPLY CURVE

Contrary to the short-run case, the long-run supply curve does not depend on the shape of firms' marginal cost curves. Rather, the zero-profit condition centers· attention on the low point of the long-run average cost curve as the factor most relevant to long-run price determination. In the constant cost case, the position of this low point does not change as new firms enter or leave a market. Consequently, only one price can prevail in the long run regardless of how demand shifts so long as input prices do not change. The long-run supply curve is horizontal at this price.

Once the constant cost assumption is abandoned, this need not be the case. If the entry of new firms causes average costs to rise, the long-run supply curve has an upward slope. On the other hand, if entry causes average costs to decline, it is even possible for the long-run supply curve to be negatively sloped. We now discuss these possibilities.

The Increasing Cost Case

Increasing cost case
A market in which the entry of firms increases firms' costs.

The entry of new firms may cause the average cost of all firms to rise for several reasons. New firms may increase the demand for scarce inputs, thus driving up their prices. New firms may impose external costs on existing firms (and on themselves) in the form of air or water pollution; and new firms may place strains on public facilities (roads, courts, schools, and so forth), and these may show up as increased costs for all firms.

Figure 8.8 demonstrates market equilibrium for this **increasing cost case.** The initial equilibrium price is P_1. At this price, the typical firm in Figure 8.8(a) pro-

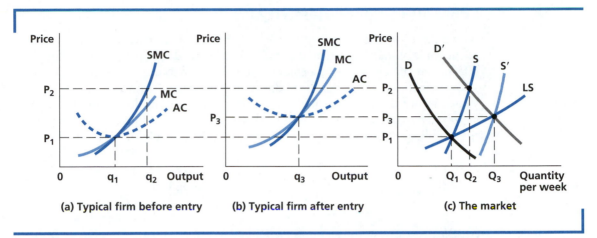

FIGURE 8.8 **Increasing Costs Result in a Positively Sloped Long-Run Supply Curve** Initially, the market is in equilibrium at P_1, Q_1. An increase in demand (to D') causes price to rise to P_2 in the short run, and the typical firm produces q_2 at a profit. This profit attracts new firms. The entry of these new firms causes costs to rise to the levels shown in (b). With this new set of curves, equilibrium is reestablished in the market at P_3, Q_3. By considering many possible demand shifts and connecting all the resulting equilibrium points, the long-run supply curve LS is traced out.

duces q_1 and total output, shown in Figure 8.8(c), is Q_1. Suppose that the demand curve for this product shifts outward to D' and the short-run supply curve (S) intersect. At this price, the typical firm produces q_2 and earns a substantial profit. This profit attracts new entrants into the market and shifts the short-run supply curve outward.

Suppose that the entry of new firms causes the cost curves of all firms to rise. The new firms may, for example, increase the demand for a particular type of skilled worker, driving up wages. A typical firm's new (higher) set of cost curves is shown in Figure 8.8(b). The new long-run equilibrium price for the industry is P_3 (here P = MC = AC), and at this price Q_3 is demanded. We now have two points (P_1, Q_1 and P_3, Q_3) on the long-run supply curve.[5] All other points on the curve can be found in an analogous way by considering all possible shifts in the demand curve. These shifts would trace out the long-run supply curve LS. Here, LS has a positive slope because of the increasing costs associated with the entry of new firms. This positive slope is caused by whatever causes average costs to rise in response to entry.[6] Still, because the supply response is more flexible in the long run, the LS curve is somewhat flatter than its short-run counterpart.

[5] Figure 8.8 also shows the short-run supply curve associated with the point P_3, Q_3. This supply curve has shifted to the right because more firms are producing now than initially.
[6] In the next chapter, we encounter another reason for a positively sloped long-run supply curve—differences in costs among firms.

Long-Run Supply Elasticity

As we have just shown, the long-run supply curve is constructed by considering all possible shifts in the demand curve for the product. In order to predict the effects that such increases in demand will have on market price, it is important to know something about the shape of the supply curve. A convenient measure for summarizing the shape of long-run supply curves is the **long-run elasticity of supply.** This concept records how proportional changes in price affect the quantity supplied, once all long-run adjustments have taken place. More formally:

Long-run elasticity of supply

The percentage change in quantity supplied in the long run in response to a 1 percent change in price.

$$\text{Long-run elasticity of supply} = \frac{\text{Percentage change in quantity supplied in long run}}{\text{Percentage change in price}} \quad (8.5)$$

An elasticity of 10, for example, would show that a 1 percent increase in price would result in a 10 percent increase in the long-run quantity supplied. We would say that long-run supply is very price elastic: The long-run supply curve would be nearly horizontal. A principal implication of such a high price elasticity is that long-run equilibrium prices would not increase very much in response to outward shifts in the market demand curve.

A small supply elasticity would have a quite different implication. If the elasticity were only 0.1, for example, a 1 percent increase in price would increase quantity supplied by only 0.1 percent. In other words, the long-run supply curve would be nearly vertical, and shifts outward in demand would result in rapidly rising prices without significant increases in quantity.

Estimating Long-Run Elasticities of Supply

Economists have devoted considerable effort to estimating long-run supply elasticities for competitive industries. Because economic growth leads to increased demands for most products (especially natural resources and other primary products), the reason for this interest is obvious. If long-run supply elasticities are high, real resource prices will not increase rapidly over time. This seems to be the case for relatively abundant resources that can be obtained with only modest increases in costs, such as aluminum or coal. Over time, real prices for these goods have not risen very rapidly in response to increasing demand. Indeed, in some cases, real prices may even have fallen because of technical improvements in production.

On the other hand, cases in which long-run supply curves are inelastic can show sharply escalating real prices in response to increased demand. Again, the ultimate causes for such an outcome relate to conditions in the market for inputs. In cases such as rare minerals (platinum, for example, which is used in automobile exhaust systems), increased demand may require the exploitation of very costly deposits. Perhaps an even more important source of increasing input costs is the market for skilled labor. When expansion of a market, such as that for medical care or computer software, creates new demand for a specialized labor input, wages for these workers may rise sharply and that gives the long-run supply curve its upward slope.

Table 8.3 summarizes a few studies of long-run supply elasticities. Although there are considerable uncertainties about some of these figures (and, in some cases, the markets may not obey all the assumptions of the perfectly competitive model), they still provide a good indication of the way in which conditions in input markets affect long-run supply elasticities. Notice, in particular, that the estimated elasticities for some natural resources are quite high—for these, the constant cost model may be approximately correct. For goods that encounter rising labor costs (medical care) or that require the use of increasingly high-cost locations (oil and farm crops), supply can be rather inelastic.

The Decreasing Cost Case

In some cases, entry may reduce costs. The entry of new firms may provide a larger pool of trained labor to draw from than was previously available, which would reduce the costs of hiring new workers. The entry of new firms may also provide a "critical mass" of industrialization that permits the development of more efficient transportation, communications, and financial networks. Whatever the exact nature of the cost reductions, the final result is illustrated in Figure 8.9. The initial market equilibrium is shown by the price quantity combination P_1, Q_1 in Figure 8.9(c). At this price, the typical firm in Figure 8.9(a) produces q_1 and earns exactly zero in economic

TABLE 8.3 Estimated Long-Run Supply Elasticities

Industry	Elasticity estimate
Agriculture	
Corn	+ 0.27
Soybeans	+ 0.13
Wheat	+ 0.03
Aluminum	Nearly infinite
Coal	+ 15.0
Medical care	+ 0.15 – + 0.60
Natural gas (U.S.)	+ 0.50
Crude oil (U.S.)	+ 0.75

Sources: Agriculture: J. S. Choi and P. G. Helmberger, "How Sensitive Are Crop Yields to Price Changes and Farm Programs?" *Journal of Agriculture and Applied Economics* (July 1993): 237–244.

Aluminum: *Critical Materials Commodity Action Analysis.* Washington, DC, U.S. Department of the Interior, 1975.

Coal: M. B. Zimmerman, "The Supply of Coal in the Long Run: The Case of Eastern Deep Coal" (Cambridge, MA: MIT Energy Laboratory Report, September 1975).

Medical care: L. Paringer and V. Fon, "Price Discrimination in Medicine: The Case of Medicare," *Quarterly Review of Economics and Business* (Spring 1988): 49–68. Estimates are based on responsiveness of medicare services to fees under the program and may overstate elasticities for the entire medical care market.

Natural gas: J. D. Khazzoom, "The FPC Staff's Model of Natural Gas Supply in the United States," *The Bell Journal of Economics and Management Science* (Spring 1971).

Crude oil: D. N. Epple, *Petroleum Discoveries and Government Policy* (Cambridge, MA: Marc Ballinger Publishing Company, 1984), Chapter 3.

MicroQuiz 8.4

Table 8.3 reports that the estimated long-run elasticity of supply for natural gas in the United States is about 0.5. Hence, over the long term we can expect each 10 percent increase in natural gas production to be accompanied by a 20 percent rise in relative price. Which interpretation (if either) of this fact is correct?

1. New firms should flock to this industry because it will be very profitable.

2. Existing firms will do very well in this market.

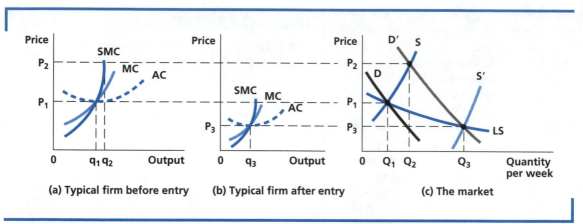

FIGURE 8.9 Decreasing Costs Result in a Negatively Sloped Long-Run Supply Curve Initially, the market is in equilibrium at P_1, Q_1. An increase in demand to D' causes price to rise to P_2 in the short run, and the typical firm produces q_2 at a profit. This profit attracts new firms. If the entry of these new firms causes costs to fall, a set of new cost curves might look like those in (b). With this new set of curves, market equilibrium is reestablished at P_3, Q_3. By connecting such points of equilibrium, a negatively sloped long-run supply curve LS is traced out.

profits. Now suppose market demand shifts outward to D'. In the short run, price increases to P_2 and the typical firm produces q_2. At this price level, positive profits are earned. These profits cause new firms to enter the market. If these entries cause costs to decline, a new set of cost curves for the typical firm might resemble those in Figure 8.9(b). Now the new equilibrium price is P_3. At this price, Q_3 is demanded. By considering all possible shifts in demand, the long-run supply curve LS can be traced out. For this **decreasing cost case**, the long-run supply curve has a negative slope. In this case, increases in demand cause price to fall. Whether this explains recent large declines in the prices of telecommunications services is examined in Application 8.4: How Do Network Externalities Affect Supply Curves?

Decreasing cost case
A market in which the entry of firms decreases firms' costs.

Infant Industries

The possibility of a negatively sloped long-run supply curve is believed to characterize some newly emerging, or "infant," industries. Initially, the costs of production of a new product may be very high. Few workers possess the skills needed to produce the good and procure other required inputs (such as communication networks or financing arrangements), which may be similarly underdeveloped. These difficulties are ameliorated as expanding production of the good yields a progressively larger pool of trained workers and a better-developed set of necessary services. Likewise, the improved availability of inputs causes the costs of all

Network externalities arise when adding additional users to a network causes costs to decline. Such externalities are common in many emerging industries in computer and Internet technology. Their presence sets the stage for declining prices as demand expands.

Metcalfe's Law

A basic property of communications networks is that they obey Metcalfe's Law, a principle named for Robert Metcalfe, a pioneer in the development of Ethernet technology. The law states that the number of interconnections possible in a given communications network expands with the square of the number of subscribers to that network.[1] This implies that the value of such a network expands much more rapidly than do the costs associated with establishing it. Such increasing returns combined with the impact of rapid change in communications technology itself have led to strong downtrends in the prices of many types of communications networks.

Some Examples

Examples of network externalities occur in the telecommunications, software, and Internet industries:

- *Telecommunications.* The benefits of having a phone or fax machine are greater the larger the number of people with whom one can communicate. Large telephone networks also facilitate other phone applications such as burglar alarm systems and mail-order operations.
- *Software.* The greater the number of users of a given software package, the greater will be the benefits to users in terms of file sharing. For this reason, Microsoft Office has come to dominate the office software business. Microsoft also benefits from network externalities with their Windows operating systems because the large number of Windows installations makes it profitable to write applications software only for that system.
- *The Internet.* Network externalities in the Internet are similar to those in telecommunications. The ability of the Internet to carry any sort of digital file enables a much wider range of interactions than is possible with traditional phone networks, however. Especially problematic has been the ability of the Internet to foster piracy of intellectual property such as music or motion pictures.

---

[1] One way to illustrate this is by picturing a matrix with all users listed both across the top and down the left side. The matrix then shows all of the ways that users may be connected. Since the number of entries in the matrix is n^2 Metcalfe's Law follows. A more precise version would eliminate entries along the main diagonal (which represent people communicating with themselves) and recognize that the communication represented by cell (i,j) is the same as that represented by (j,i). Hence, the true number of connections in the network is $n(n-1)/2$, which nevertheless increases like n^2.

(continued)

Network Externalities and Supply Curves

Because prices for telecommunications and Internet services have fallen rapidly, it is tempting to argue that the presence of network externalities in these industries gives their long-run supply curves a negative slope. Falling prices just reflect movement along this supply curve as demand expands. Unfortunately, this analysis is unconvincing because the benefits of network externalities accrue largely to demanders,[2] not to suppliers in terms of lower input costs. Yes, input prices for telecommunications have also been falling because of technical progress, but this effect is largely independent of network externalities. The prices of computers and digital watches have also been falling without reliance on significant network effects.

Economists remain undecided about the effect of network externalities on markets—especially about their impact on competition. The issue seems to be whether a firm can manage to appropriate some of the benefits of network externalities to themselves (as seems to be the case with Microsoft Windows) or whether such externalities open the way for greater competition (as seems to be the case in telephone long-distance service). Models that differentiate between these two cases are currently being developed.

To Think About

1. Because additional users of a network generate gains to existing users, some economists have argued that new users should be subsidized. Will networks be "too small" without such subsidies?

2. Switching to a new network may pose substantial costs. For example, when a company adopts a new word-processing program it must incur large training costs. What economic factors would cause users to shift from an existing network to a new one?

[2] Some authors refer to network externalities as "economies of scale on the demand side of the market."

---

firms within an infant industry to decline. For example, the development of the electronics industry in California's Silicon Valley or along Routes 128 and 495 in Boston was undoubtedly aided by such cost-reducing economies stemming from the growing concentration of related firms in these areas.

Infant industries play an important role in discussions of international trade policy. Because new industries have high costs, it is argued, they may not be able to compete against lower-cost, foreign competition. Given adequate protection (in the form of a tariff or quota), the domestic industry would grow; costs would fall; and, eventually, firms would be able to meet foreign competition. This argument undoubtedly has held some validity in the past. For example, protection of the U.S. textile industry in the early nineteenth century helped to make it become the world's largest. Today, however, the argument often is exploited by industries wanting protection from foreign competitors. Detailed research is required to determine whether they really meet the conditions of an infant industry.

SUMMARY

The model of pricing in perfectly competitive markets is probably the most widely used economic model. Even when markets do not strictly obey all of the assumptions of perfect competition, it is still possible to use that model as a reasonable approximation of how such markets work. Some of the basic features of the perfectly competitive model that are highlighted in this chapter are:

- The short-run supply curve in a perfectly competitive market represents the horizontal sum of the short-run supply curves for many price-taking firms. The upward slope of the short-run supply curve reflects these firms' increasing short-run marginal costs.
- Equilibrium prices are determined in the short run by the interaction of the short-run supply curve with the market demand curve. At the equilibrium price, firms are willing to produce precisely the amount of output that people want to buy.

- Shifts in either the demand curve or the supply curve change the equilibrium price. The extent of such a change depends on the particular shape of the two curves.
- Economic profits attract entrants into a perfectly competitive market in the long run. This entry continues until economic profits are reduced to zero. At that point, the market price equals long-run average cost and each firm is operating at the low point of its long-run average cost curve.
- Entry of new firms may have an effect on the cost of firms' inputs. In the constant cost case, however, input costs are not affected so the long-run supply curve is horizontal. If entry raises input costs, the long-run supply curve is upward sloping. If entry reduces costs, the long-run supply curve is downward sloping.

REVIEW QUESTIONS

1. Each day 1,000 fishing boats return to port with the fish that have been caught. These fish must be sold within a few hours or they will spoil. All of the fish are brought to a single marketplace, and each fisher places a price of the fish he or she has for sale.

   a. How would a fisher know that his or her price was too high?

   b. How would a fisher know that his or her price was too low?

   c. As the day progresses, what would you expect to happen to the prices posted by the fishers?

2. Many of the figures in this chapter show both an entire market and a single typical firm. How do these graphs reflect the assumption that each firm is selling the same good? How do these graphs reflect the assumption that firms are price takers for this good?

3. Why is the price for which quantity demanded equals quantity supplied called an "equilibrium

price"? Suppose, instead, we viewed a demand curve as showing what price consumers are willing to pay and a supply curve as showing what price firms want to receive. Using this view of demand and supply, how would you define an "equilibrium quantity"?

4. For markets with inelastic demand and supply curves, most short-run movements will be in prices, not quantity. For markets with elastic demand and supply curves, most movements will be in quantity, not price." Do you agree? Illustrate your answer with a few simple graphs.

5. If long-run equilibrium in a perfectly competitive industry involves zero profits, why would anyone ever start a new business? What does an entrepreneur hope to achieve by starting a new firm? How might his or her initial success undermine this goal in the long term?

6. In long-run equilibrium in a perfectly competitive market, each firm operates at minimal

average cost. Do firms also operate at minimum long-run average cost when such markets are out of equilibrium in the short run? Wouldn't firms make more in short-run profits if they opted always to produce that output level for which average costs were as small as possible?

7. Dr. D. is a critic of standard microeconomic analysis. In one of his frequent tirades, he was heard to say: "Take the argument for upward-sloping, long-run supply curves. This is a circular argument if I ever heard one. Long-run supply curves are said to be upward sloping because input prices rise when firms hire more of them. And that occurs because the long-run supply curves for these inputs are upward sloping. Hence, the argument boils down to 'long-run supply curves are upward sloping because other supply curves are upward sloping.' What nonsense!" Does Dr. D. have a point? How would you defend the analysis in this chapter?

8. Dr. E. is an environmentalist and a critic of economics. On *The Charlie Rose Show,* he attacks this book: "That text is typical—it includes all of this nonsense about long-run supply elasticities for natural resources like oil or coal. Any idiot knows that, because the earth has a finite size, all supply curves for natural resources are perfectly inelastic with respect to price. How can a rise in price for, say, oil lead to more oil when all of our oil was created eons ago? Focusing on these ridiculously high elasticity numbers just detracts from studying our real need—the need to conserve." How would you defend the analysis in this book against this tirade?

9. The long-run supply curve for gem diamonds is positively sloped because increases in diamond output increase the wages of diamond cutters. Explain why a decision by people to no longer buy diamond engagement rings would have disastrous consequences for diamond cutters but why such a trend would not really harm the owners of firms in the perfectly competitive gem diamond business.

10. "The existence of the decreasing cost case ultimately depends on the availability of inputs that also have negatively sloped supply curves. If firms themselves took actions that reduced costs, they would appropriate these cost reductions for themselves, and they would not spread to other firms." Do you agree? Or may some cost reductions not be fully appropriable by the firm that causes them?

PROBLEMS

8.1 Suppose the daily demand curve for flounder at Cape May is given by

$$Q_D = 1,600 - 600P$$

where Q_D is demand in pounds per day and P is price per pound.

a. If fishing boats land 1,000 pounds one day, what will the price be?

b. If the catch were to fall to 400 pounds, what would the price be?

c. Suppose the demand for flounder shifts outward to

$$Q_D = 2,200 - 600P$$

How would your answers to part a and part b change?

d. Graph your results.

8.2 Suppose, as in problem 8.1, the demand for flounder is given by

$$Q_D = 1,600 - 600P$$

but now assume that Cape May fishermen can, at some cost, choose to sell their catch elsewhere. Specifically, assume that the amount they will sell in Cape May is given by

$$Q_S = -1,000 + 2,000P \text{ for } Q_S \geq 0$$

where Q_S is the quantity supplied in pounds and P is the price per pound.

a. What is the lowest price at which flounder will be supplied to the Cape May market?

b. Given the demand curve for flounder, what will the equilibrium price be?

c. Suppose now, as in problem 8.1, demand shifts to

$$Q_D = 2,200 - 600P$$

What will be the new equilibrium price?

d. Explain intuitively why price will rise by less in part c than it did in problem 8.1.

e. Graph your results.

8.3 A perfectly competitive market has 1,000 firms. In the very short run, each of the firms has a fixed supply of 100 units. The market demand is given by

$$Q = 160,000 - 10,000P$$

a. Calculate the equilibrium price in the very short run.

b. Calculate the demand schedule facing any one firm in the industry. Do this by calculating what the equilibrium price would be if one of the sellers decided to sell nothing or if one seller decided to sell 200 units. What do you conclude about the effect of any one firm on market price?

8.4 Assuming the same conditions as in problem 8.3, suppose now that in the short run each firm has a supply curve that shows the quantity the firm will supply (q_i) as a function of market price. The specific form of this supply curve is given by

$$q_i = -200 + 50P$$

Using this short-run supply response, supply new solutions to part a and part b in problem 8.3. Why do you get different solutions in this case?

8.5 Widgets, Inc., is a small firm producing widgets. The widget industry is perfectly competitive; Widgets, Inc., is a price taker. The short-run total cost curve for Widgets, Inc., has the form:

$$STC = \tfrac{1}{3} q^3 + 10q^2 + 100q = 48$$

and the short-run marginal cost curve is given by

$$SMC = q^2 + 20q + 100$$

a. Calculate the firm's short-run supply curve with q (the number of widgets produced per day) as a function of market price (P).

b. How many widgets will the firm produce if the market price is P = 121? P = 169? P = 256? (Assume variable costs are covered.)

c. How much profit will Widgets, Inc., make when P = 121? P = 169? P = 256?

8.6 Suppose there are 100 identical firms in the perfectly competitive notecard industry. Each firm has a short-run total cost curve of the form:

$$STC = q^3/300 + 0.2q^2 + 4q + 10$$

and marginal cost is given by

$$SMC = .01q^2 + .4q + 4$$

a. Calculate the firm's short-run supply curve with q (the number of crates of notecards) as a function of market price (P).

b. Calculate the industry supply curve for the 100 firms in this industry.

c. Suppose market demand is given by $Q = -200P + 8,000$. What will be the short-run equilibrium price-quantity combination?

d. Suppose everyone starts writing more research papers and the new market demand is given by $Q = -200P + 10,000$. What is the new short-run price-quantity equilibrium? How much profit does each firm make?

8.7 Suppose there are 1,000 identical firms producing diamonds and that the short-run total cost curve for each firm is given by

$$STC = q^2 + wq$$

and short-run marginal cost is given by

$$SMC = 2q + w$$

where q is the firm's output level and w is the wage rate of diamond cutters.

a. If w = 10, what will be the firm's (short-run) supply curve? What is the industry's supply curve? How many diamonds will be produced at a price of 20 each? How many more diamonds would be produced at a price of 21?

b. Suppose that the wages of diamond cutters depend on the total quantity of diamonds produced and the form of this relationship is given by

$$w = .002Q$$

where Q represents total industry output, which is 1,000 times the output of the typical firm. In this situation, show that the firm's marginal cost (and short-run supply) curve depends on Q. What is the industry supply curve? How much will be produced at a price of 20? How much more will be produced at a price of 21? What do you conclude about how the shape of the short-run supply curve is affected by this relationship between input prices and output?

8.8 Wheat is produced under perfectly competitive conditions. Individual wheat farmers have U-shaped, long-run, average-cost curves that reach a minimum average cost of $3 per bushel when 1,000 bushels are produced.

a. If the market demand curve for wheat is given by

$$Q_D = 2,600,000 - 200,000P$$

where Q_D is the number of bushels demanded per year and P is the price per bushel, in long-run equilibrium what will be the price of wheat? How much total wheat will be demanded? How many wheat farms will there be?

b. Suppose demand shifts outward to

$$Q_D = 3,200,000 - 200,000P$$

If farmers cannot adjust their output in the short run (that is, suppose the SMC curve is vertical), what will market price be with this new demand curve? What will the profits of the typical farm be?

c. Given the new demand curve described in part b, what will be the new long-run equilibrium? (That is, calculate market price, quantity of wheat produced, and the new equilibrium number of farms in this new situation.)

d. Graph your results.

8.9 Gasoline is sold through local gasoline stations under perfectly competitive conditions. All gasoline station owners face the same long-run average cost curve given by

$$AC = .01q - 1 + 100/q$$

and the same long-run marginal cost curve given by

$$MC = .02q - 1$$

where q is the number of gallons sold per day.

a. Assuming the market is in long-run equilibrium, how much gasoline will each individual owner sell per day? What are the long-run average cost and marginal cost at this output level?

b. The market demand for gasoline is given by

$$Q_D = 2,500,000 - 500,000P$$

where Q_D is the number of gallons demanded per day and P is the price per gallon. Given your answer to part a, what will be the price of gasoline in long-run equilibrium? How much gasoline will be demanded and how many gas stations will there be?

c. Suppose that because of the development of solar-powered cars, the market demand for gasoline shifts inward to

$$Q_D = 2,000,000 - 1,000,000P$$

In long-run equilibrium, what will be the price of gasoline, how much total gasoline will be demanded, and how many gas stations will there be?

d. Graph your results.

8.10 A perfectly competitive painted necktie industry has a large number of potential entrants. Each firm has an identical cost structure such that long-run average cost is minimized at an output of 20 units ($q_i = 20$). The minimum average cost is $10 per unit. Total market demand is given by

$$Q = 1,500 - 50P$$

a. What is the industry's long-run supply schedule?

b. What is the long-run equilibrium price (P^*)? The total industry output (Q^*)? The output of each firm (q_i^*)? The number of firms? The profits of each firm?

c. The short-run total cost curve associated with each firm's long-run equilibrium output is given by

$$STC = .5q^2 - 10q + 200$$

where SMC = q − 10. Calculate the short-run average and marginal cost curves. At what necktie output level does short-run average cost reach a minimum?

d. Calculate the short-run supply curve for each firm and the industry short-run supply curve.

e. Suppose now painted neckties become more fashionable and the market demand function shifts upward to $Q = 2{,}000 - 50P$. Using this new demand curve, answer part b for the very short run when firms cannot change their outputs.

f. In the short run, use the industry short-run supply curve to recalculate the answers to part b.

g. What is the new long-run equilibrium for the industry?

INTERNET EXERCISES

1. *Competition and school choice.* Would introducing competition into our educational system improve the quality of our schools? This important question is explored in a collection of PBS Frontline interviews, "Competition, School Choice and Charter Schools," at *http://www.pbs.org/wgbh/pages/frontline/shows/vouchers/choice/choice.html.* Proponents of school choice claim that it would introduce competition into the school system. According to Caroline Hoxby, what are the three main benefits of introducing competition into school systems? According to your textbook, what happens in the long run to inefficient firms operating in competitive markets? Have the long-run consequences been the same for inefficient public schools? Why do several of the interviewees suggest that school failure is important to the ultimate success of our educational system? How does David Brennan respond to the criticism that school failures harm students? Does his response imply that in the absence of competition, there is little distinction between short- and long-run outcomes? Explain. Do you think it is appropriate to apply economic models of competition to education? Explain.

2. *Barriers to competition.* What do taxicab operators, hypnotherapists, attorneys, barbers, morticians, and fortune tellers have in common? Answer: They may all be subject to occupational licensing requirements. What is the impact of licensing requirements and entry restrictions on otherwise competitive markets? Let's take a look at the case of the New York City taxicab market. In New York City, each cab must be licensed by the city—the license takes the form of a visible medallion on the hood of the vehicle. The PBS Web site offers some facts and figures on the taxicab market in New York City at *http://www.pbs.org/wnet/taxidreams/data/index.html.* How many taxicabs presently operate (are licensed) in New York City? Since no new licenses have been issued, this number has been the same since 1937! In 1999, how many passengers rode in New York City taxicabs? Clearly, the demand for taxicab rides has shifted outward since 1937. Describe how the entry restrictions created by licensing alter the usual competitive long-run adjustments to an outward shift in demand. Would you expect the licensing restrictions to enable taxicab operators to earn positive profits in the long run? Explain. A potential entrant into the taxicab market must purchase an existing medallion from someone who owns one. The New York City licensing commission has data on medallion prices at *http://www.nyc.gov/html/tlc/html/value.html.* For the most recent year listed, how much must an individual owner pay for a medallion? In light of your conclusions about licensing and profitability, what do you think the price of a medallion represents?

Applying the Competitive Model

In Chapter 1, we met an educated parrot who became an economist by learning to say, "Supply and demand!" This parrot knew that practically every applied economic model starts from the competitive case we studied in the previous chapter. Here, we will look at some of the most important of these applications. An appendix to this chapter briefly describes how models of many markets can be used to give further insights into economic questions.

CONSUMER AND PRODUCER SURPLUS

A simple supply-demand analysis can often be used to assess the well-being of market participants. For example, in Chapter 3 we introduced the notion of **consumer surplus** as a way of illustrating consumers' gains from market transactions. Figure 9.1 summarizes these ideas by showing the market for, say, fresh tomatoes. At the equilibrium price of P*, individuals choose to consume Q* tomatoes. Because the demand curve D shows what people are willing to pay for one more tomato at various levels of Q, the total value of tomato purchases to buyers (relative to a situation where no tomatoes are available) is given by the total area below the demand curve from Q = 0 to Q = Q*, that is, by area AEQ*0. For this value, they pay an amount given by P*EQ*0 and hence receive a "surplus" (over what they pay) given by the gray shaded area AEP*. Possible happenings in the tomato market that change the size of this area clearly affect the well-being of these market participants.

Figure 9.1 also can be used to illustrate the surplus value received by tomato producers relative to a situation where no tomatoes are produced. This measure is based on the intuitive notion that the supply curve S shows the minimum price that producers would accept for each unit produced. At the market equilibrium

Consumer surplus
The extra value individuals receive from consuming a good over what they pay for it. What people would be willing to pay for the right to consume a good at its current price.

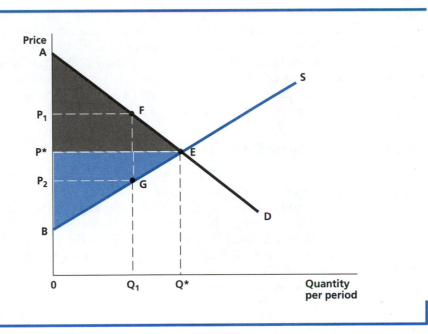

FIGURE 9.1 Competitive Equilibrium and Consumer/Producer Surplus At the competitive equilibrium (Q^*), the sum of consumer surplus (shaded gray) and producer surplus (shaded in color) is maximized. For an output level less than Q^*, say Q_1, there is a deadweight loss of consumer and producer surplus given by area FEG.

P^*, Q^*, producers receive total revenue of P^*EQ^*0. But under a scheme of selling one unit at a time at the lowest possible price, producers would have been willing to produce Q^* for a payment of BEQ^*0. At Q^*, therefore, they receive a **producer surplus** given by the colored area P^*EB. To understand the precise nature of this surplus, we must again examine the short-run/long-run distinction in firms' supply decisions.

Short-Run Producer Surplus

The supply curve S in Figure 9.1 could be either a short-run or a long-run supply curve. However, in Chapter 8, we showed that the upward slope of S has rather different causes in these two cases. In the short run, the market supply curve is the horizontal summation of all firms' short-run marginal cost curves. The curve's positive slope reflects the diminishing returns to variable inputs that are encountered as output is increased. In this case, price exceeds marginal cost (as reflected by the supply curve) at all output levels, except Q^*. Production of each of these "intramarginal" units of output generates incremental profits for suppliers. Total short-run profits, then, are given by the sum of all of these profit increments

Producer surplus
The extra value producers get for a good in excess of the opportunity costs they incur by producing it. What all producers would pay for the right to sell a good at its current market price.

(area P*EB) plus profits when Q = 0 (that is, a loss of fixed costs). Hence, area P*EB—short-run producer surplus—reflects the sum of both total short-run profits and short-run fixed costs. It includes that part of total profits that is in excess of the profits firms would have if they chose to produce nothing (in which case they would suffer a loss equal to fixed costs). In this sense, short-run producer surplus mirrors consumer surplus, which measures what consumers would lose if nothing were produced.

Long-Run Producer Surplus

In the long run, positively sloped supply curves arise because firms experience increasing input costs. When the market is in equilibrium, each firm has zero profits and there are no fixed costs. Short-run producer surplus does not exist in this situation. Instead, long-run producer surplus now reflects the increasing payments being received by the firms' inputs as output expands. The area P*EB in Figure 9.1 measures all of these increased payments relative to a situation in which the industry produces no output, in which case these inputs would receive lower prices for their services.

Ricardian Rent

Long-run producer surplus can be most easily illustrated with a situation first described by David Ricardo in the early part of the nineteenth century.[1] Assume there are many parcels of land on which tomatoes might be grown. These range from very fertile land (low costs of production) to very poor, dry land (high costs). The long-run supply curve for tomatoes is constructed as follows. At low prices, only the best land is used to produce tomatoes and few are produced. As output increases, higher-cost plots of land are brought into production because higher prices make it profitable to grow tomatoes on this land. The long-run supply curve for tomatoes is positively sloped because of the increasing costs associated with using less-fertile land. Notice that this is a different reason than we discussed in Chapter 8. There, firms had identical cost curves and every forms' costs were affected by rising input prices.

MicroQuiz 9.1

The study of long-run producer surplus is one of the most important ways in which microeconomics ties together effects in various markets. Why are the following relationships true?

1. If the peanut harvesting industry is a price taker for *all* of the inputs it hires, there will be no long-run producer surplus in this industry.

2. If the only "scarce" resource in the potato harvesting industry is land for growing potatoes, total long-run producer surplus in this industry will be measured by total economic rents earned by potato-land owners. Do these rents "cause" high potato prices?

[1] See David Ricardo, *The Principles of Political Economy and Taxation* (1817; reprint, London: J. M. Dent and Son, 1965), Chapter 2 and Chapter 32.

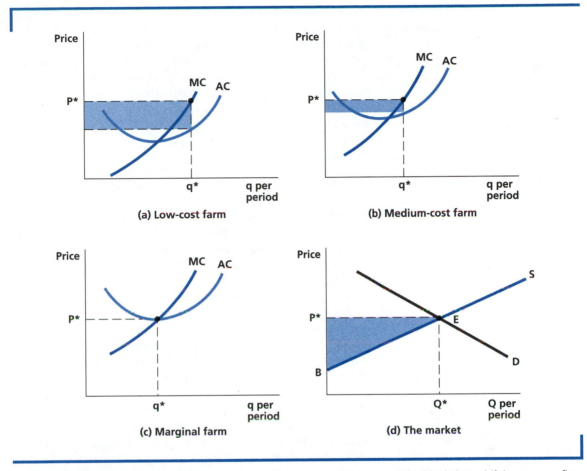

FIGURE 9.2 Ricardian Rent Low-cost and medium-cost farms can earn long-run profits (shaded areas) if these costs reflect ownership of unique resources. Total Ricardian rent represents producer surplus—area P*EB in (d). Ricardian rents are usually capitalized into resource prices.

In the Ricardian example, firms' costs differ and costs of the marginal firm increase as more firms enter a market.

Market equilibrium in this situation is illustrated in Figure 9.2. At an equilibrium price of P*, both the low-cost and the medium-cost farms earn (long-run) profits. The "marginal farm" earns exactly zero economic profits. Farms with even higher costs stay out of the market because they would incur losses at a price of P*. Profits earned by the intramarginal farms can persist in the long run, however, because they reflect returns to a rare resource—low-cost land. Free entry cannot erode these profits even over the long term. The sum of these long-run profits constitutes total producer surplus as given by area P*EB in Figure 9.2(d).

The long-run profits illustrated in Figure 9.2 are sometimes referred to as **Ricardian rent.** They represent the returns obtained by the owners of scarce resources (in this case, fertile tomato-growing land) in a marketplace. Often these rents are "capitalized" into the prices of these resources; in short, fertile land sells for higher prices than does poor land. Similarly, rich gold mines have higher prices than poor mines, favorably located retail space in malls rents for more than out-of-the-way space, and airport landing slots at Chicago's O'Hare are more valuable than slots at airports in the Yukon.

Economic Efficiency

This description of producer and consumer surplus also provides a simple proof of why economists believe competitive markets produce "efficient" allocations of resources. Although a more detailed examination of that topic requires that we look at many markets (which we do in the appendix to this chapter), here we can return to Figure 9.1 as a simple illustration. Any output level for tomatoes other than Q^* in this figure is inefficient in that the sum total of consumer and producer surplus is not as large as possible. If Q_1 tomatoes were produced, for example, a total surplus of area FEG would be forgone. At Q_1 demanders are willing to pay P_1 for another tomato, which would cost only P_2 to produce. That gap suggests that there exists a mutually beneficial transaction (such as producing one more tomato at a price of P^*) that could benefit both demanders (who would get the tomato for less than they were willing to pay) and suppliers (who would get more for the tomato than it would cost to produce). Only at Q^* are all such mutually beneficial transactions consummated and only then is the sum of consumer and producer surplus as large as possible.[2] Output level Q^* is said to be an **economically efficient allocation of resources**—a term we explore further in the appendix to this chapter. Application 9.1: Does Buying Things on the Internet Improve Welfare? shows how the extra welfare from expanding markets can be measured. Before turning to a number of other applications, a numerical example may help illustrate the efficiency concept.

A Numerical Illustration

In Chapter 8, we looked at a hypothetical market for cassette tapes in which demand was represented by

$$Q = 10 - P \tag{9.1}$$

and supply by

$$Q = P - 2 \tag{9.2}$$

---

[2] Producing more than Q^* would also reduce total producer and consumer surplus since consumers' willingness to pay for extra output would fall short of the costs of producing that output.

Technical innovations together with significant network externalities have reduced sharply the transactions costs associated with conducting business over the Internet. This promises to transform the retailing process in many industries.

The Gains to Internet Trade

Figure 1 illustrates the nature of the gains from reduced transactions costs of Internet trading. The demand and supply curves in the figure represent con-sumers' and firms' behavior vis-à-vis any good that might be bought and sold over the Internet. Prior to the decline in Internet costs, per-unit transactions costs exceeded $P_2 - P_1$. Hence, no trading was conducted; buyers and sellers preferred traditional retail outlets. A fall in these costs increased Internet business. Assuming that the per-unit cost of making trans-actions fell to zero, the market would show a large increase in Internet trad-ing, settling at the competitive equi-librium, P^*, Q^*.

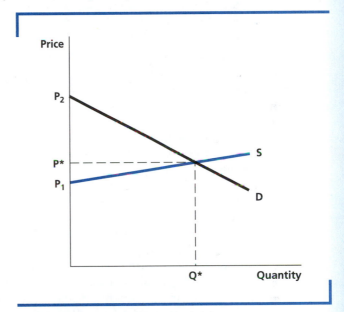

Some Early Evidence

Although Internet retailing has only just begun, early growth has been remarkable. In 2001, electronic retail-ing directly to consumers totaled about $20 billion, with business-to-business sales representing another $50 to 75 bil-lion. The most important early inroads by Internet sales have been in travel-related goods (airline and resort reser-

FIGURE 1 Reduced Transaction Costs Promote Internet Commerce When transaction costs for Internet trading exceed $P_2 - P_1$, no transactions occur. As transaction costs decline, equilibrium approaches P^*, Q^*.

vations), on-line financial services, and some narrow categories of consumer goods (for exam-ple, books sold by Amazon.com). These are goods for which Internet trading represented some of the largest reductions in transactions costs relative to traditional outlets.

Retailers as Infomediaries

One major question raised by the growth of Internet commerce is whether there is a sepa-rate role for retailing. If the Internet allows producers to reach customers directly, why would any role for "middlemen" remain? The answer to this query lies in the nature of services that e-retailers might provide. The main role of Internet retailers may be as "infomediaries"— the primary good they provide is information. For example, Internet automobile sellers (such

(continued)

as carsdirect or autotrader) not only provide comparative information about the features of various models, but can also point to the dealer that gives the best price. Internet airline services can search for the lowest price or for the most convenient departure. More advanced retailing sites make use of customer profiles to suggest items they might like to buy. For example, Amazon.com uses a customer's past book purchases to suggest potential new ones. At LandsEnd.com you can "try on" clothes. How all this will evolve in the future is anyone's guess.

To Think About

1. How will expansion of Internet retailing affect traditional retailers such as WalMart or Sears? What special services can these retailers offer that the Internet cannot?
2. In 1998, the U.S. Congress enacted a statute that prohibited taxes on Internet commerce for 3 years, and this ban was renewed in 2001. What would be the effect of, say, subjecting Internet commerce to state sales taxes?

We showed that equilibrium in this market occurs at $P^* = \$6$ and $Q^* = 4$ tapes per week. Figure 9.3 repeats Figure 8.6 by providing an illustration of this equilibrium. At point E, consumers are spending $\$24 (= 6 \cdot 4)$ per week for tapes. Total consumer surplus is given by the gray triangular area in the figure and amounts to $\$8 (= \frac{1}{2} \text{ of } 4 \cdot 4)$ per week. At E, producers also receive revenues of $\$24$ per week and gain a producer surplus of $\$8$ per week as reflected by the colored triangle. Total consumer and producer surplus is therefore $\$16$ per week.

The inefficiency of other potential tape output levels can also be illustrated with the help of Figure 9.3. If price remains at $\$6$ but output is only three tapes per week, for example, consumers and producers each receive $\$7.50$ per week of surplus in their transactions. Total consumer and producer surplus is $\$15$ per week—a reduction of $\$1$ from what it is at E. Total surplus would still be $\$15$ per week with output of three tapes per week at any other price we might have chosen. Once output is specified, the price at which transactions occur affects only the distribution of surplus between consumers and producers. The transaction price does not affect the total amount of surplus, which is always given by the area between the demand curve and the supply curve.

Output levels greater than four tapes per week are also inefficient. For example, production of five tapes per week at a transaction price of $\$6$ would again generate consumer surplus of $\$7.50$ ($\$8$ for the four tapes transaction less a loss of $\$.50$ on the sale of the fifth tape, since the tape sells for more than people are willing to pay). Similarly, a producer surplus of $\$7.50$ would occur, representing a loss of $\$.50$ in the production of the fifth tape. Total surplus at this point is now $\$15$ per week, one dollar less than at the market equilibrium. Again, the actual price assumed here doesn't matter—it is the fact that costs (reflected by the supply curve S) exceed individuals' willingness to pay (reflected by the demand curve D) for output levels greater than four tapes per week that results in the loss of total surplus value.

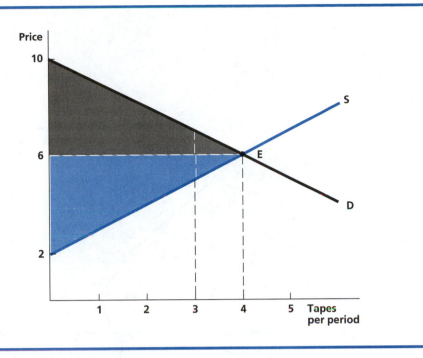

FIGURE 9.3 Efficiency in Tape Sales Equilibrium in the cassette tape market yields a price of $6 and a quantity of four tapes per week. Consumer surplus (shaded gray) and producer surplus (shaded in color) are each $8. An output of three tapes per week would reduce the sum of consumer and produces surplus from $16 to $15.

PRICE CONTROLS AND SHORTAGES

Sometimes governments seek to control prices at below-equilibrium levels. Although adoption of such policies is usually claimed to be based on noble motives, frequently the controls deter long-run supply responses and create welfare losses for both consumers and producers. A simple analysis of this possibility is provided by Figure 9.4. Initially, the market is in long-run equilibrium at P_1, Q_1 (point E). An increase in demand from D to D' would cause the price to rise to P_2 in the short run and encourage entry by new firms. Assuming this market is characterized by increasing costs (as reflected in the long-run supply curve LS), price would fall somewhat as a result of this entry, ultimately settling at P_3. If these price changes were regarded as undesirable, the government could, in principle, prevent them by imposing a legally enforceable ceiling price of P_1. This would cause firms to continue to supply their previous output (Q_1); and, because at P_1 demanders now want to purchase Q_4, there will be a shortage, given by $Q_4 - Q_1$.

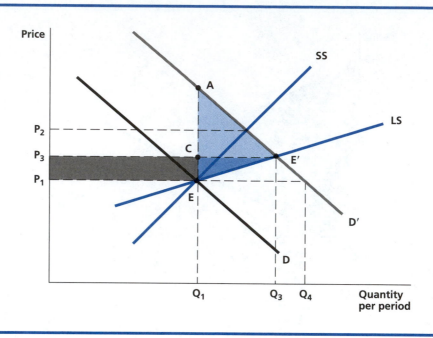

FIGURE 9.4 Price Controls and Shortages A shift in demand from D to D′ would raise price to P_2 in the short run. Entry over the long run would yield a final equilibrium of $P_3 Q_3$. Controlling the price at P_1 would prevent these actions and yield a shortage of $Q_4 - Q_1$. Relative to the uncontrolled situation, the price control yields a transfer from producers to consumers (shaded gray) and a deadweight loss of forgone transactions given by the two areas shaded in color.

The welfare consequences of this price-control policy can be evaluated by comparing consumer- and producer-surplus measures prevailing under this policy to those that would have prevailed in the absence of controls. First, the buyers of Q_1 gain consumer surplus given by the gray area P_3CEP_1, because they can buy this good at a lower price than would exist in an uncontrolled market. This gain reflects a pure transfer to these buyers from the producer surplus that would exist without controls. What current consumers have gained from the lower price, producers have lost. Though this transfer does not represent a loss of overall welfare, it does clearly affect the relative well-being of the market participants.

Second, the lightly colored area $AE′C$ represents the value of additional consumer surplus that would have been attained without controls. Similarly, the darkly colored area $CE′E$ reflects additional producer surplus available in the uncontrolled situation. Together these two areas (that is, area $AE′E$) represent the total value of mutually beneficial transactions between willing buyers and sellers that are prevented by the government policy of controlling price. This is, therefore, a measure of the pure welfare costs of that policy (as distinct from its transfer effects).

Finally, the welfare analysis associated with Figure 9.4 also provides some insights about the politics of any price-control policy. Buyers who are able to get output Q_1 at a price of P_1 will be big supporters of the policy because they obtain substantial welfare benefits. Those benefits, however, come at the expense of producers of Q_1 who, because they earn less than they might, would likely oppose the policy. Both producers and consumers who wish to make transactions for amounts greater than Q_1 lose and they might also oppose the policy. They might, in fact, seek ways around the price controls by engaging in illegal transactions at prices higher than P_1. All of these likelihoods are supported by the analysis of Application 9.2: Rent Control: Why This Bad Idea Never Dies, which looks at the most widespread price-control policy.

TAX INCIDENCE

Another important application of the perfectly competitive model is to the study of the effects of taxes. Not only does the model permit an evaluation of how taxation alters the allocation of resources, but it also highlights the issue of who bears the actual burden of various taxes. By stressing the distinction between the legal obligation to pay a tax and the economic effects that may shift that burden elsewhere, **tax incidence theory** helps to clarify the ways in which taxes actually affect the well-being of market participants.

Figure 9.5 illustrates this approach by considering a "specific tax" of a fixed amount per unit of output that is imposed on all firms in a constant cost industry. Although legally the tax is required to be *paid* by the firm, this view of things is very misleading. To demonstrate this, we begin by showing that the tax can be analyzed as a shift downward in the demand curve facing this industry from D to D'. The vertical distance between the curves measures the amount of the per unit tax, t. For any price that consumers pay (say, P) firms get to keep only P – t. It is that after-tax demand curve D', then, that is relevant to firms' behavior. Consumers continue to pay a "gross" price as reflected by the demand curve D. The tax creates a "wedge" between what consumers pay and what firms actually get to keep.

The short-run effect of the tax is to shift the equilibrium from its initial position P_1, Q_1 to the point where the new demand curve D' intersects the short-run supply curve S. That intersection occurs at output level Q_2 at an after-tax price to the firm of P_2. Assuming this price exceeds average variable costs, the typical firm now produces output level q_2 at a loss.

Tax incidence theory
The study of the final burden of a tax after considering all market reactions to it.

MicroQuiz 9.2

Suppose a local government placed price controls on prescription drugs in expectation of a large increase in demand.

1. What aspect of drug firms' costs would determine the difference between the short-run and the long run impact of this policy?

2. Explain how the losses of producer surplus from this policy would differ between the short run and the long run.

In Application 1.6: Do Economists Ever Agree? we showed that the vast majority of economists agree with the statement, "Rent controls reduce the quantity of housing." In this application we look at the research underlying this belief and survey some recent thinking on the topic.

History of Rent Control

In response to rapidly rising rents during World War II, rent controls were adopted in many U.S. and European cities. Following the war, these controls were scrapped in many places but continued in effect in New York City and several European countries, including Great Britain, France, and Sweden. Rent controls also have long been used in many Canadian provinces.

Rapid inflation in the late 1970s led to a revived interest in rent controls. Large cities, such as Boston and San Francisco, introduced new, ostensibly more flexible regulations. Many smaller cities in Massachusetts, California, Connecticut, and New Jersey followed suit. Since that time, however, interest in rent control has waned and many cities have relaxed or abandoned their laws. Still, by some estimates, more than 10 percent of the U.S. stock of rental units remains subject to some form of control.

Rent Control and Housing Quality

Figure 9.4 provides a starting place for a study of the effects of rent control. The prediction that such controls will benefit current tenants and harm landlords and new tenants has been confirmed in many studies of the World War II controls. For example, research on Swedish controls during the 1950s showed that waiting times for new apartments reached more than 3 years because of the shortages of rental units.[1]

Still, the analysis of Figure 9.4 misses the most important effect of rent control—its effect on housing quality. Because controls apply to specific rental units, landlords can effectively reduce the supply of housing by reducing the quality of their units. That is, they can adopt only minimal maintenance procedures and make needed repairs only grudgingly. Of course, tenants may employ various strategies to get landlords to provide better upkeep. But, in the absence of monetary incentives to do so, this is often a long, futile battle. Indeed, the deterioration in housing quality occasioned by rent control has sometimes been compared to the effects of bombing. Particularly quotable is Vietnamese Foreign Minister Nguyen C. Thach, who is reported to have said, "The Americans couldn't destroy Hanoi by bombing, but we have done the job with low rents."[2]

Effects of the "New" Rent-Control Laws

New rent-control ordinances tend to be more flexible than their World War II predecessors. Most allow for cost pass-through for increases in taxes or utility costs. And many have provisions for "vacancy decontrol" so that when present tenants leave, rents can be raised toward market levels. A few economists have argued that this type of flexible control may

---

[1] S. Rydenfelt, "Rent Control after Thirty Years," in *Verdict on Rent Control* (London: Institute for Economic Affairs, 1972).

[2] Quoted in *Fortune,* February 27, 1989: 14.

be beneficial in helping new tenants to cope with the uncertainties they face in searching for living space or in confronting the market power that some landlords may have in certain locations. Most economists have not been persuaded by such theoretical possibilities, however. They doubt that the political process would lead to the kinds of carefully crafted rent control ordinances that might improve welfare in conditions of imperfect competition. Empirical evidence with which to appraise the new rent control laws has been especially hard to obtain because localities differ in many aspects besides whether or not they have rent control.[3]

To Think About

1. Some people have blamed rent control for the increasing levels of homelessness observed in the United States. How would you construct such an argument? What aspects of homelessness would argue against such an interpretation?
2. Tenants who live in rent-controlled apartments may be able to take advantage of their position. How could they thwart the purpose of vacancy decontrol through subleasing? Even if a tenant gives up a rent-controlled lease, how might he or she capitalize on the deal?

[3] See R. Arnott, "Time for Revision on Rent Control," *Journal of Economic Perspectives* (Winter 1993): 99–120.

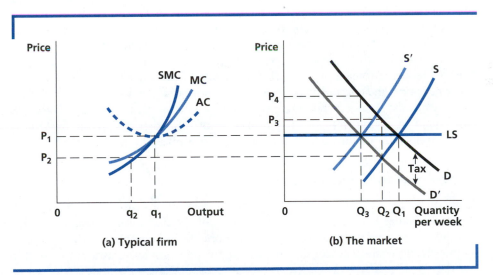

FIGURE 9.5 Effect of the Imposition of a Specific Tax on a Perfectly Competitive, Constant Cost Industry A specific commodity tax of amount t lowers the after-tax demand curve to D'. With this "new" demand curve, Q_2 will be produced in the short run at an after-tax price of P_2. In the long-run, firms will leave the industry and the price will return to P_1. The entire amount of the tax is shifted onto consumers in the form of a higher market price. (P_4).

I N F O T R A C©
COLLEGE EDITION
Exclusively from Gale Group and Thomson Learning

www.infotrac-college.com
Keywords: Consumer surplus,
Producer surplus, Economic
efficiency, Price controls, Rent
control, Tax incidence

Consumers will pay P_3 for output level Q_2. The graph reveals that $P_3 - P_2 = t$; so, in the short run, the tax is borne partially by consumers (who see the price they pay rise from P_1 to P_3) and partially by firms, which are now operating at a loss because they are receiving only P_2 (instead of P_1) for their output.

Long-Run Shifting of the Tax

In the long run, firms do not continue to operate at a loss. Some firms leave the market bemoaning the role of oppressive taxation in bringing about their downfall. The industry short-run supply curve shifts leftward because fewer firms remain in the market. A new long-run equilibrium is established at Q_3 where the after-tax price received by firms still in the industry enables them to earn exactly zero in economic profits. Those firms remaining in the industry return to producing output level q_1. The price paid by buyers in the market is now P_4. In the long run, the entire amount of the tax has been shifted into increased prices. Even though the firm ostensibly *pays* the tax, the long-run burden is borne completely by the consumers of this good.[3]

Long-Run Incidence with Increasing Costs

In the more realistic case of increasing costs, both producers and consumers pay a portion of this tax. Such a possibility is illustrated in Figure 9.6. Here, the long-run supply curve (LS) has a positive slope because the costs of various inputs are bid up as industry output expands. Imposition of the tax, t, shifts the after-tax demand curve inward to D′, and this brings about a fall in net price over the long run from P_1 to P_2. Faced with the lower price, P_2, firms leave this industry, which has the effect of reducing some inputs' prices. Long-run equilibrium is reestablished at this lower net price, and consumers now pay a gross price of P_3, which exceeds what they paid previously. Total tax collections are given by the gray area $P_3ARE_2P_2$. These are partly paid by consumers (who pay P_3 instead of P_1) and partly by the owners of firms' inputs who are now paid based on a lower net price, P_2, instead of P_1.[4]

Incidence and Elasticity

A bit of geometric intuition suggests that the relative sizes of the price changes shown in Figure 9.6 depend on the elasticities of the demand and supply curves. Intuitively, the market participant with the more-elastic response is able more easily to "get out of the way" of the tax, leaving the one with less-elastic response still

---

[3] Notice that owners of firms leaving the industry incur no long-run burden because they were initially earning zero economic profits, and, by assumption, can earn the same return elsewhere.
[4] Notice again that the firms' owners, per se, experience no losses here since they earned zero profits before the tax. Rather, the producer's share of the tax burden is borne by the owners of those inputs that have fallen in price.

in place to pay the most. We have already illustrated a special case of this principle in Figure 9.5. In that figure, the long-run elasticity of supply was infinite because of the constant-cost nature of the industry. Because the price received by firms (and by the inputs the firm employs) does not vary as output contracts as a result of the tax, the entire tax burden is shifted onto consumers. This outcome may be quite common in situations of some state or local taxes for which the good being taxed constitutes such a small portion of the national total that local supply is infinitely elastic. For example, a small town that tries to impose a large tax on its restaurants may find that the tax is quickly reflected in the price of restaurant meals. Some restaurant owners can avoid the tax by going elsewhere.

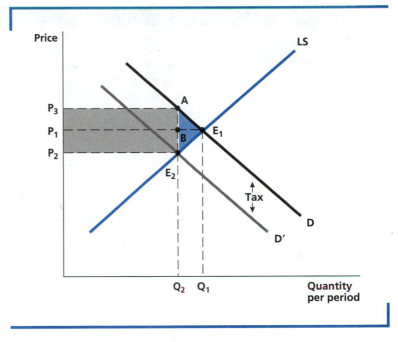

FIGURE 9.6 Tax Incidence in an Increasing Cost Industry The initial equilibrium (E_1) is shifted to E_2 by the imposition of a tax. Total tax revenues (shaded gray) are partly paid by consumers, partly by producers. There is a deadweight loss (excess burden) from the tax shown by the area shaded in color.

More generally, if demand is relatively inelastic whereas supply is elastic, demanders pay the bulk of a tax in the form of higher prices. Alternatively, if supply is relatively inelastic but demand is elastic, producers pay most of the tax. Indeed, in this case, we can push the analysis further by noting that the producer's share is paid primarily by those inputs that have inelastic supply curves because it is these inputs that experience the greatest drop in price when demand for their services declines. For example, the producer's share of a tax on gold or silver would be largely paid by mine owners because the supply of mining land to this industry may be very inelastic. The supply of mining machinery or mine workers may be more elastic, however, because these inputs may have good alternative sources of employment. Hence, they would pay little of the tax. Of course, taking account of all of these repercussions of a tax in various markets is sometimes very difficult and simple models of supply and demand may not be up to the task. Modern analyses of the tax incidence question use computer models of general equilibrium so that effects on many markets can be studied simultaneously. A brief look at these types of models is provided in the appendix to this chapter. Application 9.3: The Tobacco Settlement Is Just a Tax looks at the impact of the large liability costs that have ostensibly been imposed on the tobacco companies in recent years.

The Tobacco Settlement Is Just a Tax

In June of 1997, attorneys general from most U.S. states reached an agreement with the largest tobacco companies to settle a series of lawsuits based on the harmful effects of cigarette smoking. That settlement required that the tobacco companies pay about $360 billion to the states over the next 25 years in exchange for limiting future suits against the companies. Because of this limitation on future suits, the settlement required approval by the U.S. Congress—an approval that became embroiled in politics and never happened. Subsequently, in November 1998, the states reached a series of more modest agreements with the tobacco companies that amounted to about $200 billion and did not require Congressional approval. The economics of this settlement are almost as interesting as the politics.

The Tobacco Settlement as a Tax Increase

Probably the most accurate way to think about this settlement is as an increase in cigarette taxes. The companies play the role of tax collector, but there may be significant shifting of the tax depending on the elasticities involved. Table 4.4 provides an estimate of the price elasticity of demand for cigarettes of −0.35. The state settlements added about $0.30 per pack, a 15 percent increase on an initial price of $2.00 per pack. Hence, the quantity of cigarettes sold would be expected to fall by about 5.25 percent (0.35 × 0.15) from about 24 billion packs per year to 22.75 billion packs. Total "tax collections" would be $6.8 billion per year ($0.30 × 22.75 billion). Tobacco consumers will pay virtually all of this cost. Assuming that tobacco companies continue to earn about $0.25 in profits per pack,[1] the 1.25 billion-pack reduction in annual sales will cost them only about $300 million per year. Because tobacco consumers tend to have relatively low incomes, the settlement amounts to a very regressive form of taxation for the states.

Other Effects of the Settlements

A primary goal of the tobacco settlements was to reduce smoking by young people. The resulting price increases may well have that effect. Some empirical evidence suggests that young smokers may have larger price elasticities than adult smokers (perhaps in the −0.5 range), and there is strong evidence that individuals who do not start smoking as teenagers are much less likely to take it up later. But the price increases brought about by the settlements are relatively modest, so the impact from prices alone may not be large. Several other components of the settlements required that tobacco companies sharply restrict marketing practices aimed at young people (Joe Camel was a casualty of the settlement, for example). The overall effectiveness of these measures remains uncertain.

As for most legislation, several special interests also gained from the tobacco settlement. Many states adopted special programs to aid tobacco farmers and other workers who might be affected by the decline in tobacco sales. The settlement was tailored so that

---

[1] The accuracy of these incidence assumptions depends on the precise structure of the tobacco industry. Given that four firms control practically all sales is seems likely that their profit rates per pack and the pre-tax price of cigarettes will be little changed by the settlement. For a more detailed discussion see. J. Bulow and P. Klemperer, "The Tobacco Deal," *Brookings Papers on Economic Activity, Microeconomics Annual 1998*, 323–394.

the smallest tobacco company (Liggett) would be rewarded because of the evidence it provided against the other firms in the earlier lawsuits. Because Liggett would benefit from the increase in cigarette prices without having to pay the settlement costs, its profits could easily double. Finally, of course, tort lawyers working on various smoking cases were well rewarded by the settlement. A standard "contingent fee" of 30 percent would have provided them with nearly $2 billion per year, but this unseemly amount was cut to about $750 million per year in the final settlements by the states. Still, the lawyers will not go hungry. By some estimates each will get between $1 million and $2 million *per year* for the foreseeable future.

To Think About

1. The state settlements actually require tobacco companies to pay a fixed number of dollars each year. How would the analysis of this type of fixed revenue tax differ, if at all, from the approach taken in this application?
2. The primary argument of the states in their lawsuits was that smoking cost them money in terms of Medicaid and other health-related expenses. How would you decide whether this is true?

Taxation and Efficiency

Because taxation reduces the output of the taxed commodity, there is a reallocation of production to other areas. This reallocation implies that some previously mutually beneficial transaction is forgone and that taxation reduces overall economic welfare. This loss can also be illustrated in Figure 9.6. The total loss in consumer surplus as a result of the tax is given by area $P_3AE_1P_1$. Of this area, P_3ABP_1 is transferred into tax revenues for the government and area AE_1B is simply lost. Similarly, the total loss of producer surplus is given by area $P_1E_1E_2P_2$ with area $P_1BE_2P_2$ being transferred into tax revenues and area BE_1E_2 being lost. By the standard of resource allocation efficiency, the effect of the transfer into tax revenues (which amounts in total to area $P_3AE_2P_2$) is ambiguous. Whether this reduces the welfare of consumers and producers as a whole depends on how wisely government funds are spent—a thorny issue, to say the least. There is no ambiguity about the loss given by the colored area AE_1E_2. This is a **deadweight loss** for which there are no compensating gains. Sometimes this loss is referred to as the "excess burden" of a tax; it represents the additional losses that consumers and producers incur as a result of a tax, over and above the actual tax revenues paid.

MicroQuiz 9.3

Suppose that a per-unit tax is imposed on the perfectly competitive golf-tee industry.

1. Why would you expect consumers to pay a larger share of this tax in the long run than in the short run?

2. How would you determine who pays the producer's share of this tax in the long run?

Deadweight loss
Losses of consumer and producer surplus that are not transferred to other parties.

A Numerical Illustration

The effects of an excise tax can be illustrated by returning once again to our example of supply-demand equilibrium in the market for cassette tapes. Suppose the government implements a $2 per tape tax that the retailer adds to the sales price for each tape sold. In this case, the supply function for tapes remains

$$\text{Supply: } Q = P - 2 \qquad (9.3)$$

where P is now the net price received by the seller. Demanders, on the other hand, must now pay P + t for each tape so their demand function becomes

$$\text{Demand: } Q = 10 - (P + t) \qquad (9.4)$$

or, since t = 2 here,

$$Q = 10 - (P + 2) = 8 - P \qquad (9.5)$$

Notice, as we have shown graphically, that the effect of the tax is to shift the net demand curve (that is, quantity demanded as a function of the net price received by firms) inward. Equating supply and demand in this case yields

$$\text{Supply} = P - 2 = \text{Demand} = 8 - P \qquad (9.6)$$

or P* = 5, Q* = 3. At this equilibrium, consumers pay $7 for each tape and total tax collections are $6 per week (= $2 per tape times three tapes per week). As we showed previously, an output of three tapes per week generates a total consumer and producer surplus of $15 per week of which $6 is now transferred into tax revenues. In this particular case, these revenues are half paid by firms (who see the net price fall from $6 to $5). In other cases, of course, one party or the other might bear a relatively greater burden. Here the excess burden of taxation is $1 per week. This represents the loss in total consumer and producer surplus that is not collected in tax revenue.

Transactions Costs

Although we have developed this discussion in terms of tax incidence theory, models incorporating a wedge between buyers' and sellers' prices have a number of other applications in economics. Perhaps the most important of these concern costs associated with making market transac-

---

MicroQuiz 9.4

Graph this numerical illustration of taxation and use your graph to answer the following questions:

1. What is the value of consumer and producer surplus after the tax is imposed? How do you know that the area of the "deadweight loss triangle" is $1 here?

2. Suppose that the tax were raised to $4. How much in extra tax revenue would be collected? How much bigger would the deadweight loss be?

3. How large a tax would foreclose all trading in cassette tapes.? What would tax collections be in this case? What would the deadweight loss be?

tions. In some cases, these may be explicit. Most real estate transactions, for example, take place through a third-party broker, who charges a fee for the service of bringing buyer and seller together. Similar explicit transactions fees occur in the trading of stocks and bonds, boats and airplanes, and practically everything that is sold at auction. In all of these instances, buyers and sellers are willing to pay a fee to an agent or broker who facilitates the transaction. In other cases, transactions costs may be largely implicit. Individuals trying to purchase a used car, for example, spend considerable time and effort reading classified advertisements and examining vehicles. These activities amount to an implicit cost of making the transaction.

To the extent that transactions costs are on a per-unit basis (as they are in the real estate, securities, and auction examples), our previous taxation example applies exactly. From the point of view of the buyers—and sellers—it makes little difference whether t represents a per-unit tax or a per-unit transactions fee, since the analysis of the fee's effect on the market is the same. That is, the fee is shared between buyers and sellers, depending on the specific elasticities involved. Output in these markets is also lower than in the absence of such fees.[5]

A somewhat different analysis would hold, however, if transactions costs were a lump-sum amount per transaction. In that case, people would seek to reduce the number of transactions made. But existence of the charge would not affect the total amount bought over the long term. For example, driving to the supermarket is mainly a lump-sum transaction cost on shopping for groceries. Existence of such a charge may not significantly affect the price of food items nor the amount of food consumed (unless it tempts people to grow their own). But the charge will cause individuals to shop less frequently, to buy larger quantities on each trip, and to hold larger inventories of food in their homes than would be the case if getting to the store were costless.

TRADE RESTRICTIONS

Restrictions on the flow of goods in international commerce have effects similar to those we just examined for taxes. Impediments to free trade may reduce mutually beneficial transactions and cause a variety of transfers among the various parties involved. Once again, the competitive model of supply and demand is frequently used to study these effects.

Gains from International Trade

Figure 9.7 illustrates the domestic demand and supply curves for a particular good, say, shoes. In the absence of international trade, the domestic equilibrium price of shoes would be P_D and quantity would be Q_D. Although this equilibrium

---

[5] One shortcoming of this analysis is its failure to consider the possible benefits obtained from brokers. To the extent these services are valuable to the parties in the transaction, demand and supply curves shift outward to reflect this value. Hence, output may in some cases expand from the availability of agents that facilitate transactions (see Application 9.1).

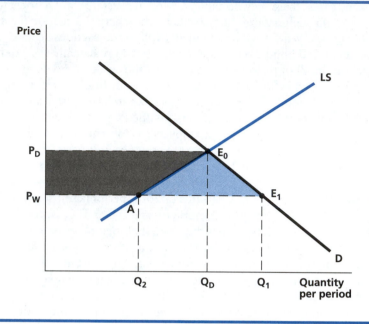

FIGURE 9.7 Opening of International Trade Increases Total Welfare Opening of international trade lowers price from P_D to P_W. At P_W, domestic producers supply Q_2 and demanders want to buy Q_1. Imports amount to Q_1 2 Q_2. The lower price results in a transfer from domestic producers to consumers (shaded gray) and a net gain of consumer surplus (shaded in color).

would exhaust all mutually beneficial transactions between domestic shoe producers and domestic demanders, opening of international trade presents a number of additional options. If the world shoe price, P_W, is less than the prevailing domestic price, P_D, the opening of trade will cause prices to fall to this world level.[6] This drop in price will cause quantity demanded to increase to Q_1, whereas quantity supplied by domestic producers will fall to Q_2. Imported shoes will amount to $Q_1 - Q_2$. In short, what domestic producers do not supply at the world price is instead provided by foreign sources.

The shift in the market equilibrium from E_0 to E_1 causes a large increase in consumer surplus given by area $P_D E_0 E_1 P_W$. Part of this gain reflects a transfer from domestic shoe producers (area $P_D E_0 A P_W$, which is shaded in gray), and part represents an unambiguous welfare gain (the colored area $E_0 E_1 A$). The source of consumer gains here is obvious—buyers get shoes at a lower price than was previously available in the domestic market. As in our former analyses, losses of producer surplus are experienced by those inputs that give the long-run supply curve

---

[6] Throughout our analysis, we assume that this country is a price taker in the world market and can purchase all of the imports it wishes without affecting the price, P_W. If the country could affect world prices, there might be situations in which it could take advantage of this position by departing from free-trade policies.

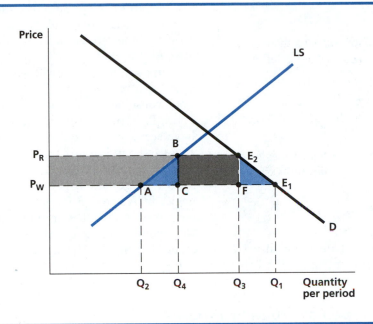

FIGURE 9.8 Effects of a Tariff Imposition of a tariff of amount t raises price to $P_R = P_W + t$. This results in collection of tariff revenue (dark gray), a transfer from consumers to producers (light gray), and two triangles measuring deadweight loss (shaded in color). A quota has similar effects, though in this case no revenues are collected.

its upward slope. If, for example, the domestic shoe industry experiences increasing costs because shoemaker wages are driven up as industry output expands, then the decline in output from Q_D to Q_2 as a result of trade will reverse this process, causing shoemaker wages to fall.

Tariff Protection

Shoemakers are unlikely to take these wage losses lying down. Instead, they will press the government for protection from the flood of imported footwear. Since the loss of producer surplus is experienced by relatively few individuals whereas consumer gains from trade are spread across many shoe buyers, shoemakers may have considerably greater incentives to organize opposition to imports than consumers would have to organize to keep trade open. The result may be adoption of projectionist measures.

Historically, the most important type of protection employed has been a **tariff,** that is, a tax on the imported good. Effects of such a tax are shown in Figure 9.8. Now comparisons begin from the free trade equilibrium E_1. Imposition of a per-unit tariff on shoes for domestic buyers of amount t raises the effective price to $P_W + t = P_R$. This price rise causes quantity demanded to fall from Q_1 to Q_3 whereas domestic production expands from Q_2 to Q_4. The total quantity of shoe imports falls from

Tariff
A tax on an imported good. May be equivalent to a quota or a nonquantitative restriction on trade.

$Q_1 - Q_2$ to $Q_3 - Q_4$. Since each imported pair of shoes is now subject to a tariff, total tariff revenues are given by the dark gray area, BE_2FC, that is, by $t(Q_3 - Q_4)$.

Imposition of the tariff on imported shoes creates a variety of welfare effects. Total consumer surplus is reduced by area $P_RE_2E_1P_W$. Part of this reduction, as we have seen, is transferred into tariff revenues and part is transferred into increased domestic producer's surplus (area P_RBAP_W, shown in light gray). The two colored triangles BCA and E_2E_1F represent losses of consumer surplus that are not transferred to anyone; these are a deadweight loss from the tariff and are similar to the excess burden imposed by any tax. All of these areas can be measured if reliable empirical estimates of the domestic supply and demand curves for shoes are available.

Other Types of Trade Protection

In recent years, tariffs have come to play a reduced role in international trade. They have been gradually negotiated downward under the General Agreement on Tariffs and Trade (GATT). The decline in tariffs has not necessarily meant a decline in protectionism, however. In their place are a number of restrictive measures including quotas, "voluntary" export restraints, and a series of nonquantitative restrictions such as those incorporated into seemingly beneficial health, safety, and environmental regulations. Many of these new types of restrictions can be illustrated by adapting the tariff diagram we have already developed in Figure 9.8.

A quota that limits imports to $Q_3 - Q_4$ would have effects that are very similar to those shown in the figure: Market price would rise to P_R; a substantial transfer from consumers to domestic producers would occur (area P_RBAP_W); and there would be deadweight losses represented by the colored triangles. With a quota, however, no revenues are collected by the government, so the loss of consumer surplus represented by area BE_2FC must go elsewhere. Often, governments are in the position to decide who the winners from quotas will be through import license programs. In Application 9.4: The Endless Saga of Steel Protectionism, we look at a situation in which a wide variety of protectionist devices have been used.

Nonquantitative restrictions such as health or other inspections also impose cost and time delays that are often treated as an "implicit" tariff on imports. For example, some European nations have tried to restrict U.S. beef imports, claiming that the growth hormones fed to American steers are harmful. Japan restricts many foreign pharmaceuticals until they are tested on Japanese patients. Figure 9.8 can easily be adapted to illustrate the effects of these costly impediments to trade.

On March 6, 2002, President Bush announced that the United States would adopt a "temporary" tariff on steel imports. This tariff amounted to 30 percent on many major steel products such as flat rolled steel and steel bars. Other products were to be taxed at somewhat lower rates—ranging from 8 to 15 percent. Two reasons were stated for the adoption of such large tariffs: (1) that some relief from foreign competition was needed to give the U.S. industry time to adapt to new market realities; and (2) that many foreign governments subsidize their steel industries and that tariffs were needed to "level the playing field." Before discussing whether either of these arguments will withstand scrutiny, let's look at the history of protectionism in this industry.

Using Every Trick in the Protectionist Book

It would be hard to find an industry that has had the degree of special protection from trade pressures that has characterized the U.S steel industry. Over the past 30 years, U.S. steel producers have succeeded in getting the following protectionist measures enacted: (1) import quotas; (2) minimum price agreements with exporters; (3) "voluntary" export restraints by nations that import into the United States; and (4) temporary tariffs. In addition, steel firms have filed any number of lawsuits against exporting nations alleging "unfair" trade practices and the firms themselves have been the beneficiaries of various loan guarantee and other subsidy programs. Often, such policies have been supported on the basis of the "importance" of the steel industry to the U.S. economy—sometimes stressing the national defense uses of steel. Because these arguments have been used many times before and are wearing a bit thin, they did not characterize the debate in 2002, however.

Assessing New Arguments for Steel Protection

The argument that the steel industry needs "breathing room" from foreign competition in order to adapt its technology to new market realities seems to be fallacious. The industry is indeed plagued by old-style blast furnace technology. But adopting tariffs will simply raise prices and allow firms that own this old technology to cover average costs. In the absence of such protection, the older plants would be closed and U.S. firms would have an incentive to adopt newer technologies that focus mainly on recycling scrap steel. The notion that foreign producers are selling steel in the United States at below cost is equally bogus. As a matter of economic logic, foreign firms would have no interest in serving a market where price did not cover average (or, perhaps, marginal) cost. On more practical grounds, U.S. "antidumping" laws are notorious for their poor methodologies used to measure whether prices really do exceed costs. And purported "subsidies" by foreign governments (to the extent they exist at all) are probably much smaller than the subsidies U.S. firms receive.

Effects of the Tariffs

Economists who study the steel industry have concluded that the costs[1] of the 2002 tariffs to the overall economy could be quite large. Estimated tariff revenues are about $900 million

---

[1] All of the figures here are calculated from G. C. Hufbauer and B. Goodrich, "Time for a Grand Bargain in Steel?" Institute for International Economics, 2002. The precise value of these estimates depends importantly on the details of how the steel tariffs were enacted—details that were not known when the estimates were made The full report is available on the IIE Web site *http://www.iie.com*

(continued)

annually, and the gains in domestic producer surplus might amount to another $700 million. Balanced against this would be estimated losses of about $2.5 billion in consumer surplus. Overall then, there might be an annual deadweight loss of perhaps $900 million from the tariffs. One popular way of conceptualizing what these numbers might mean is to compare them to the increased employment in the steel industry as a result of the tariffs. A median estimate of this employment gain is about 5,000. Hence, the tariff package costs consumers about $500,000 per "job saved." Of course, some of this loss will flow back to the government in the form of tariff revenue and to producers in the form of profits. The overall deadweight loss to the economy then amounts to about $140,000 per job.

To Think About

1. It the steel tariffs are such an economic mistake, why do you think President Bush supported them?
2. Steel firms argue that they have large "legacy costs" in terms of pensions promised to workers at their older plants. Tariffs would help them to pay those costs. How might the promise of tariff protection affect bargaining for pension benefits in the future?

SUMMARY

In this chapter we have shown how the competitive model of supply and demand can be used to investigate a wide range of actual economic activities and policies. Some of the general lessons from these applications include:

- The concepts *consumer* and *producer surplus* provide useful ways of analyzing the effects of economic changes on the welfare of market participants. Changes in consumer surplus represent changes in the overall utility consumers receive from consuming a particular good. Changes in producer surplus represent changes in the returns producers receive.

- In the short run, producer surplus represents the coverage of fixed costs plus whatever profits are received. In the long run, producer surplus represents the extra returns that inputs enjoy relative to a situation where no output of the good is produced.

- Ricardian rent is one type of producer surplus in which owners of low-cost firms receive long-run profits.

- In some cases, the long-run competitive equilibrium represents an economically efficient allocation of resources—it maximizes the sum of consumer and producer surplus.[7]

- Price controls involve both transfers between producers and consumers and losses of transactions that could benefit both consumers and producers.

- Tax incidence analysis concerns the determination of which market participants ultimately bear the burden of a tax. In general this incidence falls mainly on participants who exhibit inelastic responses to price changes. Taxes also involve deadweight losses in addition to the burden imposed by the actual tax revenues collected.

- Trade restrictions create both transfers between consumers and producers and deadweight losses of economic welfare. The effects of many types of trade restrictions can be modeled as being equivalent to a tariff.

[7] This conclusion is expanded upon in the appendix to this chapter.

REVIEW QUESTIONS

1. Early in Chapter 1, we defined *economics* as "the study of the allocation of scarce resources among alternative end uses." How does the observation that a competitive equilibrium exhausts all mutually beneficial transactions relate to this definition? What "scarce resources" are being allocated by competitive markets? How are "alternative end uses" reflected by demand and supply curves?

2. A fledgling microeconomics student is having some trouble grasping the concept of short-run producer surplus. In exasperation, he blurts out, "This is absolute nonsense. I can understand that producer surplus is a good thing for firms because it measures the improvement in their welfare relative to a situation where they cannot participate in the market. But then I'm told that fixed costs are a component of short-run producer surplus. Aren't fixed costs a bad thing? They must be paid! How can they be one component of a good thing?" Can you set this student straight? (*Hint:* When is short-run producer surplus zero?)

3. "The size of producer surplus in the long run is ultimately determined by the elasticity of supply for the inputs to an industry." Use a series of graphs of both inputs' and goods' markets to explain this statement.

4. Suppose that all operators of fast-food restaurants must rent the land for their establishments from other landowners. All other aspects of the costs of fast-food establishments are identical. Why would rents differ among fast-food locations? Would these differences in rents necessarily cause differences in the prices of fast food? What do you make of the claim by Mr. Z that "I simply can't make a go of my McDonald's outlet on the interstate—the landowner just wants too much rent"?

5. Would price controls involve welfare losses even in the constant cost case? What economic process would such controls short-circuit even in this case? Who would experience the welfare losses you describe?

6. "Firms don't pay taxes, only people pay taxes" is a favorite slogan of *The Wall Street Journal*. But our analysis in this chapter shows that in the long run (with an upward-sloping supply curve) at least some portion of a unit tax is paid out of producer surplus. Is *The Wall Street Journal* wrong in this case?

7. Use a graphical analysis similar to Figure 9.6 to show that the allocation resulting from a per-unit subsidy also results in a deadweight loss. Explain in detail who loses what in this case.

8. It is difficult if not impossible to rent television sets in the United States. But this is a market for which standard supply-demand analysis surely applies. How might you explain the absence of this presumably beneficial market? (*Hint:* Why might transactions costs be high in the television rental case? Why is there a limit to the transactions costs that the market might absorb?)

9. Figure 9.8 shows that some part of the loss consumers suffer as a result of a tariff is transferred to domestic producers. Exactly how does this happen? Who gains from tariff protection? More specifically, who will gain from the steel tariffs discussed in Application 9.4.

10. Suppose that a nation institutes a costly inspection program on one of its imported goods. How would this affect equilibrium in the imported goods market? Explain how the various areas identified in Figure 9.8 should be interpreted in this circumstance.

PROBLEMS

9.1 Suppose that the demand for broccoli is given by

$$\text{Demand: } Q = 1,000 - 5P$$

where Q is quantity per year measured in hundreds of bushels and P is price in dollars per hundred bushels. The long-run supply curve for broccoli is given by

$$\text{Supply: } Q = 4P - 80$$

a. Show that the equilibrium quantity here is Q = 400. At this output, what is the equilibrium price? How much in total is spent on broccoli? What is consumer surplus at this equilibrium? What is producer surplus at this equilibrium?
b. How much in total consumer and producer surplus would be lost if Q = 300 instead of Q = 400?
c. Show how the allocation of the loss of total consumer and producer surplus between suppliers and demanders described in part b depends on the price at which broccoli is sold. How would the loss be shared if P = 140? How about if P = 95?
d. What would the total loss of consumer and producer surplus be if Q = 450 rather than Q = 400? Show that the size of this total loss also is independent of the price at which the broccoli is sold.
e. Graph your results.

9.2 The handmade snuffbox industry is composed of 100 identical firms, each having short-run total costs given by

$$\text{STC} = 0.5q^2 + 10q + 5$$

and short-run marginal costs by

$$\text{SMC} = q + 10$$

where q is the output of snuffboxes per day.
a. What is the short-run supply curve for each snuffbox maker? What is the short-run supply curve for the market as a whole?
b. Suppose the demand for total snuffbox production is given by

$$Q = 1,100 - 50P$$

What is the equilibrium in this marketplace? What is each firm's total short-run profit?
c. Graph the market equilibrium and compute total producer surplus in this case.
d. Show that the total producer surplus you calculated in part c is equal to total industry profits plus industry short-run fixed costs.

9.3 The perfectly competitive videotape copying industry is composed of many firms who can copy five tapes per day at an average cost of $10 per tape. Each firm must also pay a royalty to film studios, and the per-film royalty rate (r) is an increasing function of total industry output (Q) given by

$$r = .002Q$$

a. Graph this royalty "supply" curve with r as a function of Q.
b. Suppose the daily demand for copied tapes is given by

$$\text{Demand: } Q = 1,050 - 50P$$

Assuming the industry is in long-run equilibrium, what is the equilibrium price and quantity of copied tapes? How many tape firms are there? What is the per-film royalty rate? (Hint: Use P = AC. Now AC = 10 + .002Q.)
c. Suppose that the demand for copied tapes increases to

$$\text{Demand: } Q = 1,600 - 50P$$

Now, what is the long-run equilibrium price and quantity for copied tapes? How many tape firms are there? What is the per-film royalty rate?
d. Graph these long-run equilibria in the tape market and calculate the increase in producer surplus between the situations described in part b and part c.
e. Use the royalty supply curve graphed in part a to show that the increase in producer surplus is precisely equal to the increase in royalties paid as Q expands incrementally from its level in part b to its level in part c.

9.4 Consider again the market for broccoli described in problem 9.1.

a. Suppose demand for broccoli shifted outward to

Demand: $Q = 1,270 - 5P$

What would be the new equilibrium price and quantity in this market?

b. What would be the new levels of consumer and producer surplus in this market?

c. Suppose the government had prevented the price of broccoli from rising from its equilibrium level of problem 9.1. Describe how the consumer- and producer-surplus measures described in part b would be reallocated or lost entirely.

d. Return now to the original demand curve in Problem 9.1. Suppose that the government instituted a $45-per-hundred-bushel tax on broccoli.

   i. How would this tax affect equilibrium in the broccoli market?

   ii. How would this tax burden be shared between buyers and sellers of broccoli?

   iii. What is the excess burden of this tax?

9.5 Suppose that the government imposed a $3 tax on snuffboxes in the industry described in problem 9.2.

a. How would this tax change the market equilibrium?

b. How would the burden of this tax be shared between snuffbox buyers and sellers?

c. Calculate the total loss of producer surplus as a result of the taxation of snuffboxes. Show that this loss equals the change in total short-run profits in the snuffbox industry. Why don't fixed costs enter into this computation of the change in short-run producer surplus?

9.6 Suppose that the government institutes a $5.50-per-film tax on the film copying industry described in problem 9.3.

a. Assuming that the demand for copied films is that given in part c of problem 9.3, how does this tax affect the market equilibrium?

b. How is the burden of this tax allocated between consumers and producers? What is the loss of consumer and producer surplus?

c. Show that the loss of producer surplus as a result of this tax is borne completely by the film studios. Explain your results intuitively.

9.7 The domestic demand for portable radios is given by

Demand: $Q = 5,000 - 100P$

where price P is measured in dollars and quantity Q is measured in thousands of radios per year. The domestic supply curve for radios is given by

Supply: $Q = 150P$

a. What is the domestic equilibrium in the portable radio market?

b. Suppose portable radios can be imported at a world price of $10 per radio. If trade were unencumbered, what would the new market equilibrium be? How many portable radios would be produced domestically? How many portable radios would be imported?

c. If domestic portable radio producers succeeded in getting a $5 tariff implemented, how would this change the market equilibrium? How much would be collected in tariff revenues? How much consumer surplus would be transferred to domestic producers? What would the deadweight loss from the tariff be?

d. Graph your results.

e. How would your results for this problem be changed if the government reached an agreement with foreign suppliers to limit "voluntarily" the portable radios they export to 1,250,000 per year? Explain how this differs from the case of a tariff.

Note: Problem 9.8 through problem 9.10 use the simple general equilibrium model described in the Appendix to Chapter 9.

9.8 Suppose the production possibility frontier for cheeseburgers (C) and milk shakes (M) is given by

$C + 2M = 600$

a. Graph this function.

b. Assuming that people prefer to eat two cheeseburgers with every milkshake, how much of each product will be produced? Indicate this point on your graph.

c. Given that this fast-food economy is operating efficiently, what price ratio (P_C/P_M) must prevail?

9.9 Suppose the production possibility frontier for guns (X) and butter (Y) is given by

$$X^2 + 2Y^2 = 900$$

a. Graph this frontier.

b. If individuals always prefer consumption bundles in which Y = 2X, how much X and Y will be produced?

c. What price ratio will cause production to take place at the point described in part b? This slope should be approximated by considering small changes in X and Y around the optimal point.

d. Show your solution on the figure from part a.

9.10 Robinson Crusoe obtains utility from the quantity of fish he consumes in one day (F), the quantity of coconuts he consumes that day (C), and the hours of leisure time he has during the day (H) according to the utility fuction

$$Utility = F^{1/4} C^{1/4} H^{1/2}$$

Robinson's production of fish is given by

$$F = \sqrt{L_F}$$

(where L_F is the hours he spends fishing), and his production of coconuts is determined by

$$C = \sqrt{L_C}$$

(where L_C is the time he spends picking coconuts). Assuming that Robinson decides to work an 8-hour day (that is, H = 16), graph his production possibility curve for fish and coconuts. Show his optimal choices of those goods.

INTERNET EXERCISES

1. *Price controls in the market for human organs.* In August 1999, many visitors to the eBay auction site were astounded to see a listing by a Florida man auctioning off one of his kidneys. The starting bid was $25,000; and, within a week, the bid had reached almost $6 million dollars! Since the National Organ Transplant Act of 1984 prohibits the sale of human organs for transplantation, eBay quickly removed the listing. Effectively, by banning the sale of organs, the National Organ Transplant Act established a price ceiling on organs of zero. Of course, one can still donate an organ for free. In his April 18, 2001, *Reason Magazine* article, "The Case for Selling Human Organs," at *http://reason.com/rb/rb041801.shtml.* Ronald Bailey argues for a free-market solution to the shortage of organ availability. In 2000, how many organs were transplanted in the United States? How many people are on the organ donor transplantation list? On average, how many people die daily due to the shortage of organs? Using a supply and demand graph, show how the price ceiling of zero creates a shortage of human organs for transplantation. Since the quantity demanded for organs exceeds the quantity supplied with the price ceiling, a mechanism is required by which the available (donor) organs are allocated. This mechanism has been one based on urgency of need. Bailey suggests that we apply the "normal way to handle shortages" to the case of organs. Referring to your graph, explain what he means. Under Bailey's solution, do all those in need of organs receive them? What is the allocation mechanism in Bailey's proposal? Compare this mechanism to the existing one and discuss why it may explain strong resistance by some to Bailey's proposal.

2. *Tariffs.* When you last purchased a pair of sneakers, did you realize that you probably paid a higher price for them because of tariffs and other trade restrictions? Many goods imported into the United States are subjected to tariffs, particularly agricultural items. The U.S. International Trade Commission (ITC) publishes a comprehensive database of tariff rates and trade data. Go to the ITC home page at *http://www.usitc.gov.* Click on

DataWeb, then click on the Tariff Database for the most recent year. Click on "yes" to proceed to the database. First, in the box for listing items, type in "sweet corn." Then click on List Items. Look at the details for "sweet corn, fresh or chilled." What is the normal trade relations (or MFN) tariff rate for sweet corn? Now do the same for "eggs" (look at details for "birds' eggs, in shell, fresh, preserved, or cooked); "golf clubs"; and "sparkling wine." For sparkling wine, what was the customs value of imports for the most recent year given? What percentage of the total value came from France? Italy? Spain? Estimate the tariff revenue from sparkling wine imports (multiply the ad valorem equivalent by the total customs value). Use a graph similar to Figure 9.8 in your text to illustrate and explain how producer and consumer surplus and government revenue in the United States would be affected if the United States removed the tariff on sparkling wine. How would overall social welfare be affected?

General Equilibrium

In Chapter 8 and Chapter 9, we looked only at a single competitive market in isolation. We were not concerned with how things that happened in that one market might affect other markets. For many economic issues, this narrowing of focus is helpful—we need only look at what really interests us. For other issues, however, any detailed understanding requires that we look at how many related markets work. For example, if we wished to examine the effects of all federal taxes on the economy, we would need to look not only at a number of different product markets but also at markets for workers and for capital. Economists have developed both theoretical and empirical (computer) models for this purpose. These are called **general equilibrium models** because they seek to study market equilibrium in many markets at once. The models in Chapter 8 and Chapter 9, on the other hand, are called **partial equilibrium models** because they are concerned with studying equilibrium in only a single market. In this appendix, we take a very brief look at general equilibrium models. One purpose of this examination is to clarify further the concept of economic efficiency that we introduced in Chapter 9.

General equilibrium model
An economic model of a complete system of markets.

Partial equilibrium model
An economic model of a single market.

A PERFECTLY COMPETITIVE PRICE SYSTEM

The most common type of general equilibrium model assumes that the entire economy works through a series of markets like those we studied in Chapter 8 and Chapter 9. Not only are all goods allocated through millions of competitive markets but also all inputs have prices that are established through the workings of supply and demand. In all of these many markets, a few basic assumptions are assumed to hold:

- All individuals and firms take prices as given—they are price takers.
- All individuals maximize utility.
- All firms maximize profits.
- All individuals and firms are fully informed, there are no transactions costs, and there is no uncertainty.

These assumptions should be familiar to you. They are ones we have been making throughout this book. One consequence of the assumptions (and a few others) is that it can be shown that when all markets work this way they establish equilibrium prices[1] for all goods. That is, at these prices, quantity supplied equals quantity demanded in every market.

WHY IS GENERAL EQUILIBRIUM NECESSARY?

To see why we need a general model of this type, consider the market for tomatoes that we studied at the start of Chapter 9. Figure 9A.1(a) shows equilibrium in this market by the intersection of the demand curve for tomatoes (D) with the supply curve for tomatoes (S). Initially, the price of tomatoes is given by P_1. Figure 9A.1 also shows the markets for three other economic items that are related to the tomato market: (b) the market for tomato pickers; (c) the market for cucumbers (a substitute for tomatoes in salads); and (d) the market for cucumber pickers. All of these markets are initially in equilibrium. The prices in these various markets do not change unless something happens to shift one of the curves.

Disturbing the Equilibrium

Suppose now that such a change does occur. Imagine a situation where the government announces that tomatoes have been found to cure the common cold so everyone decides to eat more of them. An initial consequence of this discovery is that the demand for tomatoes will shift outward to D'. In our analysis in Chapter 8 and Chapter 9, this shift would cause the price of tomatoes to rise and that would be, more or less, the end of the story. Now, however, we wish to follow the repercussions of what has happened in the tomato market into the other markets shown in Figure 9A.1. A first possible reaction would be in the market for tomato pickers. Because tomato prices have risen, the demand for labor used to harvest tomatoes increases. The demand curve for labor in Figure 9A.1(b) shifts to D'. This tends to raise wages of tomato pickers, which, in turn, raises the costs of tomato growers. The supply curve for tomatoes (which, under perfect competition, just reflects growers' marginal costs) shifts to S'.

What happens to the market for cucumbers? Because people have an increased desire for tomatoes, they may reduce their demands for cucumbers because these tomato substitutes don't cure colds. The demand for cucumbers shifts inward to D', and cucumber prices fall. That reduces the demand for cucumber workers, and the wage associated with that occupation falls.

---

[1] Competitive markets can only establish relative, not absolute, prices. That is, these markets can only determine that one apple trades for two oranges, not whether apples and oranges cost $.50 and $.25 or $20 and $10. Absolute prices in an economy are determined by monetary factors that are usually studied in macroeconomics.

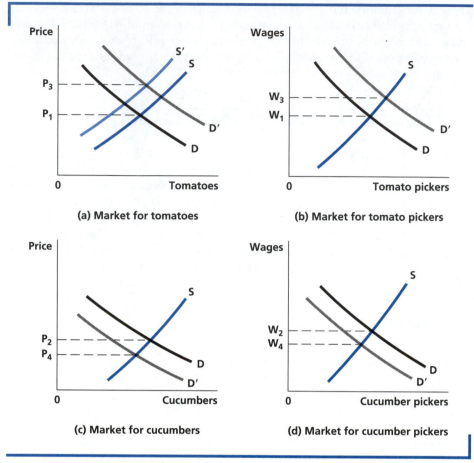

FIGURE 9A.1 The Market Cost for Tomatoes and Several Related Markets Initially, the market for tomatoes is in equilibrium (at P_1) as are the markets for tomato pickers, cucumbers, and cucumber pickers. An increase in demand for tomatoes disturbs these equilibria. Virtually all the supply and demand curves shift in the process of establishing a new general equilibrium.

Reestablishing Equilibrium

We could continue this story indefinitely. We could ask how the lower price of cucumbers affects the tomato market. Or we could ask whether cucumber pickers, discouraged by their falling wages, might consider picking tomatoes, shifting the supply of labor curve in Figure 9A.1(b) outward. To follow this chain of events further or to examine even more markets related to tomatoes would add little to out story. Eventually we would expect all four markets in Figure 9A.1 (and all the other markets we have not shown) to reach a new equilibrium, such as that illustrated by the lighter supply and demand curves in the figure. Once all the repercussions have been worked out, the final result would be a rise in tomato prices (to P_3), a rise in the wages of tomato pickers (to w_3), a fall in cucumber prices (to P_4), and a fall in the wages of cucumber pickers (to w_4). This is what we mean then by a smoothly working system of perfectly competitive markets. Following any disturbance, all the markets can eventually reestablish a new set of equilibrium prices at which quantity demanded is equal to quantity supplied in each market. These interconnections between markets are the subject of this appendix.

> **MicroQuiz 9A.1**
>
> Why are there two supply curves in Figure 9A.1(a)? How does this illustrate "feedback" effects? Why would a partial equilibrium analysis of the effect of an increase in demand for tomatoes from D to D' give the wrong answer?

A SIMPLE GENERAL EQUILIBRIUM MODEL

One way to give the flavor of general equilibrium analysis is to look at a simple model of two goods—the ever-popular X and Y. The "supply" conditions for these two goods are shown by the production possibility frontier PP' in Figure 9A.2. This curve shows the various combinations of X and Y that this economy can produce if its resources are employed efficiently.[2] Figure 9A.2 also shows a series of indifference curves representing the preferences of the consumers in this simple economy for the goods X and Y. These indifference curves represent the "demand" conditions in our model. Clearly, in this model, the best use of resources is achieved at point E where production is X*, Y*. This point provides the maximum utility that is available in this economy given the limitations imposed by scarce resources (as represented by the production possibility frontier). As in Chapter 9, we define this to be an **economically efficient allocation of resources.** Notice that this notion of efficiency really has two components. First, there is a "supply" component—X*, Y* is on the production possibility frontier. Any point inside the frontier would be inefficient because it would provide less utility than can be achieved in this situation. The efficiency of X*, Y* also has a "demand" component because, from among all those points on PP', this allocation of resources provides greatest utility. This reinforces the notion that the goal of economic activity is to improve the welfare of people. Here, people decide for themselves which allocation is the best.

Economically efficient allocation of resources
An allocation of resources in which the sum of consumer and producer surplus is maximized. Reflects the best (utility-maximizing) use of scarce resources.

---

[2] All of the points on PP' are sometimes referred to as being "technically efficient" in the sense that available inputs are fully employed and are being used in the right combinations by firms. For a detailed discussion of the conditions that must hold for such technical efficiency, see W. Nicholson, *Microeconomic Theory: Basic Principles and Extensions,* 8th ed. (Cincinnati: South-Western/ Thomson Learning, 2002): 423–430.

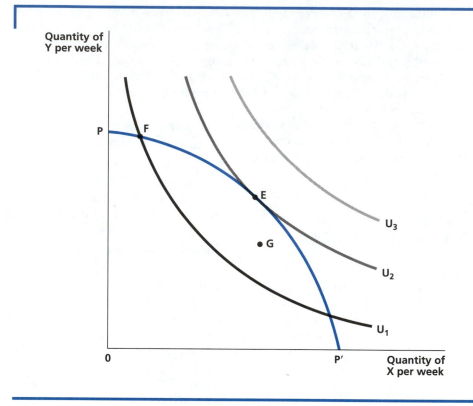

FIGURE 9A.2 **Efficiency of Output Mix** In this economy, the production possibility frontier represents those combinations of X and Y that can be produced. Every point on it is efficient in a technical sense. However, only the output combination at point E is a true utility maximum for the typical person. Only this point represents an economically efficient allocation of resources.

THE EFFICIENCY OF PERFECT COMPETITION

Fundamental theorem of welfare economics
A perfectly competitive price system will bring about an economically efficient allocation of resources.

In this simple model, the "economic problem" is how to achieve this efficient allocation of resources. One of the most important discoveries of modern welfare economics is to show that, under certain conditions, competitive markets can bring about this result. Because of the importance of this conclusion, it is sometimes called the **fundamental theorem of welfare economics**. This "theorem" is simply a generalization of the efficiency result we described in Chapter 9 to many markets. Although a general proof of the theorem requires a lot of mathematics, we can give a glimpse of that proof by seeing how the efficient allocation shown in Figure 9A.2 might be achieved through competitive markets.

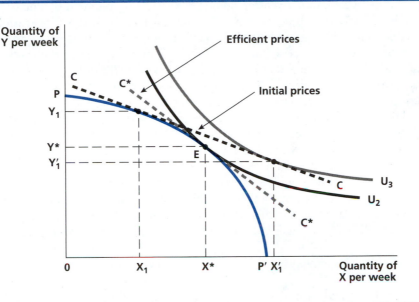

FIGURE 9A.3 How Perfectly Competitive Prices Bring about Efficiency With an arbitrary initial price ratio, firms will produce X_1, Y_1 society's budget, constraint will be given by line CC. With this budget constraint, individuals demand X_1', Y_1 that is, there is an excess demand for good X_1 ($X_1' - X_1$) and an excess supply of good Y_1 ($Y_1 - Y_1'$). The workings of the market will move these prices toward their equilibrium levels P_x^*, P_y^*. At those prices, society's budget constraint will be given by the line C*C* and supply and demand will be in equilibrium. The combination X^*, Y^* of goods will be chosen, and this allocation is efficient.

In Figure 9A.3, we have redrawn the production possibility frontier and indifference curves from Figure 9A.2. Now assume that goods X and Y are traded in perfectly competitive markets and that the initial prices of the goods are P_X and P_Y, respectively. With these prices, profit-maximizing firms will choose to produce X_1, Y_1 because, from among all the combinations of X and Y on the production possibility frontier, this one provides maximum revenue and profits.[3]

Suppose that an economy produces only the two goods, left shoes (X) and right shoes (Y). Individuals only want to consume these in combinations for which X = Y.

1. Which point (points) on the production possibility frontier would be economically efficient?

2. Why would a point on the production possibility frontier for which X = 2Y be inefficient?

[3] The point provides maximum revenue because the prices of X and Y determine the slope of the line CC, which represents total revenue for the firm ($P_X X + P_Y Y$), and this line is as far from the origin as possible given that production must take place on PP'. But the production possibility frontier assumes that input usage is fixed everywhere on and inside the frontier. Hence, maximization of revenue also amounts to maximization of profits.

On the other hand, given the budget constraint represented by line CC, individuals collectively will demand X_1', Y_1'.[4] Consequently, at this price ratio, there is excess demand for good X (people want to buy more than is being produced), whereas there is an excess supply of good Y. The workings of the marketplace will cause P_X to rise and P_Y to fall. The price ratio P_X/P_Y will rise; the price line will move clockwise along the production possibility frontier. That is, firms will increase their production of good X and decrease their production of good Y. Similarly, people will respond to the changing prices by substituting Y for X in their consumption choices. The actions of both firms and individuals eliminate the excess demand for X and the excess supply of Y as market prices change.

Equilibrium is reached at X^*, Y^* with an equilibrium price ratio of P_X/P_X. With this price ratio, supply and demand are equilibrated for both good X and good Y. Firms, in maximizing their profits, given P_X and P_Y, will produce X^* and Y^*. Given the income that this level of production provides to people, they will purchase precisely X^* and Y^*. Not only have markets been equilibrated by the operation of the price system, but the resulting equilibrium is also economically efficient. As we showed previously, the equilibrium allocation X^*, Y^* provides the highest level of utility that can be obtained given the existing production possibility frontier. Figure 9A.3 provides a simple two-good general equilibrium proof of the first fundamental theorem of welfare economics.

MicroQuiz 9A.3

Draw simply supply and demand curve models for determining the prices of X and Y in Figure 13.4. Show the "disequilibrium" points X_1 and X_1' on your diagram for good X and points Y1 and Y_1' on your diagram for good Y. Describe how *both* of these markets reach equilibrium simultaneously.

Prices, Efficiency, and Laissez-Faire Economics

We have shown that a perfectly competitive price system, by relying on the self-interest of people and of firms and by utilizing the information carried by equilibrium prices, can arrive at an economically efficient allocation of resources. This finding provides some "scientific" support for the laissez-faire position taken by many economists. For example, take Adam Smith's assertion that

The natural effort of every individual to better his own condition, when suffered to exert itself with freedom and security, is so powerful a principle that it is alone,

---

[4] It is important to recognize why the budget constraint has this location. Because P_X and P_Y are given, the value of total production is

$$P_X \cdot X_1 + P_Y \cdot Y_1$$

This is the value of total output in the simple economy pictured in Figure 9A.3. Because of the accounting identity "value of income = value of output," this is also the total income accruing to people in society. Society's budget constraint passes through X_1, Y_1 and has a slope of $-P_X/P_Y$. This is precisely the line labeled CC in the figure.

and without any assistance, not only capable of carrying on the society to wealth and prosperity, but of surmounting a hundred impertinent obstructions with which the folly of human laws too often encumbers its operations. . . .[5]

This statement has been shown to have considerable theoretical validity. As Smith noted, it is not the public spirit of the baker that provides bread for people to eat. Rather, bakers (and other producers) operate in their own self-interest in responding to market signals (Smith's invisible hand). In so doing, their actions are coordinated by the market into an efficient, overall pattern. The market system, at least in this simple model, imposes a very strict logic on how resources are used.

That efficiency theorem raises many important questions about the ability of markets to arrive at these perfectly competitive prices and about whether the theorem should act as a guide for government policy (for example, should governments avoid interfering in international markets as suggested by Application 9A.1: Gains from Free Trade and the NAFTA Debate?).

WHY MARKETS FAIL TO ACHIEVE ECONOMIC EFFICIENCY

Showing that perfect competition is economically efficient depends crucially on all of the assumptions that underlie the competitive model. In this section we examine some of the conditions that may prevent markets from generating an efficient allocation.

Imperfect Competition

Imperfect competition in a broad sense includes all those situations in which economic actors (that is, buyers or sellers) exert some market power in determining price. The essential aspect of all such situations is that marginal revenue is different from market price since the firm is no longer a price taker. Because of this, relative prices will no longer accurately reflect marginal costs and the price system no longer carries the information about costs necessary to ensure efficiency. The deadweight loss from monopoly that we study in Chapter 10 is a good measure of this inefficiency.

Imperfect competition
A market situation in which buyers or sellers have some influence on the prices of goods or services.

Externalities

A price system can also fail to allocate resources efficiently when there are relationships among firms or between firms and people that are not adequately represented by market prices. Examples of such occurrences are numerous. Perhaps

[5] Adam Smith, *The Wealth of Nations* (1776; reprint, New York: Random House, Modern Library ed., 1937), 508.

Gains from Free Trade and the NAFTA Debate

Following the Napoleonic Wars, high tariffs on grain imports were imposed by the British government. Debate over the effects of these "Corn Laws" dominated politics in Great Britain from 1820 to 1845. A principal focus of the debate concerned the effect that elimination of tariffs would have on the welfare of British consumers and on the incomes of various groups in society. This debate was repeated more than 150 years later with regard to passage of the North American Free Trade Agreement (NAFTA).

Theory of the Corn Laws Debate

The production possibility frontier in Figure 1 shows those combinations of grain (X) and manufactured goods (Y) that could be produced, say, by English factors of production. Assuming (somewhat contradictory to fact) that the Corn Laws completely prevented trade, market equilibrium would be at E with the domestic, pretrade price ratio shown in the figure. Removal of the tariffs would reduce this price ratio to the price ratio that prevailed in the rest of the world. Given that new ratio, England would produce combination A and consume combination B. Grain imports would amount to $X_B - X_A$ and these would be financed by exporting manufactured goods equal to $Y_A - Y_B$. Overall, the opening of trade increases the level of utility from U_2 to U_3. Hence, there may be substantial welfare gains from trade.

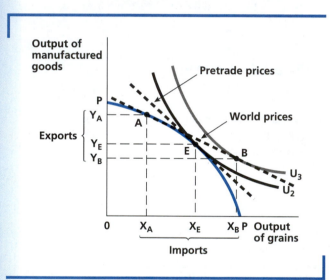

FIGURE 1 **Analysis of the Corn Laws Debate** Reduction of tariff barriers on grain would cause production to be reallocated from point E to point A. Consumption would be reallocated from E to B. If grain production were relatively capital intensive, the relative price of capital would fall as a result of these reallocations.

The movement from point E to point A in Figure 1 may also affect input prices. If we assume that grain production is relatively capital intensive (that is, it uses a lot of land), the movement from A to E causes the ratio of land to labor to rise in both industries. This will, in turn, cause the relative price of land to fall (since, effectively, each acre of land now has fewer workers on it). Hence, this analysis suggests that repeal of the Corn Laws would be harmful to landowners and helpful to workers. It is not surprising, therefore, that landed interests fought repeal of these laws.

Modern Resistance to Trade

That trade policies may affect the relative incomes of various factors of production continues to exert a major influence on political debates about such policies. In the United States, for example, exports tend to be intensive in their use of skilled labor, whereas imports tend to be intensive in unskilled labor input. By analogy to our discussion of the Corn Laws, it might be expected that freer trade policies would result in rising relative wages for skilled workers and in falling relative wages for unskilled workers. It is not surprising that unions representing skilled workers (such as machinists, agricultural equipment workers, and petroleum and atomic workers) tend to favor free trade, whereas unions of unskilled workers (those in textiles, shoes, and related businesses) tend to oppose it.

Adjustment Costs

There is another reason why workers in firms that produce imported goods may be opposed to movement toward more open world trade. The reallocation of production from point E to point A in Figure 1 requires that factors of production be transferred out of X (import) production into Y (export) production. Making such a reallocation may impose costs on workers. They may have to move to new communities, search for new jobs, or learn new skills. All of these activities are costly to the individuals involved. Even though society as a whole benefits from trade expansion (overall utility increases from U_2 to U_3), individual workers may not be so lucky.

The NAFTA Debate

Issues that arose in the debate over the Corn Laws have surrounded every major change in trade policy since then. A recent example is the 1993 debate over adoption of the North American Free Trade Agreement (NAFTA). Perhaps the most dramatic confrontation was the televised debate between Vice President Albert Gore and Ross Perot on the Larry King Show. In that debate, Perot again made reference to the "giant sucking sound" of jobs being drawn to Mexico as a result of the agreement. Not to be outdone, Gore presented the "protectionist" Perot with a framed picture of the sponsors of the notorious (and damaging) Smoot-Hawley Tariff of 1930. Our analysis suggests that each participant had a point. The agreement may indeed negatively affect low-wage workers as the United States increasingly imports goods produced by less-skilled workers. But it also promises welfare improvements to all consumers who can obtain such goods at lower prices. Most studies of these effects have found the agreement's positive effects are much larger than its negative ones. Indeed, some computer models suggest the increased trade brought about under the agreement may even improve the prospects of many low-wage workers in the United States by making labor markets more competitive.[1]

To Think About

1. The preceding example shows that the typical consumer gains from the opening of trade. Use Figure 1 to discuss under what circumstances these gains would be relatively large. When might they be small or nonexistent? Is it possible that the opening of trade might actually make the typical consumer worse off?
2. Figure 1 shows that a nation will tend to export goods that have a lower relative price domestically than they do in the international market (in this case, good Y). What will determine such differences in relative prices—that is, what factors determine a country's "comparative advantage" in international trade?

[1]See Nora Lustig, Barry Bosworth, and Robert Lawrence, eds., *North American Free Trade* (Washington, DC: The Brookings Institution, 1992).

the most common is the case of a firm that pollutes the air with industrial smoke and other debris. This is called an **externality.** It is an effect of the firm's activities on people's well-being that is not taken directly into account through the normal operation of the price system. The basic problem with externalities is that firms' private costs no longer correctly reflect the social costs of production. In the absence of externalities, the costs a firm incurs accurately measure social costs. The prices of the resources the firm uses represent all the opportunity costs involved in production. When a firm creates externalities, however, there are additional costs—those that arise from the external damage. The fact that pollution from burning coal to produce steel causes diseases and general dirt and grime is as much a cost of production as are the wages paid to the firm's workers. However, the firm responds only to private input costs of steel production in deciding how much steel to produce. It disregards the social costs of its pollution. This results in a gap between market price and (social) marginal cost and therefore leads to a misallocation of resources. In Chapter 16, we look at this issue in some detail.

Externality
The effect of one party's economic activities on another party that is not taken into account by the price system.

Public Goods

A third failure of the price system to yield an efficient allocation of resources stems from the existence of goods that can be provided to users at zero marginal cost and must be provided on a nonexclusive basis to everyone. Such goods include national defense, control of infectious diseases, provision of justice, and pest control. The distinguishing features of these goods are that providing benefits to one more person costs nothing (the goods are "nonrival") and that they provide benefits to everyone. Once the goods are produced, it is impossible (or at least very costly) to exclude anyone from benefiting from them. In such a case, price cannot equal marginal cost (which is zero) since then the fixed cost of providing the good would not be covered. There is also an incentive for each person to refuse to pay for the good in the hope that others will purchase it and thereby provide benefits to all. The pervasive nature of this incentive ensures that not enough resources are allocated to public goods. To avoid this underallocation, communities (or nations) may decide to have the government produce these goods and finance this production through compulsory taxation. For that reason, such goods are frequently termed **public goods.** In Chapter 16, we also treat the problems raised by public goods in detail.

Public goods
Goods that are both nonexclusive and nonrival.

Imperfect Information

Throughout our discussion of the connection between perfect competition and economic efficiency, we have been implicitly assuming that the economic actors involved are fully informed. The most important kind of information they are assumed to have is a knowledge of equilibrium market prices. If for some reason markets are unable to establish these prices or if demanders or suppliers do not know what these prices are, the types of "invisible hand" results we developed may not hold. Consider, for example, the problem that any consumer faces in trying to buy a new television receiver. Not only does he or she have to make some kind of judgment about the quality of various brands (to determine what the available "goods" actually are) but this would-be buyer also faces the problem of finding out what various sellers are charging for a particular set. All of these kinds of problems have been assumed away so far by treating goods as being homogeneous and having a universally known market price. As we will see in Chapter 15, if such assumptions do not hold, the efficiency of perfectly competitive markets is more problematic.

EFFICIENCY AND EQUITY

So far in this chapter we have discussed the concept of economic efficiency and whether an efficient allocation of resources can be achieved through reliance on market forces. We have not mentioned questions of **equity** or fairness in the way goods are distributed among people. In this section, we briefly take up this question. We show not only that it is very difficult to define what an equitable distribution of resources is but also that there is no reason to expect that allocations that result from a competitive price system (or from practically any other method of allocating resources, for that mater) will be equitable.

> **Equity**
> The fairness of the distribution of goods or utility.

Defining and Achieving Equity

A primary problem with developing an accepted definition of "fair" or "unfair" allocations of resources is that not everyone agrees as to what the concept means. Some people might call any allocation "fair" providing no one breaks any laws in arriving at it—these people would call only acquisition of goods by theft "unfair." Others may base their notions of fairness on a dislike for inequality. Only allocations in which people receive about the same levels of utility (assuming these levels could be measured and compared) would be regarded as fair. On a more practical level, some people think the current distribution of income and wealth in the United States is reasonably fair whereas others regard it as drastically unfair. Welfare economists have devised a number of more specific definitions, but these tend to give conflicting conclusions about which resource allocations are or are not equitable. There is simply no agreement on this issue.[6]

---

[6] For a discussion of some recent thinking on this topic, see Amartya Sen's 1998 Nobel Prize Speech, reprinted in A. Sen, "The Possibility of Social Choice," *American Economic Review* (June 1999): 349–378.

Equity and Competitive Markets

Even if everyone agreed on what a fair allocation of resources (and, ultimately, of people's utility) is, there would still be the question of how such a situation should be achieved. Can we rely on voluntary transactions among people to achieve fairness, or will something more be required? Some introspection may suggest why voluntary solutions will not succeed. If people start out with an unequal distribution of goods, voluntary trading cannot necessarily erase that inequality. Those who are initially favored will not voluntarily agree to make themselves worse off. Similar lessons apply to participation in competitive market transactions. Since these are voluntary, they may not be able to erase initial inequalities, even while promoting efficient outcomes. In the next section, we look at a model that shows this importance of initial endowments.

Adopting coercive methods to achieve equity may involve problems too. For example, in several places in this book, we have shown how taxes may affect people's behavior and result in efficiency losses that arise from this distortion. Using government's power to transfer income may therefore be a costly activity; achieving equity may involve important losses of efficiency. Making decisions about equity-efficiency trade-offs is a major source of political controversy throughout the world.

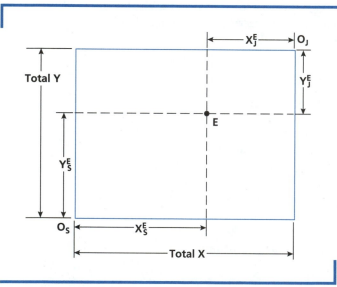

FIGURE 9A.4 Edgeworth Box Diagram The Edgeworth box diagram permits all possible allocations of two goods (X and Y) to be visualized. If we consider the corner O_S to be Smith's "origin" and O_J to be Jones's, then the allocation represented by point E would have Smith getting X_S^E and Y_S^E, and Jones would receive what is left over (X_J^E, Y_J^E). One purpose of this diagram is to discover which of the possible locations within the box can be reached through voluntary exchange.

THE EDGEWORTH BOX DIAGRAM FOR EXCHANGE

Problems in achieving equity voluntarily can be illustrated with a graphic device called the Edgeworth box diagram. In this diagram, a box is used that has dimensions given by the total quantities of two goods (we'll call these goods simply X and Y). The horizontal dimension of the box represents the total quantity of X available, whereas the vertical height of the box is the total quantity of Y. These dimensions are shown in Figure 9A.4. The point O_S is considered to be the origin for the first person (call her Smith). Quantities of X are measured along the horizontal axis rightward from O_S; quantities of Y, along the vertical axis upward from O_S. Any point in the box can be regarded as some allocation of X and Y to Smith. For example, at point E, Smith gets X_S^E and Y_S^E. The useful property of the Edgeworth box is that the quantities received by the second person (say, Jones) are also recorded by point E. Jones simply gets that part of the total quantity that is left over. In fact, we can regard Jones's quantities as being measured from the origin O_J. Point E therefore also corresponds to the quantities X_J^E and Y_J^E for Jones. Notice that the quantities assigned to Smith and Jones in this manner exactly exhaust the total quantities of X and Y available.

Mutually Beneficial Trades

Any point in the Edgeworth box represents an allocation of the available goods between Smith and Jones, and all possible allocations are contained somewhere in the box. To discover which of the allocations offer mutually beneficial trades, we must introduce these people's preferences. In Figure 9A.5, Smith's indifference curve map is drawn with origin O_S. Movements in a northeasterly direction

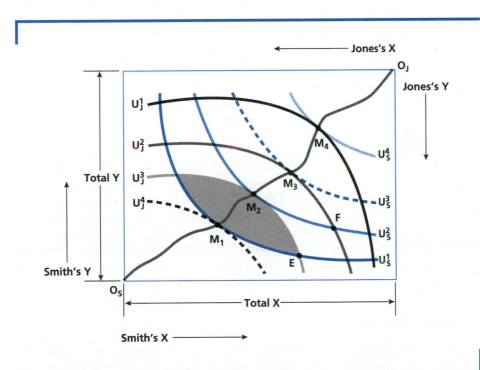

FIGURE 9A.5 Edgeworth Box Diagram of Pareto Efficiency in Exchange The points on the curve O_S, O_J are efficient in the sense that at these allocations Smith cannot be made better off without making Jones worse off, and vice versa. An allocation such as E, on the other hand, is inefficient because both Smith and Jones can be made better off by choosing to move into the shaded area. Notice that along O_S, O_J the MRS for Smith is equal to that for Jones. The line O_S, O_J is called the *contract curve*.

represent higher levels of utility to Smith. In the same figure, Jones's indifference curve map is drawn with the corner O_J as an origin. We have taken Jones's indifference curve map, rotated it 180 degrees, and fit it into the northeast corner of the Edgeworth box. Movements in a southwesterly direction represent increases in Jones's utility level.

Using these superimposed indifference curve maps, we can identify the allocations from which some mutually beneficial trades might be made. Any point for which the MRS for Smith is unequal to that for Jones represents such an opportunity. Consider an arbitrary initial allocation such as point E in Figure 9A.5. This point lies on the point of intersection of Smith's indifference curve U^1_S and Jones's indifference curve U^3_J. Obviously, the marginal rates of substitution (the slopes of the indifference curves) are not equal at E. Any allocation in the oval-shaped area in Figure 9A.5 represents a mutually beneficial trade for these two people—they can both move to a higher level of utility by adopting a trade that moves them into this area.

Efficiency in Exchange

When the marginal rates of substitution of Smith and Jones are equal, however, such mutually beneficial trades are not available. The points M_1, M_2, M_3, and M_4 in Figure 9A.5 indicate tangencies of these individuals' indifference curves, and movement away from such points must make at least one of the people worse off. A move from M_2 to E, for example, reduces Smith's utility from U^2_S to U^1_S, even though Jones is made no worse off by the move. Alternatively, a move from M_2 to F makes Jones worse off but keeps the Smith utility level constant. In general, then, these points of tangency do not offer the promise of additional mutually beneficial trading. Such points are called **Pareto efficient allocations** after the Italian scientist Vilfredo Pareto (1878–1923), who pioneered in the development of the formal theory of exchange. Notice that the Pareto definition of efficiency does not require any interpersonal comparisons of utility; we never have to compare Jones's gains to Smith's losses or vice versa. Rather, individuals decide for themselves whether particular trades improve utility. For efficient allocations, there are no such additional trades to which both parties would agree.

Pareto efficient allocation
An allocation of available resources in which no mutually beneficial trading opportunities are unexploited. That is, an allocation in which no one person can be made better off without someone else being made worse off.

Contract curve
The set of efficient allocations of the existing goods in an exchange situation. Points off that curve are necessarily inefficient, since individuals can be made unambiguously better off by moving to the curve.

Contract Curve

The set of all the efficient allocations in an Edgeworth box diagram is called the **contract curve**. In Figure 9A.5, this set of points is represented by the line running from O_S to O_J and includes the tangencies M_1, M_2, M_3, and M_4 (and many other such tangencies). Points off the contract curve (such as E or F) are inefficient, and mutually beneficial trades are possible. But, as its name implies, moving onto the contract curve exhausts all such mutually beneficial trading opportunities. A move along the contract curve (say, from M_1 to M_2) does not represent a mutually beneficial trade since there will always be a winner (Smith) and a loser (Jones).

Efficiency and Equity

The Edgeworth box diagram not only permits a graphic description of efficiency, but also allows us to illustrate the problematic relationship between efficiency and equity. Suppose, for example, that everyone agreed that the only fair allocation is one of equal utilities. Perhaps everyone remembers his or her childhood experiences in dividing up a cake or candy bar where equal shares seemed to be the only reasonable solution. This desired allocation might be represented by point E in the Edgeworth exchange box in Figure 9A.6. On the other hand, suppose Smith and Jones start out at point A—at which Smith is in a fairly favorable situation. As we described previously, any allocation between M_2 and M_3 is preferable to point A because both people would be

> **MicroQuiz 9A.4**
>
> What would the contract curve look like in the following situations:
>
> **1.** Smith likes only good X and Jones likes only good Y.
>
> **2.** Smith and Jones both view X and Y as perfect complements.
>
> **3.** Smith and Jones are both always willing to substitute one unit of X for one unit of Y and remain equally well-off.

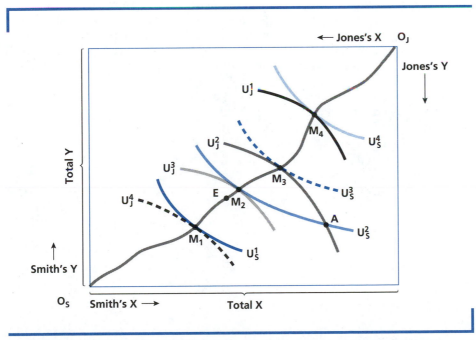

FIGURE 9A.6 Voluntary Transactions May Not Result in Equitable Allocations This Edgeworth box diagram for exchange is taken from Figure 9A.5. Point E represents a "fair" sharing of the available goods (assuming that can be defined). If individuals' initial endowments are at point A, voluntary transactions cannot be relied on to reach point E since such an allocation makes Smith worse off than at A.

Appendix

Initial endowments
The initial holdings of goods from which trading begins.

better off by voluntarily making such a move. In this case, however, the point of equal utility (E) does not fall in this range. Smith would not voluntarily agree to move to point E since that would make her worse off than at point A. Smith would prefer to refrain from any trading rather than accept the "fair" allocation E. In the language of welfare economics, the **initial endowments** (that is, the starting place for trading) of Smith and Jones are so unbalanced that voluntary agreements will not result in the desired equal allocation of utilities. If point E is to be achieved, some coercion (such as taxation) must be used to get Smith to accept it.

SUMMARY

This very brief introduction to general equilibrium theory suggests a few important conclusions that should be kept in mind as we look at the variety of single-market models in the remainder of this book:

- Any change in the equilibrium in one market can result in changes in the equilibria in many other markets. A general equilibrium model is required to study such interconnections among markets.
- An economically efficient allocation of resources in a situation with many goods consists of choosing that point on the production possibility frontier that provides greatest utility to people.
- Under certain conditions, the operations of a perfectly competitive price system yield an economi-

cally efficient allocation of resources. This is the fundamental theorem of welfare economics.

- Many factors may cause competitive markets to fail to achieve efficiency. These include: (1) imperfect competition—that is, non-price-taking behavior; (2) externalities; (3) public goods; and (4) imperfect information. We study all of these impediments to efficiency later in this book.
- Defining "equity" in the allocation of resources is difficult and subject to various interpretations. There are no mechanisms under perfect competition that guarantee equity (however defined) will be achieved.

10

Monopoly

A market is described as a monopoly if it has only one producer. This single firm faces the entire market demand curve. Using its knowledge of this demand curve, the monopoly makes a decision on how much to produce. Unlike the single competitive firm's output decision (which has no effect on market price), the monopoly output decision will completely determine the good's price.

CAUSES OF MONOPOLY

The reason monopoly markets exist is that other firms find it unprofitable or impossible to enter the market. **Barriers to entry** are the source of all monopoly power. If other firms could enter the market, there would, by definition, no longer be a monopoly. There are two general types of barriers to entry: technical barriers and legal barriers.

Barriers to entry
Factors that prevent new firms from entering a market.

Technical Barriers to Entry

A primary technical barrier to entry is that the production of the good in question exhibits decreasing average cost over a wide range of output levels. That is, relatively large-scale firms are more efficient than small ones. In this situation, one firm finds it profitable to drive others out of the industry by price cutting. Similarly, once a monopoly has been established, entry by other firms is difficult because any new firm must produce at low levels of output and therefore at high average costs. Because this barrier to entry arises naturally as a result of the technology of production, the monopoly created is sometimes called a **natural monopoly**.

Natural monopoly
A firm that exhibits diminishing average cost over a broad range of output levels.

329

The range of declining average costs for a natural monopoly need only be "large" relative to the market in question. Declining costs on some absolute scale are not necessary. For example, the manufacture of concrete does not exhibit declining average costs over a broad range of output when compared to the total U.S. market. In any particular small town, however, declining average costs may permit a concrete monopoly to be established. The high costs of transporting concrete tend to create local monopolies for this good.

Another technical basis of monopoly is special knowledge of a low-cost method of production. In this case, the problem for the monopoly firm fearing entry by other firms is to keep this technique uniquely to itself. When matters of technology are involved, this may be extremely difficult, unless the technology can be protected by a patent (discussed subsequently). Ownership of unique resources (such as mineral deposits or land locations) or the possession of unique managerial talents may also be a lasting basis for maintaining a monopoly.

Legal Barriers to Entry

Many pure monopolies are created as a matter of law rather than as a matter of economic conditions. One important example of a government-granted monopoly position is the legal protection provided by a patent. Intel processing chips and most prescription drugs are just two notable examples of goods that would-be competitors may be prevented from copying by patent law. Because the basic technology for these products was assigned by the government to only one firm, a monopoly position was established. The rationale of the patent system, originally put forth by Thomas Jefferson, is that it makes innovation more profitable and therefore encourages technical advancement. Whether or not the benefits of such innovative behavior exceed the cost of creating monopolies is an open question.

A second example of a legally created monopoly is the awarding of an exclusive franchise or license to serve a market. These are awarded in cases of public utility (gas and electric) services, communication services, the post office, some airline routes, some television and radio station markets, and a variety of other businesses. The (often dubious) argument usually put forward in favor of creating these monopolies is that having only one firm in the industry is more desirable than open competition.

In some instances, it is argued that restrictions on entry into certain industries are needed to ensure adequate quality standards (licensing of physicians, for example) or to prevent environmental harm (franchising businesses in the national parks). In many cases, there are sound reasons for such entry restrictions but, in some cases, as Application 10.1: Should You Need a License to Shampoo a Dog? shows, the reasons are obscure. The restrictions act mainly to limit the competition faced by existing firms and seem to make little economic sense.

State governments license many occupations and impose stiff legal penalties on people who run a business without a license. For some of these occupations, licensing is clearly warranted—no one wants to be treated by a quack doctor, for example. However, in other cases, licensing restrictions may go too far?. Many states license such occupations as embalmers, dog groomers appliance repairers, or golf course designers. Here we look in more detail at three specific cases of how such licensing creates monopoly.

Dry Cleaning

One rationale for licensing is that existing firms find it in their interest to promote entry restrictions to reserve the market for themselves. A good illustration is provided by dry cleaners in California.[1] In order to enter the business, a would-be cleaner must pass examinations in a variety of specialties (fur cleaning, hat renovating, spot removal, and so forth). To do so, one must usually attend a dry-cleaning school. Those who try to skirt the process and do laundry on the side face stiff fines and even jail sentences for "practicing dry cleaning without a license." Whether Californians have cleaner clothes than the rest of us in the United States as a result of all of this is unclear, though several studies have found that profits in the industry are higher in California than in other states.

Liquor Stores and Wine on the Web

Following the repeal of Prohibition, states adopted a variety of restrictions on how alcoholic beverages can be sold. Currently, 16 states operate liquor-store monopolies. In these states, consumers must purchase such beverages from a "state store," and usually they pay extra. In 34 other states, liquor stores are licensed and subject to restrictions on pricing, advertising and wholesale distribution. There is considerable evidence that alcoholic beverages are more expensive in states with the most restrictive entry laws. Recently, local liquor monopolies have been challenged by the emergence of a number of Internet sites that sell wine. Although a few states have amended their Prohibition-era laws to accommodate this innovation, a number have made it very tough for residents to buy wine over the Web (for example, by requiring that orders be placed at the winery in person). One implausible reason given for such restrictions is to prevent teenagers from buying cabernet and merlot over the Web. A more likely rationale is simply to protect the profits of local sellers.

Taxicabs

Many cities limit the number of taxicabs allowed on their streets. Ostensibly, the purpose of such regulation is to control unscrupulous cab drivers who may overcharge passengers who are new to town. This rationale is not wholly consistent with evidence that tends to show that taxi fares are higher in regulated markets. One study of Toronto, for example, found that prices are about 225 percent higher than would prevail in an unregulated market.[2] In

[1] This example is based on David Kirp and Eileen Soffer, "Taking Californians to the Cleaners," *Regulation* (September/October 1985): 24–26. The puns in the article are highly recommended.
[2] D. W. Taylor, "The Economic Effects of the Direct Regulation of Taxicabs in Metropolitan Toronto," *Logistics and Transportation Review* (June 1989): 169–182.

(continued)

2002, considerable controversy broke out in London when the Taxi Commission suggested making it easier for drivers to pass an onerous knowledge test. In order to sell the plan, the commission granted a large price increase to present taxi drivers, making fares in London some of the highest in the world. Existing drivers still oppose relaxing strict entry standards on cab sizes and driver qualifications, so it seems likely that these high fares are here to stay.

To Think About

1. Can you think of good reasons for regulating entry into the businesses described in this application? Is licensing needed to ensure quality or to achieve other goals? How would you determine whether these goals are met?
2. Why do you think some states or countries have chosen to license certain occupations, whereas other states have not? Who are the gainers and losers under the current arrangement as compared to a competitive market?

PROFIT MAXIMIZATION

To maximize profits, a monopoly chooses to produce that output level for which marginal revenue is equal to marginal cost. Because the monopoly, in contrast to a perfectly competitive firm, faces a downward-sloping demand curve for its product, marginal revenue is less than market price. To sell an additional unit, the monopoly must lower its price on all units to be sold in order to generate the extra demand necessary to find a taker for this marginal unit. In equating marginal revenue to marginal cost, the monopoly produces an output level for which price exceeds marginal cost. This feature of monopoly pricing is the primary focus of our analysis of the negative effect of monopoly on resource allocation later in this chapter.

A Graphic Treatment

The profit-maximizing output level for a monopoly is given by Q^* in Figure 10.1.[1] For that output, marginal revenue is equal to marginal costs, and profits are as large as possible given these demand and cost characteristics. If a firm produced slightly less than Q^*, profits would fall since the revenue lost from this cutback (MR) would exceed the decline in production costs (MC). A decision to pro-

---

[1] In Figure 10.1 and in the other diagrammatic analyses in this chapter, no distinction is made between the behavior of a monopoly in the short run and in the long run. The analysis is the same in both cases, except that different sets of cost curves would be used depending on the possibilities for adjustment that would be feasible for the firm. In the short run, the monopoly follows the same shutdown rule as does a competitive firm. Notice also that we use a capital Q for the monopoly output level because, by a definition, this firm serves the entire market.

duce more than Q* would also lower profits since the additional costs from increased production would exceed the extra revenues from selling the extra output. Consequently, profits are at a maximum at Q*, and a profit-maximizing monopoly will choose this output level.

Given the monopoly's decision to produce Q*, the demand curve D indicates that a market price of P* will prevail. This is the price that demanders as a group are willing to pay for the output of the monopoly. In the market, an equilibrium price-quantity combination of P*, Q* will be observed.[2] This equilibrium will persist until something happens (such as a shift in demand or a change in costs) to cause the monopoly to alter its output decision.

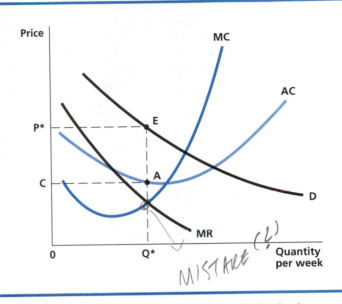

FIGURE 10.1 **Profit Maximization and Price Determination in a Monopoly Market** A profit-maximizing monopolist produces that quantity for which marginal revenue is equal to marginal cost. In the diagram, this quantity is given by Q*, which yields a price of P* in the market. Monopoly profits can be read as the rectangle P*EAC.

Monopoly Supply Curve

In the theory of perfectly competitive markets we presented earlier, it was possible to speak of an industry supply curve. We constructed this curve by allowing the market demand curve to shift and observing the supply curve that was traced out by the series of equilibrium price-quantity combinations. This type of construction is not possible for monopoly markets. With a fixed market demand curve, the supply "curve" for a monopoly is only one point—namely, the

> **MicroQuiz 10.1**
>
> Monopoly behavior can also be modeled as a problem of choosing the profit-maximizing price.
>
> **1.** Why can a monopoly choose either price or quantity for its output but not both?
>
> **2.** How should the marginal revenue–marginal cost rule be stated when the monopolist is treated as a price setter?

[2] This combination must be on an elastic section of the demand curve. This is so because MC is positive, so for a profit maximum MR must also be positive. But, if marginal revenue is positive, demand must be elastic, as we showed in Chapter 7. One conclusion to be drawn is that markets that are found to operate along an inelastic portion of the demand curve probably are not characterized by strong monopoly power.

point corresponding to the quantity at which MR = MC (point E in Figure 10.1). If the demand curve should shift, the marginal revenue curve would shift along with it and a new profit-maximizing output would be chosen. However, to connect the resulting series of equilibrium points would have little meaning and would not represent a supply curve. The set of points might have a very strange shape, depending on how the market demand curve's elasticity (and its associated MR curve) changed as the curve was shifted outward. In this sense, a monopoly market has no well-defined supply curve. Instead, each demand curve represents a unique profit-maximizing opportunity for the monopoly firm and each has to be studied independently.

Monopoly Profits

Economic profits earned by the monopolist can be read directly from Figure 10.1. These are shown by the rectangle P*EAC and again represent the profit per unit (price minus average cost) times the number of units sold. These profits will be positive when, as in the figure, market price exceeds average total cost. Since no entry is possible into a monopoly market, these profits can exist even in the long run. For this reason, some authors call the profits that a monopolist earns in the long run **monopoly rents.** These profits can be regarded as a return to the factor that forms the basis of the monopoly (such as a patent, a favorable location, or the only liquor license in town). Some other owner might be willing to pay that amount in rent for the right to operate the monopoly and obtain its profits. The huge prices paid for television stations or baseball franchises reflect the capitalized values of such rents.

MicroQuiz 10.2

Suppose there is an increase in the demand for *Two Towers* battle swords (a monopoly good):

1. Why might you expect both price and quantity to increase?

2. Could price and quantity move in opposite directions in some cases?

Monopoly rents
The profits that a monopolist earns in the long run.

WHAT'S WRONG WITH MONOPOLY?

Firms that have a monopoly position in a market can be criticized for a variety of reasons. Here, we look at two specific complaints: the profitability of monopoly and the effect of monopoly on resource allocation.

Profitability

Because perfectly competitive firms earn no economic profits in the long run, a firm with a monopoly position in a market can earn higher profits than if the market is competitive. This does not imply, however, that monopolies necessarily earn huge profits. Two equally strong monopolies may differ greatly in their profitability. It is the ability of monopolies to raise price above *marginal* cost that

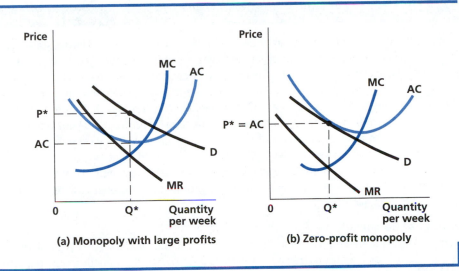

FIGURE 10.2 Monopoly Profits Depend on the Relationship between the Demand and Average Cost Curves Both of the monopolies in this figure are equally "strong" in that they have similar divergences between market price and marginal cost. Because of the location of the demand and average cost curves, however, it turns, out that the monopoly in graph (a) earns high profits, whereas that in graph (b) earns no profits. The size of profits is not a measure of the strength of a monopoly.

reflects their monopoly power. Since profitability reflects the difference between price and *average* cost, profits are not necessarily a clear sign of monopoly power.

Figure 10.2 exhibits the cost and demand conditions for two firms with essentially the same degree of monopoly power (that is, the divergence between price and marginal cost is the same in both graphs). The monopoly in Figure 10.2(a) earns a high level of profits, whereas the one in Figure 10.2(b) actually earns zero in profits since price equals average cost. Hence, excess profitability is not inevitable, even for a strong monopoly. Indeed, if monopoly rents accrue mainly to the inputs a monopoly uses (for example, rent on a favorably located piece of land), the monopoly itself may appear to make no profits.

More than the size of monopoly profits, people are likely to object to the distribution of these profits. If the profits go to relatively wealthy owners at the expense of less-well-to-do consumers, there may be valid objections to monopoly profits no matter what their size. Profits from a monopoly may not necessarily always go to the wealthy, however. For example, consider the decision of Navajo blanket makers to form a monopoly to sell their products to tourists at the Grand Canyon. In this situation, the monopoly profits make the income distribution more equal by transferring income from more wealthy tourists to low-income Navajos. Application 10.2: Who Makes Money at Casinos? describes how many groups have tried to make money from gambling.

Who Makes Money at Casinos?

Casino gambling is a big business in many countries. In the United States, casinos take in about $50 billion each year in gross revenues and these revenues have been growing faster than the overall economy as more areas legalize casino operations. In some markets, casinos operate quite competitively. There are so many casinos in Las Vegas, for example, that it is unlikely that any one of them has much power to set prices monopolistically. Profits from Las Vegas casinos are similarly in line with what owners might earn on their capital in many other business ventures. However, many other locales have adopted such restrictions on the numbers and sizes of casinos that are permitted that owners of these establishments are able to capture substantial monopoly rents. Two illustrations are provided by riverboat casinos and by so-called "Indian gaming."

Riverboat Gambling[1]

A number of states along the Mississippi River (Illinois, Iowa, Louisiana, and Mississippi) permit casino gambling only on riverboats. The number of riverboats is strictly regulated, as are many features of their operations. For example, some states have mandatory "cruising" requirements. Under such requirements, the riverboats must actually leave port and cruise along the river. Patrons must participate in the complete cruise and once the cruise ends they must leave the boat. This might be contrasted to land-based casinos where patrons can come-and-go as they like. The purported reason for this cruise requirement (as for many other seemingly odd regulations) is to limit compulsive gambling, but there is little evidence that the regulations have this effect.

One clear impact of the way that riverboat gambling is regulated is to provide monopoly rents to a number of different parties. States are a prime beneficiary—they usually tax net profits from riverboats at more than 30 percent—so obviously they have an incentive to adopt regulations that prevent the outbreak of competition. Some regulations themselves also create monopoly rents. For example, compulsory cruising rules benefit a variety of firms and workers engaged in river transportation who would not earn anything from stationary riverboats. Finally, the owners of the riverboats make monopoly rents. Riverboat licenses are highly sought after commodities and have sometimes been the fodder for major political scandals when bribes were involved in obtaining them.

Indian Gaming

The Indian Gaming Regulatory Act of 1988 clarified the relationship between states and the Indian tribes living within their borders, making it possible for these tribes to offer casino gambling under certain circumstances. Since the passage of the Act, more than 120 tribes have adopted some form of legalized gambling. Revenue from this gambling amounts to more than 15 percent of all such spending in the United States. Indian gambling establishments range from slot machines in gas stations or card tables in trailers to the luxurious Foxwoods Casino in Connecticut that employs more than 20,000 people and takes in nearly

[1] This section is based in part on W. R. Eadington "The Economics of Casino Gambling," *Journal of Economic Perspectives* (Summer 1999): 173–192.

$1 billion in gambling revenues per year. Overall, revenues from legalized gambling have become an important source of income for many Indian tribes.

The distributional consequences of Indian gaming are generally beneficial. The tribes offering gambling include some of the poorest people in the United States. A number of studies have documented significant declines in welfare numbers with the introduction of gaming.[2] Still, the income from gambling can be quite unequally distributed, especially in the cases of smaller tribes (interestingly, the largest U.S. tribe, the Navajo, does not operate casinos). The very few Indian owners of the Foxwoods Casino probably make many millions of dollars each annually. Assorted lawyers, consultants, and local officials also probably share significantly in the booty.

To Think About

1. Much of the gambling in the United States is illegal. How does the presence of illegal gambling options affect the monopoly power of legalized gambling operations?
2. How do the details of casino licensing affect which party makes the money? Could casino workers ever be the primary recipients of casino monopoly rents?

[2] For a discussion, see G. C. Anders, "Indian Gaming: Financial and Regulatory Issues," *Annals of the American Academy of Political and Social Science* (1998): 98–108

Distortion of Resource Allocation

Economists (who tend to worry about such matters) raise a second objection to monopolies: Their existence distorts the allocation of resources. Monopolies intentionally restrict their production in order to maximize profits. The discrepancy between price and marginal cost shows that, at the monopoly's profit-maximizing output level, consumers are willing to pay more for an extra unit of output than it costs to produce that output. From a social point of view, output is too low and some mutually beneficial transactions are being missed.

Figure 10.3 illustrates this observation by comparing the output produced in a market characterized by perfect competition with the output produced in the same market when it contains only one firm. The figure assumes that the monopoly produces under conditions of constant marginal cost[3] and that the competitive industry also exhibits constant costs with the same minimum long-run average cost as the monopolist—an assumption we question in the next section. In this situation, a perfectly competitive industry would choose output level Q*, where long-run supply and demand intersect. At this point, price is equal to average and marginal cost. A monopoly would choose output level Q**, for which marginal revenue is equal to marginal cost. The restriction in output

[3] This assumption might be justified as reflecting the case of a multiplant monopoly that changes output by changing the number of plants it operates.

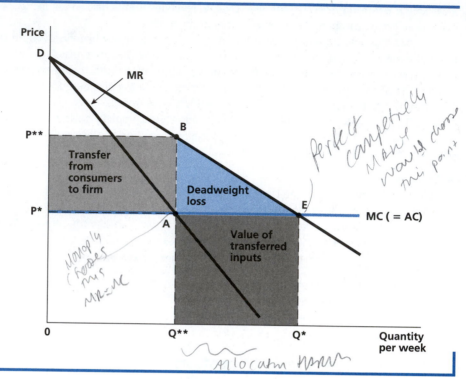

FIGURE 10.3 Allocational and Distributional Effects of Monopoly A perfectly competitive industry would produce output level Q* at a price of P*. A monopolist would opt for Q** at a price of P**. Consumer expenditures and productive inputs worth AEQ*Q** are reallocated into the production of other goods. Consumer surplus equal to P**BAP* is transferred into monopoly profits. There is a deadweight loss given by BEA.

(Q*—Q**) is then some measure of the allocation harm done by monopoly. At Q** people would be willing to pay P** for additional output, which would only cost MC. However, the monopolist's market control and desire to maximize profits prevent the additional resources from being drawn into the industry to fill this demand.

As an admittedly inane example of this distortion, suppose a local hamburger joint has a monopoly in the production of chili dogs because its cook is the only one in town capable of concocting them. To maximize profits, the owner of the monopoly restricts chili dog output to a point at which each dog sells for $2.00 but, at the margin, costs only $1.00 in terms of ingredients and the cook's time. Why is this inefficient? Because the well-being of both the cook and chili dog consumers could be improved. If the cook agreed to sell chili dogs at $1.50 to people who came around to the back door, overall welfare would be improved. Consumers would be better off (since they would save $.50 per dog over what they would be willing to pay), and the cook would be better off (by effectively getting a higher wage). Of course, the owner would prevent these illicit sales because they would undercut the profits being made. But the fact that such unexploited mutually beneficial trading opportunities exist is clear evidence that resources (here, the cook's time) are not being used efficiently.

MONOPOLISTIC DISTORTIONS AND TRANSFERS OF WELFARE

Monopolies cause an artificial restriction in output together with an increase in price and thereby distort the allocation of resources. We can explore this distortion a bit further by looking at the changes involved. Figure 10.3 shows that, when the market is competitively organized, Q^* is produced at a price of P^*. As we showed before, the total value to consumers of this output level is given by the area under the demand curve (that is, by area DEQ^*0), for which they pay P^*EQ^*0. Total consumer surplus is given by the triangle DEP^*.

Allocational Effects

If this market is monopolized, only Q^{**} is produced and the price of this output is P^{**}. The restriction in output and consequent price rise has had several effects. The total value of this good that consumers receive has been reduced in Figure 10.3 by the area BEQ^*Q^{**}. This reduction is not a complete loss, however, because consumers previously had to pay AEQ^*Q^{**} for these goods and they may now spend this money elsewhere. Since the monopoly produces less, it needs to hire fewer inputs. These released inputs will be used to produce those other goods that consumers buy. The loss of consumer surplus given by the area BEA is, however, an unambiguous reduction in welfare as a result of the monopoly. Some authors refer to triangle BEA as the "deadweight loss" since it represents losses of mutually beneficial transactions between demanders and the suppliers of inputs (where opportunity costs are measured by MC). This loss is similar to the excess burden from a tax, which we illustrated in Chapter 9. It is the best single measure of the allocational harm caused by monopoly.

Distributional Effects

In addition to the allocational effect of monopolization of a market, there is a distributional effect, which can also be seen in Figure 10.3. At the monopoly's

> ### MicroQuiz 10.3
>
> What is lost from the "deadweight loss" that results from the monopolization of a market? Who loses this? Do the monopoly's profits make up for the deadweight loss?

output level of Q**, there exist monopoly profits given by the area P**BAP*. In the case of perfect competition, this area was a part of the consumer surplus triangle. If the market is a monopoly, that portion of consumer surplus is transferred into monopoly profits. The area P**BAP* in Figure 10.3 does not necessarily represent a loss of social welfare. It does measure the redistributional effects of a monopoly, and these may or may not be undesirable.

Monopolists' Costs

Figure 10.3 assumes that monopolists and competitive firms have essentially the same costs of production. Further thought suggests this may not in fact be the case. Monopoly profits, after all, provide a tantalizing target for firms, and they may spend real resources to achieve those profits. They may, for example, adopt extensive advertising campaigns or invest in ways to erect barriers to entry against other firms and hence obtain monopoly profits. Similarly, firms may seek special favors from the government in the form of tariff protection, restrictions on entry through licensing, or favorable treatment from a regulatory agency. Costs associated with these activities (such as lobbyists' salaries, legal fees, or advertising expenses) may make monopolists' costs exceed those in a competitive industry.

The possibility that costs may be different (and presumably higher) for a monopolist than for a firm in a competitive industry creates some complications for measuring monopolistic distortions to the allocation of resources. In this case, some potential monopoly profits are dissipated into monopoly-creating costs, and it is possible that some of those costs (advertising, for example) may even shift the demand curve facing the producer. Such effects seriously complicate Figure 10.3, and we do not analyze them in detail here.[4] Researchers who have tried to obtain empirical estimates of the dollar value of welfare losses from monopoly have found that these are quite sensitive to the assumptions made about monopolists' costs. Trivial figures of less than 0.5 percent of GDP have been estimated under the assumption that monopolists are not cost increasing. Much more significant estimates (perhaps 5 percent of GDP) have been derived under rather extreme assumptions about monopolists' higher costs. Despite the variation in these estimates, concern about potential losses from monopolization plays a large role in the actual regulation of business through antitrust laws. Application 10.3: Pricing Problems in Dallas shows that a firm's ability to control prices can be a sometimes thing.

---

[4] For a relatively simple treatment, see R. A. Posner, "The Social Costs of Monopoly and Regulation," *Journal of Political Economy* (August 1975): 807–827.

Antitrust regulators look first at pricing in order to detect monopoly influences in a market. Much as Goldilocks discovered that soup can be either too hot or too cold, some firms have discovered that their prices can be too high or too low.

The Infamous Phone Call

Adam Smith noted that "people in the same trade seldom meet together, even for merriment and diversion, but the conversation ends . . . in some contrivance to raise prices."[1] Smith's skepticism was shown to have been justified by an infamous 1982 phone call between American Airlines CEO Robert Crandall and Braniff Airways CEO Howard Putnam about the pricing of flights to and from Dallas. Unfortunately for Mr. Crandall, the conversation was taped by Mr. Putnam and portions of it later appeared in *The Wall Street Journal*.[2] One particularly colorful part of the conversation went:

> *Crandall. I think it's dumb . . . to sit here and pound the *** out of each other . . . neither one of us making a *** dime.*
> *Putnam. Do you have a suggestion for me?*
> *Crandall. Yes. . . . Raise your *** fares 20 percent. I'll raise mine the next morning!*

Such a "suggestion" represents a clear violation of Section I of the U.S. Sherman Antitrust Act, which forbids all "conspiracies in restraint of trade." A subsequent investigation by the Justice Department, however, could find no evidence that American and Braniff ever carried out Crandall's plan.

Predatory Pricing in Dallas?

Sixteen years later, American Airlines' pricing policies in Dallas made the news again. This time the Justice Department charged American Airlines with illegally forcing smaller competitors out of Dallas by slashing ticket prices. According to the suit (filed in May 1999), after the small carriers left the market, American then boosted fares and reduced service. If true, this behavior might be illegal under Section II of the Sherman Act, which forbids "attempts to monopolize."

To bolster its claim of such predatory pricing,[3] the Justice Department looked at four specific routes, including the Dallas-to-Kansas City route on which American competed with Vanguard Airlines. They showed that American dropped its $113 fare to $83 when Vanguard entered the market, only to raise it to $125 once the firm left the market. The question, of course, is whether such behavior is illegal or simply what might have been expected in competitive markets.

---

[1] Adam Smith, *The Wealth of Nations* (New York: Modern Library, 1937), 128.
[2] February 24, 1983.
[3] One of the first applications of this term was to the behavior of Standard Oil Company in the late nineteenth century. For a further discussion, see Application 12.5.

Throwing in the Towel

Whatever the legality of American's pricing policy, the airline has discovered that the only way to compete with low-fare airlines is to reduce its costs. In August 2002, the firm announced that it would overhaul its entire route system and reduce the number of types of planes it flies.[4] In Dallas, American's primary hub, the plan would remove peaks in arrivals and departures, spreading flights more evenly over the day. Such a plan (which was pioneered by Southwest Airlines) would significantly reduce costs by permitting the airline to use fewer planes together with higher passenger loads in each plane.

To Think About

1. Do airline executives really need to talk on the phone in order to figure out how to rig prices? Can't the firms coordinate their prices through computerized reservation systems?

2. Why could American Airlines operate for many years with higher costs than some of their rivals? Who benefited from these higher costs?

[4] See "American Airlines Will Retrench in Bid to Beat Discount Carriers," *The Wall Street Journal,* August 13, 2002.

A NUMERICAL ILLUSTRATION OF DEADWEIGHT LOSS

As a numerical illustration of the types of calculations made by economists in studying the effects of monopoly, consider again the example of cassette tape sales introduced in Chapter 7 and Chapter 9. Table 10.1 repeats some of the information about this market. Assume now that tapes have a marginal cost of $3 per tape. Under a situation of marginal cost pricing, tapes would also sell for $3 each and, as Table 10.1 shows, seven tapes per week would be bought. Consumer surplus can be computed as the amount people were willing to pay for each tape less what they actually pay ($3). For example, someone who was willing to pay $9 for the first tape sold paid only $3. He or she received a consumer surplus of $6. The sixth column of Table 10.1 makes a similar computation for each level of output from one to seven tapes. As the table shows, total consumer surplus is $21 per week when price is equal to marginal cost.

Suppose now that the tape market is monopolized by a single local merchant with a marginal cost of $3. This profit-maximizing firm will supply four tapes per week since at this level of output marginal revenue equals marginal cost. At this level of sales, price will be $6 per tape, profit per tape will be $3, and the firm will have total profits of $12. These profits represent a transfer of what was previously consumer surplus for the first four buyers of tapes. The seventh column of Table 10.1 computes consumer surplus figures for the monopolized situation. With a price of $6, for example, the buyer of the first tape now receives a con-

TABLE 10.1 Effects of Monopolization on the Market for Cassette Tapes

	Demand Conditions				Consumer Surplus		
Price	Quantity (tapes per week)	Total revenue	Marginal revenue	Average and marginal cost	Under perfect competition	Under monopoly	Monopoly profits
$9	1	$9	$9	$3	$6	$3	$3
8	2	16	7	3	5	2	3
7	3	21	5	3	4	1	3
6	4	24	3	3	3	0	3
5	5	25	1	3	2	—	—
4	6	24	−1	3	1	—	—
3	7	21	−3	3	0	—	—
2	8	16	−5	3	—	—	—
1	9	9	−7	3	—	—	—
0	10	0	−9	3	—	—	—
				Totals	$21	$6	$12

☐ Competitive equilibrium: (P = MC). ☐ Monopoly equilibrium: (MR = MC).

sumer surplus of only $3 ($9 − $6); the other $3 he or she enjoyed under marginal cost pricing has been transferred into $3 of profits for the monopoly. As Table 10.1 shows, total consumer surplus under the monopoly amounts to only $6 per week. When combined with the monopolist's profits of $12 per week, it is easy to see that there is now a deadweight loss of $3 per week ($21 − $18). Some part of what was previously consumer surplus has simply vanished with the monopolizing of the market.

PRICE DISCRIMINATION

So far in this chapter we have assumed that a monopoly sells all its output at one price. The firm was assumed to be unwilling or unable to adopt different prices for different buyers of its product. There are two consequences of such a policy. First, as we illustrated in the previous section, the monopoly must forsake some transactions that would in fact be mutually beneficial if they could be conducted at a lower price. The total value of such trades is given by area BEA in Figure 10.4 (which repeats Figure 10.3). Second, although the monopoly does succeed in transferring a portion of consumer surplus into monopoly profits, it still leaves some consumer surplus to those individuals who value

INFOTRAC©
COLLEGE EDITION
Exclusively from Gale Group and Thomson Learning

www.infotrac-college.com
Keywords: Monopoly, Natural monopoly, Barriers to entry, Deadweight loss, Price discrimination

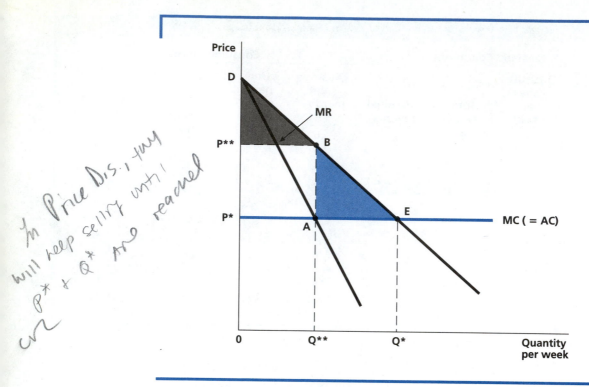

In Price Dis, they will keep selling until P & Q* are reached*

FIGURE 10.4 Targets for Price Discrimination The monopolist's price-output choice (P**, Q**) provides targets for additional profits through successful price discrimination. It may obtain a portion of the consumer surplus given by area DBP** (shaded gray) through discriminatory entry fees, whereas it can create additional mutually beneficial transactions (area BEA, shaded in color) through quantity discounts.

the output more highly than the price that the monopolist charges (area DBP** in Figure 10.4). The existence of both of these areas of untapped opportunities suggests that a monopoly has the possibility of increasing its profits even more by practicing **price discrimination**—that is, by selling its output at different prices to different buyers. In this section, we examine some of these possibilities.

Price discrimination
Selling identical units of output at different prices.

Perfect Price Discrimination

In theory, one way for a monopoly to practice price discrimination is to sell each unit of its output for the maximum amount that buyers are willing to pay for that particular unit. Under this scheme, a monopoly faced with the situation described in Figure 10.4 would sell the first unit of its output at a price slightly below 0D, the second unit at a slightly lower price, and so forth. When the firm has the ability to sell one unit at a time in this way, there is no reason now to stop at output level Q**. Because it can sell the next unit at a price only slightly below P** (which still exceeds marginal and average cost by a considerable margin), it might as well do so. Indeed, the firm will continue to sell its output one unit at a time until it reaches output level Q*. For output levels greater than Q*, the price that buyers are willing to pay does not exceed average and marginal cost; hence, these sales would not be profitable.

The result of this **perfect price discrimination**[5] scheme is the firm's receiving total revenues of 0DEQ*, incurring total costs of 0P*EQ*, and, therefore, obtaining total monopoly profits given by area P*DE. In this case, all of the consumer surplus available in the market has been transferred into monopoly profits. Consumers have had all the extra utility they might have received by consuming this good wrung out of them by the monopolist's price discrimination scheme.

Perhaps somewhat paradoxically, this perfect price discrimination scheme results in an equilibrium that is economically efficient. Because trading proceeds to the point at which price is equal to marginal cost, there are no further unexploited trading opportunities available in this marketplace. Of course, this solution requires that the monopoly know a great deal about the buyers of its output in order to determine how much each is willing to pay. It also requires that no further trading occur in this good in order to prevent those who buy it at a low price from reselling to those who would have paid the most to the monopoly. The pricing scheme will not work for goods like toasters or concert tickets, which may easily be resold; but, for some services, such as medical office visits or personalized financial or legal planning, providers may have the required monopoly power and may know their buyers well enough to approximate such a scheme. Application 10.4: Financial Aid at Private Colleges looks at another area in which pricing policies are used to extract consumer surplus from unsuspecting students.

Perfect price discrimination
Selling each unit of output for the highest price obtainable. Extracts all of the consumer surplus available in a given market.

Quantity Discounts

One way to differentiate among buyers' willingness to pay is by offering quantity discounts. These have the advantage of retaining some sales at the monopolist's preferred price (P** in Figure 10.4) but earning additional profits for quantities greater than Q** sold at a lower price to consumers with lower marginal evaluations of the good. For example, the Pizza Hut restaurant chain offers customers a second pizza for much less than what it charges for the first one. Hungry consumers are tempted to make the additional purchase at a price that still yields profits for the restaurant. Similar quantity discounts occur with respect to supermarket coupons, video rental packages, and frequent-flier programs.

As for other price discrimination schemes, an important problem for the monopolist utilizing quantity discounts is to prevent further transactions between

---

[5] Some authors refer to perfect price discrimination as "first-degree price discrimination." In this (relatively unhelpful) terminology, quantity discounts and two-part tariffs where each individual faces the same pricing menu are referred to as "second-degree price discrimination" and market-separating strategies are referred to as "third-degree price discrimination."

Financial Aid at Private Colleges

In recent years, private colleges and universities have adopted increasingly sophisticated methods for allocating financial aid awards. The result of such practices is to charge a wide variety of net prices to students for the same education. Of course, most colleges are not profit-maximizing institutions, and financial aid policies are claimed to have more socially redeeming goals than simple price discrimination. Still, an investigation of the complexity of this topic can provide useful insights about price discrimination in other markets.

The 1991 Antitrust Case

Prior to the 1990s, most private colleges used a fairly straightforward methodology to determine financial aid awards to their students.[1] The U.S. government proposed a formula to determine a student's need, and schools with sufficient resources would offer such aid. Because the formula was applied somewhat differently among schools, net prices (that is, the "family contribution") still varied. In order to reduce that variance, 23 of the nation's most prestigious private colleges and universities formed the Overlap Group to negotiate the differences. The result was that these schools offered identical net prices to individual student applicants. In 1991 the U.S. Justice Department challenged this arrangement as illegal price fixing. In their defense, the schools argued that the overlap arrangement made it possible for them to aid more needy students. The schools settled the case by signing a consent decree in early 1992,[2] though ultimately their conduct was exempted from the antitrust laws under the Higher Education Act passed later that year. However, the turmoil created by the case and increasing competitive pressures in higher education generally led to the adoption of a vast variety of pricing schemes in the 1990s.

A Different Price for Every Student?

Pricing variants introduced during the 1990s took several forms. Some modest innovations among the most prestigious private schools were focused on the old government methodology for determining aid. Several schools (notably Princeton) unilaterally adopted more generous interpretations of the methodology—essentially cutting prices for certain categories of middle-class students. Other schools adopted "preferential packaging" in which the division of their aid between loans and pure grants was tailored to attract specific kinds of students. And many schools experimented with "merit" aid as they added extra financial support (above that suggested by their formulas) for top students.

Even more innovative pricing strategies began to be adopted during the 1990s by schools that needed to cut the costs of their financial aid operations. Admissions directors frequently gained new job titles ("enrollment managers") and began to worry about decreasing the average "discount rate" that resulted from their financial aid policies. Some schools adopted sophisticated statistical models of applicants' decisions and used them to

---

[1] Of course, athletic scholarships were always a separate category, awarded on the basis of on-the-field promise. And, prior to the 1960s, financial aid was often based on academic performance.

[2] MIT refused to sign the consent decree and went to trial. It was found guilty of price fixing, but that decision was overturned on appeal.

tailor a pricing policy that minimized the financial aid award necessary to get a particular student to accept an offer of admission.[3] By using information on the student's intended major, whether he or she applied early, and even on whether the student made a visit to the campus, these models try to estimate the student's elasticity of demand for attending the particular institution. Schools using this approach, therefore, come very close to employing the kind of information-intensive technology that would be required to practice perfect price discrimination.

To Think About

1. Is the approach to college pricing taken in this application too cynical? After all, these are nonprofit institutions, seeking to do good in the world. Is it reasonable even to discuss them in a section on monopoly pricing practices?

2. How can the differences in net price that result from financial aid policies persist? Could other industries (say, automobile sellers) try the same approach using computer models of prior consumer buying patterns to set price? What would limit this type of price discrimination in other industries?

[3] See "Expensive Lessons: Colleges Manipulate Financial-Aid Offers, Shortchanging Many," *The Wall Street Journal*, April 11, 1996.

customers who pay a low price and those who pay a high price. In the case of Pizza Hut and others, such resale is discouraged by custom; restaurant patrons seldom offer to buy a pizza for someone sitting at the next table (though a mutually beneficial transaction could probably be arranged). In the case of frequent-flier coupons, however, resales can be a major problem for airlines, and they take many precautions (not always successfully) to prevent low-cost tickets from competing with their more profitable ticket sales.

Two-Part Tariffs

Another way of increasing profits through price discrimination is to adopt a two-part pricing scheme under which consumers must pay an entry fee for the right to purchase the good being sold. The traditional example is popcorn pricing at movie theaters. The entry fee for the movie itself is the first part of this pricing scheme. Entry fees should be set in a way so as to extract as much of the available consumer surplus as possible from moviegoers. Presumably, this should involve a variety of quantity discount schemes coupled with special charges for very popular films. Popcorn itself should be priced in a way that maximizes admissions subject to the constraint that it cannot be sold below cost; that is, it should be priced at marginal cost, since this expands the pool of consumers paying entry fees.

Theater owners price popcorn well above marginal cost because it is impossible to extract all available consumer surplus through entry price schemes. It is

more profitable to raise popcorn prices above marginal cost and lose movie attendance revenue extracted from some popcorn lovers with relatively little interest in
movies; the hope is to make up for this loss by extracting additional consumer
surplus from movie lovers who also buy popcorn.

Presenting a full analysis of optimal two-part pricing schemes is beyond our
intentions here; but the prevalence of many kinds of pricing policies at restaurants, video stores, and resorts suggests that the topic is a fascinating one.
Application 10.5: Pricing at the Magic Kingdom illustrates how Disney has
tried many schemes to draw consumer surplus from the demanders of its unique
offerings.

Market Separation

A final way in which a monopoly firm may be able to practice price discrimination for a single output is to separate its potential customers into two or more
categories and to charge different amounts in these markets. If buyers cannot
shift their purchasing from one market to another in response to price differences, this practice may increase profits over what is obtainable under a single-
price policy.

Such a situation is shown graphically in Figure 10.5. The figure is drawn so
that the market demand and marginal revenue curves in the two markets share

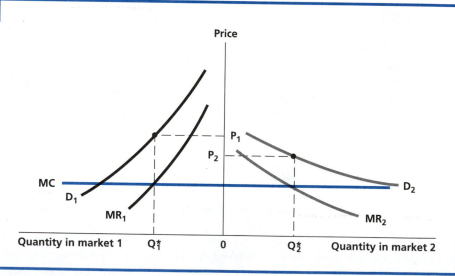

FIGURE 10.5 Separated Markets Raise the Possibility of Price Discrimination If two markets
are separate, a monopolist can maximize profits by selling its product at different prices in the two
markets. The firm would choose that output for which MC = MR in each of the markets. The diagram
shows that the market that has a less-elastic demand curve is charged the higher price by the price
discriminator.

Disneyland and Disney World are unique entertainment attractions. Amusement park aficionados (including this author) agree there are few substitutes for Disney's products. The company occupies a clear monopolistic position with regard to its pricing decisions.

The Disneyland Passport

Prior to the 1980s, Disney used a complicated multipart pricing schedule for its rides.[1] Under that schedule, Disneyland patrons had to purchase a "passport" containing a ticket for admission to the park together with coupons for admission to the rides themselves. (The contents of your author's old passport are summarized in Table 1.) Disney enjoyed a great deal of pricing flexibility with the passport arrangement. It could vary the basic price of a passport; it could vary the composition of tickets contained in a passport; it could redefine which rides required which tickets; and it could alter the prices of extra tickets. Notice, for example, that the price of extra tickets for "E" rides was quite high (certainly well above marginal cost). This pricing policy was consistent with the low price elasticity of "E" ride fanatics.

Changes in Pricing Policy

Labor costs were substantially higher under the passport system (since many ticket collectors and salespersons were needed) than under the single price admission policy followed at other amusement parks. Consequently, in the early 1980s, Disney moved away from individual tickets for rides and toward a single entry fee with zero marginal prices for all rides. This single fee still provided the company with numerous opportunities for price discrimination, such as the ability to charge reduced prices for multiday tickets and to charge lower rates for local residents.

TABLE 1 Structure of a Typical Disneyland Passport

Item	Example	Number of tickets in passport	Price of extra ticket
Admission	—	1	$4.00
"A" ride	Shooting Gallery	2	.25
"B" ride	Dumbo, train	3	.50
"C" ride	Peter Pan's Flight	3	.75
"D" ride	Autopia	2	1.00
"E" ride	Space Mountain	5	1.50

Source: Author's 1978 passport.

[1] For the first analytical treatment of these points, see W. Y. Oi, "A Disneyland Dilemma: Two-Part Tariffs for a Mickey Mouse Monopoly," *Quarterly Journal of Economics* (February 1971): 77–96.

Pricing at Disney World

The ever-growing number of attractions at Disney World in Orlando, Florida, has made it possible for Disney to return to pricing methods similar to those used prior to the 1980s. With three major theme parks (Magic Kingdom, EPCOT, and Disney-MGM Studios) and many additional features (River Country, Typhoon Lagoon, and so forth), the company can develop passports that offer any combination of these for differing lengths of time. Development of newer ticket technology (especially optical scanners) has allowed Disney to achieve economies of scale associated with its discriminatory pricing schemes.

To Think About

1. Can you offer other examples of theme park price discrimination? How is food priced? How about hotel accommodations?
2. Price discrimination schemes can work only if further trading among buyers is prevented. How do the Disney pricing schemes prevent such additional transactions?

the same vertical axis, which records the price charged for the good in each market. As before, the figure also assumes that marginal cost is constant over all levels of output. The profit-maximizing decision for the monopoly firm is to produce Q_1^* in the first market and Q_2^* in the second market; these output levels obey the MR = MC rule for each market. The prices in the two markets are then P_1 and P_2, respectively. It is clear from the figure that the market with the less-elastic demand curve has the higher price.[6] The price-discriminating monopolist charges a higher price in that market in which quantity purchased is less responsive to price changes.

Whether a monopoly is successful in this type of price discrimination depends critically on its ability to keep the markets separated. In some cases, that separation may be geographic. For example, book publishers tend to charge higher prices in the United States than abroad because foreign markets are more competitive and subject to illegal copying. In this case, the oceans enforce market separation; few people travel abroad simply to buy books. Such a discriminatory policy

> **MicroQuiz 10.4**
>
> Explain why the following versions of a profit-maximizing approach to market separation are not correct.
>
> **1.** A firm with a monopoly in two markets and the same costs of serving them should charge a higher price in that market with a higher demand.
>
> **2.** A firm with a monopoly in two markets with different marginal costs should always charge a higher price in the market with the higher marginal costs.

---

[6] *Proof:* Since MR = P(1 + 1/e), $MR_1 = MR_2$ implies that $P_1(1 + 1/e_1) = P_2(1 + 1/e_2)$. If $e_1 > e_2$ (i.e., if the demand in market 1 is less elastic), then P_1 must exceed P_2 for this equality to hold.

would not work if transportation costs were low, however. As chain stores that charge different prices in different parts of a town have discovered, people flock to where the bargains are.

Price discrimination by time of sale may also be possible. For example, tickets to late-night or afternoon showings of motion pictures are usually cheaper than for evening shows. Discriminating against those who wish to attend prime-time shows succeeds because the good being purchased cannot be resold later. A firm that tried to sell toasters at two different prices during the day might discover itself to be in competition with savvy customers who bought when the price was low and undercut the firm by selling to other customers during high-price periods. If customers themselves can alter when they shop, a discriminatory policy may not work. A firm that offers lower post-Christmas prices may find its pre-Christmas business facing stiff competition from those sales. As always, arrival of competition (even from a monopoly's other activities) makes it impossible to pursue pure monopoly pricing practices.

Pricing for Multiproduct Monopolies

If a firm has pricing power in markets for several related products, a number of additional price discrimination strategies become possible. All of these involve coordinating the prices of the goods in ways that convert more of available consumer surplus into profits than would be possible if the goods were priced independently. In some cases, firms can extend monopoly power directly by requiring that users of one product also buy a related, complementary product. For example, some producers of coffee machines require that replacement filters be bought through them and some makers of sophisticated lighting fixtures are the only sources of bulbs for them. Of course, a would-be buyer of such a product usually knows that the firm has a monopoly in replacement parts, so the firm must be careful not to scare off customers with exorbitant prices for those parts. It must also beware of potential entrants who may undersell it on the parts.

Other multiproduct schemes involve the creative pricing of bundles of goods. Automobile producers create various options packages, laptop computer makers configure their machines with specific components, and Chinese restaurants offer combination lunches. The key to the profitability of such bundling arrangements is to take advantage of differences among consumers in their relative preference for various items in the bundle. For example, some buyers of Chinese lunches may have a strong preference for appetizers and never eat dessert whereas others may skip the appetizers but never skip dessert. But a properly priced "complete lunch" package may tempt appetizer fanciers to buy dessert and vice versa. The restaurant can then obtain higher revenues (and profits) than if it only sold appetizers and desserts separately. Application 10.6: Bundling of Cable and Satellite Television Offerings illustrates how such bundling provisions can be quite intricate in some cases.

The huge expansion in television offerings made possible by improvements in satellite technology has created the possibility for many bundling options by providers.

Theory of Program Bundling

Figure 1 illustrates the theory of program bundling in a very simple case. The figure shows four consumers' willingness to pay for either sports or movie programming. Consumers A and D are true devotees, willing to pay $20 per month for sports (A) or movies (D) and nothing for the other option. Consumers B and C are more diverse in their interests, though their preferences are still rather different from each other. Here, the revenue-maximizing strategy is to charge $15 for each package if sold separately, which would yield $60 to the firm. A bundling scheme, however, that charges $20 for each package if bought individually, but $23 if both were bought, would yield $86.[1] Bundling has yielded a substantial increase in revenue to the provider.

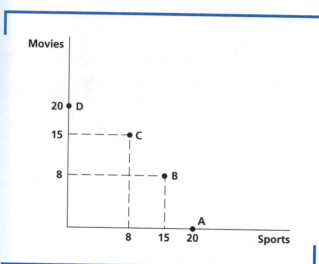

FIGURE 1 Four consumers have different preferences for movie and sports programming, making bundling profitable.

TABLE 1 Sample Direct TV Program Options

Package	Cost ($/mo.)	Incremental cost
Total Choice Plus	35.99	—
TCP + 1 option	47.99	12.00
TCP + 3 options	66.99	31.00
TCP + 5 options	81.99	46.00
Total Choice Premium	81.99	46.00

Source: http://www.directtv.com

Bundling by Direct TV, Inc.

These features of bundling are illustrated by Direct TV's price schedule for mid-2002 (see Table 1). Subscribers can add up to five options (which include the Sports Pack, HBO, and three other entertainment packages) to the basic package. The incremental cost to adding the first option ($12) is significantly higher than the per-option cost of adding subsequent options. This provision of the schedule allows

[1] With such a scheme, A and D would opt for single packages, and B and C would buy the combination.

Direct TV to capture revenue from viewers who have very definitive viewing preferences (i.e., they like only sports). After purchasing the first option, incremental costs decline, thereby encouraging subscribers to add more options. But there are no additional gains from purchasing the Premium Bundle (which includes all five options), perhaps because Direct TV believes that some subscribers will simply opt for "the works" without any careful weighing of marginal benefits and costs.

To Think About

1. Our hypothetical data and the actual data from Direct TV suggest that bundling is profit maximizing only when consumers have divergent preferences for the items being bundled. Why do you think that is the case?
2. Why isn't bundling more extensive in retailing? For example, could supermarkets gain by offering shoppers pre-filled shopping bags at modestly reduced prices?

REGULATION OF NATURAL MONOPOLIES

The regulation of natural monopolies is an important subject in applied economic analysis. The utility, communications, and transportation industries are highly regulated in most countries; and devising regulatory procedures that cause these industries to operate in a socially desirable way is an important practical problem. Here, we look at a few aspects of the regulation of monopolies that relate to pricing policies.

Marginal Cost Pricing and the Natural Monopoly Dilemma

By analogy to the perfectly competitive case, many economists believe that it is important for the prices charged by regulated monopolies to accurately reflect marginal costs of production. In this way, the deadweight loss from monopolies is minimized. The principal problem raised by a policy of marginal cost pricing is that it may require natural monopolies to operate at a loss.

Natural monopolies, by definition, exhibit decreasing average costs over a broad range of output levels. The cost curves for such a firm might look like

> **MicroQuiz 10.5**
>
> Does the regulatory pricing dilemma apply to a monopoly with a U-shaped average cost curve? Under what conditions would a regulated policy of marginal cost pricing create losses for the monopoly? Could the policy cause the monopoly to shut down?

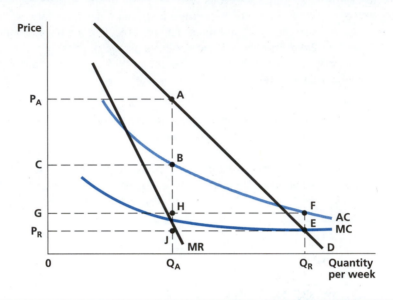

FIGURE 10.6 Price Regulation for a Natural Monopoly Because natural monopolies exhibit decreasing average cost, marginal costs fall below average cost. Enforcing a policy of marginal cost pricing entails operating at a loss. A price of P_R, for example, achieves the goal of marginal cost pricing but necessitates an operating loss of $GFEP_R$.

those shown in Figure 10.6. In the absence of regulation, the monopoly would produce output level Q_A and receive a price of P_A for its product. Profits in this situation are given by the rectangle $P_A ABC$. A regulatory agency might set a price of P_R for this monopoly. At this price, Q_R is demanded, and the marginal cost of producing this output level is also P_R. Consequently, marginal cost pricing has been achieved. Unfortunately, because of the declining nature of the firm's cost curves, the price P_R (= marginal cost) falls below average costs. With this regulated price, the monopoly must operate at a loss of $GFEP_R$. Since no firm can operate indefinitely at a loss, this poses a dilemma for the regulatory agency: Either it must abandon its goal of marginal cost pricing, or the government must subsidize the monopoly forever.

Two-Tier Pricing Systems

One way out of the marginal cost pricing dilemma is a two-part pricing system. Under this system, the monopoly is permitted to charge some users a high price while maintaining a low price for "marginal" users. In this way, the demanders paying the high price in effect subsidize the losses of the low-price customers.

Such a pricing scheme can be illustrated with Figure 10.6. The regulatory commission might decide to permit the firm to charge one class of buyers the monopoly price P_A. At this price, Q_A is demanded. Other users (those who find this good less valuable to them) would be offered a marginal cost price of P_R and would demand $Q_R = Q_A$. With total output of Q_R, average costs are given by 0G. With this two-tier price schedule, profits earned from those who pay the high price (given by the size of the rectangle P_AAHG) balance the losses incurred on sales to those who pay the low price (these losses are given by the area HFEJ). Here, the "marginal user" does indeed pay a price equal to marginal cost and the losses this entails are subsidized by profits from the "intra-marginal user."

Although in practice it may not be so simple to establish pricing schemes that maintain marginal cost pricing and cover operating costs, many regulatory commissions do use multipart price schedules that intentionally discriminate against some users to the advantage of others. Application 10.7: Can Anyone Understand Telephone Pricing? illustrates how this was done for many years in the telephone industry and caused major problems in moving to a more competitive situation.

Rate of Return Regulation

Another approach to setting the price charged by a natural monopoly that is followed in many regulatory situations is to permit the monopoly to charge a price above average cost that will earn a "fair" rate of return on investment. Much analytical effort is then spent on defining the "fair" rate and on developing how it might be measured. From an economic point of view, some of the most interesting questions about this procedure concern how the regulatory activity affects the firm's decisions. If, for example, the allowed rate of return exceeds what an owner might earn under competitive circumstances, the firm will have an incentive to use relatively more capital input than needed to truly minimize costs. If regulators typically delay in making rate decisions, firms may be given incentives to minimize costs that would not otherwise exist since they cannot immediately recover their costs through higher rates. Although it is possible to develop a formal analysis of all these possibilities, we do not do so here.

Can Anyone Understand Telephone Pricing?

In 1974, the Department of Justice filed an antitrust suit against the American Telephone and Telegraph (AT&T) Company charging unlawful monopolization of the markets for telephone equipment and long-distance service. At the time, AT&T controlled virtually all of the telephone business in the United States and was regulated at both the federal and state levels. Filing an antitrust suit against a regulated natural monopoly is rarely done, and legal wrangling over the suit lasted into the 1980s. A settlement was reached in late 1982; and, on January 1, 1984, AT&T formally divested itself of its seven local Bell Operating Companies (Ameritech, Atlantic Bell, Bell South, NYNEX, Pacific Telesis, Southwestern Bell, and U.S. West). AT&T retained its long-distance operations. The goal of this huge restructuring was to improve the performance and competitiveness of the U.S. telephone industry, but these gains have sometimes proven difficult to obtain.

Subsidization of Local Phone Service

Prior to the breakup, AT&T had been forced by regulators to provide local residential phone service at prices below average cost, making up these losses by charging above-average cost for long-distance calls (see Figure 10.6). Over the years immediately prior to the breakup, the subsidies had grown larger as technical improvements (such as fiber-optics cables) sharply reduced the costs of long-distance service. But regulators chose to keep long-distance rates high and local rates low. By the early 1980s, residential service was estimated to cost about $26 per month, but the typical charge was only $11 per month. Subsidies from long distance and other sources made up the $15-per-month difference. After the breakup, state regulators were faced with the politically unappealing prospect of implementing huge increases in residential telephone rates. Not surprisingly, local regulators instead opted for a continuation of subsidies from AT&T (and, to a lesser extent, from other long-distance companies such as MCI or Sprint) to the local operators.

The Telecommunications Act of 1996

One route to lower local phone prices might be increasing competition in those monopoly markets. Under the Telecommunications Act of 1996, the government specified a number of steps that local providers should take to increase such competition.[1] Not surprisingly, the local firms have fought the implementation of many of these provisions in court, thereby making it very costly for any would-be local competitor seeking to enter the marketplace. Local, fixed-line phone service remains very much a monopoly enterprise.

Technology Does Not Stand Still

Relentless improvement in telecommunications technology has not permitted phone markets to stand still, however. By 2002, overcapacity in fiber-optics cable, together with new phone transmission technology, had significantly reduced the profitability of long-distance service. This led to the bankruptcy of some major providers (most notably, the WorldCom corporation). It also further reduced the ability of regulators to cross-subsidize local service.

[1] For a discussion of some of these provisions, see R. G. Harris and C. J. Kraft, "Meddling Through: Regulating Local Telephone Competition in the United States," *Journal of Economic Perspectives* (Fall 1997): 93–112.

In addition, the rapid growth of cellular phone networks and a sharp decline in their costs called into question the continued viability of any sort of fixed-line phone service. Whether regulators can (or should) catch up with all of this is an open question.

To Think About

1. Why should local phone service be subsidized? Are there socially desirable benefits from ensuring that phone service is available to practically everyone? If so, who should pay the subsidy?

2. The logic of the initial AT&T breakup was to treat the long-distance market as competitive and the local exchange as a natural monopoly. Have future changes in technology supported that view?

SUMMARY

A market in which there is a single seller is called a monopoly. In a monopoly situation, the firm faces the entire market demand curve. Contrary to the case of perfect competition, the monopolist's output decision completely determines market price. The major conclusions about pricing in monopoly markets are:

- The profit-maximizing monopoly firm will choose an output level for which marginal revenue is equal to marginal cost. Because the firm faces a downward-sloping demand curve, market price will exceed both marginal revenue and marginal cost.

- The divergence between price and marginal cost is a sign that the monopoly causes resources to be allocated inefficiently. Buyers are willing to pay more for one more unit of output than it costs the firm to produce it, but the monopoly prevents this

beneficial transaction from occurring. This is the deadweight loss of welfare from a monopoly.

- Because of barriers to entry, a monopoly may earn positive long-run economic profits. These profits may have undesirable distributional effects.

- A monopolist may be able to increase profits further by practicing price discrimination. Adoption of such schemes depends on the specific nature of demand in the market the monopoly serves.

- Governments may choose to regulate the prices charged by monopoly firms. In the case of a natural monopoly (for which average costs decline over a broad range of output), this poses a dilemma. The regulatory agency can opt for marginal cost pricing (in which case the monopoly will operate at a loss) or for average cost pricing (in which case an inefficient quantity will be produced).

REVIEW QUESTIONS

1. In everyday discussions, people tend to talk about monopoly firms "setting high prices," but in this chapter we have talked about choosing a profit-maximizing level of output. Are these two approaches saying the same thing? What kind of rule would a monopoly follow if it wished to choose a profit-maximizing price? Why not charge the highest price possible?

2. Why are barriers to entry crucial to the success of a monopoly firm? Explain why all monopoly profits will show up as returns to the factor or factors that provide the barrier to entry.

3. "At a monopoly firm's profit-maximizing output, price will exceed marginal cost simply because price exceeds marginal revenue for a downward-sloping demand curve." Explain

why this is so and indicate what factors will affect the size of the price-marginal cost gap.

4. The following conversation was overheard during a microeconomics cram session:

   Student A. "In order to maximize profits, a monopolist should obviously produce where the gap between price and *average* cost is the greatest."

   Student B. "No, that will only maximize profit per unit. To maximize total profits, the firm should produce where the gap between price and *marginal* cost is the greatest since that will maximize monopoly power and hence profits."

   Can you make any sense out of this drivel? Which concepts, if any, have these students not grasped sufficiently?

5. "Monopolies perpetuate inflation. When wages rise, a monopoly simply passes on the increased cost in its price. Competitive firms would not be able to do that." Do you agree? What are the differences between how a monopoly and a competitive firm respond to cost increases?

6. Figure 10.3 illustrates the "deadweight loss" from the monopolization of a market. What is this a loss of? In the chili-dog cook example, what is the world missing out on?

7. Describe some of the transactions costs that must be present if a monopoly is to be able to practice price discrimination successfully. Are different types of costs more relevant to the practice of third-degree (market separation) price discrimination than to second-degree (price schedule) price discrimination?

8. Ronald Coase has conjectured that a monopoly that produces a durable good (one that lasts more than a single period) has less monopoly power than a monopoly that produces a good that is consumed quickly because the durable good monopoly must face competition from its own used goods. Explain the general types of considerations that a monopoly producer of a durable good would have to consider in choosing a profit-maximizing output level.

9. Suppose that the government instituted a per-unit tax on the output of a monopoly firm. How would you graph this situation? What would happen to the market equilibrium after implementation of such a tax? How would you analyze the tax incidence question—that is, how would you show which economic actor pays most of the tax?

10. What is a "natural monopoly"? Why does electric power distribution or local telephone service have the characteristics of a natural monopoly? Why might this be less true for electric power generation or long-distance telephone service?

PROBLEMS

10.1 A monopolist can produce at constant average and marginal costs of $AC = MC = 5$. The firm faces a market demand curve given by $Q = 53 - P$. The monopolist's marginal revenue curve is given by $MR = 53 - 2Q$.

a. Calculate the profit-maximizing price-quantity combination for the monopolist. Also calculate the monopolist's profits and consumer surplus.

b. What output level would be produced by this industry under perfect competition (where price = marginal cost)?

c. Calculate the consumer surplus obtained by consumers in part b. Show that this exceeds the sum of the monopolist's profits and consumer surplus received in part a. What is the value of the "deadweight loss" from monopolization?

10.2 A monopolist faces a market demand curve given by

$$Q = 70 - P$$

The monopolist's marginal revenue curve is given by

$$MR = 70 - 2Q$$

a. If the monopolist can produce at constant average and marginal costs of $AC = MC = 6$, what output level will the monopolist choose in order to maximize profits? What is the price at this output level? What are the monopolist's profits?

b. Assume instead that the monopolist has a cost structure where total costs are described by

$$TC = 0.25Q^2 - 5Q + 300$$

and marginal cost is given by

$$MC = 0.5Q - 5$$

With the monopolist facing the same market demand and marginal revenue, what price-quantity combination will be chosen now to maximize profits? What will profits be?

c. Assume now that a third cost structure explains the monopolist's position with total costs given by

$$TC = 0.333Q^3 - 26Q^2 + 695Q - 5,800$$

and marginal costs given by

$$MC = Q^2 - 52Q + 695$$

Again, calculate the monopolist's price-quantity combination that maximizes profits. What will profits be? (Hint: Set MC = MR as usual and use the quadratic formula or simple factoring to solve the equation for Q.)

d. Graph the market demand curve, the MR curve, and the three marginal cost curves from part a, part b, and part c. Notice that the monopolist's profit-making ability is constrained by (1) the market demand curve it faces (along with its associated MR curve) and (2) the cost structure underlying its production.

10.3 A single firm monopolizes the entire market for Nixon masks and can produce at constant average and marginal costs of

$$AC = MC = 10$$

Originally, the firm faces a market demand curve given by

$$Q = 60 - P$$

and a marginal revenue curve given by

$$MR = 60 - 2Q$$

a. Calculate the profit-maximizing price-quantity combination for the firm. What are the firm's profits?

b. Now assume that the market demand curve becomes steeper and is given by

$$Q = 45 - .5P$$

with the marginal revenue curve given by

$$MR = 90 - 4Q$$

What is the firm's profit-maximizing price-quantity combination now? What are the firm's profits?

c. Instead of the assumptions of part b, assume that the market demand curve becomes flatter and is given by

$$Q = 100 - 2P$$

with the marginal revenue curve given by

$$MR = 50 - Q$$

What is the firm's profit-maximizing price-quantity combination now? What are the firm's profits?

d. Graph the three different situations of part a, part b, and part c. Using your results, explain why there is no meaningful "supply curve" for this firm's mask monopoly.

10.4 Suppose that the market for hula hoops is monopolized by a single firm.

a. Draw the initial equilibrium for such a market.

b. Suppose now that the demand for hula hoops shifts outward slightly. Show that, in general (contrary to the competitive case), it will not be possible to predict the effect of this shift in demand on the market price of hula hoops.

c. Consider three possible ways in which the price elasticity of demand might change as the demand curve shifts outward—it might increase, it might decrease, or it might stay the same. Consider also that marginal costs for the monopolist might be rising, falling, or constant in the range where MR = MC. Consequently, there are nine different combinations of types of demand shifts and marginal cost slope configurations. Analyze each of these to determine for which cases it is possible to make a definite prediction about the effect of the shift in demand on the price of hula hoops.

10.5 Suppose a company has a monopoly on a game called Monopoly and faces a demand curve given by

$$Q_T = 100 - P$$

and a marginal revenue curve given by

$$MR = 100 - 2Q_T$$

where Q_T equals the combined total number of games produced per hour in the company's two factories ($Q_T = q_1 + q_2$). If factory 1 has a marginal cost curve given by

$$MC_1 = q_1 - 5$$

and factory 2 has a marginal cost curve given by

$$MC_2 = 0.5q_2 - 5$$

how much total output will the company choose to produce and how will it distribute this production between its two factories in order to maximize profits?

10.6 Suppose a textbook monopoly can produce any level of output it wishes at a constant marginal (and average) cost of $5 per book. Assume that the monopoly sells its books in two different markets that are separated by some distance. The demand curve in the first market is given by

$$Q_1 = 55 - P_1$$

and the curve in the second market is given by

$$Q_2 = 70 - 2P_2$$

a. If the monopolist can maintain the separation between the two markets, what level of output should be produced in each market and what price will prevail in each market? What are total profits in this situation?
b. How would your answer change if it only cost demanders $5 to mail books between the two markets? What would be the monopolist's new profit level in this situation? How would your answer change if mailing costs were 0? (Hint: Show that for a downward-sloping linear demand curve, profits are maximized when output is set at $Q^*/2$, where Q^* is the output level that would be demanded when $P = MC$. Use this result to solve the problem.)

10.7 Suppose a perfectly competitive industry can produce Roman candles at a constant marginal cost of $10 per unit. Once the industry is monopolized, marginal costs rise to $12 per unit because $2 per unit must be paid to politicians to ensure that only this firm receives a Roman candle license. Suppose the market demand for Roman candles is given by

$$Q_D = 1,000 - 50P$$

and the marginal revenue curve by

$$MR = 20 - Q/25$$

a. Calculate the perfectly competitive and monopoly outputs and prices.
b. Calculate the total loss of consumer surplus from monopolization of Roman candle production.
c. Graph and discuss your results.

10.8 Consider the following possible schemes for taxing a monopoly:

i. A proportional tax on profits
ii. A tax on each unit produced
iii. A proportional tax on the gap between price and marginal cost

a. Explain how each of these taxes would affect the monopolist's profit-maximizing output choice. Would the tax increase or decrease the deadweight loss from monopoly?
b. Graph your results for these three cases.

10.9 Show that with a linear demand curve imposition of a per unit tax on a monopoly will cause price to rise by less than the tax. Would this be true for a constant elasticity demand curve?

10.10 Suppose a monopoly produces its output in a large number of identical plants, each characterized by a U-shaped long-run average cost curve. How should the firm decide how much to produce and how many plants to utilize? Will each plant be operated at the low point of its average cost curve? Does this imply that production is efficient in this situation? How might a regulatory body enforce efficiency in this situation?

INTERNET EXERCISES

1. *Price Discrimination.* Imagine a vending machine that charges a different price for a can of soda depending on how hot it is outside! Well, that's exactly what Coca-Cola had in mind when it was considering putting thermostats in their vending machines. Read the article entitled "Mean Vending Machines" at *http://economics.about.com* (in the search field, type in Mean Vending Machines). Use a graph similar to Figure 10.5 in the text to illustrate and discuss the economic rationale behind Coca-Cola's pricing scheme. Be sure to apply the notion of elasticity. Which consumers would be made better off and which would be made worse off by this pricing scheme? Suppose instead of the thermostats, Coca-Cola installed a mechanism that would increase the price of the soda as the number of cans left in the machine decreases. Would this be a form of price discrimination? Explain why or why not.

2. *"High-Tech" Monopolies.* Read the August 31, 2000, speech by Orson Swindle, a commissioner at the Federal Trade Commission, entitled, "Government and the Tech World: Friends or Foes" at *http://www.ftc.gov/speeches/swindle/ fedhightech96.htm.* What is the proper goal of antitrust law? Why does Swindle suggest that it is more challenging to apply our antitrust laws to high-tech than to low-tech industries? Why does Swindle believe that it is particularly important in high-tech industries that one look beyond mere market share in assessing the ability of a firm to exercise market power? What are network effects, and why can they create a barrier to entry into an industry? On November 5, 1999, Judge Thomas Penfield Jackson released his findings of fact in the Microsoft case. He found that Microsoft "enjoys monopoly power" in the market for PC operating systems. How important do you think network effects might have been in Microsoft's attainment of its monopoly position? Judge Thomas Penfield Jackson also found that the Microsoft monopoly created significant harm since "some innovations that would truly benefit consumers never occur." What are some potential criticisms of this finding, in light of Swindle's discussion of the special challenges in determining the harm to consumers from monopoly in high-tech industries?

11

Imperfect Competition

This chapter discusses pricing in markets that fall between the polar extremes of perfect competition and monopoly. Although no single model can explain all possible types of such imperfect competition, we look at a few of the basic elements that are common to many of the models in current use. To that end, we focus on three topics: (1) pricing of homogeneous goods in markets in which there are relatively few firms; (2) product differentiation in these markets; and (3) how entry and exit affect long-run outcomes in imperfectly competitive markets. A related topic, strategy in the competition between firms, is taken up in Chapter 12.

PRICING OF HOMOGENEOUS GOODS

This section looks at pricing in markets in which relatively few firms each produce the same good. As before, we assume that the market is perfectly competitive on the demand side; that is, there are assumed to be many demanders, each of whom is a price taker. We also assume that there are no transactions or informational costs, so that the good in question obeys the law of one price. That is, we can accurately talk about *the* price of this good. Later in this chapter, we relax this assumption to consider cases where firms sell products that differ slightly from each other and may therefore have different prices.

Quasi-competitive model

A model of oligopoly pricing in which each firm acts as a price taker even though there may be few firms.

Quasi-Competitive Model

The possible outcomes for prices when there are few firms are uncertain; they depend on how the firms react to their competitors. At one extreme is what we might call a **quasi-competitive model.** In this case, each firm acts as a price taker. For example, a new gas station operator would be a price taker if he or she assumed that opening the station would not affect the local price of gasoline either directly (because opening the station doesn't change the local supply very much) or indirectly (because nearby stations will not change their prices in the face of the new competition). The price-taker assumption may not always be valid, especially in volatile, cut-throat markets such as local gasoline sales, but this assumption is a useful place to start.

If a firm acts as a price taker, it produces, as before, where price equals long-run marginal cost. The market solution in this case resembles a competitive one even though relatively few firms may be involved. Figure 11.1 shows a particularly simple market solution of this type. The figure assumes that marginal cost (and average cost) is constant for all output levels. Consequently, market price (P_C) must equal this marginal cost. Under this quasi-competitive solution, Q_C is produced and market equilibrium

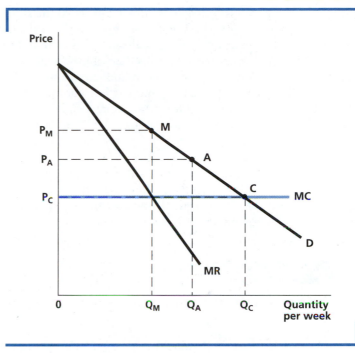

FIGURE 11.1 Pricing under Imperfect Competition Market equilibrium under imperfect competition can occur at many points on the demand curve. In this figure (which assumes that marginal costs are constant over all output ranges), the quasi-competitive equilibrium occurs at point C and the cartel equilibrium at point M. Many solutions (such as A) may occur between points M and C, depending on the specific assumptions made about how firms complete.

occurs at point C. This equilibrium represents the highest quantity and lowest price that can prevail in the long term with the demand curve D. A price lower than P_C would not cover firms' average cost, so it would not be sustainable in the long run.

Cartel Model

The assumption of price-taking behavior may be inappropriate in concentrated industries in which each firm's decisions have an effect on price. An alternative assumption might be that firms as a group recognize that they can affect price and coordinate their decisions to achieve monopoly profits. This case can be described by a **cartel model** in which the cartel acts as a multiplant monopoly and produces in each of its "plants" (that is, in each firm in the cartel) where marginal revenue equals marginal cost. Assuming, as before, that these marginal costs are

Cartel model
A model of pricing in which firms coordinate their decisions to act as a multiplant monopoly.

equal and constant for all firms, the output choice is indicated by point M in Figure 11.1. Because this coordinated plan requires a specific output level for each firm, the plan also dictates how monopoly profits earned by the cartel are to be shared by its members. In the aggregate, these profits are as large as possible, given the market demand curve and the industry's cost structure.

Maintaining this cartel solution poses three problems for the firms involved. First, cartel formations may be illegal. In the United States, for example, Section I of the Sherman Act of 1890 outlaws "conspiracies in restraint of trade," so would-be cartel members may expect a visit from the FBI. Similar laws exist in many other countries. A second problem with the cartel solution is that it requires that a considerable amount of information be available to the directors of the cartel—specifically, they must know the market demand function and each firm's marginal cost function. This information may be costly to obtain, and some cartel members may be reluctant to provide it. Finally, and most important, the cartel solution may be fundamentally unstable. Since each cartel member will produce an output level for which price exceeds marginal cost, each will have an incentive to expand output to increase its own profits. If the directors of the cartel are not able to police such "chiseling," this pricing solution may collapse. As Application 11.1: The De Beers Cartel illustrates, even the famous De Beers cartel occasionally finds itself unable to control its market.

MicroQuiz 11.1

Explain why each of the following is an alternative way of explaining the instability of cartels:

1. Each firm in a cartel faces a more elastic demand curve for its output than does the entire cartel itself.

2. Marginal revenue for an individual cartel member exceeds marginal revenue for the cartel as a whole.

Other Pricing Possibilities

The quasi-competitive and cartel models of pricing tend to determine the outer limits between which actual prices in an imperfectly competitive market are set (one such intermediate price is represented by point A in Figure 11.1). This band of outcomes may be very wide, so economists have tried to develop models to predict where market equilibrium will actually occur within these limits.[1] Developing these models is very difficult. For example, imagine developing a systematic description of how people play poker complete with betting strategies, bluffing, and each player guessing what the other players are doing. No model can predict such behavior with complete accuracy. The outcomes depend on the skills of the players, the way the cards are running, and even on seemingly

---

[1] Under a quasi-competitive solution, P = MC. Under a cartel solution, the relation between P and MC depends on the elasticity of demand. Because $MR = P(1 + 1/e)$ and $MR = MC$, $P/MC = e/(1+e)$. For example, if $e = -2$, $P = 2MC$—that is, price under monopoly is twice what it would be under competition. A model that can predict prices only within a 100 percent range is not very useful.

Although diamonds have been bought and sold throughout most of recorded history, it was not until the latter part of the nineteenth century that the diamond market became fully developed on a worldwide scale. The discovery of rich diamond fields in South Africa in the 1870s vastly expanded the world's diamond supply, which led eventually to the major gem and industrial markets that exist today. At first, diamond mining in South Africa was a very competitive enterprise—practically any prospector with a shovel could enter the market. Throughout the early 1880s, however, the richest diamond mines around the city of Kimberley were unified under the ownership of Cecil Rhodes. By 1888, Rhodes incorporated his holdings into De Beers Consolidated Mines, which at that time controlled about 90 percent of the world's total supply of diamonds. To this day, De Beers continues to dominate the world diamond trade.

Operation of the De Beers Cartel

Since the 1880s, diamonds have been found in many other places such as Namibia, Australia, and Siberia. De Beers did not make most of these discoveries, nor does the firm actually own the resulting mines. Instead, the mine owners (often governments) have found it profitable to sell their output only to De Beers, which then markets diamonds to final consumers through its central selling organization (CSO) in London. By carefully regulating the flow of diamonds into the market, the CSO manages to maintain high prices and ensure significant profits for itself and its fellow cartel members. It is De Beers's ability to add to its large diamond inventory if market conditions weaken that enables it to avoid the periodic swings in prices that the random nature of diamond finds might cause. By some estimates, high-quality gem diamonds sold by De Beers are priced at a multiple of as much as one thousand times actual marginal production cost.

Dealing with Threats to the Cartel

Because of this gap between price and marginal cost, any new diamond discovery is a potential threat to the De Beers cartel. Historically, De Beers has used its marketing strength to control any would-be chiselers. For example, when industrial diamonds from the former Soviet Union and Zaire started to enter the market in the early 1980s, De Beers quickly flooded the market from its own inventory, thereby driving down prices and quickly convincing these newcomers of the wisdom of joining the cartel. Similarly, two very large diamond finds in Australia in the mid-1980s hardly disturbed the market at all; the owners found it more profitable to market through the CSO rather than fight it. The latest threat to De Beers is the discovery of diamond-bearing kimberlite pipes under several lakes in northern Canada. Although environmental concerns may delay the development of Canadian mines for some time, discussions are already starting about whether their output will be marketed through the CSO.

The Glamour of De Beers

De Beers sponsors practically all print and television advertising of gem diamonds. The cartel invented the slogan "Diamonds Are Forever" and is credited with one of the major

(continued)

marketing coups of all times—convincing Japanese couples to adopt the western habit of buying engagement rings. Some diamond producers fear that any weakening of the cartel would leave a vacuum for such marketing activity—why should De Beers advertise if the resulting sales would primarily benefit their competitors? De Beers has also been experimenting with ways to develop a brand image for the cartel. By etching a microscopic logo into its diamonds, it hopes that consumers may come to believe that De Beers diamonds are superior to those of other producers.[1]

To Think About

1. How does the fact that diamonds are durable affect the ability of De Beers to control diamond prices? Could a cartel of producers of a perishable commodity (say, tomatoes or fish) be equally successful? How does CSO's ownership of a large inventory of diamonds help it enforce its pricing decisions?

2. Why would the owner of a large new source of diamonds voluntarily join the De Beers cartel?

[1] As reported in *The Economist,* December 19, 1998.

---

irrelevant factors like the time of night or the temperature of the room. Exactly the same types of problems arise in creating a model of pricing in markets with relatively few firms. In this case, the outcome depends entirely on how the firms play the game. In Chapter 12, we take up such strategic questions. Here, we look at two very simple models that have been widely used.

THE COURNOT MODEL

One of the first people to use mathematics in economics was the nineteenth-century French economist Augustin Cournot.[2] Among other advances, Cournot devised what we now know as the concept of marginal revenue and used this both to discuss profit maximization by a monopoly and to develop a model in which two firms compete for the same market. Since a formal development of the **Cournot model** can become quite mathematically complex, a simple numerical example may suffice.

Cournout model
A model of duopoly in which each firm assumes the other firm's output will not change if it changes its own output level.

Market Conditions

Cournot began his study by looking at a very simple situation in which a single owner of a costless but healthful spring has to decide how to price its water. Early

[2] Augustin Cournot, *Researches into Mathematical Principles of the Theory of Wealth,* trans. N. T. Bacon (New York: Macmillan, 1897).

on, he recognized that the owner must contend with a downward-sloping demand for spring water—adoption of too high a price might be as unprofitable as adoption of too low a price. Suppose, for example, the demand for spring water in terms of thousands of gallons per week (Q) depends on water price (P) according to the equation

$$Q = 120 - P \qquad \text{(11.1)}$$

This demand curve is shown in Figure 11.2. Because water itself is costless to this firm, profits (and revenues) are maximized by proceeding to the point where marginal revenue equals zero. That is, the owner of the spring monopoly should produce Q = 60. At this output level, P is $60 and revenues are $3,600 (= $60 × 60). For the future development of a duopoly model, it is important to note how the profit-maximizing output level is chosen. In this particular case, Q is chosen to be one-half of that quantity that would be demanded at a price of zero (that is, half of 120).[3] Using this conclusion, we now turn to an examination of how two independent firms might respond to this market situation.

Duopoly Model

In devising his model of his situation, Cournot assumed that each of the two firms in the market took the other firm's activities into account in only a very limited way. In particular, Cournot theorized that firm A, say, chooses its output level (q_A) on the assumption that the output of firm B (q_B) is fixed and will not be adjusted in response to firm A's actions. Total market output is then given by

$$Q = q_A + q_B = 120 - P \qquad \text{(11.2)}$$

Assuming that q_B is fixed, the demand curve facing firm A is given by

$$q_A = (120 - q_B) - P \qquad \text{(11.3)}$$

This simply says that some portion of market demand is assumed to be taken by firm B and firm A makes its choice from what is left. Using the rule discussed in footnote 3, it is obvious that firm A's profit-maximizing output level would be given by

$$q_A = \frac{120 - q_B}{2} \qquad \text{(11.4)}$$

[3] This result follows since, for a linear demand curve, the marginal revenue curve is twice as steep as the demand curve. Because both curves have the same P-intercept, the MR curve always bisects the horizontal distance between the price axis and the demand curve.

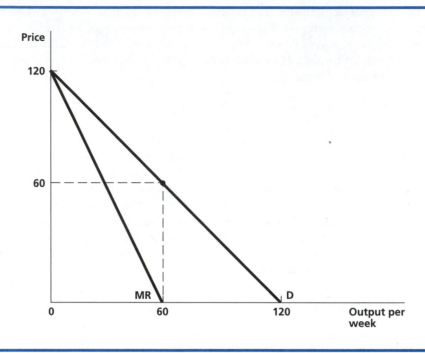

FIGURE 11.2 Spring Monopolist's Output Choice Given the market demand curve Q = 120 – P, a zero-cost monopolist would produce that output (60) for which marginal revenue is equal to 0. At this output, a price of $60 would prevail and profits would be $3,600. Notice that MR = 0 at an output level of $\frac{1}{2}Q_0$ (where Q_0 is the quantity demanded at P = 0). This result holds for any linear demand curve.

In other words, firm A produces half the output demanded at a price of zero after allowing for firm B's production. Consequently, the output level actually chosen by firm A will depend on the level of output that firm B is assumed to produce. For example, if firm B chooses to produce 60 units, firm A would choose 30 [= (120 – 60) ÷ 2]. Equation 11.4 is called the **reaction function** for firm A because it demonstrates how this firm reacts to firm B's actions. This reaction function is shown graphically in Figure 11.3.

Reaction function
In the Cournot model, a function or graph that shows how much one firm will produce given what the other firm procedures.

Firm B can perform the same analysis and arrive at a reaction function that expresses q_B as a function of q_A of the form

$$q_B = \frac{120 - q_A}{2} \tag{11.5}$$

This reaction function is also shown in Figure 11.3.

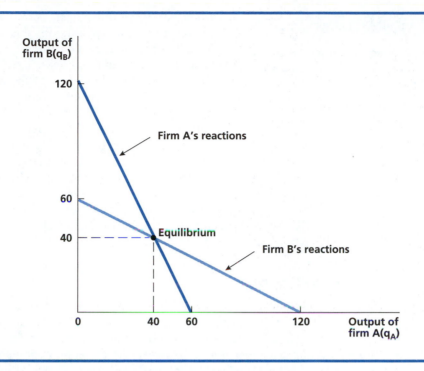

FIGURE 11.3 Cournot Reaction Functions in a Duopoly Market The reaction function for firm A shows how that firm will react on the assumption that firm B's output choice is not affected by the level of q_A produced. The function for firm B shows a similar reaction for firm B. Only at the point of intersection of the two curves ($q_A = 40$; $q_B = 40$) will both of the firms' assumptions be realized. This point of intersection is called the Cournot equilibrium point.

Cournot Equilibrium

So far, we know how firm A reacts to firm B's decisions and how firm B reacts to firm A's decisions. These decisions are consistent with each other only at the point where the two lines intersect. At all other points, the two firms' output choices are inconsistent because each firm expects the other to be producing at some output level other than what it actually is. The point of intersection is the only **Cournot equilibrium** that can prevail in this two-firm market. It is easy to show that this point of intersection is given by

$$q_A = 40$$

$$q_B = 40 \qquad\qquad (11.6)$$

At the Cournot equilibrium, both firms produce 40, total output is 80, and the market price is \$40 (= 120 − 80). This Cournot equilibrium solution is stable because each firm has adjusted its output to the actual output level being

Cournot equilibrium A solution to the Cournot model in which each firm makes the correct assumption about what the other firm will produce.

produced by the other firm. Total industry revenues and profits in this case ($3,200 – $1,600 for each firm) are lower than under the monopoly case ($3,600). This is a result of the failure of the firms in the duopoly situation to coordinate their actions perfectly. Only if the firms collude will they be able to achieve the full monopoly profits possible from the market demand curve for spring water. Otherwise, the uncertainties in the market lead to a greater level of production than in the cartel case, though price still remains well above the competitive solution (which here would require P = MC = 0).

INFOTRAC®
COLLEGE EDITION
Exclusively from Gale Group and Thomson Learning

www.infotrac-college.com
Keywords: Imperfect competition, Cournot, Cartel, Duopoly

Generalizations

It is relatively easy to generalize the Cournot equilibrium concept to cases involving more complex cost assumptions or to situations with three or more firms.[4] Often such models provide a good starting point for examining outcomes that lie between the cartel and competitive equilibria. However, the basic weakness of all such models is in the assumption that each firm takes no account of how its actions affect those of its rival. It would take a particularly obtuse owner of spring B, say, not to recognize that its decisions were affecting what the owner of spring A does. As we will see in Chapter 12, making more realistic assumptions about firms' strategies can involve a number of complications. Still, the Cournot model itself is widely used, as Application 11.2: Cournot in California shows.

PRICE LEADERSHIP MODEL

Price leadership model
A model in which one dominant firm takes reactions of all other firms into account in its output and pricing decisions.

A second model of pricing in markets with few sellers is called the **price leadership model.** This model resembles many real-world situations. In some markets, one firm or group of firms is looked upon as the leader in pricing, and all firms adjust their prices to what this leader does. Historical illustrations of this kind of behavior include the leadership of U.S. Steel Corporation during the early post–World War II period and the pricing "umbrella" of IBM in the formative years of the computer industry.

---

[4] With more firms, the Cournot equilibrium approaches the competitive case where P = MC.

Wholesale markets for electric power have been increasingly deregulated in many countries. In the United States, the process has evolved rather slowly because each state has a separate regulatory apparatus and moves toward deregulation have generated considerable political controversy. In California, the largest power market in the United States, deregulation of wholesale electricity sales was first authorized in 1996 and actual trading of day-ahead electricity sales began in early 1998. Early attempts to model this process reached cautionary conclusions about the possibilities for market power in this trading. Subsequent events have tended to confirm these predictions.

Modeling Spot Markets in Electricity

Perhaps the most elaborate attempt at modeling the impact of electricity deregulation in California can be found in an important paper by Borenstein and Bushnell.[1] In this paper, the authors focus on the competition between the three major electricity-generating firms in the state (Pacific Gas and Electric, Southern California Edison, and San Diego Gas and Electric) together with a group of smaller in-state and out-of-state suppliers. They argue that the smaller suppliers can be treated as competitive suppliers but that the major in-state producers behave in the way assumed in the Cournot model. That is, each major supplier is assumed to choose its output levels (or, more precisely, its levels of electricity-generating capacity) in a way that treats output by other producers as fixed. The authors then study the resulting Cournot equilibrium under various assumptions about electricity demand and the behavior of out-of-state suppliers.

Results of the Modeling

Borenstein and Bushnell show that under certain circumstances there is substantial market power in California wholesale electricity markets. One way to measure that power is by the Lerner Index, defined as the ratio $(P - MC/P)$; that is, the Index measures the gap between price and marginal cost expressed as a ratio of price. In periods of normal demand, the authors calculate values for this Index in the range of 0.10 or less; the price-MC gap is less than 10 percent of price. However, during peak hours of electric usage or during peak months (i.e., September), the Index rises to well over 0.50; the price-MC gap is more than half of price. Hence, during such peak periods, equilibrium in these markets is far from the competitive ideal. Interestingly, the authors also show that market power can be significantly restrained by larger price elasticities of demand for electricity. But they point out that actual policies in California tend to keep price elasticities small by preventing increases in the wholesale price of electricity from being passed on to consumers.

Actual Price "Spikes" in California

Seldom has an economic model proven to be right so quickly. In the summer of 2000, California experienced a relatively modest shortfall in electric power availability because

[1] S. Borenstein and J. Bushnell, "An Empirical Analysis of the Potential for Market Power in California's Electricity Industry," *Journal of Industrial Economics* (September 1999): 285–323.

(continued)

droughts in the Pacific Northwest reduced the supply of hydroelectric power. The result was a rapid spiking in the wholesale price of electricity in the late summer and fall. From a normal price of perhaps $50 per megawatt-hour in 1999, peak prices rose to over $500 per megawatt-hour and sometimes reached over $1,000. These increases were, more or less, in line with what had been predicted by Borenstein and Bushnell. Because large California electric utilities had not been allowed to sign long-term power contracts, they had little choice but to buy at these prices. But the firms could not pass on these higher prices to their customers so there were only modest reductions in demand. By 2001, several of California's largest utilities had filed for bankruptcy and had been forced to sell off major portions of their electricity distribution networks to the state.

To Think About

1. The model described in this application assumes that the major suppliers of electricity to California engaged in Cournot-type competition when electricity supplies were tight. Could the large price increases in 2000 also be explained with a competitive model?

2. One result of price spikes in the California electricity market was the filing of many lawsuits against suppliers. Should firms engaged in Cournot-type competition be found guilty of a "conspiracy in restraint of trade"?

Competitive fringe

A group of firms that act as price takers in a market dominated by a price leader.

A formal model of pricing in a market dominated by a leading firm is presented in Figure 11.4. The industry is assumed to be composed of a single price-setting leader and a **competitive fringe** of firms who take the leader's price as given in their decisions. The demand curve D represents the total demand curve for the industry's product, and the supply curve SC represents the supply decisions of all the firms in the competitive fringe. Using these two curves, the demand curve (D') facing the industry leader is derived as follows. For a price of P_1 or above, the leader sells nothing since the competitive fringe would be willing to supply all that is demanded. For prices below P_2, the leader has the market to itself since the fringe is not willing to supply anything. Between P_2 and P_1, the curve D' is constructed by subtracting what the fringe will supply from total market demand. That is, the leader gets that portion of demand not taken by the fringe firms.

Given the demand curve D', the leader can construct a marginal revenue curve for it (MR') and then refer to its own marginal cost curve (MC) to determine the profit-maximizing output level, Q_L. Market price is then P_L. Given that price, the competitive fringe produces Q_C and total industry output is $Q_T (= Q_C + Q_L)$.

This model does not answer such important questions as how the price leader in an industry is chosen or what happens when a member of the fringe decides to challenge the leader for its position (and profits). The model does

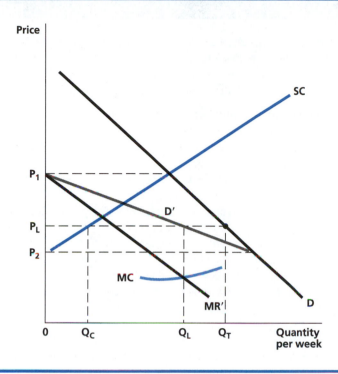

FIGURE 11.4 Formal Model of Price Leadership Behavior The curve D′ shows the demand curve facing the price leader. It is derived by subtracting what is produced by the competitive fringe of firms (SC) from market demand (D). Given D′, the firm's profit-maximizing output level is Q_L, and a price of P_L will prevail in the market.

show how elements of both the perfectly competitive and the monopoly theories of price determination can be woven together to produce a model of pricing under imperfectly competitive conditions. Such a model may explain industry behavior in some important markets, as Application 11.3: Price Leadership in Financial Markets illustrates.

MicroQuiz 11.3

In the market equilibrium illustrated in Figure 11.4, does the leader earn long-run profits? Do members of the competitive fringe earn long-run profits? What do these profit levels suggest about the long-run stability of this equilibrium?

PRODUCT DIFFERENTIATION

Up to this point, we have assumed the firms in an imperfectly competitive market all produce the same good. Demanders are indifferent about which firm's output they buy, and the law of one price holds. These assumptions may not be true in

Price Leadership in Financial Markets

Many financial markets are dominated by a few large firms. Because of the volatility of prices in these markets, smaller firms tend to look to these large firms in setting their own prices. In this application, we show how markets in both the United States and Germany tend to behave much like those illustrated in Figure 11.4.

The Prime Rate at New York Commercial Banks

Major New York commercial banks quote a "prime rate," which purports to be the interest rate that they charge on loans to their most creditworthy customers. Although recent research suggests that the actual pricing of such loans is much more complex than this description implies, it is still true that the banks' prime rates provide a visible and influential indicator of what they charge.

Banks' costs of funds change on a day-to-day basis. The prime rate, however, tends to be rather sluggish, changing only occasionally by rather large amounts (say 0.25 percent or more). It is when changes are needed that price leadership patterns are most clearly visible. One of the major banks (Citicorp or Morgan-Chase) will announce a new prime rate on a trial basis to see whether it will "stick." In a few days, either most other banks will have joined the new rate or the initiator will be forced to go back to the old rate. Because of the uncertainties involved in this procedure, the prime rate will tend to remain relatively stable for extended periods.

Figure 11.4 suggests that price leadership can be profitable for the leaders, and some evidence on the prime rate tends to confirm that possibility. Specifically, researchers have found an asymmetry in banks' changes in their prime rates: Rates tend to rise very soon after an increase in banks' costs but decline only slowly when costs fall. Banks' stock prices also tend to reflect this pattern.[1] A rise in the prime rate tends to hurt the stock prices of banks because such an increase is a signal that profits are being squeezed by costs. On the other hand, a fall in the prime rate tends to be good for bank stocks because it indicates a period of profitability on their loans.

Price Leadership in the Foreign Exchange Market

The market for world currencies is very large and very volatile. It is dominated by major financial institutions and is heavily influenced by the "intervention" of various nations' central banks in the market for their own currencies. Because such central bank intervention is usually not announced in advance, traders who are particularly well informed may have an informational advantage in the market. One might expect, therefore, other firms to look to these firms as price leaders in particular currencies.

This presumption is supported by a recent study of trading in German Marks (DM).[2] In this study, the author looked at every major transaction in trading DMs for U.S. dollars over a one-year period (1.5 million separate transactions). She found that one bank, the Deutsche Bank (the 13th largest bank in the world), tended to play the role of leader in

---

[1] For an analysis, see P. G. Nabar, S. Y. Park, and A. Saunders, "Prime Rate Changes: Is There an Advantage to Being First?" *Journal of Business* (January 1993): 69–92.

[2] B. Peiers, "Informed Traders, Intervention, and Price Leadership: A Deeper View of the Microstructure of the Foreign Exchange Market," *Journal of Finance* (September 1997): 1589–1614.

setting the DM/$ exchange rate for these transactions. This leadership role arose because of the bank's ability to foresee intervention by the German central bank (the Bundesbank) in exchange markets. Specifically, the author shows that changes in the exchange rate quoted by Deutsche Bank made between 25 minutes and 60 minutes before such intervention tended to be copied by many other large banks. These other banks presumably believed that Deutsche Bank had superior information about central bank intervention and were willing to follow that bank's pricing based on this belief. As the actual time of Bundesbank intervention approached, however, the information became more widely diffused, so no clear patterns emerged in price setting within 25 minutes of the intervention.

To Think About

1. Why do large commercial banks tend to converge to a single prime rate? Shouldn't there be some variation in this rate among banks to reflect differences in their costs of funds and other operating characteristics?
2. Can you think of other situations where informational advantages about upcoming financial events may yield a price leadership position to a financial institution?

many real-world markets. Firms often devote considerable resources to make their products different from those of their competitors through such devices as quality and style variations, warranties and guarantees, special service features, and product advertising. These activities require firms to use additional resources, and firms choose to do so if profits are thereby increased. Product variation also results in a relaxation of the law of one price, since now the market consists of goods that vary from firm to firm and consumers may have preferences about which supplier to patronize.

Market Definition

That possibility introduces a certain fuzziness into what we mean by the "market for a good," since now there are many closely related, but not identical, products. For example, if toothpaste brands vary somewhat from supplier to supplier, should we consider all these products to be in the same market or should we differentiate among fluoridated products, gels, striped toothpaste, smokers' toothpaste, and so forth? Although this question is of great practical importance in industry studies, we do not pursue it here. Instead, we assume that the market is composed of a few firms, each producing a slightly different product but that these products can usefully be considered a single **product group**. That is, each firm produces a product that is highly substitutable for that of its rivals. More precisely, cross-price elasticities of demand are very large for the products in a group. Although this definition has its own ambiguities (arguments about the definition of a product group often dominate antitrust lawsuits, for example), it should suffice for our purposes.

Product group
Set of differentiated products that are highly substitutable for one another.

Firms' Choices

Let us assume that there are a few firms competing within a particular product group. Each firm can choose the amount to spend on differentiating its product from those of its competitors. Again, the profit-maximization model provides some insight about how firms will do this: They incur additional costs associated with differentiation up to the point at which the additional revenue brought in by such activities equals each activity's marginal cost. With this view, producing differentiated products involves the same types of marginal decisions that firms use in selecting any input.

Market Equilibrium

Although this description of firms' choices seems straightforward, the choices are actually quite complex. Because the demand curve facing any one firm depends on the prices and product differentiation activities of its competitors, that demand curve may shift frequently, and its position at any particular time may only be partly understood. The firm must make some assumptions in order to make decisions; and, whatever one firm decides to do may affect its competitors' actions. For example, Nike's touting of the air pockets in its basketball shoes caused its competitors to adapt their product lines. It is quite difficult to generalize about the precise nature of market equilibrium in such situations. Application 11.4: Competition in Breakfast Space illustrates one of the simpler models used to look at product differentiation.

ENTRY BY NEW FIRMS

The possibility of new firms entering an industry plays an important part in the theory of perfectly competitive price determination. Free entry ensures that any long-run profits are eliminated by new entrants and that firms produce at the low points of their long-run average cost curves. With relatively few firms, the first of these forces continues to operate. To the extent that entry is possible, long-run profits are constrained. If entry is completely costless, long-run economic profits are zero (as in the competitive case).

Monopolistic Competition

Whether firms in an imperfectly competitive industry with free entry are directed to the low point of their average cost curves depends on the nature of the demand curve facing them. If firms are price takers, the analysis given for the competitive case carries over directly. Because $P = MR = MC$ for profit maximization and $P = AC$ if entry is to result in zero profits, production takes place where $MC = AC$ (that is, at minimum average cost).

On average, U.S. consumers eat about 50 boxes of breakfast cereal each year. The market for cereals is dominated by three firms (Kellogg, General Foods, and General Mills). Each of these firms produces a huge variety of specific brands. In 1972, the U.S. Federal Trade Commission brought a formal complaint against these producers claiming that their actions tended to establish monopoly-like pricing and profits. Specifically, the complaint was that the major firms so proliferated their brands of cereals that they left "no room" for potential competitors to enter the marketplace.

Salop's Model of Competition in "Space"

One way of illustrating this contention uses a model of "spatial competition" first developed by S. Salop.[1] In this model, the market for a particular class of goods is pictured as a circle, as shown in Figure 1. Consumers are evenly distributed around this circle. Firms locate on the circle to serve these consumers. This circle may be viewed as representing an actual geographic area where consumers care about how close they are to a firm. For example, commuting costs mean that consumers prefer discount stores close to them to those far away. But this model can also represent a commodity "space" that describes a consumer product for which consumers care about how "close" the characteristics of an actual product are to their most preferred choice. In the breakfast cereal context, the circle would represent consumer preferences among cereal types with regard to, say, sweetness, crunchiness, or flavor. Firms position their products to meet the preferences of as large a number of consumers as possible.

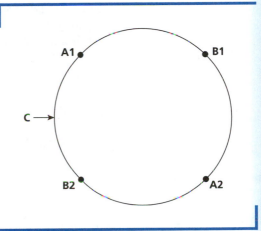

FIGURE 1 Salop's Model of Spatial Competition
Consumers are evenly located along this circle, which may represent an actual geographic space or a product space. Presence of two firms (A and B) with two products each deters entry by C.

Brand Proliferation

Figure 1 illustrates the brand proliferation argument for two firms (A and B), each producing two products (A1, A2, B1, B2). The firms have positioned these products around the cereal market to maximize profits; it seems reasonable that a strategy of equal-sized market shares (as shown in the figure) might do that. The problem for a would-be entrant into the cereal market is that there is "nowhere to go." Consider an attempt to enter at point C. This might take some business from brand A1 and brand B2, but there are simply not

[1] S. Salop, "Monopolistic Competition with Outside Goods," *Bell Journal of Economics* (Spring 1979): 141–156.

(continued)

enough consumers with preferences close to C to warrant any substantial expenditures to enter this marketplace. By creating additional brands, firm A and firm B have been able to deter entry by C.

A Flimsy Legal Case

Showing that the sort of competition illustrated in Figure 1 violated any explicit U.S. law proved to be quite difficult. After all, firm A and firm B did not consciously conspire to keep C out of the market. Ultimately, the legal case was dropped in 1982. Still, the breakfast cereal market remains very profitable in the United States and the limited entry there has been (say, in the form of supermarket generic cereals) has not significantly eroded those profits.

To Think About

1. What role do economies of scale explain in explaining why firm C cannot enter the market illustrated in Figure 1?
2. Is the equilibrium shown in Figure 1 with only two firms efficient?

Monopolistic competition

Market in which each firm faces a negatively sloped demand curve and there are no barriers to entry.

If firms have some control over the price they receive (perhaps because each produces a slightly differentiated product), each firm faces a downward-sloping demand curve and the competitive analysis may not hold. Entry still can reduce profits to zero, but now production at minimum average cost is not assured. This situation, which is sometimes termed **monopolistic competition** because it has features of both perfect competition and monopoly, is illustrated in Figure 11.5. Initially, the demand curve facing the typical firm is given by d and economic profits are being earned. New firms are attracted by these profits, and their entry shifts d inward (because now a larger number of firms are contending for a given market). Indeed, entry can reduce profits to zero by shifting the demand curve to d'. The level of output that maximizes profits with this demand curve, q', is not, however, the same as that level at which average costs are minimized, q_m. Rather, the firm produces less than that output level and exhibits "excess capacity," given by $q_m - q'$. Some economists have hypothesized that this outcome characterizes such industries as service stations, convenience stores, and fast-food franchisers, where product differentiation is prevalent but entry is relatively costless.[5]

Sustainability of Monopolistic Competition

The conclusion that a zero-profit equilibrium with price above marginal cost (such as that pictured in Figure 11.5) is sustainable in the long run has been challenged by some economists. They argue that the model neglects the effects of potential entry on market equilibrium by focusing only on the behavior of actual

---

[5] This analysis was originally developed by E. H. Chamberlain, *The Theory of Monopolistic Competition* (Cambridge, MA: Harvard University Press, 1950).

entrants. This argument introduces the distinction first made by
Harold Demetz between competition *in* the market and competition *for* the market by showing
that the latter concept provides a
more appropriate perspective for
analyzing the free entry assumption.[6] Within this broader perspective, the "invisible hand" of
competition places even more
restriction on firms' behavior, and
perfectly competitive-type results
are more likely to emerge.

To see why the equilibrium
illustrated in Figure 11.5 may not
be sustainable, suppose that a
potential entrant reasoned as follows: "I could certainly take all of
this firm's market by charging
slightly below P'. In itself, that
would lead to a loss. But, because
other firms are also pricing above

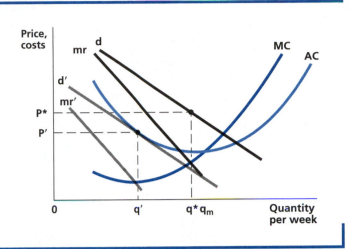

FIGURE 11.5 **Entry Reduces Profitability in Oligopoly** Initially the
demand curve facing the firm is d. Marginal revenue is given by mr, and q*
is the profit-maximizing output level. If entry is costless, new firms attracted
by the possibility for profits may shift the firm's demand curve inward to d',
where profits are zero. At output level q', average costs are not at a
minimum and the firm exhibits excess capacity given by $q_m - q'$.

marginal cost, I can sell a few extra units to their customers and make incremental profits on those sales to cover my losses." Although this entrant may not actually enter the market to do this, the threat of its doing so undermines any equilibrium in which price exceeds marginal cost. Hence, even in the absence of
price-taking behavior, the only sustainable equilibrium is one in which P = MC =
AC (as in the competitive model).

Determination of Industry Structure

We can take one step further by showing how industry structure is determined. If, as
in Chapter 8, we let q* represent that output level for which average costs are minimized and let Q* represent the total market for the commodity when price equals
marginal (and average) cost, then the number of firms in the industry, n, is given by

$$n = \frac{Q^*}{q^*} \qquad\qquad (11.7)$$

Contrary to the perfectly competitive case, this number of firms may be quite
small. In Figure 11.6, for example, exactly four firms can supply the market

---

[6] Harold Demetz, "Why Regulate Utilities?" *Journal of Law and Economics* (April 1968): 55–65.

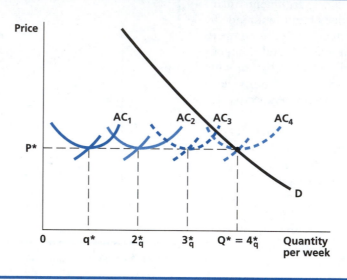

FIGURE 11.6 Contestability and Industry Structure In a contestable market, equilibrium requires that P = MC = AC. The number of firms is determined by market demand (Q*) and by the output level that minimizes average cost (q*).

MicroQuiz 11.4

Is each of the four firms pictured in Figure 11.6 a price taker? If not, why do they produce where price equals marginal cost?

demand at P*. The threat of potential entrants to seize any marginal opportunities for profit sharply constrains the types of behavior that are possible and thereby provides a well-defined equilibrium market structure. One of the most important industries that seems to have such characteristics is the airline industry; and, in Application 11.5: Airline Deregulation Revisited, we look at its recent history.

Barriers to Entry

All the analysis presented so far in this section has assumed free entry and exit. When various barriers prevent such flexibility, these results must be modified. Barriers to entry include all of those already discussed in connection with monopoly in Chapter 10. They also include those arising specifically out of some features of imperfectly competitive markets. Product differentiation, for example, may raise entry barriers by promoting strong brand loyalty. The possibility of strategic pricing decisions may also deter entry if existing firms use them to convince firms wishing to enter that it would be unprofitable to do so. Firms may, for a time, adopt lower, entry-deterring prices in order to accomplish this goal, with the intent of raising prices once potential entrants disappear (assuming they do). In Chapter 12, we look more closely at the logic behind these various possibilities.

In Application 7.2, we showed how the passage of the Airline Deregulation Act of 1978 caused major changes in the way airlines operate. Here, we look at the market repercussions of these activities. Especially interesting is the light that these experiences shed on the model of monopolistic competition.

Airlines' Entry

In many respects, the airline industry represents a perfect illustration of the free-entry assumption. Because the industry's principal capital assets (planes) are mobile, they can in principle be quickly moved into any market that promises excess profitability. The possibility of such hit-and-run entry by potential competitors should keep prices at competitive levels even in markets with relatively few actual competitors.

The prediction that the monopolistic competition equilibrium is unstable for airlines is not ironclad, however. A portion of airlines' capital is invested in terminal facilities and is, therefore, committed to a specific market. Similarly, many fliers tend to prefer to patronize a specific airline (perhaps they belong to its frequent-flier club), so they may not be willing to respond very quickly to differences in price. Finally, some airports (Chicago's O'Hare; Washington, D.C.'s Ronald Reagan; and New York's LaGuardia) are operating very close to capacity and have restricted possibilities for new landing slots.

Effects of Deregulation

Most studies of airline deregulation have found that fares declined dramatically after 1978. For example, S. Morrison and C. Winston looked at over 800 city pairs for flights and calculated that by 1983 travelers and airlines had yearly gains of about $8.6 billion from the passage of the deregulation act.[1] They note that such estimated gains would be even larger if potential benefits to aircraft manufacturers and to travelers on buses and trains (from lower fares on these modes) were also taken into account. Still, the authors find that, even after deregulation, the airline industry has some elements of imperfectly competitive behavior. Further annual welfare gains of about $2.5 billion might be obtainable if airline markets more closely approximated perfect competition. Some of these gains might be obtainable by adopting better ways of rationing landing slots at major airports or by making airline computer reservation systems more competitive, since existing systems may aid in price collusion among major airlines.

Trends in Airline Competition

One result of airline deregulation was a remarkable shake-up in the structure of the industry. At first, many new firms entered the industry, but often these were quickly consolidated into the larger carriers. In other cases, some major airlines (such as Eastern and Pan-American) fell on hard times and were broken up among existing airlines. Adding to this increasing concentration in the air travel market were significant changes in the ways airlines organize their flight networks. By developing hub-and-spoke designs, airlines have been able to economize on total distance traveled and to encourage passengers to make

---

[1] S. Morrison and C. Winston *Economic Effects of Airline Deregulation* (Washington, DC: The Brookings Institution, 1986).

(continued)

their trips on a single carrier. One undesirable side effect of this reorganization is an increasing dominance of one or two airlines in hub cities. For example, Delta Airlines provides most of the traffic at the Atlanta airport; the Dallas–Fort Worth airport is dominated by American. Because several studies have found that concentration of the traffic at a single airport is correlated with higher fares, there is some concern that such changes in the airline market may eventually reverse some of the gains from deregulation.

To Think About

1. Who were the principal gainers from air fare deregulation? Who, if any, were the losers?
2. How might hub-and-spoke operations undercut the predictions of the contestable markets model in air travel markets? What would determine the limits on how much price might rise above marginal cost?

SUMMARY

Many real-world markets resemble neither of the polar cases of perfect competition and monopoly. Rather, such markets are characterized by relatively few firms that have some effect on market price—they are not price takers—but no single firm exercises complete market control. In these circumstances, there is no generally accepted model of market behavior. Aspects of both competitive and monopoly theory must be used, together with particular institutional details of the market in question, in order to develop a realistic picture of how price and output decisions are made. Some of the main points about the models covered in this chapter are the following:

- The competitive and monopoly models set bounds for the equilibrium in any specific market. In many cases, these bounds may be quite large. For example, predicted prices under monopoly may be two or three times what they would be under perfect competition.
- There may be large benefits in the form of monopoly profits that can be earned by firms who are

able to form a cartel. Because monopoly pricing results in a situation in which P > MC, however, cartels may be unstable as each member has an incentive to cheat.

- The Cournot and Price Leadership models provide illustrations of market equilibria that differ from the polar cases of monopoly and perfect competition. Outcomes in these models depend importantly on how firms view the strategic relationship among themselves.
- With differentiated products, market outcomes may be quite complicated because each firm has a variety of strategies it can use to affect the demand for its product.
- Free entry forces any market toward a zero-profit equilibrium. Under monopolistic competition, this equilibrium results in a situation in which price exceeds marginal cost. In some circumstances, this equilibrium may not be sustainable, however, and competitive-type results may emerge.

REVIEW QUESTIONS

1. One way of categorizing various market structures is by the nature of the demand curve that faces the individual firm. What kind of demand curve faces a firm in a perfectly competitive industry? What demand curve faces a monopolist? How do the demand curves in the price leadership and monopolistic competition models represent a mixture of these two extremes?

2. "No cartel in history has ever succeeded for very long. There is just too much opportunity to cheat." What does it mean for a cartel member to "cheat"? What would a member of, say, the OPEC cartel actually do if it were to cheat? Why would this undermine the cartel? Why don't members of the DeBeers cartel cheat (at least not very much)?

3. What does the Cournot model assume about the way a firm treats its rival's output decision? Is this assumption consistent with profit maximization by the rival?

4. How does the price leader in an industry compute the "residual demand" curve facing it? In making this computation, what does the leader assume about the behavior of other firms? What might happen if two firms in an industry both tried to employ such a strategy?

5. "Profit maximization always dictates setting marginal revenue equal to marginal cost for anything that a firm might do." Explain why this statement is true and then describe how it might be applied to the following two situations:
   • A firm must decide how much to spend on devising a spiffy new bottle for its shampoo.
   • A firm must decide how much to spend on advertising its newly packaged shampoo.

6. An antitrust lawyer was heard to complain: "All this concern with defining a product group by economists is silly. I can tell what goods constitute a 'market' without ever learning how to define the cross-price elasticity of demand."

How might this lawyer want to define a 'market' and why might he or she be better off to rely on empirically measured cross-price elasticities than on intuition?

7. In Figure 11.5, the demand curve facing a firm in a monopolistically competitive industry is shown as being tangent to its average cost curve at q'. Explain why this is a long-run equilibrium position for this firm. That is, why does marginal revenue equal marginal cost and why are long-run profits zero?

8. Suppose that the market for gasoline sales along a busy highway attained an equilibrium similar to that pictured in Figure 11.5. How might a would-be entrant threaten this equilibrium by building a large "discount" gas station?

9. "The only way that participants in a market can create entry barriers that keep other firms out is to enlist the aid of a friendly government." Explain how a government might in fact aid in the creation of such entry barriers. Are there ways in which firms could achieve the same result from their own actions?

10. Concentration ratios are one of the most frequently used measures of market structure. These show the fraction of an industry's output produced by, say, the four largest firms. Under what conditions would such ratios be fairly good indicators of the kind of pricing behavior that occurs in an industry? When might such measures be a poor predictor of pricing behavior?

PROBLEMS

11.1 Suppose there are two firms selling ice cream cones in a small town. The prices charged by the firms are given by P_1 and P_2. Because the firms sell different types of cones, their goods are only partial substitutes for one another. The demand facing firm 1 is given by

$$q_1 = 10 - P_1 + 0.5P_2$$

and that facing firm 2 is

$$q_2 = 10 - P_2 + 0.5P_1$$

Both firms have a constant marginal cost of $2 per cone.

a. Suppose each firm sets a price equal to marginal cost. How many cones will each sell and what will each firm's profits be?

b. Suppose firm 1 believes firm 2 will have a price of $2 per cone. How much should this firm charge to maximize profits? (*Hint:* Price should be halfway between P = MC and the price for which $q_1 = 0$.) What is this firm's profits if $P_2 = 2$?

c. Suppose firm 2 also follows the strategy described in part b. What price does it charge and what are its profits if $P_1 = 2$?

d. Are the decisions in part b and part c consistent with each other? How might the firms choose their prices in a consistent way?

e. Suppose the two firms merge. What pricing policy would maximize their total joint profits? (*Hint:* Assume they should each charge the same price.)

11.2 A carrot monopolist can produce at constant average (and marginal) costs of AC = MC = 5. The firm faces a weekly market demand curve for carrots given by

$$Q = 53 - P$$

a. Calculate the profit-maximizing price-quantity combination for this monopolist. Also calculate the monopolist's profits. (*Hint:* Use footnote 3 of this chapter.)

b. Suppose that a second firm enters the carrot market. Let q_A be the output of firm A and q_B the output of firm B. Market demand now is given by

$$q_A + q_B = 53 - P$$

On the assumption that firm B has the same costs as firm A, calculate the profits of firm A and firm B as functions of q_A and q_B.

c. Suppose (as in the Cournot model) that each of these two firms chooses its level of output so as to maximize profits on the assumption that the other's output is fixed. Calculate each firm's reaction function (which expresses desired output of one firm as a function of the other's output).

d. On the assumption in part c, what is the only level for q_A and q_B with which both firms will be satisfied (what q_A, q_B combination satisfies both reaction curves)?

e. With q_A and q_B at the equilibrium level specified in part d, what will be the market price of carrots, the profits for each firm, and the total profits earned?

11.3 Some critics contend that U.S. automobile companies pursue a strategy of planned obsolescence: That is, they produce cars that are intended to become obsolete in a few years. Would that strategy make sense in a monopoly market? How would the presence of other firms affect profitability of this strategy?

11.4 Suppose advertising expenditures are able to increase a firm's sales. How should a firm decide on the profit-maximizing level of advertising? What marginal rule should it use?

11.5 Under monopolistic competition, each firm sells a product that is slightly different from that of its competitors. Suppose two firms in this industry merged. Would they continue to produce two different goods? Or should they focus on a single product? How would the characteristics of market demand affect this decision?

11.6 In the 1945 Alcoa case, Judge Learned Hand was faced with deciding whether Alcoa had a monopoly in aluminum production. A crucial issue concerned the distribution between "primary" aluminum production (P) and "secondary" (recycled) production (S). Three different market-share measures were used to evaluate Alcoa's position:

$$I = P_A/P$$
$$II = P_A/(P + S)$$
$$III = (P_A - F)/(P + S)$$

where P_A = Alcoa's primary production (Alcoa was not significantly engaged in recycling) and F = the amount of Alcoa's primary production that it used for its own fabricated products.

a. Which of these definitions seems to provide the best approximation for the market for aluminum production?

b. How would you answer part a if you were an Alcoa attorney? How would you answer if you were a government attorney?

c. The figures showed the following results for each of the three market-share measures:

$$I = .90$$
$$II = .64$$
$$III = .33$$

If you were Judge Hand, how would you rule on the charge that Alcoa had a monopoly? How did the judge actually rule?

11.7 In the Clorox case, Procter & Gamble was alleged to be a potential entrant into the liquid bleach market and was therefore prevented from buying Clorox Company. Can you devise a way to use firms' cost curves and the demand curves facing the firms to differentiate among actual entrants? Potential entrants? Nonentrants? Use your analysis to suggest what the court should have looked for in this antitrust case.

11.8 Suppose that the total market demand for crude oil is given by

$$Q_D = -2,000P + 70,000$$

where Q is the quantity of oil in thousands of barrels per year and P is the dollar price per barrel. Suppose also that there are 1,000 identical small producers of crude oil, each with marginal costs given by

$$MC = q + 5$$

where q is the output of the typical firm.

a. Assuming that each small oil producer acts as a price taker, calculate the typical firm's supply curve (q = ...), the market supply curve (Q_S = ...), and the market equilibrium price and quantity (where $Q_D = Q_S$).

b. Suppose a practically infinite supply of crude oil is discovered in New Jersey by a would-be price leader and that this oil can be produced at a constant average and marginal cost of AC = MC = $15 per barrel. Assume also that the supply behavior of the competitive fringe described in part a is not changed by this discovery. Calculate the demand curve facing the price leader.

c. Assuming that the price leader's marginal revenue curve is given by

$$MR = -Q/1,500 + 25$$

how much should the price leader produce in order to maximize profits? What price and quantity will now prevail in the market?

d. Graph your result indicating the market demand curve, the supply curve for the competitive fringe, and the price leader's demand, MR, and MC curves.

e. Does consumer surplus increase as a result of the New Jersey oil discovery? How does consumer surplus after the discovery compare to what would exist if the New Jersey oil were supplied competitively?

11.9 Suppose a firm is considering investing in research that would lead to a cost-saving innovation. Assuming the firm can retain this innovation solely for its own use, will the additional profits from the lower (marginal) costs be greater if the firm is a competitive price taker or if the firm is a monopolist? Develop a careful graphical argument. More generally, develop a verbal analysis to suggest how market structure may affect the adoption of cost-saving innovations.

11.10 Suppose a firm facing a downward-sloping demand curve for its product can shift that demand curve outward by undertaking an advertising campaign that involves a certain additional level of fixed costs (that is, the level of advertising does not depend on the amount produced).

a. Show that, if the firm is a monopoly, this advertising campaign will definitely increase the amount the monopoly chooses to produce.

b. Show that, if this firm is initially in equilibrium in an industry characterized by monopolistic competition, the advertising campaign will also cause it to increase output. Will this firm operate closer to minimum average cost than was previously the case?

INTERNET EXERCISES

1. *International cartels.* Since the mid- to late 1990s, the Department of Justice (DOJ) has significantly increased its international cartel enforcement efforts. Most notable, perhaps, was their prosecution of the international vitamin cartel, which was said to have cost U.S. consumers over $1 billion in damages. Read the 11/20/2000 DOJ report entitled, "Antitrust in the Twenty-First Century: Status Report on International Cartel Enforcement" at *http://www.usdoj.gov/atr/public/speeches/7086.htm* by Belinda A. Barnett. What proportion of the antitrust division's activity is directed toward

international cartel activity? What is the reason cited for the success and longevity of the vitamin cartel? What collusive practices were employed by the vitamin cartel? How pervasive was the resulting harm to consumers? In the graphite electrode case, by how much did prices rise in the United States as a result of the cartel? In the Lysine case, how were cartel members deterred from selling more than their cartel allotment? Should the entire harm to consumers from cartel/monopoly pricing be included in the deadweight loss of monopoly? Explain (it may be helpful to review Chapter 10 here).

2. *Concentration ratios.* One measure of the degree of industrial concentration (the degree to which industry output is concentrated in the hands of a few large firms) is the concentration ratio. The concentration ratio (CR "N") tells us the market share of the leading N firms in an industry. The CR4, therefore, measures the combined market share of the leading four firms in an industry; that is, a CR4 of 20 would imply that the leading four firms produce 20 percent of the market share. Higher concentration ratios are typically representative of an increasing degree of market concentration and imperfect competition. The Census Bureau publishes concentration ratios for industries as categorized by the North American Industry Classification System (NAICS). Go to the Concentration Ratio site at *http://www. census.gov/epcd/www/concentration.html*. Click on Manufacturing. Go to Table 2: Share of Value of Shipments Accounted for by the 4, 8, 20, and 50 Largest Companies (these are the concentration ratios). The lefthand column gives the NAICS codes for the industries. Increasing digits of the NAICS code represents increasing narrowness of industry definition. For example, the NAICS four-digit code 3121 represents general beverage manufacturing, but the more narrow six-digit code 312111 represents specifically soft drink manufacturing. Find and list three industries defined at the six digit NAICS level with CR4s in each of the following categories: (1) CR4 < 10 (2) 20 < CR4 < 40 (3) 60 < CR4 < 80 (4) CR4 > 80 . Do you think there is a critical value of the concentration ratio above which an industry can be regarded as imperfectly competitive? What other considerations do you think might be important?

12

Strategy and Game Theory

One of the primary tools that economists use to study the strategic choices that firms make is *game theory*. This subject was originally developed during the 1920s and grew rapidly during World War II in response to the need to develop formal ways of thinking about military strategy.[1] In this chapter, we provide a brief introduction to the use of game theory in explaining pricing and entry behavior in imperfectly competitive markets.

BASIC CONCEPTS

Game theory models seek to portray complex strategic situations in a simplified setting. Much like the previous models in this book, a game theory model abstracts the details of a problem to arrive at its mathematical representation. The greatest strength of this type of modeling is that it enables us to get to the heart of the problem.

Any situation in which individuals must make strategic choices and in which the final outcome depends on what each person chooses to do can be viewed as a *game*. All games have three basic elements: (1) players, (2) strategies, and (3) payoffs. Games may be *cooperative*, in which players can make binding agreements, or *noncooperative*, where such agreements are not possible. Here we are concerned primarily with noncooperative games.

---

[1] Much of the pioneering work in game theory was done by the mathematician John von Neumann. The main reference is J. Von Neumann and O. Morgenstern, *The Theory of Games and Economic Behavior* (Princeton, NJ: Princeton University Press, 1944).

Players

Each decision maker in a game is called a *player*. The players may be individuals (as in poker games), firms (as in imperfectly competitive markets), or entire nations (as in military conflicts). All players are characterized as having the ability to choose among a set of possible actions. Usually, the number of players is fixed throughout the "play" of a game and games are often characterized by the number of players (that is, two-player, three-player, or *n*-player games). In this chapter, we primarily study two-player games and denote these players (usually firms) by A and B. An important assumption usually made in game theory (as in most of economics) is that the specific identity of players is irrelevant. There are no "good guys" or "bad guys" in a game, and players are not assumed to have any special abilities or shortcomings. Each player is simply assumed to choose the course of action that promises the most favorable outcome.

Strategies

Each course of action open to a player in a game is called a *strategy*. Depending on the game being examined, a strategy may be a very simple action (taking another card in blackjack) or a very complex one (building a laser-based antimissile defense, for example), but each strategy is a well-defined, specific course of action. Although some games offer the players many different strategies, several important results can be illustrated for situations in which each player has only two strategies available.[2] In noncooperative games, players cannot reach agreements with each other about what strategies they will play; each player is uncertain about what the other will do.

Payoffs

The final returns to the players of a game at its conclusion are called *payoffs*. Payoffs are usually measured in levels of utility obtained by the players, although frequently monetary payoffs (say, profits for firms) are used instead. Payoffs incorporate all aspects associated with outcomes of a game; these include both explicit monetary payoffs and the implicit feelings of the players about the outcomes, such as whether they are embarrassed or they gain self-esteem. Naturally, players prefer payoffs that offer more utility to those that offer less. In some games, the payoffs are simply transfers among the players—what one player wins, the other loses. Most of the games we look at are not of this zero-sum type, however. Instead, some outcomes may offer higher payoffs to all players than do others.

---

[2] Players may also adopt "mixed" strategies by choosing to play their pure strategies randomly (say, by flipping a coin). We analyze this possibility only briefly in footnotes.

EQUILIBRIUM CONCEPTS

In our examination of the theory of markets, we developed the concept of equilibrium in which both suppliers and demanders were content with the market outcome. Given the equilibrium price and quantity, no market participant has an incentive to change his or her behavior. The question therefore arises whether there are similar equilibrium concepts in game theory models. Are there strategic choices that, once made, provide no incentives for the players to further alter their behavior? Do these equilibria then offer believable explanations of market outcomes?

The most frequently used approach to defining equilibrium is similar to that originally proposed in the nineteenth century by Cournot (see Chapter 11) and generalized in the early 1950s by J. Nash (of *A Beautiful Mind* fame). Under this procedure, a pair of strategies, say (a*, b*), is defined to be a **Nash equilibrium** if a* represents player A's best move when B plays b* and b* represents B's best move when A plays a*. Even if one of the players reveals the (equilibrium) strategy he or she will use, the other player cannot benefit from knowing this. For nonequilibrium strategies, as we shall see, this is not the case. If one player knows what the other's strategy will be, he or she can often benefit from that knowledge and, in the process, take actions that reduce the payoff received by the player who has revealed his or her strategy.

Not every game has a Nash equilibrium. And, in some cases, a game may have many different Nash equilibria, some of which are more plausible than others. Some Nash equilibria may not be especially desirable to the players in a game. And, in some cases, other equilibrium concepts may be more reasonable than those proposed by Nash. Hence, there is a rather complex relationship between game theory equilibria and more traditional market equilibrium concepts. Still, the concept provides an initial working definition of equilibrium with which to start our study of game theory.

Nash equilibrium
A pair of strategies (a*, b*) in a two-player game such that a* is an optimal strategy for A against b* and b* is an optimal strategy for B against a*.

AN ILLUSTRATIVE ADVERTISING GAME

As a way of illustrating the game theoretic approach to strategic modeling, we examine a simple example in which two firms (A and B) must decide how much to spend on advertising. Each firm may adopt either a high (H) budget or a low (L) budget, and we wish to examine possible equilibrium choices in this situation. It should be stressed at the outset that this game is not especially realistic—it is intended only to illustrate some ideas.

The Game in Extensive Form

Figure 12.1 shows the specific details of the advertising game. In this game "tree," the action proceeds from left to right, and each "node" represents a

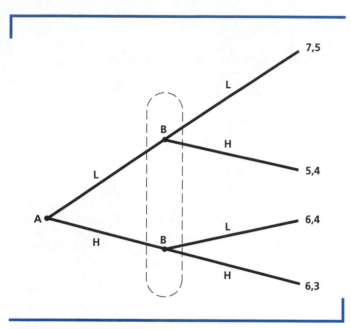

FIGURE 12.1 The Advertising Game in Extensive Form In this game, A chooses a low (L) or a high (H) advertising budget, then B makes a similar choice. The oval surrounding B's nodes indicates that they share the same (lack of) information—B does not know what strategy A has chosen. Payoffs (with A's first) are listed at the right.

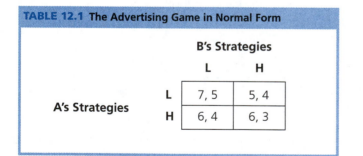

TABLE 12.1 The Advertising Game in Normal Form

		B's Strategies	
		L	H
A's Strategies	L	7, 5	5, 4
	H	6, 4	6, 3

decision point for the firm indicated there. The first move in this game belongs to firm A: It must choose its level of advertising expenditures, H or L. To indicate that firm B's decisions occur after A's, the tree places B's decisions to the right of A's. At this stage, two versions of the game are possible depending on whether B knows what choice A has made. First, we look at the case where B does not have this information. The larger oval surrounding B's two decision nodes indicates that both nodes share the same (lack of) information. Firm B must choose H or L without knowing what A has done. Later, we examine the case where B knows A's choice.

The numbers at the end of each tree branch indicate payoffs, here measured in thousands or millions of dollars of profits. Each pair of payoffs lists A's profits first. For example, the payoffs in Figure 12.1 show that, if firm A chooses H and firm B chooses L, profits will be 6 for A and 4 for B. Other payoffs are interpreted similarly.

The Game in Normal Form

Although the game tree in Figure 12.1 offers a useful visual presentation of the complete structure of a game, sometimes it is more convenient to describe games in tabular (or "normal") form. Table 12.1 provides such a presentation for the advertising game. In the table, firm A's strategies (H or L) are shown at the left and B's strategies are shown across the top. Payoffs (again with firm A's coming first) corresponding to the various strategic choices are shown in the body of the table. The reader should check that Figure 12.1 and Table 12.1 convey the same information about this game.

Dominant Strategies and Nash Equilibria

Table 12.1 makes clear that adoption of a low advertising budget is a **dominant strategy** for firm B. No matter what A does, the L strategy provides greater profits to firm B than does the H strategy. Of course, since the structure of the game is assumed to be known to both players, firm A recognizes that B has such a dominant strategy and opts for the strategy that does the best against it; that is, firm A also chooses L. Considerations of strategy dominance, therefore, suggest that the (A: L, B: L) strategy choice will be made and that the resulting payoffs will be 7 (to A) and 5 (to B).

The (A: L, B: L) strategy choice also obeys the Nash criterion for equilibrium. If A knows that B will play L, its best choice is L. Similarly, if B knows A will play L, its best choice is also L (indeed, since L is a dominant strategy for B, this is its best choice no matter what A does). The (A: L, B: L) choice, therefore, meets the symmetry required by the Nash criterion.

To see why the other strategy pairs in Table 12.1 do not meet the Nash criterion, let us consider them one at a time. If the players announce (A: H, B: L), this provides A with a chance to better its position—if firm A knows B will opt for L, it can make greater profits by choosing L. The choice (A: H, B: L) is therefore not a Nash equilibrium. Neither of the two outcomes in which B chooses H meets the Nash criterion because, as we have already pointed out, no matter what A does, B can improve its profits by choosing L instead. Since L strictly dominates H for firm B, no outcome in which B plays H can be a Nash equilibrium.

> **Dominant strategy**
> A strategy that is optimal regardless of the strategy adopted by an opponent.

Nature of Nash Equilibria

Although the advertising game illustrated in Figure 12.1 contains a single Nash equilibrium, that is not a general property of all two-person games.[3] Table 12.2 illustrates two familiar games that reflect differing possibilities for Nash equilibria. In part (a) of the table, the children's finger game "Rock, Scissors, Paper" is depicted. The zero payoffs along the diagonal show that if players adopt the same strategy, no payments are made. In other cases, the payoffs indicate a $1 payment from loser to winner under the usual hierarchy (Rock breaks Scissors, Scissors cut Paper, Paper covers Rock). As anyone who has played this game knows, there is no equilibrium. Any strategy pair is unstable because it offers at least one of the players an incentive to adopt another strategy. For example, (A: Scissors, B: Scissors) provides an incentive for either A or B to choose Rock. Similarly (A: Paper, B: Rock) obviously encourages B to choose Scissors. The irregular cycling behavior exhibited in the play of this game clearly indicates the absence of a Nash equilibrium.

---

[3] Nash equilibria always exist in certain types of games. This is true for games with "continuous" strategies and for games that permit "mixed" strategies that allow players to choose pure strategies with various probabilities.

TABLE 12.2 Two Simple Games

(a) Rock, Scissors, Paper—No Nash Equilibria

		B's Strategies		
		Rock	Scissors	Paper
A's Strategies	Rock	0, 0	1, −1	−1, 1
	Scissors	−1, 1	0, 0	1, −1
	Paper	1, −1	−1, 1	0, 0

(b) Battle of the Sexes—Two Nash Equilibria

		B's Strategies	
		Mountain	Seaside
A's Strategies	Mountain	2, 1	0, 0
	Seaside	0, 0	1, 2

MicroQuiz 12.1

Let's look at the Cournot springs model from Chapter 11 in terms of game theory.

1. Is the Cournot equilibrium (in which each firm produces an output of 40) also a Nash equilibrium?

2. Is the cartel solution (in which each firm produces 30) a Nash equilibrium?

In the "Battle of the Sexes" game, a husband (A) and wife (B) are planning a vacation. A prefers mountain locations; B prefers the seaside. Both players prefer a vacation spent together to one spent apart. The payoffs in part (b) of Table 12.2 reflect these preferences. Here, both of the joint vacations represent Nash equilibria. With (A: Mountain, B: Mountain), neither player can gain by taking advantage of knowing the other's strategy. Similar comments apply to (A: Seaside, B: Seaside). Hence, this is a game with two Nash equilibria. Application 12.1: Nash Equilibrium on the Beach looks at how the Nash concept can be applied to firms' decisions about "locations."

Prisoner's Dilemma

A game in which the optimal outcome for the players is unstable.

THE PRISONER'S DILEMMA

The **Prisoner's Dilemma** was first introduced by A. W. Tucker in the 1940s. Its name stems from the following game situation. Two people are arrested for a crime. The district attorney has little evidence in the case and is anxious to extract

Some of the most important applications of the Nash equilibrium concept concern the location of economic activity—that is, *where* firms choose to operate rather than how much they will produce.

Hotelling's Beach

In Application 11.4, we showed how spatial competition can be modeled along a circle. An earlier model of this type was developed by H. Hotelling in the 1920s. In this case, the author pictured competition as occurring along a linear "beach" as shown in Figure 1. If two ice cream stands (A and B) seek to locate on this beach, each will draw the nearest customers (because ice cream will melt before a buyer gets back to his or her umbrella). Under

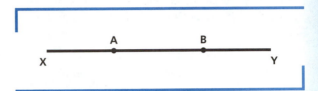

FIGURE 1 **Hotelling's Beach** Consumers are located uniformly along beach X–Y. Firms A and B wish to place ice cream stands at locations that are profit maximizing. A variety of Nash equilibria are possible in this game.

certain circumstances, it can be shown that the Nash equilibrium is for the stands to locate either at the middle of the beach or at each end.[1] Neither of these equilibria is efficient for consumers.

Milk Marketing in Japan

A recent study of the market for milk on the southern Japanese island of Kyushu illustrates how these ideas can be applied.[2] Local marketing boards regulate the sale of fluid milk in Japan as they do in many other countries including the United States. On Kyushu there are four regional boards, each of which exercises some control over pricing and sales volume in its region. It appears that each regional board must take into account what the others are doing, because milk itself can be shipped from one region to another. After exploring several models, the authors settle on a Nash equilibrium model that is very similar to the Cournot model examined in Chapter 11. This model replicates the regional pricing of milk and shows that prices are about 30 percent above competitive levels.

Television Scheduling

Hotelling's beach model can also be applied to product characteristics. Consumers are arranged along a spectrum that represents their preferences for the characteristics of a product. Firms choose where on this spectrum they will choose to "locate." Of course, any one firm must take into account what other firms are doing, so this becomes a game theoretic problem. Nash equilibrium solutions to such marketing questions have been studied for the programming decisions of the major television networks. The networks must choose

[1] Various versions of the Hotelling model are analyzed in J. Tirole, *The Theory of Industrial Organization* (Cambridge: MIT Press, 1988), 279–282.
[2] T. Kawaguchi, N. Suzuki, and H. Kaiser, "A Spatial Equilibrium Model for Imperfectly Competitive Milk Markets," *American Journal of Agricultural Economics* (August 1997): 851–859.

(continued)

how to locate their programs along the spectrum of viewer preferences. Such preferences tend to be defined along two dimensions—program content and broadcast timing. Nash equilibrium solutions to this problem have tended to focus on central locations—that is, there is much duplication of both program types and schedule timing. This has left "room" for specialized cable channels to pick off viewers with special preferences for programs or viewing times. In many cases (for example, the scheduling of sitcoms), these equilibria tend to be rather stable from season to season. Sometimes scheduling can be quite chaotic, however. For example, the scheduling of local news programs tends to fluctuate greatly, each station jockeying to gain only temporary advantage.[3]

To Think About

1. How does a firm's location give it some pricing power among "nearby" consumers? Would such power exist if the costs of "moving" were zero?

2. How can Hotelling's model of spatial equilibrium be applied to political campaigns? How do candidates choose their locations (that is, positions on issues that matter to voters)?

[3] For an analysis of why no Nash equilibrium may exist in this situation, see M. Cancian, A. Bills, and T. Bergstrom, "Hotelling Location Problems with Directional Constraints: An Application to Television News Scheduling," *The Journal of Industrial Economics* (March 1995): 121–123.

TABLE 12.3 The Prisoner's Dilemma

		B	
		Confess	**Not confess**
A	**Confess**	A: 3 years B: 3 years	A: 6 months B: 10 years
	Not confess	A: 10 years B: 6 months	A: 2 years B: 2 years

a confession. She separates the suspects and tells each, "If you confess and your companion doesn't, I can promise you a reduced (6-month) sentence; whereas, on the basis of your confession, your companion will get 10 years. If you both confess, you will each get a 3-year sentence." Each suspect also knows that if neither of them confesses, the lack of evidence will cause them to be tried for a lesser crime for which they will receive 2-year sentences. The payoff matrix for this situation is illustrated in Table 12.3. The "confess" strategy dominates for both A and B. Hence, these strategies constitute a Nash equilibrium and the district attorney's ploy looks successful. However, an agreement by both not to confess would reduce prison terms from 3 years to 2 years. This "rational" solution is not stable, and each prisoner has an incentive to squeal on his or her colleague. This, then, is the dilemma: Outcomes that appear to be optimal from the prisoners' points of view are not stable, and cheating usually prevails.

Applications

Prisoner's Dilemma–type problems may arise in many real-world market situations. Table 12.4 contains an illustration of the dilemma in the advertising context. Here, the twin L strategies are most profitable but his choice is unstable. In this game, advertising might be regarded as "defensive" in the sense that a mutual agreement to reduce expenditures would be profitable to both parties. Such an agreement in the situation of Table 12.4 would be unstable. Either firm could increase its profits even further by cheating on the agreement. Similar situations arise in the tendency for airlines to give "bonus mileage" (there would be larger profits if all firms stopped offering free trips, but such a solution is unstable) and in the instability of farmers' cartel agreements to restrict output (it is just too tempting for an individual farmer to try to sell more milk). As is generally the case for cartels, the inability to enforce agreements can result in competitive-like results.

Cooperation and Repetition

Communication between participants can be an important part of a game. In the Prisoner's Dilemma, for example, the inability to reach a cooperative agreement not to confess leads to a second-best outcome. If the parties could agree to cooperate, they might do better. As an example of how communications can affect the outcome of a game, consider the payoff matrix shown in Table 12.5. In this version of the advertising game, the adoption of strategy H by firm A has disastrous consequences for firm B, causing a loss of –50 when B plays L and –25 when H is chosen.

TABLE 12.4 An Advertising Game with a Desirable Outcome That Is Unstable

		B's Strategies	
		L	H
A's Strategies	L	7, 7	3, 10
	H	10, 3	5, 5

TABLE 12.5 A Threat Game in Advertising

		B's Strategies	
		L	H
A's Strategies	L	20, 5	15, 10
	H	10, –50	5, –25

MicroQuiz 12.2

Explain whether or not the following everyday situations appear to have the characteristics of the Prisoner's Dilemma. How would repetition of these "games" affect your conclusions?

1. Cleaning up a four-person dormitory suite.

2. Choosing how much to take from a candy box that is being passed around.

3. Joining with a friend to study for an examination.

4. Walking across a flower bed as a shortcut.

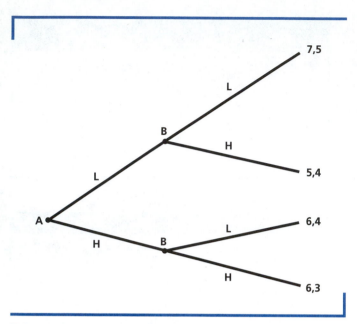

Without any communication, A would choose L (this dominates H) and B would choose H (which dominates L). Firm A would therefore end up with +15 and B with +10. However, by recognizing the potency of strategy H, A may be able to improve its situation. It can threaten to play H unless B plays L. If this threat is credible (a topic we take up later), A can increase its profits from 15 to 20.

If games are to be played many times, cooperative behavior may be fostered. In the Prisoner's Dilemma game, for example, it seems doubtful that the district attorney's ploy would work if it were used repeatedly. In this case, prisoners might hear about the method and act accordingly in their interrogations. In other contexts, firms that are continually exasperated by their inability to obtain favorable market outcomes may come to perceive the kind of cooperative behavior that is necessary. In antitrust theory, for example, some markets are believed to be characterized by "tacit collusion" among the participants. Firms act as a cartel even though they never meet to plot a common strategy. We explore the formal aspects of this problem later. Finally, repetition of the threat game (Table 12.5) offers player A the opportunity to take reprisals on B for failing to choose L. Imposing severe losses on B for "improper" behavior may be far more persuasive in getting the firm to choose the "right" strategy than simply making abstract threats.

MANY-PERIOD GAMES

These observations suggest that repeated games, perhaps with some types of communication or cooperation, may involve complex scenarios that better reflect real-world markets than do the simple single-period models we have studied so far. In order to illustrate the formal aspects of such games in a simple setting, we return to a reformulated version of the advertising game presented at the beginning of this chapter. Figure 12.2 repeats that game, but now we assume that firm B knows which advertising spending level A has chosen. In graphical terms, the oval around B's nodes has been eliminated in Figure 12.2 to indicate this additional

TABLE 12.6 Contingent Strategies in the Advertising Game

		B's Strategies			
		L,L	L,H	H,L	H,H
A's Strategies	L	7, 5	7, 5	5, 4	5, 4
	H	6, 4	6, 3	6, 4	6, 3

information. B's strategic choices now must be phrased in a way that takes the added information it has into account.

In Table 12.6, we delineate such an extension of strategies. In all, there are four such strategies covering the possible choices B might make. Each strategy is stated as a pair of actions indicating what B will do depending on its information. The strategy (L,L) indicates that B chooses L if A chooses its first strategy and L also if A chooses its second strategy. Similarly (H,L) indicates that B chooses H if A chooses its first strategy and B chooses L if A chooses is second strategy. Although this table conveys little more than did the previous illustration of the advertising game (Table 12.1), explicit consideration of contingent strategy choices does enable us to explore equilibrium notions of dynamic games.

Credible Threats

There are three Nash equilibria in this game: (1) A: L, B: (L,L); (2) A: L, B: (L,H); and (3) A: H, B: (H,L). Each of these strategy pairs meets the criterion of being optimal for each player given the strategy of the other (check this out for yourself). Pairs (2) and (3) are implausible, however, because they incorporate a noncredible threat that firm B would not carry out if it were in a position to do so. Consider, for example, the pair A: L, B: (L,H). Under this choice, B promises to play H if A plays H (its second strategy). A glance at Figure 12.2 shows that this threat is not credible—it is an "empty threat." If B is presented with the fact of A having chosen H, it will make profits of 3 if it chooses H, but 4 if it chooses L. The threat implicit in the (L,H) strategy is therefore not credible. Even though B's strategy (L,H) is one component of a Nash equilibrium, firm A should be able to infer the noncredibility of the threat implicit in it and thereby eliminate it as a possible choice B might make.

By eliminating strategies that involve empty (noncredible) threats, A can conclude that B would never play (L,H) or (H,L).[4] Proceeding in this way, the

---

[4] The process of eliminating strategies involving noncredible threats is termed "backward induction." For a more complete discussion of this topic and many of the others in this chapter, see D. Fudenberg and J. Tirole, *Game Theory* (Cambridge, MA: MIT Press, 1992).

advertising game is reduced to the payoff matrix originally shown in Table 12.1 and, as we discussed previously, in that case always playing L—that is, choosing (L,L)—is a dominant strategy for B. Firm A can recognize this and will opt for strategy L. The Nash equilibrium A: L, B: (L,L) is therefore the only one of the three in Table 12.6 that does not involve noncredible threats. Such an equilibrium is termed a **perfect equilibrium.** By using the concepts of strategic dominance, Nash equilibrium, and perfect equilibrium, we are now in a position to examine a few game theoretic models of firm behavior.

Perfect equilibrium

A Nash equilibrium in which the strategy choices of each player do not contain empty threats. That is, no strategy in such an equilibrium requires a player to carry out an action that would not be in its interest at the time.

MODELS OF PRICING BEHAVIOR

We begin our discussion of the economic applications of game theory by illustrating some of the insights that this approach can provide to the analysis of pricing. As in Chapter 11, most of the interesting results can be shown for the case of two firms (duopoly). Later in the chapter, we briefly discuss some complications involved in extending game theory models to markets that include many firms.

The Bertrand Equilibrium

Suppose there are two firms (A and B) each producing the same good at constant marginal cost, c. The demand for the good is such that all sales go to the firm with the lowest price (because the firms' outputs are perfect substitutes) and that sales are split evenly if $P_A = P_B$. The available pricing strategies here consist of choosing any price greater than or equal to c—no firm would choose to operate at a loss in the long run by choosing a price less than c.

In this case, the only Nash equilibrium is $P_A = P_B = c$. That is, the Nash equilibrium is the competitive solution with marginal cost pricing even though there are only two firms. To see why, suppose firm A chooses a price greater than c. The profit-maximizing response for firm B is to choose a price slightly less than P_A and corner the entire market. But B's price, if it exceeds c, still cannot be a Nash equilibrium since it provides A with further incentives for price cutting. Only by choosing $P_A = P_B = c$ will the two firms in this market achieve a Nash equilibrium in which they share the market equally. This pricing strategy is sometimes referred to as a "Bertrand equilibrium" after the French economist who discovered it.[5]

Two-Stage Price Games and Cournot Equilibrium

The simplicity of the Bertrand result depends crucially on the assumptions underlying the model. If firms do not have equal costs (see Problem 12.4) or if the goods produced by the two firms are not perfect substitutes, the competitive

[5] J. Bertrand, "Théorie Mathematique de la Richess Sociale," *Journal de Savants* (1883): 499–508.

result no longer holds. Other duopoly models that depart from the Bertrand result treat price competition as only the final stage of a two-stage game in which the first stage involves various types of entry or investment considerations for the firms. In Chapter 11, we examined Cournot's example of a natural spring duopoly in which each spring owner chose how much water to supply. In the present context, we might assume that each firm in a duopoly must choose a certain capacity output level for which marginal costs are constant up to that level and infinite thereafter. It seems clear that a two-stage game in which firms choose capacity first (and then price) is formally identical to the Cournot analysis. The quantities chosen in the Cournot equilibrium represent a Nash equilibrium because each firm correctly perceives what the other's output will be. Once these capacity decisions are made, the only price that can prevail is that for which total quantity demanded equals the combined capacities of the two firms.

To see why Bertrand-type price competition will result in such a solution, suppose Cournot capacities are given by $\bar{q}_A$ and $\bar{q}_B$ and that $\bar{P}$ is the price that would prevail when production is at capacity for both firms. A situation in which

$$P_A = P_B < \bar{P} \tag{12.1}$$

is not a Nash equilibrium. With this price, total quantity demanded exceeds total capacity, so firm A could increase its profits by raising price slightly and still selling $\bar{q}_A$. Similarly,

$$P_A = P_B > \bar{P} \tag{12.2}$$

is not a Nash equilibrium because now total sales fall short of capacity. At least one firm (say, firm A) is selling less than its capacity. By cutting price slightly, firm A can increase its profits by taking all possible sales up to $\bar{q}_A$. Of course, B will respond to a loss of sales by dropping its price as well. Hence, the only Nash equilibrium that can prevail is the Cournot result[6]

$$P_A = P_B = \bar{P} \tag{12.3}$$

In general, this price will fall short of the monopoly price but will exceed marginal cost. Results of this two-stage game are therefore indistinguishable from those arising from the Cournot model of the previous chapter.

Comparing the Bertrand and Cournot Results

The contrast between the Bertrand and Cournot games is striking. The former predicts competitive outcomes in a duopoly situation, whereas the latter predicts

---

[6] For completeness, it should also be noted that no situation in which $P_A \neq P_B$ can be an equilibrium since the low-price firm has an incentive to raise price and the high-price firm wishes to cut price.

monopolylike inefficiencies in which price exceeds marginal cost. This suggests that actual behavior in duopoly markets may exhibit a wide variety of outcomes depending on the precise way in which competition occurs. The principal lesson of the two-stage Cournot game is that, even with Bertrand price competition, decisions made prior to this final (price-setting) stage of a game can have an important impact on market behavior. This lesson will be reflected again in some of the game theory models of entry we describe later in this chapter. Application 12.2: How is the Price Game Played? illustrates how relatively minor factors can affect whether a market exhibits Cournot or Bertrand competition.

Tacit Collusion

Our analysis of the Prisoner's Dilemma concluded that if the game were played several times the participants might devise ways to adopt more cooperative strategic choices. A similar issue might be raised about the Bertrand game. Would repetition of this game offer some mechanism for the players to attain supracompetitive profits by pursuing a monopoly pricing policy? One possibility, discussed in Chapter 11, would be for the players to establish a cartel and explicitly set price or output targets. As we demonstrated, such explicit agreements can be difficult to enforce. Here, we adopt a noncooperative approach to the collusion question by exploring models of "tacit" collusion. That is, we use game theory concepts to see whether there exist equilibrium strategies that, though not explicitly coordinated, would allow firms to achieve monopoly profits.

Finite Time Horizon

Our initial result from the Bertrand model poses a stumbling block to achieving tacit collusion. Because the single-period Nash equilibrium in this model results in $P_A = P_B = c$, we need to ask whether this situation would change if the game were repeated during many periods. With any small number of repetitions, it seems clear that the Bertrand result remains unchanged. Any strategy in which firm A, say, chooses $P_A > c$ during the final period offers firm B the possibility of earning profits by setting $P_A > P_B > c$. The threat of charging $P_A > c$ in the last period is therefore not credible. Because a similar argument applies also to any period prior to the last one, we can conclude that the only perfect equilibrium is one in which firms charge the competitive price in every period. The assumptions of the Bertrand model make tacit collusion impossible over any finite period.

Infinite Time Horizon

If firms are viewed as having an infinite time horizon (or, at least no clear end to their game), matters change significantly. In this case there is no "final" period so there may exist collusive strategies that are not undermined by the logic of the Bertrand result. One such possibility is for firms to adopt "trigger" strategies in which each firm (again, say firm A) sets $P_A = P_M$ (where P_M is the cartel price) in every period in which firm B adopts that price also but chooses $P_A = c$ if firm B has cheated in the previous period.

Many factors may influence how the pricing "game" is played in imperfectly competitive industries. In this application, we look at two such factors.

Product Availability

Whether or not a given product is available is an important component of competition in many retail industries. Consumers who wish to avoid being disappointed have a preference for patronizing retailers who can be counted on to have a desired item in stock. Retailers know that availability is important to consumers and often stress this in their advertisements. Appliance store ads often stress that they have large stocks of air conditioners when hot weather arrives, and car dealers publicize the fact that they have lots of good deals on last year's models during the fall model change-over season.

The impact of movie availability in the video-rental industry was examined in a 2001 paper by James Dana.[1] The author's informal survey of video-rental outlets in the neighborhood of Boston University suggested that Blockbuster's prices were about 40 percent higher than at other stores. His data also showed that movies were more likely to be available at Blockbuster than elsewhere. The author argues that Blockbuster's higher price in part stems from its reputation for having movies available and in part because higher prices act as a signal to consumers that more movies are in fact available.

Whether the relationship between product availability and pricing is more like the Cournot model (where movie inventories are chosen first with prices following) or like the Bertrand model (where prices are chosen first) is hard to tell from the available data. But Dana does show that the Cournot price generally exceeds the Bertrand price. He also illustrates why free entry in the video-rental industry may not reduce price to the competitive level because consumers value availability.

Information Sharing

Firms in the same industry often share information with each other at many levels. Local retailers may get together to talk about the business climate; nationwide firms may send their sales figures to industry associations for publication; and some firms may share the same directors. It seems plausible that such information sharing could influence the nature of price competition in an industry, and a number of studies have found that is indeed the case.

For example, a 2000 study of cross-shareholding in the Dutch financial sector showed clear evidence that competition was reduced when firms had financial interests in each other's profits.[2] Prices were at least 8 percent higher in such cases when the firms behaved as specified in the Cournot model. Similar results have been reported in the United States for situations where firms own minority stakes in their competitors.

Information sharing through sales reporting can also influence price competition. A famous 1914 antitrust case found that a price list published by lumber retailers facilitated

---

[1] J. D. Dana, "Competition in Price and Availability When Availability Is Unobserved," *Rand Journal of Economics* (Winter 2001): 497–513.
[2] E. Dietzenbacher, B. Smid, and B. Volkerink, "Horizontal Integration in the Dutch Financial Sector," *International Journal of Industrial Organization* (December 2000): 1223–1242.

(continued)

higher prices by discouraging wholesalers from selling at retail. Similarly, sales reporting by movie theaters may have helped motion picture distributors to coordinate pricing (in a Cournot-like model) according to a 1939 U.S. Supreme Court decision.

To Think About

1. What are some of the other elements of "service" that retail establishments could offer that might affect how they compete on price? What kinds of problems would be encountered by a high-service retailer that tried to recoup its service costs in higher prices?

2. How might firms use the Internet to develop pricing strategies by checking what their competitors are doing?

To determine whether these firms' trigger strategies constitute a perfect equilibrium, we must discern whether they constitute a Nash equilibrium in every period. Suppose the firms have colluded for a time and firm A thinks about cheating in this period. Knowing that firm B will choose $P_B = P_M$, it can set its price slightly below P_M and, in this period, obtain the entire market for itself. It will thereby earn (almost) the entire monopoly profits (π_M) in this period. But, by doing this, firm A will lose its share of profits ($\pi_M/2$) forever after because its treachery will trigger firm B's retaliatory strategy. Because the present value[7] of these lost profits is given by

$$(\pi_M/2) \cdot \frac{1}{r} \qquad (12.4)$$

(where r is the per-period interest rate), cheating will be unprofitable if

$$\pi_M < (\pi_M/2) \cdot \frac{1}{r} \qquad (12.5)$$

MicroQuiz 12.3

Would the following situations make tacit collusion more or less likely?

1. Neither firm believes that it can last forever.

2. A monopoly cartel has ten members rather than only two.

This condition holds for values of r less than ½. We can therefore conclude that the trigger strategies constitute a perfect equilibrium for sufficiently low interest rates. The collusion implicit in these strategies is totally noncooperative. The firms never actually have to meet in seedy hotel rooms to adopt strategies that yield monopoly profits.

[7] For a discussion of the present value concept see Chapter 14 and its Appendix on compound interest.

Generalizations and Limitations

The contrast between the competitive results of the Bertrand model and the monopoly results of the tacit collusion model suggests that the viability of collusion in game theory models is very sensitive to the particular assumptions made. Two assumptions in our simple model of tacit collusion are especially important: (1) that firm B can easily detect whether firm A has cheated; and (2) that firm B responds to cheating by adopting a harsh response that not only punishes firm A but also condemns itself to zero profits forever. In more general models of tacit collusion, these assumptions can be relaxed, for example, by allowing for the possibility that it may be difficult for firm B to recognize cheating by A. Some models examine alternative types of punishment B might inflict on A—for example, B could cut price in some other market in which A also sells. Other categories of models explore the consequences of introducing differentiated products into models of tacit collusion or of incorporating reasons why the demand for a firm's product may not respond instantly to price changes by its rival. As might be imagined, results of such modeling efforts are quite varied.[8] In all such models, the notions of Nash and perfect equilibria continue to play an important role in identifying whether tacit collusion can arise from strategic choices that appear to be viable. Real-world markets often exhibit aspects of both tacit and explicit collusion, as Application 12.3: The Great Electrical Equipment Conspiracy shows.

ENTRY, EXIT, AND STRATEGY

The treatment of entry and exit in earlier chapters left little room for strategic thinking. A potential entrant was concerned only with the relationship between prevailing market price and its own (average or marginal) costs. We assumed that making that comparison involved no special problems. Similarly, we assumed that firms will promptly leave a market they find to be unprofitable. Upon closer inspection, however, the entry and exit issue can become considerably more complex. The fundamental problem is that a firm wishing to enter or leave a market must make some conjecture about how its action will affect market price in subsequent periods. Making these conjectures obviously requires the firm to consider what its rivals will do. What appears to be a relatively straightforward decision comparing price and average cost may therefore involve a number of strategic ploys, especially when a firm's information about its rivals is imperfect.

Sunk Costs and Commitment

Many game theory models of the entry process stress the importance of a firm's *commitment* to a specific market. If the nature of production requires that firms

---

[8] See J. Tirole, *The Theory of Industrial Organization* (Cambridge, MA: MIT Press, 1988), Chapter 6.

The Great Electrical Equipment Conspiracy

Even though an industry may be reasonably profitable, the lure of monopoly profits may tempt it to create cartels. The lure is especially strong when there are relatively few firms and when one member of the cartel can easily police what the other members are doing. This was the case with the electrical equipment industry in the early 1950s when it developed an elaborate price-rigging scheme. However, the scheme came under both increasing internal friction and external legal scrutiny. By the 1960s, the scheme had failed, and executives of several major companies had been imprisoned.[1]

The Markets for Generators and Switch Gear

Electric turbine generators and high-voltage switching units are sold to electric utility companies. Often they are customized to unique specifications and can cost many millions of dollars. With the rapid growth in the use of electricity after World War II, manufacturing this machinery provided a very lucrative business to such major producers as General Electric, Westinghouse, and Federal Pacific Corporations. Although these growth prospects promised good profits for the large firms in the business, the possibility of collusion in pricing proved to be even more enticing.

The Bid-Rigging Scheme

The principal problem faced by the electrical equipment firms seeking to create a cartel was that most of their sales took place through sealed bidding to large electric utilities. To avoid competition, they therefore had to devise a method for coordinating the bids each firm would make. Through a complex strategy that involved dividing the United States into bidding regions and using the lunar calendar to decide whose turn it was to "win" a bid in a region, the firms were able to overcome the secrecy supposedly guaranteed by submitting sealed bids. The practice worked quite well until the end of the decade. It probably increased total profits of electrical equipment manufacturers by as much as $100 million over the period.

Demise of the Conspiracy

Toward the end of the 1950s, the electrical equipment conspiracy came under increasing internal friction as its leaders (General Electric and Westinghouse) were asked to give a greater share of the business to other firms. New entries into the industry by importers and low-cost domestic producers also caused some problems for the cartel. The final blow to the conspiracy came when a newspaper reporter discovered that some of the bids on Tennessee Valley Authority projects were suspiciously similar. His discovery led to a series of widely publicized hearings led by Senator Estes Kefauver in 1959. These resulted in the federal indictment of 52 executives of the leading generator, switch gear, and transformer companies. Although the government recommended prison sentences for thirty of these defendants, only seven actually served time in jail. Still, the notoriety of the case and the

---

[1] For a popularized and somewhat sensationalized version of this episode, see J. G. Fuller, *The Gentlemen Conspirators* (New York: Grove Press, 1962).

personal disruption it caused to those involved probably had a chilling effect on the future establishment of other cartels of this type.

To Think About

1. Why did the electrical equipment manufacturers opt for an illegal bid-rigging scheme rather than settling for some other form of tacit collusion? What about the nature of transactions in this business made the explicit price-fixing solution a necessary one? Would tacit collusion have worked?
2. Prosecution of the electrical equipment conspirators was one of the few cases of a successful "cops and robbers" approach to antitrust law. It involved wire tapping, government informers, and so forth to collect evidence on the illegal behavior of the executives. How would the evidence differ if this had been a case of tacit collusion?

make specific capital investments in order to operate in a market and if these cannot easily be shifted to other uses, any firm that makes such investments has committed itself to being a market participant. As we saw in Chapter 6, expenditures on such investments are called *sunk costs*. Sunk costs might include expenditures on items such as unique types of equipment (for example, a newsprint-making machine) or on job-specific training for workers (developing the skills to use the newsprint machine). Sunk costs have many characteristics of fixed costs in that these costs are incurred even if no output is produced. Rather than being incurred periodically as are many fixed costs (heating the factory), these costs are incurred only once, as part of the entry process. When the firm makes such an investment, it has committed itself to the market, which may have important consequences for its strategic behavior.

First-Mover Advantages

Although at first glance it might seem that incurring sunk costs by making the commitment to serve a market puts a firm at a disadvantage, in most models that is not the case. Rather, one firm can often stake out a claim to a market by making a commitment to serve it and in the process limit the kinds of actions its rivals find profitable. Many game theory models, therefore, stress the advantage of moving first.

As a simple numerical example, consider again Cournot's example of two springs. In our discussion in Chapter 11, we assumed each firm chose its output capacity simultaneously and this resulted in a price of $40 with a total output of 80 (thousand gallons). Suppose now, instead, that firm A has the option of moving first. Because firm A can safely assume that firm B will maximize profits given what it has done, firm A can take account of this insight in its decision. Specifically, since firm A knows that firm B reacts by

$$q_B = 120 - \frac{q_A}{2} \qquad\qquad (12.6)$$

it can use this to compute the net demand for its own spring's water:

$$q_A = 120 - q_B - P = 120 - \frac{(120 - q_A)}{2} - P = 60 + \frac{q_A}{2} - P \qquad (12.7)$$

Solving for q_A gives

$$q_A = 120 - 2P \qquad (12.8)$$

Hence, marginal revenue equals zero (and total revenues are maximized) when firm A chooses a capacity of $q_A = 60$ (that is, half of 120—the quantity demanded when $P = 0$). With firm A taking advantage of its first-mover position, firm B chooses to produce

$$q_B = \frac{120 - q_A}{2} = \frac{(120 - 60)}{2} = 30 \qquad (12.9)$$

With total output of 90, spring water sells for $30 and firm A's total revenues are $1,800 (= 60 × $30)—an improvement over the $1,600 collected in the Cournot equilibrium. Firm B's revenues have correspondingly been reduced to $900—a sign of the disadvantage faced by a later mover.[9]

Entry Deterrence

In some cases, first-mover advantages may be large enough to deter all entry by rivals. Intuitively, it seems plausible that the first mover could opt for a very large capacity and thereby discourage all other firms from entering the market. The economic rationality of such a decision is not clear-cut, however. In the Cournot model, for example, the only sure way for one spring owner to deter all entry is to satisfy the total market demand at the firm's marginal and average cost; that is, firm A would have to offer $q_A = 120$ at a price of zero if it is to have a fully successful entry-deterrence strategy. Obviously, such a choice results in zero profits for the firm and would not represent profit maximization. Instead, it would be better for firm A to accept some entry.

With economies of scale in production, the possibility for profitable entry deterrence is increased. If the firm that is to move first can adopt a large enough

---

[9] Sometimes this solution is referred to as a "Stackelberg equilibrium" after the German economist who first discovered the advantage of moving first in the Cournot case.

scale of operation, it may be able to limit the scale of the potential entrant. The potential entrant will therefore experience such high average costs that there would be no way for it to earn a profit.

A Numerical Example

The simplest way to incorporate economies of scale into the Cournot model is to assume each spring owner must pay a fixed cost of operations. If that fixed cost is given by $784 (a carefully chosen number!), firm B would still find it attractive to enter if firm A moves first and opts to produce $q_A = 60$. In this case, firm B would earn profits of $116 (= $900 − $784) per period. However, if the first mover opts for $q_A = 64$, this would force firm B to choose $q_B = 28$ [= (120 − 64) ÷ 2]. At this combined output of 92, price would be $28 and firm B would break even [profits = TR − TC = (28 · 28) − 784 = 0] and choose not to enter. Firm A would now have the market to itself, obtain a price of $56 (= 120 − 64), and earn profits of $2,800 [= (56 · 64) − 784]. Economies of scale, combined with the ability to move first, provide firm A with a very profitable entry-deterring strategy. Of course, in the real world, the advantages of entering a market first may not be so clear-cut, as Application 12.4: First-Mover Advantages for Alcoa, DuPont, Procter & Gamble, and Wal-Mart illustrates.

Limit Pricing

So far, our discussion of strategic considerations in entry decisions has focused on issues of sunk costs and output commitments. A somewhat different approach to the entry-deterrence question concerns the possibility that an incumbent monopoly could deter entry through its pricing policy alone. That is, are there situations where a monopoly might purposely choose a low ("limit") price with the goal of deterring entry into its market?

In most simple cases, the limit pricing strategy does not seem to yield maximum profits nor to be sustainable over time. If an incumbent monopoly opts for a price of $P_L < P_M$ (where P_M is the profit-maximizing price), it is obviously hurting its current-period profits. But this limit price will deter entry in the future only if P_L falls short of the average cost of any potential entrant. If the monopoly and its potential entrant have the same costs (and if capacity choices do not play the role they did in the previous example), the only limit price that is sustainable in the presence of potential entry is $P_L = AC$, adoption of which would obviously defeat the purpose of being a monopoly because profits would now be zero. Hence, the basic monopoly model offers little room for limit price behavior—either there are barriers to entry that allow the monopoly to sustain P_M, or there are no such barriers and competitive pricing prevails.

INFOTRAC©
COLLEGE EDITION
Exclusively from Gale Group and Thomson Learning

www.infotrac-college.com
Keywords: Nash equilibrium, Prisoner's dilemma, Bertrand equilibrium, Sunk costs, Predatory pricing

First-Mover Advantages for Alcoa, DuPont, Procter & Gamble, and Wal-Mart

The first-mover advantages that arise in game theory are illustrated in a number of actual markets. Here, we look at two types of advantages: (1) advantages that stem from economies of scale in production and (2) advantages that arise in connection with the introduction of pioneering brands.

Economies of Scale for Alcoa and DuPont

If there are economies of scale in production, the first firm into a market may "overbuild" its initial plant in the interest of achieving low costs in the future as demand for the product expands. In this way, future entry will be deterred. One of the first instances of this behavior studied by economists concerned the expansion of the Aluminum Company of America (Alcoa) immediately after World War II. In an important antitrust suit against the company, it was claimed that Alcoa, in an effort to foreclose entry by others, built far larger plants than was justified by current demand.

A similar case occurred during the 1970s in connection with the production of titanium dioxide.[1] DuPont was the largest producer of this product (which is the primary coloring agent in white paint), but the firm worried about potential expansions by its principal competitors. In an attempt to forestall new investment, DuPont decided to embark on a major expansion in its capacity to produce titanium dioxide. Several studies of this episode have concluded that DuPont's strategy was largely successful in deterring investment by others.

Pioneering Brands for Procter and Gamble

Introducing the first brand of a new product to its market seems to give that brand considerable advantages over its later-arriving rivals. The Procter & Gamble corporation has been especially successful in garnering such advantages. For example, the introduction of Tide laundry detergent in the early 1940s gave the company an advantage in this type of product it has never lost. Similar results occurred when P&G introduced the first fluoride toothpaste (Crest) in the late 1950s.

Although traditional arguments about economies of scale in the production of these brands or in the advertising related to their introduction may explain some of these first-mover advantages, a more important reason may arise from the information problems faced by consumers.[2] Invention of a new product poses difficulty for consumers in that they don't know whether it will do what it's supposed to do. Someone who buys the product thereby exposes him- or herself to risk. If the product does work as advertised, a consumer may then decide to stick with it as other "me-too" brands are developed. Being first, therefore, has an advantage.

The Wal-Mart Advantage

The Wal-Mart retailing chain gained its prominent position both through exploiting economies of scale and from the first-mover advantages it enjoyed by its initial "small

---

[1] See E. A. Hall, "An Analysis of Preemptive Behavior in the Titanium Dioxide Industry," *International Journal of Industrial Organization* (September 1990): 469–484.
[2] For additional details, see R. Schmalensee, "Product Differentiation Advantages of Pioneering Brands," *American Economic Review* (June 1982): 349–365.

town" strategy. The firm was started by Sam Walton in the late 1960s and, at first, focused on small, mostly Southern markets. By establishing near-monopoly positions in these markets, the firm was very profitable and was able to finance a rapid expansion. As the firm grew, it gained scale economies both in terms of its ability to distribute goods to its locations and in terms of its ability to negotiate better prices with suppliers. It was not until Wal-Mart had solidified its position in smaller marketplaces that it began to make inroads into the more competitive markets in suburban areas outside of the southern United States.

To Think About

1. Are economies of scale crucial to implementation of a successful strategy of entry-deterring plant expansion? Would such expansion be a profitable strategy under conditions of constant returns to scale?
2. Why is the existence of imperfect information crucial to the first-mover advantage of pioneering brands? Would pioneering brands enjoy any advantage in a world of homogeneous products and perfect information?

Incomplete Information

Believable models of limit pricing behavior must therefore depart from traditional assumptions. The most important set of such models are those involving incomplete information. If an incumbent monopoly knows more about a particular market situation than does a potential entrant, it may be able to take advantage of its superior knowledge to deter entry. As an example, consider the game tree illustrated in Figure 12.3. Here, firm A, the incumbent monopolist, may have either "high" or "low" production costs as a result of its past decisions. Firm A does not actually choose its costs currently but, because these costs are not known to B, we must allow for the two possibilities. The profitability of B's entry into the market depends on A's costs—with high costs, B's entry is profitable ($\pi_B = 3$); whereas, if A has low costs, entry

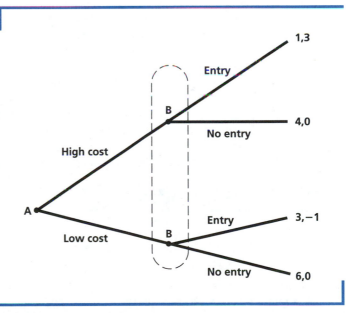

FIGURE 12.3 An Entry Game Firm A has either a "high" or a "low" cost structure that cannot be observed by B. If B believes A has high costs, it will enter; otherwise it will not. Firm A may try to influence B's assessment.

is unprofitable ($\pi_B = -1$). What is B to do? Somehow it must use whatever information it can get to guess what A's true cost situation is.

The particularly intriguing aspects of this game concern whether A can influence B's assessment. Regardless of its true costs, firm A is better off if B adopts the no-entry strategy, and one way to ensure that is for A to take steps that lead B to believe that A has low costs. For example, if A chooses a low-price policy when it serves the market as a monopoly, this may signal to B that A's costs are low and thereby deter entry. Such strategy might be profitable for A even though it would require it to sacrifice some profits. This provides a possible rationale for setting a low price as an entry-deterrence strategy.

Predatory Pricing

Tools used to study limit pricing can also shed light on the possibility for "predatory" pricing. Ever since the formation of the Standard Oil monopoly in the late nineteenth century, part of the mythology of American business is that John D. Rockefeller was able to drive his competitors out of business by charging ruinously low (predatory) prices. Although both the economic logic and the empirical facts behind this version of the Standard Oil story have generally been discounted (see Application 12.5: The Standard Oil Legend), the possibility of encouraging exit through predation continues to provide interesting opportunities for theoretical modeling.

The structure of many models of predatory behavior is similar to that used in limit pricing models; that is, the models stress asymmetric information. An incumbent firm wishes to encourage its rival to exit the market so it takes actions intended to affect the rival's view of the future profitability of market participation. The incumbent may, for example, adopt a low-price policy in an attempt to signal to its rival that its costs are low—even if they are not. Or the incumbent may adopt extensive advertising or product differentiation activities with the intention of convincing its rival that it has economies of scale. Once the rival is convinced that the incumbent firm possesses these advantages, it may recalculate the expected profitability of its production decisions and decide to exit the market. Of course, as in the limit pricing models, successful predatory strategies are not a foregone conclusion. Their viability depends crucially on the nature of information in the market. Only if the monopoly can take advantage of its better information can predatory behavior succeed.

MicroQuiz 12.5

"Dumping" is the international equivalent of predatory pricing in which imports are sold at very low prices to drive out domestic competition.

1. Explain how "dumping" is supposed to be a profitable strategy for producers of imports.

2. Is dumping more likely to be a successful strategy than domestic predatory pricing?

The Standard Oil case of 1911 was one of the landmarks of U.S. antitrust law. In that case, John D. Rockefeller's Standard Oil Company was found to have "attempted to monopolize" the production, refining, and distribution of petroleum in the United States, violating the Sherman Act. One of the ways that Standard Oil was found to have established its monopoly was through the use of predatory pricing. The government claimed that the company would cut prices dramatically to drive rivals out of a particular market and then raise prices back to monopoly levels after the rivals had left the market or had sold out to Standard Oil. This view of how Standard Oil operated was promoted by the "muckraker" author Ida Tarbell[1] and became one of the more durable beliefs about nineteenth-century business practices.

Theory of Predatory Pricing

Unfortunately, the notion that Standard Oil practiced predatory pricing policies in order to discourage entry and encourage exit by its rivals makes little sense in terms of economic theory. As we have seen, if a would-be monopolist wishes to impose costs on its rivals, it must sell its output below average cost, perhaps below marginal cost. It must also be willing to absorb the extra sales that such lowered prices would bring. The predator must, therefore, operate with relatively large losses for some time in the hope that the smaller losses this may cause rivals will eventually prompt them to give up. This strategy is clearly inferior to the strategy of simply buying smaller rivals in the marketplace. Even if such mergers were illegal, it is unclear that the predator has longer staying power than its rivals in sticking to a low-price policy—especially since rivals know that price must eventually return to a normal, profitable level.

Actual Evidence on Standard Oil

These thoughts prompted J. S. McGee to reexamine the historical record of what Standard Oil actually did. In a famous 1958 article, McGee concluded that Standard Oil neither tried to use predatory policies nor did its actual price policies have the effect of driving rivals from the oil business.[2] McGee examined over 100 refineries that were bought by Standard Oil between 1871 and 1900. He found no evidence that predatory behavior by Standard Oil caused these firms to sell out. Indeed, in many cases Standard paid quite good prices for these refineries, which themselves were reasonably profitable. McGee also looked in detail at the effect that Standard Oil's retailing activities had on the network of jobbers and small retailers who had grown up around the oil and kerosene business in the late nineteenth

---

[1] The antagonist relationship between Tarbell and Rockefeller had a major impact on the early regulation of American business. For a discussion, see the excellent biography by R. Chernow, *Titan: The Life of John D. Rockefeller* (New York: Random House, 1998).

[2] J. S. McGee, "Predatory Price Cutting: The Standard Oil Case," *Journal of Law and Economics* (October 1958): 137–169.

(continued)

century. It seems clear that Standard's retailing methods were superior to those used previously (and were quickly adopted by other firms). The use of local price cutting does not seem to have been practiced by the company, however. Hence, although Standard Oil did eventually obtain an oil-refining monopoly, which probably required some attention by policymakers, it did not appear to attain this position through predatory behavior.

To Think About

1. If the facts do not support the notion of predatory pricing by Standard Oil, why do you think the company is so widely believed to have practiced it? What kinds of market-wide trends were influencing oil pricing during the late nineteenth century? Might these have been mistaken for predatory behavior?

2. Another claim in the Standard Oil case is that Rockefeller obtained preferential rates from railroads to transport oil. Why might railroads have granted such rates to Rockefeller? Would they have an interest in refusing such rates to other shippers?

N-PLAYER GAME THEORY

All the game theory examples we have looked at in this chapter involve only two players. Although this limitation is useful for illustrating the strategic issues that arise in the play of a game (or the operation of a duopoly market), it also tends to obscure some important questions. The most important additional element added to game theory when the study moves beyond two players is the possibility for the formation of subsets of players who agree on coordinated strategies. Although the possibility for forming such **coalitions** exists in two-player games (the two firms in a duopoly could form a cartel), the number of possible coalitions expands rapidly as games with larger numbers of players are considered. In some games, simply listing the number of potential coalitions and the payoffs they might receive can be a major task.

Coalitions
Combinations of two or more players in a game who adopt coordinated strategies.

As in the formation of cartels in oligopolistic markets, the likelihood of forming successful coalitions in *n*-player games is importantly influenced by organizational costs. These costs involve both information costs associated with determining coalition strategies and enforcement costs associated with ensuring that a coalition's chosen strategy is actually followed by its members. If there are incentives for members to chat on established coalition strategies, then monitoring and enforcement costs may be high. In some cases, monitoring costs may be so high as to make the establishment of coalitions prohibitively costly. For these games, then, all *n* players operate independently and many of the insights from two-person game theory continue to hold.

SUMMARY

In this chapter, we have briefly examined the economic theory of games. We also used that theory to explain strategic behavior in duopoly markets. Some of our conclusions are:

- Concepts such as players, strategies, and payoffs are common to all games.
- Many games also possess equilibrium solutions. With a Nash equilibrium, each player's strategic choice is optimal given its rival's choice. In multi-period games, only Nash equilibria that involve credible threats are viable.
- The Prisoner's Dilemma represents a particularly instructive two-person game. In this game, the most preferred outcome is unstable; though, in repeated games, the players may adopt various enforcement strategies.

- Game theory models of duopoly pricing start from the Bertrand result that the only Nash equilibrium in a simple game is competitive (marginal cost) pricing. Consideration of capacity commitments and first-mover strategies may result in noncompetitive results, however. Tacit collusion at the monopoly price is sustainable in infinite-period games under certain circumstances.
- Much of the game theoretic modeling of entry and exit stresses the importance of information. In situations of asymmetric information, incumbent firms may be able to capitalize on superior information by adopting strategies that result in entry deterrence.

REVIEW QUESTIONS

1. In game theory, players maximize utility. Is this assumption different from the one we used in Chapters 2 through Chapter 4?

2. Express the notion of a Nash equilibrium as a utility-maximization problem. What does each player maximize? What are the constraints in the problem? What can you say about these constraints at the Nash equilibrium?

3. Explain why the Cournot equilibrium described in Chapter 11 is a Nash equilibrium in a game where firms' strategies consist of potential output levels. Why is the intersection of firms' reaction functions (Figure 11.3) a graphical illustration of the Nash equilibrium concept?

4. Which of the following activities might be represented as a zero-sum game? Which are clearly not zero-sum?
   a. Flipping a coin for $1
   b. Playing blackjack
   c. Choosing which candy bar to buy from a vendor
   d. Reducing taxes through various "creative accounting" methods and seeking to avoid detection by the IRS

   e. Deciding when to rob a particular house knowing that the residents may adopt various countertheft strategies

5. Why is the Prisoner's Dilemma a "dilemma" for the players involved? How might they solve this dilemma through pregame discussions? If you were arrested and the D.A. tried this ploy, what would you do? Would it matter whether you were very close friends with your criminal accomplice?

6. The Nash equilibrium in a Bertrand price-setting game assumes that the demand for any one firm's product is very responsive to pricing by the other firm. Why is this assumption crucial for the competitive results in the Bertrand model? How would those results be affected if a consumer had some reluctance to shift its purchases from one firm to another?

7. Why can the Cournot model from Chapter 11 be regarded as a choice of firms' "capacities"? What is "capacity" and how is this concept related to firms' cost functions?

8. "The definition of a perfect equilibrium is an exercise in the use of double negatives—how can

you expect anyone to learn what it means to be an equilibrium in which 'there are no noncredible threats'?" Can you help out this hapless student? How could you refine this definition so that it includes no negatives?

9. "The infinite horizon assumed in games that illustrate tacit collusion is another example of the nonsense of economic theory. No one thinks infinitely far into the future." Do you agree with this assessment? What role does the infinite time horizon play in the model of tacit collusion? Can

this assumption be justified without resorting to the implausible notion that firms think infinitely far into the future?

10. Explain the differences between entry deterrence through first-mover investments and entry deterrence through pricing. What assumptions are required for each of these entry-deterrence strategies to be successful? Describe a hypothetical situation under which each strategy might work for an incumbent monopolist.

PROBLEMS

12.1 The following table reports the payoff matrix for an advertising game. Explain why the strategy pair "A: high, B: low" is a Nash equilibrium in this game and all the other strategy pairs are not.

		B's Strategies	
		High	**Low**
	High	A: 5 B: 2	A: 3 B: 3
A's Strategies			
	Low	A: 4 B: 3	A: 2 B: 4

12.2 Player A and player B are engaged in a coin-matching game. Each shows a coin as either heads or tails. If the coins match, B pays A $1. If they differ, A pays B $1.

a. Write down the payoff matrix for this game, and show that it does not contain a Nash equilibrium.

b. How might the players choose their strategies in this case?

12.3 Smith and Jones are playing a number-matching game. Each chooses either 1, 2, or 3. If the numbers match, Jones pays Smith $3. If they differ, Smith pays Jones $1.

a. Describe the payoff matrix for this game, and show that it does not possess a Nash equilibrium strategy pair.

b. Show that with mixed strategies this game does have a Nash equilibrium if each player plays each number with probability 1/3. What is the expected value of this game if it is played many times?

12.4 Suppose firm A and firm B each operate under conditions of constant average and marginal cost but that $MC_A = 10$ and $MC_B = 8$. The demand for the firms' output is given by

$$Q_D = 500 - 20P$$

a. If the firms practice Bertrand competition, what will be the market price under a Nash equilibrium?

b. What will the profits be for each firm?

c. Will this equilibrium be Pareto efficient?

12.5 The entire world's supply of kryptonite is controlled by 20 people, each having a large supply of this potent material ($MC = 0$). The annual world demand for kryptonite is given by

$$Q = 10,000 - 1,000P$$

where P is the price per gram.

a. If all owners could conspire to rig the price of kryptonite, what price would they set and how much of their supply would they sell?

b. Why is the price computed in part a an unstable equilibrium?

c. Does a price for kryptonite exist that would be a stable equilibrium in the sense that no firm could gain by altering its output from that required to maintain this market price?

12.6 The game of "chicken" is played by two macho teens who speed toward each other on a single-lane road. The first to veer off is branded the chicken, whereas the one who doesn't turn gains peer group esteem. Of course, if neither veers, both die in the resulting crash. Payoffs to the chicken game are provided in the following table.

		B's Strategies	
		Chicken	Not chicken
A's Strategies	Chicken	2, 2	1, 3
	Not chicken	3, 1	0, 0

a. Does this game have a Nash equilibrium?
b. Is a threat by either not to chicken out a credible one?
c. Would the ability of one player to firmly commit to a no-chicken strategy (by, for example, throwing away the steering wheel) be desirable for that player?
d. In the 2002 film *A Beautiful Mind*, John Nash is pictured as having his most basic insight at a bar when several male students are discussing whether to approach an attractive blonde female. The film offers an extremely muddled account of what Nash is thinking, but one interpretation is that he sees approaching the blonde (rather than the other women present) as a game of "chicken." How might you interpret the situation in this way? Does this seem to get at what Nash was thinking?

12.7 Two firms (A and B) are considering bringing out competing brands of a healthy cigarette. Payoffs to the companies are as follows (A's profits are given first):

		Firm B	
		Produce	Don't produce
Firm A	Produce	3, 3	5, 4
	Don't produce	4, 5	2, 2

a. Does this game have a Nash equilibrium?
b. Does this game present any first-mover advantages for either firm A or firm B?
c. Would firm B find it in its interest to bribe firm A enough to stay out of the market?

12.8 The Wave Energy Technology (WET) company has a monopoly on the production of vibratory waterbeds. Demand for these beds is relatively inelastic—at a price of $1,000 per bed, 25,000 will be sold; whereas, at a price of $600, 30,000 will be sold. The only costs associated with waterbed production are the initial costs of building a plant. WET has already invested in a plant capable of producing up to 25,000 beds, and this sunk cost is irrelevant to its pricing decisions.

a. Suppose a would-be entrant to this industry could always be assured of half the market but would have to invest $10 million in a plant. Construct entrant's strategies (enter, don't enter). Does this game have a Nash equilibrium?
b. Suppose WET could invest $5 million in enlarging its existing plant to produce 40,000 beds. Would this strategy be a profitable way to deter entry by its rival?

12.9 An individual is thinking of going on a picnic but fears it might rain. Utilities possible in this situation are reflected in the following table:

	Rain	No rain
Picnic	0	20
No picnic	5	10

a. Suppose this individual adopts the pessimistic attitude that "whatever can go wrong will go wrong," which strategy should she choose? (Technically, this is called a maximin strategy because it is the maximum utility from all the worst outcomes.)
b. Suppose instead this individual assigns a probability of 0.6 to the likelihood of rain and opts for the strategy with the greatest expected utility (see Chapter 15). Will she go on the picnic?

12.10 Game theorists sometimes use the terms "strategic substitutes" and "strategic complements" to describe the relationship between the strategic choices made by two firms. Firms' activities are strategic substitutes if and when firm A increases the activity and firm B reduces it. The activities are strategic complements if an increase in the activity by firm A causes firm B to increase the activity as well. Use these definitions to provide intuitive proofs of the following propositions:

a. In the Cournot model, quantities (or production capacities) are strategic substitutes.

b. In the Bertrand model, prices are strategic complements.

INTERNET EXERCISES

1. *Prisoner's Dilemma.* Play Prisoner's Dilemma against a computer! Go to Morris Danielson's Prisoner's Dilemma game at *http://www.princeton. edu/~mdaniels/PD/PD.html.* Before playing, scroll down and carefully read the instructions, paying particular attention to the descriptions of Albert's possible strategies. For each of Albert's four strategies (Golden Rule, Brazen Rule, Brazen Rule 3, and Iron Rule), formulate your own strategy to play in response, keeping in mind that you wish to minimize your total jail time. Now, choose a strategy for Albert, and play the game ten times, where you will play according to the relevant strategy you have formulated. What strategy did you pick for Albert and how did you play in response? How many years must you spend in jail? Repeat the same for each of Albert's other possible strategies. Now, play the game one more time, except now choose "???" for Albert. How well did you do? Did it help you to know which strategy Albert was playing as compared to when he played "???"? Suppose you and Albert both agree to play Golden Rule. Would this be a Nash equilibrium? Why or why not?

2. *Predatory pricing.* In May 1999, the U.S. Department of Justice filed a complaint against American Airlines, alleging that American Airlines had engaged in predatory pricing to drive its competitors out of the market (you may wish to refer back to Application 10.3 in your text, which discusses the case). Read the Justice Department's complaint at *http://www.usdoj. gov/atr/cases/f2400/2438.htm.* Briefly describe the complaint against American Airlines. Next, read the American Airlines press release responding to the Justice Department's allegations at *http://www.aadoj.com/press/990513b.htm.* Briefly describe American's response. If you were judging this case, what factors would be important to you in attempting to discern between "anticompetitive predatory pricing" and "competitive pricing responses" to additional competition? The Justice Department also claimed that American's actions were also designed to deter future entry by competitors into the market. What was the Justice Department's reasoning? How does this compare and contrast to the practice of limit pricing?

Part 5

Further Topics

"In devising and choosing among social arrangements, we should have regard for the total effect."

Ronald Coase, *The Problem of Social Cost*, 1960

Although Chapter 12 completed our study of microeconomic models of pricing, the tools we developed are useful for studying a large number of additional topics. In this final part, we look at some of those applications.

Chapter 13 looks at the market for labor. We show how the desire of firms to maximize profits leads them to take wages into account in their hiring decisions; that is, firms are shown to have a downward-sloping demand curve for the workers they hire. Labor-supply decisions by individuals (which we briefly examine in the Appendix to Chapter 13) then interact with this demand curve to determine wages.

Much of the analysis of Chapter 13 is quite general—it applies equally well to any other input that firms hire. In Chapter 14, we look specifically at firms' use of capital. The chapter emphasizes the importance of interest rates in such decisions. The appendix to Chapter 14 looks at some of the mathematics associated with interest rates.

In Chapter 15, we look at the important role that uncertainty plays in economics. The principal goal of the chapter is to illustrate why people are probably averse to risk and will pay something to avoid taking such risks. Chapter 15 also briefly looks at how uncertainty may affect market outcomes.

Finally, Chapter 16 looks at two situations where markets may "fail" to perform efficiently: (1) cases involving important third-party effects (externalities); and (2) cases involving goods that have certain "public" characteristics. An important focus of the chapter is to suggest how, if at all, market forces can be modified to yield better results.

13

Labor Markets

Input prices are also determined by the forces of demand and supply. In this case, however, market roles are reversed. Now firms are on the demand side of the market, hiring inputs to meet their production needs. These inputs are supplied by individuals through the jobs they take and the capital resources that their savings provide. In this chapter, we explore some models of how wages are determined in labor markets. We begin with a fairly extensive discussion of demand, then very briefly summarize the nature of supply decisions. The remainder of the chapter is devoted to examining how demand and supply interact to determine wages. The appendix to this chapter explores questions of labor supply in somewhat more detail. Chapter 14 uses some of the tools developed in this chapter to study pricing of capital.

MARGINAL PRODUCTIVITY THEORY OF INPUT DEMAND

In Chapter 9, we looked briefly at Ricardo's theory of economic rent. This theory was an important first step in the development of marginal economics. Ricardo's notion that price is determined by the costs of the "marginal" producer in many ways represents the seed from which modern microeconomics grew. One application of his approach was the development of the "marginal productivity" theory of the demand for inputs. This section investigates that theory in detail.

Profit-Maximizing Behavior and the Hiring of Inputs

The basic concept of the marginal productivity theory of input demand was already stated in Chapter 7 when we discussed profit maximization. There we showed that one implication of the profit-maximization hypothesis is that the firm makes marginal input choices. More precisely, we showed that a profit-maximizing firm hires additional units of any input up to the point at which the additional revenue from hiring one more unit of the input is exactly equal to the cost of hiring that unit. If we use ME_K and ME_L to denote the marginal expense associated with hiring one more unit of capital and labor, respectively, and let MR_K and MR_L be the extra revenue that hiring these units of capital and labor allows the firm to bring in, then profit maximization requires that

$$ME_K = MR_K$$
$$ME_L = MR_L. \tag{13.1}$$

Price-Taking Behavior

If the firm is a price taker in the capital and labor markets, it is easy to simplify the marginal expense idea. In this case, the firm can always hire an extra hour of capital input at the prevailing rental rate (v) and an extra hour of labor at the wage rate (w). Therefore, the profit-maximizing requirement reduces to

$$v = ME_K = MR_K$$
$$w = ME_L = MR_L \tag{13.2}$$

These equations simply say that a profit-maximizing firm that is a price taker for the inputs it buys should hire extra amounts of these inputs up to the point at which their unit cost is equal to the revenue generated by the last one hired. If the firm's hiring decisions affect input prices, it has to take that into account. We look at such a situation later in this chapter.

Marginal Revenue Product

To calculate the additional revenue yielded by hiring one more unit of an input is a two-step process. First, we must ask how much output the additional input can produce. As we discussed in Chapter 5, this is given by the input's marginal physical productivity. For example, if a firm hires one more worker for an hour to make shoes, the worker's marginal physical productivity (MP_L) is simply the number of additional pairs of shoes per hour that the firm can make.

Once the additional output has been produced, it must be sold. Assessing the value of that sale is the second step in analyzing the revenue yielded by hiring one more unit of an input. We have looked at this issue quite extensively in previous chapters—the extra revenue obtained from selling an additional unit of output is, by definition, marginal revenue (MR). So, if an extra worker can produce two pairs of shoes per hour and the firm can take in $4 per pair from selling these shoes, then hiring the worker for an hour has increased the firm's revenues by $8.

This is the figure the firm compares to the worker's hourly wage to decide whether he or she should be hired. So now our profit-maximizing rules become

$$v = ME_K = MR_K = MP_K \cdot MR$$

$$w = ME_L = MR_L = MP_L \cdot MR \tag{13.3}$$

The terms on the right side of Equation 13.3 are called the **marginal revenue product** of capital and labor, respectively. They show how much extra revenue is brought in by hiring one more unit of the input. These are precisely what we need to study the demand for inputs and how the demand might change if wages or rental rates change.

Marginal revenue product
The extra revenue obtained from selling the output produced by hiring an extra worker or machine.

A Special Case—Marginal Value Product

The profit-maximizing rules for input choices can be made even simpler if the firm we are examining sells its output in a competitive market. In that case, the firm will also be a price taker in the goods market, so the marginal revenue it takes in from selling one more unit of output is the market price (P) at which the output sells. Using the result that, for a price taker in the goods market, marginal revenue is equal to price, Equation 13.3 becomes

$$v = MP_K \cdot P$$

$$w = MP_L \cdot P \tag{13.4}$$

as the conditions for a profit maximum.[1] We call the terms on the right-hand side of Equation 13.4 the **marginal value product** (MVP) of capital and labor, respectively, since they do indeed put a value on these inputs' marginal physical productivities. Our final condition for maximum profits in this simple situation is

Marginal value product (MVP)
A special case of marginal revenue product in which the firm is a price taker for its output.

$$v = MVP_K$$

$$w = MVP_L \tag{13.5}$$

---

[1] Equation 13.4 implies that this firm is minimizing costs. Dividing the two equations gives

$$MP_L/MP_K = w/v$$

but in Chapter 5 we showed that RTS (of L for K) = MP_L/MP_K. A firm that pursues a marginal productivity approach to input demand will equate

$$RTS \text{ (of L for K)} = w/v$$

and this is required for (long-run) cost minimization.

MicroQuiz 13.1

Suppose that a firm has a monopoly in the goods it sells but must hire its two inputs in competitive markets.

1. Will this monopoly hire workers up to the point at which $w = MVP_L$ and $v = MVP_K$?

2. Will this monopoly be minimizing the total costs of the output that it produces?

To see why these are required for profit maximization, consider again our shoe worker example. Suppose the worker can make two pairs of shoes per hour and that shoes sell for $4. The worker's marginal value product is $8 per hour. If the hourly wage is less than this (say, $5 per hour), the firm can increase profits by $3 by employing the worker for one more hour; profits were not at a maximum so the extra labor should be hired. Similarly, if the wage is $10 per hour, profits would rise by $2 if one less hour of labor were used. Only if the wage and labor's marginal value product are equal will profits truly be as large as possible. One way to see the consequence of this approach to input demand is to look at some cases where firms have goals other than profit maximization. Application 13.1: Hiring by Nonprofit Firms does that.

RESPONSES TO CHANGES IN INPUT PRICES

Suppose the price of any input (say, labor) were to fall. It seems reasonable that firms might demand more of this input in response to such a change. In this section, we provide a detailed analysis of why the model of a profit-maximizing firm supports this conclusion.

Single-Variable Input Case

Let's look first at the case where a firm has fixed capital input and can only vary its labor input in the short run. In this case, labor input exhibits diminishing marginal physical productivity, so labor's MVP $(= P \cdot MP_L)$ declines as increasing numbers of labor hours are hired. The downward-sloping MVP_L curve in Figure 13.1 (on page 424) illustrates this possibility. With a wage rate of w_1, a profit-maximizing firm hires L_1 labor hours.

If the wage rate were to fall to w_2, more labor (L_2) would be demanded. At such a lower wage, more labor can be hired because the firm can "afford" to have a lower marginal physical productivity from the workers it employs. If it continued to hire only L_1, the firm would not be maximizing profits because, at the margin, labor would now be capable of producing more in additional revenue than hiring additional labor would cost. When only one input can be varied, the assumption of a diminishing marginal productivity of labor ensures that a fall in the price of labor causes more labor to be hired.[2] The marginal value product curve shows this response.

[2] Because the marginal productivity of labor is positive, hiring more labor also implies that output increases when w declines.

Hiring by Nonprofit Firms

The marginal productivity theory of hiring follows directly from the assumption that firms seek to maximize profits. One way to illustrate the implications of this theory is to contrast hiring by profit-making and nonprofit firms. Here, we do so for the case of hospitals and educational/cultural institutions.

Hospitals

Most hospitals in the United States operate on a not-for-profit basis. In some cases, however, hospitals are owned by public corporations and presumably strive for maximum profits. Economists have found important differences in the labor demand of these two types of institutions. Some of these relate to what appears to be a "quality bias" for non-profit hospitals. Such hospitals seem to hire more high-wage labor (physicians) and less lower-wage labor (nurses) than do for-profit hospitals. Similar trends seem to show up in the hiring of other inputs—nonprofit hospitals are more likely to have expensive diagnostic equipment than are for-profit firms. One explanation for this result may be that nonprofit hospitals are run by physicians who may gain utility from high-quality (and high-cost) surroundings. Managers of for-profit hospitals may have a more "bottom line" mentality and may therefore pay more attention to the relationship between marginal revenue product and wage for the inputs that they hire.

Nonprofit and for-profit hospitals also seem to exhibit some differences in the way they pay their employees. One recent study[1] of managerial contracts in hospitals found that for-profit hospitals tended to be much more likely to include various incentive features such as performance-based bonuses. Contracts for managers of nonprofit hospitals had few explicit incentive provisions.

Educational and Cultural Institutions

Virtually all colleges and universities are operated as nonprofit institutions. It is not surprising therefore that faculty hiring does not follow the principles of profit maximization. For example, on most campuses, more than 50 percent of the faculty has full professor rank. In some cases (for example, one small college well known to your author), this figure may approach 70 percent or more. But, on average, full professors are paid nearly twice what assistant professors and instructors are paid. To rationalize such a pattern in a profit-making firm, one would have to believe that full professors are twice as productive as those faculty members in lower ranks. A more likely explanation is that institutions of higher education are pursuing some goal other than profits. Perhaps they are seeking a good life for their faculties by providing them with many witty companions.

Most cultural institutions such as theater, opera, or ballet companies also operate on a not-for-profit basis. They also may hire inputs in ways different from what would characterize hiring by a profit-making firm. For example, in a study of performing arts companies,

---

[1] M. J. Roomkin and B. A. Weisbrod, "Managerial Compensation and Incentives in For-Profit and Nonprofit Hospitals," *Journal of Law Economics and Organization* (October 1999): 750–781.

(continued)

J. Gapinski[2] found that the marginal value products of theater and ballet performers were only about 60 percent of the wages they were paid. In opera and symphony orchestras, the figure was even smaller—less than 40 percent of the market wage. On the other hand, the author found that marginal value products for support personnel such as janitors, ushers, and stagehands were increasing at current wage rates—implying that more of these personnel would have been employed in a profit-making firm. Again, the explanation for this pattern probably relates to the goals being pursued by the arts companies–most specifically the provision of employment to needy artists.

To Think About

1. If nonprofit hospitals operate inefficiently, why aren't they driven out of the market by profit-making competitors? What about the nature of their output may mitigate such competitive pressures?

2. Our examples suggest that both universities and arts institutions would produce at lower costs if they substituted low-cost labor for high-cost labor. What prevents these firms from doing this? Do the substitution possibilities depend on how the output of these institutions is produced?

[2] J. H. Gapinski, "The Production of Culture," *Review of Economics and Statistics* (November 1980): 578–586.

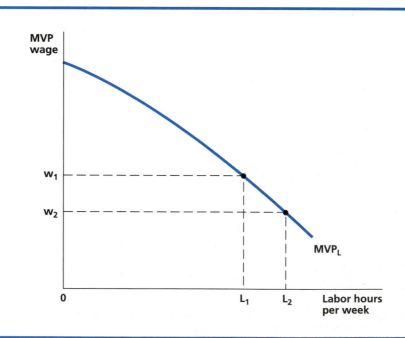

FIGURE 13.1 Change in Labor Input When Wage Falls: Single Variable Case At a wage rate w_1, profit maximization requires that L_1 labor input be hired. If the wage rate falls to w_2, more labor (L_2) will be hired because of the assumed negative slope of the MVP_L curve.

TABLE 13.1 Hamburger Heaven's Profit-Maximizing Hiring Decision

Labor input per hour	Hamburgers produced per hour	Marginal product (hamburger)	Marginal value product ($1.00 per hamburger)
1	20.0	20.0	$20.00
2	28.3	8.3	8.30
3	34.6	6.3	6.30
4	40.0	5.4	5.40
5	44.7	4.7	4.70
6	49.0	4.3	4.30
7	52.9	3.9	3.90
8	56.6	3.7	3.70
9	60.0	3.4	3.40
10	63.2	3.2	3.20

A Numerical Example

As a numerical example of these input choices, let's look again at the hiring decision for Hamburger Heaven first discussed in Chapter 5. Table 13.1 repeats the productivity information for the case in which Hamburger Heaven uses four grills (K = 4). As the table shows, the marginal productivity of labor declines as more workers are assigned to use grills each hour—the first worker hired turns out 20 (heavenly) hamburgers per hour, whereas the tenth hired produces only 3.2 hamburgers per hour. To calculate these workers' marginal value products, we simply multiply these physical productivity figures by the price of hamburgers, $1.00. These results appear in the final column of Table 13.1. With a market wage of $5.00 per hour, Hamburger Heaven should hire four workers. The marginal value product of each of these workers exceeds $5.00, so the firm earns some incremental profit on each of them. The fifth worker's MVP is only $4.70, however, so it does not make sense to add that worker.

At a wage other than $5.00 per hour, Hamburger Heaven would hire a different number of workers. At $6.00 per hour, for example, only three workers would be hired. With wages of $4.00 per hour, on the other hand, six workers would be employed. The MVP calculation provides complete information about Hamburger heaven's short-run hiring decisions. Of course, a change in the wages of burger flippers might also cause the firm to reconsider how many grills it uses—a subject we now investigate.

Two-Variable Input Case

For the case where the firm can vary two (or more) inputs, the story is more complex. The assumption of a diminishing marginal physical product of labor can be misleading here. If w falls, there is a change not only in labor input but also in

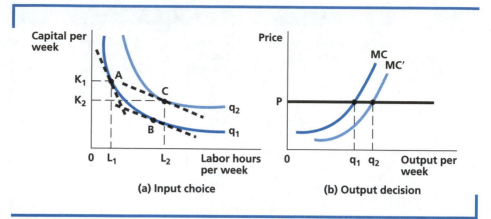

FIGURE 13.2 Substitution and Output Effects of a Decrease in Price of Labor When the price of labor falls the substitution effect causes more labor to be purchased even if output is held constant. This is shown as a movement from point A to point B in panel a. The change in w also shifts the firm's marginal cost curve. A normal situation might be for the MC curve to shift downward in response to a decrease in w, as shown in panel b. With this new curve (MC), a high-level of output (q_1) is chosen. The hiring of labor increases (to L_2) from this output effect.

capital input as a new cost-minimizing combination of inputs is chosen (see our analysis in Chapter 6). When capital input changes, the entire MP_L function shifts (workers now have a different amount of capital to work with), and our earlier picture of how wages affect hiring is incorrect. The remainder of this section presents a series of observations that establish that, even with many inputs, a fall in w leads to an increase in the quantity of labor demanded.

Substitution Effect

Substitution effect
In the theory of production, the substitution of one input for another while holding output constant in response to a change in the input's price.

In some ways, studying the two-input case is similar to our analysis of the individual's response to a change in the price of a good in Chapter 3. When w falls, we can decompose the total effect on the quantity of L hired into two components: a substitution effect and an output effect.

To study the **substitution effect,** we hold q constant at q_1. With a fall in w, there is a tendency to substitute labor for capital in the production of q_1. This effect is illustrated in Figure 13.2(a). Because the condition for minimizing the cost of producing q_1 requires that RTS = w/v, a fall in w necessitates a movement from input combination A to combination B. The firm now decides to produce q_1 in a more labor-intensive way—because labor is relatively cheaper.

Output Effect

Output effect
The effect of an input price change on the amount of the input that the firm hires that results from a change in the firm's output level.

It is, however, not correct to hold q output constant when w falls. When the firm changes its level of production—the **output effect**—the analogy to a person's utility-maximization problem breaks down. The reason for this is that consumers have budget constraints but firms do not. Firms produce as much as profit maximization requires; their need for inputs is derived from these production decisions. In order to investigate what happens to the quantity of output produced, we must investigate the firm's profit-maximizing output decision. A fall in w, because it changes relative input costs, shifts the firm's expansion path. Consequently, all the firm's cost curves are shifted and, probably, some output level other than q_1 is chosen.

Figure 13.2(b) illustrates the most common case. As a result of the fall in w, the marginal cost curve for the firm has shifted downward to MC'. The profit-maximizing level of output rises from q_1 to q_2.[3] The profit-maximizing condition (P = MC) is now satisfied at a higher level of output. Returning to Figure 13.2(a), this increase in output causes even more labor input to be demanded. The combined result of both the substitution and the output effects is to move the input choice to point C on the firm's isoquant for output level q_2. Both effects work to increase L in response to a decrease in w.[4]

Summary of Firm's Demand for Labor

We can summarize our findings about a firm's response to a fall in w by concluding that a profit-maximizing firm increases its hiring of labor for two reasons. First, the firm substitutes the now cheaper labor for other inputs that are now relatively more expensive. This is the substitution effect. Second, the wage decline reduces the firm's marginal costs, thereby causing it to increase output and to increase the hiring of all inputs including labor. This is the output effect.

This conclusion holds for any input, and it can be reversed to show that an increase in the price of an input causes the firm to hire less of that input. We have shown that the firm's demand curve for an input is unambiguously downward sloping: the lower its price, the more of the input is demanded.[5]

---

[3] If all firms in an industry were confronted with a decline in w, all would change their output levels; the industry supply curve would shift outward and, consequently, the market price of output would fall. As long as the market demand curve for the firm's output is negatively sloped, however, the analysis in this chapter would not be seriously affected by this observation because the shift in supply leads to more output being demanded.

[4] No definite statement can be made about how the quantity of capital (or any other input) changes in response to a decline in w. The substitution and output effects work in opposite directions (as can be seen in Figure 13.2), and the outcome depends on the relative sizes of these effects.

[5] Actually, a proof of this assertion is not as simple as is implied here. The complicating factor arises when the input in question is "inferior," and it is no longer true that the marginal cost curve shifts downward when the price of such an input declines. Nevertheless, it can be shown that, as long as the good that is being produced has a downward-sloping demand curve, the firm's demand for the input is also negatively sloped.

RESPONSIVENESS OF INPUT DEMAND TO PRICE CHANGES

The notions of substitution and output effects help to explain how responsive to price changes the demand for an input might be. Suppose the wage rate rises. We already know that less labor will be demanded. Now we wish to ask whether this decrease will be large or small.

Ease of Substitution

First, consider the substitution effect. The decrease in the hiring of labor from a rise in w depends on how easy it is for firms to substitute other inputs for labor. Some firms may find it relatively simple to substitute machines for workers, and for these firms the quantity of labor demanded decreases substantially. Other firms may produce with a fixed-proportions technology. For them, substitution is impossible. The size of the substitution effect may also depend on the length of time allowed for adjustment. In the short run, a firm may have a stock of machinery that requires a fixed complement of workers. Consequently, the short-run substitution possibilities are slight. Over the long run, however, this firm may be able to adapt its machinery to use less labor per machine; the possibilities of substitution may now be substantial. For example, a rise in the wages of coal miners has little short-run substitution effect since existing coal-mining equipment requires a certain number of workers to operate it. In the long run, however, there is clear evidence that mining can be made more capital intensive by designing more complex machinery. In the long run, capital can be substituted for labor on a large scale.

Costs and the Output Effect

An increase in the wage rate also raises firms' costs. In a competitive market, this causes the price of the good being produced to rise and people reduce their purchases of that good. Consequently, firms lower their levels of production; because less output is being produced, the output effect causes less labor to be demanded. In this way, the output effect reinforces the substitution effect. The size of this output effect depends on (1) how large the increase in marginal costs brought about by the wage rate increase is and (2) how much quantity demanded is reduced by a rising price. The size of the first of these components depends on how "important" labor is in total production costs, whereas the size of the second depends on how price elastic the demand for the product is.

In industries for which labor costs are a major portion of total costs and for which demand is very elastic, output effects are large. For example, an increase in wages for restaurant workers is likely to induce a large negative output effect in the demand for such workers since labor costs are a significant portion of restaurant operating costs and the demand for meals eaten out is relatively price elastic.

An increase in wages causes a big price rise, and this causes people to reduce sharply the number of meals they eat out. On the other hand, output effects in the demand for pharmaceutical workers are probably small. Direct labor costs are a small fraction of drug production costs, and the demand for drugs is price inelastic. Wage increases have only a small effect on costs, and any increases in price that do result will not reduce demand for drugs significantly. All of these features of labor demand are illustrated by Application 13.2: Controversy over the Minimum Wage.

> ## MicroQuiz 13.2
>
> Suppose that state law requires that every gasoline pump have exactly one attendant and suppose that gasoline pumps are always in use filling motorists' cars.
>
> **1.** Will a rise in attendants' wages cause fewer to be hired? Explain.
>
> **2.** Suppose attendants' wages represent one-third of the total cost of gasoline to motorists and that the price elasticity of demand for gasoline is –0.50. What is the elasticity of demand for gasoline pump attendants?

INPUT SUPPLY

Firms get their inputs from three primary sources. Labor input is provided by individuals who choose among available employment opportunities. Capital equipment is produced primarily by other firms and may be bought outright or rented for a period. Finally, natural resources are extracted from the ground and may be used directly (Exxon produces gasoline from the crude oil it extracts) or sold to other firms (DuPont buys a petroleum feedstock from Exxon). Studying the supply decisions for firms that produce capital equipment and natural resources does not require us to develop any new tools. We already know how to model this supply since nothing in our prior discussion required that firms produce their output only for consumers. Hence, we can safely assume that firms that produce inputs to be sold to other firms have upward-sloping supply curves.[6]

Studying labor supply, however, raises different issues. This input (which constitutes the majority of practically all firms' costs) is supplied by individuals, so our previous models of firms are not much help in analyzing labor supply. Indeed, individuals are also partly involved in the supply of capital. In this case, individuals provide the funds (usually channeled through banks or securities) that firms use to finance capital purchases. Again, models of firms' supply behavior do not help us to understand this process. In the appendix to this chapter, we look in detail at models of labor supply. Here, we summarize our findings as they relate to drawing labor supply curves. Issues related to savings and the supply of capital are taken up in Chapter 14.

---

[6] That is, unless these firms are monopolies, in which case our analysis in Chapter 10 would apply.

Controversy over the Minimum Wage

The Fair Labor Standards Act of 1938 established a national minimum wage of $.25 per hour. In recent years, each increase has met with considerable debate about whether such increases may be counterproductive.

A Graphic Analysis

Figure 1 illustrates the possible effects of a minimum wage. Figure 1(a) shows the supply and demand curves for labor. Given these curves, an equilibrium wage rate, w_1, is established in the market. At this wage, a typical firm hires l_1 (shown on the firm's isoquant map in Figure 1[b]). Suppose now that a minimum wage of $(w_2 > w_1)$ is imposed by law. This new wage will cause the firm to reduce its demand for labor from l_1 to l_2. At the same time, more labor (L_3) will be supplied at w_2 than was supplied at the lower wage rate. The imposition of the minimum wage will result in an excess of the supply of labor over the demand for labor of $L_3 - L_2$.

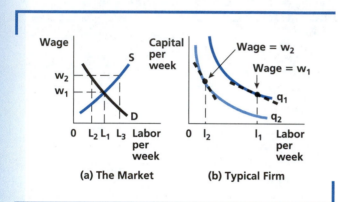

(a) The Market

(b) Typical Firm

FIGURE 1 **Effects of a Minimum Wage in a Perfectly Competitive Labor Market** The imposition of a minimum wage (w_2) causes the firm to reduce labor usage to l_2 because it will both substitute capital (and other inputs) for labor and cut back output.

Minimum Wages and Teenage Unemployment

There is some empirical evidence that changes in the minimum wage law have had serious effects in increasing teenage unemployment. Teenagers are the labor-market participants most likely to be affected by minimum wage laws, because their skills usually represent the lower end of the spectrum. Minority group members, for whom unemployment rates often exceed 30 percent, may be especially vulnerable. Although there are several factors that may account for this high rate (unstable employment opportunities, discrimination in employment), several early statistical studies suggested that hikes in the minimum wage played an important role.

Recent Disputes over the Evidence

In an influential 1994 study, David Card and Alan Krueger challenged the belief that minimum wages reduce employment opportunities.[1] By comparing employment levels at fast-food restaurants in New Jersey and Pennsylvania following increases in the New Jersey minimum wage, they concluded that there was no negative effect from the raise. That finding has not been universally accepted, however. An analysis of somewhat different data from similar fast-food franchises (Burger King, Wendy's, and KFC) in these states reached the opposite conclusion. More generally, the methods used in the Card-Krueger study have

---

[1] David Card and Alan Krueger, "Minimum Wages and Employment: A Case Study of the Fast-Food Industry in New Jersey and Pennsylvania" *American Economic Review* (September 1994): 722–793.

been subject to considerable dispute.[2] Still, although theoretical models provides the clear prediction that higher minimum wages should reduce employment, measuring this effect empirically has proven rather difficult.[3]

To Think About

1. Does a minimum wage increase or decrease total wages received by workers affected by it?
2. Would an increase in minimum wage necessarily reduce employment in every industry?

[2] The controversy over the Card-Krueger results is summarized in the July 1995 issue of *Industrial and Labor Relations Review*.

[3] For an interesting, though somewhat opinionated, summary, see A. B. Krueger, "Teaching the Minimum Wage in Econ 101 in Light of the New Economics of the Minimum Wage," *Journal of Economic Education* (Summer 2001): 243–258.

Labor Supply and Wages

For individuals, the wages they can earn represent the opportunity cost of not working at a paying job. Of course, no one works 24 hours a day, so individuals incur these opportunity costs all the time. They may refuse jobs with long hours, opt for early retirement, or choose to work in their homes. Presumably, all such decisions are made to maximize utility. That is, individuals balance the monetary rewards from working against the psychic benefits of other, nonpaid activities.

A change in the wage rate, because it changes opportunity costs, alters individuals' decisions. Although, as we show in the appendix to this chapter, the story is relatively complicated, in general we might expect that a rise in the wage would encourage market work. With higher wages, people might voluntarily agree to work overtime or to moonlight, they might retire later, or they might do less at home. In graphical terms, the supply curve for labor is positively sloped—higher wages cause more labor to be supplied.

Two additional observations should be kept in mind about labor supply. First, "wages" should be interpreted broadly to include all forms of compensation. Fringe benefits (such as health insurance), paid vacations, and firm-paid child care are important supplements to cash earnings. When we speak of the market wage w, we include all such returns to workers and these also represent costs to firms.

A second important lesson of labor supply theory is that supply decisions are based on individual preferences. If people prefer some jobs to others, perhaps because some offer a more pleasant work environment, labor supply curves differ. Similarly, if attitudes toward work change, labor supply curves shift (as seems to have been the case for married women during the 1960s and 1970s). Hence, a wide variety of "noneconomic" factors may shift labor supply curves.

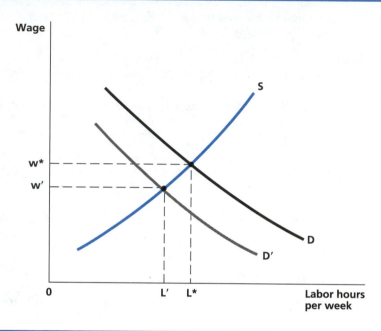

FIGURE 13.3 Equilibrium in an Input Market An equilibrium wage (w*) in the labor market is determined by demand (D) and supply (S). A shift in demand to D' would lower the wage to w' and the quantity of labor demanded to L'. If the wage does not adjust immediately, there may be some unemployment.

EQUILIBRIUM INPUT PRICE DETERMINATION

Bringing the various strands of our analysis together provides a straightforward view of how wages are determined. This process is illustrated by the familiar demand (D) and supply (S) curves in Figure 13.3. For this figure, we have chosen to diagram equilibrium wage determination in the general labor market, but the graph would serve equally well for workers with specific skills or for any other input market. Given this demand-supply configuration, the equilibrium wage is w*, and L* units of labor are employed. As for any market, this equilibrium tends to persist from period to period until demand or supply curves shift. As described earlier in Application 13.2, government wage regulation may affect this equilibrium outcome.

Shifts in Demand and Supply

Although by now you should be familiar with analyses in which demand or supply curves shift, the details of input markets are sufficiently different from those for goods markets that some review may be in order. Marginal productivity theory provides the guide for understanding shifts in demand. Any factor that shifts the firms'

TABLE 13.2 Factors That Sift Input Demand and Supply Curves

Demand	Labor Supply	Capital Supply
Demand shifts outward	**Supply shifts outward**	
Rise in output price	Decreased preference for leisure	Fall in input costs of equipment makers
Increase in marginal productivity	Increased desirability of job	Technical progress in making equipment
Demand shifts inward	**Supply shifts inward**	
Fall in output price	Increased preference for leisure	Rise in input costs of equipment makers
Decrease in marginal productivity	Decreased desirability of job	

underlying production function (such as the development of labor-saving technologies) shifts its input demand curve. In addition, since the demand for inputs is ultimately derived from the demand for the goods those inputs produce and the prices paid for such goods, happenings in product markets also can shift input demand curves. An increased demand for four-wheel-drive vehicles raises the price of such vehicles and increases the demand for workers who make them. On the other hand, a decline in the price of clothing brought on, say, by an increase in imports would reduce the demand for apparel workers. This situation can be reflected in Figure 13.3 by the shift in the demand curve to D'. The impact of such a shift would be to reduce equilibrium wages of apparel workers from w* to w' and equilibrium employment from L* to L'. If the adjustment in wages does not occur quickly (perhaps because wages are fixed by custom or long-term contract), some unemployment may be experienced in moving to this new equilibrium.

Input supply curves are shifted by a variety of factors. For inputs that are produced by other firms (power tools, railroad locomotives, and so forth), the standard supply analysis applies—supply curves are shifted by anything that affects the input producers' costs. For labor input, changes in individuals' preferences (both for "work" in general and for the characteristics of specific jobs) shift supply.

All these various reasons for shifting demand or supply curves for inputs are summarized in Table 13.2. It is important to keep these various factors in mind when you try to understand how the economy as a whole operates. Because people get their incomes from input markets, any investigation of well-being requires an understanding of these factors. Application 13.3: Why Is Wage Inequality Increasing? examines some recent trends.

INFOTRAC©
COLLEGE EDITION
Exclusively from Gale Group and Thomson Learning
www.infotrac-college.com
Keywords: Substitution effect, Wage inequality, Monopsony

MicroQuiz 13.3

In the United States, Social Security taxes of about 6 percent are levied on workers with a matching 6 percent paid by firms. What determines who *actually pays* these taxes?

Why Is Wage Inequality Increasing?

Wages earned by workers have exhibited a large degree of inequality throughout history. In *The Republic,* for example, Plato laments the fact that some workers make more than ten times what others make. In recent years, wage inequality seems to have increased throughout the world and especially in the United States.

Measuring Wage Inequality

A first step in understanding the inequality of wages among workers is to think about issues of measurement. One reason earnings differ among workers is that they work differing numbers of hours or may only have seasonal jobs. It is customary therefore to look only at "full-time, year-round" workers in studying inequality. Often researchers look only at men (or women) to try to control for the large changes in the gender composition of the workforce that have occurred in recent years. Finally, it is important to look at total wages (including fringe benefits). Otherwise, changes in the makeup of workers' pay packages can influence trends in inequality.

Studies that address these various issues tend to conclude that wage inequality increased fairly significantly in the United States over the 30 years from 1965 to 1995. One common measure compares the wages of workers at the 90th percentile of the wage distribution (about $70,000 in 1995) to those of workers at the 10th percentile ($13,000). This 90/10 ratio stood at about 4.3 in 1965 for male, full-time, year-round workers. By 1995, the ratio had risen to 5.4—clearly a significant increase in wage inequality. European countries have also experienced an increase in inequality over this period, though only the United Kingdom has had increases of the magnitude of those in the United States.

Supply-Demand Analysis

A careful consideration of demand and supply trends in the labor market is a good starting place for understanding these trends[1]. Any factor that increased the supply of low-wage workers or increased the demand for high-wage workers would be a candidate for explaining the trend. Factors that increased the supply of high-wage workers or increased the demand for low-wage workers would tend to work against the trend.

Researchers have identified two important trends in labor demand that have acted to increase inequality. First, and most important, recent years have seen a sharp increase in the relative demand for technically skilled workers, especially those with computer experience. The effects of this increase are most apparent in a rising wage premium for college graduates—especially for graduates of "elite" institutions.

A second trend affecting labor markets has been a decline in the demand for low-wage workers. Economists have identified two forces behind this trend: (1) a decline in the importance of manufacturing industries in the overall economy, and (2) sustained increases in

[1] A simple supply-demand analysis is presented in the 1997 *Economic Report of the President,* Chapter 5. For a more thorough econometric investigation, see L. F. Katz and K. M. Murphy, "Changes in Relative Wages, 1963–1987: Supply and Demand Factors," *Quarterly Journal of Economics* (February 1992): 35–78.

imports of goods that are produced mainly with unskilled labor.[2] In combination, these two forces are probably less important, however, than the increase in demand for technically skilled workers.

Trends in labor supply have also tended to exacerbate wage inequality. Large (legal and illegal) immigration in the 1990s may have increased the supply of low-wage workers, at least in some areas; and the increase in labor supply by women probably had its greatest impact on low-wage men. It appears that these relative supply effects were not as important in affecting inequality, however, as the demand factors.

To Think About

1. Although the wage premium for college graduates increased after 1980, it had been falling for the previous 15 years. How would you explain the turnaround?
2. Increasing imports have had little effect on the domestic prices of goods that compete with those imports. Explain how this finding is relevant to the pricing of low-wage labor.

[2] The relative importance of international trade in the trend is subject to considerable dispute. For a discussion of the issues, see the symposium on income inequality and trade in the summer 1995 *The Journal of Economic Perspectives*.

MONOPSONY

In many situations, a firm may not be a price taker for the inputs it buys. It may be necessary for the firm to offer a wage above that currently prevailing to attract more employees, or the firm may be able to get a better price on some equipment by restricting its purchases. To explore these situations, it is convenient to examine the polar case of **monopsony** (a single buyer) in an input market.

Monopsony
Condition in which one firm is the only hirer in a particular input market.

Marginal Expense

If there is only one buyer of an input, that firm faces the entire market supply curve for the input. In order to increase its hiring of labor, say, by one or more units, the firm must move to a higher point on this supply curve. This involves paying not only a higher wage to the last worker hired but also additional wages to those workers already employed. The marginal cost of hiring the extra unit of labor therefore exceeds its wage rate, and the price-taking assumption we made earlier no longer holds. Instead, for a monopsonist facing an upward-sloping supply curve for an input, the **marginal expense** exceeds the market price of the input. For labor input, for example, the marginal expense (ME_L) of hiring one more worker exceeds the market wage (w).

Notice the similarity between the concept of the marginal expense of an input and the marginal revenue for a monopolist. Both concepts are intended to be used when firms possess market power and their choices have an effect on prices. In

Marginal expense
The cost of hiring one more unit of an input. Exceeds the price of the input if the firm faces an upward-sloping supply curve for the input.

TABLE 13.3 Labor Costs of Hiring Bear Wardens in Yellowstone Park

Hourly wage	Workers supplied per hour	Total labor cost per hour	Marginal expense
$2	1	$2	$2
4	2	8	6
6	3	18	10
8	4	32	14
10	5	50	18
12	6	72	22
$14	7	98	26

such situations, firms are no longer price takers. Instead, firms recognize that their actions affect prices and use this information in making decisions.

A Numerical Illustration

This distinction is easiest to see with a numerical example. Suppose (as is probably the case) that the Yellowstone Park Company is the only hirer of bear wardens. Suppose also that the number of people willing to take this job (L) is a simple positive function of the hourly wage (w) given by

$$L = \frac{1}{2}\, w \qquad\qquad (13.6)$$

This relationship between the wage and the number of people who offer their services as bear wardens is shown in the first two columns of Table 13.3. Total labor costs (w·L) are shown in the third column, and the marginal expense of hiring each warden is shown in the fourth column. The extra expense associated with adding another warden always exceeds the wage rate paid to that person. The reason is clear. Not only does a newly hired warden receive the higher wage, but all previously hired wardens also get a higher wage. A monopsonist takes these extra expenses into account in its hiring decisions.

A graph can be used to help to clarify this relationship. Figure 13.4 shows the supply curve (S) for bear wardens. If Yellowstone wishes to hire three wardens, it must pay $6 per hour, and total outlays will be $18 per hour. This situation is reflected by point A on the supply curve. If the firm tries to hire a fourth warden, it must offer $8 per hour to everyone—it must move to point B on the supply curve. Total outlays are now $32 per hour, so the marginal expense of hiring the fourth worker is $14 per hour. By comparing the sizes of the total outlay rectangles, we can see why the marginal expense is higher than the wage paid to the fourth worker. That worker's hourly wage is shown by the gray rectangle—it is $8 per hour. The other three workers, who were previously earning $6 per hour, now earn $8. This extra outlay is shown in color. Total labor expenses for four wardens exceed those for three by the area of both the color and gray rectangles. In this case, marginal expense exceeds the wage since the Yellowstone Company is the sole hirer of people in this unusual occupation.

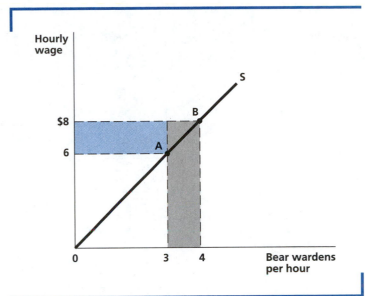

FIGURE 13.4 **Marginal Expense of Hiring Bear Wardens** Since Yellowstone Park is (probably) the only hires of bear wardens, it must raise the hourly wage offered from $6 to $8 if it wished to hire a fourth warden. The marginal expense of hiring that warden is $14—his or her wage ($8, shown in gray) plus the extra $4 per hour that must be paid to the others three wardens (shown in color).

Monopsonist's Input Choice

As for any profit-maximizing firm, a monopsonist hires an input up to the point at which the additional revenue and additional cost of hiring one more unit are equal. For the case of labor, this requires

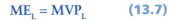

$$ME_L = MVP_L \qquad (13.7)$$

In the special case of a price taker that faces an infinitely elastic labor supply ($ME_L = w$), Equation 13.5 and Equation 13.7 are identical. However, if the firm faces a positively sloped labor supply curve, Equation 13.7 dictates a different level of input choice, as we now show.

A Graphical Demonstration

The monopsonist's choice of labor input is illustrated in Figure 13.5. The firm's demand curve for labor (D) is drawn initially on the assumption that the firm is a price taker. The ME_L curve associated with the labor supply curve (S) is constructed in much the same way that the marginal revenue curve associated with a demand curve was constructed. Because S is positively sloped, the ME_L curve always lies above S. The profit-maximizing level of labor input for the monopsonist is given by L_1. At this level of input use, marginal expense is equal to marginal value product (MVP). At L_1 the wage rate in the market is given by w_1. The quantity of labor demanded falls short of that which would be hired in a perfectly

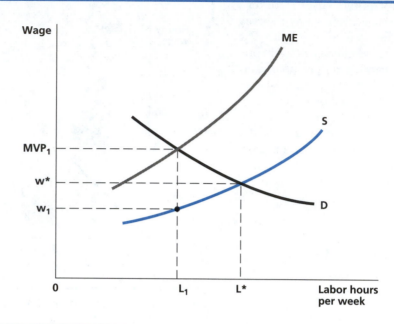

FIGURE 13.5 Pricing in a Monopsonistic Labor Market If a firm faces a positively sloped supply curve for labor (S), it bases its decisions on the marginal expense of labor curve (ME_L). Because S is positively sloped, ME_L lies above S. The curve S can be thought of as an average cost of labor curve, and the ME_L curve is marginal to S. At L_L the equilibrium condition $ME_L = MVP_L$ holds, and this quantity will be hired at a market wage rate w_1.

competitive market (L^*). The firm has restricted input demand to take advantage of its monopsonistic position in the labor market.

The formal similarities between this analysis and the monopoly analysis we presented in Chapter 10 should be clear. In particular, the actual "demand curve" for a monopsonist consists of a single point. In Figure 13.5, this point is given by L_1, w_1. The monopsonist has chosen this point as the most desirable of all those points on the supply curve S. A different point is not chosen unless some external change (such as a shift in the demand for the firm's output or a change in technology) affects labor's marginal value product.

Monopsonists and Resource Allocation

In addition to restricting its input demand, the monopsonist pays an input less than its marginal value product. This result is also illustrated in Figure 13.5. At the monopsonist's preferred choice of labor input (L_1), a wage of w_1 prevails in the market. For this level of input demand, the firm is willing to pay an amount equal to MVP_1: This is the amount of extra revenue that hiring another worker would provide to the firm. At L_1 the monopsonist pays workers less than they are "worth" to the firm. This is a clear indication that this firm uses too little labor. Total output could be increased by drawing labor from elsewhere in the econ-

MicroQuiz 13.4

Is there a deadweight loss from the monopsony pictured in Figure 13.5? How would this loss be shown graphically? Who would suffer this loss?

omy into this industry. It should be clear from Figure 13.5 that the extent of this misallocation of resources is greater the more inelastic the supply of labor is to the monopsonist. The less responsive to low wages the supply of labor is, the more the monopsonist can take advantage of this situation.

Causes of Monopsony

To practice monopsonistic behavior, a firm must possess considerable power in the market for a particular input. If the market is reasonably competitive, this cannot occur because other firms recognize the profit potential reflected in the gap between MVPs and input costs. They therefore bid for these inputs, driving their prices up to equality with marginal value products. Under such conditions, the supply of labor to any one firm is nearly infinitely elastic (because of the alternative employment possibilities available), and monopsonistic behavior is impossible.

Monopsonistic outcomes consequently are observed in real-world situations in which, for some reason, effective competition for inputs is lacking. For example, some firms may occupy a monopsonistic position by being the only source of employment in a small town. Because moving costs for workers are high, alternative employment opportunities for local workers are unattractive and the firm may be able to exert a strong effect on wages paid. Similarly, it may sometimes be the case that only one firm hires a particularly specialized type of input. If the alternative earnings prospects for that input are unattractive, its supply to the firm is inelastic, presenting the firm with the opportunity for monopsonistic behavior. For example, marine engineers with many years of experience in designing nuclear submarines must work for the one or two companies that produce such vessels. Because other jobs would not make use of these workers' specialized training, alternative employment is not particularly attractive. Since the government occupies a monopoly position in the production of a number of goods requiring specialized inputs (space travel, armed forces, and national political offices, to name a few), it would be expected to be in a position to exercise monopsony power. In other cases, a group of firms may combine to form a cartel in their hiring decisions (and, perhaps, in their output decisions too). Application 13.4: Monopsony in the Market for Sports Stars illustrates this relationship in a situation in which it is possible to obtain direct measures of workers' marginal value.

Monopsony in the Market for Sports Stars

Occasionally powerful cartels of hirers can achieve a successful monopsony. Professional sports leagues that are able to implement restrictions on interteam competition in hiring players provide several important examples.

Why Study Sports?

Although some economists may indeed be sports fanatics, that is not the primary reason they study the wages of sports stars. Rather, professional athletics represents one of the few industries in which worker productivity is directly observable. Batting averages in baseball, scoring in basketball or hockey, and defensive tackles' "sacks" in football can all be measured and (more importantly) correlated with spectator attendance and television ratings. These provide clear evidence of each person's marginal revenue product—information that is simply not available in most other labor markets.

Monopsony in Major League Baseball

Throughout much of its history, major league baseball limited competition for players among teams with a "reserve clause" that bound players to the teams that first signed them. Numerical estimates of the degree of monopsony thereby created were constructed by G. W. Scully in a famous 1974 article.[1] Scully adopted a two-step procedure to measure marginal revenue products (MRPs) for players. First, he examined the correlation between a team's winning percentage and its attendance figures. He concluded that winning did indeed produce additional revenues. Next, he analyzed which aspects of individual player performance were most closely related to a team's overall performance. These data showed that most players' MRPs exceed their salaries by substantial margins. Major stars were especially underpaid relative to the revenue they generated. For example, Sandy Koufax (the great Dodger left-hander during the 1950s and 1960s) may have been paid less than 25 percent of what he was "worth."

It was only a matter of time before players came to recognize the effect of the reserve clause and took organized action against it. A players' strike in 1972 (coupled with legal action brought by St. Louis Cardinal outfielder Curt Flood) eventually led to the adoption of a free-agent provision in players' contracts as a partial replacement of the reserve clause. Although the leagues have tried several actions to reestablish their cartel position (such as caps on team salaries and limiting league expansion), they have been unable to return to the powerful position they occupied prior to 1970.

Basketball and Michael Jordan

Similar research on professional basketball players' salaries suggests that the National Basketball Association (NBA) has at times been able to exercise monopsony power. Although the NBA never had the advantage of the reserve clause (because, unlike baseball,

---

[1] G. W. Scully, "Pay and Performance in Major League Baseball," *American Economic Review* (December 1974): 915–930. For more detail on the status of the players' labor market, see Scully's *The Business of Major League Baseball* (Chicago: University of Chicago Press, 1989).

it is not exempt from antitrust action), various draft limitations and salary cap provisions have served to restrain salaries to some extent. Early stars such as Bill Russell and Oscar Robertson were probably the most affected by such limits, but it appears that even Michael Jordan (undoubtedly the most famous sports figure of the 1990s) may have been under-paid. Of course, it is hard to feel sorry for Jordan, who was earning over $10 million a year after returning from his mediocre career as a minor league baseball player (not to mention Nike and MCI endorsements). But recent research suggests that he may have been worth over $70 million to the NBA as a whole in terms of the higher television ratings they enjoyed when he played.[2]

To Think About

1. Professional leagues argue that they need to constrain competition for players to ensure some "competitive balance." Does this rationale make sense?
2. NCAA rules prevent any student-athlete from being directly paid. Should this be regarded as an example of a monopsonistic cartel?

[2] J. A. Hausman and G. K. Leonard, "Superstars in the National Basketball Association: Economic Value and Policy," *Journal of Labor Economics* (October 1997): 586–624.

Bilateral Monopoly

In some cases, there may be monopoly power on both sides of an input market. That is, suppliers of the input may have a monopoly and the buyer of the input may be a monopsony. In this situation of **bilateral monopoly**, the price of the input is indeterminate and ultimately depends on the bargaining abilities of the parties involved.

Bilateral monopoly
A market in which both suppliers and demanders have monopoly power. Pricing is indeterminate in such markets.

Figure 13.6 illustrates this general result. Although the "supply" and "demand" curves in this diagram intersect at P^*, Q^*, this market equilibrium does not occur because neither the supplier nor the demander of the input is a price taker. Instead, the monopoly supplier of the input uses the marginal revenue curve (MR) associated with the demand curve (D) to calculate a preferred price-quantity combination of P_1, Q_1. The monopsonistic buyer of this input, on the other hand, uses the marginal expense curve (ME) to calculate a preferred equilibrium of P_2, Q_2. Although both the monopolist and monopsonist here seek to restrict the quantity hired, they differ significantly on what they think the input should be paid. This leads to some sort of bargaining between the two parties with suppliers holding out for P_1 and demanders offering only P_2. Protracted labor disputes in major industries and "holdouts" by sports and entertainment celebrities are evidence of this type of market structure.

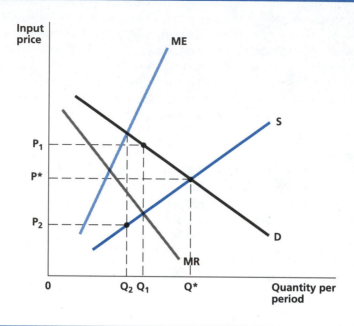

FIGURE 13.6 Bilateral Monopoly When both demanders and suppliers have monopoly power, price is indeterminate. Suppliers want P_1, Q_1 but demanders want P_2, Q_2.

SUMMARY

In this chapter, we illustrated some models of markets for inputs with particular focus on labor markets. The conclusions of this examination include:

- Firms hire any input up to the point at which the marginal expense of hiring one more unit is equal to the marginal revenue yielded by selling what that input produces.
- If the firm is a price taker in both the market for its inputs and the market for its output, profit maximization requires that it employ that level of inputs for which the market price of each input (for example, the wage) is equal to the marginal value product of that input (for example, $P \cdot MP_L$).
- If the price of an input rises, the firm hires less of it for two reasons. First, the higher price causes the firm to substitute other inputs for the one whose price has risen. Second, the higher price raises the

firm's costs and reduces the amount it is able to sell. This output effect also causes fewer units of the input to be hired.
- Input supply curves are positively sloped. Capital equipment supply is much like the supply of any good. Labor supply involves individual choices (see the appendix to this chapter).
- Equilibria in labor markets resemble those in goods markets, though reasons for shifts in supply and demand curves are somewhat different.
- If a firm is the sole hirer of labor (a monopsony), its hiring decisions affect market wages. The marginal expense associated with hiring an additional unit of labor exceeds the wage. Firms take this into account in their hiring decisions—they restrict hiring below what it would be under competitive conditions.

REVIEW QUESTIONS

1. In the supply-demand model of input pricing, who are the demanders? What types of assumptions would you use to explain their behavior? In this model, who are the suppliers? What types of assumptions would you use to explain their behavior?

2. Profit maximization implies that firms make input choices in a marginal way. Explain why the following marginal rules found in this chapter are specific applications of this general idea:

   a. $MR_L = ME_L$
   b. $MP_L \cdot MR = ME_L = w$
   c. $MVP_L = ME_L = w$
   d. $MVP_L = w$
   e. $MVP_L = ME_L > w$

   If firms follow these various rules, will they also be producing a profit-maximizing level of output? That is, will they produce when $MR = MC$? Will they also be minimizing costs if they use these rules?

3. Many textbooks label the demand curve for labor as the "marginal value product curve" or "marginal revenue product curve." Does a move along a firm's demand curve for labor in response to a change in the wage cause only the quantity of labor hired to change? Why is this labeling misleading? When might the labeling be accurate?

4. Although the substitution effect in the theory of a firm's demand for labor is straightforward, the output effect is rather complicated. Explain the sequence of events that cause a firm to change its hiring when the wage changes through output effects. On the basis of your analysis, do you agree with this statement: "ultimately the size of the output effect in any firm's demand for labor depends on the elasticity of demand for the goods it is selling"?

5. Suppose the price of an input used by firms with fixed-proportions production functions were to fall. Why would such a change not cause any

substitution effects for these firms' input demand? Would there, however, be output effects? What would determine the size of these effects?

6. What factors would cause a firm's demand for labor to shift? Be sure to use the theory of profit maximization to explain your answers.

7. In Chapter 9, we described the notions of consumer and producer surplus as they related to a competitive equilibrium. How should similar areas be interpreted in a supply-demand graph of the competitive equilibrium in a factor market?

8. In Chapter 10 we showed the relationship between marginal revenues and market price for a monopoly to be given by $MR = P\left(1 + \dfrac{1}{e}\right)$, where e is the price elasticity of demand for the product. For a monopsony, a similar relationship holds for the marginal expense associated with hiring more labor: $ME = w\left(1 + \dfrac{1}{e}\right)$, where e is the elasticity of supply of labor to the firm. Use this equation to show:

   a. that for a firm that is a price taker in the labor market, $ME = w$;
   b. that $ME > w$ for a firm facing a labor supply curve that is not infinitely elastic at the prevailing wage; and
   c. that the gap between ME and w is larger the smaller is e.

   Explain all of these results intuitively.

9. How would you measure the strength of a monopsonist in an input market? Would a monopsony necessarily be very profitable? What would you need to add to Figure 13.5 in order to show a monopsonist's profit graphically?

10. "In a situation of bilateral monopoly, the two parties are more likely to agree on quantity than on price." Explain why this is the case.

PROBLEMS

13.1 A landowner has three farms (A, B, and C) of differing fertility. The levels of output for the three farms with one, two, and three laborers employed are as follows:

Level of Output

Number of laborers	Farm A	Farm B	Farm C
1	10	8	5
2	17	11	7
3	21	13	8

For example, if one laborer were hired for each farm, the total output would be $10 + 8 + 5 = 23$. This would represent a poor allocation of labor, since if the farm C laborer were assigned to farm A the total output would be $17 + 8 = 25$.

a. If market conditions caused the landowner to hire five laborers, what would be the most productive allocation of that labor? How much would be produced? What is the marginal product of the last worker?

b. If we assume that farm output is sold in a perfectly competitive market with one unit of output priced at $1 and we assume that labor market equilibrium occurs when five workers are hired, what wage is paid? How much profit does the landowner receive?

13.2 Assume that the quantity of envelopes licked per hour by Sticky Gums, Inc., is $q = 10{,}000\sqrt{L}$ where L is the number of laborers hired per hour by the firm. Assume further that the envelope-licking business is perfectly competitive with a market price of $.01 per envelope. The marginal product of a worker is given by

$$MP_L = 5{,}000/\sqrt{L}$$

a. How much labor would be hired at a competitive wage of $10? $5? $2? Use your results to sketch a demand curve for labor.

b. Assume that Sticky Gums hires its labor at an hourly wage of $10. What quantity of envelopes will be licked when the price of a licked envelope is $.10? $.05? $.02? Use your results to sketch a supply curve for licked envelopes.

13.3 Suppose there are a fixed number of 1,000 identical firms in the perfectly competitive concrete pipe industry. Each firm produces the same fraction of total market output, and each firm's production function for pipe is given by

$$q = \sqrt{KL}$$

and for this production function

$$RTS\ (L\ for\ K) = K/L$$

Suppose also that the market demand for concrete pipe is given by

$$Q = 400{,}000 - 100{,}000P$$

where Q is total concrete pipe.

a. If $w = v = \$1$, in what ratio will the typical firm use K and L? What will be the long-run average and marginal cost of pipe?

b. In the long-run equilibrium, what will be the market equilibrium price and quantity for concrete pipe? How much will each firm produce? How much labor will be hired by each firm and in the market as a whole?

c. Suppose the market wage, w, rose to $2 while v remained constant at $1. How will this change the capital-labor ratio for the typical firm, and how will it affect its marginal costs?

d. Under the conditions of part c, what will the long-run market equilibrium be? How much labor will now be hired by the concrete pipe industry?

e. How much of the change in total labor demand from part b to part d represents the substitution effect resulting from the change in wage and how much represents the output effect?

13.4 Suppose the demand for labor is given by

$$L = -50w + 450$$

and the supply is given by

$$L = 100w$$

where L represents the number of people employed and w is the real wage rate per hour.

a. What will be the equilibrium levels for w and L in this market?
b. Suppose the government wishes to raise the equilibrium wage to $4 per hour by offering a subsidy to employers for each person hired. How much will this subsidy have to be? What will the new equilibrium level of employment be? How much total subsidy will be paid?
c. Suppose instead the government declares a minimum wage of $4 per hour. How much labor would be demanded at this price? How much unemployment would there be?
d. Graph and compare your results.

13.5 Suppose that the demand for labor in the perfectly competitive market for temporary help is given by

$$L = 750 - 25w$$

and that the supply of temporary workers is given by

$$L = 25w - 250$$

a. What are the equilibrium values for L and w in this market?
b. Suppose that the firms that hire temporary workers are considering adding a health insurance benefit. The insurance cost of this benefit is $4 per worker hour. Assuming that the health benefit affects only the demand for labor, how will this demand curve be shifted by the extra $4 cost and what will be the new equilibrium values for L and w?
c. Assume now that the health benefit is also valuable to workers. Specifically, assume that workers value the benefit at $h per hour. How will this shift the supply curve for temporary workers?
d. How will the equilibrium values for L and w be affected by the value that workers assign to the health benefit? Compute the labor market equilibrium for h = 2 and h = 4. What do you conclude about the impact of fringe benefits on labor markets?

13.6 Suppose that the supply curve for the labor to a firm is given by

$$L = 100w$$

and the marginal expense of labor curve is given by

$$ME_L = L/50$$

where w is the market wage. Suppose also that the firm's demand for labor (marginal revenue product) curve is given by

$$L = 1,000 - 100MRP_L$$

a. If the firm acts as a monopsonist, how many workers does it hire in order to maximize profits? What wage does it pay? How does this wage compare to the MRP_L at this employment level?
b. Assume now that the firm must hire its workers in a perfectly competitive labor market but it still acts as a monopoly when selling its output. How many workers does the firm hire now? What wage does it pay?
c. Graph your results.

13.7 Carl the clothier owns a large garment factory on a remote island. Carl's factory is the only source of employment for most of the islanders, and thus Carl acts as a monopsonist. The supply curve for garment workers is given by

$$L = 80w$$

and the marginal-expense-of-labor curve is given by

$$ME_L = L/40$$

where L is the number of workers hired and w is their hourly wage. Assume also that Carl's labor demand (marginal value product) curve is given by

$$L = 400 - 40MVP_L$$

a. How many workers does Carl hire in order to maximize his profits and what wage does he pay?
b. Assume now that the government implements a minimum wage law covering all garment workers. How many workers does Carl now hire and how much unemployment will there be if the minimum wage is set at $3 per hour? $3.33 per hour? $4.00 per hour?
c. Graph your results.
d. How does the imposition of a minimum wage under monopsony differ in results from a minimum wage imposed under perfect competition (assuming the minimum wage is above the market-determined wage)?

13.8 The Ajax Coal Company is the only employer in its area. It can hire any number of female workers or male workers it wishes. The supply curve for women is given by

$$L_f = 100w_f$$
$$ME_f = L_f/50$$

and for men by

$$L_m = 9w_m^2$$
$$ME_m = \frac{1}{2}\sqrt{L_m}$$

where w_f and w_m are, respectively, the hourly wage rate paid to female and male workers. Assume that Ajax sells its coal in a perfectly competitive market at $5 per ton and that each worker hired (both men and women) can mine two tons per hour. If the firm wishes to maximize profits, how many female and male workers should be hired and what will the wage rates for these two groups be? How much will Ajax earn in profits per hour on its mining machinery? How will that result compare to one in which Ajax was constrained (say, by market forces) to pay all workers the same wage based on the value of their marginal products?

Note: The following problems involve mainly material from the Appendix to Chapter 13.

13.9 Mrs. Smith has a guaranteed income of $10 per day from an inheritance. Her preferences require her always to spend half her potential income on leisure (H) and consumption (C).

a. What is Mrs. Smith's budget constraint in this situation?
b. How many hours will Mrs. Smith devote to work and to leisure in order to maximize her utility given that her market wage is $1.25? $2.50? $5.00? $10.00?
c. Graph the four different budget constraints and sketch in Mrs. Smith's utility-maximizing choices. (Hint: When graphing budget constraints, remember that when H = 24, C = 10, not 0.)
d. Graph Mrs. Smith's supply-of-labor curve.

13.10 How will Mrs. Smith's supply-of-labor curve (calculated in part d of problem 13.9) shift if her inheritance increases to $20 per day? Graph both supply curves to illustrate this shift.

INTERNET EXERCISES

1. *Monopsony.* Application 13.4 discusses monopsony in the market for professional sports stars. Let's take a look at monopsony in the world of college athletics. Go to the Birmingham Post–Herald's series entitled "Investigating the NCAA" at *http://www.postherald.com/cheating.shtml.* Scroll down and read the second article entitled "Destined to Deceive" by Taylor Bright. Why has the NCAA been called a monopsonistic cartel? Under NCAA regulations, colleges may not offer college athletes anything more than tuition, room, and board; yet, according to the article, "star athletes" can be worth much more to a school. (How much?) Is this consistent with the relationship between the wage and the marginal value product in the monopsony outcome as described in your text? Explain. Why does the relationship between the wage and the marginal value product in the monopsony outcome encourage cheating by individual colleges and universities in the monopsonistic cartel? Suppose the NCAA were disbanded and the "market" for student athletes were to become perfectly competitive. What do you predict will happen to the "wage" received by star athletes, and how will this wage compare to the athlete's marginal value product?

2. *Occupational outlook.* What is the occupational outlook for dental assistants? Real estate agents? Power plant operators? Pest control workers? The outlook for these and other occupations can be found in the Bureau of Labor Statistics' Occupational Outlook Handbook. Go to the home page of the Bureau of Labor Statistics at

http://stats.bls.gov. Under Publications and Research Papers, click on Occupational Outlook Handbook. Click on an occupational category of interest, then scroll down the list and click on a specific occupation of interest. Scroll down the page for your selected occupation and read the section on Job Outlook. How is employment expected to change in this occupation and why?

Now repeat the exercise for another occupation of interest. According to your text, what factors can cause the demand curve for labor to shift? Is either of the demand curves for labor in the occupations you selected expected to shift? Carefully explain. Do you think that the publication of such occupational outlooks can affect the future supply of labor to an occupation? Explain.

Labor Supply

In this appendix, we use the utility maximization model to study individual labor supply decisions. The ultimate goal of this discussion is to provide additional details about the labor supply curves that we used to study how wages are determined in Chapter 13.

ALLOCATION OF TIME

Part 2 studied how an individual chooses to allocate a fixed amount of income among a variety of available goods. People must make similar choices in deciding how they will spend their time. The number of hours in a day (or in a year) is absolutely fixed, and time must be used as it passes by. Given this fixed amount of time, any person must decide how many hours to work; how many hours to spend consuming a wide variety of goods, ranging from cars and television sets to operas; how many hours to devote to self-maintenance; and how many hours to sleep. Table 13A.1 shows that there is considerable variation in time use between men and women and among various countries around the world. By studying the division of time people choose to make among their activities, economists are able to understand labor supply decisions. Viewing work as only one of a number of choices open to people in the way they spend their time enables us to understand how these decisions may be adjusted in response to changing opportunities.

A Simple Model of Time Use

We assume that there are only two uses to which any person may devote his or her time: either engaging in market work at a wage rate of w per hour or not working. We refer to nonwork time as **leisure,** but to economists this word does not mean idleness. Time that is not spent in market work can be used in many productive ways: for work in the home, for self-improvement, or for consump-

Leisure
Time spent in any activity other than market work.

TABLE 13A.1 Time Allocation (Percentage of Time during Typical Week)

	Men			Women		
	U.S.	Japan	Russia	U.S.	Japan	Russia
Market work	28.3%	33.6%	35.1%	15.4%	15.3%	25.4%
Housework	8.2	2.1	7.1	18.2	18.5	16.1
Personal care and sleep	40.6	43.1	40.4	42.6	42.9	41.6
Leisure and other	22.9	21.2	17.4	23.8	23.3	16.9

Source: Adapted from F. T. Juster and F. P. Stafford, "The Allocation of Time: Empirical Findings, Behavioral Models, and Problems and Measurement," *Journal of Economic Literature* (June 1991), Table 1.

tion (it takes time to use a television set or a bowling ball).[1] All of these activities contribute to a person's well-being, and time will be allocated to them in a utility-maximizing way.

More specifically, assume that utility depends on consumption of market goods (C) and on the amount of leisure time (H) used. Figure 13A.1 shows an indifference curve map for this utility function. The diagram has the familiar shape introduced in Chapter 2. It shows those combinations of C and H that yield an individual various levels of utility.

Now we must describe the budget constraint that faces this person. If the period we are studying is one day, the individual will work (24 − H) hours. That is, he or she will work all of the hours not devoted to leisure. For this work, she or he will earn w per hour and will use this to buy consumption goods.

The Opportunity Cost of Leisure

Each extra hour of leisure this person takes reduces his or her income (and consumption) by w dollars. The hourly wage therefore reflects the opportunity cost of leisure. People have to "pay" this cost for each hour they do not work. The wage rate used to make these calculations should be a real wage in that it should represent how workers can turn their earnings into actual consumer goods. A nominal wage of $1 per hour provides the same purchasing power when the typical item costs $.25 as does a wage of $100 per hour when that item sells for $25. In either case, the person must work 15 minutes to buy the item. Alternately, in both cases, the opportunity cost of taking one more hour of leisure is to do without four consumption items. In Application 13A.1: The Opportunity Cost of Time, we look at some cases of competing uses of time and illustrate how the notion of opportunity cost can explain the choices people make.

[1] For the classic treatment of the allocation of time, See G. S. Becker, "A Theory of the Allocation of Time," *The Economic Journal* (September 1965): 493–517.

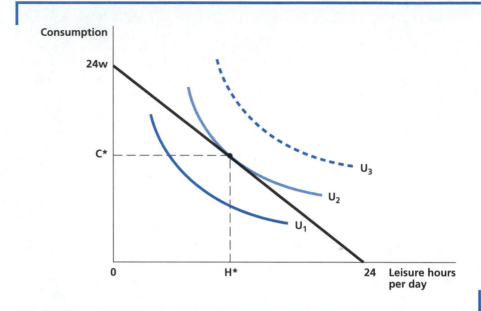

FIGURE 13A.1 Utility-Maximizing Choice of Hours of Leisure and Work Given his or her budget constraint, this person maximizes utility by choosing H* hours of leisure and consumption of C*. At this point, the rate at which he or she is willing to trade H for C (the MRS) is equal to the rate at which he or she is able to trade these in the market (the real hourly wage, w).

Utility Maximization

To show the utility-maximizing choices of consumption and leisure, we must first graph the budget constraint. This is done in Figure 13A.1. If this person doesn't work at all, he or she can enjoy 24 hours of leisure. This is shown as the horizontal intercept of the budget constraint. If, on the other hand, this person works 24 hours per day, he or she will be able to buy $(24 \cdot w)$ in consumption goods. This establishes the vertical intercept in the figure. The slope of the budget constraint is $-w$. This reflects opportunity costs—each added hour of leisure must be "purchased" by doing without w worth of consumption items. For example, if w = $10, this person will earn $240 if he or she works 24 hours per day. Each hour not worked has an opportunity cost of $10.

Given this budget constraint, this person will maximize utility by choosing to take H* hours of leisure and to work the remaining time. With the income earned from this work, he or she will be able to buy C* units of consumption goods. At the utility-maximizing point, the slope of the budget $(-w)$ is equal to the slope of indifference curve U_2. In other words, the person's real wage is equal to the marginal rate of substitution of leisure hours for consumption.

Choices that people must make among competing uses of time can often be clarified by recognizing the opportunity costs involved.

Transportation Choices

In choosing among alternative ways of getting to work, people take both time and dollar costs into account. Most studies have found that commuters are quite sensitive to time costs, especially those associated with walking to a bus or train station or with waiting for the bus or train to come.[1] By examining people's willingness to pay to avoid such waits, the studies generally conclude that people value travel time at about one-half of their market wage. For example, studies conducted in connection with the Bay Area Rapid Transit System (BART) in San Francisco concluded that fares were less than one-fourth of the total costs people faced. Far more important were the time costs involved in getting to suburban BART stations, waiting for trains, and walking from downtown BART stations to the final destination. Given the size of these costs, it is not surprising that most commuters in the Bay Area continue to use private cars for their trips.

The Economics of Childbearing

People's decisions to have children are affected by a number of social, religious, and economic factors. Economists have tended to focus primarily on the costs associated with having children and how those costs vary among individuals. One of the most important costs is the forgone wages of parents who choose to have and raise children rather than to pursue market employment. Indeed, by some estimates, this cost is far in excess of all other costs of childbearing combined. This calculation has led some economists to speculate that higher real wages earned by women in the United States since World War II are the principal reason for the decline in the birthrate during the same period. Similarly, the lower birthrates in North America and Western Europe as compared to the less-developed world might be attributed to wage-rate differences (and hence cost-of-children differences) between these regions.[2]

Job Search Theory

When seeking new jobs, people are often faced with considerable uncertainty about available openings. Consequently, they must invest some time (and possibly other resources, such as telephone calls or advertising) in finding a suitable job match. To the extent that people must reduce work time to accommodate their job search plans, the hourly cost of a search can be approximated by the market wage. The higher an individual's market wage, the more likely he or she would be to adopt search techniques that economize on time

---

[1] See, for example, T. A. Domencich and Daniel McFadden, *Urban Travel Demand* (Amsterdam: North Holland Press, 1973).

[2] For a seminal contribution to the economics of fertility, see G. S. Becker, "An Economic Analysis of Fertility," in *Demographic and Economic Change in Developed Countries* (Princeton, NJ: Princeton University Press, 1960).

(continued)

(such as using an employment agency). If, on the other hand, search time is subsidized (say, by unemployment insurance benefits), search time may be prolonged in the hope of finding a better job. By one estimate, a 10 percent increase in weekly unemployment benefits is associated with about one-half week of additional unemployment.[3]

To Think About

1. Why do empirical studies of commuting patterns find that people value their time at about one-half the market wage? Doesn't our theory suggest that the value should be the full wage rate?

2. The evidence about people's job search activities is that receipt of unemployment insurance benefits causes them to be more choosy about the jobs they take. Isn't that a good thing?

[3] For a summary of many studies of the effects of unemployment compensation, see P.M. Decker, "Incentive Effects of Unemployment Insurance," in C. O'Leary and S. Wandner, *Unemployment Insurance in the United States* (Kalamazoo, MI: Upjohn Institute, 1999).

MicroQuiz 13A.1

How would you graph the utility-maximizing choices for individuals with the following preferences?

1. Ms. Steady always works exactly 7 hours each day no matter what wage is offered to her.

2. Mr. Mellow currently doesn't work but might if the right wage were offered.

If this were not true, utility would not be as large as possible. For example, suppose a person's MRS were equal to 5, indicating a willingness to give up five units of consumption to get an additional hour of leisure. Suppose also that the real wage is $10. By working one more hour, he or she is able to earn enough to buy ten units (that is, $10 worth) of consumption. This is clearly an inefficient situation. By working one hour more, this person can buy ten extra units of consumption; but he or she required only five units of consumption to be as well-off as before. By working the extra hour, this person earns five (= 10 − 5) more units of consumption than required. Consequently, he or she could not have been maximizing utility in the first place. A similar proof can be constructed for any case in which the MRS differs from the market wage, which proves that the two trade-off rates must be equal for a true utility maximum.

INCOME AND SUBSTITUTION EFFECTS OF A CHANGE IN THE REAL WAGE RATE

A change in the real wage rate can be analyzed the same way we studied a price change in Chapter 3. When w rises, the price of leisure becomes higher—people must give up more in lost wages for each hour of leisure consumed. The substitution effect of an increase in w on the hours of leisure is therefore to reduce them. As leisure becomes more expensive, there is reason to consume less of it. However, the income effect of a rise in the wage tends to increase leisure. Because leisure is a normal good, the higher income resulting from a higher w increases the demand for it. Hence, income and substitution effects work in the opposite direction. It is impossible to predict whether an increase in w will increase or decrease the demand for leisure time. Because leisure and work are mutually exclusive ways to use time, this also shows that it is impossible to predict what will happen to the number of hours worked when wages change.

Substitution effect of a change in w
Movement along an indifference curve in response to a change in the real wage. A rise in w causes an individual to work more.

Income effect of a change in w
Movement to a higher indifference curve in response to a rise in the real wage rate. If leisure is a normal good, a rise in w causes an individual to work less.

A Graphical Analysis

Figure 13A.2 illustrates two different reactions to an increase in w. In both graphs, the initial wage rate is w_0 and the optimal choices of consumption and leisure are given by C_0 and H_0. When the wage rate increases to w_1, the utility-maximizing combination moves to C_1, H_1. This movement can be divided into two effects. The substitution effect is represented by the movement along the indifference curve U_0 from H_0 to S. This effect works to reduce the number of hours of leisure in both parts of Figure 13A.2. People substitute consumption for leisure because the relative price of leisure has increased.

The movement from S to C_1, H_1 represents the income effect of a higher real wage. Because leisure time is a normal good, increases in income cause more leisure to be demanded. Consequently, the income and substitution effects induced by the increase in w work in opposite directions. In Figure 13A.2(a), the demand for leisure is reduced by the rise in w; that is, the substitution effect outweighs the income effect. On the other hand, in Figure 13A.2(b), the income effect is stronger and the demand for leisure increases in response to an increase in w. This person actually chooses to work fewer hours when w increases. In the analysis of demand, we would have considered this result unusual—when the price of leisure rises, this person demands more of it. For the case of normal consumption goods, income and substitution effects work in the same direction, and both cause quantity to decline when price increases. In the case of leisure, however, income and substitution effects work in opposite directions. An increase in w makes a person better off because he or she is a *supplier* of labor. In the case of a consumption good, an individual is made worse off by a rise in price because he or she is a *consumer* of that good. Consequently, it is not possible to predict exactly how a person will respond to a wage increase—he or she may work more or fewer hours depending on his or her preferences.

MicroQuiz 13A.2

Suppose the the government is choosing among two types of income tax: (1) a proportional tax on wages and (2) a lump-sum tax of a fixed dollar amount. How would each of these taxes be expected to affect the labor supply of a typical person?

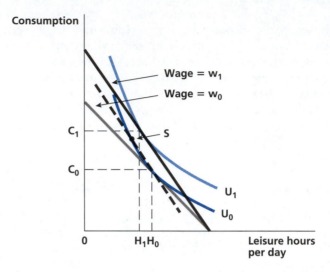

(a) Rise in wage increases work

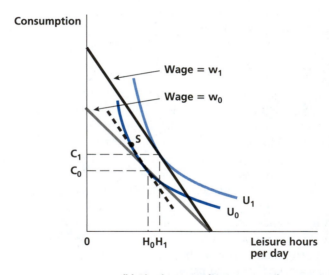

(b) Rise in wage decreases work

FIGURE 13A.2 Income and Substitution Effects of a Change in the Real Wage Rate Because the individual is a supplier of labor, the income and substitution effects of an increase in the real wage rate affect the hours of leisure demanded (or hours of work) in opposite directions. In panel a, the substitution effect (movement to point S) outweighs the income effect and a higher wage causes hours of leisure to decline to H_1. Hours of work, therefore, increase. In panel b, the income effect is stronger than the substitution effect and H increases to H_1. Hours of work in this case fall.

Appendix

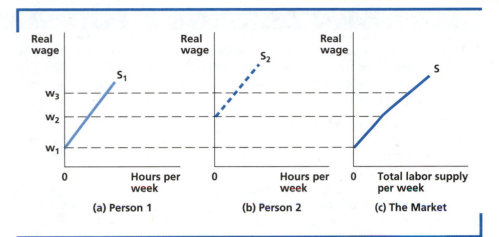

FIGURE 13A.3 Construction of the Market Supply Curve for Labor As the real wage rises, the supply of labor may increase for two reasons. First, higher real wages may cause each person to work more hours. Second, higher wages may induce more people (for example, person 2) to enter the labor market.

MARKET SUPPLY CURVE FOR LABOR

If we are willing to assume that in most cases substitution effects of wage changes outweigh income effects, individual labor supply curves will have positive slopes. We can construct a market-supply-of-labor curve from these individual supply curves by "adding" them up. At each possible wage rate, we add together the quantity of labor offered by each person in order to arrive at a market total. One particularly interesting aspect of this procedure is that, as the wage rate rises, more people may be induced to enter the labor force. That is, rising wages may induce some people who were not previously employed to take jobs. Figure 13A.3 illustrates this possibility for a simple case of two individuals. For a real wage below w_1, neither person chooses to work in the market. Consequently, the market supply curve of labor (Figure 13A.3[c]) shows that no labor is supplied at real wages below w_1. A wage in excess of w_1 causes person 1 to enter the labor market. However, as long as wages fall short of w_2, person 2 will not work. Only at a wage rate above w_2 will both people choose to take a job. As Figure 13A.3(c) shows, the possibility of the entry of these new workers makes the market supply of labor somewhat more responsive to wage rate increases than would be the case if we assumed that the number of workers was fixed. Changing wage rates may not only induce current workers to alter their hours of work but, perhaps more important, they may change the composition of the workforce. As Application 13A.2: Changing Labor Force Participation for Younger Women and Older Men shows, such effects have been especially pronounced for these two groups in the United States over the past 40 years.

Probably the two most significant trends in labor market behavior in the United States during the past three decades have been (1) the increasing tendency for women to hold paying jobs, and (2) the decline in employment of older men. Both of these trends are illustrated in Table 1.

Expanding Female Labor Force Participation

For women in the age category 25 to 34, the increase in labor force participation has been spectacular. The fraction of women age 25 to 34 who are in the workforce more than doubled between 1960 and 1985 and continued to rise during the next fifteen years. Many reasons have been proposed to explain this major social phenomenon. Economists have tended to focus on expanding job opportunities and real wages for women as a principal explanation. Because many women have good alternative uses for their time (such as working in the home versus working in the market), substitution effects from higher real wages would be expected to be large; labor supply will increase in response to higher wages. Sociologists, on the other hand, tend to attribute the increasing work by women to political and cultural factors. That is, they attribute the change to a shift in the supply curve rather than a move along it in response to higher wages. Whatever the cause, these labor force statistics show greater responsiveness in labor supply behavior of a large segment of the population than was believed likely in earlier times.

The Case of Older Men

Interestingly, the labor force trend for older men has been precisely opposite that for younger women. As Table 1 shows, between 1960 and 1985, the labor force participation rate for men over 65 fell to less than half its initial level. The pattern is all the more puzzling given the improvement in the health of older men that occurred over this period. Such improvements should have resulted in more rather than less work activity by this group.

TABLE 1 Labor Force Participation Rates, 1960–2000

Year	Females age 25–34	Males age 65 and over
1960	35.2	33.9
1970	43.1	27.7
1975	53.7	21.6
1980	65.5	19.0
1985	69.4	15.8
1990	73.5	16.3
1995	74.9	16.8
2000	76.3	17.5

Source: Statistical Abstract of the United States at http://www.census.gov

Although it is possible that the figures simply reflect a backward-bending supply of labor in response to higher wages, most economists have instead focused on issues related to retirement as being the primary cause. Most important, the rapid growth in Social Security coverage of the elderly coupled with rising real benefit amounts may have encouraged increasingly large numbers of workers to retire in recent years. Other provisions of the program (such as reduction in benefits that results when the elderly do take jobs) have had a similar effect of discouraging work. Policymakers have been especially concerned about these trends (most importantly because they threaten the financial integrity of Social Security) and have taken some steps to try to reverse them.[1]

To Think About

1. How does income taxation affect the labor supply decisions of men and women? Which group would you expect to respond most to changes in tax rates?
2. Would the availability of Social Security benefits at retirement cause people to work more or less during their prime working years?

[1] For a more complete discussion of these issues in the theory of labor supply, see R. G. Ehrenberg and R. G. Smith, *Modern Labor Economics*, 4th ed (Glenview, IL: Scott, Foresman, 1991), Chapters 6 and 7.

SUMMARY

In this appendix, we have examined the utility-maximizing model of labor supply. This model is another application of the economic theory of choice that we described earlier in this textbook. Although the results are quite similar to those we derived before, the focus here on labor supply provides a number of new insights, including:

- Labor supply decisions by individuals can be studied as one aspect of their allocation of time. The market wage represents an opportunity cost for individuals if they choose not to engage in market work.

- A rise in the market wage induces income and substitution effects into individuals' labor supply decisions. These effects operate in opposite directions. A higher wage causes a substitution effect favoring more market work but an income effect favoring more leisure.

- Construction of the labor supply curve also requires the consideration of labor force participation decisions by individuals.

14

Capital Markets

In this chapter, we look at capital markets. In some respects, this material is not very different from the discussion of labor markets in the previous chapter. Firms acquire capital equipment for the same reason that they hire workers—to maximize profits. Hence, the general rule of hiring any input up to the point at which its marginal revenue product is equal to its market rental rate continues to apply. The main new dimension added in the study of capital markets is the need to explicitly consider questions of time. Because machinery may produce valuable output for many years into the future, we need to take account of the fact that values that occur in different time periods can be compared only after taking account of the potential interest payments that might have been earned. A primary purpose of this chapter then is to show clearly how interest rates affect the rental rates on capital equipment and thereby determine how much capital is hired.

TIME PERIODS AND THE FLOW OF ECONOMIC TRANSACTIONS

Before starting our investigation, it may be best to get some conceptual issues out of the way. As everyone knows, time is continuous—it just keeps passing by, much like a river. Often, however, it is useful to divide time up into discrete intervals such as days, months, or years. This is true also for economic activity. Although economic activity (such as producing and selling cars) proceeds more or less continuously, it is often convenient to divide up this activity into discrete intervals and speak of markets as reaching an equilibrium on a per-day, per-month, or per-year basis. This is how we have proceeded in this book by, for example, noting on most graphs that they refer to "Quantity per Period." Hence, these magnitudes are a "flow" per period. Just as one might measure the flow of a river on the basis of gallons per hour, so too economic transactions are usually measured as a per-period flow. For example, gross domestic product (GDP) is measured as total output per year, and total peanut output is measured in bushels per year.

There are two important ways in which transactions can occur across periods. First, some goods may be "durable" in that they last more than one period. Most relevant to this chapter, firms buy machinery and hope to be able to use it for many periods into the future. In deciding whether to make such a purchase, firms must think about the future. Economic models that take account of these decisions are usually fairly straightforward generalizations of the models we have already studied. Many new and interesting issues do arise when such future expectations are taken into account.

A second way that transactions can occur across periods is through borrowing and lending. An individual can borrow to increase his or her spending in one period but knows that the loan must be repaid (by spending less) in the next period. Similarly, a firm may borrow in one period to buy equipment that then generates future returns with which to repay the loan. In the next section, we see how this demand and supply for loans determines the interest rate to be paid. Then we show how this interest rate becomes the primary "price" that ties together all transactions that take place over time—especially firms' investment decisions. The appendix to this chapter examines some of the mathematical concepts that relate to interest rates.

INDIVIDUAL SAVINGS—THE SUPPLY OF LOANS

When individuals save out of their current incomes, these savings have two important economic effects. First, they free up some resources that might otherwise have been devoted to their own consumption. These resources can be used to produce the kinds of investment goods (buildings and equipment) that firms need. Second, savings also provide the funds that firms can use to finance the purchase of these investment goods. Usually, individuals "lend" their funds, not directly to firms but indirectly through financial intermediaries such as banks or the stock market. In the study of how interest rates are determined, therefore, we think of individuals' savings decisions as providing the supply of loans.

Two-Period Model of Saving

Individual savings decisions can be illustrated with a simple utility-maximization model. Suppose that we are concerned only with two periods—this year and next year. Consumption this year is denoted by C_0 and consumption next year is denoted by C_1, and these are the only items that provide utility to this individual. He or she has a current income of Y dollars that can either be spent now on C_0 or saved to buy C_1 next year. Any income saved this year earns interest (at a real

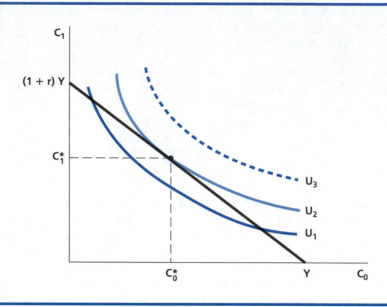

FIGURE 14.1 The Savings Decision A person with a current income of Y can either spend this on current consumption; C_0, or save it (at an interest rate of r) to buy consumption next year, C_1. Here, the person's utility-maximizing choice is C_0, C_1. Current savings are $Y - C_0^*$.

interest rate[1] of r) before it is used to buy C_1. The individual's problem then is to maximize utility given this budget constraint.

A Graphical Analysis

Figure 14.1 shows this utility-maximization process. The indifference curves show the utility obtainable from various combinations of C_0 and C_1. To understand the (intertemporal) budget constraint in this problem, consider first the case where $C_1 = 0$. Then $C_0 = Y$, and no income is saved for use in period 2. On the other hand, if all income is saved, $C_0 = 0$ and $C_1 = (1 + r)Y$. In year 2, this person can consume all of his or her income plus the interest earned on that income. For example, if $r = 0.05$ (that is, 5 percent), C_1 will be $1.05Y$. Waiting for the interest to be earned has made it possible for this person to have relatively more consumption in period 2 than in period 1.

Given the two intercepts in Figure 14.1, the entire budget constraint can be constructed as the black straight line joining them. Utility maximization is

---

[1] That is, the interest rate is adjusted for any possible change in purchasing power between the two periods. Hence, this real interest rate provides information to the consumer about how *real* consumption this year can be traded for *real* consumption next year. In Application 14.3, we look at the real interest rate concept in more detail.

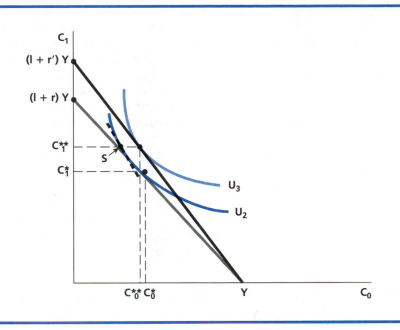

FIGURE 14.2 Effect of an Increase in r on Savings Is Ambiguous An increase in r to r' causes a substitution effect that reduces C_0 from C_0^* to S (an increase in savings) and an income effect that raises C_0 from S to C_0^{**} (a decrease in savings). In the figure, the rise in r results in a net increase in savings.

achieved at C_0^*, C_1^* at which point the marginal rate of substitution (MRS) is equal to $(1 + r)$. That is, utility maximization requires equating the rate at which the individual is willing to trade C_0 for C_1 to the rate at which he or she is able to trade these goods for each other in the market through saving. The interest rate is clearly an important part of this story because it measures the opportunity cost that the individual incurs when he or she chooses to consume now rather than in the future.

Substitution and Income Effects of a Change in r

A change in the real interest rate, r, changes the "price" of future versus current consumption. The substitution and income effects of this price change are illustrated in Figure 14.2 for an increase in r. In this case, the rise in r to r' causes this individual to move along the U_2 indifference curve to point S—this is the substitution effect. With a higher r, the opportunity cost of C_0 rises and this person substitutes C_1 for C_0—that is, he or she saves more. But the rise in r also shifts this person's budget constraint outward because he or she is made better off by this rise. This income effect causes the preferred consumption point to move from S to C_0^{**}, C_1^{**}. Assuming that both C_0 and C_1 are normal goods,

MicroQuiz 14.1

One way to study the results of Figure 14.1 and Figure 14.2 is by thinking about the "relative price" of C_1 in terms of C_0.

1. Explain why the relative price of C_1 is given by $1/(1 + r)$. If $r = 0.10$, what is the relative price of C_1? Explain the meaning of this "price."

2. Explain why an increase in r reduces the relative price of C_1. Why is the individual's reaction to such a price decline ambiguous here, whereas that was not the case in Chapter 3?

they should both be increased by this move. The final effect of an increase in r on C_0 (and hence on savings) is indeterminate—the substitution effect increases savings (C_0 falls) whereas the income effect decreases savings (C_0 rises). The net effect depends on the relative sizes of these two effects.[2] In general, economists believe that the substitution effect is probably the stronger of the two effects so that a rise in r encourages savings. This is the final result pictured in Figure 14.2. But there is considerable disagreement about the actual size of this effect as Application 14.1: Do We Need Tax Breaks for Savers? illustrates.

FIRMS' DEMAND FOR CAPITAL AND LOANS

In Chapter 13, we saw that profit-maximizing firms rent additional capital equipment up to the point at which the marginal revenue product of the equipment is equal to the rental rate on the equipment, v. To understand the connections between this demand and the demand for loans, we need to understand the nature of the determinants of this rental rate. We begin by assuming that firms rent all of the capital that they use from other firms. Cases in which firms directly own their own equipment are then easy to explain.

Rental Rates and Interest Rates

Many types of capital equipment are in fact rented in the real world. Hertz rents millions of cars each year to other firms; banks and insurance companies actually own many commercial planes that they rent to airlines; and construction firms rent specialized equipment (for example, heavy-lifting cranes) when they need it. In these cases, the per-period rate that firms have to pay to rent this equipment (v) is determined by the average costs that the rental firms (for example, Hertz) incur. Two such costs are especially important: depreciation costs and borrowing costs. Depreciation costs reflect the physical wear and tear on equipment that occurs during each period that it is used. Borrowing costs may be either explicit or implicit for the firm providing the equipment. If they have financed the purchase of their equipment with a loan, interest payments on that loan are an

[2] This ambiguity is identical to the encountered in looking at the effect on labor supply of an increase in the real wage—see the appendix to Chapter 13 for a discussion.

Personal savings rates in the United States are very low by international standards. In 2002, total personal savings amounted to only about 1 percent of disposable income. That figure represented both a steep decline from earlier savings levels in the United States and a markedly lower rate than exists in many other countries (where rates above 10 percent are common).[1] These low savings rates have prompted a variety of concerns. Some observers worry about whether individuals will have adequate savings for their own retirement or for various emergencies. Others worry that inadequate savings will fail to provide sufficient capital accumulation for future generations.

Recent Savings Incentive Plans

Many recent savings incentive plans have a similar structure. All of them allow a tax deduction for contributions to the plans.[2] Then they do not tax investment returns from assets in the plans until benefits are paid out at retirement. The three principal types of such plans are

- *Individual Retirement Accounts (IRAs)*, which are set up by individuals acting on their own. Only low-income individuals receive an income tax deduction for IRA contributions, but everyone can avoid taxation of returns from assets in the plans.
- *401(k) Plans* are set up by employers who sometimes make matching contributions to their workers' plans. Both contributions and asset returns are tax-exempt until retirement.
- *Keogh Plans* are similar to IRAs and 401(k) plans but are intended for self-employed individuals. They generally have higher contribution limits than do the other plans.

Theoretical Effects on Savings

The effect of these various tax benefits on total personal savings is, however, ambiguous. Although special tax treatment does raise the after-tax interest rate for savers, our discussion of Figure 14.2 showed that the effect of such a change on savings is ambiguous—income and substitution effects work in opposite directions. In addition, the fact that the incentives do not apply to all savings but only to contributions to specific plans gives individuals an incentive to shift their assets into the tax-favored plans without actually changing the total amount of their savings. Hence, the rapid growth of the plans should not be taken as an indication of the plans' ability to stimulate savings.

Research on Savers and Spenders

Because savings incentive plans involve significant losses in tax revenues, much research has been undertaken to determine whether the plans are achieving their goal of increasing savings. Most studies use data on individual savings behavior to detect such influences. Unfortunately, this research has been plagued by one serious problem: it appears that people have very different attitudes toward saving. Some people are serious savers who will

---

[1] To some extent the low savings rate in the United States may reflect mismeasurment. See W. G. Gale and J. Sabelhaus, "Perspectives on the Household Savings Rate," *Brookings Papers on Economic Activity*, No. 1 (1999): 181–224.

[2] Roth IRAs, which became available in 1998, do not allow current deductibility, but all income is nontaxable when received.

(continued)

accumulate assets in many forms. Other people are only spenders who never put anything aside. Individuals who participate in one of the special saving plans have shown themselves to fit into the "saver" category. But to compare their savings behavior to the behavior of those individuals without the plans runs the danger of concluding that the plans themselves increase savings. A more correct interpretation is that plan participation acts only to identify savers who are *predisposed* to save more. Researchers have been unable to resolve this difficulty, and the true impact of the special savings plans remains unknown.

To Think About

1. The taxation of interest income always distorts individuals' choices between present and future consumption. Would a move from income taxation to consumption taxation change this situation?
2. If you wanted to study the impact of the special savings plans, how would you define a "control" group to compare to individuals who participate in the plans?

explicit cost.[3] If, on the other hand, they have bought equipment with internal funds, interest payments are an implicit or opportunity cost. By having the funds tied up in the equipment, the firm is forgoing what it could have earned by putting them in the bank. Hence, interest costs are always relevant to the firm that supplies the rented equipment no matter how they have actually financed the equipment purchase.

In general, it might be expected that both depreciation and borrowing costs are proportional to the market price of the equipment being rented. If P represents that price, d is the per-period rate of depreciation, and r is the interest rate, we have the following expression for the per-period rental rate (v):

$$\text{Rental rate} = v = \text{Depreciation} + \text{Borrowing costs} = dP + rP = (d + r)P \quad \textbf{(14.1)}$$

For example, suppose Citicorp owns a Boeing 777 that it leases to United Airlines. Suppose also that the current value of the plane is $50 million, that the plane is expected to deteriorate at a rate of 10 percent each year, and that the real interest rate is 5 percent. Then Citicorp's total costs of owning the plane are $7.5 million ($5 million in depreciation and $2.5 million in interest costs). If it is to break even in its plane rental business, that is the rate it must charge United each year for the plane.

Equation 14.1 clearly shows why firms' demand for equipment is negatively related to the interest rate. When the interest rate is high, rental rates on equipment are high and firms try to substitute toward cheaper inputs. When interest

---

[3] Financing through offering stock would involve similar costs, though we do not examine that case.

rates are low, rental rates are low and firms opt to rent more equipment. Such changes in equipment rentals also bring about accompanying changes in the demand for loans with which to finance the equipment. When interest rates are high, the demand for loans contracts because there is little need to finance equipment purchases. With low interest rates, loan volume picks up as a consequence of the rental firms' needs to add to their available equipment.

Ownership of Capital Equipment

Of course, most capital equipment is owned by the firms that use it; only a relatively small portion is rented. But that distinction does not affect the validity of Equation 14.1. Firms that own equipment are really in two businesses—they produce goods and they lease capital equipment to themselves. In their role as equipment lessors, firms are affected by the same economic considerations as are firms whose primary business is leasing. The implicit rental rates that they pay are the same regardless of who owns the equipment.[4] Application 14.2: Do Taxes Affect Investment? shows how Equation 14.1 can be used to study the ways in which government tax policy can be used to influence firms' decisions to purchase capital equipment.

DETERMINATION OF THE REAL INTEREST RATE

Now that we have described the two sides of the market for loans, we are ready to describe how the real interest rate is determined. Figure 14.3 shows that the supply of loans is an upward-sloping function of the real interest rate, r. This slope reflects our assumption that individuals increase their savings (which are converted into loans by financial intermediaries) as the interest rate rises. The demand for loans is negatively sloped because of the inhibiting effect that higher interest rates have on firms' equipment rental rates. Equilibrium then occurs at r*, Q* where the quantity of loans demanded is equal to the quantity supplied. This equilibrium real interest rate provides the price that links economic periods together.

> **MicroQuiz 14.2**
>
> A "pure" inflation (in which all prices change by the same amount) should not have any real effect on firms' decisions. Use Equation 14.1 together with the theory of input demand from Chapter 13 to explain why this is so for firms' decisions about how much capital to use.

---

[4] The mathematical relationship between the present-value calculations that owners must make in deciding whether to purchase new equipment and the rental rate they implicitly pay on the equipment is examined in the appendix to this chapter.

Do Taxes Affect Investment?

Although a tax on pure economic profits would not affect firms' input choices, the actual U.S. corporate income tax departs in several ways from such a pure tax. Most important, opportunity costs of equity capital are not deductible under U.S. tax law and allowable depreciation charges for tax purposes often fall short of true economic depreciation. Equation 14.1 should be modified to take these effects of taxes into account.

$$v = (d + r)P \cdot (1 + t) \qquad \text{(i)}$$

where t is the effective tax rate per unit of capital. In the usual case, t > 0, but in some cases, the government may subsidize certain types of capital input (t < 0). Because taxes change the rental rate that firms must pay on their capital, they can obviously affect input choices.

Elements of Tax Policy

Federal tax policy toward investment has undergone many changes since 1950. Three specific elements of tax policy have been frequently adjusted:

1. The *corporate tax rate* has been reduced on several occasions. Changes in the individual income tax (such as the special treatment of capital gains) have also had the effect of reducing the overall tax on capital ownership.
2. *Accelerated depreciation* schedules have been adopted on several occasions to bring depreciation allowances more into line with actual economic depreciation. Indeed, sometimes firms have been able to depreciate a capital investment at a rate faster than its economic value declines.
3. *Investment tax credits* have been enacted and then abolished. With such credits, firms can deduct from the corporate taxes they owe a certain percentage of the dollars they invest. This also has the effect of lowering the tax rate on capital input.

Brief History of Tax Policy

Major reductions in rates of capital taxation were implemented in 1962 during the Kennedy Administration. At that time depreciation schedules, especially for producers' equipment, were made more generous. A temporary 7 percent investment tax credit was also enacted. According to some estimates, these changes may have increased total purchases of capital equipment by as much as 20 percent.[1]

Similar changes were instituted early in the Reagan Administration (1981). Especially important were the adoption of more generous depreciation schedules for buildings and longer-lived equipment. In some cases, these allowances may have resulted in a subsidy for these investments. But the initial Reagan policies were significantly modified in 1982, so the most generous of the policies had little time to influence investment behavior, which remained sluggish through much of the 1980s.

[1] R. E. Hall and D. W. Jorgenson, "Tax Policy and Investment Behavior," *American Economic Review* (June 1967): 391–414.

Policy changes instituted during the Clinton Administration primarily involved investment tax credits. Such credits were adopted for research and development expenditures and for smaller firms' new investments.

Effects of Tax Policies

Although it seems clear in principle that changes in tax policies can affect rental rates on capital, the evidence about whether tax changes have had important effects on firms' input choices is quite ambiguous. Economic theory suggests that one reason that the impacts may be rather small is that tax benefits for investment may also raise the prices of capital equipment therefore largely offsetting their direct effect on lowering rental rates (see Equation i). There is some empirical evidence supporting this possibility.[2] Another possibility is that the piecemeal nature of investment incentives may only have caused firms to change what they buy, but not their overall level of investment.

To Think About

1. Why would the government wish to adopt tax policies that encourage investment? Which kinds of investment (if any) should be encouraged?
2. Much of the discussion of tax policy toward capital focuses on depreciation allowances. Once an investment is made, why should the rules for allocating its costs over the years matter?

[2] See A. Goolsbee, "Investment Tax Incentives, Prices, and the Supply of Capital Goods," *Quarterly Journal of Economics* (February 1999): 121–149.

Changes in the Real Interest Rate

This simple theory of how the real interest rate is determined also provides some insights about why that interest rate might change. On the one hand, any factor that increases firms' demand for capital equipment also increases the demand for loans. Such factors include technical progress that makes equipment more productive, declines in the actual market prices of such equipment, or more optimistic views by firms about the strength of demand for their products in the future. All such effects shift the demand for loans outward, increasing the real interest rate. On the other hand, any factor that affects individual savings affects the supply of loans. For example, availability of government-provided pension benefits in the future may reduce individuals' current savings, thereby raising real interest rates. Similarly, reductions in taxes on savings may increase the supply of loans and reduce the real interest rate. Application 14.3. Inflation-Indexed Bonds looks at one way in which changes in real interest rates might actually be measured.

INFOTRAC©
COLLEGE EDITION
Exclusively from Gale Group and Thomson Learning

www.infotrac-college.com
Keywords: Supply of loans, Tax policy and investment, Firms' demand for capital

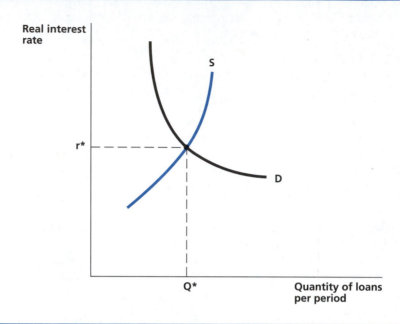

FIGURE 14.3 The Real Interest Rate Is Determined in the Market for Loans Individuals supply loans by saving. Firms demand loans to finance capital equipment. These two forces determine the equilibrium real interest rate, r*.

PRESENT DISCOUNTED VALUE

Probably the most important lesson from studying the economics of decision making over time is that interest rates must be taken into account. Transactions that take place at different times cannot be compared directly because of interest that was or might have been earned (or paid) between the two dates. For example, a promise to pay a dollar today is not the same as a promise to pay a dollar in one year. The dollar today is more valuable because it can be invested at interest for the year. In order to bring comparability to transactions that occur over time, actual dollar amounts must always be adjusted for such possibilities.

Single-Period Discounting

With only two periods, this process is very simple. Because any dollar invested today grows by a factor of $(1 + r)$ next year, the present value of a dollar that is not received until next year is $1/(1 + r)$ dollars. For example, if $r = 0.05$, an investment of $1 today will grow to $1.05 next year. Hence, the promise of $1 next year is worth about $0.95 today.[5] That is, investing $0.95 today will yield $1 in

---

[5] To be precise, $1/(1.05) = 0.95238$.

Most government bonds take no explicit account of economy-wide inflation. They make nominal interest payments and allow the market for the bonds to take inflationary expectations into account. In recent years, however, a number of nations have begun to offer "inflation-indexed" bonds that adjust payments for changes in the overall price level. These bonds therefore, in principle, pay a real interest rate. The government of Israel is the most significant issuer of inflation-indexed bonds. In that country, over 80 percent of all government bonds are indexed. Australia, Turkey, and Brazil are also significant issuers of such bonds. The U.S. Treasury began issuing inflation-indexed bonds in 1997, although these bonds make up a very small portion of government debt.

Real and Nominal Interest Rates

Exploring the relationship between real and nominal interest rates requires a bit of math. Suppose you are promised a (nominal) interest rate of i for making a one-period loan of $1 but that you expect the price level to increase by π^e percent next year. Then the real value of your repayment will be

$$\text{Real value of repayment} = (1 + i)/(1 + \pi^e) \tag{i}$$

But, as we have already seen, this real payment is also given by $(1 + r)$, where r is the real interest rate. So,

$$1 + r = (1 + i)/(1 + \pi^e) \tag{ii}$$

and, when all of these rates are reasonably small, Equation ii can be approximated as

$$r = i - \pi^e \tag{iii}$$

That is, nominal and real interest rates differ by the expected rate of inflation, π^e. Looked at in another way, Equation iii also gives a way of estimating general inflationary expectations. For example, on October 1, 2002, the nominal yield on a 30-year U.S. Treasury bond was 4.82 percent. The yield on a 30-year indexed bond was 2.60 percent, so it appears that, on this date, individuals were expecting inflation rates to average a bit over 2 percent per year over the next 30 years.

The Design of Inflation-Indexed Bonds[1]

One should be cautious in using this method for assessing expectations about inflation, however, because it depends crucially on the assumption that inflation-indexed bonds actually pay a *real* interest rate. In the United States, inflation adjustment is accomplished by adjusting both the annual interest payment and the final redemption value of the bond each year to changes in the Consumer Price Index (CPI). That approach at first seems unobjectionable. Indeed, it seems generous given the general belief that the CPI may overstate actual inflation (see Application 3.2). However, the U.S. Internal Revenue Service has

---

[1] This section is based on R. W. Kopcke and R. C. Kimball, "Inflation-Indexed Bonds: The Dog That Didn't Bark" *New England Economic Review* (January–February 1999): 3–24. Also available at *http://www.bos.frb.org/economic/neer/neer.htm*

(continued)

decided that both the higher interest payments caused by inflation adjustment and the annual increase in the redemption value of the bond represent currently taxable income. Hence, the actual, after-tax real interest rate promised by inflation-indexed bonds may be much lower than reported.

A second complexity involved in using Equation iii to compute expected inflation is that nominal and inflation-indexed bonds are subject to differing risk factors. For nominal bonds, of course, the greatest risk is inflation. So nominal bonds might be expected to pay higher interest rates simply to compensate investors not only for expected inflation but also for the variability associated with that expectation (see Chapter 15 for a discussion of individual's aversion to risk). For inflation-indexed bonds, most risks relate to fears about changes in government policy toward them. The bonds would seem to be especially vulnerable to possible changes in the way the CPI is computed.

To Think About

1. Equations i–iii look only at interest rates and inflation over a single period. Do you think that the relationship embodied in Equation iii would be changed if one were interested in multiple-year compounding?
2. Why are inflationary adjustments to indexed bonds taxed? Do these represent real income to the bondholders? Is this simply a mistaken policy or is it done to be consistent with other aspects of income taxation in the United States?

Present value
Discounting the value of future transactions back to the present day to take account of the effect of potential interest payments.

one year. The discount factor $1/(1 + r)$ must always be applied to calculate the **present value** of funds to be paid 1 year in the future. The first row of Table 14.1 illustrates this discount factor for various interest rates—clearly, the higher the interest rate, the smaller the discount factor.

Multiperiod Discounting

Generalizing the discounting concept to any number of periods is easy. As we show in the appendix to this chapter, the present value of $1 that is not to be paid until n years in the future is given by

$$\text{Present value of \$1 in n years} = \$1/(1 + r)^n \qquad (14.2)$$

This discounting factor allows the user to take into account the compound interest that is forgone by waiting for n years to obtain funds, rather than obtaining them immediately. The entries in Table 14.1 show how this discount term depends both on the interest rate (r) and on the number of years until payment is received (n). For high values of r and/or high values of n, this factor can be very small. For example, the promise of $1 in 10 years with an interest rate of 10 percent is worth only $0.39 today. If payment is delayed for 100 years (again with a 10 percent interest rate), its present value is worth less than one hundredth of a

TABLE 14.1 Present Discounted Value of $1 for Various Time Periods and Interest Rates

Years until payment is received	Interest rate			
	1 percent	3 percent	5 percent	10 percent
1	$.99010	$.97087	$.95238	$.90909
2	.98030	.94260	.90703	.82645
3	.97059	.91516	.86386	.75131
5	.95147	.86281	.78351	.62093
10	.90531	.74405	.61391	.38555
25	.78003	.47755	.29531	.09230
50	.60790	.22810	.08720	.00852
100	.36969	.05203	.00760	.00007

cent! Such calculations make clear that the present value of payments long into the future may be very low so we should not be surprised that such distant payments play a rather small part in most economic decisions.

Present Value and Economic Decisions

When looking at economic decisions over time, the concepts of utility maximization by individuals and profit maximization by firms continue to be relevant. But they must be restated to allow for the discounting that should be done in all multiperiod situations. For firms, this reformulation is easy to understand. Instead of assuming that firms "maximize profits," we now assume that they "maximize the present value of all future profits." Virtually all of the results of the theory of profit maximization continue to hold under this revised formulation.[6] For example, profit maximization requires that firms whose revenues and costs may not occur at the same time choose that output level for which the *present value* of marginal revenue equals the *present value* of marginal cost. Similarly, such firms should hire inputs up to the point at which the *present value* of the marginal revenue product is equal to the *present value* of the input's cost. Sometimes economists state the profit-maximization assumption a little differently when speaking

> **MicroQuiz 14.3**
>
> A state lottery is currently offering a Power Ball payoff of $20 million, which it will pay to the lucky winner in 20 annual $1 million installments. Is this really a $20 million prize? How would you decide its actual value?

[6] For some illustrations, see Review Question 14.8. In the theory of corporate finance, some issues do arise in choosing which interest rate to use to compute the present value of future profits, but we do not pursue those issues here.

about decisions over time—they assume that firms make decisions that seek to "maximize the present value of the firm." But this amounts to just another version of profit maximization, because a firm is only worth the future profits that it generates.

Present-value concepts are also important to individuals. Although we do not explore these connections here, Problem 14.8 and Problem 14.9 provide you with some practice in avoiding common deceptive sales practices that are based on a failure of consumers to understand how interest rates work. Application 14.4: Discounting Cash Flows and Derivative Securities shows a few more complicated illustrations of present-value calculations that can confuse even the most astute investor.

PRICING OF EXHAUSTIBLE RESOURCES

One important way in which considerations of time and interest rates enter into economics is in the pricing of natural resources—especially those that are not renewable. Ever since Robert Malthus was worrying about population growth in nineteenth-century England, there have been recurrent concerns that we are "running out" of such resources and that market pressures may be accelerating that process. In this section, we try to shed some light on this important issue by focusing on the ways in which resource scarcity might be expected to affect the current pricing of those resources.

Scarcity Costs

What makes the production of nonrenewable resources different from the production of other types of economic goods is that the current production from a finite stock of the resource reduces the amount that is available in the future. This contrasts with the usual case in which firms' production decisions during one year have no effect on the next year's production. Firms involved in the production of an exhaustible resource must therefore take an additional cost into account: the opportunity cost of not being able to make some sales in the future. These extra costs are defined as the **scarcity costs.** Of course, recognition of these costs does not mean that a firm thinking about producing from a finite resource stock always opts to produce nothing, constantly hoarding its resource holdings for sale at some future date. But the firm must be careful to incorporate all opportunity costs into its decisions.

Scarcity costs
The opportunity costs of future production forgone because current production depletes exhaustible resources.

The implications of scarcity costs are illustrated in Figure 14.4. In the absence of scarcity costs, the industry supply curve for the resource would be given by S. This curve reflects the marginal costs of actually producing the resource (that is, the costs of drilling, mining, and/or refining). Scarcity costs shift firms' marginal cost curves upward because of the extra opportunity cost of forgone future sales that they represent. The new market supply curve is therefore S' and the gap between S and S' represents scarcity costs. Current output falls from Q* to Q'

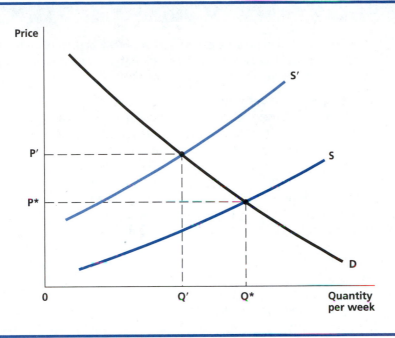

FIGURE 14.4 Scarcity Costs Associated with Exhaustible Resources Firms that produce exhaustible resources take into account both current marginal production costs and the opportunity costs of forgone future production. The market supply curve for such firms (S′ is above their marginal cost curves to the extent of those scarcity costs.

and market price rises from P* to P′ once these costs are taken into account. These changes effectively encourage "conservation" of the resource—firms withhold some extra resources from the market, intending to sell them sometime in the future.

The Size of Scarcity Costs

The actual value of scarcity costs depends on firms' views about what prices for the resource will be in the future. Knowledge of these prices is required if resource owners are to be able to calculate correctly the present value of revenues that will be forgone by producing the resource now out of their currently available stock.[7] As a simple example, suppose that the owner of a copper mine believes that copper will sell for $1 per pound in 10 years. Hence, selling a pound today means forgoing a $1 sale in 10 years because the supply of copper

[7] If the firm does not actually own the resource (suppose it is mining on public land, for example), it may not take scarcity costs into account because it may believe that it will not have access to the resource in the future. In Chapter 16, we explicitly consider the externalities created when resources are "owned" in common.

Discounting Cash Flows and Derivative Securities

The concept of present value can be applied to any pattern of cash inflows or outflows. This provides a general way to think about transactions that are really quite complex. Here, we look at two examples.

Mortgage-Backed Securities

Mortgages on houses are probably the most prevalent type of individual loan. Such loans commit homeowners to pay a fixed monthly charge, typically for 30 years. Most mortgages also permit early repayments with no penalties. Because mortgages are so long-lived, an active secondary market in them has been developed that permits the initial lender to sell the mortgage to someone else. Often, many mortgages are bundled together in order to achieve economies of scale in buying and selling. Recent innovations in financial markets have carried this process one step further by creating new securities that represent only one portion of the cash flow from a pool of mortgages. These new securities are called "collateralized mortgage obligations" (CMOs). For example, one CMO might promise only the monthly interest payments from a given pool of mortgages. Another might promise all of the repayments from the same pool.

Calculation of the present value of a CMO is in principle a straightforward application of Equation 14A.25 in the appendix to this chapter. Each expected cash flow must be appropriately discounted to the present day. Unfortunately, the variability in individuals' repayment patterns can make the actual calculation subject to considerable uncertainty in practice.

The Fannie Mae Mismatch

An illustration of the problems that can be caused by mortgage repayments came in the fall of 2002. The decline in interest rates throughout 2001–2002 caused many people to pay off long-term mortgages. This posed special problems for Fannie Mae—the largest dealer in mortgage-backed securities in the United States. The expected timing of the firm's receipts from mortgages became much shorter than the timing of payments they owed to their bondholders. This timing mismatch posed special risks for the company because its net worth (the present value of assets minus the present value of liabilities) might drop precipitously if interest rates were to fall farther.[1]

Derivatives and Hedging Risks

CMOs are one example of a "derivative security"—a security whose value "derives" from some other asset. Because such securities are very complex, firms need to be especially careful that they have not exposed themselves to too much risk in taking derivative positions. One way that they seek to do that is to aggregate all of the expected cash flows from the many derivatives that they own into a single stream of expected payments and receipts. Then they can use a version of Equation 14A.25 to see how the present values of their overall position might be affected by various happenings. They can then buy or sell securities with payment streams that offset the risks that they discover. Usually this procedure works well; but it has spawned a few major failures.

[1] See "Can Fannie Make Repairs to Its Investment Portfolio?" *The Wall Street Journal* (1 October 2002).

The Long-Term Capital Management Fiasco

This type of risk assessment was practiced extensively by the Long-Term Capital Management hedge fund—a fund run in part by two recent Nobel prize winners in economics. Although the fund thought that it had most scenarios accounted for, the summer of 1998 proved to be devastating, primarily because cash flows did not follow previous historical relationships in the spread between interest rates on high-risk and low-risk foreign bonds. Ultimately, the U.S. Federal Reserve had to orchestrate a multibillion-dollar bailout for the fund despite the sophistication with which it approached risk assessment. The value of the procedure proved to be only as good as the data the firm had.[2]

To Think About

1. Although any cash flow, no matter how complex, can be converted to a single value by discounting using Equation 14A.25, there still is the matter of which interest rate to use in the computation. How would you choose an interest rate?
2. For a simple derivative security (such as a repayment CMO) how would you evaluate the relationship between the cash flows promised and other economic data (such as general interest rates or income growth)?

[2] The Long-Term Capital story is told in the fascinating video "The Trillion-Dollar Gamble" (WGBH Videos, 1999).

---

in the mine is fixed. With a real interest rate of, say, 5 percent, Table 14.1 shows that the present value of this opportunity cost is about $0.61. Assuming that the owner of the mine is indifferent about whether the copper is sold today or in 10 years, the current market price should be about $0.61 because that is the only price that reflects an equilibrium between present and future sales. If the actual marginal cost of copper production is, say, $0.35 per pound, then scarcity costs would be $0.26 per pound. Price would exceed the actual marginal cost of production by $0.26 per pound. In this case, the fact that price exceeds marginal cost is not a sign of inefficiency as it has been in several other situations we've looked at. Instead, the price here reflects efficiency in resource use in that consumers are paying all of the costs associated with the current production of the resource.

> **MicroQuiz 14.4**
>
> Suppose that kryptonite is discovered on Earth and that one firm owns the entire world supply.
>
> **1.** Should the monopoly firm take scarcity costs into account?
>
> **2.** Will the monopoly produce less kryptonite than would a competitive industry?

Time Pattern of Resource Prices

An important implication of this discussion is that, in the absence of any change in real production costs or in firms' expectations about future prices, the relative

The question "Are any resources scarce?" is, of course, intentionally provocative. After all, Earth is of finite size so (barring mining in space) the total quantity of natural resources is ultimately fixed. Any production today necessarily reduces the amount that can be produced tomorrow. By this test, all natural resources are scarce. The economic consequence of this scarcity, however, is not obvious.

Resource Price Trends

During the past century, the primary trend for natural resource prices has been downward in real terms. As Table 1 shows, annual rates of decline between 1 and 2 percent characterize the price histories for such diverse resources as petroleum, coal, and aluminum. Similarly, farmland prices seem to have declined in real terms, though at a slower rate than natural resources. It is, however, difficult to infer actual scarcity values from these figures since declining relative costs of extraction and development may have masked rising scarcity costs. Since 1970, the decline in real resource prices appears to have slowed and this may indeed indicate an increasing relevance of scarcity costs. Nevertheless, the prospect of rising real resource prices driven by scarcity is not yet a forgone conclusion.

Implications of Scarcity

Even if real prices of natural resources were to follow a rising path indicating their scarcity, market reactions to the trend could be quite complex. The ultimate effect on overall output (GDP) would depend on such factors as the ability of firms to substitute inputs that have stable prices for those that were rising in price; the tendency of rising resource prices to induce various types of resource-saving technical innovations; and the willingness of consumers to reduce their consumption of resource-intensive goods. Modeling all of these various reactions is a formidable undertaking. One fairly careful estimate suggests that resource scarcity might reduce real economic growth rates by about 0.3 percent by the year

TABLE 1 Real Prices for Natural Resources (1990 = 100)

Resource	1870	1910	1950	1970	1990
Petroleum	700	250	150	80	100
Coal	550	350	200	110	100
Copper	1,000	500	250	160	100
Iron ore	1,000	750	200	120	100
Aluminum	—	800	180	110	100
Farmland	200	375	80	105	100

Source: Adapted from W. D. Nordhaus, "Lethal Model 2: Limits to Growth Revisited," *Brookings Papers on Economic Activity,* no. 2 (1992): 24–26.

2050 with more than half of the decline being attributed to the increasing scarcity of energy resources.[1] Whether this relatively modest effect will prove accurate is, of course, anyone's guess.

To Think About

1. How should changing costs of resource extraction be factored into an explanation of market prices? In what way might such changes mask changing scarcity values? What is the maximum effect that changing relative extraction costs might be expected to have?
2. Why do economists and environmentalists have such different views on resource scarcity? Don't environmentalists understand that the price system works to mitigate the effects of scarcity? Or is it economists who mistakenly disregard the sharp discontinuities and irreversibilities that environmentalists fear?

[1] W. D. Nordhaus, "Lethal Model 2: Limits to Growth Revisited," *Brookings Papers on Economic Activity*, no. 2 (1992): 1–43.

---

price of resources should be expected to rise over time at the real rate of interest. In our previous example, because the real rate of interest was assumed to be 5 percent, real copper prices would be expected to rise at 5 percent per year. Only by following that time path would prices always be equal to the present value of $1 in 10 years.

This result can be shown intuitively from another perspective. Any firm that owns some supply of a finite natural resource evaluates that holding in the way it evaluates any other investment. Since the real interest rate represents the rate of return on such alternative investments, only if resource prices rise at this rate do they provide a competitive return to the owner. If prices were rising more slowly than the real rate of interest, natural resources would be an inferior investment and firms should put their funds elsewhere. A rate of increase in prices faster than the real interest rate is also unsustainable because investors would quickly bid up the current price of resources to attempt to capture those desirable returns. This important result about resource pricing can be used to study a variety of important economic issues, as Application 14.5: Are Any Resources Scarce? shows.

SUMMARY

In this chapter, we have examined economic issues associated with decisions that are made over time in capital markets. The discussion focused primarily on the role of the real interest rate (r) in providing a "price" that connects one period to the next. Some of the important results of this examination included:

• Real interest rates affect individuals' savings decisions. Although income and substitution effects of a change in the real interest rate work in opposite directions, it is generally believed that the (intertemporal) substitution effect is stronger. Hence, an increase in r causes savings (and loans) to increase.

- The real interest rate represents a cost of capital to firms regardless of whether they rent or own their equipment. An increase in r raises the rental rate on capital equipment and reduces its usage. This also reduces the demand for loans.
- Real interest rates are determined by the supply and demand for loans. Loans are supplied by individuals through their savings decisions. Loans are demanded by firms to finance their purchases of capital equipment.

- Expenditures or receipts in different periods cannot be compared directly because of the opportunity cost of interest payments. Such flows must be discounted so that they can be compared on a common, present-value basis. Investment decisions are an especially important situation where discounting is required.
- Production of finite resources involves additional costs reflecting resource scarcity. These costs arise because current production involves an opportunity cost in terms of forgone future sales.

REVIEW QUESTIONS

1. Some economic variables are "stocks" in that they represent the total value of something at a point in time, rather than a per-period "flow." Explain the connection between the following flow and stock variables:

Flow	Stock
Individual savings	Individual wealth
Firm investment	Firm capital
Education	Human capital
Gold production	Gold

2. Explain why the intertemporal budget constraint pictured in Figure 14.1 can be interpreted as requiring that individuals choose C_0 and C_1 so that the present value of this consumption is equal to their current income.

3. Suppose that an individual obtains the same utility from a given level of consumption regardless of whether it is consumed now or next period. Suppose also that the marginal utility of consumption is diminishing. Why would you expect this person to be "impatient," that is, always choosing C_0 to be greater than C_1? (Hint: What is the relative "price" of C_1 in terms of C_0?)

4. Sometimes retirement planners suggest that people set a "target" for retirement income. For example, the advice might be, "Be sure to have accumulated $1,000,000 by the time you are 60." Assuming that the target remains unchanged, how would an increase in the real interest rate affect a person's level of savings to reach this target? Is it

appropriate to hold the target constant when the real interest rate changes?

5. P. T. Blowhard is the CEO of Ditch Industries. He was heard to make the following statement about his choice of inputs for digging ditches: "We borrowed $100,000 to buy this DitchWitch and we're still paying $8,000 per year in interest on that loan even though the machine is now essentially worthless. We could save money by borrowing $70,000 to buy a new DitchKing machine that would do the same job with only $5,600 in interest." What do you make of this argument? Assuming the machines are perfect substitutes, costs would be minimized by using the one with the lower rental rate. Which one has the lower rental rate?

6. CEO Blowhard continues his economic wisdom by discussing his rationale for calculating the present value of the rents he might save by purchasing a building to house his firm: "We could save $25,000 per year in rent by purchasing our own building. Over a 25-year horizon, Nicholson's Table 14A.3 [see Appendix to Chapter 14] tells me that the present value of these savings is about $350,000 using a real interest rate of 5 percent. But that is clearly an understatement since our rents are bound to rise because of general inflation. Hence, I'm sure it would be worthwhile for us to purchase a building costing up to at least $400,000." Has the CEO got it right now? How should he take into account the expected inflationary increases in rent in the future?

7. Figure 14.3 shows how the real interest rate is determined by the supply and demand for loans. Explain why this process also determines the rate of return that any capital owner should expect to earn on investments in physical capital. That is, how do you reconcile a "loanable funds" theory of interest rates with a "return of capital" theory of interest rates? If you are adventuresome, you might also seek to reconcile these theories with whatever theory of interest rates you learned in macroeconomics.

8. Suppose that a monopoly farmer of Wonder Grain must pay all of its costs of production in this year but that it must wait until next year to sell its output. Why would the farm's profit-maximizing output be the level for which $MR = MC(1 + r)$? Explain why this profit-maximizing condition takes *all* costs into account. Would this farmer produce more or less output if he or she could defer paying costs until next period? Explain why the firm should also hire any input, such as labor, up to the point at which $MRP_L = w(1 + r)$.

9. Why do scarcity costs occur only in the case of finite resources? Do producers of renewable resources such as fish or trees also incur scarcity costs? Explain the differences between these cases.

10. Our theory of the pricing of exhaustible resources concludes that the prices of such resources should increase (relative to prices of other goods) at a rate equal to the real rate of interest. What does this conclusion assume about the costs involved in actually producing natural resources?

   a. That they are constant
   b. That they increase at the overall rate of inflation
   c. That they also increase relative to prices of other goods at the real rate of interest

   Explain your answer and discuss how resource prices would be expected to move if your assumption were not true.

PROBLEMS

14.1 The budget constraint facing an individual planning his or her consumption over two periods is an intertemporal one in which the present value of consumption expenditures must equal the present value of incomes in the two periods:

$$C_0 + C_1/(1 + r) = Y_0 + Y_1/(1 + r)$$

where Y and C represent income and consumption respectively and the subscripts represent the two time periods.

a. Explain the meaning of this constraint.
b. If $Y_0 > C_0$, this individual is saving in period 0. Why does this imply that $Y_1 < C_1$?
c. If this individual is saving in period 0, why is $Y_0 - C_0$ less than $C_1 - Y_1$?

14.2 Flexible Felix views present and future consumption as perfect substitutes. He does, however, discount future consumption by a bit to reflect the uncertainties of his life. His utility function is therefore given by

$$U(C_0, C_1) = C_0 + C_1/(1 + \delta)$$

where δ (which is positive) is the "discount rate" he applies to C_1.

a. Graph Felix's indifference curve map.
b. Show that if r (the real interest rate) exceeds δ, then $C_0 = 0$.
c. Show that if $r < \delta$, then $C_1 = 0$.
d. What do you conclude about the relationship between a person's saving behavior and his or her "impatience"?

14.3 Two roommates, Prudence and Glitter, graduate from college and get identical jobs that pay them $50,000 this year and $55,000 next year. The roommates have different utility functions so that the marginal rates of substitution are given by

$$\text{MRS for Prudence} = C_1/3C_0$$
$$\text{MRS for Glitter} = 3C_1/C_0$$

Assume that the real interest rate is 10 percent.

a. What is the present value of each student's income?

b. Focusing first on Prudence, what is her condition for utility maximization?

c. How should Prudence choose C_0 and C_1 so as to satisfy the condition for utility maximization and so that the present value of her consumption equals the present value of her income? How much will Prudence borrow or save in period 0?

d. Answer part c and part d for Glitter.

14.4 The Robotics Corporation produces cuddly toys using only computer-driven robots. The quantity of toys (T) produced per year is given by $T = 10\sqrt{R}$ where R is the number of robots used during each year of production.

a. If the market price of robots is $2,000, the real interest rate is 0.05, and the depreciation rate on robots is 0.10, what is the firm's implicit rental rate for robot use?

b. What is the firm's total cost function for production of T?

c. If cuddly toys sell for $60, how many will this firm choose to produce? (Hint: If Total Cost = kT^2 then calculus shows that Marginal Cost = 2kT.)

d. How many robots will the firm employ for the year?

14.5 Acme Landfill Company is considering the purchase of 10 better trash collection trucks. Each truck costs $50,000 and will last 7 years. The firm estimates that the purchase will increase its annual avenues by $100,000 per year for as long as the trucks last. If the real interest rate is 10 percent, should the firm buy the 10 trucks? Would your answer change if the real interest rate fell to 8 percent?

14.6 Scotch whiskey increases in value as it ages, at least up to a point. For any period of time, t, the value of a barrel is given by $V = 100t - 6t^2$. This function implies that the proportional rate of growth of the value of the scotch is $(100 - 12t)/V$.

a. Graph this scotch value function.

b. At what value of t is the barrel of scotch most valuable?

c. If the real interest rate is 5 percent, when should this distiller bottle the scotch for immediate sale?

d. How would the distiller's decision change if the real interest rate were 10 percent? (Hint: You will have to use the quadratic equation to solve part d here.)

14.7 In order to calculate scarcity costs for any finite resource, a price at some future date must be assumed. Suppose, for example, that the real price of platinum will be $1,000 per ounce in 25 years.

a. If the real interest rate is 5 percent and no change is expected in the real costs of producing platinum over the next 25 years, what should the equilibrium price be today?

b. If the current cost of producing platinum is $100 per ounce, what are current scarcity costs?

c. What will scarcity costs be in 25 years?

d. Assuming that resource markets are in equilibrium and that real production costs for platinum continue to remain constant, what is the real equilibrium price of the metal in 50 years?

Note: Problems 14.8–14.10 make more extensive use of the material on compound interest that is in the appendix to this chapter.

14.8 A persistent life insurance salesman makes the following pitch: "At your age (40) a $100,000 whole life policy is a much better buy than a term policy. The whole life policy requires you to pay $2,000 per year for the next 4 years but nothing after that. A term policy will cost you $400 per year for as long as you own it. Let's assume you live 35 more years—that means you'll end up paying $8,000 for the whole life policy and $14,000 for the term policy. The choice is obvious!"

a. Is the choice so obvious? How does the best buy depend on the interest rate?

b. If the interest rate is 10 percent, which policy is the best buy?

14.9 A car salesman once made the following pitch to your author: "If you buy this $10,000 car with cash you will lose at least $1,500 over the next 3 years in forgone interest (assumed to be 5 percent per year). If you take one of our low-cost auto loans you only have to pay $315 per month for the next 3 years. That amounts to $11,340—$10,000 for the car and $1,340 in interest. With our car loan you will actually save $160 in interest." What do you make of this argument?

14.10 Although perpetual bonds are illegal, sometimes it is easiest to assume that interest payments last forever to show some simple results based on Equation 14A.24. Use that equation to show that

a. Assuming no inflation, the value of a bond that pays $10 per year is $200 with a real rate of interest of 5 percent.
b. If inflation is 3 percent per year and interest payments rise at that rate, the current value of the perpetual bond is still $200.

c. If inflation is 3 percent per year and the bond's payments are fixed at $10, that the current value of the perpetual bond is $125 can be shown in two ways:
 i. By assuming that the nominal rate of interest is 8 percent and using that rate for discounting
 ii. By adjusting the $10 payment for inflation in each period and using a real discount rate of 5 percent (Hint: This latter proof is easiest if you use the approximation $(1 + r)(1 + i) \approx 1 + r + i$ for small values of r [the real interest rate] and i [the inflation rate].)

INTERNET EXERCISES

1. *Present value.* Congratulations! You have just won a $1 million grand prize! Prize officials have notified you that you have a choice of payment options. You can choose to have the $1 million paid out in annual payments of $50,000 for each of the next 20 years, or you can choose to receive a one-time lump sum payment today of $560,000. As you've learned from Chapter 14, future dollars are worth less than present dollars due to interest rates. For example, let's calculate the present value of the *final* $50,000 payment that you would receive in 20 years under the first payment option. Financial Players Center, Inc., has useful on-line financial calculators at *http://www.financialplayerscenter.com/Overview. html#calculators.* First, click on Future Value Calculator. Use this calculator to calculate the present value of the $50,000 payment in the 20th year, using an interest rate of 6 percent (since we assume no compounding, enter one period per year). Next, calculate the present value of the $50,000 payment you would receive in the 10th year. Explain why the present value is higher in the 10th year versus the 20th year. Now, to determine which payment option you should choose for your grand prize, you need to calculate the present value of the *entire* payment stream over the 20 years. Go back to the Financial Players Center, Inc., list of calculators. Now, click on Payment Calculator. This calculator will compute the present value of a stream of payments over

time. Still using an interest rate of 6 percent, what is the present value of $50,000 annually for each of the next 20 years? Which payment option for your grand prize will you choose? Explain. Would your decision be any different if the interest rate were 8 percent? Carefully explain.

2. *Bonds.* The concept of present value is very important to understanding the way bond markets work. Investopedia.com at *http://www.investopedia.com* offers an excellent tutorial on the basics of bond investing. Link to the main site, and then click on Tutorials. From there, click on Bond and Debt Basics. Read through the tutorial at least up through Part 5, Different Types of Bonds. Next, read the formal definition of yield-to-maturity at Moneychimp's Web site at *http://www.moneychimp.com/articles/finworks/fmbondytm.htm.* Let's calculate the current yield and the yield-to-maturity for a hypothetical bond using Moneychimp's on-line bond yield calculator. Click on the bond yield calculator. Consider a bond with a current price of $860, par value of $1,000, and a coupon rate of 6 percent. The bond matures in 8 years. What are the values of the current yield and the yield-to-maturity? Suppose the price of the bond increases to $1,050.00. Now what are the values of the current yield and the yield-to-maturity? Explain why the price increase has caused the current yield and the yield-to-maturity to change as they have.

Compound Interest

People encounter compound interest concepts almost every day. Calculating returns on bank accounts, deciding on the true cost of an automobile loan, and buying a home with a mortgage all involve the use of interest rate computations. This appendix shows how some of those computations are made. The methods introduced are useful not only in economics classes but in many personal economic decisions too.

INTEREST

Interest

Payment for the current use of funds.

Interest is payment for the time value of money. A borrower gets to use funds for his or her own purposes for a time and in return pays the lender some compensation. Interest rates are usually stated as some percentage of the amount borrowed (the principal). For example, an annual interest rate of 5 percent would require someone who borrowed $100 to pay $5 per year in interest.

Throughout this appendix, we assume that the market has established an annual interest rate, i, and that this interest rate will persist from one year to the next. It is a relatively simple matter to deal with interest rates that change from one period to another, but we do not consider them here. We are also not particularly interested in whether i is a "nominal" interest rate (such as a rate quoted by a bank) or a "real" interest rate that has been adjusted for any inflation that may occur over time.[1] The mathematics of compound interest is the same for both nominal and real interest rates.

---

[1] For a discussion of the relationship between nominal and real interest rates see Application 14.3.

COMPOUND INTEREST

If you hold funds in a bank for more than one period, you receive **compound interest**—that is, you receive interest not only on your original principal but also on the interest that you earned in prior periods and left in the bank. Compounding is relatively complicated and results in rather dramatic growth over long periods.

Compound interest
Interest paid on prior interest earned.

Appendix

Interest for 1 Year

If you invest $1 at the interest rate of i, at the end of 1 year you will have

$$\$1 + \$1 \cdot i = \$1 \cdot (1 + i) \qquad \text{(14A.1)}$$

For example, if i is 5 percent, at the end of 1 year, you will have

$$\$1 + \$1 \cdot (.05) = \$1 \cdot (1.05) = \$1.05 \qquad \text{(14A.2)}$$

Interest for 2 Years

If at the end of the first year you leave your money in the bank, you will now earn interest on both the original $1 and on your first year's interest. At the end of 2 years you will therefore have

$$\$1 \cdot (1 + i) + \$1 \cdot (1 + i) \cdot i = \$1 \cdot (1 + i)(1 + i)$$
$$= \$1 \cdot (1 + i)^2 \qquad \text{(14A.3)}$$

To understand this equation, it is helpful to expand the term $(1 + i)^2$. Remember from algebra that

$$(1 + i)^2 = 1 + 2i + i^2 \qquad \text{(14A.4)}$$

At the end of 2 years, $1 will grow to

$$\$1 \cdot (1 + i)^2 = \$1 \cdot (1 + 2i + i^2)$$
$$= \$1 + \$1 \cdot (2i) + \$1 \cdot i^2 \qquad \text{(14A.5)}$$

At the end of 2 years, you will have the sum of three amounts:

1. Your original $1
2. Two years' simple interest on your original $1, that is, $1 \cdot 2i$
3. Interest on your first year's interest, that is, $[(\$1 \cdot i) \cdot i] = \$1 \cdot i^2$

If, again, the interest rate is 5 percent, at the end of 2 years you will have

$$\$1 \cdot (1.05)^2 = \$1 \cdot (1.1025) = \$1.1025 \tag{14A.6}$$

This represents the sum of your original $1, 2 years' interest on the $1 (that is, $.10), and interest on the first year's interest (5 percent of $.05, which is $.0025). The fact that you will have more than $1.10 is a reflection of compounding. As we look at longer and longer periods of time, the effects of this compounding become much more pronounced.

Interest for 3 Years

If you now leave these funds, which after 2 years amount to $1 \cdot (1 + i)^2$, in the bank for another year, at the end of this third year you will have

$$\$1 \cdot (1 + i)^2 + \$1 \cdot (1 + i)^2 \cdot i = \$1 \cdot (1 + i)^2(1 + i)$$
$$= \$1 \cdot (1 + i)^3 \tag{14A.7}$$

For an interest rate of 5 percent, this amounts to

$$\$1 \cdot (1 + 0.05)^3 = \$1 \cdot 1.157625 = \$1.157625 \tag{14A.8}$$

The fact that you get more than your original $1 and 3 years' simple interest ($.15) again reflects the effects of compounding.

A General Formula

By now the pattern should be clear. If you leave your $1 in the bank for any number of years, n, you will have, at the end of that period,

$$\text{Value of } \$1 \text{ compounded for n years} = \$1 \cdot (1 + i)^n \tag{14A.9}$$

With a 5 percent interest rate and a period of 10 years, you would have

$$\$1 \cdot (1.05)^{10} = \$1 \cdot 1.62889 \ldots$$
$$= \$1.62889 \tag{14A.10}$$

Without compounding you would have had $1.50—your original $1 plus 10 years' interest at $0.05 per year. The extra $0.12889 comes about through compounding.

To illustrate the effects of compounding further, Table 14A.1 shows the value

MicroQuiz 14A.1

The term $(1 + i)^3$ can be expanded to be $1 + 3i + 3i^2 + i^3$. Carefully explain why each of these terms is required in order to reflect the complete effects of compounding. You may have to do some factoring to make your explanation clear.

TABLE 14A.1 Effects of Compound Interest for Various Interest Rates and Time Periods with an Initial Investment of $1

	Interest Rate			
Years	1 percent	3 percent	5 percent	10 percent
1	$1.01	$1.03	$1.05	$1.10
2	1.0201	1.0609	1.1025	1.2100
3	1.0303	1.0927	1.1576	1.3310
5	1.051	1.159	1.2763	1.6105
10	1.1046	1.344	1.6289	2.5937
25	1.282	2.094	3.3863	10.8347
50	1.645	4.384	11.4674	117.3909
100	2.705	19.219	131.5013	13,780.6123

of $1 compounded for various time periods and interest rates.[2] Notice how compounding becomes very important for long periods. For instance, the table shows that, at a 5 percent interest rate, $1 grows to be $131.50 over 100 years. This represents the original $1, simple interest of $5 ($.05 per year for 100 years), and a massive $125.50 in interest earned on prior interest. At higher interest rates, the effect of compounding is even more pronounced since there is even more prior interest on which to earn interest. At a 1 percent interest rate, only about 26 percent of the funds accumulated over 100 years represents the effects of compounding. At a 10 percent interest rate, more than 99.9 percent of the huge amount accumulated represents the effects of compounding.

Compounding with Any Dollar Amount

The use of $1 in all of the computations we have made so far was for convenience only. Any other amount of money grows in exactly the same way. Investing $1,000 is just the same as investing a thousand one-dollar bills—at an interest rate of 5 percent this amount would grow to $1,050 at the end of 1 year [$1,000 · (1.05)]; it would grow to $1,629 at the end of 10 years [$1,000 · (1.629)]; and to $131,501 at the end of 100 years [$1,000 · 131.501].

Algebraically, D dollars invested for n years at an interest rate of i will grow to

$$\text{Value of \$D invested for n years} = \$D \cdot (1 + i)^n \qquad \textbf{(14A.11)}$$

Application 14A.1: Compound Interest Gone Berserk illustrates some particularly extreme examples of using this formula.

---

[2] All calculations in this appendix were done on a Hewlett-Packard financial calculator—a device that is highly recommended.

Compound Interest Gone Berserk

The effects of compounding can be truly gigantic if a sufficiently long period is used. Here are three of your author's favorite examples.

Manhattan Island

Legend has it that in 1623 Dutch settlers purchased Manhattan Island from the Native Americans living there for trinkets worth about $24. Suppose these Native Americans had invested this $24 at 5 percent interest for the 377 years between 1623 and 2000. Using Equation 14A.11, in 2000 they would have had

$$\$24 \cdot (1.05)^{377} = \$24 \cdot (97,356,679) = \$2,336,560,296$$

Over 377 years, their $24 would have grown to more than $2.3 billion! With a higher interest rate (say 10 percent) the figure would be much larger—probably exceeding by far the entire actual value of Manhattan Island today.

Horse Manure

In the 1840s, the horse population of Philadelphia was growing at nearly 10 percent per year. Projecting this growth into the future, the city fathers began to worry about excessive crowding and potential pollution of the streets from manure. So they passed restrictions on the number of horses allowed in the city. It's a good thing! If the horse population of 50,000 had continued to grow at 10 percent per year there would have been quite a few by the year 2000:

$$\text{Number of horses} = 50,000 \cdot (1 + i)^{150} = 50,000 \cdot (1.10)^{150} = 80,886,000,000$$

With these 81 billion horses, the manure problem would have been severe—amounting to perhaps 500 feet deep per year over the entire city. The City of Brotherly Love (the author's hometown) was spared this fate through timely governmental action.

Rabbits

Rabbits were first introduced into Australia in the early 1860s. There they found a country free of predators and highly conducive to rabbit multiplication. By some estimates, the rabbit population grew at 100 percent per year during the 1860–1880 period. Assuming there were only two rabbits to start, by 1880 there would have been

$$\text{Number of rabbits} = 2\,(1 + i)^{20} = 2(1 + 1)^{20} = 2(2)^{20} = 2,097,152$$

Continuing this growth for the next 100 years would have resulted in more than 10^{36} rabbits in Australia by 1980—or over a trillion rabbits per square foot.

To Think About

1. The tongue-in-cheek nature of these examples suggests there is probably something wrong with such simplistic applications of compound interest. For each of the examples explain carefully why the calculations are pure nonsense.
2. As the rabbit problem shows, with high interest rates, compounding can produce spectacular results even for relatively short time periods. In the late 1970s, for example, it was possible to invest in bonds that yielded 15 percent per year. How much would you have to invest now at 15 percent to have $1 million in, say, 45 years when you retire? Do you think this calculation is "reasonable"? What does it overlook?

PRESENT DISCOUNTED VALUE

Because interest is paid on invested dollars, a dollar you get today is more valuable than one you won't receive until next year. You could put a dollar you receive today in a bank and have more than a dollar in 1 year. If you wait a year for the dollar, you will do without this interest that you could have earned.

Economists use the concept of present discounted value—or, more simply, **present value**—to reflect this opportunity cost notion. The present discounted value of the dollar you will not get for 1 year is simply the amount you would have to put in a bank now to have $1 at the end of 1 year. If the interest rate is 5 percent, for example, the present value of $1 to be obtained in 1 year is about $.95—if you invest $.95 today, you will have $1 in 1 year, so $.95 accurately reflects the present value of $1 in 1 year.

Present value
Discounting the value of future transactions back to the present day to take account of the effect of potential interest payments.

An Algebraic Definition

More formally, if the interest rate is i, the present discounted value of $1 in 1 year is $1/(1 + i) since

$$\frac{\$1}{1+i} \cdot (1+i) = \$1 \qquad \text{(14A.12)}$$

If i = 5 percent, the present discounted value (PDV) of $1 in 1 year is

$$PDV = \frac{\$1}{1.05} = \$0.9524 \qquad \text{(14A.13)}$$

and

$$\$0.9524 \cdot 1.05 = \$1 \qquad \text{(14A.14)}$$

A similar computation would result for any other interest rate. For example, the PDV of $1 payable in 1 year is $0.971 if the interest rate is 3 percent, but $0.909 when the interest rate is 10 percent. With a higher interest rate, the PDV is lower because the opportunity costs involved in waiting to get the dollar are greater.

Waiting 2 years to get paid involves even greater opportunity costs than waiting 1 year since now you forgo 2 years' interest. At an interest rate of 5 percent, $0.907 will grow to be $1 in 2 years—that is, $1 = $0.907 \cdot (1.05)^2$. Consequently, the present value of $1 payable in 2 years is only $0.907. More generally, for any interest rate, i, the present value of $1 payable in 2 years is

$$\text{PDV of \$1 payable in 2 years} = \$1/(1+i)^2 \qquad \text{(14A.15)}$$

and, for the case of a 5 percent interest rate,

$$\begin{aligned} \text{PDV of \$1 payable in 2 years} &= \$1/(1.05)^2 \\ &= \$1/1.1025 \\ &= \$0.907 \qquad \text{(15A.16)} \end{aligned}$$

General PDV Formulas

The pattern again should be obvious. With an interest rate of i, the present value of $1 payable after any number of years, n, is simply

$$\text{PDV of \$1 payable in n years} = \$1/(1 + i)^n \qquad \textbf{(14A.17)}$$

Calculating present values is the reverse of computing compound interest. In the compound interest case (Equation 14A.9), the calculation requires multiplying by the interest factor $(1 + i)^n$ whereas in the present discounted value case (Equation 14A.17) the calculation proceeds by dividing by that factor. Similarly, the present value of any number of dollars ($D) payable in n years is given by

$$\text{PDV of \$D payable in n years} = \$D/(1 + i)^n \qquad \textbf{(14A.18)}$$

Again, by comparing Equation 14A.11 and Equation 14A.18, you can see the different ways that the interest factor $(1 + i)^n$ enters into the calculations.

In Table 14A.2, the author has again put his calculator to work to compute the present discounted value of $1 payable at various times and for various interest rates. The entries in this table are the reciprocals of the entries in Table 14A.1 because compounding and taking present values are different ways of looking at the same process. In Table 14A.2, the PDV of $1 payable in some particular year is smaller the higher the interest rate. Similarly, for a given interest rate, the PDV of $1 is smaller the longer it is until the $1 will be paid. With a 10 percent interest rate, for example, a dollar that will not be paid for 50 years is worth less than 1 cent ($0.00852) today. Application 14A.2: Zero-Coupon Bonds shows how such PDV calculations apply to a popular type of financial asset.

TABLE 14A.2 Present Discounted Value of $1 for Various Time Periods and Interest Rates

Year until payment is received	Interest Rate			
	1 percent	3 percent	5 percent	10 percent
1	$0.99010	$0.97087	$0.95238	$0.90909
2	0.98030	0.94260	0.90703	0.82645
3	0.97059	0.91516	0.86386	0.75131
5	0.95147	0.86281	0.78351	0.62093
10	0.90531	0.74405	0.61391	0.38555
25	0.78003	0.47755	0.29531	0.09230
50	0.60790	0.22810	0.08720	0.00852
100	0.36969	0.05203	0.00760	0.00007

Note: These amounts are the reciprocals of those in Table 14A.1.

Federal Treasury bonds sometimes include coupons that promise the owner of the bond a specified semiannual interest payment. For example, a 30-year $1 million bond issued in 2000 with a 6 percent interest rate would include 60 semiannual coupons that represent the government's promise to pay $30,000 (that is, half of 6 percent of $1 million) on January 1 and July 1 of each year. The image of a Scrooge-like "coupon clipper" collecting regular interest payments in this way is a popular figure for financial cartoonists.

The Invention of Zero-Coupon Bonds

Unfortunately, this form of bond is not particularly convenient for investors. Bonds (and their attached coupons) may be lost, cashing the coupon necessitates a trip to the bank, and there is no easy way to reinvest interest payments to obtain the benefits of compounding. As a remedy for some of these problems, in the late 1970s some financial firms began to introduce *zero-coupon bonds* based on the Treasury obligations. These worked as follows: A brokerage firm would buy a bond (say, the $1 million bond described in the preceding paragraph). Then it would "strip" the coupons from the bond and sell these as separate investments. For example, it would sell a coupon representing a $30,000 interest payment on July 1, 2022, to an investor who wished to invest his or her funds until then.

Applying the PDV Formula

How much would such a stripped coupon be worth? The present discounted value formula gives the answer. If the interest rate is 5 percent, the present value of $30,000 payable in 2022 (20 years from July 1, 2002) is

$$\frac{\$30{,}000}{(1+i)^{20}} = \frac{\$30{,}000}{(1+0.05)^{20}} = \frac{\$30{,}000}{2.653} = \$11{,}308$$

So the coupon would sell for $11,308 and would grow to nearly three times this amount by 2022 when it was redeemed. Such a financial investment offers considerable advantages to an investor who does not want to be bothered with semiannual coupons, and zero-coupon bonds have proven to be quite popular. Prices for Treasury strips are now quoted daily in all financial newspapers.

A Specific Example

The Wall Street Journal on September 30, 2002, reported that a Treasury strip worth $1,000 in August of 2022 had a current value of $397.57. An investor thinking of retiring on that date could invest $398 and be assured of $1,000 in 20 years, earning a yield of 4.7 percent.

To Think About

1. Does an investor who buys a zero-coupon bond have to leave his or her funds in that investment until the payment is due? Would someone who sells before this due date lose all interest earned? Are zero-coupon investments more risky than ordinary bonds?
2. Do the financial institutions offering zero-coupon bonds have to use Treasury coupons for their promises of future payments? Couldn't they just make the promises themselves and sell them in the market? What advantages are offered by using Treasury bond coupons as the basis for zero-coupon investment?

DISCOUNTING PAYMENT STREAMS

Dollars payable at different points of time have different present values. One must be careful in calculating the true worth of streams of payments that occur at various times into the future—simply adding them up is not appropriate. Consider a situation that has irritated the author for some time. Many state lotteries promise grand prizes of $1 million (or, sometimes, much more) that they pay to the winners over 25 years. But $40,000 per year for 25 years is not "worth" $1 million. Indeed, at a 10 percent interest rate, the present value of such a stream is only $363,200—much less than half the amount falsely advertised by the state. This section describes how such a calculation can be made. There is really nothing new to learn about discounting streams of payments—performing the calculations always involves making careful use of the general discounting formula. However, repeated use of that formula may be very time-consuming (if a stream of income is paid, say, at one hundred different times in the future), and our main purpose here is to present a few shortcuts.

MicroQuiz 14A.2

If the interest rate is 5 percent, would you rather have $1,000 in 5 years or $3,000 in 25 years? Would your answer change if the interest rate were 10 percent?

An Algebraic Presentation

Consider a stream of payments that promises $1 per year starting next year and continuing for 3 years. By applying Equation 14A.18, it is easy to see that the present value of this stream is

$$PDV = \frac{\$1}{1+i} + \frac{\$1}{(1+i)^2} + \frac{\$1}{(1+i)^3} \qquad (14A.19)$$

If the interest rate is 5 percent, this value would be

$$\frac{\$1}{1.05} + \frac{\$1}{(1.05)^2} + \frac{\$1}{(1.05)^3} = \$0.9523 + \$0.9070 + \$0.8639$$
$$= \$2.7232 \qquad (14A.20)$$

Consequently, just as for the lottery, $1 a year for 3 years is not worth $3 but quite a bit less because of the need to take forgone interest into account in making present value calculations. If the promised stream of payments extends for longer than 3 years, additional terms should be added to Equation 14A.19. The present value of $1 per year for 5 years is

$$PDV = \frac{\$1}{1+i} + \frac{\$1}{(1+i)^2} + \frac{\$1}{(1+i)^3} + \frac{\$1}{(1+i)^4} + \frac{\$1}{(1+i)^5} \qquad (14A.21)$$

TABLE 14A.3 Present Value of $1 per Year for Various Time Periods and Interest Rates

Years of payment	Interest Rate			
	1 percent	3 percent	5 percent	10 percent
1	$.99	$.97	$.95	$.91
2	1.97	1.91	1.86	1.74
3	2.94	2.83	2.72	2.49
5	4.85	4.58	4.33	3.79
10	9.47	8.53	7.72	6.14
25	22.02	17.41	14.09	9.08
50	39.20	25.73	18.26	9.91
100	63.02	31.60	19.85	9.99
Forever	100.00	33.33	20.00	10.00

which amounts to about $4.33 at a 5 percent interest rate. Again, $1 per year for 5 years is not worth $5.

The PDV equation can be generalized to any number of years (n) by just adding the correct number of terms:

$$PDV = \frac{\$1}{1+i} + \frac{\$1}{(1+i)^2} + \ldots + \frac{\$1}{(1+i)^n} \qquad (14A.22)$$

Table 14A.3 uses this formula to compute the value of $1 per year for various numbers of years and interest rates. Several features of the numbers in this table are important to keep in mind when discussing present values. As noted previously, none of the streams is worth in present value terms the actual number of dollars paid. The figures are always less than the number of years for which $1 will be paid. Even for low interest rates the difference is substantial. With a 3 percent interest rate, $1 per year for 100 years is worth only $31 in present value. At higher interest rates, the effect of discounting is even more pronounced. A dollar each year for 100 years is worth (slightly) less than $10 in present value terms with an interest rate of 10 percent.

Perpetual Payments

The value of a stream of payments that goes on "forever" at $1 per year is reported as the final entry in each column of Table 14A.3. To understand how this is calculated, we can pose the question in a slightly different way. How much

($X) would you have to invest at an interest rate of i to yield $1 a year forever? That is, we wish to find $X that satisfies the equation

$$\$1 = i \cdot \$X \qquad\qquad \textbf{(14A.23)}$$

But this just means that

$$\$X = \$1/i \qquad\qquad \textbf{(14A.24)}$$

Perpetuity

A promise of a certain number of dollars each year, forever.

which is the way the entries in the table were computed. For example, the present value of $1 per year forever with an interest rate of 5 percent is $20 (= $1/0.05). With an interest rate of 10 percent the figure would be $10 (= $1/0.10). Such a permanent payment stream is called a **perpetuity.** Although these are technically illegal in the United States (however, many people set up "permanent" endowments for cemetery plots, scholarships, and prize funds), other countries do permit such limitless contracts to be written. In the United Kingdom, for example, perpetuities originally written in the 1600s are still bought and sold. Equation 14A.24 shows that, even though such perpetuities in effect promise an infinite number of dollars (since the payments never cease), in present-value terms they have quite modest values. Indeed, for relatively high interest rates, there isn't much difference between getting $1 a year for 25 or 50 years and getting it forever. At an interest rate of 10 percent, for example, the present value of a perpetuity (which promises an infinite number of dollars) is only $0.92 greater than a promise of a dollar a year for only 25 years. The infinite number of dollars to be received after year 25 are only worth $0.92 today.[3]

---

[3] Using the formula for perpetuities provides a simple way of computing streams that run for only a limited number of years. Suppose we wished to evaluate a stream of $1 per year for 25 years at a 10 percent interest rate. If we used Equation 14A.22, we would need to evaluate 25 terms. Instead, we could note that a 25-year stream is an infinite stream less all payments for year 26 and beyond. The present value of a perpetual stream is

$$\frac{\$1}{i} = \frac{\$1}{0.10} = \$10$$

whereas the present value of a perpetual stream that starts in year 25 is

$$\frac{\$10}{(1+i)^{25}} = \frac{\$10}{(1+0.10)^{25}} = \frac{\$10}{10.83} = \$0.92$$

The value of a 25-year stream is

$$\$10 - \$0.92 = \$9.08$$

which is the figure given in Table 14A.3.

More generally, a stream of $1 per year for n years at the interest rate i has a present value of

$$PDV = \frac{\$1}{i} - \frac{\$1/i}{(1+i)^n} = \frac{\$1}{i}\left(1 - \frac{1}{(1+i)^n}\right)$$

Varying Payment Streams

The present value of a payment stream that consists of the same number of dollars each year can be calculated by multiplying the value of $1 per year by that amount. In the lottery illustration with which we began this section, for example, we calculated the present value of $40,000 per year for 25 years. This is 40,000 times the entry for $1 per year for 25 years at 10 percent from Table 14A.3 (40,000 · $9.08 = $363,200). The present value of any other constant stream of dollar payments can be calculated in a similar fashion.

When payments vary from year to year, the computation can become more cumbersome. Each payment must be discounted separately using the formula given in Equation 14A.18. We can show this computation in its most general form by letting D_i represent the amount to be paid in any year i. Then the present value of this stream would be

$$PDV = \frac{D_1}{1+i} + \frac{D_2}{(1+i)^2} + \frac{D_3}{(1+i)^3} + \ldots + \frac{D_n}{(1+i)^n} \qquad (14A.25)$$

Here, each D could be either positive or negative depending on whether funds are to be received or paid out. In some cases the computations may be very complicated, as we saw in Application 14.4. Still, Equation 14A.25 provides a uniform way to approach all present value problems.

Calculating Yields

Equation 14A.25 can also be used to compute the **yield** promised by any payment stream. That is, we can use the equation to compute the interest rate that discounts any payment stream to the present price that a buyer must pay for the rights to the stream. If we let P be the price of the payment stream and if we know the periodic payments to be made ($D_1 \ldots D_n$), then Equation 14A.25 becomes

Yield
The effective (internal) rate of return promised by a payment stream that can be purchased at a certain price.

$$P = PDV = \frac{D_1}{(1+i)} + \frac{D_2}{(1+i)^2} + \ldots + \frac{D_n}{(1+i)^n} \qquad (14A.26)$$

where now i is an unknown to be computed. Solving this equation can be clarified if we let $\delta = 1/(1+i)$. Then Equation 14A.26 can be written as

$$P = \delta D_1 + \delta^2 D_2 + \ldots + \delta^n D_n \qquad (14A.27)$$

which is simply a polynomial in the unknown δ. This polynomial equation can usually be solved for δ and hence for the yield (or "internal rate of return") on the flow of payments, i.

Reading Bond Tables

One of the most common applications of this type of calculation is the computation of yields on bonds. Most ordinary bonds promise to pay a stream of annual interest payments for a given number of years and to make a final repayment of principal when the bond matures. For example, the bond tables in *The Wall Street Journal* list a "5.5% Bond maturing in August 2028," which currently sells for $1,095. This bond is simply a promise to pay 5.5 percent of its initial face amount ($1,000) each year and then to repay the $1,000 principal when interest payments end in 26 years. The yield on this bond is found by solving[4] the following equation for δ [and, also for $i = (1 - \delta)/\delta$]:

$$1,095 = 55\delta + 55\delta^2 + \ldots + 55\delta^{26} + 1,000\delta^{26} \qquad \textbf{(14A.28)}$$

The result of this calculation is given as 4.85 percent—that is the yield on this particular bond. Notice that in this case the yield is less than the interest rate quoted on the bond, in part because the bond's current price is greater than $1,000.

MicroQuiz 14A.3

For the bond described in the text, how would the yield be affected by

1. Increasing the annual interest payment from $55 to $60?

2. Increasing the repayment amount from $1,000 to $1,100?

3. Shortening the maturity date from 2028 to 2025?

FREQUENCY OF COMPOUNDING

So far we have talked only about interest payments that are compounded once a year. That is, interest is paid at the end of each year and does not itself start to earn interest until the next year begins. In the past, that was how banks worked. Every January, depositors were expected to bring in their bank books so that the past year's interest could be added. People who withdrew money from the bank prior to January 1 often lost all the interest they had earned so far in the year.

Since the 1960s, however, banks and all other financial institutions have started to use more frequent, usually daily, compounding. This has provided some extra interest payments to investors, because more frequent compounding means that prior interest earned begins itself to earn interest more quickly. In this section, we use the tools we have developed so far to explore this issue.

Semiannual Compounding

As before, assume the annual interest rate is given by i (or in some of our examples 5 percent). But now suppose the bank agrees to pay interest two times a

---

[4] The actual calculation is a bit more complicated than described here because adjustments have to be made for the actual dates at which interest and principal payments are to be made. Typically, interest payments are made semiannually.

year—on January 1 and on July 1. If you deposit $1 on January 1, by July 1 it will have grown to be $1 · (1 + i/2) since you will have earned half a year's interest. With an interest rate of 5 percent, you will have $1.025 on July 1. For the second half of the year, you will earn interest on $1.025, not just on $1. At the end of the year, you will have $1.025 · 1.025 = $1.05063, which is slightly larger than the $1.05 you would have with annual compounding. More generally, with an interest rate of i, semiannual compounding would yield

$$\$1(1 + i/2)(1 + i/2) = \$1(1 + i/2)^2 \qquad \text{(14A.29)}$$

at the end of 1 year. That this is superior to annual compounding can be shown with simple algebra:

$$\$1 \cdot (1 + i/2)^2 = \$1(1 + i + i^2/4) = \$1 \cdot (1 + i) + \$1 \cdot i^2/4 \qquad \text{(14A.30)}$$

which is clearly greater than $1 · (1 + i). The final term in Equation 14A.30 reflects the interest earned in the first half of the year, $1 · (i/2), times the interest rate in the second half of the year (i/2). This is the bonus earned by semiannual compounding.

A General Treatment

We could extend this algebraic discussion to more frequent compounding—quarterly, monthly, or daily—but little new information would be added. More frequent compounding would continue to increase the effective yield that the 5 percent annual interest rate actually provides. Table 14A.4 shows how the frequency of compounding has this effect over time periods of various durations. The gains of using monthly rather than annual compounding are relatively large, especially

TABLE 14A.4 **Value of $1 at a 5 Percent Annual Interest Rate Compounded with Different Frequencies and Terms**

	Frequency			
Years on deposit	Annual	Semiannual	Monthly	Daily
1	$1.0500	$1.0506	$1.0512	$1.0513
2	1.1025	1.1038	1.1049	1.1052
3	1.1576	1.1596	1.1615	1.1618
5	1.2763	1.2801	1.2834	1.2840
10	1.6289	1.6386	1.6471	1.6487
25	3.3863	3.4371	3.4816	3.4900
50	11.4674	11.8137	12.1218	12.1803
100	131.5013	139.5639	146.9380	148.3607

over long periods of time when small differences in effective yields can make a big difference. Gains in going from monthly to daily compounding are fairly small, however. The extra yield from compounding even more frequently (every second?) are even smaller. Application 14A.3: Continuous Compounding shows that, for some purposes, using such frequent compounding can make calculations much easier.

THE PRESENT DISCOUNTED VALUE APPROACH TO INVESTMENT DECISIONS

The present discounted value concept provides an alternative way of approaching the theory of capital demand that we discussed in Chapter 14. When a firm buys a machine, it is in effect buying a stream of net revenues in future periods. In order to decide whether to purchase the machine, the firm must assign some value to this stream. Because the revenues will accrue to the firm in many future periods, the logic of the preceding pages suggests that the firm should compute the present discounted value of this stream. Only by doing so will the firm have taken adequate account of the opportunity costs associated with alternative assets it might have bought.

Consider a firm in the process of deciding whether to buy a particular machine. The machine is expected to last n years and will give its owner a stream of real returns (that is, marginal value products) in each of the n years. Let the return in year i be represented by R_i. If r is the real interest rate on alternative investments, and if this rate is expected to prevail for the next n years, the present discounted value (PDV) of the machine to its owner is given by

$$PDV = \frac{R_1}{1+r} + \frac{R_2}{(1+r)^2} + \ldots + \frac{R_n}{(1+r)^n} \qquad (14A.31)$$

This represents the total value of the stream of payments that is provided by the machine, once adequate account is taken of the fact that these payments occur in different years. If the PDV of this stream of payments exceeds the price (P) of the machine, the firm should make the purchase. Even when opportunity costs are taken into account, the machine promises to return more than it will cost to buy and firms would rush out to buy machines. On the other hand, if P exceeds the machine's PDV, the firm would be better off investing its funds in some alternative that promises a rate of return of r. When account is taken of forgone returns, the machine does not pay for itself. No profit-maximizing firm would buy such a machine.

In a competitive market, the only equilibrium that can persist is one where the price of a machine is exactly equal to the present discounted value of the net revenues it provides. Only in this situation will there be neither an excess demand

As a limiting case, it is useful to look at the mathematics of compounding when interest is paid continuously—that is, at every instant of time. Of course, financial institutions do not actually pay interest that frequently. But the case of continuous compounding often provides a very useful approximation.

The Amazing Properties of e

One of the most important constants in mathematics is "e," the designation applied to the base of natural logarithms (= 2.71828) by Euler in 1727. This constant seems to turn up everywhere, arising in such phenomena as the equations for spiral shells, for hanging power lines, and for the normal distribution (the bell curve) that characterizes many natural populations. In the mathematics of compound interest, e is used in formulas for continuous compounding. This arises because it can be shown that the limit of the compound interest expression $(1 + i/n)^n$ as n gets infinitely large (that is, as interest is compounded more and more frequently) is simply e^i. Hence, e^i is the one-period result of having \$1 compounded instantaneously. If, for example, i is 0.05, then $e^{0.05} = 1.05127$, which is approximately the value for daily compounding given in Table 14.4. If compounding extends for t years, the value of \$1 becomes $\$1 \cdot e^{it}$ and the value of \$D is $\$D \cdot e^{it}$.

The Rule of 70

One simple application of continuous compounding is a way to compute doubling times for any interest rate. To find the doubling time, we solve for t the equation

$$e^{it} = 2 \qquad \text{(i)}$$

Taking natural logarithms of both sides gives

$$t^* = \frac{\ln 2}{i} \qquad \text{(ii)}$$

Because ln2 is approximately 0.70 (actually it is 0.6913), doubling time can be found by dividing 70 by the interest rate, in percent. For example, anything growing at 5 percent per year will double in 14 years (= 70/5).

Products and Ratios

Exponential growth also provides a simple way for computing growth rates of the product or ratio of two variables. For example, suppose x is growing at rate r_1, and y at rate r_2. Then, if z is the product of x times y, it is growing at

$$z = x \cdot y = e^{r_1 t} \, e^{r_2 t} = e^{(r_1 + r_2)t} \qquad \text{(iii)}$$

That is, the growth rate of z is the *sum* of r1 and r2. For example, if the price of a product is growing at 3 percent per year and quantity is growing at 7 percent per year, total revenue is growing at 10 percent per year. Similarly, if w is the ratio of x to y, we have

$$w = x/y = e^{r_1 t}/e^{r_2 t} = e^{(r_1 - r_2)t} \qquad \text{(iv)}$$

So, the growth rate in w is the *difference* between the growth rate in x and the growth rate in y. If nominal GDP is growing at 4 percent per year and inflation is 2 percent per year, then real GDP is growing at 2 percent per year.

(continued)

Discounting

If interest is compounded continuously, the appropriate discount factor is e^{-it}. Hence, any continuous stream of payments can be discounted by multiplying it by this term. Summing the payments requires calculus (because of the continuous nature of the interest payments). For example, suppose that you are promised $10 per year for 20 years and wish to know the present value of this promise. By treating the $10 as being paid continuously over the year, the calculation becomes

$$\text{Value} = \int_0^{20} 10e^{-0.05t}dt \tag{v}$$
$$= 200\,(1 - e^{-1})$$
$$= 126.42$$

which, at least to this author, is much easier than remembering the formula in Footnote 3 of this appendix.

To Think About

1. If a variable is growing exponentially as in the expression $y = e^{it}$, what does its graph (with y on the vertical axis, t on the horizontal axis) look like?
2. In Equation v, payments of $10 lasted for 20 years. How would this expression change if the payments had gone on forever?

for machines nor an excess supply of machines. Hence, market equilibrium requires that

$$P = PDV = \frac{R_1}{1 + r} + \frac{R_2}{(1 + r)^2} + \ldots + \frac{R_n}{(1 + r)^n} \tag{14A.32}$$

Present Discounted Value and the Rental Rate

For simplicity, assume now that machines do not depreciate and that the marginal value product is the same in every year. This uniform return will then also equal the rental rate for machines (v), since that is what another firm would be willing to pay for the machine's use during each period. With these simplifying assumptions, we may write the present discounted value from machine ownership as

$$PDV = \frac{v}{1 + r} + \frac{v}{(1 + r)^2} + \ldots + \frac{v}{(1 + r)^n} + \ldots \tag{14A.33}$$

where the dots (. . .) indicate that payments go on forever. But because in equilibrium P = PDV, our earlier discussion of perpetuities gives

$$P = \frac{v}{r} \qquad \text{(14A.34)}$$

or

$$v = rP \qquad \text{(14A.35)}$$

which is the same as Equation 14.1 when d = 0. For this case, the present discounted value criterion gives results identical to those outlined earlier using the rental rate approach. In equilibrium, a machine must promise owners the prevailing rate of return.

MicroQuiz 14A.4

Equation 14A.33 assumes that machines do not depreciate. How should the equation be changed if the machine deteriorates at the rate of d per year? If the machine still lasts forever (even though it will be very deteriorated), will its rental rate be given by the formula in Chapter 14—that is, $v = (r + d)P$?

SUMMARY

This appendix surveys mathematical calculations involving compound interest concepts. Dollars payable at different points in time are not equally valuable (because those payable in the distant future require the sacrifice of some potential interest), and it is important to be careful in making comparisons among alternative payment schedules. Discussing this issue we show:

- In making compound interest calculations, it is necessary to take account of interest that is paid on prior interest earned. The interest factor $(1 + i)^n$—where n is the number of years over which interest is compounded—reflects this compounding.
- Dollars payable in the future are worth less than dollars payable currently. To compare dollars that are payable at different dates requires using present discounted value computations to allow for the opportunity costs associated with forgone interest.
- Evaluating payment streams requires that each individual payment be discounted by the appropriate interest factor. It is incorrect simply to add together dollars payable at different times.
- More frequent compounding leads to higher effective returns because prior interest paid begins to earn interest more quickly. There is an upper limit to the increased yield provided, however.
- The present discounted value formula provides an alternative approach to investment decisions that reaches the same result already derived in Chapter 14.

Uncertainty and Information

So far in this book, we have assumed that people's and firms' choices do not involve any degree of uncertainty; once they decide what to do, they get what they have chosen. That is not always the way things work in many real-world situations. When you buy a lottery ticket, invest in shares of common stock, or play poker, what you get back is subject to chance. Many choices involve incomplete information (such as deciding which used car is a lemon and which isn't), and these choices must be made somewhat "in the dark." In this chapter, we look at four questions raised by economic problems involving uncertainty: (1) Why do people generally dislike risky situations? (2) What can people do to avoid or reduce risks? (3) How can the problem of uncertainty be treated more generally as one of incomplete information? and (4) How does incomplete information affect the market equilibria we have studied?

PROBABILITY AND EXPECTED VALUE

The study of individual behavior under uncertainty and the mathematical study of probability and statistics have a common historical origin in games of chance. Gamblers who try to devise ways of winning at blackjack and casinos trying to keep the game profitable are modern examples of this concern. Two statistical concepts that originated from studying games of chance, *probability* and *expected value,* are very important to our study of economic choices in uncertain situations.

Probability
The relative frequency with which an event occurs.

The **probability** of an event happening is, roughly speaking, the relative frequency with which it occurs. For example, to say that the probability of a head coming up on the flip of a fair coin is ½ means that if a coin is flipped a large number of times, we can expect a head to come up in approximately one-half of the flips. Similarly, the probability of rolling a "2" on a single die is ⅙. In approximately one out of every six rolls, a "2" should come up. Of course, before a coin is flipped or a die is rolled, we have no idea what will happen, so each flip or roll has an uncertain outcome.

The **expected value** of a game with a number of uncertain outcomes (or prizes) is the size of the prize that the player will win on average. Suppose Jones and Smith agree to flip a coin once. If a head comes up, Jones will pay Smith $1; if a tail comes up, Smith will pay Jones $1. From Smith's point of view, there are two prizes or outcomes (X_1 and X_2) in this game: If the coin is a head, $X_1 = +\$1$; if a tail comes up, $X_2 = -\$1$ (the minus sign indicates that Smith must pay). From Jones's point of view, the game is exactly the same except that the signs of the outcomes are reversed. The expected value of the game is then

Expected value
The average outcome from an uncertain gamble.

$$\frac{1}{2}X_1 + \frac{1}{2}X_2 = \frac{1}{2}\,(\$1) + \frac{1}{2}\,(-\$1) = 0 \qquad (15.1)$$

The expected value of this game is zero. If the game were played a large number of times, it is not likely that either player would come out very far ahead.

Now suppose the prizes of the game were changed so that, from Smith's point of view, $X_1 = \$10$, and $X_2 = -\$1$. Smith will win $10 if a head comes up but will lose only $1 if a tail comes up. The expected value of this game is $4.50:

$$\frac{1}{2}X_1 + \frac{1}{2}X_2 = \frac{1}{2}\,(\$10) + \frac{1}{2}\,(-\$1) = \$5 - \$0.50 = \$4.50 \qquad (15.2)$$

If this game is played many times, Smith will certainly end up the big winner, averaging $4.50 each time the coin is flipped. The game is so attractive that Smith might be willing to pay Jones something for the privilege of playing. She might even be willing to pay as much as $4.50, the expected value, for a chance to play. Games with an expected value of zero and games that cost their expected values for the right to play (here, $4.50) are called **fair games**. If fair games are played many times, the monetary losses or gains are expected to be rather small. Application 15.1: Blackjack Systems shows the importance of the expected-value concept in the game of blackjack, a game in which players and casinos struggle to gain an advantage.

Fair games
Games that cost their expected value.

MicroQuiz 15.1

What is the actuarially fair price for each of the following lotteries?

1. Winning $1,000 with probability 0.5 and losing $1,000 with probability 0.5

2. Winning $1,000 with probability 0.6 and losing $1,000 with probability 0.4

3. Winning $1,000 with probability 0.7, winning $2,000 with probability 0.2, and losing $10,000 with probability 0.1

Blackjack Systems

The game of blackjack (or twenty-one) provides an illustration of the expected-value notion and its relevance to people's behavior in uncertain situations. Blackjack is a very simple game. Each player is dealt two cards (with the dealer playing last). The dealer asks each player if he or she wishes another card. The player getting a hand that totals closest to 21, without going over 21, is the winner. If the receipt of a card puts a player over 21, that player automatically loses.

Played in this way, blackjack offers a number of advantages to the dealer. Most important, the dealer, who plays last, is in a favorable position because other players can go over 21 (and therefore lose) before the dealer plays. Under the usual rules, the dealer has the additional advantage of winning ties. These two advantages give the dealer a margin of winning of about 6 percent on average. Players can expect to win 47 percent of all hands played, whereas the dealer will win 53 percent of the time.

Betting Systems

Because the rules of blackjack make the game unfair to players, casinos have gradually eased the rules in order to entice more people to play. At many Las Vegas casinos, for example, dealers must play under fixed rules that allow no discretion depending on the individual game situation; and, in the case of ties, rather than winning them, dealers must return bets to the players. These rules alter fairness of the game quite a bit. By some estimates, Las Vegas casino dealers enjoy a blackjack advantage of as little as 0.1 percent, if that. In fact, in recent years a number of systems have been developed by players that they claim can even result in a net advantage for the player. The systems involve card counting, systematic varying of bets, and numerous other strategies for special situations that arise in the game. Computer simulations of literally billions of potential blackjack hands have shown that careful adherence to a correct strategy can result in an advantage to the player of as much as 1 or 2 percent. Actor Dustin Hoffman illustrated these potential advantages in his character's remarkable ability to count cards in the 1989 movie *Rain Man*.

Casino's Response

It should come as no surprise that players' use of these blackjack systems is not particularly welcomed by those who operate Las Vegas casinos. The casinos have made several rule changes (such as using multiple card decks to make card counting more difficult) in order to reduce system players' advantages. They have also started to refuse admission to known system players. Dustin Hoffman's and Tom Cruise's characters in *Rain Man* were rudely ejected from the casino after their big win using card-counting systems. Recent books on blackjack systems have long sections on how players can avoid detection when counting cards.

All of this turmoil illustrates the importance of small changes in expected values for a game such as blackjack that involves many repetitions. System players pay little attention to the variability of outcomes on a single hand. Instead, they focus on improving the average outcome of many hours at the card table.

To Think About
1. If blackjack systems increase people's expected winnings, why doesn't everyone use them? Who do you expect would be most likely to learn how to use the systems?
2. Casinos make money by gearing their games of chance to result in a positive expected value for them. With many players, they are, therefore, assured of making a profit. Explain how the house manages to win, on average, with slot machines, craps, roulette, and stud poker games.

RISK AVERSION

Economists have found that, when people are faced with a risky but fair situation, they usually choose not to participate.[1] A major reason for this **risk aversion** was first identified by the Swiss mathematician Daniel Bernoulli in the eighteenth century. In his early study of behavior under uncertainty, Bernoulli theorized that it is not the monetary payoff of a game that matters to people. Rather, it is the expected utility (what Bernoulli called the *moral value*) associated with the game's prizes that is important for people's decisions. If differences in a game's money prizes do not completely reflect utility, people may find that games that are fair in dollar terms are in fact unfair in terms of utility. Specifically, Bernoulli (and most later economists) assumed that the utility associated with the payoffs in a risky situation increases less rapidly than the dollar value of these payoffs. That is, the extra (or marginal) utility that winning an extra dollar in prize money provides is assumed to decline as more dollars are won.

Risk aversion
The tendency of people to refuse to accept fair games.

Diminishing Marginal Utility

This assumption is illustrated in Figure 15.1, which shows the utility associated with possible prizes (or incomes) from $0 to $15,000. The concave shape of the curve reflects the assumed diminishing marginal utility of these prizes. Although additional income always raises utility, the increase in utility resulting from an increase in income from $1,000 to $2,000 is much greater than the increase in utility that results from an increase in income from $14,000 to $15,000. It is this assumed diminishing marginal utility of income (which is in some ways similar to the assumption of a diminishing MRS introduced in Chapter 2) that gives rise to risk aversion.

---

[1] The games we discuss here are assumed to yield no utility in their play other than the prizes. The observation that many people gamble at unfair odds (for instance, in the game of roulette, there are 38 possible outcomes but the house pays only 36 to 1 for a winning number) is not necessarily a refutation of risk aversion. These people can reasonably be assumed to derive some utility from the circumstances associated with the play of the game (perhaps playing the game makes them feel like James Bond). Because economists wish to focus on the purely risk-related aspects of a situation, they must abstract from such consumption-type behavior.

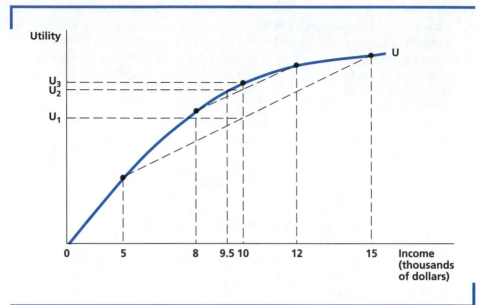

FIGURE 15.1 **Risk Aversion** An individual characterized by the utility-of-income curve U will obtain a higher utility (U_3) from a risk-free income of $10,000 than from a 50-50 chance of winning or losing $2,000 ($U_2$). He or she will be willing to pay up to $500 to avoid having to take this bet. A fair bet of $5,000 provides even less utility (U_1) than the $2,000 bet.

A Graphical Analysis of Risk Aversion

Figure 15.1 illustrates risk aversion. The figure assumes that three options are open to this person. He or she may (1) retain the current level of income ($10,000) without taking any risk; (2) take a fair bet with a 50-50 chance of winning or losing $2,000; or (3) take a fair bet with a 50-50 chance of winning or losing $5,000. To examine the person's preferences among these options, we must compute the expected utility available from each.

The utility received by staying at the current $10,000 income is given by U_3. The U curve shows directly how the individual feels about this current income. The utility level obtained from the $2,000 bet is simply the average of the utility of $12,000 (which the individual will end up with by winning the game) and the utility of $8,000 (which he or she will end up with when the game is lost). This average utility is given by U_2.[2] Because it falls short of U_3, we can assume that the per-

[2] This average utility can be found by drawing the chord joining U($12,000) and U($8,000) and finding the midpoint of that chord. Since the vertical line at $10,000 is midway between $12,000 and $8,000, it will also bisect the chord.

son will refuse to make the $2,000 bet. Finally, the utility of the $5,000 bet is the average of the utility from $15,000 and the utility from $5,000. This is given by U_1, which falls below U_2. In other words, the person likes the risky $5,000 bet even less than the $2,000 bet.

Willingness to Pay to Avoid Risk

Diminished marginal utility of income, as shown in Figure 15.1, means that people will be averse to risk. Among options with the same expected dollar values ($10,000 in all of our examples), people will prefer risk-free incomes to risky options because the gains such risky options offer are worth less in utility terms than the losses. In fact, a person would be willing to give up some amount of income to avoid taking a risk. In Figure 15.1, for example, a risk-free income of $9,500 provides the same utility as the $2,000 gamble ($U_2$). The individual is willing to pay up to $500 to avoid taking that risk. There are a number of ways this person might spend these funds to reduce the risk or avoid it completely.

METHODS FOR REDUCING RISK

In many situations, taking risks is unavoidable. Even though driving a car or eating a meal at a restaurant subjects an individual to some uncertainty about what will actually happen, short of becoming a hermit, there is no way all risks can be avoided. Our analysis in the previous section suggests, however, that people are generally willing to pay something to reduce these risks. In this section, we examine two methods for doing so—insurance and diversification.

Insurance

Each year, people in the United States spend more than half a trillion dollars on insurance of all types. Most commonly, they buy coverage for their own life, for their home and automobiles, and for their health care costs. But, insurance can be bought (perhaps at a very high price) for practically any risk imaginable. For example, many people in California buy earthquake insurance, outdoor swimming pool owners can buy special coverage for injuries to falling parachutists, and surgeons or basketball players can insure their hands. In all of these cases, individuals are willing to pay a premium to an insurance company in order to be assured of compensation if something goes wrong.

The underlying motive for insurance purchases is illustrated in Figure 15.2. Here, we have repeated the utility-of-income curve from Figure 15.1, but now we assume that during the next year this person with a $10,000 current income (and consumption) faces a 50 percent chance of having $4,000 in unexpected medical bills, which would reduce his or her consumption to $6,000. Without insurance, this person's utility would be U_1—the average of the utility from $10,000 and the utility from $6,000.

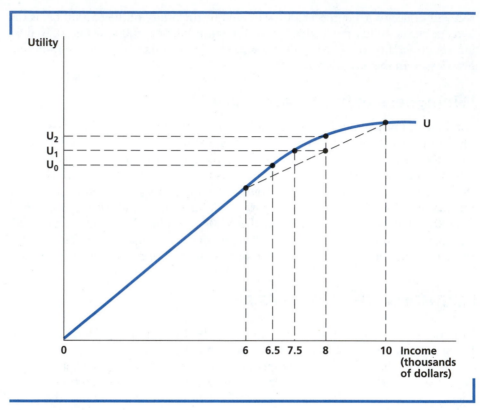

FIGURE 15.2 Insurance Reduces Risk A person with $10,000 in income who faced a 50-50 chance of $4,000 in medical bills would have an expected utility of U_1. With fair insurance (which costs $2,000), utility would be U_2. Even unfair insurance costing $2,500 would still yield the same utility (U_1) as facing the world uninsured. But a premium of $3,500, which provides a utility of only U_0, would be too costly.

Fair Insurance

Fair insurance
Insurance for which the premium is equal to the expected value of the loss.

This person would clearly be better off with an actuarially **fair insurance** policy for his or her health care needs. Such a policy would cost $2,000—the expected value of what insurance companies would have to pay each year in health claims. A person who bought the policy would be assured of $8,000 in consumption. If he or she bought the policy and stayed well, income would be reduced by the $2,000 premium. If this person suffered the illness, the insurance company would pay the $4,000 in medical bills but this person would have paid the $2,000 premium so consumption would still be $8,000. As Figure 15.2 shows, the utility from a certain income of $8,000 ($U_2$) exceeds that attainable from facing the world uninsured, so the policy represents a utility-enhancing use for funds.

Unfair Insurance

No insurance company can afford to sell insurance at actuarially fair premiums. Not only do such companies have to pay benefits, but they must also maintain records, collect premiums, and investigate claims to ensure they are not fraudulent. Hence, a would-be insurance purchaser can always expect to pay more than an actuarially fair premium. Still, a buyer may decide that the risk reduction that insurance provides is worth the extra charges. In the health care illustration in Figure 15.2, for example, this person would be willing to pay up to $2,500 for health insurance since the risk-free consumption stream of $7,500 that buying such "unfair" insurance would yield provides as much utility (U_1) as does facing the world uninsured. Of course, even a desirable product such as insurance can become too expensive. At a price of $3,500, the utility provided with full insurance (U_0) falls short of what would be obtained from facing the world uninsured. In this case, this person is better off taking the risk of paying his or her own medical bills than accepting such an actuarially unfair insurance premium.

Uninsurable Risks

The preceding discussion shows that risk-averse individuals will always buy insurance against risky outcomes unless insurance premiums exceed the expected value of a loss by too much. Three types of factors may result in such high premiums and thereby cause some risks to become uninsurable. First, some risks may be so unique or difficult to evaluate that an insurer may have no idea how to set the premium level. Determining an actuarially fair premium requires that a given risky situation must occur frequently enough so that the insurer can both estimate the expected value of the loss and rely on being able to cover expected payouts with premiums from individuals who do not suffer losses. For rare or very unpredictable events such as wars, nuclear power plant mishaps, or invasions from Mars, would-be insurers may have no basis for establishing insurance premiums and therefore refrain from offering any coverage.

Two other reasons for absence of insurance coverage relate to the behavior of the individuals who want to buy insurance. In some cases, these individuals may know more about the likelihood that they will suffer a loss than does an insurer. Those who expect large losses will buy insurance, whereas those who expect small ones will not. This **adverse selection** results in the insurer paying out more in losses than expected unless the insurer finds a way to control who buys the policies offered. As we will see later, in the absence of such controls, no insurance would be provided even though people would willingly buy it.

The behavior of individuals once they are insured may also affect the possibility for insurance coverage. If having insurance makes people more likely to incur losses, insurers' premium calculations will be incorrect and again, they may be forced to charge premiums that are too unfair in an actuarial sense. For example, if people who have insurance on the cash they carry in their pockets are far more likely to lose it through carelessness than those who do not have insurance, insurance premiums to cover such losses may have to be very high. This **moral hazard** in people's behavior means that insurance against accidental losses of cash will not be available on any reasonable terms. The moral hazard problem is especially important in the study of health insurance, as Application 15.2: Do HMO Patients Need a Bill of Rights? illustrates.

Adverse selection
When buyers and sellers have different information, market outcomes may exhibit adverse selection—the quality of goods or services traded will be biased toward market participants with better information.

Moral hazard
The effect that having insurance has on the behavior of the insured.

Do HMO Patients Need a Bill of Rights?

The arrival of prepaid medical plans such as Health Maintenance Organizations (HMOs) has created much annoyance among consumers of medical care. These were captured in a famous scene from the 1998 film *As Good as it Gets* in which the character played by Helen Hunt refers to her HMO as "that ..*!@!* company"—a statement met with approval both in the film and by audiences viewing the film. Such feelings have led many states to adopt strong "Bills of Rights" for HMO customers. Much of the controversy over HMOs can be clarified by considering how the issue of moral hazard operates in health insurance markets.

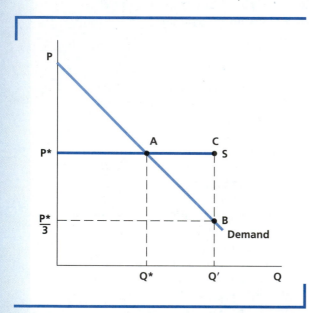

FIGURE 1 Moral Hazard in the Medical Care Market
Because insured people pay only one-third the price of medical care, they will demand Q' rather than Q* and cause a welfare loss of ABC.

Losses from Moral Hazard

Figure 1 illustrates the moral hazard dilemma as it applies to medical care. The figure shows the demand for medical care together with a horizontal long-run supply curve. In the absence of insurance, people would buy Q* units of medical care at a price of P*. Because most medical care purchases are insured, however, consumers do not pay P* for their care. Instead, they may pay only, say, one-third of the market price for the care received and they therefore increase the quantity demanded to Q'. Because the value of this extra care to consumers is less than the marginal cost of the care (assumed to be P*), there will be a deadweight loss from insurance given by area ABC.

We can get a rough idea of the size of this deadweight loss by using the findings from the Rand Experiment (Application 4.4), which showed that the price elasticity of demand for medical care is about −0.18. Hence, a typical 66 percent reduction in net price because of insurance will increase demand by about 12 percent (0.18 × 0.66). Because U.S. consumers currently spend more than $1 trillion per year on medical care services that are covered by insurance, this expansion is huge in dollar terms—considerably more than $100 million per year. The deadweight loss would be about one-half this amount. Of course, consumers gain something from the reduced risk that health insurance provides, but the inefficiency shown in Figure 1 represents a tempting target for those who would seek to economize on health care spending.

HMOs and the "Underprovision" of Care

Because HMOs and other prepaid plans operate with predetermined budget constraints, they have an incentive to be sure that the care they provide meets some sort of cost-benefit standard. They may therefore be reluctant to provide care up to the amount that insured consumers want to buy (Q′). They may believe (perhaps correctly) that, at the margin, the value of such care falls short of its cost. These firms will therefore tend to push the quantity of care toward Q*—a level of care for which marginal benefit is equal to marginal cost. Much of the consumer dissatisfaction with HMOs may reflect the fact that established (pre-HMO) spending patterns were already exaggerated by the prevalence of insurance in medical care markets.

To Think About
1. Suppose that patients could sue their HMOs for negligence if they were providing "inadequate" care. How should a court determine the legal meaning of "inadequate"? Should the court opt for Q* or Q′ as the expected level of care?
2. Most decisions about medical care are made by physicians (see Application 7.4). How might the managers of an HMO seek to influence those decisions? Should the government ensure that physicians are not bound by such influences?

Diversification

A second way for risk-averse individuals to reduce risk is by diversifying. This is the economic principle underlying the adage, "Don't put all your eggs in one basket." By suitably spreading risk around, it may be possible to raise utility above that provided by following a single course of action. This possibility is illustrated in Figure 15.3, which shows the utility of income for an individual with a current income of $10,000 who must invest $4,000 of that income in risky assets.

For simplicity, assume there are only two such assets, shares of stock in company A or company B. One share of stock in either company costs $1, and the investor believes that the stock will rise to $2 if the company does well during the next year; if the company does poorly, however, the stock will be worthless. Each company has a 50-50 chance of doing well. How should this individual invest the $4,000? At first, it would seem that it does not matter since the two companies' prospects are identical. But, if we assume the company's prospects are unrelated to one another, it is possible to show that holding both stocks will reduce this person's risks.

Suppose this person decides to plunge into the market by investing only in 4,000 shares of company A. Then he or she has a 50 percent chance of having $14,000 at the end of the year and a 50 percent chance of having $6,000. This undiversified investment strategy will therefore yield a utility of U_1.

Let's consider a diversified strategy in which the investor buys 2,000 shares of each stock. There are now four possible outcomes depending on how each company does. These are illustrated in Table 15.1 together with the individual's income in each of these eventualities. Each of these outcomes is equally likely. Notice that the diversified strategy only achieves very good or very bad results

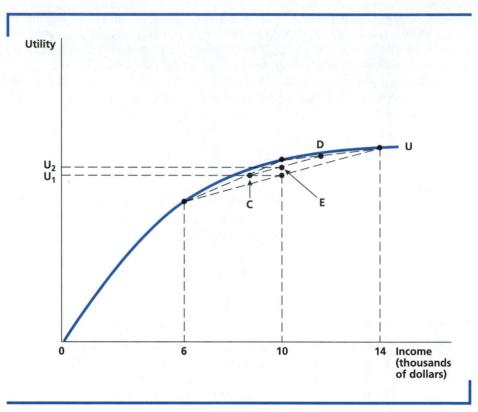

FIGURE 15.3 Diversification Reduces Risk Here, an investor must invest $4,000 in risky stocks. If he or she invests in only one stock, utility will be U_1. Although two unrelated stocks may promise identical returns, investing in both of them can, on average, reduce risk and raise utility to U_2.

TABLE 15.1 Possible Outcomes from Investing in Two Companies

		Company B's Performance	
		Poor	**Good**
Company A's	**Poor**	$6,000	$10,000
Performance	**Good**	10,000	14,000

when both companies do well or poorly, respectively. In half the cases illustrated, the gains in one company's shares balance the losses in the other's, and the individual ends up with the original $10,000. The diversified strategy, although it has the same expected value ($10,000) as the single stock strategy, is less risky.

Illustrating the utility gain from this reduction in risk requires a bit of ingenuity because we must average the utilities from the four outcomes shown in Table 15.1. We do so in a two-step process. Point C in Figure 15.3 represents the average utility for the case where company B does poorly (the average of the utility from $6,000 and $10,000) whereas point D represents the average utility when company B does well ($10,000 and $14,000). The final average of points C and D is found at point E, which represents a utility level of U_2. Because U_2 exceeds U_1, it is clear that this individual has gained from diversification.

The conclusion that spreading risk through **diversification** can increase utility applies to a number of situations. The reasoning in our simple illustration can be used, for example, to explain why individuals opt to buy mutual funds that invest in many stocks rather than choosing only a few stocks on their own (see Application 15.3: Mutual Funds). It also explains why people invest in many kinds of assets (stocks, bonds, cash, precious metals, real estate, and durable goods such as automobiles) rather than in only one. Individuals may also choose to diversify their earnings stream by obtaining skills that can be used in many kinds of jobs or by choosing jobs whose success does not depend on the fortunes of a single product. In all of these cases, our analysis shows that individuals will not only obtain higher utility levels because of the risk reduction from diversification but that they might even be willing to pay something (say, mutual fund fees or educational costs) to obtain these gains.

Diversification
The spreading of risk among several options rather than choosing only one.

> **MicroQuiz 15.3**
>
> Explain why the following are examples of diversification—that is, explain why each choice specified offers the same expected value though the preferred choice is lower in risk.
>
> **1.** Preferring to bet $100 on each of 10 coin flips over $1,000 on a single flip
>
> **2.** Preferring single feed lines at banks to lines for each teller
>
> **3.** Preferring basketball to soccer if a single game is to determine the best team (this example may reflect a peculiarity of your author)

PRICING OF RISK IN FINANCIAL ASSETS

Because people are willing to pay something to avoid risks, it seems as if one should be able to study this process directly. That is, we could treat "risk" like any other commodity and study the factors that influence its demand and supply. One result of such a study would be to be able to say how much risk there is in the economy and how much people would be willing to pay to have less of it. Although, as we shall see, there are several problems with this approach,

Mutual Funds

One of the most convenient ways for individuals to invest in commons stocks is by purchasing mutual fund shares. Mutual funds pool money from many investors to buy shares in several different companies. For this service, individuals pay an annual management fee of about 1 to 1.5 percent of the value of the money they have invested.

Diversification and Riskiness of Funds

Although mutual fund managers often sell their services on the basis of their supposed superiority in picking stocks, the diversification that funds offer probably provides a better explanation of why individuals choose them. Any single investor who tried to purchase shares in, say, 100 different companies would find that most of his or her funds would be used for brokerage commissions with little money left over to buy the shares themselves. Because mutual funds deal in large volume, brokerage commissions are lower. It then becomes feasible for an individual to own a proportionate share in the stocks of many companies. For the reasons illustrated in Figure 15.3, this diversification reduces risk.

Still, investing in stocks generally is a risky enterprise, so mutual fund managers offer products that allow investors to choose the amount of risk they are willing to tolerate. Money market and short-term bond funds tend to offer little risk; balanced funds (which consist of both common stocks and bonds) are a bit riskier; growth funds offer the greatest risk. On average, the riskier funds have tended to yield a somewhat higher return for investors. For example, one well-known study of mutual fund performance during the 1960s found that each 10 percent increase in riskiness resulted in an increase in average total yield from the funds of about one percentage point.[1]

Portfolio Management

Managers of mutual funds can reduce risk further by the choices they make when purchasing specific stocks. Our numerical illustration of the benefits of diversification assumed that the returns on the shares of the two companies were independent of each other; it was that fact that resulted in the benefits from diversification. Further benefits in terms of risk reduction can be achieved if mutual fund managers find investments whose returns tend to move in opposite directions (that is, when one does well, the other does not, and vice versa). For example, some fund managers may choose to hold some of their funds in mining companies because precious metal prices tend to rise when stock prices fall. Another way to achieve this balancing of risk is to purchase stocks from companies in many countries. Such global mutual funds and international funds (which specialize in securities from individual countries) have grown rapidly in recent years. More generally, fund managers may even be able to develop complex strategies involving short sales or stock options that allow them to hedge their returns from a given investment even further. Recent financial innovations such as standardized put and call options, stock index options, interest rate

---

[1] M. Jensen, "Risk, the Pricing of Capital Assets, and the Evaluation of Investment Performance," *Journal of Business* (April 1969).

futures, and a bewildering variety of computer-program trading schemes illustrate the increasing demand for such risk-reduction vehicles.

To Think About

1. Most studies of mutual fund performance conclude that managers cannot consistently exceed the average return in the stock market as a whole. Why might you expect this result? What does it imply about investors' motives for buying mutual funds?
2. Some mutual funds are managed by computer so as to have a performance that precisely duplicates the performance of a particular stock market average (e.g., the Standard and Poor's 500 Stock Average). Why would an investor want to buy shares in such an "index" fund? Alternatively, given that such funds tend to have low management costs (in some cases as low as 0.2 percent per year), why would an investor buy into any other kind of fund?

---

financial markets do indeed provide a good place to get useful information about the pricing of risk.

With financial assets, the risks people face are purely monetary and relatively easy to measure. One can, for example, study the history of the price of a particular financial asset and determine whether this price has been stable or volatile. Presumably, less-volatile assets are more desirable to risk-averse people so they should be willing to pay something for them. Economists are able to get some general idea of people's attitudes toward risk by looking at differences in financial returns on risky versus non-risky assets.

Investors' Market Options

Figure 15.4 shows a simplified illustration of the market options open to a would-be investor in financial assets. The vertical axis of the figure shows the expected annual return that the investor might earn from an asset, whereas the horizontal axis shows the level of risk associated with each asset. The points in the figure represent the options available. For example, point A represents a risk-free asset such as money in a checking account. Although this asset has (practically) no risks associated with its ownership, it promises a very low annual rate of return. Asset B, on the other hand represents a relatively risky stock—this asset promises a high annual rate of return, but any investor must accept a high risk to get that return. All of the other points in Figure 15.4 represent the risks and returns associated with assets that an investor might buy.

Because investors like high annual returns but dislike risk, they will choose to hold combinations of these available assets that lie on their "northwest" periphery. By mixing various risky assets with the risk-free asset (A), they can choose any point along the line AC. This line is labeled the **market line** because

Market line
A line showing the relationship between risk and annual returns that an investor can achieve by mixing financial assets.

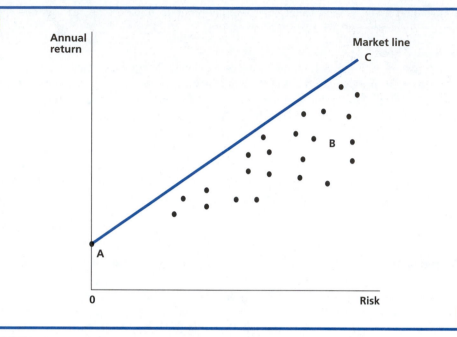

FIGURE 15.4 **Market Options for Investors** The points in the figure represent the risk/return features of various assets. The market line shows the best options a risk-averse investor can obtain by mixing risk assets with the risk-free asset A.

it shows the possible combinations of annual returns and risk that an investor can achieve by taking advantage of what the market offers.[3] The slope of this line shows the trade-off between annual returns and risk that is available from financial markets. By studying the terms on which such trade-offs can be made in actual financial markets, economists can learn something about how those markets price risks. Application 15.4: The Equity Premium Puzzle illustrates these calculations but also highlights some of the uncertainties that arise in making them.

Choices by Individual Investors

The market line shown in Figure 15.4 provides a constraint on the options that financial markets provide to individual investors. These investors then choose among the available options on the basis of their own attitudes toward risk. This

---

[3] The actual construction of the market line is relatively complicated. For a discussion, see W. Nicholson, *Microeconomic Theory: Basic Principles and Extensions,* 8th ed. (Mason, OH: Thomson Learning, 2002): 221–224. See also Internet Exercise 2 for this chapter, which illustrates the Capital Asset Pricing Model—the basic theoretical underpinning for Figure 15.4.

As shown in Figure 15.4, differences in the rates of return of financial assets reflect, in part, the differing risks associated with those assets. The historical data show that stocks have indeed had higher returns than bonds to compensate for that risk. In fact, returns on common stock have been so favorable that they pose a puzzle to economists.

Historical Rates of Return

Table 1 illustrates the most commonly used rate of return data for U.S. financial markets, published by the Ibbotson firm in Chicago. These data show that over the period 1926–1994,[1] stocks provided average annual rates of return that exceeded those on long-term government bonds by 7 percent per year. Average returns on short-term government bonds fell short of those on stocks by a whopping 8.5 percent. Indeed, given the rate of inflation during this period (averaging 3.2 percent per year), the very low real return on short-term government bonds—about 0.5 percent per year—is a bit of a puzzle.

One way to measure the risk associated with various assets uses the "standard deviation" of their annual returns. This measure shows the range in which roughly two-thirds of the returns fall. For the case of, say, common stocks, the average annual return was 12.2 percent, and the standard deviation shows that in two-thirds of the years the average was within ±20.2 percent of this figure. In other words, in two-thirds of the years, common stocks returned more than –8 percent and less than +32.4 percent. Rates of return on stocks were much more variable than those on bonds.

The Excess Return on Common Stocks

Although the qualitative findings from data such as those in Table 1 are consistent with risk aversion, the quantitative nature of the extra returns to common stock holding are inconsistent with many other studies of risk. These other studies suggest that individuals would accept the extra risk that stocks carry for an extra return of between 1 and 2 percent per year—significantly less than the 7 percent extra actually provided.

TABLE 1 Total Annual Returns, 1926–1994

Financial asset	Average annual rate of return	Standard deviation of rate of return
Common stocks	12.2%	20.2%
Long-term government bonds	5.2	8.8
Short-term government bonds	3.7	3.3

Source: Stocks, Bonds, Bills, and Inflation: 1995 Yearbook (Chicago: Ibbotson Associates, 1995).

[1] Years after 1994 were eliminated here so as not to bias the results by the very strong performance of stocks in the period 1996–2000.

(continued)

One set of explanations focuses on the possibility that the figures in Table 1 understate the risk of stocks. The risk individuals really care about is changes in their consumption plans. If returns on stocks were highly correlated with the business cycle, then they might pose extra risks because individuals would face a double risk from economic downturns—a fall in income and a fall in returns from investments. However, it does not appear that the correlation between stocks' returns and the business cycle is high enough for this extra risk to be very large.

Other suggested explanations for the high return on common stocks include the possibility that there are much higher transactions costs on stocks (hence, the returns are necessary to compensate) and that only people whose incomes are excessively affected by the business cycle buy stocks. Again, however, neither of these explanations has survived closer scrutiny.[2]

To Think About

1. Holding stocks in individual companies probably involves greater risks than are reflected in the data for all stocks in Table 1. Do you think these extra risks are relevant to appraising the extra rate of return that stocks provide?
2. The real return on short-term government bonds implied by Table 1 is less than 1 percent per year. Why do people save at all if this relatively risk-free return is so low?

[2] For an extensive discussion, see N. R. Kocherlakota, "The Equity Premium: It's Still a Puzzle," *Journal of Economic Literature* (March 1996): 42–71.

process is illustrated in Figure 15.5. The figure shows a typical indifference curve for three different types of investors. Each of these indifference curves has a positive slope because of the assumption that investors are risk averse—they can be induced to take on more risk only by the promise of a higher return. The curves also have a convex curvature on the presumption that investors will become increasingly less willing to take on more risk as the overall riskiness of their positions increases.

The three investors illustrated in Figure 15.5 have different attitudes toward risk. Investor I has a very low tolerance for risk. He or she will opt for a mix of investments that includes a lot of the risk-free option (point L). Investor II has a modest toleration for risk, and he or she will opt for a combination of assets that is reasonably representative of the overall market (M). Finally, investor III is a real speculator. He or she will accept a very risky combination of assets (N)—more risky than the overall market. One way for this investor to do that is to borrow to invest in stocks. The impact of any fluctuations in stock prices will then be magnified in its impact on this investor's wealth. Actual financial markets therefore accommodate a wide variety of risk preferences by providing the opportunity to choose various mixes of asset types.

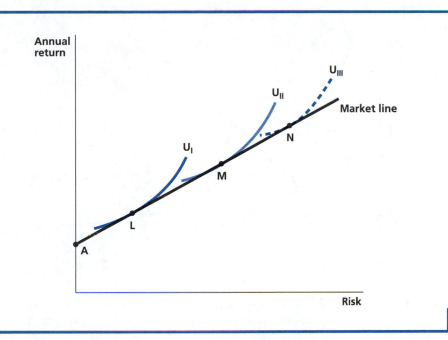

FIGURE 15.5 Choices by Individual Investors Points L, M, and N show the investment choices made by three different investors. Investor I is very risk averse and has a high proportion of the risk-free asset. Investor II has modest toleration for risk and chooses the "market" portfolio. Investor III has a great toleration for risk and leverages his/her position.

THE ECONOMICS OF INFORMATION

In a sense, all individual behavior in uncertain situations can be regarded as a response to a lack of information. If people knew that a coin was going to come up a head, or knew how their investments would fare next year, they would be better off. They may even be willing to pay for additional information to reduce uncertainty, and probably will do so as long as the expected gains from this information exceed its cost. For example, someone trying to decide whether to buy a used car may pay an impartial mechanic to evaluate the car's condition before buying it; someone wishing to buy a color television may check around to find the best price. They may also consult *Consumer Reports* magazine, which gives its subscribers detailed information on various consumer goods. Similarly, farmers may use information about the weather to make decisions about what to grow and when to harvest their crops. In this section, we look briefly at a model that can be used to study such activities.

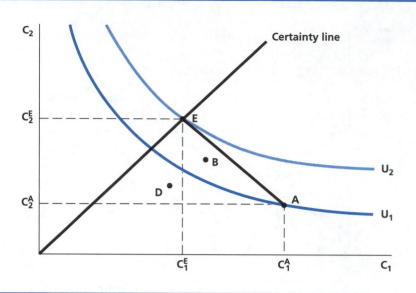

FIGURE 15.6 **Utility Maximization under Uncertainty** The individual faces two possible situations, and the axes record consumption under each of them. If insurance costs are reflected by the slope of AE, this person will opt for complete insurance ($C_1 = C_2$) and raise utility to U_2. Opportunities to acquire information may either raise utility (point B) or reduce utility (point D).

A Utility-Maximizing Model

Many of the issues that arise in studying the economics of information can be examined by using a utility-maximizing model similar to the one we presented in Chapters 2 and 3. The basic outline of the model is presented in Figure 15.6. For this model, an individual is assumed to face two possible outcomes (sometimes called *states of the world*), but he or she does not know which outcome will occur. The individual's consumption in the two states is denoted by C_1 and C_2, and possible values for these are recorded on the axes in Figure 15.6. A particular risk such as point A in the figure promises C_1^A if state 1 occurs and C_2^A if state 2 occurs.

In the situation illustrated at point A, this person has considerably more consumption in state 1 than in state 2. If there were ways to give up some consumption from state 1 to increase consumption in state 2, this person might jump at the chance. He or she could then avoid the possibility of ending up impoverished should state 2 occur. Insurance, as we learned in the previous section, is one mechanism that might be used for this purpose. By paying an insurance premium, this person reduces C_1 (consumption during a good time when things don't go wrong) in order to increase C_2 (consumption when things do go wrong). For example, if the terms at which insurance can be bought are reflected by the slope of the line AE, this person can increase utility from U_1 to U_2 by purchasing complete insurance and moving to point E where $C_1 = C_2$. This outcome is similar to the complete insurance solution examined in Figure 15.2. In other words, by paying a premium of $C_1^A - C_1^E$, this person has assured enough additional consumption when things go wrong ($C_2^E - C_2^A$) that consumption is the same no matter what happens. Buying complete insurance has allowed this person to obtain C_1^E (which equals C_2^E) with certainty.

There are many other ways in which the person pictured in Figure 15.6 might improve his or her situation. For example, if insurance were more costly than indicated by the slope of the line AE, some utility improvement might still be possible. In this case, the budget line would be flatter than AE (because more expensive insurance means that obtaining additional C_2 requires a greater sacrifice of C_1) and this person could not attain utility level U_2. He or she might not opt for complete insurance, selecting instead a point where C_1 still exceeded C_2. But achieving a utility level greater than U_1 might still be possible.

Balancing the Gains and Costs of Information

Another way that this person might better his or her situation would be to gather additional information. The key question, of course, is whether such actions are worth the cost and effort they may entail. Consulting *Consumer Reports* when buying a new automobile might make sense because the cost is low and the potential gains (in terms of getting a better car for one's money) may be significant. Similarly, investing in a few phone calls to discount stores may be worth the time before buying a new television. On the other hand, visiting every store in town to find a lower-priced candy bar clearly carries the information search too far.

These ideas can also be illustrated with the model in Figure 15.6. For an individual initially facing the prospects represented by point A, the issue is whether acquiring information will raise utility above U_1. Because most information is costly to obtain, gathering it will usually result in lower consumption in favorable situations. Reading *Consumer Reports* or checking around for low prices won't improve your consumption prospects if you would have chosen correctly in any case; moreover, the magazine or phone calls cost both time and money. But, gathering the information will probably raise C_2 because the information makes it possible to be a wiser consumer when things go wrong. Point B, for example, represents a utility-improving investment in information acquisition. For that point, the sacrifice of C_1 is more than compensated for by the rise in C_2 and utility rises above U_1. An investment in information that yielded point D would be a poor one, however. Even though the information does have value (C_2 rises), its cost in terms of C_1 is too great and utility would fall below U_1. Again, visiting every store in town in search of a cheaper candy bar is a poor use of time.

Information Differences among Economic Actors

Our discussion suggests two observations about acquiring information. First, the level of information that an individual acquires will depend on how much the information costs. Unlike market prices for most goods (which are usually assumed to be the same for everyone), there are many reasons to believe that information costs may differ significantly among individuals. Some people may possess specific skills relevant to information acquisition (they may be trained mechanics, for example), whereas others may not possess such skills. Some individuals may have other types of experiences that yield valuable information while others may lack that experience. For example, the seller of a product will usually know more about its limitations than will a buyer because the seller knows precisely how the good was made and what possible problems might arise. Similarly, large-scale repeat buyers of a good may have greater access to information about it than do first-time buyers. Finally, some individuals may have invested in some types of information services (for example, by having a computer link to a brokerage firm or by subscribing to *Consumer Reports*) that make the cost of obtaining additional information lower than for someone without such an investment.

Differing preferences provide a second reason why information levels may differ among buyers of the same good. Some people may care a great deal about getting the best buy. Others may have a strong aversion to seeking bargains and will take the first model available. As for any good, the trade-offs that individuals are willing to make are determined by the nature of their preferences.

The possibility that information levels will differ among people raises a number of difficult problems about how markets operate. Although it is customary to assume that all buyers and sellers are fully informed, in a number of situations this assumption is untenable. In the next section, we look at that possibility. In Application 15.5: Safe Driver Insurance Policies, we examine one specific case where these differences can pose major problems in adverse selection for insurance companies.

INFORMATION AND ECONOMIC EFFICIENCY

Existence of imperfect information calls into question the correspondence between competitive prices and economic efficiency. Our proof of the efficiency of competitive prices in Chapter 9 assumed that these equilibrium prices were known to all economic actors. If some actors are not fully informed about

The notion that actuarially fair insurance can increase the utility of risk-averse individuals implies that individuals who face very different probabilities of loss should pay different insurance premiums. The difficulty faced by insurers in this situation is in estimating an individual's probability of loss so that insurance can be correctly priced. When insurers possess less information than do insurance buyers, adverse selection may undermine the entire insurance market.

A Theoretical Model

This possibility is illustrated in Figure 1, which assumes that two individuals initially face identical consumption prospects represented by point A. If person 1 has a relatively low risk of incurring state 2, costs of insurance will be low and this individual's budget constraint is given by AE. If insurance is fairly priced, this risk-averse individual would choose to fully insure by moving to point E on the certainty line. For person 2, losses are more likely. Fair insurance costs are represented by AF. This person too might choose to be fully insured by moving to point F. If the insurance company cannot tell how risky a particular customer is, however, this twin solution is unstable. Person 2 will recognize that he or she can gain utility by purchasing a policy intended for person 1. The additional losses this implies means that the insurer will lose money on policy AE and will have to

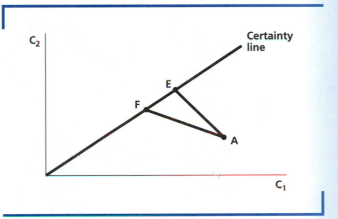

FIGURE 1 Adverse Selection in Insurance Markets Two individuals face identical consumption prospects at A. Low-risk individuals can buy insurance at a rate reflected by AE; high-risk individuals must pay the rate reflected by AF. If insurers cannot distinguish among individuals, high-risk people will choose AE type policies and cause them to be unprofitable. Low-risk individuals will be made worse off by the absence of such policies.

increase its price, thereby reducing person 1's utility. Whether there is a final solution to this type of adverse selection is a complex question. It is possible that person 1 may choose to face the world uninsured rather than buy an unfairly priced policy.[1]

Safe Driver Policies

Traditionally, insurers have used accident data to devise group rating factors that assign higher premium costs to groups such as young males and urban dwellers, who tend to be

[1] For one of the original discussions of this issue, see M. Rothschild and J. Stiglitz, "Equilibrium in Competitive Insurance Markets: An Essay on the Economics of Imperfect Information," *Quarterly Journal of Economics* (November 1976): 629–650.

(continued)

more likely to have accidents. Recently, however, this rate-setting procedure has come under attack as unfairly lumping both safe and unsafe drivers together. A 1989 ballot initiative in California, for example, sharply limited the use of rating factors by requiring them to be primarily individual-based rather than group-based. Because data on individuals is hard to obtain and not very good at predicting accidents, the main result has been to force rates together for all groups. The main beneficiary of the law seems to have been young male drivers in Los Angeles. Figure 1 suggests that individuals in safer groups (females and rural California residents) may have been the losers.

To Think About

1. How are low-risk individuals made worse off by adverse selection?
2. Can you think of other types of situations where risk ratings might differ among individuals? How would you decide which risk differences should be reflected in differences in rates and which should not?

prevailing prices, or (what amounts to the same thing) if information about product quality is not freely available, Adam Smith's invisible hand may not be very effective. Incorrect decisions based on faulty information about price or quality can result in an inefficient allocation of resources.

A vast number of economic models seek to explore the consequences of imperfect information about prices. Here, we briefly review some of these models that are based on a competitive framework (that is, models with large numbers of buyers and sellers).

Asymmetric Information and the "Lemons" Problem

Asymmetric information
A situation in which buyer and sellers have different amounts of information about a market transaction.

A particularly intriguing problem involving imperfect information occurs when the parties to a transaction possess significantly different—**asymmetric**—amounts of **information.** Because this situation was first examined in detail for the case of used cars by George Akerlof, it is sometimes called the "lemons" problem.[4] Suppose used cars are of two types (good cars and lemons) and only the owner of a car knows for certain into which category that vehicle falls. Since buyers cannot differentiate between good cars and lemons, all used cars of a particular type will sell for the same price—somewhere between the true worth of the two types. The owner of a car will choose to keep his or her car if it is a good one (since a good car is worth more than the prevailing market price) but will sell the car if it is a lemon (since a lemon is worth less than the market price). Consequently, only

[4] G. A. Akerlof, "The Market for 'Lemons': Quality Uncertainty and the Market Mechanism," *Quarterly Journal of Economics* (August 1970): 488–500.

lemons will be brought to the used-car market, and the quality of cars traded will be less than expected. Of course, this erosion in quality may be retarded by trustworthy used-car dealers, by development of car-buying expertise by the general public, or by sellers providing proof that their cars are trouble-free. But anyone who has ever shopped for a used car knows the problem of potential lemons is a very real one.

Adverse Selection

In formal terms, the lemons problem is an example of adverse selection in the marketplace. Adverse selection in the used-car market is mirrored in many other markets for used durable goods. Indeed, in some cases (trading between individuals in precious gems, for example), the problem may be so severe as to foreclose practically all exchanges. As we saw earlier, the problem arises in insurance markets when buyers of health or life insurance know more about their own health than do sellers of such insurance. In this case, only high-risk individuals may choose to buy insurance since those who know they are low risk may find insurance too costly. In markets for inputs, adverse selection may be manifested if firms are less able to judge productivity than is the inputs' supplier. Especially productive workers may have no way to illustrate their skills to would-be hirers and may turn down job offers based on employers' perceptions of the average skills of only "typical" workers. In all of these cases, therefore, informational asymmetries may cause competitively determined prices to depart from economic efficiency.

Acquisition and Provision of Information

In many situations, however, these conclusions drawn from the lemon model may be premature because they take no account of possible actions by market participants to improve the information they have. The inefficiency inherent in the adverse selection outcomes provides a powerful incentive for economic actors to acquire information. It might, therefore, be expected that Smith's invisible hand would also be operating in the market for information. In the used-car case, for example, potential buyers might spend both time and money to appraise used cars they are considering. Sellers might also attempt to provide information by showing maintenance records or by offering limited warranties. That is, they will attempt to "signal" the quality of the car they wish to sell. Of course, information may not always be accurate. One might, for example, be skeptical about a 10-year-old car with 45,000 miles on the odometer. Still, as Application 15.6: Looking for Lemons shows, quality deterioration is not a foregone conclusion. It all depends on what information is available.

Looking for Lemons

Economists have spent some time trying to find markets in which the quality deterioration predicted by the lemons model is apparent. Here, we look at three such investigations.

Pickup Trucks

Although used pickup trucks might be expected to exhibit quality deterioration because of asymmetric information between buyers and sellers, that does not appear to be the case. A 1982 study of pickup purchases during the 1970s found that about 60 percent of such trucks were bought used.[1] After controlling for the mileage that trucks had traveled, the author found no difference in the repair records for trucks purchased new versus those purchased used. The author offered two explanations for the relatively good quality of used pickups. First, pickup buyers may have some expertise in truck repair or can gain that expertise by looking at several pickups before buying. Second, it seems possible that, in some cases, sellers provide repair records in order to get good prices for their trucks.

Free Agents in Baseball

Professional baseball players become "free agents" after playing a certain number of years with the teams that initially sign them. Because a player's present team may know much more about his physical conditions and general skills than does a would-be hirer, the market for "used players" may provide another case where asymmetric information leads to quality deterioration. Consistent with this idea, one study found that free agents hired by a new team spent almost twice as many days on baseball's disabled list as did those who were re-signed by their own teams.[2] Of course, teams undoubtedly recognize the adverse incentives inherent in the trading of free agents. So, detailed physical examinations and other kinds of tryouts have become commonplace in recent years. No team wants to be saddled with a multimillion-dollar "dud" if that can be avoided.

Thoroughbreds

Many racehorse "yearlings" are sold at auction. One of the largest of these is the Keeneland auction that is held in September near Lexington, Kentucky. A recent article examined the sale prices from this auction in 1994 for evidence that lemons may appear among the Thoroughbreds.[3] The authors divided sellers at the auction into two groups—those stables that both breed and race horses and those that are only in the breeding business. They reasoned that breeder-only stables would bring all of their yearlings to the auction but that those stables that also raced would have an incentive to keep the best horses for themselves. Although a would-be buyer has relatively little information about the racing quality of any yearling, he or she does know the nature of the stable from which it comes and therefore is in a position to suspect that the racers' offerings will contain relatively more lemons.

---

[1] E. W. Bond, "A Direct Test of the 'Lemons' Model: The Market for Used Pickup Trucks," *American Economic Review* (September 1982): 836–840.
[2] K. Lehn, "Information Asymmetries in Baseball's Free Agent Market," *Economic Inquiry* (January 1984): 37–44.
[3] B. Chezum and D. Wimmer, "Roses or Lemons: Adverse Selection in the Market for Thoroughbred Yearlings," *Review of Economics and Statistics* (August 1997): 521–526.

Evidence on auction prices tended to confirm these expectations. The authors found that, after holding constant such factors as the quality of the yearlings' parents, yearlings from stables that are heavily involved in racing tended to have lower prices than did those from breeder-only stables. Specifically, the authors estimated that each race that a stable entered in 1993 tended to reduce the price of its 1994 yearlings by nearly one percentage point. Apparently, buyers at the Keeneland auction were cautious about buying yearlings from breeders who may have incentives to take the best horses out of their offerings.

To Think About

1. Each of these examples suggests that buyers may take steps to address problems raised by asymmetric information. Do sellers have similar incentives to provide information to buyers?
2. The late 1990s saw a huge number of initial offerings of common stock by Internet start-up companies. How might the lemons model be applied to these initial offerings? Did subsequent events bear out the model?

SUMMARY

In this chapter, we have briefly surveyed the economic theory of uncertainty and information. From that survey, we reached several conclusions that have relevance throughout the study of microeconomics.

- In uncertain situations, individuals are concerned with the expected utility associated with various outcomes. If individuals have a diminishing marginal utility for income, they will be risk averse. That is, they will generally refuse bets that are actuarially fair in dollar terms but result in an expected loss of utility.
- Risk-averse individuals may purchase insurance that allows them to avoid participating in fair bets. Even if the premium is somewhat unfair (in an actuarial sense), they may still buy insurance in order to increase utility.

- Diversification among several uncertain options may reduce risk. Such risk spreading may sometimes be costly, however.
- Financial markets allow people to choose the risk-return combination that maximizes their utility. These markets therefore provide evidence on how risk is priced.
- New information is valuable because it may permit individuals to make new choices that increase expected utility. However, individuals may face differing costs of obtaining information and may therefore acquire different amounts of it.
- With asymmetric information, adverse selection may result in economically inefficient allocations, at least in models with no information acquisition possibilities.

REVIEW QUESTIONS

1. What does it mean to say we expect a fair coin to come up heads about half the time? Would you expect the fraction of heads to get closer to exactly 0.5 as more coins are flipped? Explain how this law of large numbers applies to the risks faced by casinos or insurance companies.

2. Why does the assumption of diminishing marginal utility of income imply risk aversion? Can you think of other assumptions that would result in risk-averse behavior (such as the purchase of insurance) but would not require the difficult-to-verify notion of diminishing marginal utility?

3. "The term *moral hazard* is entirely inappropriate since it maligns individuals' reactions to economic incentives provided by insurance that in other circumstances are regarded as perfectly normal." Do you agree? Explain.
4. The diversification example illustrated in Table 15.1 and Figure 15.3 requires that returns on the two stocks be independent. Explain what "independent" means in this context and why independence of returns provides opportunities for diversification. Why would such opportunities be limited if the returns on the stocks in the example moved together?
5. In order to understand the market line shown in Figure 15.4, it is easiest to assume there are only two assets: a risk-free asset (A) and a risky asset (M). Explain why an individual who mixes these assets in various proportions will be located along the market line. What will determine where on the line he or she actually is?
6. Explain why the slope of the market line in Figure 15.4 and Figure 15.5 shows how risk is "priced" in this market. How might the data in Application 15.4 be plotted to determine this slope?
7. "The model in Figure 15.6 differs from other models because the individual does not ultimately consume both C_1 and C_2; rather, these are the two possible outcomes from one random event." Explain exactly how this model does differ from the one in Chapters 2 and 3 and provide a simple example of how Figure 15.6 might apply to an actual situation.
8. Our analysis in this chapter suggests that individuals have a utility-maximizing amount of information. Explain why some degree of ignorance is optimal.
9. What kinds of information do demanders and suppliers need to make "informed" market transactions? Suppose you set out to hire someone to tutor you in microeconomics. Is the price of this transaction all you need to know, or should more go into your decision? Is the price all the tutor needs to know, or might he or she care about other aspects of the transaction?
10. What does "judge quality by price" or "you get what you pay for" mean? Can you name some goods for which this approach to buying seems reasonable? What about the market for these goods suggests such a strategy may be reasonable? Suggest some situations where the strategy might backfire.

PROBLEMS

15.1 Suppose a person must accept one of three bets:

Bet 1: Win $100 with probability 1/2; lose $100 with probability 1/2.
Bet 2: Win $100 with probability 3/4; lose $300 with probability 1/4.
Bet 3: Win $100 with probability 9/10; lose $900 with probability 1/10.
a. Show that all of these are fair bets.
b. Graph each bet on a utility of income curve similar to Figure 15.1.
c. Explain carefully which bet will be preferred and why.

15.2 Two fast-food restaurants are located next to each other and offer different procedures for ordering food. The first offers five lines leading to a server, whereas the second has a single line leading to five servers, with the next person in the line going to the first available server. Use the assumption that most individuals are risk averse to discuss which restaurant will be preferred.

15.3 A person purchases a dozen eggs and must take them home. Although making trips home is costless, there is a 50 percent chance that all of the eggs carried on one trip will be broken during the trip. This person considers two strategies:

Strategy 1: Take all 12 eggs in one trip.
Strategy 2: Make two trips, taking six eggs in each trip.

a. List the possible outcomes of each strategy and the probabilities of these outcomes. Show that, on average, six eggs make it home under either strategy.
b. Develop a graph to show the utility obtainable under each strategy.
c. Could utility be improved further by taking more than two trips? How would the desirability of this possibility be affected if additional trips were costly?

15.4 Suppose there is a 50-50 chance that a risk-averse individual with a current wealth of $20,000 will contract a debilitating disease and suffer a loss of $10,000.

a. Calculate the cost of actuarially fair insurance in this situation and use a utility-of-income graph (Figure 15.2) to show that the individual will prefer fair insurance against this loss to accepting the gamble uninsured.
b. Suppose two types of insurance policies were available:
   1. A fair policy covering the compete loss
   2. A fair policy covering only half of any loss incurred

   Calculate the cost of the second type of policy and show that the individual will generally regard it as inferior to the first.
c. Suppose individuals who purchase cost-sharing policies of the second type take better care of their health, thereby reducing the loss suffered when ill to only $7,000. In this situation, what will be the cost of a cost-sharing policy? Show that some individuals may now prefer this type of policy. (This is an example of the moral hazard problem in insurance theory.)

15.5 Ms. Fogg is planning an around-the-world trip. The utility from the trip is a function of how much she spends on it (Y) given by

$$U(Y) = \log Y$$

Ms. Fogg has $10,000 to spend on the trip. If she spends all of it, her utility will be

$$U(10,000) = \log 10,000 = 4$$

(In this problem, we are using logarithms to the base 10 for ease of computation.)

a. If there is a 25 percent probability that Ms. Fogg will lose $1,000 of her cash on the trip, what is the trip's expected utility?
b. Suppose that Ms. Fogg can buy insurance against losing the $1,000 (say, by purchasing traveler's checks) at an actuarially fair premium of $250. Show that her utility is higher if she purchases this insurance than if she faces the chance of losing the $1,000 without insurance.
c. What is the maximum amount that Ms. Fogg would be willing to pay to insure her $1,000?
d. Suppose that people who buy insurance tend to become more careless with their cash than those who don't, and assume that the probability of their losing $1,000 is 30 percent. What will be the actuarially fair insurance premium? Will Ms. Fog buy insurance in this situation?

15.6 Losing one's watch can be quite traumatic. Not only does the loss entail giving up an attractive piece of wristwear but it also can result in missing important engagements.

a. Use a diagram similar to Figure 15.6 to show an individual's consumption possibilities in the two states: (1) keep watch and (2) lose watch.
b. What are some of the things a person might do to move toward the certainty line in your diagram? What would determine whether these actions were undertaken or not?
c. If it were possible to buy watch loss insurance that guaranteed an immediate replacement upon loss, how might this raise utility? Indicate this possibility on your diagram.
d. Suppose blue-eyed people are more likely to lose their watches than are brown-eyed people but that, otherwise, such individuals are identical. If insurance companies could tell the color of people's eyes, show how the situations of blue-eyed and brown-eyed people would differ.
e. What difficulties might arise if insurance companies could not know the color of people's eyes but each individual knows the color of his or her own eyes (and therefore the likelihood of watch loss)?

15.7 Suppose Molly Jock wishes to purchase a high-definition television to watch the Olympic Greco-Roman wrestling competition in Beijing. Her current income is $20,000, and she knows where she can buy the television she wants for $2,000. She had heard the rumor that the same set can be bought at Crazy Eddie's (recently out of bankruptcy) for $1,700 but is unsure if the rumor is true. Suppose this individual's utility is given by

$$\text{Utility} = \ln(Y)$$

where Y is her income after buying the television.

a. What is Molly's utility if she buys from the location she knows?
b. What is Molly's utility if Crazy Eddie's really does offer a lower price?
c. Suppose Molly believes there is a 50-50 chance that Crazy Eddie does offer the lower-priced television, but it will cost her $100 to drive to the discount store to find out for sure (the store is far away and has had its phone disconnected). Is it worth it to her to invest the money in the trip? (Hint: To calculate the utility associated with part c, simply average Molly's utility from the two states: [1] Eddie offers the television; [2] Eddie doesn't offer the television.)

15.8 Suppose there are two types of workers, high-ability workers and low-ability workers. Workers' wages are determined by their ability—high-ability workers earn $50,000 per year; low-ability workers earn $30,000. Firms cannot measure workers' abilities, but they can observe whether a worker has a high school diploma. Workers' utility depends on the difference between their wages and the costs they incur in obtaining a diploma.

a. If the cost of obtaining a high school diploma is the same for high-ability and low-ability workers, can there be a separating equilibrium in this situation in which high-ability workers get high-wage jobs and low-ability workers get low wages?
b. What is the maximum amount that a high-ability worker would pay to obtain a high school diploma? Why must a diploma cost more than this for a low-ability person if having a diploma is to permit employers to identify high-ability workers?

15.9 Investment in risky assets can be examined in the state-preference framework by assuming that W^* dollars invested in an asset with a certain return, r,

will yield $W^* (1 + r)$ in both states of the world, whereas investment in a risky asset will yield $W^* (1 + r_g)$ in good times and $W^* (1 + r_b)$ in bad times (where $r_g > r > r_b$).

a. Graph the outcomes from the two investments.
b. Show how a "mixed portfolio" containing both risk-free and risky assets could be illustrated in your graph. How would you show the fraction of wealth invested in the risky asset?
c. Show how individuals' attitudes toward risk will determine the mix of risk-free and risky assets they will hold. In what case would a person hold no risky assets?[5]

15.10 The used-care supply in Metropolis consists of 10,000 cars. The values of these cars range from $5,000 to $15,000 with exactly one car being worth each dollar amount between these two figures. Used-car owners are always willing to sell their cars for what they are worth. Demanders of used cars in Metropolis have no way of telling the value of a particular car. Their demand depends on the average value of cars in the market ($\bar{P}$) and on the price of the cars themselves (P) according to the equation

$$Q = 1.5\,\bar{P} - P$$

a. If demanders base their estimate of $\bar{P}$ on the entire used-car market, what will its value be and what will be the equilibrium price of used cars?
b. In the equilibrium described in part a, what will be the average value of used cars actually traded in the market?
c. If demanders revise their estimate of $\bar{P}$ on the basis of the average value of cars actually traded, what will be the new equilibrium price of used cars? What is the average value of cars traded now?
d. Is there a market equilibrium in this situation at which the actual value of $\bar{P}$ is consistent with supply-demand equilibrium at a positive price and quantity?

---

[5] This problem is taken from J. E. Stiglitz, "The Effects of Income, Wealth, and Capital Gains Taxation in Risk Taking," *The Quarterly Journal of Economics* (May 1969): 263–283.

INTERNET EXERCISES

1. *Expected value.* State lotteries have become a significant source of revenue in many states. For example, in fiscal year 2001, the Massachusetts State Lottery generated $864,464,920 in net revenue. Let's calculate your expected value from playing Mass Cash, a Massachusetts state lottery game. With Mass Cash, you choose a total of five numbers between 1 and 35. The state then draws its own five numbers. If you have three or more numbers that match the state's, you win. Go to the homepage of the Massachusetts State Lottery Commission: *http://www.masslottery.com.* Click on Games, and then click on Mass Cash. How much do you win if you have five matching numbers? Four? Three? Now click on Odds. What are the odds of having five matching numbers? Four? Three? Calculate your expected value of a single play of Mass Cash. Given that each play costs $1, what are your expected net winnings from a single play of Mass Cash? Is Mass Cash a fair game? Explain. Assuming that on average, one million tickets for Mass Cash are sold each week, what is the expected weekly net revenue to the State of Massachusetts from Mass Cash? Suppose the State of Massachusetts were to increase from 35 to 40 the total numbers from which the five are chosen. How will this affect your expected net winnings from playing Mass Cash? Explain. Can you determine unambiguously how the state's expected weekly net revenue will be affected? Explain.

2. *The Capital Asset Pricing Model (CAPM).* In 1990, William F. Sharpe was awarded the Nobel Memorial Prize in Economic Science for his contribution to financial economics (he shared the award with two other leaders in the area, Harry Markowitz and Merton Miller). Professor Sharpe developed the Capital Asset Pricing Model of modern portfolio theory, which is a model describing the relationship between the riskiness of an asset and the asset's required return. Very readable presentations of the basic theory can be found at *http://investopedia.com/university/concepts/concepts8.asp* and at *http://teachmefinance.com/capm.html*. First, read the presentations of the CAPM model at these sites. Now, let's find the beta values for a few specific companies. Go to Multex Investor's Marketguide at: *http://www.marketguide.com/home.asp*. In the search field, type in Microsoft (or its stock ticker, MSFT). Then, in the pull-down menu just below it, choose Snapshot Report. Scroll down the page to the chart showing Key Ratios and Statistics. Under Price and Volume, you will see Microsoft's beta. What is its value? Now repeat the exercise for the following companies: Kellogg (K), Exxon-Mobil (XOM), Nike (NKE), and AOL Time Warner (AOL). Use these betas to sort the companies from least to most risky. Which company's volatility most closely parallels that of the overall market? Explain. Supposing that the risk-free rate of return is 5 percent and the expected return on the overall stock market is 12 percent, use the CAPM model to compute for each company the rate of return required to compensate investors for the riskiness of their investment.

Externalities and Public Goods

Although markets can often yield economically efficient allocations, in many important cases they fail to do so. In this chapter, we look at two specific examples. We begin by describing the general problem of "externalities"—that is, situations where the production or consumption of certain kinds of goods affects third parties not actually involved in the transaction. We also look at various ways that problems raised by externalities in private markets might be addressed. The concluding sections of the chapter then focus on a specific type of externality—the benefits that individuals receive from public goods. Our particular interest there is on asking how well various methods of public decision making (for example, voting) allocate resources to this kind of good.

DEFINING EXTERNALITIES

Externality
The effect of one party's economic activities on another party that is not taken into account by the price system.

An **externality** is an effect of one economic actor's activities on another actor's well-being that is not taken into account by the normal operations of the price system. This definition stresses the direct, nonmarket effect of one actor on another, such as soot falling out of the air or toxic chemicals appearing in drinking water. The definition does not include effects that take place through the market. If I buy a shirt that is on sale before you get there, I may keep you from getting it and thereby affect your well-being. That is not an externality in our sense because the effect took place in a market setting.[1] Its occurrence does not affect the ability of markets to allocate resources efficiently since whether you or I get the shirt is only a distributional question. Real externalities can occur between

---

[1] Sometimes such effects are called "pecuniary" externalities to distinguish them from the "technological" externalities we will be discussing.

any two economic actors. Here, we first illustrate negative (harmful) and positive (beneficial) externalities between firms. We then consider externalities between people and firms and conclude with a few externalities between people.

Externalities between Firms

Consider two firms—one producing eyeglasses, another producing charcoal (this is an actual example from nineteenth-century English law). The production of charcoal is said to have an external effect on the production of eyeglasses if the output of eyeglasses depends not only on the amount of inputs chosen by the eyeglass firm but also on the level at which the production of charcoal is carried on. Suppose these two firms are located near each other, and the eyeglass firm is downwind from the charcoal firm. In this case, the output of eyeglasses may depend not only on the level of inputs the eyeglass firm uses itself but also on the amount of charcoal in the air, which affects its precision grinding wheels. The level of pollutants, in turn, is determined by the output of the charcoal firm. Increases in charcoal output would cause fewer high-quality eyeglasses to be produced even though the eyeglass firm has no control over this negative effect.[2]

The relationship between two firms may also be beneficial. Most examples of positive externalities are rather bucolic in nature. Perhaps the most famous, proposed by James Meade, involves two firms, one producing honey by raising bees and the other producing apples.[3] Because the bees feed on apple blossoms, an increase in apple production will improve productivity in the honey industry. The beneficial effects of having well-fed bees is a positive externality to the beekeeper. Similarly, bees pollinate apple crops and the beekeeper provides an external benefit to the orchard owner. Later in this chapter, we examine this situation in greater detail because, surprisingly enough, the beekeeper–apple grower relationship has played an important role in economic research on the significance of externalities.

Externalities between Firms and People

Firms may impact directly on individuals' well-being. A cement firm that spews dust into the air imposes costs on people living near the plant in the form of ill health and increased dirt and grime. Similar effects arise from firms' pollution of water (for example, mining firms that dump their waste into Lake Superior, reducing the lake's recreational value to people who wish to fish there), misuse of land (strip mining that is an eyesore and may interfere with water supplies), and production of noise (airports that are located near major cities). In all of these

---

[2] We will find it necessary to redefine the assumption of "no control" considerably as the analysis of this chapter proceeds.
[3] James Meade, "External Economies and Diseconomies in a Competitive Situation," *Economic Journal* (March 1952): 54–67.

cases, at least on first inspection, it seems that firms will not take any of these external costs into account when deciding how much to produce.

Of course, people may also have external effects on firms. Drivers' auto pollution harms the productivity of citrus growers, cleaning up litter and graffiti is a major expense for shopping centers, and the noise of Saturday night rock concerts on college campuses probably affects motel rentals. In these cases, there may be no simple way for the affected parties to force the people who generate the externalities to take the full costs of their actions into account.

Externalities between People

Finally, the activity of one person may affect the well-being of someone else. Playing a radio too loud, smoking cigars, or driving during peak hours are all consumption activities that may negatively affect the utility of others. Planting an attractive garden or shoveling the snow off one's sidewalk may, on the other hand, provide beneficial externalities. Often, however, these activities will not be reflected in market transactions among the people involved.

Reciprocal Nature of Externalities

Although these examples of externalities picture one actor as the cause of the problem and some other actor as the helpless victim (or beneficiary), that is not a very useful way of looking at the problem. By definition, externalities require (at least) two parties and in a sense each should be regarded as the "cause." If the producer of eyeglasses had not located its factory near the charcoal furnace, it would not have suffered any negative effects on its grinding wheels; if individuals didn't live below airport flight paths, noise would only be a minor problem; and if you were out of earshot, it wouldn't matter that someone else had the radio's volume turned up. Recognizing these reciprocal relationships is not intended to exonerate polluters, only to clarify the nature of the problem. In all of these cases, two economic actors are seeking to use the same resource, and (as we illustrate in Application 16.1: Secondhand Smoke) there are no unambiguous economic principles for deciding whose claim is stronger.

EXTERNALITIES AND ALLOCATIONAL EFFICIENCY

It has traditionally been argued that the presence of externalities such as those we have just described can cause a market to operate inefficiently. We discussed the reasons for this briefly in the Appendix to Chapter 9 and repeat these reasons here using the example of eyeglass and charcoal producers. Production of eyeglasses produces no externalities but is negatively affected by the level of charcoal output. We now show that resources may be allocated inefficiently in this situation. Remember that for an allocation of resources to be efficient price must be

Many of the economic issues that arise in cases of externalities are illustrated in recent controversies over secondhand smoke. The term *secondhand smoke* (more formally, *environmental tobacco smoke,* or *ETS*) refers to the effects of smokers' consumption of cigarettes and other tobacco products on third-party bystanders. This is a separate issue from the harmful effects of smoking on smokers themselves—an activity that generally does not involve externalities, strictly defined.

Health Effects of Secondhand Smoke

Although few doubt that secondhand smoke is annoying, the question of whether ETS has serious health consequences is quite controversial. The Environmental Protection Agency estimates that approximately 2,200 people die annually as a result of the increased incidence of lung cancer among those exposed to ETS. The agency suggests that the figure could be much higher if possible effects of ETS on heart disease were also taken into account. But these estimates, as is the case for many such epidemiological calculations, are based on relatively simple comparisons between individuals who live or work in proximity to smokers and those who do not. Many unbiased observers believe that the case against ETS remains unproved.

Reciprocal Nature of the ETS Externality

As for all externalities, the ETS externality involves reciprocal effects. Smokers harm bystanders with their smoke, but attempts to limit the "rights" of smokers impose inconveniences that need not arise if the bystanders were not present. Although such effects are seldom discussed, they are not necessarily trivial. For example, one study of the potential impact of workplace restrictions on smoking calculates a loss in smokers' consumer surplus of approximately $20 billion per year.[1] Of course, such estimates may be as far off the mark as are those for the health effects of ETS. The fact that any specification of rights will significantly affect the welfare of the parties involved makes the issue a controversial one in deciding how a particular resource (air) should be used.

Private Actions

For many years, decisions regarding secondhand smoke were handled through private transactions. Railroads designated smoking cars; airlines and restaurants had smoking sections; and workers would negotiate among themselves over whether smoking on the job would be permitted. Such private restrictions on smoking have been tightened in recent years, mainly in response to market pressures. For example, all airlines have banned smoking from all flights, and many restaurants have gone smoke free. A few restaurants and theaters offer a "smoke-free card" that provides discounts to nonsmokers. And many hotel chains have begun segregating smokers and nonsmokers by floors.

Public Actions

Concern about ETS has also been reflected in the demand for government regulation. The Occupational Safety and Health Administration has proposed banning all workplace

[1] W. K. Viscusi, "Secondhand Smoke: Facts and Fantasy," *Regulation,* no. 3 (1995): 42–49.

(continued)

smoking in public areas, and recent polls suggest that the public would support a broader ban on smoking in all public places. Some economists have asked whether such additional restrictions (beyond those adopted privately) are really necessary. They ask for clear evidence that private choices by smokers and nonsmokers have not been adequate for ameliorating most of the adverse effects of smoking externalities. Given the declining number of smokers and the increasing aggressiveness with which nonsmokers pursue their rights, however, it seems likely that smoking regulations will become increasingly restrictive.

To Think About

1. Some analysts argue that smokers create additional externalities in their behavior by driving up health care and insurance costs for nonsmokers. Are such effects "externalities"? How, if at all, do they distort the allocation of resources?
2. Nonsmokers can often avoid ETS through their own behavior (for example, by refusing to patronize establishments that permit smoking). How, if at all, should such actions be taken into account in defining an optimal policy toward ETS?

equal to true social marginal cost in each market. If the market for eyeglasses is perfectly competitive (as we assume both markets to be), their price will indeed be equal to this good's private marginal cost. Since there are no externalities in eyeglass production, there is no need to make a distinction between private and social marginal cost in this case.

For charcoal production, the story is more complex. The producer of charcoal will still produce that output for which price is equal to private marginal cost. This is a direct result of the profit-maximization assumption. However, because of the negative effect that production of charcoal has on eyeglass production, it will not be the case that private and social marginal costs of charcoal production are equal. Rather, the **social cost** of charcoal production is equal to the private cost *plus* the cost that charcoal production imposes on eyeglass firms in terms of reduced or inferior output. The charcoal-producing firm does not recognize this effect and produces too much charcoal. Society would be made better off by reallocating resources away from charcoal production and toward the production of other goods.

Social costs
Costs of production that include both input costs and costs of the externalities that production may cause.

A Graphical Demonstration

Figure 16.1 illustrates the misallocation of resources that results from the externality in charcoal production. Assuming that the charcoal producer is a price taker, the demand curve for its output is a horizontal line at the prevailing market price (say, P*). Profits are maximized at q* where price is equal to the private marginal cost of producing charcoal (MC). Because of the externality that charcoal production imposes on eyeglass makers, however, the social marginal cost of

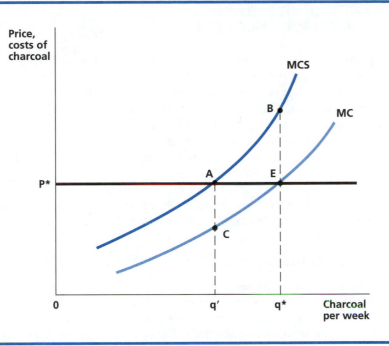

FIGURE 16.1 An Externality in Charcoal Production Causes an Inefficient Allocation of Resources Because production of charcoal imposes external costs on eyeglass makers, social marginal costs (MCS) exceed private marginal costs (MC). In a competitive market, the firm would produce q* at a price of P*. At q*, however, MCS > P* and resource allocation could be improved by reducing output to q'. With bargaining among the parties, however, output level q' may be arrived at voluntarily.

this production (MCS) exceeds MC as shown in Figure 16.1. The vertical gap between the MCS and the MC curves is a measure of the harm that producing an extra unit of charcoal imposes on eyeglass makers. At q*, the social marginal cost of producing charcoal exceeds the price people are willing to pay for this output (P*). Resources are misallocated, and production should be reduced to q' where social marginal cost and price are equal. In making this reduction, the reduction in total social costs (area ABq*q') exceeds the reduction in total spending on charcoal (given by area AEq*q'). This comparison shows that the allocation of resources is improved by a reduction in charcoal output because social costs are reduced to a greater extent than are consumers' expenditures on charcoal. Consumers can reallocate their spending toward something else that involves lower social costs than charcoal does.

MicroQuiz 16.1

At several places in previous chapters we have illustrated "deadweight loss" triangles. Explain why the triangle ABE in Figure 16.1 represents exactly the same kind of deadweight loss as in the monopoly case.

PROPERTY RIGHTS, BARGAINING, AND THE COASE THEOREM

The conclusion that externalities always distort the allocation of resources should not be accepted uncritically. To explore the issue further, we need to introduce the concept of property rights to show how these rights might be traded voluntarily between the two firms. Simply put, **property rights** are the legal specification of who owns a good and of the types of trades that the current owner is allowed to make. Some goods may be defined as **common property** that is owned by society at large and may be used by anyone; others may be defined as **private property** that is owned by specific people. Private property may either be *exchangeable* or *nonexchangeable,* depending on whether the good in question may or may not be traded to someone else. In this book, we have been primarily concerned with exchangeable private property and we consider these types of property rights here.

Property rights
The legal specification of who owns a good and the trades the owner is allowed to make with it.

Common property
Property that may be used by anyone without cost.

Private property
Property that is owned by specific people who may prevent others from using it.

Costless Bargaining and Competitive Markets

For the purposes of the charcoal-eyeglass eternality, it is interesting to consider the nature of the property right that might be attached to the air shared by the charcoal and eyeglass firms. Suppose property rights were defined so as to give sole rights to use of the air to one of the firms, but that the firms were free to bargain over exactly how the air might be used. At first, you might think that if rights to the air were given to the charcoal producer, pollution would result; whereas, if rights were given to the eyeglass firm, the air would remain pure and grinding machines would work properly. This might not be the case, because your snap conclusion disregards the bargains that might be reached by the two parties. Indeed, some economists have argued that if there are no transactions (bargaining) costs, the two parties left on their own will arrive at the efficient output (q'), and this result will be true regardless of who "owns" the rights to use the air.

Ownership by the Polluting Firm

Suppose the charcoal firm owns the right to use the air as it wishes. It must then add the costs (if any) related to this ownership into its total costs. What are the costs associated with air ownership? Again, the opportunity cost notion provides the answer. For the charcoal firm, the costs of using the air as a dumping place for its dust are what someone else is willing to pay for this resource in its best alternative use. In our example, only the eyeglass maker has some alternative uses for the air (to keep it clean), and the amount that this firm would be willing to pay for clean air is precisely equal to the external damage done by charcoal pollution. If the charcoal firm calculates its costs correctly, its marginal cost curve (including the implicit cost of air use rights) becomes MCS in Figure 16.1. The firm will therefore produce q' and sell the remaining air use rights to the eyeglass maker for a fee of some amount between AEC (the lost profits from producing q' rather than q* tons of charcoal) and ABEC (the maximum amount the eyeglass maker would pay to avoid having charcoal output increased from q' to q*).

Ownership by the Injured Firm

A similar result would occur if eyeglass makers owned the rights to use the air as they pleased. In this case, the charcoal producer would be willing to pay up to its total profits for the right to pollute the air (assuming, as we have all along, that there is no less damaging way to make charcoal). The eyeglass maker will accept these payments as long as they exceed the costs imposed on it by the charcoal firm's pollution. The ultimate result of bargaining will be for the charcoal firm to offer a payment for the right to "use" the air to dispose of the amount of soot and ash associated with output level q'. The eyeglass maker will not sell the rights to undertake any further pollution into "its" air because, beyond q', what the charcoal firm would be willing to pay (P* − MC) falls short of the cost of this additional pollution (MCS − MC). Again, as when the charcoal firm had the property rights for air usage, an efficient allocation can be reached by relying on voluntary bargaining between the two firms. In both situations, some production of charcoal takes place, and there will therefore be some air pollution. Having no charcoal output (and no pollution) would be inefficient in the same sense that producing q* is inefficient—scarce resources would not be efficiently allocated. In this case, there is some "optimal level" of air pollution that may be achieved through bargains between the firms involved.

The Coase Theorem

We have shown that the two firms left on their own can arrive at the efficient output level (q'). Assuming that making such transactions is costless, both parties will recognize the advantages of striking a deal. Each will be led by the "invisible hand" to the same output level that would be achieved through an ideal merger. That solution will be reached no matter how the property rights associated with air use are assigned. The pollution-producing firm has exactly the same incentives to choose an efficient output level as does the injured firm. The ability of the two firms to bargain freely causes the true social costs of the externality to be recognized by each in its decisions. This result is sometimes referred to as the **Coase theorem** after the economist Ronald Coase, who first proposed it in this form.[4]

Coase theorem
If bargaining is costless, the social cost of an externality will be taken into account by the parties, and the allocation of resources will be the same no matter how property rights are assigned.

Distributional Effects

There are distributional effects that do depend on who is assigned the property rights to use the air. If the charcoal firm is given the air rights, it will get the fee

[4] See Ronald Coase, "The Problem of Social Cost," *Journal of Law and Economics* (October 1960): 1–44.

paid by the eyeglass maker, which will make the charcoal producer at least as well off as it was producing q*. If the eyeglass firm gets the rights, it will receive a fee for air use that at least covers the damage the air pollution does. Because, according to the Coase result, the final allocation of resources will be unaffected by the way in which property rights are assigned,[5] any assessment of the desirability of the various possibilities might be made on equity grounds. For example, if the owners of the charcoal firm were very wealthy and those who make eyeglasses were poor, we might argue that ownership of the air use rights should be given to eyeglass makers on the basis of distributional equity. If the situation were reversed, one could argue for giving the charcoal firm the rights. The price system may often be capable of solving problems in the allocation of resources caused by externalities, but, as always, it will not necessarily achieve equitable solutions. Such issues of equity in the assignment of property rights arise in every allocational decision, not only in the study of externalities, however.

MicroQuiz 16.2

The Coase theorem requires both that property rights be fully specified and that there be no transactions costs.

1. Would efficiency be achieved if transactions costs were zero but property rights did not exist?

2. Would efficiency be achieved if transactions costs were high but property rights were fully defined? Would your answer to this question depend on which party was assigned the property rights?

The Role of Transactions Costs

The result of the Coase theorem depends crucially on the assumption of zero transactions costs. If the costs of striking bargains were high, the workings of this voluntary exchange system might not be capable of achieving an efficient result. In the next section, we examine situations where transactions costs are high and show that competitive markets will need some help if they are to achieve efficient results. Still, as Application 16.2: Property Rights in Nature shows, the market system often has a surprising power to handle certain types of externalities.

EXTERNALITIES WITH HIGH TRANSACTIONS COSTS

When transactions costs are high, externalities may cause real losses in economic welfare. The fundamental problem is that, with high transactions costs, economic actors face no pressure to recognize the third-party effects they have. All solutions to externality problems in these cases must therefore find some way to get the actors to "internalize" the third-party effects they cause. In this section, we look at three such methods, each of which has both advantages and disadvantages.

---

[5] Assuming that the wealth effects of how property rights are assigned do not affect demand and cost relationships in the charcoal market.

The notion that the specification and enforcement of private property rights may aid in coping with externalities has provided a number of surprising insights. Some of the most picturesque of these involve natural surroundings.

Bees and Apples

Bees pollinate apple trees, and apple blossoms provide nectar with which bees produce honey. Despite the seeming complexity of these externalities, it appears that markets function quite well in this situation. In many locales, contractual bargaining between beekeepers and orchard owners is well developed. Standard contracts provide for the renting of bees for the pollination of many crops. Research has shown that the rents paid in these contracts accurately reflect the value of honey that is yielded from the rentals. Apple growers, for example, must pay higher rents than clover growers because apple blossoms yield considerably less honey.[1] Because bargaining among those affected by these externalities is relatively costless, this seems to be one case where the Coase theorem applies directly.

Shellfish

Overfishing results from an externality—no single fisher takes into account the fact that his or her catch will reduce the amounts that others can catch. In the open seas, there is no easy solution to this sort of externality. But in coastal situations, where property rights can be effectively policed, the harmful effects of overfishing can be ameliorated. When these rights are defined and enforced, private owners will recognize how their harvesting practices affect their own fish stocks.

This possibility has been especially well documented for coastal shellfish, such as oysters and lobsters. In cases where property rights to specific fishing grounds are well defined, average catches are much higher over the long run. For example, one comparison of oyster yields in Virginia and Maryland during the 1960s found that catches were nearly 60 percent higher in Virginia. The authors attributed this finding to the fact that Virginia state law made it much easier to enforce private coastal fishing rights than did Maryland law.[2] Similar results have been found by comparing harvest yields between family-owned and communal lobster beds on the Maine coast.

Elephants

The potential conservationist value of property rights enforcement has recently been discovered by African nations who are seeking to preserve their elephant herds. In the past, ivory hunters have been ruthless in their killing of elephants. Strong, international sanctions have been largely ineffective in preventing the carnage. During the 1980s, for example, elephant populations declined by more than 50 percent in East African countries, such as Kenya.

---

[1] The classic examination of this question is S. N. S. Cheung, "The Fable of the Bees: An Economic Investigation," *Journal of Law and Economics* (April 1973): 11–33.

[2] R. J. Agnello and L. P. Donnelly, "Property Rights and Efficiency in the Oyster Industry," *Journal of Law and Economics* (October 1975): 521–533.

(continued)

Several southern African nations, such as Botswana, have taken a different approach to elephant preservation. These countries have allowed villages to capitalize on their local elephant herds by giving them the right to sell a limited number of elephant hunting permits and by encouraging them to develop tourism in protected elephant areas. Essentially, the elephants have been converted into the private property of villages, which now have an incentive to maximize the value of this asset. Elephant herds have more than doubled in Botswana.

To Think About

1. In the bees-apples case, considerable bargaining may be required to reach a satisfactory contract, and, in some instances, the bees may wander out of their contracted areas. What factors would determine whether private property contracts will be developed in natural settings?

2. Isn't the notion of "privatizing wildlife" (as Botswana has done for elephants) crass commercialism? Wouldn't a better solution be to develop a conservationist ethic under which everyone agreed to nurture the planet's wild heritage?

Legal Redress

The operation of the law may sometimes provide a way for taking externalities into account. If those who are injured by an externality have the right to sue for damages in a court of law, the possibility of such suits may lead to internalization. For example, if the charcoal producer shown in Figure 16.1 can be sued for the harm that it does to eyeglass makers, payment of damages will increase the costs associated with charcoal production. Hence, the charcoal marginal cost curve will shift upward to MCS and an efficient allocation of resources will be achieved.

This discussion suggests that different types of law might be applied in cases of externalities depending on whether transactions costs are high or low. When transactions costs are low, careful specification of rights under property law can be used to achieve efficient results because the Coase theorem applies. When transactions costs are high, the law of "torts" (harms) should be used because lawsuits can get those who create externalities to recognize the damage that they do. Hence, the possibility of legal redress provides an important complement to the Coase theorem.[6]

Of course, using the legal system requires real resources. Lawyers, judges, and expert witnesses do not come cheap. These costs may

---

[6] These insights were first noted in G. Calabresi and A. D. Melamed, "Property Rules, Liability Rules, and Inalienability," *Harvard Law Review* (March 1972): 1089–1128. Notice that the lawsuits described here are intended only to recover "compensatory damages" that compensate for the harm that externalities do.

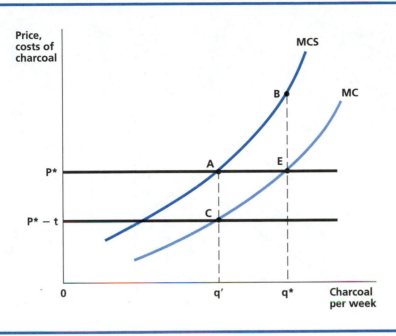

FIGURE 16.2 Taxation Solution to the Externality Problem An excise tax of amount t would reduce the net price of charcoal to P* − t. At that price, the firm would choose to produce the socially optimal level of charcoal output (q′).

multiply rapidly as the number of injured parties increases. Hence, any full assessment of the desirability of using the law to obtain market-like solutions to the externality problem must take the costs of using the law into account. Still, it seems clear that in many cases of externalities, such as automobile accidents or other types of personal injuries, use of the legal system may prove to be expeditious.

Taxation

A second way to achieve internalization is through taxation. This remedy was first suggested by the welfare economist A. C. Pigou[7] in the 1920s, and it remains the standard economists' solution for many types of externalities.

The taxation solution is illustrated in Figure 16.2. Again, MC and MCS represent the private and social marginal costs of charcoal production, and the market price of charcoal is given by P*. An excise tax of amount t would reduce the net price received by the firm to P* − t, and at that price the firm would choose to produce q′. The tax causes the firm to reduce its output to the socially optimal

[7] A. C. Pigou, *The Economics of Welfare*, 4th ed. (London: Macmillan, 1946); Pigou also stressed the desirability of providing subsidies to firms that produce beneficial externalities.

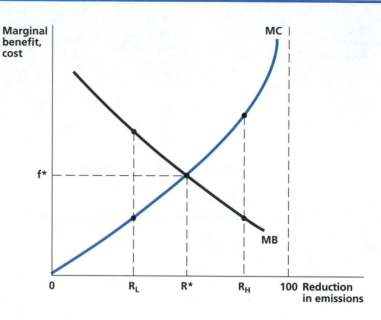

FIGURE 16.3 Optimal Pollution Abatement The MB and MC curves show the marginal benefits and marginal costs, respectively, of pollution abatement. R* represents an optimal allocation of resources to this purpose. Such an outcome may be attained through the imposition of an effluent fee of f*, through the sale of marketable pollution permits, or through direct controls.

amount. At q′, the firm incurs private marginal costs of P* − t and imposes external costs on eyeglass makers of t per unit. The per-unit tax is therefore exactly equal to the extra costs that charcoal producers impose on eyeglass producers.[8] The problem then for government regulators is to decide on the proper level for such a **Pigovian tax**.

Pigovian tax
A tax or subsidy on an externality that brings about an equality of private and social marginal costs.

Regulation of Externalities

A third set of ways to control externalities in situations of high transactions costs is through regulation. In order to look at some of the issues that arise in regulation, let's consider the case of policy toward environmental pollution. The horizontal axis in Figure 16.3 shows percentage reductions in environmental pollu-

[8] If the charcoal firm here represents an entire industry, then the tax would, as in Chapter 8, raise the market price of charcoal. If the industry exhibited constant costs, in the long run, price would rise by the exact amount of the tax, and demand would be reduced to the socially optimal level by that price rise. In this case, the tax would be fully paid by charcoal consumers in the long run. If charcoal production exhibited increasing costs, some portion of the Pigovian tax would be paid by suppliers of inputs to the charcoal industry.

tion from some source below what would occur in the absence of any regulation. The curve MB in the figure shows the additional social benefits obtained by reducing such pollution by one more unit. These benefits consist of possibly improved health, the availability of additional recreational or aesthetic benefits, and improved production opportunities for other firms. As for most economic activities, this provision of benefits is assumed to exhibit diminishing returns— the curve MB slopes downward to reflect the fact that the marginal benefits from additional reductions in pollution decline as stricter controls are implemented.

The curve MC in Figure 16.3 represents the marginal costs incurred in reducing environmental emissions. The positive slope of this curve reflects our usual assumptions of increasing marginal costs. Controlling the first 50 or 60 percent of pollutants is a relatively low-cost activity, but controlling the last few percentage points is rather costly. As reductions in emissions approach 100 percent, marginal costs rise very rapidly.

Optimal Regulation

Given this configuration, it is clear that R^* is the optimal level of pollution reduction. For reductions less than R^* (say, R_L), the marginal benefits associated with further tightening of environmental controls exceed the marginal cost of achieving lower pollution levels, so emissions should be reduced further. Reductions in excess of R^* are also inefficient—environmental control can be pushed too far. At R_H, the marginal cost of emissions control exceeds the marginal benefits obtained, so less-strict regulation may be desirable. To noneconomists, the notion that there is an optimal level of pollution (that R^* is less than 100 percent) may sound strange, but this result reflects the general principles of efficient resource allocation we have been studying throughout this book.

Fees, Permits, and Direct Controls

There are three general ways that emissions reductions of R^* might be attained through regulatory policy. First, the government may adopt a Pigovian-type "effluent fee" of f^* for each percent that pollution is not reduced. Faced with such a charge, the polluting firm will choose the optimal emissions reduction level, R^*. For reductions less than R^*, the fee exceeds the marginal cost of pollution abatement, so a profit-maximizing firm will opt for abatement. Reductions in emissions of more than R^* would be unprofitable, however, so the firm will opt to pay the fee on $(100 - R^*)$ of its pollutants. One important feature of the fee approach is that the firm itself is free to choose whatever combination of output reduction and adoption of pollution control technology achieves R^* at minimal cost.

A similar allocational result would be attained if governmental regulators issued permits that allow firms to "produce" $(100 - R^*)$ percent of their unregulated emissions levels. Figure 16.3 implies that, if such permits were freely tradable, they would sell for a price of f^*. In this case, a competitive market for pollution permits ensures that the optimal level of emissions reductions will be attained at minimal social cost.

A third regulatory strategy would be simply to implement reductions of R* through direct controls. In this case, which tends to be the one most often followed in the United States, firms would be told the level of emissions they would be allowed. Such a direct approach can, in principle, duplicate the allocations provided by lawsuits, Pigovian taxation or marketable permits. If, as is often the case, direct control is also accompanied by specification of the precise mechanism by which R* is to be achieved (for example, through the installation of a special kind of pollution-control equipment) the cost-minimization incentives incorporated in the other approaches may be lost. Application 16.3: Regulating Power Plant Emissions looks at a situation where a variety of regulatory strategies have been used.

MicroQuiz 16.3

Suppose that the government does not have detailed information about the costs of the firms that produce pollution.

1. Why are the three methods described here for attaining R* superior to a regulatory strategy that requires firms to install a specific technology that would allow them to attain R*?

2. How do the three strategies minimize the information that the government needs?

PUBLIC GOODS

The activities of governments can have important externalities. For many of the goods that governments provide, the benefits are shared by all citizens. For example, one of the primary functions of all governments is the provision of a common defense. All citizens benefit from this whether or not they pay taxes for it. More generally, the government establishes such things as property rights and laws of contract that create a legal environment in which economic transactions occur. Benefits arising from this environment are, again, shared by all citizens.

One way of summarizing these observations is to conclude that the government provides many *public goods* to its citizens. In a sense, governments are not very different from other organizations such as labor unions, professional associations, or even fraternities and sororities. They provide benefits to and impose obligations on their members. Governments differ primarily because they may be able to achieve economies of scale by virtue of their all-inclusive character and because they have the ability to finance their activities through compulsory taxation.

Attributes of Public Goods

The preceding discussion of public goods is circular—governments are defined as producers of public goods, and public goods are defined as the stuff governments produce. Many economists (starting with Paul Samuelson) have tried to attach a

The majority of electric power plants throughout the world burn coal for fuel. This burning results in the emission of a variety of unhealthy byproducts. Most important, burning combines the sulfur in the coal with oxygen to produce sulfuric acid. This pollutant has been associated with the creation of the "acid rain" that harms the lakes and forests of the eastern United States and Canada. The acidification problem is even more severe in Europe, and its effects have recently been found in many areas of Russia and China.

Regulation of Production Technology

Most power-plant regulation in the United States has followed a "command-and-control" (CAC) approach. Under this approach, air quality standards are defined by law, and plants are required to install specific equipment that enables them to meet the standards. To achieve the defined goal, most large power plants must install "scrubbers" that clean the exhaust fumes in their stacks.

A variety of studies have found that these regulations are not especially cost-effective. A primary reason for the extra costs is the inflexibility of the regulations—plants are not free to adapt the required technology to prevailing meteorological or geographical realities. One survey of studies of cost-effectiveness concludes that, nationwide, costs may have exceeded a least-cost ideal by a factor of two or more.[1]

Emission Charges

An alternative, more efficient approach favored by many economists would follow Pigou's proposal by imposing a tax on power plants for their emissions. With such a charge, utility owners would be free to choose any technology that promised emissions reductions at a marginal cost that is equal to or less than this charge. Computer simulations of the effect suggest that it would be considerably more cost-effective. Both Japan and France have made significant use of the emissions-charge approach.

Emissions Trading

The Clean Air Act amendments of 1990 incorporated an innovation in regulatory procedures that may improve the cost-effectiveness of the CAC procedures used in the United States. Under this new plan, power plants that reduce their pollution levels below those specified by the air quality standards would achieve "credits" for doing so. They would then be permitted to sell those credits to other firms. The purchasing firm can exceed air quality standards by the extent of its credits. In principle, this should reduce the overall costs associated with achieving any particular air quality standards, because those firms that can achieve additional reductions at the lowest marginal cost will do so. Early results from studies of such emissions trading suggest that cost savings of approximately 50 percent are being achieved over what would prevail under a pure CAC framework.[2]

[1] T. Tietenberg, *Environmental and Natural Resource Economics,* 3rd ed. (New York: Harper-Collins, 1992): 402–405.
[2] R. Rico, "The U.S. Allowance Trading System for Sulfur Dioxide: An Update on Market Experience," *Energy and Resource Economics* (March 1995): 115–129.

(continued)

CO_2 and Global Warming

Although most of the focus on regulating power plant emissions has focused on SO_2, there are growing concerns that carbon dioxide emissions from such plants may be equally harmful, primarily because they may contribute to global warming. Under the Kyoto Protocol, nations would be required to reduce their CO_2 emissions significantly and, although the United States and most developing countries have not adopted this plan, a few states (such as California) have opted to do so on their own. As with SO_2 regulation, a number of approaches have been suggested for CO_2 reduction including direct regulation, institution of a Pigovian-like carbon tax, and adopting various emissions trading schemes.[3]

To Think About

1. Would a tax on coal output have the same effects on firms' input choices as a tax on emissions themselves?
2. Emissions trading credits have sometimes been purchased by environmental groups. Does this subvert the goal of the program?

[3] For a discussion of these possibilities, see the extended survey in *The Economist,* July 4, 2002.

---

more specific, technical definition to the term *public good.*[9] The purpose of such a definition is to differentiate those goods that are public by nature from those that are suitable for private markets. The most common definitions of public goods stress two attributes that seem to characterize many of the goods governments produce: nonexclusivity and nonrivalry.

Nonexclusivity

One property that distinguishes many public goods is whether people may be excluded from the benefits the goods provide. For most private goods, exclusion is indeed possible. I can easily be excluded from consuming a hamburger if I don't pay for it. In some cases, exclusion is either very costly or impossible. National defense is the standard example. Once an army or navy is set up, everyone in a country benefits from its protection whether they pay for it or not. Similar comments apply on a local level to such goods as mosquito control or inoculation programs against disease. In these cases, once the programs are implemented, all of the residents of a community benefit from them and no one can be excluded from those benefits, regardless of whether he or she pays for them. These **nonexclusive goods** pose problems for markets because people are tempted to "let the other guy do it" and benefit from this person's spending.

Nonexclusive goods
Goods that provide benefits that no one can be excluded from enjoying.

[9] See Paul A. Samuelson, "The Pure Theory of Public Expenditure," *Review of Economics and Statistics* (November 1954): 387–389. Usually the implication is that governments should not produce goods because competitive markets will do a better job.

Nonrivalry

A second property that characterizes many public goods is nonrivalry. **Nonrival goods** are goods for which benefits can be provided to additional users at zero marginal social cost. For most goods, consumption of additional amounts involves some marginal costs of production. Consumption of one more hot dog, for example, requires that various resources be devoted to its production. For some goods, however, this is not the case. Consider one more automobile crossing a highway bridge during an off-peak period. Because the bridge is already there anyway, one more vehicle crossing it requires no additional resources and does not reduce consumption of anything else. One more viewer tuning into a television channel involves no additional cost even though this action would result in additional consumption taking place. Consumption by additional users of such a good is nonrival in that this additional consumption involves zero marginal social costs of production; such consumption does not reduce other people's ability to consume. Again, goods with the nonrival property pose problems for markets because the efficient price (= marginal cost) is zero.

Nonrival goods
Goods that additional consumers may use at zero marginal costs.

Categories of Public Goods

The concepts of nonexclusivity and nonrivalry are in some ways related. Many goods that are nonexclusive are also nonrival. National defense and mosquito control are two examples of goods for which exclusion is not possible and for which additional consumption takes place at zero marginal cost. Many other instances might be suggested.

These concepts are not identical. Some goods may possess one property but not the other. It is, for example, impossible (or at least very costly) to exclude some fishing boats from ocean fisheries, yet one more boat imposes social costs in the form of a reduced catch for all concerned. Similarly, use of a bridge during off-peak hours may be nonrival, but it is possible to exclude potential users by erecting toll booths. Table 16.1 presents a cross-classification of goods by their

TABLE 16.1 Types of Public and Private Goods

		Exclusive	
		Yes	**No**
Rival	**Yes**	Hot dogs, automobiles, houses	Fishing grounds, public grazing land, clean air
	No	Bridges, swimming pools, scrambled satellite television signals	National defense, mosquito control, justice

possibilities for exclusion and their rivalry. Several examples of goods that fit into each of the categories are provided. Many of the examples in boxes other than the upper left corner in the table are often produced by the government. Nonrival goods are sometimes privately produced—there are private bridges, swimming pools, and highways that consumers must pay to use even though this use involves zero marginal cost. Nonpayers can be excluded from consuming these goods, so a private firm may be able to cover its costs.[10] Still, even in this case, the resulting allocation of resources will be inefficient because price will exceed marginal cost.

Public goods

Goods that are both nonexclusive and nonrival.

For simplicity we define **public goods** as having both of the properties listed in Table 16.1. That is, such goods provide nonexclusive benefits and can be provided to one more user at zero marginal cost. Public goods are both nonexclusive and nonrival.

PUBLIC GOODS AND MARKET FAILURE

The definition of public goods suggests why private markets may not produce them in adequate amounts. For exclusive private goods, the purchaser of that good can appropriate the entire benefits of the good. If Smith eats a pork chop, for example, that means the chop yields no benefits to Jones. The resources used to produce the pork chop can be seen as contributing only to Smith's welfare, and he or she is willing to pay whatever this is worth.

INFOTRAC®
COLLEGE EDITION
Exclusively from Gale Group and Thomson Learning

www.infotrac-college.com
Keywords: Public goods and market failure

For a public good, this will not be the case. In buying a public good, any one person will not be able to appropriate all the benefits the good offers. Because others cannot be excluded from benefiting from the good and because others can use the good at no cost, society's potential benefits from the public good will exceed the benefits that accrue to any single buyer. However, the purchaser will not take the potential benefits of this purchase to others into account in his or her expenditure decisions. Consequently, private markets will tend to underallocate resources to public goods.

A Graphical Demonstration

One way to show this result is by looking at the demand curve associated with such goods. In the case of a private good, we found the market demand curve (see Chapter 4) by summing people's demands horizontally. At any price, the quantities demanded by each person are summed up to calculate the total quantity

---

[10] Nonrival goods that permit imposition of an exclusion mechanism are sometimes referred to as *club goods* since provision of such goods might be organized along the lines of private clubs. Such clubs might then charge a "membership" fee and permit unlimited use by members. The optimal size of a club is determined by the economies of scale present in the production process for the club good. For an analysis, see R. Cornes and T. Sandler, *The Theory of Externalities, Public Goods, and Club Goods* (Cambridge, England: Cambridge University Press, 1986).

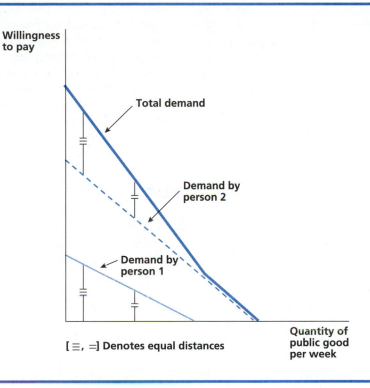

Willingness to pay

Total demand

Demand by person 2

Demand by person 1

[☰, ꞊] Denotes equal distances

Quantity of public good per week

FIGURE 16.4 Derivation of the Demand for a Public Good Because a public good is nonexclusive, the price that people are willing to pay for one more unit (their marginal valuations) is equal to the sum of what each individual would pay. Here person 1's willingness to pay is added vertically to person 2's to get the total demand for the public good.

demanded in the market. The market demand curve shows the marginal evaluation that people place on an additional unit of output. For a public good (which is provided in about the same quantity to everyone), we must add individual demand curves vertically. To find out how society values some level of public good production, we must ask how each person values this level of output and then add up these valuations.

This idea is represented in Figure 16.4 for a situation with only two people. The total demand curve for the public good is the vertical sum of each person's demand curve. Each point on the curve represents what person 1 and person 2 together are willing to pay for the particular level of public good production. Producing one more unit of the public good would benefit both people; so, to evaluate this benefit, we must add up what each person would be willing to pay. This is shown in Figure 16.4 by adding what person 1 is willing to pay to what person 2 is willing to pay. In private markets, on the other hand, the production of one more unit benefits only the person who ultimately consumes it. Because each person's demand curve in Figure 16.4 is below the total demand for the public good, no single buyer is willing to pay what the good is worth to society as a whole. Therefore, in many cases, private markets may undervalue the benefits of public goods because they take no account of the externalities the goods create. Hence, resources will be under-allocated to them.

SOLUTIONS TO THE PUBLIC GOODS PROBLEM

Because private markets will not allocate resources efficiently to the production of public goods, some other mechanism must be found. Unfortunately, as anyone who tries to organize a picnic (or get his or her children to clean their rooms) quickly discovers, getting people to provide public goods voluntarily is a difficult task. Because people know that they will benefit from the good regardless of whether or not they contribute to its production, everyone will have an incentive to be a **free rider.** That is, they will refrain from contributing to production in the hope that someone else will. In general, this will result in the underproduction of the public good in question.

Free rider
A consumer of a nonexclusive good who does not pay for it in the hope that other consumers will.

Nash Equilibrium and Underproduction

One approach that illustrates this underproduction relies on the concept of Nash equilibrium, first introduced in Chapter 12. Consider the situation of two roommates illustrated in Table 16.2. Each roommate may either clean the room or not. A clean room provides more utility than a dirty room to both of the players in this game. But each player would also prefer to have a clean room cleaned by his or her roommate to one in which the cleaning is shared. On the other hand, each roommate prefers a dirty room to one that he or she has had to clean alone. In this game (which resembles the Prisoner's Dilemma game in Chapter 12), the only Nash equilibrium is for neither player to clean the room. Any choice by one

TABLE 16.2 Utilities from Room Cleaning: The Nash Equilibrium Underproduces Public Goods

		B's Strategies	
		Clean	Do not clean
A's Strategies	Clean	A:2 B:2	A:0 B:3
	Do not clean	A:3 B:0	A:1 B:1

player to clean would induce the other to shirk. But this dirty equilibrium is inferior to a situation where both players clean the room—a solution that would require some degree of coercion to enforce.

Compulsory Taxation

Although this illustration is a trivial one in comparison to issues of public good production that involve national defense or providing for public health, the nature of the problem is the same for any public good. The free-rider problem is inescapable. Hence, some compulsory mechanism must be found to ensure efficient production. Most often, this solution relies on some form of tax-like measures. That is, members of a group who are expected to benefit from a public good must in some way be forced to pay for it in the optimal amounts. The fact that there can be an efficient equilibrium with compulsory taxation was first illustrated by the Swedish economist Erik Lindahl in 1919. Lindahl's argument can be illustrated graphically for a society with only two individuals (again, the ever-popular Smith and Jones). In Figure 16.5, the curve labeled SS shows Smith's demand for a particular public good. Rather than using the price of the public good on the vertical axis, we instead record the share of a public good's cost that Smith must pay (which varies from 0 percent to 100 percent). The negative slope of SS indicates that, at a higher tax "price" for the public good, Smith will demand a smaller quantity of it.

Jones's demand for the public good is derived in much the same way. Now, however, we record the proportion paid by Jones on the right-hand vertical axis on Figure 16.5 and reverse the scale so that moving up the axis results in a lower tax price paid. Given this convention, Jones's demand for the public good (JJ) has a positive slope.

The Lindahl Equilibrium

The two demand curves in Figure 16.5 intersect at C, with an output level of 0E for the public good. At this output level Smith is willing to pay, say, 60 percent of the good's cost whereas Jones pays 40 percent. That point C is an equilibrium is suggested by the following argument. For output levels less than 0E, the two people combined are willing to pay more than 100 percent of the public good's cost. They will vote to increase its level of production (but see the warnings about this statement in the next section). For output levels greater than 0E, the people are not willing to pay the total cost of the public good being produced and may vote for reductions in the amount being provided. Only for output level 0E is there a **Lindahl equilibrium** where the tax shares precisely pay for the level of public good production undertaken by the government.

Not only does this allocation of tax responsibilities result in an equilibrium in people's demands for public goods, but it is also possible to show that this equilibrium is efficient. The tax shares introduced in Lindahl's solution to the public goods problem play the role of "pseudo prices" that mimic the functioning of a competitive price system in achieving efficiency. Unfortunately, for reasons we now examine, this solution is not a very realistic one.

Lindahl equilibrium
Balance between people's demand for public goods and the tax shares that each must pay for them.

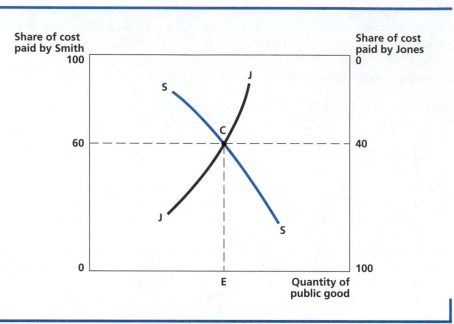

FIGURE 16.5 Lindahl Equilibrium in the Demand for a Public Good The curve SS shows that Smith's demand for a public good increases as the tax share that Smith must pay falls. Jones's demand curve for the public good (JJ) is constructed in a similar way. The point C represents a Lindahl equilibrium at which OE of the public good is supplied with Smith paying 60 percent of the cost. Any other quantity of the public good is not an equilibrium since either too much or too little funding would be available.

REVEALING THE DEMAND FOR PUBLIC GOODS

Although the Lindahl equilibrium is efficient, computation of the optimal tax shares requires knowledge of individuals' demands for public goods. A major problem is how to get people to reveal those demands. In usual market transactions, people reveal their demands by either choosing to buy or not to buy a given product. If I really like Steven Spielberg movies, I reveal that by renting them. By declining to rent Oliver Stone films, I reveal that they are not worth the price (though for many other people that is not the case). Getting people to reveal their demands for public goods is much more difficult, however, because of the free-rider problem. If each person knows that his or her tax share will be based on his or her personal demand for public goods, there is a clear incentive to try to hide this true demand. Of course, the government may try any number of clever schemes to try to induce people to show their true preferences; but, often, this proves to be a very frustrating task. Application 16.4: Why Is There So Much Fund-Raising on Public Broadcasting? describes one such situation that is probably very familiar to many of you. In the end, any government will probably have to depart from the Lindahl ideal and resort to more pragmatic ways of determining how much will be spent on public goods.

The creation of public radio and television broadcasting corporations in the United States in the 1960s was viewed as a revolution in media design. Rather than being financed solely by the government (as is the case in many other countries), public radio and television in the United States were intended to be supported primarily by their listeners and viewers through voluntary contributions.

Why Is There So Much Fund-Raising on Public Broadcasting?

Is Public Broadcasting a Public Good?

Over-the-air television and radio broadcasting would seem to meet the strict definition of a public good. Broadcasting is nonexclusive in that no listener or viewer can be excluded for using what is "on the air." And the good is nonrival because costs are not increased if an additional user tunes in. However, thriving commercial markets in both television and radio should raise some caution in jumping to the conclusion that such broadcasting is underproduced.

It is the complementary relationship between advertising and broadcasting that mitigates the problems raised by the public-good nature of broadcasting. Viewed as a mechanism for delivering advertising messages, broadcasting is both exclusive (those who do not pay cannot advertise) and rival (when one advertiser buys a time slot, no one else can use it). Hence, a general underprovision of broadcasting seems unlikely. Instead, the rationale for public broadcasting must rest on the notion that certain types of programming (i.e., children's, cultural, or public affairs) will be unattractive to advertisers and will therefore be underprovided in private markets.[1] It is this type of programming that was intended to be supported through government grants and voluntary public contributions.

The Consequences of Free Riders

Unfortunately, the free-rider problem common to most public goods has tended to undermine this voluntary support. By most estimates, fewer than 10 percent of the viewers of public television make voluntary contributions. Approximately the same percentage applies to public radio as well.[2] Although the broadcasters have tried to encourage contributions through extensive fund-raising campaigns and more subtle pressures to make noncontributors feel guilty, these have met with, at best, partial success. Hence, public broadcasting has had to turn increasingly to advertising—a funding source that was originally considered to be contrary to its philosophy. Today, most public television shows are preceded by a series of short advertising messages and the viewer is reminded of these at the end of the show. Public radio has been under somewhat less pressure to advertise, but in this case too the time devoted to advertising has been lengthening in recent years.

Technology and Public Television

The situation of public television has been aggravated in recent years by the spread of cable television. Because cable access substantially increases the number of viewing

---

[1] Judging whether the market would have provided such programming is difficult because public broadcasting can also crowd out private options. For a discussion, see S. T. Berry and J. Waldfogel, "Public Radio in the United States: Does It Correct Market Failure or Cannibalize Commercial Stations?" *Journal of Public Economics* (February 1999): 189–211.

[2] For a discussion of direct evidence on free riding in public radio, see E. J. Brunner, "Free Riders or Easy Riders? An Examination of Voluntary Provision of Public Radio," *Public Choice* (December 1998): 587–604.

(continued)

options, the notion that there are untapped areas of viewer preferences that public broadcasting might serve has become increasingly dubious. Public television shows have become indistinguishable from those offered by such commercial cable networks as A&E, The Learning Channel, History Channel, and House and Garden Television. Indeed, these new networks have been increasingly competing with public television for the same shows, drawing several popular offerings into the commercial venue. Voluntary support for public television has been declining (at least in some areas) and the long-run viability of this "public good" remains in doubt.

To Think About

1. Is there a conflict between what advertisers will support and what viewers wish to see on television?
2. In many countries, public broadcasting is supported through direct taxation. Does this solve the problem of free riders? Does such direct government support improve welfare?

Local Public Goods

Some economists have suggested that the problem of revealing the demand for public goods may be more tractable on a local than on a national level.[11] Because people are relatively free to move from one locality to another, they may indicate their preferences for local public goods by choosing to live in communities that offer them utility-maximizing public-goods taxation packages. "Voting with one's feet" provides a mechanism for revealing demand for public goods in much the same way that "dollar voting" reveals demand for private goods. People who want high-quality schools or a high level of police protection can "pay" for them by choosing to live in highly taxed communities. Those who prefer not to receive such benefits can choose to live elsewhere. These observations suggest that some decentralization of government functions may be desirable.

DIRECT VOTING AND RESOURCE ALLOCATION

Voting is used to decide questions about the production and financing of public goods in many institutions. In some instances, people vote directly on policy questions. That is the case in New England town meetings and many statewide referenda (such as those discussed later in Application 16.5) and for many of the public policies adopted in Switzerland. Direct voting also characterizes the social decision procedure used for many smaller groups and clubs such as farmers'

[11] See C. M. Tiebout, "A Pure Theory of Local Expenditures," *Journal of Political Economy* (October 1956): 416–424.

cooperatives, university faculties, or the local Rotary Club. In other cases, societies have found it more convenient to utilize a representative form of government in which people directly vote only for political representatives, who are then charged with making decisions on policy questions.

To study how decisions about public goods are made, we begin with an analysis of direct voting. Direct voting is important, not only because such a procedure may apply to some cases but also because elected representatives often engage in direct voting (such as in the U.S. Congress), and the theory we illustrate applies to those instances also. Later in the chapter, we take up special problems of representative government.

Majority Rule

Because so many elections are conducted by majority rule, we often tend to regard that procedure as a natural and, perhaps, optimal one for making social choices. But a quick examination suggests that there is nothing particularly sacred about a rule requiring that a policy obtain 50 percent of the vote to be adopted. In the U.S. Constitution, for example, two-thirds of the states must adopt an amendment before it becomes law; and 60 percent of the U.S. Senate must vote to limit debate on controversial issues. Indeed, in some institutions (Quaker meetings, for example), unanimity may be required for social decisions. Our discussion of the Lindahl equilibrium concept suggests that there does indeed exist a distribution of tax shares that would obtain unanimous support in voting for public goods. But arriving at such unanimous agreements poses difficult information problems and may be subject to strategic ploys and free-rider behavior by the voters involved. To examine in detail the forces that lead societies to move away from unanimity and to choose some other determining fraction would take us too far afield here. We instead assume throughout our discussion of voting that decisions are made by majority rule. You may be able to think of some situations that might call for a decisive proportion other than 50 percent.

The Paradox of Voting

In the 1780s, the French social theorist M. De Condorcet observed an important peculiarity of majority-rule voting systems—they may not arrive at an equilibrium but instead may cycle among alternative options. Condorcet's paradox is illustrated for a simple case in Table 16.3. Suppose there are three voters (Smith, Jones, and Fudd) choosing among three policy options. These policy options represent three levels of spending on a particular public good (A = low, B = medium, and C = high). Preferences of Smith, Jones, and Fudd among the three policy options are indicated by the order listed in the table. For example, Smith prefers option A to option B and option B to option C, but Jones prefers option B to option C and option C to option A. The preferences described in Table 16.3 give rise to Condorcet's paradox.

TABLE 16.3 Preferences That Produce the Paradox of Voting			
Voter	**Order of preferences**		
Smith	A	B	C
Jones	B	C	A
Fudd	C	A	B

A = Low-spending policy. B = Medium-spending policy. C = High-spending policy.

Consider a vote between options A and B. Option A would win, because it is favored by Smith and Fudd and opposed only by Jones. In a vote between options A and C, option C would win, again by two votes to one. But in a vote of option C versus option B, the previously defeated option B would win, and consequently social choices would cycle. In subsequent elections, any choice that was initially decided upon could later be defeated by an alternative, and no decision would ever be reached. In this situation, the option finally chosen will depend on such seemingly unimportant issues as when the balloting stops or how items are ordered on an agenda rather than being derived in some rational way from the preferences of voters.

Single-Peaked Preferences and the Median Voter Theorem

Condorcet's voting paradox arises because of the degree of irreconcilability in the preferences of voters. We might ask whether restrictions on the types of preferences allowed might yield situations where equilibrium voting outcomes are more likely. A fundamental result about this probability was discovered by Duncan Black in 1948.[12] Black showed that equilibrium voting outcomes can always occur in cases where the issue being voted upon is one-dimensional (such as how much to spend on public goods) and where voters' preferences are "single-peaked."

To understand what *single-peaked* means, consider again Condorcet's paradox. In Figure 16.6, we illustrate the preferences that gave rise to the paradox by assigning hypothetical utility levels to options A, B, and C that are consistent with the preferences recorded in Table 16.3. For Smith and Jones, preferences are single-peaked—as levels of public goods' expenditures rise, there is only one local utility-maximizing choice (A for Smith, B for Jones). Fudd's preferences, on the other hand, have two local peaks (A and C). It is these preferences that produced the cyclical voting pattern. If, instead, Fudd had preferences represented by the dashed line in Figure 16.6 (where C is now the only local peak), there would be no paradox. In that case, option B would be chosen since that option would defeat both A and C by votes of two to one. Here, B is the preferred choice of the *median voter* (Jones) whose preferences are "between" the preferences of Smith and the opposing preferences of Fudd.

Black's result is quite general and applies to any number of voters. If choices are one-dimensional and preferences are single-peaked, majority rule will result

[12] Duncan Black, "On the Rationale of Group Decision Making," *Journal of Political Economy* (February 1948): 23–24.

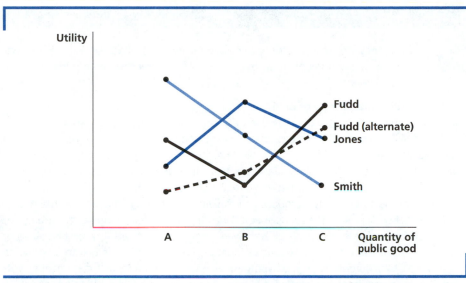

FIGURE 16.6 Single-Peaked Preferences and the Median Voter Theorem This figure illustrates
the preferences in Table 16.3. Smith's and Jones's preferences are single-peaked, but Fudd's have two
peaks, and these yield the voting paradox. If Fudd's instead had been single-peaked (the dashed
lines), option B would be chosen as the preferred choice of the median voter (Jones).

in selection of that project that is most favored by the **median voter.** Therefore, that
voter's preference will determine what social choices are made. Application 16.5:
Referenda on Public Spending looks at some of the problems in using actual voting results to infer voters' attitudes.

Median voter
A voter whose pref-
erences for a public
good represent the
middle point of all
voters' preferences
for the good.

Voting and Resource Allocation

Voting does in fact determine the allocation of resources to the production of
public goods in many cases. The important economic question is whether that
allocation is efficient or whether it results in misallocations that might be as bad
as leaving the production of public goods to private markets. Unfortunately,
economists have found relatively little correspondence between the efficient allocations called for by the Lindahl approach to public goods demand and the actual
allocations that will be adopted under a median voter approach. For example,
virtually every Western country has seen an increase in the share of GDP devoted
to the production of public goods since World War II. Undoubtedly, this reflects,
at least in part, the attitudes of the median voters in these countries; but there is
no agreement among economists about whether this trend reflects a move toward
greater efficiency as previously unmet demands for public goods are satisfied or
some failure in voting mechanisms that causes public goods to be overproduced.

One of the primary problems with voting for public goods as a method of
allocating resources is simply that votes by themselves do not provide enough

Referenda on Public Spending

In recent years, many states have passed tax-limitation statutes, and several constitutional amendments have been proposed to serve the same purpose at the federal level.

California's Proposition 13

The tax-limitation idea largely originated in California with the passage of Proposition 13 in 1977. This ballot initiative, which passed by a two-to-one margin, required that property in California be taxed at a maximum rate of 1 percent of the 1975 fair market value and imposed sharp limits on tax increases in future years. It resulted in a decline in local property tax revenues of nearly 60 percent between fiscal 1978 and 1979.

Two hypotheses have been proposed to explain why voters demanded such a drastic change in policy. The first views Proposition 13 as a demand for changing the sources of local tax revenues. Under this view, citizens were largely content with the existing levels of local services but wanted state tax sources (primarily income and sales tax) to take over a larger share of the burden. A second hypothesis views Proposition 13 as a statement by voters that local government had grown too large and that voters wished to see a cutback.

Extensive research on Proposition 13 finds support for both of these propositions.[1] California voters have raised other state taxes and some other local sources of revenue while cutting back on local property taxes. But there is also evidence that spending is significantly lower than it would have been in the absence of Proposition 13. Outcomes such as government employment and the wages of government employees also seem to have been curtailed.

Massachusetts and Michigan

Evidence from studies of other tax-limitation initiatives tends to be somewhat contradictory as to voters' motivations. For example, Ladd and Wilson used personal survey data to examine voter patterns in Massachusetts in connection with the 1980 passage of "Proposition 2½"— a proposal very similar to Proposition 13.[2] Consistent with the California study, they also found evidence to contradict the notion that voters simply wanted to shift the source of local revenues (say, from the property tax to the income tax). But voters feared the loss of "vital" services and did not seem to want large cutbacks. Instead, they preferred "greater efficiency" in government but seemed to be quite vague as to what actual policies that might require. Similar conclusions have been obtained by studying voters' opinions in connection with voting in Michigan on the "Headler Amendment" to limit state taxes.

Home Rule in Illinois

A study of the decisions of communities in Illinois to adopt "Home Rule," thereby eliminating state-level restrictions on spending, sheds additional light on voters' motivations.[3] In this

---

[1] See "Forum on Proposition 13," *National Tax Journal* (March 1999): 99–138.

[2] H. Ladd and J. B. Wilson, "Why Voters Support Tax Limitations—Proposition 2 1/2," *National Tax Journal* (June 1982): 127–148.

[3] J. A. Temple, "Community Composition and Voter Support for Tax Limitations: Evidence from Home-Rule Elections," *Southern Economic Journal* (April 1996): 1002–1016.

case, the author shows that more heterogeneous communities seem to prefer to keep restrictions on local spending whereas those communities with more homogeneous populations are willing to forsake the restrictions. An interpretation of this finding is that, as Tiebout's model of local public goods suggests, members of relatively homogeneous communities may have similar views about the proper size and functions of government. But, in heterogeneous communities, voters fear that those favoring spending will get the upper hand. These voters therefore feel the need for some sort of outside constraint.

To Think About

1. Since World War II, the fraction of GDP devoted to government has risen in virtually every Western country. How do you explain this rise?
2. Some American politicians favor a balanced budget amendment to the U.S. Constitution. Does the analysis of this chapter provide any reasons for thinking this amendment is a good idea? Would a limit on the fraction of GDP devoted to government be better?

information for the proper guiding of resource allocation. Because resources have real costs, any proper allocational mechanism must in some way reveal the willingness of people to pay those costs. But voting does not offer voters any way to indicate the intensity with which they desire specific public goods. Nor are the options presented to voters usually very explicit about potential trade-offs involved in choosing one good over another. Economists and political scientists have proven to be quite innovative in dreaming up more informative voting schemes that give people some say on how strongly they feel about public spending options. But none of these, so far, has been especially effective in getting people to reveal their demands for public goods. The market mechanism has proven to be a remarkably effective way of gathering this sort of information with regard to allocating resources to the production of private goods, but it has been much more difficult to find a similarly effective method for allocations to public goods.

Representative Government and Bureaucracies

In large, complex societies, the problem of allocating resources to public goods production is made even more complex by the necessity of operating many governmental functions through representative legislative bodies or through administrative bureaucracies. Both elected representatives and people who work in government departments can be viewed as agents for voters who are the ultimate demanders of public goods. But, as in any principal/agent relationship, there may be important differences in motives between voters and the people they have chosen to represent them. As was the case in the situations we studied in Chapter 7, agents may be able to take advantage of the informational asymmetries between themselves and the principals they represent (here, the voters) in ways that increase their own utility but distort the allocation of resources away from the voters' true demands for public goods. Hence, just as private markets may fail to provide efficient allocations in the presence of public goods, so too may governments fail in the provision of such goods. For example, many economics actors may find it in their interests to use the government to obtain monopoly gains for themselves that would not otherwise be obtainable without government help. They may, for example, enlist the government's aid in limiting competition in their markets or they may seek spending that benefits them alone. Through such **rent-seeking behavior** they may be able to get governmental agents to distort the allocations of resources away from what the voters would actually prefer if their preferences could be measured directly. To study all of the ways in which this might happen would, however, take us far beyond the intended subject matter of this book.

Rent-seeking behavior
Firms or individuals influencing government policy to increase their own welfare.

SUMMARY

We began this chapter with a demonstration of the misallocation of resources that may be created by an externality. We then proceeded to look at a number of consequences of this observation.

- When transactions costs are low and property rights are fully specified, no governmental intervention may be required to cope with an externality. Private negotiations between the parties may result in an efficient allocation regardless of how the property rights are assigned (the Coase theorem).

- Some externalities, such as those associated with environmental pollution, involve high transactions costs. In this case, legal redress or governmental regulation may be required to achieve an efficient allocation (although regulation does not guarantee such a result).

- The traditional method for correcting the allocational harm of an externality, first proposed by A. C. Pigou, is to impose an optimal tax on the firm creating the externality.

- Environmental regulation can proceed through the use of fees, pollution permits, or direct control. In

the simplest case, these can have identical outcomes. In actuality, however, the incentives incorporated under each may yield quite different results.

- Pure public goods have the property of nonexclusivity and nonrivalry—once the good is produced, no one can be excluded from receiving the benefits it provides, but additional people may benefit from the good at zero cost. These properties pose a problem for private markets because people will not freely choose to purchase such goods in economically efficient amounts. Resources may be underallocated to public goods.

- In theory, compulsory taxation can be used to provide public goods in efficient quantities by charging taxpayers what the goods are worth to each of them. However, measuring this demand may be very difficult because each person has an incentive to act as a free rider by understating his or her demands.

- Direct voting may produce paradoxical results. However, in some cases, majority rule will result in the adoption of policies favored by the median voter.

REVIEW QUESTIONS

1. If one firm raises the costs of another firm by bidding against it for its inputs, that is not an externality by our definition. But, if a firm raises the costs of another firm by polluting the environment, that is an externality. Explain the distinction between these two situations. Why does the second lead to an inefficient allocation of resources but the first does not?

2. Our general definition of economic efficiency focuses on mutually beneficial transactions. Explain why the presence of externalities may result in some mutually beneficial transactions being forgone. Illustrate these using Figure 16.1.

3. The proof of the Coase theorem requires that firms recognize both the explicit and implicit costs of their decision. Explain a situation where a firm's failure to curtail pollution may cause it to incur implicit costs. Why is the assumption of zero bargaining costs crucial if the firm is to take account of these costs?

4. Explain why the level of emissions control R^* in Figure 16.3 is economically efficient. Why would the levels of abatement given by R_L and R_H result in inefficiency? What kinds of inefficient trades would be occurring at these levels of abatement?

5. Figure 16.3 shows that an emissions fee can be chosen that attains the same level of pollution reduction as does direct control. Explain why firms would make the same choices under either control method. Would this equivalence necessarily hold if government regulators did not know the true marginal costs of emissions control?

6. For each of the following goods, explain whether it possesses the nonexclusive property, the nonrival property, or both. If the good does not have the characteristics of a public good but is, nevertheless, produced by the government, can you explain why?

   a. Television receivers
   b. Over-the-air television transmissions
   c. Cable television transmissions
   d. Elementary education
   e. College education
   f. Electric power
   g. Delivery of first-class mail
   h. Low-income housing

7. The Lindahl solution to the public goods problem promises economic efficiency on a voluntary basis. Why would each person voluntarily agree to the tax assessments determined under the Lindahl solution? What choice is he or she being asked to make?

8. Why is the "paradox of voting" a paradox? What, if anything, is undesirable about a voting scheme that cycles? How will issues be decided in such cases?

9. "Under perfect competition, voting with dollars achieves economic efficiency, but democratic voting (one person—one vote) offers no such promise." Do you agree? Why does the specification of one vote per person interfere with the ability to achieve economic efficiency?

10. Why would individuals or firms engage in rent-seeking behavior? How much will they spend on such behavior? What are the externalities associated with rent seeking?

PROBLEMS

16.1 A firm in a perfectly competitive industry has patented a new process for making widgets. The new process lowers the firm's average costs, meaning this firm alone (although still a price taker) can earn real economic profits in the long run.

a. If the market price is $20 per widget and the firm's marginal cost curve is given by $MC = 0.4q$

where q is the daily widget production for the firm, how many widgets will the firm produce?

b. Suppose a government study has found that the firm's new process is polluting the air and estimates the social marginal cost of widget production by this firm to be $MCS = 0.5q$. If the market price is still $20, what is the socially optimal level of production for the firm? What should the amount of a government-imposed excise tax be in order to bring about this optimal level of production?

16.2 On the island of Pago-Pago, there are two lakes and 20 fishers. Each fisher gets to fish on either lake and gets to keep the average catch on that lake. On Lake X, the total number of fish caught is given by

$$F^X = 10L_X - \frac{1}{2}L_X^2$$

where L_X is the number of fishers on the lake. The amount an additional fisher will catch is $MP_X = 10 - L_X$. For Lake Y, the relationship is

$$F^Y = 5L_Y$$

a. Under this organization of society, what will the total number of fish caught be? Explain the nature of the externality in this equilibrium.
b. The chief of Pago-Pago, having once read an economics book, believes that she can raise the total number of fish caught by restricting the number of fishers allowed on Lake X. What is the correct number of fishers on Lake X to allow in order to maximize the total catch of fish? What is the number of fish caught in this situation?
c. Being basically opposed to coercion, the chief decides to require a fishing license for Lake X. If the licensing procedure is to bring about the optimal allocation of labor, what should the cost of a license be (in terms of fish)?

16.3 Suppose that the oil industry in Utopia is perfectly competitive and that all firms draw oil from a single (and practically inexhaustible) pool. Each competitor believes that he or she can sell all the oil he or she can produce at a stable world price of $10 per barrel and that the cost of operating a well for one year is $1,000.

Total output per year (Q) of the oil field is a function of the number of wells (N) operating in the field. In particular,

$$Q = 500N - N^2$$

and the amount of oil produced by each well (q) is given by

$$q = \frac{Q}{N} = 500 - N$$

The output from the Nth well is given by

$$MP_N = 500 - 2N$$

a. Describe the equilibrium output and the equilibrium number of wells in this perfectly competitive case. Is there a divergence between private and social marginal cost in the industry?
b. Suppose that the government nationalizes the oil field. How many oil wells should it operate? What will total output be? What will the output per well be?
c. As an alternative to nationalization, the Utopian government is considering an annual license fee per well to discourage overdrilling. How large should this license fee be to prompt the industry to drill the optimal number of wells?

16.4 The law of product safety raises the issue of whether the Coase theorem may apply. Two polar legal regimes might be termed *caveat emptor* (let the buyer beware) and *caveat vendor* (let the seller beware). Under the former scheme, producers would have no responsibility for the safety of their products: buyers would absorb all losses. Under the latter scheme, this liability assignment would be reversed; firms would be completely responsible under law for losses incurred from unsafe products. Using simple supply and demand analysis, discuss how the assignment of such liability might affect the allocation of resources. Would safer products be produced if firms were strictly liable under law? How do the results of this problem depend on whether buyers and sellers are fully informed?

16.5 As an illustration of the apple-bee externality, suppose that a beekeeper is located next to a 20-acre apple orchard. Each hive of bees is capable of pollinating 1/4 acre of apple trees, thereby raising the value of apple output by $25.

a. Suppose the market value of the honey from one hive is $50 and that the beekeeper's marginal costs are given by

$$MC = 30 + .5Q$$

where Q is the number of hives employed. In the absence of any bargaining, how many hives will the beekeeper have and what portion of the apple orchard will be pollinated?

b. What is the maximum amount per hive the orchard owner would pay as a subsidy to the beekeeper to prompt him or her to install extra hives? Will the owner have to pay this much to prompt the beekeeper to use enough hives to pollinate the entire orchard?

16.6 A government study has concluded that the marginal benefits from controlling cow-induced methane production are given by

$$MB = 100 - R$$

where R represents the percentage reduction from unregulated levels. The marginal cost to farmers of methane reduction (through better cow feed) is given by

$$MC = 20 + R$$

a. What is the socially optimal level of methane reduction?
b. If the government were to adopt a methane fee that farmers must pay for each percent of methane they do not reduce, how should this fee be set to achieve the optimal level of R?
c. Suppose there are two farmers in this market with differing costs of methane reduction. The first has marginal costs given by

$$MC_1 = 20 + \frac{2}{3}R_1$$

whereas the second has marginal costs given by

$$MC_2 = 20 + 2R_2$$

Total methane reduction is the average from these two farms. If the government mandates that each farm reduce methane by the optimal amount calculated in part a, what will the overall reduction be and what will this reduction cost (assuming there are no fixed costs to reducing methane)?
d. Suppose, instead, that the government adopts the methane fee described in part b. What will be the total reduction in methane and what will this reduction cost?
e. Explain why part c and part d yield different results.

16.7 Suppose there are only two people in society. The demand curve for person A for mosquito control is given by

$$q_A = 100 - P$$

For person B, the demand curve for mosquito control is given by

$$q_B = 200 - P$$

a. Suppose mosquito control is a nonexclusive good—that is, once it is produced everyone benefits from it. What would be the optimal level of this activity if it could be produced at a constant marginal cost of $50 per unit?
b. If mosquito control were left to the private market, how much might be produced? Does your answer depend on what each person assumes the other will do?
c. If the government were to produce the optimal amount of mosquito control, how much would this cost? How should the tax bill for this amount be allocated between the individuals if they are to share it in proportion to benefits received from mosquito control?

16.8 Suppose there are three people in society who vote on whether the government should undertake specific projects. Let the net benefits of a particular project be $150, $140, and $50 for persons A, B, and C, respectively.

a. If the project costs $300 and these costs are to be shared equally, would a majority vote to undertake the project? What would be the net benefits to each person under such a scheme? Would total net benefits be positive?
b. Suppose the project cost $375 and again costs were to be shared equally. Now would a majority vote for the project and total net benefits be positive?
c. Suppose (presumably contrary to fact) votes can be bought and sold in a free market. Describe what kinds of results you might expect in part a and part b.

16.9 The town of Pleasantville is thinking of building a swimming pool. Building and operating the pool will cost the town $5,000 per day. There are three groups of potential pool users in Pleasantville: (1) 1,000 families who are each willing to pay $3 per day for the pool; (2) 1,000 families who are each willing to pay $2 per day for the pool; and (3) 1,000 families who are each willing to pay $1 per day for the pool. Suppose also that the intended pool is large enough so that whatever number of families come on any day will not affect what people are willing to pay for the pool.

a. Which property of public goods does this pool have? Which does it not have?

b. Would building the pool be an efficient use of resources?

c. Consider four possible prices for family admission to the pool: (1) $3; (2) $2; (3) $1; and (4) $0. Which of these prices would result in covering the cost of the pool? Which of the prices would achieve an efficient allocation of resources?

d. Is there any pricing scheme for admission to this pool that would both cover the pool's cost and achieve an efficient allocation of resources?

e. Suppose that this pool has a capacity of only 2,000 families per day. If more than 2,000 families are admitted, the willingness to pay of any family (with children or not) falls to $0.50 per day. Now what is the efficient pricing scheme for the pool?

16.10 The demand for gummy bears is given by

$$Q = 200 - 100P$$

and these confections can be produced at a constant marginal cost of $.50.

a. How much will Sweettooth, Inc., be willing to pay in bribes to obtain a monopoly concession from the government for gummy bear production?

b. Do the bribes represent a welfare cost from rent seeking?

c. What is the welfare cost of this rent-seeking activity?

INTERNET EXERCISES

1. *Externalities.* The acid rain problem is a good example of an externality. The Environmental Protection Agency (EPA) Web site offers a good description of the problem and some measures taken to address it. Go to the EPA's acid rain Web site at *http://www.epa.gov/airmarkets/arp.* Click on the blue "acid rain" link in the introductory paragraph. Read the sections entitled "What Is Acid Rain and What Causes It?" and "What Are Acid Rain's Effects?" Then, using an appropriate graph, provide a brief economic analysis of the acid rain problem using the concept of externalities (be sure to describe some of the external costs and use your graph to show how these costs can lead to an inefficient allocation of resources). Next, return to the main page of the EPA's Acid Rain Program. Under Sulphur Dioxide (SO2) Allowances, click on the Allowances Fact Sheet. Briefly describe how the allowance trading program works. Next, return once again to the main page of the Acid Rain Program. From there, click on Allowance Auctions and then click on Bids for the Spot Auction. Using the most recent auction results, what was the range of successful bids? Which organization purchased the most allowances? How many allowances in total were sold? Why does the creation of a market for SO2 emissions help internalize the acid rain externality? What are the benefits of the trading program over direct regulation by a governing agency?

2. *Public goods.* Intellectual property goods, such as computer software, can be said to have public goods characteristics. Do you think software is a nonrival good? A nonexclusive good? Explain your answers. Is the problem of software piracy related to the free-rider problem? Explain. Let's take a look at the magnitude of the software piracy problem. Go to the Software and Information Industry Association's Anti-Piracy Web site at: *http://www.spa.org/piracy/default. asp.* Click on Publications, and then click on Reports and Publications. Read the 2000 (or most recent) Global Software Piracy Report (just read the Press Overview). What is the most recent estimate of global piracy losses? What is the estimate of the piracy loss from North America alone? What is the estimated piracy rate in Russia? China? The United States? What is the likely impact of piracy on the incentive for firms to develop new software applications? Do you think piracy has any social benefits? Explain.

Solutions to Odd-Numbered Problems

This section contains relatively brief solutions to the text's odd-numbered problems. Complete solutions to all of the problems are contained in the *Instructor's Manual*.

Chapter 1

1.1 a.

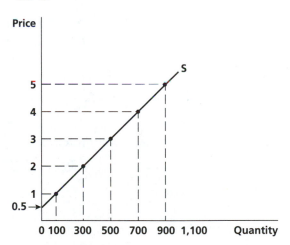

b. The points seem to be on a straight line. Use $\Delta P/\Delta Q$ for slope = 1/200.
If $P = a + bQ = a + 1/200Q$ at $P = 2$, $Q = 300$, $2 = a + 1.5$, or $a = 0.5$.
Hence, the equation is $P = 0.5 + 1/200Q$ or $Q = 200P - 100$.

c. Using $Q = 200P - 100$:
If $P = 0$, $Q = -100$.
If $P = 6$, $Q = 1,100$.

1.3 a. Supply: $Q = 200P - 100$
Demand: $Q = -100P + 800$
Supply = demand: $200P - 100 = -100P + 800$
$300P = 900$ or $P = 3$
When $P = 3$, $Q = 500$.

b. At $P = 2$, demand = 600, and supply = 300.
At $P = 4$, demand = 400, and supply = 700.

c.

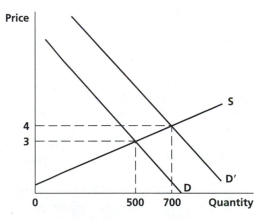

d. New demand is $Q = -100P + 1,100$.

e. Supply = demand: $200P - 100 = -100P + 1,100$
$300P = 1,200$
$P = 4$, $Q = 700$.

1.5

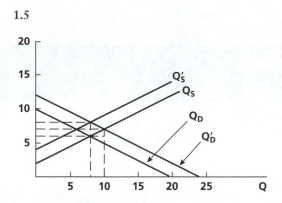

The algebraic solution proceeds as follows:

a. $Q_D = -2P + 20$.
   $Q_S = 2P - 4$.
   Set $Q_D = Q_S$: $-2P + 20 = 2P - 4$
   $\qquad\qquad\qquad 24 = 4P$
   $\qquad\qquad\qquad P = 6$.
   Substituting for P gives: $Q_D = Q_S = 8$.

b. Now $Q_D' = -2P + 24$.
   Set $Q_D = Q_S$: $-2P + 24 = 2P - 4$
   $\qquad\qquad\qquad 28 = 4P$
   $\qquad\qquad\qquad P = 7$.
   Substituting gives: $Q_D = Q_S = 10$.

c. $P = 8$, $Q = 8$ (see graph).

1.7 a.

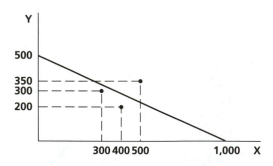

b. Both these points lie below the frontier.

c. This point lies beyond the frontier.

d. Opportunity cost of 1Y is 2X no matter how much is produced.

1.9 a. $X^2 + 4Y^2 = 100$.
   If $X = Y$, then $5X^2 = 100$, and $X = \sqrt{20}$ and $Y = \sqrt{20}$.

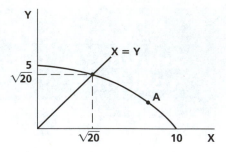

b. If only X is produced, $X = 10$. So can trade any combination for which $X + Y = 10$.

c. Because consumers wish X and Y in equal amounts, should have $X = Y = 5$.

d. Costs of forgone trade would be a loss of X of $5 - \sqrt{20} \approx 0.53$. Loss in Y would be the same.

Chapter 2

2.1 a. $\dfrac{\$8.00}{\$.40/apple} = 20$ apples can be bought.

b. $\dfrac{\$8.00}{\$.10/orange} = 80$ oranges can be bought.

c. 10 apples cost:
   10 apples · \$.40/apple = \$4.00, so there is \$8.00 − \$4.00 = \$4.00 left to spend on oranges, which means $\dfrac{\$4.00}{\$.10/orange} = 40$ oranges can be bought.

d. One less apple frees \$.40 to be spent on oranges, so $\dfrac{\$.40}{\$.10/orange} = 4$ more oranges can be bought.

e. \$8.00 = \$.40 · number of apples + \$.10 · number of oranges = .40A + .10O.

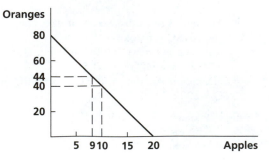

2.3 a. If $U = \sqrt{C \cdot D}$ indifference curves are hyperbolas

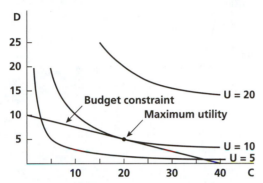

b. Budget constraint is $200 = 5C + 20D$ shown on graph

c. With 200 can buy 10D. With D = 10, C = 0, and U = 0

d. See graph. If, say, spend 100 on C and 100 on D can only buy C = 20, D = 5. Well below U = 20.

e. With C = 20, D = 5, U = 10

f. To show solution in e is highest, try
$C = 40, D = 0, U = 0$
$C = 24, D = 4, U = \sqrt{96} < 10$
$C = 16, D = 6, U = \sqrt{96} < 10$
$C = 0, D = 10, U = 0$
so C = 20, D = 5, looks like maximum

2.5

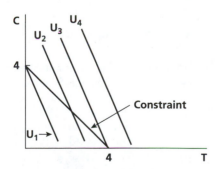

Her indifference curves are straight lines: Slope of these lines is −4/3. Therefore, MRS = 4/3—this person is willing to give up 4/3 units of C to get one more T. She would buy where her budget constraint intersects her indifference curve

(maximizing U), which is at T = 4, C = 0. If she had more income, she would not buy more coffee (she would maximize utility by buying more tea). If the price of coffee fell to $2, she would buy all coffee maximizing her utility at $U = 3C + 4T = 3(6) + 4(0) = 18$.

2.7

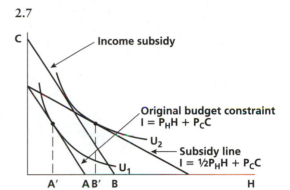

Income subsidy is cheaper since AB < A′B′

2.9

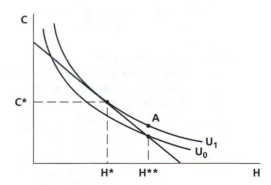

The figure shows that an unconstrained choice will yield utility level U_1 with choices of C^*, H^*. If the government requires purchase of H^{**}, utility would fall to U_0. Low-income consumers are most likely to be constrained by $H \geq H^{**}$. To return to U_1, budget constraint must allow this person to reach point A.

Chapter 3

3.1 a. $I = \$200$; $S = J$.
$P_S S + P_J J = 20S + 20S = 200$; $40S = 200$
$S = 5$, $J = 5$

b. $P_S S + P_J J = I$; $20S + 30S = 200$; $50S = 200$.
$S = 4$, $J = 4$

c.

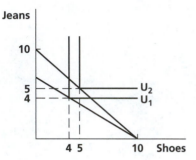

Elizabeth's indifference curves are L-shaped since she only gains utility when shoes and jeans are purchased in a one-to-one proportion. Ten shoes and five pairs of jeans yield the same utility as five sweaters and five pairs of jeans.

d. The change from U_2 to U_1 is entirely attributable to the income effect. There is no substitution effect due to Elizabeth's insistence on a fixed proportion of jeans and shoes.

3.3 a. Demand functions are
$P_F F = I/3$ or $F = I/3 P_F$
$P_S S = 2I/3$ or $S = 2I/3 P_S$.
If I, P_F and P_S all change by the same a proportion, quantities of F and S demanded will not change.
If $I = 20,000$

$$F = \frac{20,000}{3P_F}$$

$$S = \frac{40,000}{3P_F}$$

If $Z = 50,000$

$$F = \frac{50,000}{3P_F}$$

$$S = \frac{100,000}{3P_F}$$

b.

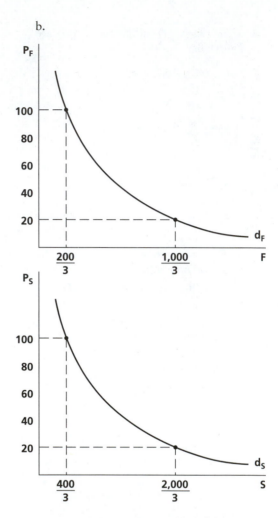

c. Increase in income would shift both d_F and d_S outward.

d. Part a shows that P_F does not enter into the shelter demand function. Since food always constitutes one-third of income, a change in P_F with no change in I does not change spending on either food or shelter. Since P_S has not changed, S does not change.

3.5 These are compensating price changes. 100($.40) + 80 ($–.50) = 0. Pete Moss can continue to purchase 100 units of fertilizer and 80 units of grass seed, although he may substitute some grass seed for fertilizer. He will not choose to buy more fertilizer and less grass seed, however, because such a choice was affordable at the previous prices and Pete chose not to consume it.

3.7

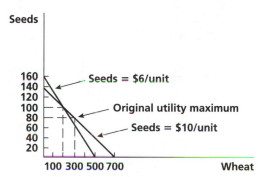

a. Started with 200 wheat, 100 sunflower seeds. Since he sells 20 units of sunflower seeds, he can buy 100 more units of wheat (will consume 300 in all).

b. If he continues to sell 20 units of sunflower seeds, he will only be able to get an additional $120/$2 = 60 units of wheat, so he'd be worse off. It is clear from the graph the new constraint is northeast (Sam can be better off) of the old one only where Sam consumes more sunflower seeds than he produces; so he must sell wheat and buy sunflower seeds with the new prices.

c. In this case, the income effect is not the usual one. The lower sunflower seed price does not imply a higher real income, as in the usual case, since Sam's income is a function of the price of sunflower seeds. (Graphically, the lower price causes a rotation around the point 200 wheat, 100 sunflower seeds rather than around the wheat intercept.)

3.9

a. This is simply a matter of definition—starting from a specific utility-maximizing point, the regular demand curve examines the consequence of changing price, holding income and other prices constant. The compensated demand curve examines the consequences of changing price, holding utility and other prices constant.

b. The compensated demand curve does not incorporate income effects. Therefore, the impact of a given price change is smaller than would be the case with a regular demand curve (assuming the good is a normal good).

c. Because the construction of a compensated demand curve can be based on any utility level and because utility levels vary along the regular demand curve, any point on the regular demand curve can be a basis for constructing a unique compensated demand curve.

d. There are no substitution effects in Irving's demand for chianti. His compensated demand curve is perfectly inelastic at the prevailing level of chianti consumption. A change in chianti consumption would change utility and represent a different compensated demand curve. Irving's regular demand curve for chianti is not perfectly inelastic because it also involves income effects when the price of this wine changes.

Chapter 4

4.1 Q = 500 – 50P.

a. If P = 2, Q = 400.
   P = 3, Q = 350.
   P = 4, Q = 300.
   P = 0, Q = 500.

b.

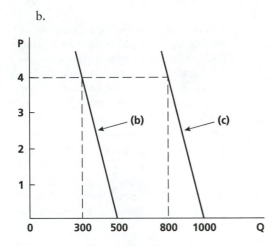

c. $Q = 1000 - 50P$.
   If $P = 2$, $Q = 900$.
   $P = 3$, $Q = 850$.
   $P = 4$, $Q = 800$.
   $P = 0$, $Q = 1000$.

4.3 a. Demand function (Q)

	(i)	(ii)	(iii)
$P = 1$	100	100	100
$P = 1.1$	90.9	95.3	86.7

b. Demand function (i) has $e = -1$.
    Demand function (ii) has $e = -0.5$.
    Demand function (iii) has $e = -1.5$.
    Note: Values are not exact because of the rel-
    atively large price change. Elasticities would
    more closely predict changes in Q for smaller
    changes.

c. Demand function (Q)

	(i)	(ii)	(iii)
$P = 4$	25	50	12.5
$P = 4.4$	22.7	47.7	10.8

These results mirror those in part a and
show the constant elasticity of the demand
functions.

4.5 a.

	Tom	**Dick**	**Harry**	**Total**
$P = 50$	0	0	0	0
$= 35$	30	20	0	50
$= 25$	50	60	25	135
$= 10$	80	120	100	300
$= 00$	100	160	150	410

b. "Total" column in part a.

c.

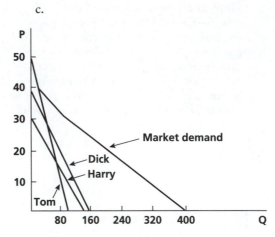

d. Above graph.

4.7 a. P falls by 10 percent, so purchases will
         increase by $10(1.3) = 13$ percent.

b. I rises by 5 percent, so purchases will
    increase by $5(1.7) = 8.5$ percent.

c. P' falls by 20 percent, so purchases fall by
    $20(0.8) = 16$ percent.

d. Summing all the changes gives $+13 + 8.5 -
    16 = +5.5$ percent increase in purchases.

4.9 a. Compensated demand is totally inelastic:
         $e_S = 0$.

b. Since there are only two goods to buy,
    $e_{EI} = 1$.

c. $s_F = 1/3$.

d. $e_{EP} = -1/3$. If P_F rises by, say, 3 percent, one
    will have to reduce spending on both food
    and shelter by 1 percent to compensate for
    the price rise. Hence $e_{EP} = -1$ percent/
    $+3$ percent $= -1/3$.

e. $e_{EP} = e_S - s_F e_{EI}$
    $-1/3 = 0 - 1/3(1)$

f. $F = I/3 P_F$.

g. Here $e_{EP} = -1$, $s_F = 1/3$, $e_{EI} = 1$.
    $e_S = e_{EP} + s_F e_{EI} = -1 + 1/3(1) = -2/3$.
    Now there is some substitution effect in
    food purchases.

h. Denote shelter by H. With fixed propor-
    tions, $e_S = 0$, $e_{H,I} = 1$, $s_H = 2/3$
    $e_{H,P} = 0 - 2/3(1) = -2/3$.

If $H = 2I/3P_H$, $e_{H,P} = -1$, $s_H = 2/3$, $e_{H,I} = 1$
$e_s = -1 + 2/3(1) = -1/3$.

Chapter 5

5.1 a. $K = 6$, $q = 6K + 4L = 6(6) + 4L = 36 + 4L$.
If $q = 60$, $4L = 60 - 36 = 24$, $L = 6$.
If $q = 100$, $4L = 100 - 36 = 64$, $L = 16$.

b. $K = 8$, $q = 6K + 4L = 6(8) + 4L = 48 + 4L$.
If $q = 60$, $4L = 60 - 48 = 12$, $L = 3$.
If $q = 100$, $4L = 100 - 48 = 52$, $L = 13$.

c. RTS = 2/3. If L increases by 1 unit, q can remain constant by decreasing K by 2/3 units.

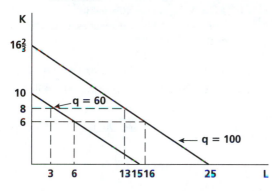

5.3 a.

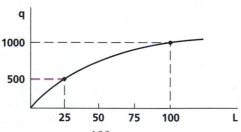

b. $AP_L = \dfrac{q}{L} = \dfrac{100}{\sqrt{L}}$

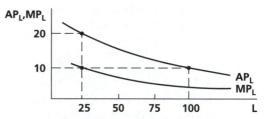

c. Graph above. Since the AP_L is everywhere decreasing, then each additional worker must be contributing less than the average of the existing workers, bringing the average down. Therefore, the marginal productivity must be lower than the average.

Here $MP_L = \dfrac{1}{2} AP_L$.

5.5 a.

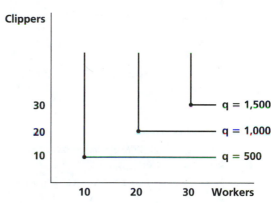

Will operate at the vertex of the isoquants.

b. Hire 20 workers, $q = 1,000$.

c. Depends on whether grapes can be sold for a price exceeding average cost.

d.

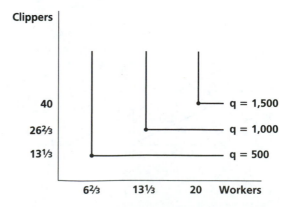

Choice would depend on clipper costs and wages for ambidextrous workers.

5.7 a. In 5.4, $a = b = 1/2$.

b. If we use 2K, 2L, have $q = (2K)^a(2L)^b = 2^{a+b}K^aL^b$ and if $a + b = 1$, this is twice K^aL^b.

c,d. From b, it follows that output will less than double or more than double if $a + b < 1$ or $a + b > 1$.

e. Function can exhibit any returns to scale desired depending on the values of a and b.

5.9 a. $q = 100\sqrt{KL} = 1{,}000$, so $\sqrt{KL} = 10$, or, $K \cdot L = 100$.

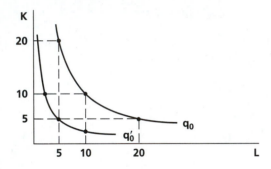

b. K = 10, L = 10
$AP_L = q/L = 1{,}000/10 = 100$ boxes per hour per worker.

c. If $q = 200\sqrt{KL} = 1{,}000$, $\sqrt{KL} = 5$, or KL $= 25$.
Isoquant shifts to q'_0. Now, if K = 10, L = 2.5. $AP_L = q/L = 1{,}000/2.5 = 400$ boxes per hour per worker.

Chapter 6

6.1 a.

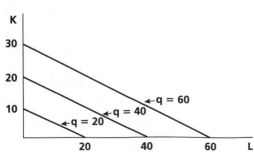

RTS = 1/2 since, if L is increased by one, K can be reduced by 1/2 while holding q constant.

b. Since RTS = 1/2 < w/v = 1, the manufacturer will use only K. For q = 20, K = 10; q = 40, K = 20; q = 60, K = 30. The manufacturer's expansion path is simply the K-axis.

c. If v = \$3, RTS = 1/2 > w/v = 1/3, the manufacturer will use only L. For q = 20, L = 20; q = 40, L = 40; q = 60, L = 60. Now the manufacturer's expansion path is the L-axis.

6.3 a. This is a cubic cost curve. It resembles Figure 6.3(d).

b. $AC = TC/q = q^2 - 40q + 430$
This is a parabola. It reaches a minimum at the axis of symmetry:
$q = -(-40)/2 = 20$
At q = 20, $AC = 400 - 800 + 430 = 30$.

c. At q = 20, $MC = 3(400) - 1{,}600 + 430 = 30$.

d.

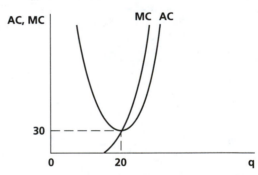

6.5 a. $q = 2\sqrt{K \cdot L}$. K = 100, $q = 2\sqrt{100 \cdot L}$.

$q = 20\sqrt{L}$. $\sqrt{L} = \dfrac{q}{20} \cdot L = \dfrac{q^2}{400}$

$STC = vK + wL = 1(100) + 4\dfrac{(q^2)}{400}$

$= 100 + \dfrac{q^2}{100}$.

$SAC = \dfrac{STC}{q} = \dfrac{100}{q} + \dfrac{q}{100}$

b. $SMC = \dfrac{q}{50}$.

If $q = 25$, STC $= 100 + \dfrac{(25)^2}{100} = 106.25$.

SAC $= \dfrac{100}{25} + \dfrac{25}{100} = 4.25$.

SMC $= \dfrac{25}{50} = .5$.

If $q = 50$, STC $= 100 + \dfrac{(50)^2}{100} = 125$.

SAC $= \dfrac{100}{50} + \dfrac{50}{100} = 2.50$.

SMC $= \dfrac{50}{50} = 1$.

If $q = 100$, STC $= 100 + \dfrac{(100)^2}{100} = 200$.

SAC $= \dfrac{100}{100} + \dfrac{100}{100} = 2$.

SMC $= \dfrac{100}{50} = 2$.

If $q = 200$, STC $= 100 + \dfrac{(200)^2}{100} = 500$.

SAC $= \dfrac{100}{200} + \dfrac{200}{100} = 2.50$.

SMC $= \dfrac{200}{50} = 4$.

c.

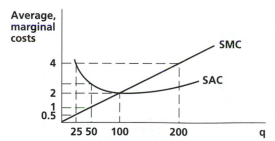

d. As long as the marginal cost of producing one more unit is below the average cost curve, average costs will be falling. Similarly, if the marginal cost of producing one more unit is higher than the average cost, then average costs will be rising. Therefore, the SMC curve must intersect the SAC curve at its lowest point.

6.7 Minimizing costs requires equal marginal productivities of labor in each plant. If labor were more productive in one plant than another, costs could be lowered by moving workers.

a. $MP_{L_1} = MP_{L_2}$. $5/2\sqrt{L_1} = 5/\sqrt{L_2}$.

$2\sqrt{L_1} = \sqrt{L_2}$. $L_2 = 4L_1$.

$q_1 = 5\sqrt{L_1}$; $q_2 = 10\sqrt{L_2} = 10\sqrt{4L_1} = 20\sqrt{L_1}$.

Hence $q_2 = 4q_1$.

b. $4q_1 = q_2$, so $q_1 = 1/5q$. $q_2 = 4/5q$ where q is total output.

STC (Plant 1) $= 25 + wL_1 = 25 + \dfrac{q_1^2}{25}$

STC (Plant 2) $= 100 + wL_2 = 100 + \dfrac{q_2^2}{100}$

STC $=$ STC (Plant 1) $+$ STC (Plant 2)

$= 25 + \dfrac{q_1^2}{25} + 100 + \dfrac{q_2^2}{100}$

$= 125 + \dfrac{(1/5q)^2}{25} + \dfrac{(4/5q)^2}{100}$

$= 125 + \dfrac{1/25q^2}{25} + \dfrac{16/25q^2}{100}$

$= 125 + \dfrac{20/25q^2}{100}$

$MC = \dfrac{2q}{125}$. $AC = \dfrac{125}{q} + \dfrac{q}{125}$.

$MC (100) = \dfrac{200}{125} = \$1.60$.

$MC (125) = \$2.00$ $MC (200) = \$3.20$.

c. Because of constant returns to scale, in the long run one can change K. It is really not important where production occurs. Production could be split evenly or produced all in one plant.
$TC = K + L = 2q$. $AC = 2 = MC$.

d. If there were decreasing returns to scale, then each firm should have equal share of production. AC and MC, no longer constant, are increasing functions of q preventing either plant from being too large.

6.9 a. Now K = L, so q = 20L.
TC = vK + wL = 5K + 5L = 10L,
so TC = 0.5q
AC = TC/q = 0.5
MC = ΔTC/Δq = 0.5.
These costs are half what they were before.

b. All costs will fall at the rate of r per year.

Chapter 7

7.1 a. Set P = MC, 20 = .2q + 10. Q = 50.

b. Maximum profits = TR – TC
= (50 · 20) – [.1(50)^2 + 10(50) + 50]
= 1000 – 800 = 200.

c.

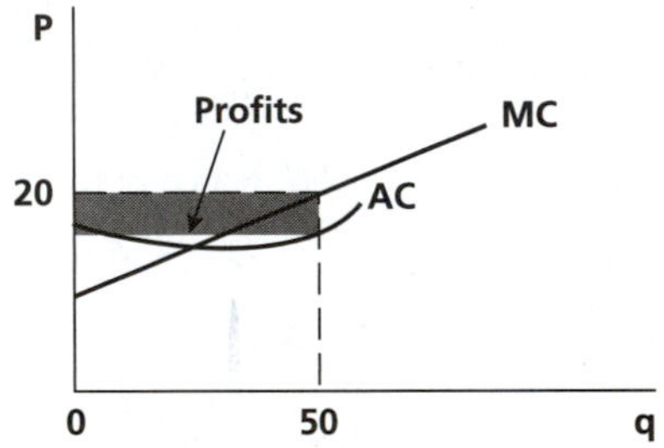

7.3

q	P	TR (= Pq)	MR	MC	AC	TC	π (= TR – TC)
1	9	9	9	3	3	3	6
2	8	16	7	3	3	6	10
3	7	21	5	3	3	9	12
4	6	24	3	3	3	12	12
5	5	25	1	3	3	15	10
6	4	24	–1	3	3	18	6
7	3	21	–3	3	3	21	0
8	2	16	–5	3	3	24	–8
9	1	9	–7	3	3	27	–18
10	0	0	–9	3	3	30	–30

Maximum profits occur at q = 4. At q = 4, the additional revenue of producing one more unit (3) is exactly equal to the cost of that added unit, and therefore it is profitable. For q > 4, profits fall and become negative for q ≥ 8.

7.5 a. Since q = 60 – 2P, solving for P yields
2P = 60 – q or P = 30 – q/2.
Hence, TR = P · q = q(30 – q/2), so
TR = 30q – q^2/2

b. That MR = 30 – q can be shown through calculus. A tabular proof is illustrated in the following table.

P	q = 60 – 2P	P_q	MR	MR = 30 – q
20	20	400		
19.5	21	409.5	9.5	9
19	22	418	8.5	8
18.5	23	425.5	7.5	7
18	24	432	6.5	6
17.5	25	437.5	5.5	5
17	26	442	4.5	4
16.5	27	445.5	3.5	3
16	28	448	2.5	2
15.5	29	449.5	1.5	1
15	30	450	0.5	0

Hence MR is approximately that given by the equation MR = 30 – q.

c. To maximize profits set MC = MR, .2q = 30 – q, so q = 150 – 5q, 6q = 150. Hence, q = 25, P = 17.5, MR = MC = 5.

d. The graph shows the linear D, MR, and MC curves.

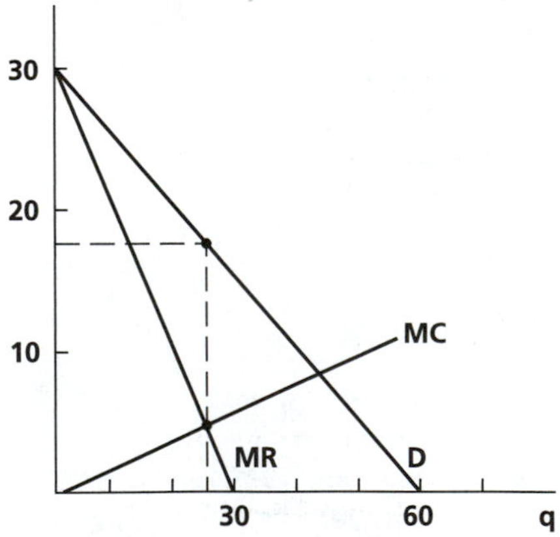

7.7 a. John's supply function is q = 5P – 50.
If P = 15, q = 25.
If P = 25, q = 75.

b. When P = 15, π = 15 · 25 – 362.5 = 375 – 362.5 = 12.5.
When P = 25, π = 25 · 75 – 1,362.5 = 1,875 – 1,362.5 = 512.5.
Average π = (512.5 + 12.5) ÷ 2 = 262.5.

c. If P = 20, q = 50, π = 1,000 – 800 = 200.
The father's deal makes John worse off.

d.

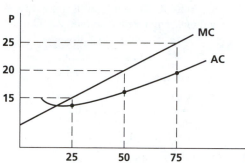

Since high profits are associated with high P, q combination, it's more profitable to let price fluctuate.

7.9 a. $STC = vK + wL$

$= 10 \cdot 100 + wL$

$= 1,000 + 5L,$

but $q = 10\sqrt{L}$, so $L = \dfrac{q^2}{100}$.

Hence, $STC = 1,000 + q^3/20$.

b. Use $P = MC$.

$20 = .1q$, so $q = 200$.

$L = q^2/100$, so $L = 400$.

c. If $P = 15$, $P = MC$ implies $15 = .1q$ or $q = 150$, $L = 225$.

d. Cost will be 175 to reduce L from 400 to 225. With $q = 150$, Profits $= TR - TC = 15(150) - (1,000 + .05q^2) = 2,250 - (1,000 + 1,125) = 125$. After paying severance cost of 175, the firm will incur a loss of 50. Note that if the firm continues to hire 400 workers it will have no severance costs and profits of TR − TC $= 15(200) - [1,000 + .05(200)^2] = 3,000 - (1,000 + 2,000) = 0$, which is better than in part d. An output level of 180 (L = 324) would yield an overall profit for the firm.

Chapter 8

8.1 a. Set supply equal to demand to find equilibrium price:

$Q_S = 1,000 = Q_D = 1,600 - 600P$.

$1,000 = 1,600 - 600P.$

$600 = 600P$

$P = 1/\text{pound}$

b. $Q_S = 400 = 1,600 - 600P$.

$600P = 1,200.$

$P = 2/\text{pound}$

c. $Q_S = 1,000 = 2,200 = 600P$.

$1,200 = 600P.$

$P = 2/\text{pound}$

$Q_S = 400 = 2,200 - 600P$.

$600P = 1,800.$

$P = 3/\text{pound}$

d.

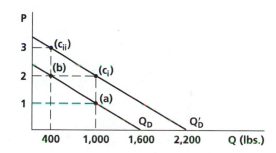

8.3 a. Supply = 100,000. In equilibrium,

$100,000 = Q_S = Q_D = 160,000 - 10,000P$,

or $P = 6$.

b. For any one firm, quantity supplied by other firms is fixed at 99,900. Demand curve is

$Q'_D = 160,000 - 10,000P - 99,900$

$= 60,100 - 10,000P.$

If quantity supplied is 0, $Q'_S = 0 = Q'_D = 60,100 - 10,000P$, or $P = 6.01$.

If quantity supplied is 200, $Q'_S = 200 = Q'_D = 60,100 - 10,000P$, or $P = 5.99$.

Elasticity = Slope of demand $\cdot$ P/Q for market.

$$e_{Q,P} = -10,000 \cdot \frac{6}{100,000} = -0.6.$$

For a single firm, demand is much more elastic:

$$e_{q,P} = -10,000 \cdot \frac{6}{100} = -600.$$

A change in quantity supplied does not affect price very much.

8.5 a. Short run: MR = P, so P = MC.

$P = q^2 + 20q + 100.$

$P = (q + 10)^2.$

$\sqrt{P} = q + 10$. $q = \sqrt{P} - 10$.

b. $P = 121$, $q = \sqrt{121} - 10 = 1$.
$P = 169$, $q = \sqrt{169} - 10 = 3$.
$P = 256$, $q = \sqrt{256} - 10 = 6$.

c. $\pi = TR - TC$. $P = 121$.
$\pi = 1 \cdot (121) - [.33(1)^3 + 10(1)^2 + 100(1) + 48]$.
$= 121 - 158.33 = 037.33$.
$P = 169$.
$\pi = 3(169) - [.33(3)^3 + 10(3)^2 + 100(3) + 48]$.
$= 507 - 447 = 60$.
$P = 256$.
$\pi = 6(256) - [.33(6)^3 + 10(6)^2 + 100(6) + 48]$.
$= 1,536 - 1,080 = 456$.

8.7 $STC = q^2 + wq = q^2 + .002Qq$

a. If $w = 10$, $STC = q^2 + 10q$. $SMC = 2q + 10 = P$.
Hence, $q = P/2 - 5$.

Industry Supply: $Q = \sum_1^{1,000} q = 500P - 5,000$.

At $P = 20$, $Q = 5,000$; at $P = 21$, $Q = 5,500$.

b. Here $MC = 2q + .002Q$. Set $= P$.
$q = P/2 - .001Q$.

Total $Q = \sum_1^{1,000} q = 500P - Q$.

Therefore, $Q = 250P$.
$P = 20$, $Q = 5,000$.
$P = 21$, $Q = 5,250$.
Supply is more steeply sloped in this case of interactions—increasingly production bids increase the wages of diamond cutters.

8.9 a. In long-run equilibrium, $AC = P$ and $MC = P$, so $AC = MC$.

$.01q - 1 + \dfrac{100}{q} = 0.2q - 1$.

$\dfrac{100}{q} = 0.1q$.

$\dfrac{10,000}{q} = q$, so $q^2 = 10,000$.

$q = 100$ gallons.

$AC = .01(100) - 1 + \dfrac{100}{100} = 1 - 1 + 1 = 1$.

$MC = .02(100) - 1 = 2 - 1 = 1$.

b. In the long run, $P = MC$; $P = \$1$.
$Q_D = 2,500,000 - 500,000(1) = 2,000,000$ gallons. The market supplies 2,000,000 gallons, so $\dfrac{2,000,000 \text{ gallons}}{100 \text{ gallons/station}} = 20,000$ gas stations.

c. In the long run, $P = \$1$ still since the AC curve has not changed. Q_D
$= 2,000,000 - 1,000,000(1)$
$= 1,000,000$ gallons.
$\dfrac{1,000,000 \text{ gallons}}{100 \text{ gallons/station}} = 10,000$ gas stations.

Chapter 9

9.1 a. With $Q = 400$, demand curve yields $400 = 1,000 - 5P$, or $P = 120$. For supply, $400 = 4P - 80$, or $P = 120$. Hence, P is an equilibrium price. Total spending on broccoli is $400 \cdot 120 = 48,000$.

On the demand curve when $Q = 0$, $P = 200$. Hence, area of the consumer surplus triangle is $.5(200 - 120)(400) = 16,000$.

On the supply curve, $P = 20$ when $Q = 0$. Producer surplus is then $.5(120 - 20)(400) = 20,000$.

b. With $Q = 300$, the total loss of surplus would be given by the area of the triangle between the demand and supply curves, which is $.5(140 - 95)(100) = 2,250$.

c. With $P = 140$, consumer surplus is $.5(200 - 140)(300) = 9,000$.
Producer surplus is $.5(95 - 20)(300) + 45(300) = 24,750$.
Consumers lose 7,000, producers gain 4,750, net loss is 2,250.
With $P = 95$, consumer surplus is $.5(200 - 140)(300) + 45(300) = 22,500$.
Producer surplus is $.5(95 - 20)(300) = 11,250$.
Consumers gain 6,500, producers lose 8,750; again net loss is 2,250.

d. With $Q = 450$, demand price would be 110, supply price is 132.50. Total loss of surplus is $.5(132.5 - 110)(5) = 562.50$.

Net loss is shared depending on where price falls between 110 and 132.5.

e.

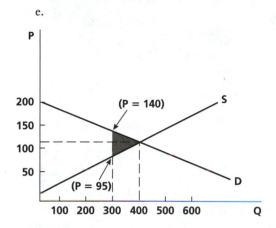

9.3   a.

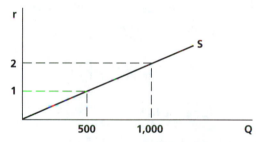

b. Since P = AC = 10 + r = 10 + .002Q, substitute this into demand: Q = 1,050 − 50P = 1,050 − 500 − .1Q, or 1.1Q = 550, Q = 500.
Since each firm produces 5 tapes, there will be 100 firms. Royalty is r = .002(500) = 1, so P = 11.

c. With Q = 1,600 − 50P, same substitution gives Q = 1,600 − 500 − .1Q or 1.1Q = 1,100, Q = 1,000.
So now there are 200 firms and r = .002(1,000) = 2, so P = 12.

d.

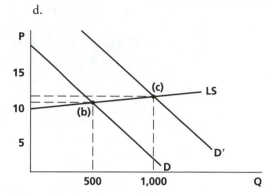

Producer surplus when P = 11 is .5(11 − 10)(500) = 250. When P = 12, it is .5(12 − 10)(1,000) = 1,000.

e. Royalties when Q = 500 are 500. Increment when Q rises from 500 to 500 is (2 − 1)(500) + .5(2 − 1)(1,000 − 500) = 500 + 250 = 750, which is precisely the increase in producer surplus in part d.

9.5   a. From 9.2, supply curve is Q = 100P − 1,000 and initial equilibrium is P = 14, Q = 400. Producer surplus is 800, composed of profits of 300 and fixed costs of 500. With a tax of 3, supply is Q = 100P − 1,000; demand is Q = 1,100 − 50(P + 3). Setting supply = demand yields 950 − 50P = 100P − 1,000. P = 13, P + 3 = 16, Q = 300.

b. Total tax collections are 900—consumers pay 600, firms pay 300.

c. Producer surplus is now .5(13 − 10)(300) = 450, a loss of 350. Short-run profits are (P − AC) · 300. STC = 39.5, SAC = 39.5/3. π = (13 − 39.5/3) · 300 = −50. Since profits before were 300, this is a loss of 350, which is the same as the loss of total producer surplus from 800 to 450. Fixed costs remain at 500 since there are a fixed number of firms.

9.7 a. Set quantity supply equal to quantity demanded.

$$150P = 5{,}000 - 100P;\ P = 20,\ Q = 3{,}000.$$

b. P will fall to 10. $Q_D = 4{,}000$, $Q_S = 1{,}500$. 2,500 radios will be imported.

c. Price would now rise to 15. $Q_D = 3{,}500$, $Q_S = 2{,}250$. Imports are now 1,250. Tariff revenue is $5(1{,}250) = 6{,}250$. With free trade, consumer surplus is $.5(50 - 10)(4{,}000) = 80{,}000$. Domestic producer surplus is $.5(10)(1{,}500) = 7{,}500$. With the tariff, consumer surplus is $.5(50 - 15)(3{,}500) = 61{,}250$, a loss of 18,750. Producer surplus is now $.5(15)(2{,}250) = 16{,}875$, a gain of 9,375. Deadweight loss is $18{,}750 - 6{,}250 - 9{,}375 = 3{,}125$, as can be found by the deadweight loss triangles measuring triangles.

d.

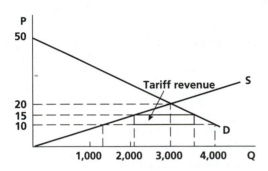

e. A "voluntary" import limit of 1,250,000 would have the same effect as the tariff on domestic price and quantity. Whoever had the right to import radios would receive rents of $5 per radio.

9.9 a. The frontier is a quarter ellipse:

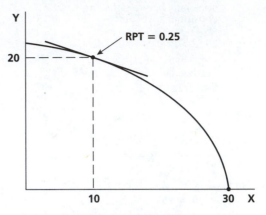

b. If $Y = 2X$, $X^2 + 2(2X)^2 = 900$. $9X^2 = 900$; $X = 10$, $Y = 20$. This point is shown on the frontier in part a.

c. If $X = 9$ on the production possibility frontier $Y = \sqrt{\dfrac{819}{2}} = 20.24.$

If $X = 11$ on the frontier, $Y = \sqrt{\dfrac{779}{2}} = 19.75.$

Hence, the RPT is $-\dfrac{\Delta Y}{\Delta X} = \dfrac{.50}{2} = 0.25.$

Chapter 10

10.1 a. $P = 53 - Q$.

For maximum profits, set MR = MC.

$MR = 53 - 2Q = MC = 5.$

$Q = 24,\ P = 29.$

$\pi = TR - TC = 24 \cdot 29 - 24 \cdot 5$
$= 696 - 120 = 576.$

Consumer surplus $= \dfrac{1}{2}(53 - 29) \cdot 24 = 288.$

b. MC = P = 5, P = 5, Q = 48.

c. Consumer surplus = $\frac{1}{2}(48)^2 = 1{,}152$.

1,152 > Profits + consumer surplus = 576 + 288 = 864.
Deadweight loss = 1,152 − 864 = 288.
Also $1/2\Delta Q \cdot \Delta P = 1/2(24)(24)$.

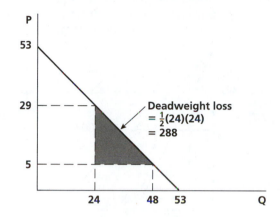

d.

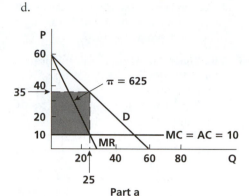

10.3 a. AC = MC = 10, Q = 60 − P, MR = 60 − 2Q.
For profit maximization, MC = MR.
10 = 60 − 2Q, 2Q = 50, Q = 25,
P = 35.
$\pi = TR − TC = (25)(35) − (25)(10)$
= 625.

b. AC = MC = 10, Q = 45 − .5P. MR= 90 − 4Q.
For profit maximization, MC = MR, 10 = 90 − 4Q, 80 = 4Q, Q = 20, P = 50.
$\pi = (20)(50) − (20)(10) = 800$.

c. AC = MC = 10, Q = 100 − 2P, MR = 50 − Q.
For profit maximization, MC = MR,
10 = 50 − Q, Q = 40, P = 30.
$\pi = (40)(30) − (40)(10) = 800$.

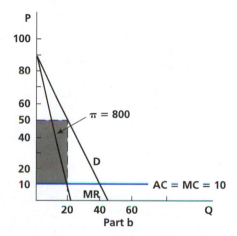

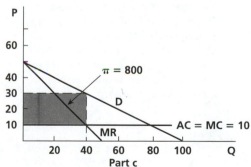

The supply curve for a monopoly is the single point on the demand curve that corresponds to profit maximization. Any attempt to connect equilibrium points (price/quantity points) on the market demand curves has little meaning and brings about a strange shape. One reason for this is that as the demand curve shifts, its elasticity (and its MR curve) often changes, bringing about widely varying price and quantity combinations.

10.5 A multiplant monopolist will still produce where MR = MC and will equalize MC among factories.

$MR = 100 - 2(q_1 + q_2)$ and $MC_1 = MC_2$
$q_1 - 5 = .5q_2 - 5$. $Q_1 = .5q_2$
$MR = 100 - 2(.5q_2 + q_2)$.
$MR = MC_2$, $100 - 2(1.5q_2) = .5q_2 - 5$.
$3.5q2 = 105$.
$q_2 = 30$ and $q_1 = 15$, so $Q_T = 45$.

10.7 $Q_D = 1,000 - 50P$; $MR = 20 - Q/25$ MC = 10 under PC; MC = 12 under monopoly

a. *Perfect competition:*
$P = MC = 10$.
$Q_D = 1,000 - 50(10) = 500 = Q_s$.
Monopoly:
$MC = MR$
$12 = 20 - Q/25$
$300 = 500 - Q$
$Q = 200$;
$200 = 1,000 - 50P$;
$50P = 800$; $P = 16$

b. Loss of consumer surplus due to monopolization can easily be obtained from the graph (shaded portion). Area of shaded portion = $(16 - 10)(200) + 1/2 (16 - 10)(500 - 200)$ = $1,200 + 900 = 2,100$. This area is much larger than loss of consumer surplus if monopolist's MC = 10.

c.

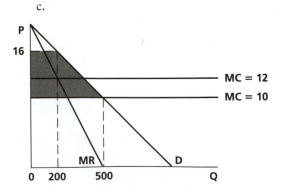

10.9 With a constant marginal cost, the graph shows that the rise in price will be less than the rise in marginal revenue as shown in the attached graph. The reason for this is that the MR curve is steeper than the demand curve so that a given fall in quantity causes a smaller vertical move along the demand curve. With an increasing marginal cost curve, the increase in price would be even smaller because MR increases by only a portion of the tax.

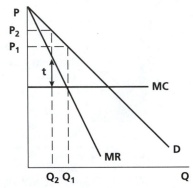

With a constant elasticity demand curve, the case is reversed, at least with constant MC.

Since $MR = P\left(1 + \dfrac{1}{e}\right)$ or $P^* = \dfrac{MC}{1 + \dfrac{1}{e}}$. With

constant MC, a unit tax will raise price to:

$$P^{**} = \dfrac{MC + t}{1 + \dfrac{1}{e}} = P^* + \dfrac{t}{1 + \dfrac{1}{e}} > P^* + t$$

because $e < -1$. An upward sloping MC curve will complicate matters, however, because the first term in this expression will fall with the implementation of the tax.

Chapter 11

11.1 a. When each firm sets a price of $2, $q_1 = 9$ and $q_2 = 9$.
Profits of each are zero since P = AC.

b. Now $q_1 = 11 - P_1$. According to the hint to Problem 10.6 for profit, maximization should set $P = 1/2(11 + 2) = 6.5$.
Now $q_1 = 4.5$, $\pi = 4.5(6.5 - 2) = 20.25$.

c. Same as (b): $P_2 = 6.5$, $q_2 = 4.5$.

d. Section (b) and (c) are inconsistent because firms do not set price as expected. One needs to use Cournot reaction functions.

e. With a single price policy, $q_1 = 10 - 1/2P$. $q_2 = 10 - 1/2P$. So, $q_1 + q_2 = 20 - P$. For maximum profits, set $P = 1/2(20 + 2) = 11$. Now $q_1 = q_2 = 4.5$. Profits of each $= 4.5(11 - 2) = 40.5$. Note the improvement over the noncooperative outcomes.

11.3 Most literature suggests that "planned obsolescence" is a profitable strategy for a monopoly, but not so under perfect competition since entrants would produce more durable commodities. The difficult part of the theory of durability is how to treat the market for used goods and the degree of substitutability between new and used goods. Under some conditions, the used-good market can constrain the monopoly to behave competitively.

11.5 Might still produce different goods depending on nature of demand and cost conditions since the firm would now have a monopoly in the production of several related products.

11.7 Might compare low point of AC curve to what price would be if firm producing that output were to enter the industry. If the resulting price is below the low point of its AC curve, the firm will not enter.

11.9

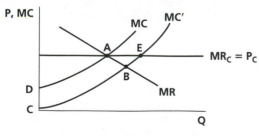

The traditional answer was provided by William Fellner who gives the following analysis:
$MR_C = P_C$ is demand facing competitive firm. MR is the marginal revenue curve for the monopolist.

Innovation shifts MC to MC′. Potential profits for competitive firms are CDAE. For monopoly, CDAB. Hence, innovation is more profitable for the competitive firm. It is more likely to adopt the innovation.

Chapter 12

12.1 Against A: high, B's best strategy is low; against B: low, A's best strategy is high. Any other strategy choice gives one player an incentive to switch.

12.3 a. Payoffs from Smith's perspective are +3, −1.

		Jones' Strategies		
		1	2	3
Smith's Strategy	1	+3	−1	−1
	2	−1	+3	−1
	3	−1	−1	+3

There is no Nash equilibrium in this game since any strategy announced by one player gives the other an incentive to switch.

b. Expected payoff to mixed strategy is for Smith:
⅓(3) + ⅓(−1) + ⅓(−1) = ⅓.
For Jones it is:
⅓(−3) + ⅓(1) + ⅓(1) = −⅓.
This mixed strategy is an equilibrium since neither player has an incentive to depart from it even if he or she knows what the other is doing (assuming the strategy choices are truly random; if not, player A can take advantage of any nonrandomness in B's choices).

12.5 a. If owners act as a cartel, they will maximize total revenue. $Q = 10,000 - 1,000P$. Hence, $P = 5$; $Q = 5,000$. For each owner, $q = 250$; Revenues = 1,250.

b. $P = 5$ is unstable since if one firm produces 251, $Q = 5,001$ and $P = 4.999$. Revenues = 1,254.7, so chiseling increases revenues for that firm.

c. With a suitably low price, there will be no incentive to cheat. With P = .30, for example, Q = 9,700 and q = 485. Revenues per firm = 145.50. If q = 486, P = .299. Revenues = 145.31, so there is no incentive to cheat. Notice that with fewer cartel members, this stable price is higher. With two firms, for example, if P = 3, Q = 7,000, and q = 3,500. Revenues per firm = 10,500. If q = 3,501, P = 2.999. Revenues for the firm = 10,499.50, so there is no incentive to chisel. Still, this stable price is well below the cartel price calculated in part a.

12.7 a. This game has two Nash equilibria:
(1) A = produce; B = don't produce
(2) A = don't produce; B = produce.

b. If A moves first, it can dictate that Nash equilibrium (1) is chosen. Similarly, if B goes first, it can assure that Nash equilibrium (2) is chosen.

c. Firm B could offer a bribe of 1 to firm A not to enter (if it is A's move first). This would yield identical profits, however, to those obtained when A moves first anyway.

12.9 a. With a maximin strategy, this person will choose "no picnic" since this assures a utility of at least 5.

b. U(picnic) = .6(0) + .4(20) = 8
U(no picnic) = .6(5) + .4(10) = 7
Using subjective probabilities, he or she will choose to go on picnic.

Chapter 13

13.1 a. With five workers, put each successively where its MP_L is greatest. First worker goes to A, second goes to B, third goes to A, fourth goes to C, fifth goes to A. Output = 21 + 8 + 5 = 34. MP of last worker is 4.

b. $P \cdot MP_L = \$1.00 \cdot 4 = \$4.00 = w$. With five workers, the wage bill is wL = $20. Profits are $\pi = TR - TC = PQ - wL = \$34 - \$20 = \$14$.

13.3 a. w = v = $1, so K and L will be used in a one-to-one ratio.
TC = (v · L) + (w · K) = L + K = 2L, so
$$AC = \frac{2L}{q} = \frac{2L}{\sqrt{KL}} = \frac{2L}{\sqrt{LL}} = 2 \text{ and}$$
MC = 2.

b. Since P = 2, quantity demanded is q = 400,000 − 100,000(2) = 200,000 pipe.
$$q = \frac{200,000 \text{ pipe}}{1,000 \text{ firms}} = 200 \text{ pipe/firm}.$$
$q = 200 = \sqrt{L \cdot K} = L$, so 200 workers are hired per firm, 200,000 by the industry.

c. When w = $2 and v = $1, cost minimization requires K/L = 2.
TC = wL + vK, so = 2L + K = 4L = $2\sqrt{2} \cdot q$, so AC = MC = $2\sqrt{2}$.

d. $P = 2\sqrt{2}$, Q = 400,000 − $100,000(2\sqrt{2})$ = 117,157.

$$L = \frac{200,000}{\sqrt{2}} = 141,000 \text{ workers hired by}$$
the industry.

e. If Q = 200,000 at the new wage,
$$L = \frac{200,000}{\sqrt{2}} = 141,000 \text{ workers would}$$
have been hired by the industry.
So if Q were unchanged, 59,000 fewer workers would have been hired = substitution effect. The remaining 58,000 fewer workers (141,000 − 83,000) are the result of the lower output; that is, the output effect.

13.5 a. 750 − 25w = 25w − 250 or w = 20, L = 250.

b. Demand for labor is now L = 750 − 25(w + 4) = 650 − 25w. Setting supply and demand equal yields w = 18, L = 200.

c. Now supply curve is L = 25(w + h) − 250. Positive values for h will shift the supply curve outward.

d. Setting the supply function in part c equal to the demand function in part b yields $650 - 25w = 25(w + h) - 250$ or $900 - 25h = 50w$. If $h = 2$, $w = 17$, $L = 225$. If $h = 4$, $w = 16$, $L = 250$. Notice that in this final case L is the same as in part a and the wage simply falls by 4 to represent the portion of wages received in fringe benefits.

13.7 Supply: $L = 80w$. $ME_L = \dfrac{L}{40}$.

Demand: $L = 400 - 40\,MVP_L$

a. For monopsonist $ME_L = MVP_L$.
$$L = 400 - 40MVP_L.$$
$$40MVP_L = 400 - L.$$
$$MVP_L = 10 - \frac{L}{40}.$$

Using the profit maximizing condition,
$$\frac{L}{40} = 10 - \frac{L}{40} \cdot \frac{2L}{40} = 10.$$
$$L = 200.$$
Get w from supply curve:
$$w = \frac{L}{80} = \frac{200}{80} + \$2.50.$$

b. For Carl, the marginal expense of labor now equals the minimum wage, and, in equilibrium, the marginal expense of labor will equal the marginal revenue product of labor.
$$W_m = ME_L = MVP_L.$$
$$W_m = \$3.00.$$

Carl's Demand	Supply
$L = 400 - 40MVP_L$	$L = 80w$
$L = 400 - 40(3)$	$L = 80(3)$
$L = 280$.	$L = 240$.

Demand > supply. Carl will hire 240 workers, with no unemployment. To study effects of minimum, try $3.33 and $4.00.
$W_m = \$3.33$
$$L = 400 - 40(3.33) \qquad L = 80(3.33)$$
$$= 267. \qquad\qquad\quad = 267.$$
Demand = supply, Carl will hire 267 workers, with no unemployment.
$W_m = \$4.00$
$$L = 400 - 40(4.00) \qquad L = 80(4.00)$$
$$= 240. \qquad\qquad\quad = 320.$$
Supply > demand, Carl will hire 240 workers, unemployment = 80.

c.

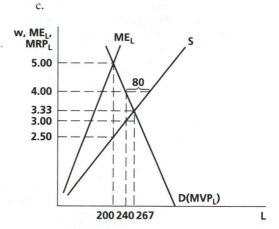

d. Under perfect competition, a minimum wage means higher wages but fewer workers employed. Under monopsony, a minimum wage may result in higher wages and more workers employed as shown by some of the cases studied in part b.

13.9 a. Budget constraint: $C = w(24 - H) + 10$.

b. Due to Mrs. Smith's preferences, she insists on spending half of potential income ($w \cdot 24 + 10$) on consumption and half on leisure. This means value of consumption = value of leisure (i.e., $w \cdot H$) for all wage rates.
$$C = wH$$
Substituting for C:
$$w(24 - H) + 10 = wH$$
$$24 - H + 10/w = H$$
$$2H = 24 + 10/w$$
$$H = 12 + 5/w$$
For $w = \$1.25$; $H = 16$; $C = 1.25(24 - 16) + 10 = 20$.
For $w = \$2.50$; $H = 14$; $C = 2.50(24 - 14) + 10 = 35$.
For $w = \$5.00$; $H = 13$; $C = 5.00(24 - 13) + 10 = 65$.
For $w = \$10.00$; $H = 12.5$; $C = 10.00(24 - 12.5) + 10 = 125$.

c. The graph shows Mrs. Smith's changing choices as the wage rises. Hours of leisure H fall toward 12 as w rises.

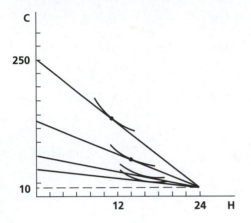

d. Mrs. Smith's labor supply curve can be constructed directly from the data in part b. It is upward sloping, being asymptotic to 12 hours as w rises.

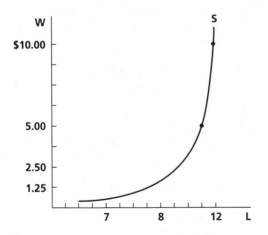

Chapter 14

14.1 a. The budget constraint shows that spending must equal income in present-value terms, but income and consumption are not constrained to be equal in either period.

    b. If this individual saves in period zero, consumption will of necessity exceed income in period 1.

    c. Because period 0 savings $(= Y_0 - C_0)$ earn interest, more can be spent in terms of dis-saving $(= C_1 - Y_1)$ in period 1.

14.3 a. Present value of income is $50,000 + 55,000/(1 + r) = 50,000 + 55,000/1.1 = 100,000$

    b. Prudence has MRS = $1 + r$, or $C_1/3\,C_0 = 1.1$.

    c. Budget constraint in present value terms is $100,000 = C_0 + C_1/1.1$.
Using the utility maximizing condition from part b gives
$100,000 = C_0 + 3.3\,C_0/1.1$.
Hence $C_0 = 25,000$. Savings in period 0 are 25,000. With these savings $C_1 = 55,000 + 25,000\,(1.1) = 82,500$.

    d. For Glitter, MRS = $3\,C_1/C_0 = 1.1$.
Substitution into budget constraint (Prudence and Glitter have the same budget constraint) yields
$100,000 = C_0 + 1.1\,C_0/3.3 = 4\,C_0/3$.
Hence, for her, $C_0 = 75,000$. Savings in period 0 are $-25,000$. Glitter borrows 25,000 and repays $25,000\,(1.1) = 27,500$. Hence $C_1 = 27,500$.

14.5 a. Assuming revenues are received at the end of each year gives a present value of $486,841 when $r = 0.1$. This falls short of the current purchase price of $500,000 for the ten trucks. When $r = 0.08$, the present value of future revenue is $520,637, which means that the investment would be profitable.

14.7 a. Price should be $1,000/(1.05)^{25} = 1,000/3.3864 = 295.30$.

    b. Scarcity costs = $295.30 - 100 = 195.30$

    c. Assuming real production costs stay at $100, scarcity costs in 25 years are $900.

    d. In 50 years price is $295.30(1.05)^{50} = 1,000(1.05)^{25} = 3,386$.

14.9 The fallacy here is that the calculation assumes that you have borrowed $10,000 for all 3 years. Since the repayment plan includes some repayment of the $10,000 too, the effective amount borrowed is only about half that amount. The actual effective interest rate on the loan, assuming that the $315 payments are made at the start of each month, is about 8.7 percent, well above the 5 percent opportunity cost.

Chapter 15

15.1 a. $E(1) = .50(100) + .50(-100) = 0$
$E(2) = .75(100) + .25(-300) = 0$
$E(3) = .90(100) + .10(-900) = 0$

b. Assume current income is $1,000.

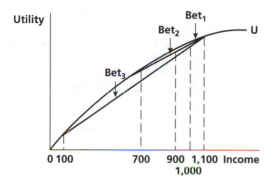

c. Bet 1 will be preferred since it has smaller variability.

15.3 a. Strategy one:

Outcome	Probability
12 eggs	.5
0 eggs	.5

Expected value = $.5 \cdot 12 + .5 \cdot 0 = 6$
Strategy two:

Outcome	Probability
12 eggs	.25
6 eggs	.5
0 eggs	.25

Expected value = $(0.25 \cdot 12) + (0.5 \cdot 6) + (0.25 \cdot 0) = 3 + 3 = 6$.

b.

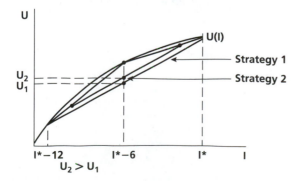

c. Gains from diversification are offset by costs of extra trips, so there may be an optimal number of such trips.

15.5 a. $E(U) = .75 \log(10,000) + .25 \log(9,000) = 3.9886$

b. $E(U)$ with insurance = $\log(9,750) = 3.9890$
∴ $U_w > U_{w.o}$.

c. Will pay up to point where $U_w = U_{w.o}$. So want $3.9886 = \log(10,000 - P)$ where P is the premium cost.
$10^{3.9886} = 10,000 - P = 9.741$
$P_{max} = \$259$.

d. Fair insurance: $E(L) = .30 \cdot 1,000 = \$300$
Since $\$300 > \$259$, she will not buy this insurance even though this is fair insurance. This is an example of moral hazard.

15.7 a. $U = \ln(\$18,000) = 9.798$

b. $U = \ln(\$18,300) = 9.815$

c. If Molly invests $100 in the trip, she will have a wealth of $17,900 if Crazy Eddie does not have the set and $18,200 if he does. $E(U) = .5\ln(17,900) + .5\ln(18,200) = 9.801$. Since this exceeds the utility from part a, it is worth the trip.

15.9 a. See graph.

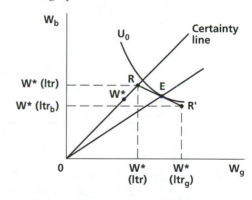

Risk-free option is R, risk option is R′.

b. Locus RR′ represents mixed portfolios.

c. Risk aversion as represented by curvature of indifference curves will determine equilibrium on RR′ (say E). If this person is very risk averse, he or she will have L-shaped indifference curves and choose point R.

Chapter 16

16.1 a. $MC = .4q$. $P = \$20$. Set $P = MC$. $20 = .4q$, $q = 50$.

b. $MCS = .5q$. Set $P = MCS$. $20 = .5q$. $q = 40$. At optimal production level of $q = 40$, the marginal cost of production is $MC = .4q = .4(40) = 16$, so the excise tax $t = 20 - 16 = \$4$.

c.

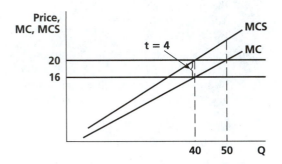

16.3 $AC = MC = 1,000/\text{well}$.

a. Produce where revenue/well $= 1,000 = 10q = 5,000 - 10N$. $N = 400$. There is an externality here because drilling another well reduces output in *all* wells.

b. Produce where $MVP = MC$ of well. Total value $= 5,000N - 10N^2$. $MVP = 5,000 - 20N = 1,000$. $N = 200$.

c. Let Tax $= X$. Want revenue/well $- X = 1,000$ when $N = 200$. At $N = 200$, average revenue per well $= 3,000$. Charge $X = 2,000$.

16.5 a. For profit maximization, set $P = MC$, $50 = 30 + .5Q$. Hence $Q = 40$ hives. There will be enough bees only to pollinate 10 acres.

b. Orchard owner would pay up to $25 per hive. A $20 subsidy would result in total receipts per hive of 70, and profit maximization would dictate $70 = 30 + 5Q$ or $Q = 80$—enough hives to pollinate the entire 20 acres.

16.7 a. Marginal valuation for person $A = P = 100 - q_A$; for B, Marginal valuation $= P = 200 - q_B$. Because of the public good nature of mosquito control, these should be added "vertically." Marginal value $= 300 - 2q$ (since $q_A = q_B$). Set this equal to marginal cost of 50, which gives $q = 125$.

b. Free-rider problem could result in having no production. Each person would let the other do it.

c. Total cost $= 50 \cdot 125 = \$6,250$. Area under demand curve for A $= \$4,688$, for B $= \$17,188$. One solution would be to share costs in proportion to these values.

16.9 a. This pool is excludable, unlike many public goods. It is nonrival, however, because there is a zero marginal cost for one more user.

b. Families as a whole are willing to pay $6,000 per day for the pool, which would cost only $5,000 per day. Building the pool would improve the allocation of resources.

c. None of these prices would cover the cost of the pool. A price of either $1 or $0 would be efficient but would require the pool to operate at a loss.

d. An efficient pricing scheme would require those who value the pool most to pay more. There is no single price policy that both covers the pool's cost and yields an efficient allocation.

e. The economic value of the pool is maximized when it is used by 2,000 families. To avoid operating at a loss, however, it still will be necessary for those who value the pool at $3 to pay that amount.

Brief Answers to MicroQuizzes

1.1 The curve is a "frontier" because it shows *the most* of one good that can be produced if the output of the other good is held fixed (assuming that resource availability is also held constant). With a *concave* shape, the opportunity cost of producing, say, X increases as X output increases. If the frontier were *convex,* the opportunity cost of producing more X would fall as X output expanded. That might happen, for example, if X production exhibited major economies of scale.

1.2 Supply and demand curves show economic actors' voluntary reactions to alternative prices. At the intersection of these curves, therefore, both parties to the transaction are satisfied. Any other P, Q combination would not lie at the intersection, so at least one party would not be at a position voluntarily chosen.

1.3 Consumer income, the prices of goods related to computers, or people's preferences for computing could all shift the demand. Supply would be shifted by anything that affects the costs of making computers. The price of computers *does not* shift either curve because the curves themselves reflect demanders' and suppliers' reactions to all possible prices.

1A.1 The intercept is in the same units as the dependent variable—100,000 pounds per week. The slope is the change in the dependent variable for a unit change in the independent variable—5,000 pounds per week for each one

dollar per pound increase in the price. If flounder were measured in pounds and price in cents, the equation would be: Q = 100,000 + 50P.

1A.2 If Y = −5X/6 + 10, Y = 0 when X = 12. Comparison of the graphs shows that the same change in X-intercept can come about through parallel shifts by suitably changing the Y-intercept.

1A.3 Here, each extra worker hour increases the grape harvest by 20 pounds per hour. The average productivity is given by Q/L = 100/L + 20. The value of this expression is 30 for L = 10, 25 for L = 20, and 22 for L = 50.

1A.4 All three sets of contour lines are the same. This shows that certain transformations of the function Y = X · Z have no effect on the appearance of the contour lines.

1A.5 The shift outward in Figure 1A.6 comes about because the intercept in the equation X + Y = 3 changes to 5. This is a change in one of the factors held constant under *ceteris paribus.* Figure 1A.6 resembles a market in which there has been an increase in demand, perhaps from an increase in consumers' incomes.

1A.6 Approach 1 fails because the demand curve will reflect several different curves depending on the incidence of DVD player ownership in each city. Approach 2 fails because the differing points used to estimate demand in fact reflect differing supply conditions. Thus, reasons for shifting demand may be confounded with reasons for differing supply.

2.1 Completeness implies that all of the points in the positive quadrant of the graph can be ranked. If, say, point X_1, Y_1 is preferred to X^*, Y^*, then any other point in the "?" areas for which $X \geq X_1$ and $Y \geq Y_1$ will also be preferred to X^*, Y^*.

2.2 Positively sloped indifference curves would imply that an increase in the amount of X consumed would have to be met by an *increase* in the amount of Y consumed to keep the individual equally well-off. But this would imply that an increase in either X or Y alone would diminish utility—a contradiction to the definition of economic "goods." The MRS cannot be computed at E or F because the indifference curve is not known at those points. All that is known is that E lies above U_1, F below it.

2.3 The budget constraint in this case would be a straight line with intercepts of 5 on the Frisbee axis and 10 on the beach ball axis. A doubling of income would double both of these intercepts. When Frisbees cost $25, the Frisbee intercept becomes 4 and the beach ball intercept remains at 10.

2.4 With these prices, an individual can forgo one movie DVD and buy an additional 1.7 music CDs or give up 1.7 CDs to get a DVD. If the MRS is 2 CDs for 1 DVD, he or she is willing to give up more CDs than required to get a DVD. Hence, he or she should buy fewer CDs and more DVDs in order to maximize utility.

2.5 1. In Figure 2.8(c), utility maximization requires that if $MRS > P_X/P_Y$ even when Y = 0, then Y = 0 is the best choice. In Figure 2.9(c), the MRS is 1 since these are identical goods, so if $P_X/P_Y > 1$ should choose X = 0. This author never eats lima beans because $P_{limas}/P_Y > MRS$ even when limas = 0. Because limas sell at a positive price, however, someone must like these dreadful vegetables.

2. The equilibrium in Figure 2.9(d) will exist at the vertex of the indifference curves for any price ratio. No matter what the separate prices are of left and right shoes, this person will always consume them in pairs (unless he or she cannot afford a single pair).

3.1 In the first case, housing and other goods will both increase directly in proportion to income. In the second, the goods will increase in proportion to income until housing reaches an "adequate" level; then, no more will be bought, and all extra income will be used to purchase other goods.

3.2 In Figure 2.5(d), there are no substitution effects. This person only changes consumption because of changes in purchasing power. In Figure 2.5(c), substitution effects are (infinitely) large. A small change in the price ratio from $P_X/P_Y > 1$ to $P_X/P_Y < 1$ will cause this person to change from consuming only Y to consuming only X. Changes in price that do not cross the 1.0 "threshold" will have no substitution effects, however.

3.3 A decrease in the price of tea will have a substitution effect that reduces coffee purchases but an income effect that increases coffee purchases (assuming coffee is a normal good). A decrease in the price of cream will increase coffee purchases because the goods are complementary. It will also increase coffee purchases because of a positive income effect (again, assuming that coffee is a normal good). The income effects are in the same direction in both of these cases, but the substitution effects are in different directions.

3.4 Reporter 1 confuses a movement along the demand curve for oranges (the freeze raises price causing such a move) and a shift of a curve. The curve does not shift, so there are no "lower prices" as a result. Reporter 2 also makes the confusion by implying that demand falls and remains low. The freeze-induced movement along the demand curve can be reversed by a more normal crop. Notice how all of this could be clarified by graphing the events described.

3.5   Consumer surplus is measured on a demand curve for which the axes are price (in dollars, say, per unit) and quantity (units). Therefore, areas are measured in $/unit · units = $—consumer surplus is a monetary measure that can be compared to other monetary figures. If price rose by 10 percent and quantity remained unchanged, consumer surplus would fall by 10 percent. When there is some nonzero price elasticity of demand, quantity would fall, so the decline in consumer surplus would be greater than 10 percent.

4.1   Case 1 would shift the demand for nutmeg *outward* so that at each price quantity demanded would increase by 2 million pounds per year. That is, the curve would be shifted to the right by an amount of 2 million pounds measured horizontally. Case 2 would shift the demand for nutmeg *upward* by $1 at each quantity. That is, the curve would shift upward in a vertical direction by $1.

4.2   Producer 1 would benefit from the lower price if the demand for theater seats were elastic. In this case, it is safe to assume that the costs of running the movie theater are not affected by the price charged. For Producer 2, the tax increases marginal costs by 0.10 at each level of output. Price should also increase by that amount if demand were totally inelastic, but the increase would be less if demand were somewhat elastic. If the demand facing the firm were completely elastic, there would be no increase in price because of the tax increase (unless that increase were paid by all other firms in the marketplace as well).

4.3   If every good had an income elasticity of demand greater than 1, then a 1 percent increase in income would cause total spending to rise by more than 1 percent—an impossibility given the budget constraint. If every income elasticity of demand were less than 1, then a 1 percent increase in income would increase total spending by less than 1 percent—leaving some income unspent (which would not maximize utility in a one-period model). If 95 percent of income were spent on housing, a high income elasticity of demand would result in housing expenditures quickly exhausting income when income rises. For example, suppose a consumer had an income of $100,

spending $95 on housing. If the income elasticity of demand for housing were 2, then a 10 percent increase in income (to $110) would cause a 20 percent increase in spending on housing (to $114). Hence, housing spending would now exceed income, an impossibility.

4.4   A fall in the price of beer will cause consumers to substitute beer for pizza. But it will also increase overall purchasing power, which will tend to increase pizza purchases. The substitution and income effects work in opposite directions. Because a 10 percent increase in all prices and income must leave demand unchanged, the sum of these three elasticities must be zero.

5.1   In Case 1, the marginal product of labor is 50 apples per hour. The average productivity of labor declines as L increases because the fixed term, "10," is divided by progressively larger amounts of labor. In Case 2, the marginal product of labor is five books dusted per minute. The average productivity of labor increases as L increases because the "−10" term is divided by progressively larger amounts of labor input.

5.2   The RTS here is: ½ hour of labor time can be substituted for an increase in shovel size. The one-hole isoquant is two points: (a) 1 hour, small shovel; (b) ½ hour, large shovel. A worker using a small shovel can dig ½ the hole in ½ an hour. If he or she then switches to the large shovel, the hole can be completed in ¼ an hour. Hence, this production technique would use ¾ an hour of labor time.

5.3   Probably constant returns to scale—twice as many teachers with twice as many books can educate twice as many students. There probably is some substitution possible between teachers and books.

5.4   1. At least in part technical progress, though some substitution also
        2. At least in part technical progress, though some substitution also
        3. Almost exclusively substitution of capital for labor
        4. Almost entirely technical progress

6.1 Rent payments are for housing services. Someone who lives in his or her own house similarly pays for such services in the form of forgone earnings on the funds invested. So, the key question is which form of housing consumption provides the services at lower costs (including opportunity costs). Paying off the mortgage converts explicit interest costs into implicit ones (the forgone earnings one could obtain by investing funds tied up in the house). If opportunity costs are the same as mortgage costs, burning the mortgage has no significance.

6.2 1. With fixed proportions, it will take 10 labor hours and 20 hours of capital services to produce 100 units of output. Total cost will be $10 \cdot 10 + 20 \cdot 4 = 180$. If capital rental rates rise to 10, the firm will continue to use the same fixed proportions but its total costs will increase to 300.

   2. With this production function, the RTS (L for K) is 2. That is, an extra unit of labor can substitute for two units of capital. With $w = 10$ and $v = 4$, cost minimization requires that the firm use only capital: if it hires 20 units to produce 100 units of output, total costs are 80 (they would be 100 if only labor were used). If v increases to 10, labor becomes the less expensive input. The firm will use $L = 10$ and incur total costs of 100.

6.3 1. Average will be $(80 \cdot 5 + 60 \cdot 2)/7 = 520/7 = 74.3$.

   2. Need $(520 + 3x)/10 = 80$, $3x = 280$, $x = 93.3$.

   3. When the marginal score falls below the average, the average falls. When the marginal score exceeds the average, the average rises.

6.4 1. SAC exceeds AC for every output level except q*, because at all other output levels the firm is using a level of capital input that is not cost minimizing.

   2. SMC exceeds MC for q > q*, because there are more significant diminishing returns to variable inputs in the short run (when some inputs are fixed) than in the long run.

3. An increase in K above K* would shift the SAC and SMC rightward along the AC curve.

6.5 The larger the fraction of total costs that are attributable to labor, the greater will be the effect of the increase in wages on total costs. If the firm is able to substitute capital for labor, the extent of this cost increase may be ameliorated.

7.1 1. Profit per unit is greatest when the gap between average revenue and average cost is greatest. That may not be where marginal revenue and marginal costs are equal. Even if application of the MR = MC rule reduces profit per unit, it will increase *total* profits.

   2. Since price is equal to "average revenue," the proposed rule would indeed maximize profit per unit. When average revenue is fixed, minimizing average cost would achieve this goal. For the reasons listed in 1, however, this would not maximize *total* profits.

7.2 1. The demand for any one crossing is elastic. When all crossings are taken together, however, the demand is inelastic.

   2. The same argument applies here. The demand for meals in any one town may be elastic, but, if the tax increase is statewide, consumers cannot so easily escape it.

7.3 1. Equation 7.9 implies that $MR/P = 1 + 1/e$. Hence, the less elastic is the demand (assuming $e < -1$), the smaller will be the ratio MR/P.

   2. Equation 7.9 implies that the *percentage* change in P will be the same as the *percentage* change in MR if e does not change. If e changes, the two percentages may differ.

7.4 1. An increase in fixed costs will affect neither the SMC curve nor the shutdown point.

   2. The fine could be treated as a fixed, cost and therefore would have no effect on supply decisions. A daily fine would still be treated as a fixed cost in Whopper supply decisions. But it might provide an incentive to the firm to adopt new, less littering packaging materials.

7.5 1. If you are knowledgeable, you can monitor the mechanics behavior more effectively.
2. With many mechanics, honest ones will have an incentive to signal their quality to potential buyers, perhaps by advertising testimonials.

8.1 1. When only 100 paddles are in the air
2. When paddles in the air increase to 100 (Are these two prices the same?)

8.2 1. The farmer cannot get the $3.25, even though his or her costs may require that, because any buyer can get all the corn desired at $3.
2. No seller will sell to the soup kitchen at $2.75 if he or she can make $3 elsewhere (unless the seller derives utility from helping the poor).

8.3 1. The price would rise to $7. Demand would be 3 and supply would be $5 - 2 = 3$.
2. Trial and error using Table 8.3 suggests that a price to buyers of $8 and to sellers of $4 would create the necessary tax "wedge." In this case, the quantity demanded and supplied would be 2.

8.4 1. Assuming the industry as perfectly competitive, economic profits will be zero despite the price rise, since costs will rise too (rising costs are the explanation of the noninfinite elasticity of supply).
2. Existing firms will also continue to earn zero profits because their costs too will rise.

9.1 1. If expansion of the industry does not lead to increases in the prices of any inputs, the long-run supply curve will be perfectly elastic.
2. As the demand for potato land increases, its price will rise. This will be the sole reason for rising potato prices. Producer surplus will be the extra rents earned by potato landowners. The rents do not "cause" the price increase—rather, they are a result of it.

9.2 1. The short-run impact would depend on the extent of the increase in demand and on the supply response that was prevented by the price control. The size of the latter effect would depend on the short-run elasticity of supply, which in turn is determined by diminishing returns in the short run. The long-run impact would depend on the long-run elasticity of supply, which depends on the possibility of rising input costs (e.g., for research inputs).
2. In the short run, firms would lose producer surplus in the form of short-run profits. In the long run, the losses would accrue to the inputs that, in the absence of the price control, would have increased in price.

9.3 1. Because short-run supply is less elastic than long-run supply
2. One would need to examine the reasons for the upward slope in the long-run supply curve. Owners of inputs that cause the upward slope would pay the producer's share of the tax.

9.4 1. Consumer surplus is $\frac{1}{2}(10 - 7)(3) = 4.5$. Producer surplus is $\frac{1}{2}(5 - 2)(3) = 4.5$. Taxes are 6. Hence, total surplus plus taxes amount to 15. Prior to the tax, consumer surplus was 8 and producer surplus was 8. With the tax, there is a deadweight loss of 1. That can also be computed as $\frac{1}{2}(t)(\Delta Q) = \frac{1}{2}(2)(1) = 1$.
2. With a tax of 4, $P - 2 = 10 - (P + 4)$, or $P = 4$; $P + t = 8$; and $Q = 2$. Deadweight loss is $\frac{1}{2}(t)(\Delta Q) = \frac{1}{2}(4)(2) = 4$. Consumer surplus $= \frac{1}{2}(10 - 8)(2) = 2$, producer surplus $= \frac{1}{2}(4 - 2)(2) = 2$, and tax collections are 8. Adding the three gives 12, a loss of 4 from total surplus when there are no taxes.
3. With a tax of, say, 8, $Q = 0$. All producer and consumer surplus would be lost. There would be no tax collected.

9.5 1. Relative to a situation of free trade, domestic producers pay none of this tax. Assuming that the foreign supply curve is infinitely elastic, foreign producers pay none of the tax either. The tariff is paid solely by domestic consumers.
2. The increase in producer surplus from the tariff goes to those inputs that give rise to the positively sloped long-run supply curve.
3. Both areas are losses of consumer surplus that are not captured by firms nor by the government.

9A.1 The primary reason for the second supply curve is to allow for repercussions in labor markets that serve the tomato industry. The rise in tomato pickers' wages shifts the supply curve. A model that looked at the effect of the shift in demand without considering these labor market effects would underpredict the impact of the increase in demand on tomato prices.

9A.2 1. Only the point for which X = Y on the frontier would be economically efficient.
2. A point for which X = 2Y on the frontier is inefficient because utility can be improved by producing more Y and less X until a point where X = Y is reached.

9A.3 The initial price of X would be below equilibrium. The initial price for Y would be above equilibrium. Raising P_X and lowering P_Y would restore equilibrium in both markets simultaneously.

9A.4 1. The only efficient point is where Smith gets all the X and Jones gets all the Y.
2. In this case, only the points on the diagonal of the box would be efficient.
3. In this case, all of the points in the box would be efficient.

10.1 1. The monopoly is constrained by the demand curve for its product. That curve provides a menu of price-quantity combinations—once one variable is chosen, the other is defined as well.
2. The profit maximization rule for price setting must still focus on the MR/MC idea. The price should be chosen so that the extra revenue from lowering the price slightly (this amount must be positive because the monopoly will only operate where demand is elastic) is just equal to the extra costs involved in producing the extra output that is sold.

10.2 1. The increase in demand will shift the marginal revenue curve outward. If MC is positively sloped, quantity will increase. Since MR has also increased, P will increase unless the elasticity of demand changes greatly (see part 2).

2. Although quantity will always rise when MR shifts outward along a positively sloped MC curve, price itself could fall if demand became much more elastic. Since MR = P(1 + 1/e), a large enough increase in (1 + 1/e) could allow P to fall even though MR increases.

10.3 The deadweight loss of consumer surplus is fundamentally a loss of utility to consumers—they receive less utility than they would if the market were competitive. Monopoly profits are a transfer from consumer surplus to the monopoly. They are not part of the deadweight loss.

10.4 1. The notion of "higher demand" is meaningless. It is elasticity of demand that matters.
2. The monopoly should set MR = MC in both markets. If the elasticities in the markets differ, this need not imply that the market with higher MC will have a higher price.

10.5 With U-shaped average costs, there is no regulatory dilemma—the regulator can set P = MC = minimum AC and achieve efficiency with zero economic profits. If P is set below AC, losses will result. Clearly, P could also be set below the shutdown price.

11.1 1. This statement implies that a lower price for a single firm will generate extra revenues for that firm that exceed the share of extra revenues they would obtain if the entire cartel expanded output.
2. Again, this means that the extra revenue obtained by a cartel member acting alone exceeds what the cartel member would receive if the cartel acted in unison.

11.2 1. Yes—if Firm B knows that Firm A will produce 40, its optimal choice is also to produce 40.
2. No—if Firm B knows A's reaction function, it can take advantage of that knowledge (see the discussion of this possibility in Chapter 12).

11.3 In the price leadership model, the competitive fringe earns zero long-run profits. The leader can, however, earn long-run economic profits.

These provide a target to other firms that might wish to become the leader.

11.4 The four firms are not price takers. They are forced to operate at the low points of their average cost curves by the free entry assumption. When P = minimum AC, however, it is also true that P = MC.

12.1 1. The Cournot solution is a Nash equilibrium because each participant's choice of strategy is optimal given the other participant's strategy.
2. The cartel solution is not a Nash equilibrium because, say, $q_A = 30$ is not optimal against $q_B = 30$.

12.2 1. A Prisoner's Dilemma (PD) because any agreement to clean up offers incentives to cheat
2. Not a PD because there is no unstable equilibrium strategy choice
3. Not a PD because both may have incentives to stick to fully cooperative strategies (though the precise incentives to cooperate depend on how grades are awarded)
4. Possibly a PD since an agreement to take the long route is unstable

Repetition of the room-cleaning game may yield cooperation because of the negative consequences of failing to do so. It is unclear that repetition of the shortcut game would yield cooperative behavior because the number of players is not well defined. Repetition of the candy and studying games may also yield different behavior than exhibited in single plays.

12.3 1. If either believes that it has only a finite horizon, tacit collusion is less likely—indeed impossible within the simple trigger-price model.
2. A greater number of members also reduces the likelihood of tacit collusion because the share of monopoly profits falls as the number of firms expands, but each firm can still capture the entire market for a period by cheating.

12.4 Firm B would perform the same analysis as A and opt for $q_B = 60$. With a combined output of 120, price would fall to zero.

12.5 1. Dumping is supposed to drive out domestic competitors. Once these firms depart the industry, the foreign firm can raise price to the monopoly level.
2. Although dumping will also be an unsuccessful strategy if reentry by firms is costless, possible informational asymmetries between domestic and foreign firms may make some game-theory scenarios more likely to support the dumping strategy.

13.1 1. The monopoly will hire labor up to the point at which $w = MR \cdot MP_L$ and capital up to the point at which $v = MR \cdot MP_K$. Because $MR < P$, $w < MVP_L$, $v < MVP_K$.
2. Even for the monopoly, $w/v = MP_L/MP_K$ (the MR term cancels out), so the firm is minimizing cost.

13.2 1. There will be no substitution effects from the wage increase. But the wage increase may cause a rise in gasoline prices and therefore a fall in the demand for gasoline and for attendants to pump it.
2. Because of the fixed-proportions nature of production, again there is no need to worry about substitution effects. A 10 percent rise in wages will raise gasoline prices by 3.33 percent. That will result in a decline in purchases of 1.67 percent and a similar decline in hiring of attendants. Hence, the elasticity of demand is $-0.167 (= -1.67/10)$.

13.3 As for any tax, the actual incidence of the 12 percent total tax depends on the elasticities of supply and demand.

13.4 Yes, there is a deadweight loss triangle in Figure 13.5 that is similar to the deadweight loss from monopoly. Part of the loss is suffered by suppliers who receive lower wages than they would under competition; part is suffered by demanders who cannot convert all of the surplus they would enjoy under competition into monopsony profits.

13A.1 1. The indifference curves have income and substitution effects of increases in w always precisely balanced at 7 hours of work.

2. The indifference curve map intersects the leisure axis with a slope steeper than the prevailing wage rate.

13A.2 The proportional tax on wages effectively reduces the wage rate, inducing income and substitution effects in labor supply—the substitution effect would favor less work, the income effect more work. A lump-sum tax would have no substitution effect, only an income effect favoring more work.

14.1 1. C_1 is effectively "cheaper" than C_0 because interest can be earned before C_1 is purchased. If $r = 0.10$, the relative price of C_1 is $1/1.1 = 0.909$. Refraining from buying 0.909 units of C_0 permits this person to buy one unit of C_1.
2. An increase in r reduces $1/(1 + r)$. For example, if $r = 0.15$, the relative price of C_1 is 0.870, a reduction from 0.909. This price decline has both income and substitution effects that favor consuming more C_1. The ambiguity is in the effect on C_0: a higher relative price of C_0 creates substitution effects causing C_0 to fall but income effects causing C_0 to rise (because the higher interest rate increases the person's purchasing power in this case).

14.2 A pure inflation would not affect the real interest rate nor the depreciation rate in Equation 15.1. It would raise the price of machinery, P, and the price of the firm's output, P*, both by the same amount. Hence, in the equation $MVP_K = P^*MP_K = v = P(r + d)$, the effects of inflation would appear on both sides and would cancel out, leaving the firm's capital use decision unchanged.

14.3 Clearly, the present value of the payments is not $20 million. To calculate the present value, one would need to assume a specific nominal interest rate (nominal because the lottery payments are nominal). At 5 percent, for example, $1 million per year for 20 years has a present value of $12.5 million, significantly less than $20 million. At a 10 percent interest rate, the present value is only $8.5 million.

14.4 1. The finite nature of the resource poses the same sort of opportunity cost for the monopoly as for a competitive firm.
2. If the future price is assumed to be the same for the monopoly and the competitive firm, the result that the resource price must rise at the rate of interest implies that the monopoly price will be identical to the competitive price in all time periods. The firm cannot exercise its monopoly power.

14A.1 If $1 is invested for 3 years, the terms in the expansion have the following meanings:
a. 1—the original dollar is returned.
b. $3i$—interest is earned on the original dollar in each year.
c. $3i^2$—interest earned on Year 1's interest in Year 2 (i^2) plus interest on Year 1's interest in Year 3 (i^2) plus interest on Year 2's interest in Year 3 (i^2), which equals $3i^2$ in all.
d. i^3—interest earned in Year 3 on the interest earned in Year 2 on Year 1's interest.

14A.2 With a 5 percent interest rate, the present value of $1,000 in 5 years is $784 (see Table 15A.2). The value of $3,000 in 25 years is $3(295) = $885, so it is worth the wait. If the interest rate is 10 percent, the $1,000 has a present value of $621, and the $3,000 has a present value of $277: With the higher interest rate, the wait is clearly not worthwhile.

14A.3 1. Increasing the annual payment to $60 would raise the yield to 5.32 percent.
2. Increasing the maturity value to $1,100 would raise the yield to 5.03 percent.
3. Reducing the maturity to 23 years would lower the yield to 4.81 percent (because the capital loss from $1,095 to $1,000 now occurs sooner).

14A.4 Depreciation can be handled by assuming that the machine's rental rate deteriorates at the rate d per period. Hence, in Period n, the numerator to Equation 14A.33 should be $v/(1 + d)^n$. The equation therefore becomes $\sum_1^n v/(1 + r)^i (1 + d)^i$. Because $(1 + r)(1 + d) \approx (1 + r + d)$, this can be approximated by

$\sum_{1}^{n} v/(1 + r + d)^i$, and taking n to infinity yields

$P = v/(r + d)$, which is Equation 14.1.

15.1 1. 0
2. $200
3. $100

15.2 If the utility of wealth function were linear, the person would be risk neutral. He or she would prefer risk if the function were convex (rather than concave as shown in Figure 15.1).

15.3 1. The expected value of the bet is zero in either case, but the variability of outcomes is much higher with the single flip.
2. The expected time to be served is the same under either approach, but the variability is higher with lines for each teller (the feeling that one has chosen the wrong line is universal).
3. Your author feels that any scoring in sports involves some randomness. Hence, sports in which many goals are scored will be more likely to reveal the best team than sports where only a few goals are scored (true, soccer fans will probably disagree).

15.4 1. There is no risk because C is the same no matter which state of the world occurs.
2. The actuarially fair slope is $-0.6/0.4 = -1.5$—this person should be able to trade 1 unit of
C_1 for 1.5 units of C_2 because State 1 is more likely to occur.
3. The slope of the indifference curve is determined by the expected MRS, which is also given by the ratios of the expected marginal utility of C_1 to the expected marginal utility of C_2.
4. If the probabilities of State 1 and State 2 are 0.6 and 0.4 respectively, then the expected MRS is $0.6MU(C_1)/0.4MU(C_2)$. Setting this

equal to the actuarially fair price ratio (0.6/0.4) implies that $MU(C1) = MU(C_2)$. If the marginal utility function is the same for both states of the world, this implies $C_1 = C_2$—that the person is on the Certainty Line.

16.1 These deadweight losses are losses of utility that would have gone to consumers under an alternative market equilibrium, just as in the monopoly case.

16.2 1. In the absence of enforceable property rights, Coase-type exchanges would not occur because neither party could be sure that the other would stick to the agreement.
2. With high transactions costs, property rights' assignments matter. The rights should be assigned to the party most likely to internalize the externality. This observation is crucial to the study of law and economics.

16.3 1. Under all three strategies, firms are left on their own to choose cost-minimizing control strategies. The requirement of specific technologies for all firms would not be likely to result in cost minimization.
2. The government does not need to know anything about the specific cost functions of firms under any of the three market-based strategies.

16.4 1. Free riding arises because individuals obtain benefits from the public good without paying for them. That requires nonexclusion. If exclusion were possible (even if the good were nonrival), production could take place in "clubs."
2. To achieve efficiency with nonrival goods requires that the price for each use be zero. Without effective policing of this use, free riders may still benefit.

Glossary

A

accounting cost The concept that inputs cost what was paid for them. (p. 188)

adverse selection When buyers and sellers have different information, market outcomes may exhibit adverse selection—the quality of goods or services traded will be biased toward market participants with better information. (p. 507)

asymmetric information A situation in which buyers and sellers have different amounts of information about a market transaction. (p. 522)

average cost Total cost divided by output; a common measure of cost per unit. (p. 197)

average effect The ratio of Y to X at a particular value of X. (Also the slope of the ray from the origin to the function.) (p. 36)

B

barriers to entry Factors that prevent new firms from entering a market. (p. 329)

bilateral monopoly A market in which both suppliers and demanders have monopoly power. Pricing is indeterminate in such markets. (p. 441)

budget constraint The limit that income places on the combinations of goods that an individual can buy. (p. 70)

C

cartel model A model of pricing in which firms coordinate their decisions to act as a multiplant monopoly. (p. 363)

ceteris paribus **assumption** In economic analysis, holding all other factors constant so that only the factor being studied is allowed to change. (p. 56)

coalitions Combinations of two or more players in a game who adopt coordinated strategies. (p. 412)

Coase theorem If bargaining is costless, the social cost of an externality will be taken into account by the parties, and the allocation of resources will be the same no matter how property rights are assigned. (p. 537)

common property Property that may be used by anyone without cost. (p. 536)

competitive fringe A group of firms that act as price takers in a market dominated by a price leader. (p. 372)

complements Two goods such that when the price of one increases, the quantity demanded of the other falls. (p. 108)

complete preferences The assumption that an individual is able to state which of any two options is preferred. (p. 59)

composite good Combining expenditures on several different goods whose relative prices do not change into a single good for convenience in analysis. (p. 81)

compound interest Interest paid on prior interest earned. (p. 483)

constant cost case A market in which entry or exit has no effect on the cost curves of firms. (p. 269)

consumer surplus The extra value individuals receive from consuming a good over what they pay for it. What people would be willing to pay for the right to consume a good at its current price. (pp. 116, 284)

contour lines Lines in two dimensions that show the sets of values of the independent variables that yield the same value for the dependent variable. (p. 43)

contract curve The set of all efficient allocations of the existing goods in an exchange situation. Points off that curve are necessarily inefficient, since individuals can be made unambiguously better off by moving to the curve. (p. 326)

Cournot equilibrium A solution to the Cournot model in which each firm makes the correct assumption about what the other firm will produce. (p. 369)

Cournot model A model of duopoly in which each firm assumes the other firm's output will not change if it changes its own output level. (p. 366)

cross-price elasticity of demand The percentage change in the quantity demanded of a good in response to a 1 percent change in the price of another good. (p. 144)

D

deadweight loss Losses of consumer and producer surplus that are not transferred to other parties. (p. 299)

decreasing cost case A market in which the entry of firms decreases firms' costs. (p. 276)

demand function A representation of how quantity demanded depends on prices, income, and preferences. (p. 89)

dependent variable In algebra, a variable whose value is determined by another variable or set of variables. (p. 29)

diminishing returns Hypothesis that the cost associated with producing one more unit of a good rises as more of that good is produced. (p. 16)

diversification The spreading of risk among several options rather than choosing only one. (p. 511)

dominant strategy A strategy that is optimal regardless of the strategy adopted by an opponent. (p. 391)

E

economic cost The amount required to keep an input in its present use; the amount that it would be worth in its next best alternative use. (p. 188)

economic profits (π) The difference between a firm's total revenues and its total economic costs. (p. 191)

economically efficient allocation of resources An allocation of resources in which the sum of consumer and producer surplus is maximized. Reflects the best (utility-maximizing) use of scarce resources. (pp. 288, 315)

economics The study of the allocation of scarce resources among alternative final uses. (p. 4)

economies of scope Reductions in the costs of one product of a multiproduct firm when the output of another product is increased. (p. 210)

Edgeworth box diagram A graphic device for illustrating all of the possible allocations of two goods (or two inputs) that are in fixed supply.

elasticity The measure of the percentage change in one variable brought about by a 1 percent change in some other variable. (p. 131)

equilibrium price The price at which the quantity demanded by buyers of a good is equal to the quantity supplied by sellers of the good. (pp. 17, 254)

equity The fairness of the distribution of goods or utility. (p. 323)

expansion path The set of cost-minimizing input combinations a firm will choose to produce various levels of output (when the prices of inputs are held constant). (p. 195)

expected value The average outcome from an uncertain gamble. (p. 501)

externality The effect of one party's economic activities on another party that is not taken into account by the price system. (pp. 322, 530)

F

fair games Games that cost their expected value. (p. 501)

fair insurance Insurance for which the premium is equal to the expected value of the loss. (p. 506)

firm Any organization that turns inputs into outputs. (p. 157)

firm's short-run supply curve The relationship between price and quantity supplied by a firm in the short run. (p. 236)

fixed costs Costs associated with inputs that are fixed in the short run. (p. 205)

fixed-proportions production function A production function in which the inputs must be used in a fixed ratio to one another. (p. 174)

free rider A consumer of a nonexclusive good who does not pay for it in the hope that other consumers will. (p. 550)

functional notation A way of denoting the fact that the value taken on by one variable (Y) depends on the value taken on by some other variable (X) or set of variables. (p. 29)

fundamental theorem of welfare economics A perfectly competitive price system will bring about an economically efficient allocation of resources. (p. 316)

G

general equilibrium model An economic model of a complete system of markets. (p. 312)

Giffen's paradox A situation in which an increase in a good's price leads people to consume more of the good. (p. 102)

H

homogeneous demand function Quantity demanded does not change when prices and income increase in the same proportion. (p. 90)

I

imperfect competition A market situation in which buyers or sellers have some influence on the prices of goods or services. (p. 319)

income effect (in demand theory) The part of the change in quantity demanded that is caused by a change in real income. (p. 94)

income effect of a change in w Movement to a higher indifference curve in response to a rise in the real wage rate. If leisure is a normal good, a rise in w causes an individual to work less. (p. 453)

income elasticity of demand The percentage change in the quantity demanded of a good in response to a 1 percent change in income. (p. 141)

increase or decrease in demand The change in demand for a good caused by changes in the price of another good, in income, or in preferences. Graphically represented by a shift of the entire demand curve. (p. 114)

increase or decrease in quantity demanded The increase or decrease in quantity demanded caused by a change in the good's price. Graphically represented by the movement along a demand curve. (p. 114)

increasing cost case A market in which the entry of firms increases firms' costs. (p. 272)

independent variable In an algebraic equation, a variable that is unaffected by the action of another variable and may be assigned any value. (p. 29)

indifference curve A curve that shows all the combinations of goods or services that provide the same level of utility. (p. 61)

indifference curve map A contour map that shows the utility an individual obtains from all possible consumption options. (p. 64)

individual demand curve A graphic representation of the relationship between the price of a good and the quantity of it demanded by a person, holding all other factors constant. (p. 110)

inferior good A good that is bought in smaller quantities as income increases. (p. 93)

initial endowments The initial holdings of goods from which trading begins. (p. 328)

intercept The value of Y when X equals zero. (p. 31)

interest Payment for the current use of funds. (p. 482)

isoquant A curve that shows the various combinations of inputs that will produce the same amount of output. (p. 163)

isoquant map A contour map of a firm's production function. (p. 163)

L

leisure Time spent in any activity other than market work. (p. 448)

Lindahl equilibrium Balance between people's demand for public goods and the tax shares that each must pay for them. (p. 551)

linear function An equation that is represented by a straight-line graph. (p. 31)

long run The period of time in which a firm may consider all of its inputs to be variable in making its decisions. (p. 202)

long-run elasticity of supply The percentage change in quantity supplied in the long run in response to a 1 percent change in price. (p. 274)

M

marginal cost The additional cost of producing one more unit of output. (p. 198)

marginal effect The change in Y brought about by a one unit change in X at a particular value of X. (Also the slope of the function.) (p. 36)

marginal expense The cost of hiring one more unit of an input. Exceeds the price of the input if the firm faces an upward-sloping supply curve for the input. (p. 435)

marginal product The additional output that can be produced by adding one more unit of a particular input while holding all other inputs constant. (p. 160)

marginal rate of substitution (MRS) The rate at which an individual is willing to reduce consumption of one good when he or she gets one more unit of another good. The negative of the slope of an indifference curve. (p. 62)

marginal rate of technical substitution (RTS) The amount by which one input can be reduced when one more unit of another input is added while holding output constant. The negative of the slope of an isoquant. (p. 165)

marginal revenue The extra revenue a firm receives when it sells one more unit of output. (p. 224)

marginal revenue curve A curve showing the relation between the quantity a firm sells and the revenue yielded by the last unit sold. Derived from the demand curve. (p. 231)

marginal revenue product The extra revenue obtained from selling the output produced by hiring an extra worker or machine. (p. 421)

marginal value product (MVP) A special case of marginal revenue product in which the firm is a price taker for its output. (p. 421)

market demand The total quantity of a good or service demanded by all potential buyers. (p. 126)

market demand curve The relationship between the total quantity demanded of a good or service and its price, holding all other factors constant. (p. 126)

market line A line showing the relationship between risk and annual returns that an investor can achieve by mixing financial assets. (p. 513)

market period A short period of time during which quantity supplied is fixed. (p. 254)

median voter A voter whose preferences for a public good represent the middle point of all voters' preferences for the good. (p. 557)

microeconomics The study of the economic choices individuals and firms make and of how those choices create markets. (p. 4)

models Simple theoretical descriptions that capture the essentials of how the economy works. (p. 4)

monopolistic competition Market in which each firm faces a negatively sloped demand curve and there are no barriers to entry. (p. 378)

monopoly rents The profits that a monopolist earns in the long run. (p. 334)

monopsony Condition in which one firm is the only hirer in a particular input market. (p. 435)

moral hazard The effect that having insurance has on the behavior of the insured. (p. 507)

N

Nash equilibrium A pair of strategies (a*, b*) in a two-player game such that a* is an optimal strategy for A against b* and b* is an optimal strategy for B against a*. (p. 389)

natural monopoly A firm that exhibits diminishing average cost over a broad range of output levels. (p. 329)

nonexclusive goods Goods that provide benefits that no one can be excluded from enjoying. (p. 546)

nonrival goods Goods that additional consumers may use at zero marginal costs. (p. 547)

normal good A good that is bought in greater quantities as income increases. (p. 91)

O

opportunity cost The cost of a good as measured by the alternative uses that are forgone by producing the good. (pp. 5, 187)

output effect The effect of an input price change on the amount of the input that the firm hires that results from a change in the firm's output level. (p. 426)

P

Pareto efficient allocation An allocation of available resources in which no mutually beneficial trading opportunities are unexploited. That is, an allocation in which no one person can be made better off without someone else being made worse off. (p. 326)

partial equilibrium model An economic model of a single market. (p. 312)

perfect equilibrium A Nash equilibrium in which the strategy choices of each player do not contain empty threats. That is, no strategy in such an equilibrium requires a player to carry out an action that would not be in its interest at the time. (p. 398)

perfect price discrimination Selling each unit of output for the highest price obtainable. Ex-

tracts all of the consumer surplus available in a given market. (p. 345)

perfectly competitive price system An economic model in which individuals maximize utility, firms maximize profits, there is perfect information about prices, and every economic actor is a price taker.

perpetuity A promise of a certain number of dollars each year, forever. (p. 492)

Pigovian tax A tax or subsidy on an externality that brings about an equality of private and social marginal costs. (p. 542)

positive-normative distinction Distinction between theories that seek to explain the world as it is and theories that postulate the way the world should be. (p. 22)

present value Discounting the value of future transactions back to the present day to take account of the effect of potential interest payments. (pp. 470, 487)

price discrimination Selling identical units of output at different prices. (p. 344)

price elasticity of demand The percentage change in the quantity demanded of a good in response to a 1 percent change in its price. (p. 131)

price leadership model A model in which one dominant firm takes reactions of all other firms into account in its output and pricing decisions. (p. 370)

price taker A firm or individual whose decisions regarding buying or selling have no effect on the prevailing market price of a good. (p. 226)

principal-agent relationship An economic actor (the principal) delegating decision-making authority to another party (the agent). (p. 237)

Prisoner's Dilemma A game in which the optimal outcome for the players is unstable. (p. 392)

private property Property that is owned by specific people who may prevent others from using it. (p. 536)

probability The relative frequency with which an event occurs. (p. 500)

producer surplus The extra value producers get for a good in excess of the opportunity costs they incur by producing it. What all producers would pay for the right to sell a good at its current market price. (p. 285)

product group Set of differentiated products that are highly substitutable for one another. (p. 375)

production function The mathematical relationship between inputs and outputs. (p. 157)

production possibility frontier A graph showing all possible combinations of goods that can be produced with a fixed amount of resources. (p. 4)

property rights The legal specification of who owns a good and the trades the owner is allowed to make with it. (p. 536)

public goods Goods that are both nonexclusive and nonrival. (pp. 322, 548)

Q

quasi-competitive model A model of oligopoly pricing in which each firm acts as a price taker even though there may be few firms. (p. 362)

R

reaction function In the Cournot model, a function or graph that shows how much one firm will produce given what the other firm produces. (p. 368)

rental rate (v) The cost of hiring one machine for one hour. (p. 189)

rent-seeking behavior Firms or individuals influencing government policy to increase their own welfare. (p. 560)

returns to scale The rate at which output increases in response to proportional increases in all inputs. (p. 167)

Ricardian rent Long-run profits earned by owners of low-cost firms. May be capitalized into the prices of these firms' inputs. (p. 288)

risk aversion The tendency of people to refuse to accept fair games. (p. 503)

S

scarcity costs The opportunity costs of future production forgone because current production depletes exhaustible resources. (p. 472)

short run The period of time in which a firm must consider some inputs to be fixed in making its decisions. (p. 202)

short-run elasticity of supply The percentage change in quantity supplied in the short run in response to a 1 percent change in price. (p. 261)

short-run market supply curve The relationship between market price and quantity supplied of a good in the short run. (p. 257)

shutdown price The price below which the firm will choose to produce no output in the short run. Equal to minimum average variable cost. (p. 237)

simultaneous equations A set of equations with more than one variable that must be solved together for a particular solution. (p. 44)

slope The direction of a line on a graph; shows the change in Y that results from a unit change in X. (p. 32)

social costs Costs of production that include both input costs and costs of the externalities that production may cause. (p. 534)

statistical inference Use of actual data and statistical techniques to determine quantitative economic relationships. (p. 49)

substitutes Two goods such that if the price of one increases, the quantity demanded of the other rises. (p. 108)

substitution effect (in demand theory) The part of the change in quantity demanded that is caused by substitution of one good for another. A movement along an indifference curve. (p. 94)

substitution effect (in production theory) The substitution of one input for another while holding output constant in response to a change in the input's price. (p. 426)

substitution effect of a change in w Movement along an indifference curve in response to a change in the real wage. A rise in w causes an individual to work more. (p. 453)

sunk cost Expenditure that once made cannot be recovered. (p. 188)

supply-demand model A model describing how a good's price is determined by the behavior of the individuals who buy the good and of the firms that sell it. (p. 14)

supply response The change in quantity of output supplied in response to a change in demand conditions. (p. 253)

T

tariff A tax on an imported good. May be equivalent to a quota or a nonquantitative restriction on trade. (p. 303)

tax incidence theory The study of the final burden of a tax after considering all market reactions to it. (p. 293)

technical progress A shift in the production function that allows a given output level to be produced using fewer inputs. (p. 175)

testing assumptions Verifying economic models by examining the validity of the assumptions on which they are based. (p. 19)

testing predictions Verifying economic models by asking if they can accurately predict real-world events. (p. 21)

theory of choice The interaction of preferences and constraints that causes people to make the choices they do. (p. 55)

transactions costs Costs involved in making market transactions and in gathering information with which to make those transactions. (p. 538)

transitivity of preferences The property that if A is preferred to B, and B is preferred to C, then A must be preferred to C. (p. 59)

U

utility The pleasure or satisfaction that people get from their economic activity. (p. 55)

V

variable costs Costs associated with inputs that can be varied in the short run. (pp. 29, 205)

variables The basic elements of algebra, usually called X, Y, and so on, that may be given any numerical value in an equation. (p. 29)

W

wage rate (w) The cost of hiring one worker for one hour. (p. 188)

Y

yield The effective (internal) rate of return promised by a payment stream that can be purchased at a certain price. (p. 493)

Index

Boldface denotes glossary term

A

Accelerated depreciation, 466
Accounting costs, 188
Accounting fraud, and stock
    options, 244–245
Adverse selection, 507,
    521–522, 523
Advertising game illustration,
    389–392, 395–397
African exports, 20–21
Agency relationship, 237, 239–245
Agreement among economists, 23–24
Agriculture, and prices, 136–137
Airline deregulation, 381–382
Airline prices, 3
Airline regulations (international),
    and costs, 203–204
Akerlof, G.A., "The Market for
    Lemons: Quality Uncertainty
    and the Market Mechanism,"
    522n.4
Alcoa, 408
Alcohol and licenses, 331
Alcohol taxes as drunk driving
    policy, 148–149
Alternate minimum tax (AMT), 130
Amazon, 256
American Airlines' pricing policy,
    341–342
AMT. See Alternate minimum tax
Animals and economics, 7–8
Antitrust, and Microsoft, 12–13

Asymmetric information, 522–525
Average cost curves, 199–202
Average costs (AC), 197
Average effect, 36, 38–39
Average product, 162, 178–179

B

Band wagon effects, 115
Banks, and economies of scope, 211
Barriers to competition, 283
Barriers to entry, 329–332, 380
Barriers to trade, and African
    exports, 20–21
Baseball
    and free agents, 524
    and monopsony, 440
Basketball, and monopsony, 440–441
Battle of the sexes game, 392
Bay Area Rapid Transit System
    (BART), 451
Becker, G.S.
    "A Theory of the Allocation of
        Time," 449n.1
    "An Economic Analysis of
        Fertility," 451n.2
Beer consumption, 148–149
Beer production, 172–173
Bell, F.W., "The Pope and the Price
    of Fish," 115n.1
Bentham, Jeremy, *Introduction to
    the Principles of Morals and
    Legislation,* 53
Bertrand, J., "Théorie Mathematique
    de la Richess Sociale," 398n.5

Bertrand equilibrium, 398–401
Bilateral monopoly, 441–442
Black, Duncan, "On the Rationale
    of Group Decision Making,"
    556n.12
Blackjack systems, 502–503
Blockbuster, demand for videos,
    11–12
Bonds, 481
    inflation-indexed, 469–470
    reading bond tables, 494
    zero-coupon, 489
Bono, economics according to,
    20–21
Borenstein, S. and Bushnell, J., "An
    Empirical Analysis of the
    Potential for Market Power in
    California's Electricity
    Industry," 371n.1
Borenstein, S. and Rose, N.L.,
    "Competition and Price
    Dispersion in the U.S. Airline
    Industry," 233n.2
Brand loyalty, 134–135
Brand proliferation, 377–378
Brazil, and ethanol subsidies, 266
Budget constraints, 70–72,
    81–82
    and income taxes, 87
    See also Utility and choice
Bureaucracies, 559–560
"Buy Prices in Online Auctions:
    Irrationality on the Internet?"
    (Budish and Takeyama),
    256n.1

C

Cable and satellite television offerings, 352–353
Calabresi, G. and Melamed, A.D., "Property Rules, Liability Rules, and Inalienability," 540n.6
Calculus, and marginalism, 39, 41
California's Proposition 13, 558
Capital
  and energy, 168–169
  holding input constant, 204–205
Capital costs, 188–189
Capital equipment ownership, 465
Capital markets, 458–481
  firms' demand for capital and loans, 462, 464–467
    ownership of capital equipment, 465–467
    rental rates and interest rates, 462, 464–465
  individual savings and the supply of loans, 459–464
    graphical analysis, 460–461
    substitution and income effects of a change in r, 461–464
    two-period model of saving, 459–460
  present discounted value, 468, 470–474
    multiperiod discounting, 470–471
    present value and economic decisions, 471–474
    single-period discounting, 468, 470
  pricing of exhaustible resources, 472, 474–477
    scarcity costs, 472, 474–475
    size of scarcity costs, 474–475
    time pattern of resource prices, 475, 477
  real interest rate determination, 465, 467–468
    changes in real interest rate, 467–468
  time periods and the flow of economic transactions, 458–459
  See also Compound interest

Card, David and Krueger, Alan, "Minimum Wages and Employment: A Case Study of the Fast-Food Industry in New Jersey and Pennsylvania," 430n.1
Cartel model, 363–366
Casinos, 336–337
Certainty line, 518–519
Ceteris paribus assumption, 48, 50–51, 55–56, 110, 113, 145, 162
Chamberlain, E.H., *The Theory of Monopolistic Competition*, 378n.5
Cheung, S.N.S., "The Fable of the Bees: An Economic Investigation," 539n.1
Childbearing, economics of, 451
Choice. *See* Utility and choice; Model of choice
Choice theory, 55
Clean air, valuing, 118–119
Clean Air Act, 545
Coase, Ronald, "The Problem of Social Cost," 417, 537n.4
Coase theorem, 537–538
Cobb-Douglas production function, 177n.1
Coca-Cola, 134
College education, and opportunity costs, 9–10
Command-and-control (CAC) approach, 545
Common property, 536
Common stocks, 515–516
Compaq, 13
Competition
  barriers to, 283
  and school choice, 283
  See also Competitive model (applying); Imperfect competition; Perfect competition
Competitive fringe, 372
Competitive model (applying), 284–311
  consumer and producer surplus, 284–291
    economic efficiency, 288
    long-run producer surplus, 286

  numerical illustration, 288, 290–291
  Ricardian rent, 286–288
  short-run producer surplus, 285–286
  price and controls and shortages, 291–295
  tax incidence, 293, 295–301
    and efficiency, 299
    and elasticity, 296–297
    long-run incidence with increasing costs, 296
    long-run shifting of the tax, 296
    numerical illustration, 300
    transactions costs, 300–301
  trade restrictions, 301–306
    gains from international trade, 301–303
    tariff protection, 303–304
Complements, 107–108
Complete preferences, 59
Composite goods, 81, 83
Compound interest, 483–486
  for 1 year, 483
  for 2 years, 483–484
  for 3 years, 484–485
  with any dollar amount, 485
  continuous compounding, 497–498
  discounting payment streams, 490–494
    algebraic presentation, 490–491
    calculating yields, 493
    perpetual payments, 491–492
    reading bond tables, 494
    varying payment streams, 493
  frequency of compounding, 494–498
    semiannual, 494–495
  "gone berserk," 486
  present discounted value, 487–489
    algebraic definition, 487
    general formulas, 488–489
    and the rental rate, 498–499
  present discounted value approach to investment decisions, 496, 498–499
Concentration ratios, 386
Condorcet's paradox, 555–556

Constant cost case, 269–270
Consumer Demand in the United States (Houthakker and Taylor), 146
Consumer Price Index (CPI), biases of, 100–102
Consumer Reports, 517, 519–520
Consumer surplus, 114, 116–120, 284, 284–285, 288, 290–291
  demand curves and, 116–117
  and utility, 117, 119–120
Consumption, balance in, 63–64
Continuous compounding, 497–498
Contour lines, 43, 44
Contract curves, 325–326
Cooperative games, 387
"Corn Laws," 320
Cornes, R. and Sandler, T., *The Theory of Externalities, Public Goods, and Club Goods,* 548n.10
Corporate Average Fuel Economy (CAFE) standards, 109–110
Corporate profits, and employee stock options, 249
Corporate profits tax, 249
Corporate tax rate, 466
Cost curves. *See* Costs
Cost minimization, 191–195
  and input inflexibility, 205–206
Costless bargaining, 536
Costs, 187–220
  accounting cost, 188
  average, 197
  capital costs, 188–189
  congestion costs on the Internet, 220
  cost curves, 195–202
    average cost curves, 199–202
    findings on firms' costs, 201–202
    marginal cost curves, 198–200
    total cost curves, 195–197
  cost-minimizing input choice, 192–195
    firm's expansion path, 194–195
    graphic presentation, 192–194
  distinction between short and long run, 202, 204–206
  economic cost, 188
  economic profits and cost minimization, 191–192
  employee compensation, 220
  entrepreneurial costs, 189
  holding capital input constant, 204–205
  input inflexibility and cost minimization, 205–206
  labor costs, 188
  marginal, 197–198
  monopolists, 340
  numerical example, 212–216
    long-run cost curves, 214
    short-run costs, 214–215
  opportunity cost, 187–188
  and output effect, 428–431
  per-unit short-run cost curves, 206–207
  shifts in cost curves, 209–210
    changes in input prices, 209–210
    economies of scope, 210–212
    technological innovation, 210
  short-run, 205
  social, 534
  stranded costs and electricity deregulation, 190–191
  transportation and time, 451
  two-input case, 189, 191
Cournot, Augustin, *Researches into Mathematical Principles of the Theory of Wealth,* 366n.2
Cournot equilibrium, 369–370, 398–401
Cournot model, 366–372
  in California, 371–372
CPI. *See* Consumer Price Index
Credible threats, 397–398
Cross-price elasticity of demand, 144
Cultural institutions, hiring by, 423–424

D

Darwin, Charles, 7
De Beers cartel, 365–366
Deadweight loss, 299, 342–343
Decreasing cost case, 275–276, 276
Dell, 13
Demand
  Blockbuster, 11–12
  curve from real-world data, 49
  empirical studies of, 144–149
    cross-price elasticity estimates, 147
  elasticity estimates, 145–147
  estimating demand curves, 145
  See also Utility and choice
Demand curves
  and consumer surplus, 116–117
  marginal revenue for downward-sloping, 226–227
  and price elasticity, 132, 137–141
  shape of, 112
  shifts in, 260–267
  See also Individual demand curves; Market demand curves
Demand functions, 89–90
Demand model. *See* Supply-demand model
Dependent variable, 29
Depreciation, accelerated, 466
Deregulation
  and airline industry, 233–234
  and electricity, 190–191
Derivatives, 39, 41, 473
Diamonds, 365–366
Diminishing marginal utility, 503
Diminishing returns, 15–16
Direct TV, Inc., 352
Discounting, 468, 470–474, 498
  discounting payment streams, 490–494
  See also Compound interest
Dismal science, 16
Disney, 134
Disneyland pricing, 349–350
Distributional effects, 537–538
  and monopoly, 339–340
Diversification, 509–513, 511
Dominant strategy, 391
Donor preferences, 106
Double taxation, 223
Drunk driving, and alcohol taxes, 148–149
Dry cleaning licenses, 331
Dumping, 410
Duopoly, 366–369
DuPont, 408
DVDs, 11, 271–272

E

e, 497–498
eBay, 256
Econometrics, 48
Economic bad, 65, 68

Economic costs, 188
Economic Effects of Airline Deregulation (Morrison and Winston), 381n.1
Economic efficiency, 288
Economic good, 59–60
Economic profits, 191
and cost minimization, 191–192
Economically efficient allocation of resources, 288, 315
Economics, 4
positive vs. normative, 23
Economics of Welfare, The (Pigou), 541n.7
Economies of scope, 210–212
Economist, The, 20n.1
Edgeworth box diagram for exchange, 324–327
Educational institutions, hiring by, 423
Efficiency, 288, 315–328
and equity, 323–328
and externalities, 532, 534–535
information and economic efficiency, 520, 522–525
prices and laissez-faire economics, 318–319
and taxation, 299
Elasticity, 130–131
and alcohol duties, 154
and bus fares, 154
cross-price elasticity of demand, 144
demand curves and, 137–141
empirical cross-price estimates, 147
empirical estimates of, 145–147
income elasticity of demand, 141, 143
long-run supply, 274–275
and marginal revenue, 228–231
price elasticity of demand, 131–141
short-run supply, 260–261
and taxes, 296–297
See also Price elasticity of demand
Electrical equipment conspiracy, 404–405
Electricity deregulation, and stranded costs, 190–191
Emission charges, 545
Emissions trading, 545

Empirical microeconomics, 46–51
Employee compensation, and costs, 220
Energy, and capital, 168–169
Engel's law, 92–93, 143
Engineering and economics, 168–169
Entrepreneurial costs, 189
Entry and exit, in long run, 268
Entry by new firms, and imperfect competition, 376, 378–382
Entry deterrence, 406–407
Equilibrium, 376
Bertrand, 398
comparing Bertrand and Cournot results, 399–400
Cournot, 369–370
and input price determination, 432–435
Lindahl, 551–552
in long run, 267
perfect, 398
two-stage price games and Cournot, 398–399
See also General equilibrium; Market equilibrium; Nash equilibrium
Equilibrium price, functions of, 258–259
Equity, 323
and efficiency, 323–328
Equity premium, 515–516
Ethanol subsidies, 265–266
Evolution, and scarcity, 7–8
Expansion path (firm's), 194–195
Expected value, 501, 529
Externalities, 319, 322, 530, 530–544, 564
and allocational efficiency, 532, 534–535
graphical demonstration, 534–535
between firms, 531
between firms and people, 531–532
between people, 532
with high transactions costs, 538, 540–546
legal redress, 540–541
taxation, 541–542
network, 277–278
property rights, 536–538
reciprocal nature of, 532
regulation of, 542–546
See also Public goods

F

Fads, 115
FAIR Act. *See* Federal Agricultural Improvement and Reform Act
Fair games, 501
Fair insurance, 506
Fannie Mae, 473
Farm prices, 136–137
Farm subsidies, 3
Federal Agricultural Improvement and Reform (FAIR) Act, 136
Federal Trade Commission, 377
Feedback effects, 314–315
Financial aid at private colleges, 346–347
Financial assets, pricing risk of, 511, 513–517
Firms, 157, 159–160
goals of, 222
nature of, 221–222
variety of, 159–160
Firm's costs, findings on, 201–202
Firms' demand for capital and loans, 462, 464–467
See also Capital markets
Firm's expansion path, 194–195
Firm's short-run supply curve, 236
First-mover advantages, 405–406, 408–409
Fixed costs, 205
Fixed-proportion production function, 173–174
Flat taxes, 40–41
Flood, Curt, 440
Food stamp program, 124–125
Foraging for food, 7–8
Foraging Theory (Stephens and Krebs), 7n.1
Foreign exchange market, 374–375
401(k) plans, 463
Franchising, principals and agents in, 242
Fraud, accounting, 244–245
Free agency, 440, 524
Free riders, 550
and public broadcasting, 553
Frequent-flier programs, 82–83
Friedman, Milton
Essays in Positive Economics, 22n.1
A Theory of the Consumption Function, 129n.1

Functional notation, 29
Fundamental theorem of welfare
    economics, 316

G

Gains from trade, 301–303,
    320–321
Gambling, 336–337, 500
Game theory, 387–416
    advertising game, 389–392,
        395–397
        dominant strategies and Nash
            equilibria, 391–392
        in extensive form, 389–390
        in normal form, 390
    cooperative, 387
    entry, exit, and strategy, 403,
        405–412
        entry deterrence, 406–407
        first-mover advantages,
            405–406, 408–409
        incomplete information,
            409–410
        limit pricing, 407
        predatory pricing, 410–412
        sunk costs and commitment,
            403, 405
    N-player game theory, 412
    Nash equilibrium, 389, 391–394
        battle of the sexes, 391–392
        rock, scissors, paper,
            391–392
    noncooperative, 387
    payoffs, 388
    players, 388
    pricing behavior models,
        398–405
        Bertrand and Cournot
            comparison, 399–400
        Bertrand equilibrium, 398
        tacit collusion, 400, 402
        two-stage price games and
            Cournot equilibrium,
            398–399
    prisoner's dilemma, 392,
        394–396
    strategies, 388
GATT. See General Agreement on
    Tariffs and Trade
General Agreement on Tariffs and
    Trade (GATT), 304
General Electric, 404

General equilibrium, 312–328
    efficiency and equity, 323–328
        contract curve, 326
        Edgeworth box diagram for
            exchange, 324–327
        efficiency in exchange, 326
        equity and competitive
            markets, 324
        equity defined, 323
        initial endowments, 328
        mutually beneficial trades,
            325–326
        Pareto efficient allocation,
            325–326
    efficiency of perfect competition,
        316–319
        prices, efficiency, and laissez-
            faire economics, 318–319
    markets failing to achieve
        economic efficiency, 319,
        322–323
        externalities, 319, 322
        imperfect competition, 319
        imperfect information,
            322–323
        public goods, 322
    perfectly competitive price
        system, 312–313
General equilibrium model, 312
General Foods, 377
General Mills, 377
Giffen's paradox, 99, 102
Global warming, 546
Goods
    budget constraint for two, 70–71
    composite, 81–83
    economic, 59–60
    many, 78, 80
    useless, 65, 68
    utility from consuming two,
        56–57
    See also Public goods

H

Hamer v. Sidway, 79–80
Happiness, and health and income,
    58–59
Harley-Davidson, 134
Health, and income, 58–59
Health insurance, experiment in,
    142–143
Health scares, 115–116

Hewlett-Packard financial
    calculator, 485n.2
Hicks, J.R., Value and Capital,
    108n.3
Higher Education Act, 346
Hiring, by nonprofit firms, 423
Historical rates of return, 515
HMOs and patients' bill of rights,
    508–509
Home Rule in Illinois, 558–559
Homogeneity demand function, 90
Hospitals
    and economies of scope, 211–212
    hiring by, 423
Hotel chains, 66
Hotelling's beach, 393–394
Houthakker, H.S. and Taylor, L.D.,
    Consumer Demand in the
    United States, 146
Human organs, price controls, 310

I

Imperfect competition, 319,
    362–386
    Cournot model, 366–372
        duopoly, 366–369
        equilibrium, 369–370
        generalizations, 370
        market conditions, 366–367
        reaction function, 368–369
    entry by new firms, 376,
        378–382
        barriers to entry, 380
        determination of industry
            structure, 379–382
        monopolistic competition,
            376, 378–379
    price leadership model, 370,
        372–375
    pricing of homogeneous goods,
        362–366
        cartel model, 363–366
        quasi-competitive model,
            362–363
    product differentiation, 373,
        375–378
        firm's choices, 376
        market definition, 375
        market equilibrium, 376
    See also Game theory
Imperfect information, 322–323
Implicit costs, 189

Implicit tariffs, 304
Import quotas, 304
In-kind programs, 105–106
Incentive contracts, 240–243
Income
    changes in, 90–94
    and happiness, 58–59
    and health, 58
Income effect, 94, 95–99
Income effect of a change in r,
    461–462
Income effect of a change in w,
    453, 452–454
Income elasticity of demand,
    141, 143
Income grants, 105
Incomplete information, 409–410
Increasing cost case, 272–273
Independent variable, 29
Indian gaming, 336–337
Indian Gaming Regulatory Act
    (1988), 336
Indifference curve maps, 64, 64–68
    illustrating preferences, 65,
        67–68
        economic bad, 65, 68
        perfect complements, 67–68
        perfect substitutes, 67–68
        useless good, 65, 68
    See also Utility and choice
Indifference curves, 61, 60–62
    diminishing marginal rate of
        substitution (MRS), 62, 64
    See also Utility and choice
Individual demand curves, 89–125
    changes in a good's price,
        94–102
        Giffen's paradox, 99, 102
        substitution and income effects
            for a normal good, 98
        substitution and income effects
            for inferior goods, 98–99
        substitution and income effects
            from a fall in price, 94–96
        substitution and income effects
            from an increase in price,
            97–98
    changes in income, 90–94
        inferior goods, 93–94
        normal goods, 91
    changes in the price of another
        good, 106–108
        substitutes and complements,
            107–108

    construction of, 108, 110–112
        shape of the demand curve,
            112–114
    consumer surplus, 114, 116–120
        demand curves and consumer
            surplus, 116–117
        and utility, 117, 119–120
    demand functions, 89–90
        homogeneous demand
            function, 90
        lump-sum principle, 103–106
        terminology, 114
Individual Retirement Accounts
    (IRAs), 463
Inefficiency, 6
Infant industries, 276, 278
Inferior goods, 93–94
    substitution and income effects
        for, 98–99
Inflation-indexed bonds, 469–470
Information and economic
    efficiency, 520, 522–525
    acquisition and provision of
        information, 523
    adverse selection, 523
    asymmetric information and the
        "lemons" problems, 522–523
Information economics, 517–522
    balancing the gains and costs of
        information, 519–520
    information differences among
        economic actors, 520
    utility-maximizing model,
        518–519
Information sharing, 401
Informediaries, 289–290
InfoTrac Web site keywords
    Alfred Marshall, 16
    asymmetric information, 505
    barriers to entry, 343
    Bertrand equilibrium, 407
    capital costs, 189
    cartel, 370
    Coase theorem, 540
    consumer surplus, 296
    cost minimizing, 189
    Cournot, 370
    deadweight loss, 343
    dismal science, 16
    distributional effects, 540
    duopoly, 370
    economic efficiency, 296
    ethanol subsidies, 263
    externalities, 540

    farm prices, 145
    firms' demand for capital, 467
    gains from trade, 304
    Giffen goods, 99
    imperfect competition, 370
    import quotas, 304
    indifference curves, 69
    input substitution, 171
    Internet auctions, 263
    labor costs, 189
    managers' incentives, 239
    marginal cost, 239
    marginal product, 171
    marginal revenue, 239
    microeconomics, 16
    monopoly, 343
    monopsony, 433
    moral hazard, 145, 505
    multifactor productivity, 171
    Nash equilibrium, 407
    natural monopoly, 343
    perfect competition, 263
    predatory pricing, 407
    price controls, 296
    price discrimination, 343
    price elasticity, 145
    prisoner's dilemma, 407
    producer surplus, 296
    production costs, 189
    profit maximization, 239
    public goods and market
        failure, 548
    Rand health insurance
        experiment, 145
    rent controls, 296
    returns to scale, 171
    risk aversion, 505
    shutdown decision, 239
    substitution effect, 99, 433
    sunk costs, 407
    supply of loans, 467
    supply response, 263
    tariff protection, 304
    tax incidence, 296
    tax policy and investment, 467
    theory of choice, 69
    theory of utility, 69
    transaction costs, 304
    uninsurable risks, 505
    utility maximization, 69
    wage inequality, 433
Initial endowments, 328
Input choices, and
    marginalism, 226

Input demand, and price changes, 428–431
Input inflexibility, and cost minimization, 205–206
Input price determination, and equilibrium, 432–435
Input prices, changes in, 209–210, 422, 424–427
Input substitution, 171, 176–174
  fixed-proportions production function, 173–174
  relevance of, 174
  vs. technical progress, 175–176
Input supply, 429, 431
Inputs, 189, 191
  hiring of, 419–420
Insurance, 505–509
  fair, 506
  safe driver policies, 521–522
  unfair, 506–507
  uninsurable risks, 507
Intercepts, 31, 34–36
  changes in, 34–36
Interest, 482
  See also Compound interest
Interest rates
  determining real, 465, 467–468
  and rental rates, 462, 464–465
  See also Compound interest
International cartels, 385–386
International trade, 301–303
Internet
  auctions, 256–257
  buying and welfare, 289–290
  liquor stores and wine on, 331
Internet exercises
  barriers to competition, 283
  bonds, 481
  budget constraints and income taxes, 87
  Capital Asset Pricing Model (CAPM), 529
  competition and school choice, 283
  concentration ratios, 386
  congestion costs on the Internet, 220
  corporate profits and employee stock options, 249
  corporate profits tax, 249
  economic jokes, 28
  elasticity and alcohol duties, 154
  elasticity and bus fares, 154

employee compensation costs, 220
expected value, 529
externalities, 564
food stamp program, 124–125
"high-tech" monopolies, 361
household production, 185–186
international cartels, 385–386
labor productivity: international comparisons, 185
monopsony, 446
occupational outlook, 446–447
opportunity costs, 28
predatory pricing, 416
present value, 481
price controls in market for human organs, 310
price discrimination, 361
price indexes and cost of living, 125
prisoner's dilemma, 416
public goods, 564
rationing, 88
tariffs, 310–311
Investment
  and taxes, 466–467
  See also Capital markets
Investment tax credits, 466
Iraq, and oil prices, 47–48
Isoquant, 163
Isoquant maps, 163, 165–167, 179

J

Japan
  and auto production, 164–165
  milk marketing in, 393
Jensen, M., "Risk, the Pricing of Capital Assets, and the Evaluation of Investment Performance," 512n.1
Job search theory, 451–452
Jordan, Michael, 134, 440–441

K

Kefauver, Estes, 404
Kellogg, 377
Keogh plans, 463
Kinked budget constraint, 82
Koufax, Sandy, 440

L

Labor costs, 188
Labor markets, 419–457
  equilibrium input price determination, 432–435
  shifts in demand and supply, 432–435
  firm's demand for labor summary, 427
  input supply, 429, 431
  labor supply and wages, 431
  marginal productivity theory of input demand, 419–424
  marginal revenue product, 420–421
  marginal value product, 421–422
  price-taking behavior, 420
  profit-maximizing behavior and the hiring of inputs, 419–420
  monopsony, 435–442
    bilateral monopoly, 441–442
    causes of, 439–441
    graphical demonstration, 437–438
    marginal expense, 435–436
    monopsonist's input choice, 437
    numerical illustration, 436–437
    and resource allocation, 438–439
    and sports stars, 440–441
  responses to changes in input prices, 422, 424–427
    numerical example, 425
    output effect, 426–427
    single-variable input case, 422, 424
    substitution effect, 426
    two-variable input case, 425–426
  responsiveness of input demand to price changes, 428–431
    costs and output effect, 428–431
    ease of substitution, 428
Labor productivity, international comparisons, 185
Labor supply, 448–457
  income and substitution effects of a change in the real wage rate, 452–454
  graphical analysis, 453–454

market supply curve for labor, 455–457
time allocation, 448–452
  opportunity cost of leisure, 449–452
  time use model, 448–449
  utility maximization, 450, 452
  younger women and older men, 456–457
Laissez-faire economics, 318–319
Legal barriers to entry, 330–332
Legal redress, and externalities, 540–541
Leisure, 448–449
  opportunity cost of, 448–452
"Lemons" problem, 522–523
Leveraged buyout craze, 223–224
Licenses, 330–332
Lindahl equilibrium, 551–552
Linear demand curves, and price elasticity, 137–140
Linear functions, 31, 30–38
Local public goods, 554
Long run, 267–269
  perfect competition, 267–269
  vs. short run, 202, 204–206
Long-run cost curves, 214
Long-run elasticity of supply, 274–275
Long-run equilibrium, perfect competition, 268–269
Long-run producer surplus, 286
Long-run shifting of tax, 296
Long-run supply, constant cost case, 269–270
Long-run supply curves, 270
  shape of, 272–278
Long-run tax incidence with increasing costs, 296
Lump-sum principle, 103–106

M

McDonald's Corporation, 242
Majority rule, 555
Managers' incentives, 237, 239–245
Many-period games, 396–398
Marginal cost curves, 198–200
Marginal costs (MC), 17, 197–198, 208
  and airline deregulation, 233–234

Marginal effect, 36, 38–39
Marginal expense (ME), 435–436
Marginal product, 158, 160–163, 178–179
  diminishing, 160–161
Marginal product curve, 161
Marginal productivity theory of input demand, 419–424
  See also Labor markets
Marginal rate of substitution (MRS), 62–64
  diminishing, 62, 64
  indifference curves and, 62
Marginal rate of technical substitution (RTS), 165–167
  diminishing, 166–167
  and marginal products, 166
Marginal revenue, 224, 226–231
  and airline deregulation, 233
  for a downward-sloping demand curve, 226–227
  and price elasticity, 228–231
Marginal revenue/marginal cost rule, 224–226
Marginal revenue curve, 231–232
  shifts in demand and, 231–232
Marginal revenue product (MRP), 420–421
Marginal utility, diminishing, 503
Marginal value product (MVP), 421–422
Marginalism, 16–17, 222
  and calculus, 39, 41
  in input choices, 226
Market definition, 375
Market demand, 126
  effect of an increase in, 260
Market demand curves, 126–130
  construction of, 126–127
  shifts in, 127–128
  simplified notation, 128, 130
Market equilibrium, 17–18
  for constant cost case, 269–270
  See also Equilibrium
Market line, 513, 514
Market period, 254
Market separation, 348, 350–351
Marketing, product positioning in, 66–67
Marriott Corporation, 66

Marshall, Alfred
  Principles of Economics, 1, 17, 29
  supply and demand model, 16–19
Massachusetts's tax-limitation initiative, 558
Median voter, 556–557
Medicine, principals and agents in, 242–243
Metcalfe's law, 277
Michigan's tax-limitation initiative, 558
Microbreweries, growth of, 172–173
Microeconomics, 4
  empirical, 46–51
  mathematics used in, 29–51
  uses of, 8–14
Microsoft and antitrust, 12–13
Middleware, 13
Milk marketing in Japan, 393
Mill, J.S., Principles of Political Economy, 155
Minimum wage controversy, 430–431
Model of choice, 74, 76–81
Models, 4
Monopolistic competition, 376, 378–379
Monopoly, 329–361
  causes of, 329–330
    legal barriers to entry, 330
    technical barriers to entry, 329–330
  complaints about, 334–335, 337–339
    distortion of resource allocation, 337–339
    profitability, 334–335
  deadweight loss numerical illustration, 342–343
  distortions and transfers of welfare, 339–340
    allocational effects, 339
    distributional effects, 339–340
    monopolists' costs, 340
  price discrimination, 343–353
    market separation, 348, 350–351
    perfect, 344–345
    pricing for multiproduct monopolies, 351

quantity discounts, 345, 347
two-part tariffs, 347–348
profit maximization, 332–334
graphically, 332–333
profits, 334
supply curve, 333–334
regulation of natural, 353–357
marginal cost pricing,
353–354
rate of return regulation, 355
two-tier pricing systems, 355
Monopoly rents, 334
Monopsony, 435–442, 446
bilateral monopoly, 441–442
causes of, 439–441
graphical demonstration,
437–438
input choice, 437
marginal expense, 435–436
in the market for sports stars,
440–441
numerical illustration, 436–437
and resource allocation, 438–439
Moral hazard, 142, 507
losses from, 508
Mortgage-backed securities, 473
Movie rentals, 271–272
MRP. *See* Marginal revenue
product
Multifactor productivity, 177–178
Mutual funds, 512–513

N

N-player game theory, 412
Nash equilibrium, 389, 391–394
and underproduction, 550–551
See also Game theory
National Basketball Association
(NBA), 440
National Football League, 75
Natural monopolies, 190n.1, 329
regulation of, 353–357
See also Monopolies; Technical
barriers to entry
Nature, property rights in,
539–540
Nominal interest rate, 482
Noncooperative games, 387
Nonequilibrium outcomes, 18
Nonexclusive goods, 546
Nonlinear functions, 30–31, 36
Nonprofit firms, hiring by, 423–424

Nonrival goods, 547
Normal goods, 91
substitution and income effects
for, 98
North American Free Trade
Agreement (NAFTA), and
gains from free trade, 320–322

O

Occupational outlook, 446–447
Oil, drilling for, 238–239
Oil prices, 3
and Iraq, 47–48
O'Neill, Paul, 20
Opportunity costs, 5, 6, 187–188
and college education, 9–10
Internet exercise, 28
of leisure, 449–452
Ordinary least squares, 50n.4
Output decision, 222, 224
Output effect, 426–427
and costs, 428–431
Overlap Group, 346

P

Paradox of agriculture, 136
Pareto efficient allocation, 325, 326
Partial equilibrium model, 312
Patents, 330
Paternalism, 106
Patients' bill of rights, 508–509
Payoffs, 388
Perfect competition, 253–283
the long run, 267–269
entry and exit, 268
equilibrium conditions, 267
equilibrium in, 268–269
profit maximization, 268
the long-run supply: constant
cost case, 269–270
long-run supply curve, 270
market equilibrium, 269–270
shift in demand, 269–270
long-run supply curve shape,
272–278
decreasing costs, 275–276
and increasing costs,
272–273
infant industries, 276, 278
long-run supply elasticity,
274–275

pricing in the very short run,
254–255
applicability of the very short-
run model, 254–255
shifts in demand: price as a
rationing device, 254–255
shifts in supply and demand
curves, 260–267
numerical illustration, 264,
266–267
shifts in demand curves and
the importance of the shape
of the supply curve,
263–264
shifts in supply curves and the
importance of the shape of
the demand curve, 261–262
short-run supply elasticity,
260–261
short-run price determination,
258–260
effect of an increase in market
demand, 260
equilibrium price, 258–259
short-run supply, 255, 257–258
short-run supply curve
construction, 257–258
timing of a supply response, 253
Perfect complements, 67–68
Perfect equilibrium, 398
**Perfect price discrimination,
344–345**
Perfect substitutes, 67–68
Permanent income hypothesis, 129
Perpetual payments, 491–492
Perpetuity, 492
Pickups, and lemons, 524
Pigou, A.C., *The Economics of
Welfare,* 541n.7
Pigovian tax, 542
Players, 388
Pollution, 536–537
Portfolio management, 512–513
Positive-normative distinction, 22–24
Poverty, and cash, 105–106
Power plant emissions, regulating,
545–546
Predatory pricing, 410–412, 416
Preferences
illustrating, 65, 67–68
properties of, 57, 59
See also Indifference curve maps;
Utility and choice

Present discounted value, 468, 470–474, 487–489
  and investment decisions, 496, 498–499
  and the rental rate, 498–499
  See also Capital markets; Compound interest
Present value, 129, 470–472, **470,** 481, **487**
Price
  changes in a good's, 94–102
  changes in the price of another, 106–108
  as rationing device, 254–255
Price controls and shortages, 291–295
Price determination models, 3–24
Price discrimination, 343–353, **344,** 361
  See also Monopoly
Price elasticity and demand curves, 137–141
  linear demand curves, 137–140
  unitary elastic curve, 140–141
Price elasticity of demand, 131–141
  and marginal revenue, 228–231
  and the shape of the demand curve, 132
  and the substitution effect, 132–133
  and time, 133
  and total expenditures, 133, 135, 137
  values of, 132
  See also Elasticity
Price indexes and cost of living, 125
Price leadership in financial markets, 374–375
Price leadership model, 370, 372–375
Price takers, 226, 312, 420
Price-taking firm, supply decision of, 232, 234–237
Pricing
  at Disneyland, 349–350
  of homogeneous goods, 362–366
  for multiproduct monopolies, 351
  predatory, 410–412
  telephone, 356–357
Pricing behavior models, 398–405
  See also Game theory

Principal-agent relationship, 237, 239–245
Prisoner's dilemma, 392, 394–396, 416
Private property, 536
Probability, 500–501
Procter and Gamble, 408
Producer surplus, 284–291, **285**
Product availability, 401
Product differentiation, 373, 375–378
Product group, 375
Product positioning in marketing, 66–67
Production, 157–186
  appraising the marginal product concept, 162–163
  average product, 162
  changes in technology, 174–176
    technical progress vs. input substitution, 175–176
  children, 160
  diminishing marginal product, 160–161
  health, 159
  household, 159, 185–186
  housing services, 159
  input substitution, 171, 173–174
  isoquant maps, 163, 165–167
  marginal product, 158, 160–163, 160
  marginal product curve, 161
  marginal rate of technical substitution (RTS), 165–167
    diminishing, 166–167
    and marginal products, 166
  multifactor, 177–178
  numerical example, 176, 178–181
    average and marginal productivities, 178–179
    the isoquant map, 179
    the production function, 176
    technical progress, 180–181
  production functions, 157–158, 157
  returns to scale, 167, 169–171
  two-input production function, 158
Production differentiation, and growth of microbreweries, 172–173

Production functions, 157–158, 176
  Cobb-Douglas, 177n.1
  fixed-proportion, 173–174
  See also Production
Production possibility frontier, 4, 5, 316
Profit maximization, 222–226, 312
  and hiring of inputs, 419–420
  and leveraged buyout craze, 223–224
  in long run, 268
  and managers' incentives, 237, 239–245
  marginal revenue, 226–231
    for a downward-sloping demand curve, 226–227
    numerical example, 227–228
    and price elasticity, 228–231
  marginal revenue/marginal cost rule, 224–226
  marginal revenue curve, 231–232
    and shifts in demand, 231–232
  marginalism, 222
  marginalism in input choices, 226
  and monopolies, 332–334
  output decision, 222, 224
  supply decision of a price-taking firm, 232, 234–237
    short-run profit maximization, 234–235
    short-run supply curve, 236
    showing profits, 235–236
    shutdown decision, 236–237
  and taxes, 223
Profits
  corporate, 223–224
  and monopolies, 334
  showing, 235–236
Progressive, taxes, 40–41
Property rights, 536–538
  in nature, 539–540
Property tax assessment, 37–38
Public broadcasting, 553–554
Public goods, 322, 544, **548,** 546–554, 564
  attributes of, 544, 546
  categories of, 547–548
  demand for public goods, 552–554
  and market failure, 548–550
  graphical demonstration, 548–550

nonexclusivity, 546
nonrivalry, 547
solutions to the public goods
    problem, 550–552
    compulsory taxation, 551
    Lindahl equilibrium, 551–552
    Nash equilibrium and
        underproduction, 550–551
voting and resource allocation,
    554–560
    majority rule, 555
    paradox of voting
        (Condorcet's paradox),
        555–556
    rent-seeking behavior, 560
    representative government and
        bureaucracies, 559–560
    single-peaked preferences and
        the median voter theorem,
        556–557
See also Externalities
Public spending referenda, 558–559

Q

Quadratic functions, 30–31, 38–39
Quantity discounts, 82–83, 345, 347
Quasi-competitive model, 362–363
Quotas, 304

R

Rand experiment, 142–143
Random influences, 49–50
Rate of return regulation, 355
Rationing, 88
Reaction function, 368–369
Real interest rate, 482
    changes in, 467–468
    determining, 465, 467–468
Rent control, 294–295
Rent-seeking behavior, 560
Rental rate (v), 189
Rental rates
    and interest rates, 462, 464–465
    and present discounted value,
        498–499
Representative government, 559–560
Reserve clause, 440
Resource allocation
    and monopoly, 337–339
    and monopsony, 438–439
    and voting, 554–560

Returns to scale, 167, 169–171,
    196–197
    Adam Smith on, 167
    in beer brewing, 172–173
    defined, 169
    graphic illustrations, 169–171
Ricardian rent, 286–288
Ricardo, David
    and diminishing returns, 15–16
    The Principles of Political
        Economy and Taxation,
        286n.1
Risk aversion, 503–505
    diminishing marginal utility, 503
    graphical analysis of, 504–505
    willingness to pay to avoid
        risk, 505
Risk pricing in financial assets,
    511, 513–517
    choices by individual investors,
        514, 516–517
    investors' market options,
        513–516
Risk-reducing methods, 505–511
    diversification, 509–513
    insurance, 505–509
Riverboat gambling, 336
Robertson, Oscar, 441
Rock, scissors, paper game,
    391–392
Rockefeller, John D., 411
RTS. See Marginal rate of technical
    substitution
Rule of 70, 497
Russell, Bill, 441

S

Salop's model of competition in
    "space," 377–378
Samuelson, Paul A., "The Pure
    Theory of Public
    Expenditure," 546n.9
Savings
    individual and the supply of
        loans, 459–464
    and tax breaks for savers,
        463–464
    See also Capital markets;
        Compound interest
Scarcity, 5–6
    and evolution, 7–8
Scarcity costs, 472, 474–477

Seasonality, 115
Secondhand smoke, 533–534
Sen, Amartya, "The Possibility of
    Social Choice," 323n.6
Sherman Antitrust Act, 13, 341,
    364, 411
Short run
    pricing in the very short run,
        254–255
    profit maximization in, 234–235
    short-run supply, 255, 257–258
    vs. long run, 202, 204–206
Short-run cost curves, 206–207
Short-run costs, 205, 214–215
Short-run elasticity of supply, 261
Short-run price determination,
    258–260
Short-run producer surplus,
    285–286
Short-run supply curve, 236,
    257–258
Shortages and price controls,
    291–295
Shutdown decision, 236–237
Simultaneous equations, 44–46
Single-peaked preferences and the
    median voter theorem,
    556–557
Slopes, 32, 31–34
    changes in, 33–34
    of nonlinear functions, 36
    and units of measurement, 33
Smith, Adam
    on laissez-faire economics,
        318–319
    on returns to scale, 167
    The Theory of Moral Sentiments,
        69n.4
    The Wealth of Nations, 14, 239,
        251, 319n.5, 341n.1
Social costs, 534
Solar water heating, 168
Sothebys, 256
Spatial competition, 377
Sport-utility vehicles (SUVs),
    109–110
Sports stars' compensation,
    440–441
Spring monopolist's output
    choice, 368
Stackelberg equilibrium, 406n.9
Standard Oil, 411–412
States of the world, 518

Statistical inferences, 49
Steel protectionism, 305–306
Stock options, effects of, 244–245, 249
Stocks, 515–516
Stranded costs, 190–191
Strategies, 388
   See also Game theory
Subsidies
   and African exports, 20–21
   ethanol, 265–266
Substitutes, 107–108
Substitution effect, 94–99, 426
   and price elasticity, 132–133
Substitution effect of a change in r, 461–462
Substitution effect of a change in w, 453, 452–454
Sunk costs, 188, 403, 405
Supply curves
   and externalities, 277–278
   for labor, 455–457
   and monopolies, 333–334
   shifts in, 260–267
Supply response, 253
Supply-demand models, 1–24, 14

T

Tacit collusion, 400
Tarbell, Ida, 411
Tariffs, 303–306, 310–311
   two-part, 347–348
Tax cuts, of 2001, 129–130
   and permanent income, 129–130
Tax incidence, 293, 295–301
   and efficiency, 299
   and elasticity, 296–297
   long-run shifting of the tax, 296
   long-run with increasing costs, 296
   numerical illustration, 300
   transaction costs, 300–301
Tax-limitation initiatives, 558–559
Tax policy
   effects of, 467
   elements of, 466
   history of, 466–467
Taxes
   affecting investment, 466–467
   alcohol, 148–149
   and breaks for savers, 463–464
   and corporate profits, 223, 249

and externalities, 541–542
   flat taxes and progressive rates, 40–41
   property tax assessment, 37–38
   and tobacco settlement, 298–299
Taxicab licenses, 331–332
Technical barriers to entry, 329–330
   See also Natural monopolies
Technical progress, 176, 180–181
Technically efficient, 315n.2
Technological innovation, 210
Technology
   changes in, 174–176
   and movie rentals, 271–272
   and public television, 553–554
Teenage unemployment and minimum wage, 430
Telephone pricing, 356–357
Television scheduling, 393–394
Testing assumptions, 19, 21
Testing predictions, 21–22
Theory of choice, 55
Thoroughbreds, and lemons, 524–525
Ticket scalping, 75–76
Tiebout, C.M., "A Pure Theory of Local Expenditures," 554n.11
Time
   allocation of, 448–452
   and price elasticity, 133
   time pattern of resource prices, 475, 477
   time periods and the flow of economic transactions, 458–459
Time horizons, 400, 402
Tirole, J., The Theory of Industrial Organization, 393n.1, 403n.8
Tobacco settlement, as tax, 298–299
Tolls, 208–209
Total cost curves. See Cost curves
Total costs (TC), 198
Total expenditures, and price elasticity, 133, 135, 137
Trade
   gains to Internet, 289
   mutually beneficial trades, 325–326
   See also Gains from trade

Trade restrictions, 301–306
   gains from international trade, 301–303
   General Agreement on Tariffs and Trade (GATT), 304
   tariff protection, 303–304
Traffic snarls, 208–209
Transaction costs, 312
   and externalities, 538, 540–546
   and taxation, 300–301
Transfers of welfare, and monopoly, 339–340
Transivity of preferences, 59
Transportation, and time costs, 451
Trucks, quantity of, 109–110
Tucker, A.W., 392
Two-part tariffs, 347–348
Two-period model of saving, 459–460
Two-tier pricing systems, 355

U

Uncertainty, 312
Unfair insurance, 506–507
Uninsurable risks, 507
Unitary elastic curves, 140–141
Useless good, 65
Utility, and consumer surplus, 117, 119–120
Utility and choice, 55–88
   balance in consumption, 63–64
   basic properties of preferences, 57, 59
   diminishing marginal rate of substitution (MRS), 62
   economic good, 59–60
   graphic analysis of utility maximization, 70–74
      the budget constraint, 70–72
      the budget constraint algebra, 71–72
   indifference curve maps, 64–68
      economic bad, 65, 68
      perfect complements, 67–68
      perfect substitutes, 67–68
      useless goods, 65, 68
   indifference curves, 60–68
   indifference curves and the marginal rate of substitution (MRS), 62

measuring utility, 57
model of choice, 74, 76–78
    complicated budget
        constraints, 81
    composite goods, 81, 83
    many goods, 78, 80
utility from consuming two
    goods, 56–57
utility maximization, 68–78
    choices are constrained, 69
    example, 69–70
Utility maximization, 312
    and leisure, 450, 452
    See also Utility and choice
Utility-maximizing model, 518–519

V

Value and Capital (Hicks), 108n.3
Variable costs, 205
Variables, 29
    functions of one, 29–41
    functions of two or more, 41–44

graphing functions of one, 31–39
graphing functions of two
    variables, 42–44
VCRs, 11, 271
Volatile prices, 136–137
Voluntary trades, 60–68
    See also Indifference curves
Von Neumann, J. and
    Morgenstern, O., *The Theory
    of Games and Economic
    Behavior,* 387n.1
Voting and resource allocation,
    554–560
    See also Public goods

W

Wage rate (w), 188
Wages
    and labor supply, 431
    minimum, 430–431
    wage inequality, 434–435
Wal-Mart, 408–409

Wealth of Nations, The (Smith), 14
Welfare
    and the Internet, 289–290
    transfers of and monopoly,
        339–340
Westinghouse, 404
Willig, R.D., "Consumer's Surplus
    without Apology," 120n.5
Windows, 13
Winston, C., "U.S. Industry
    Adjustment to Economic
    Deregulation," 233
Wold, H. and Jureen, L., *Demand
    Analysis,* 146

Y

Yield, 493

Z

Zero-coupon bonds, 489